Innovations in Maritime Education

Andi Asrifan
https://orcid.org/0000-0002-9934-6129
Universitas Negeri Makassar, Indonesia

Syahruddin Syahruddin
https://orcid.org/0000-0002-1667-2405
Universitas Negeri Makassar, Indonesia

IGI Global
Scientific Publishing
Publishing Tomorrow's Research Today

Vice President of Editorial	Melissa Wagner
Director of Acquisitions	Mikaela Felty
Director of Book Development	Jocelynn Hessler
Production Manager	Mike Brehm
Cover Design	Jose Rosado

Published in the United States of America by
IGI Global Scientific Publishing
701 East Chocolate Avenue
Hershey, PA, 17033, USA
Tel: 717-533-8845 | Fax: 717-533-7115
Website: https://www.igi-global.com E-mail: cust@igi-global.com

Library of Congress Cataloging-in-Publication Data

LCCN: 2025046646 (CIP Data Pending)
ISBN13: 9798337366708
Isbn13Softcover: 9798337366715
EISBN13: 9798337366722

British Cataloguing in Publication Data
A Cataloguing in Publication record for this book is available from the British Library.

Table of Contents

Detailed Table of Contents

Artificial Intelligence (AI) is transforming Maritime Education and Training (MET) through data-driven personalization, intelligent tutoring, and predictive analytics. This study explores the evolution of maritime learning from traditional, standardized instruction to adaptive, competency-based systems powered by AI. It highlights the ethical, pedagogical, and infrastructural challenges accompanying digital transformation, including data privacy, automation bias, and institutional readiness. The analysis underscores the importance of designing human-centered, AI-integrated curricula and developing policy frameworks that balance innovation with accountability. By proposing a roadmap for human–AI co-learning ecosystems, the discussion envisions maritime institutions as dynamic environments that blend automation with experiential learning—ensuring the next generation of seafarers remain competent, ethical, and adaptable in an increasingly intelligent maritime world.

This research examines the amalgamation of mobile learning and micro-credentialing as innovative approaches for continuous maritime education. It shows how digital technologies, modular learning, and competency-based frameworks can make the maritime industry more accessible, adaptable, and relevant to professionals. The conversation looks at the best practices, governance models, and policy directions from around the world that support learning ecosystems that are both sustainable and open to everyone. To improve workforce mobility and ongoing professional development, the focus is on digital infrastructure, collaboration among stakeholders, and interoperability between regions. The proposed framework envisions a globally connected maritime education system that promotes innovation, equity, and environmental responsibility, ensuring seafarers remain competent and future-ready in the era of digital and green transformation.

The maritime industry, handling over 80% of global trade, faces rapid changes due to digitalization, automation, and sustainability pressures. However, many maritime education systems focus primarily on technical skills, neglecting the integration of business, management, and economic knowledge. This chapter discusses the need for curriculum reform in maritime education to align with the evolving global maritime industry. It highlights the importance of interdisciplinary skills like logistics analytics, environmental economics, and digital trade management. The chapter also proposes strategies such as integrating sustainability, interdisciplinary learning, and simulation technologies to prepare students for the challenges and opportunities of the modern maritime economy.

This study investigates the execution of Competency-Based Education (CBE) at maritime training institutions by evaluating the identification, structuring, delivery, and assessment of competencies to satisfy current industry requirements. It emphasizes the amalgamation of occupational analysis, performance metrics, simulation-based pedagogy, and ongoing evaluation to improve learners' operational preparedness. The discourse examines quality assurance tools, including tracer studies, audit cycles, and industry input, as well as institutional difficulties such as resource constraints, instructor readiness, and technical deficiencies. Future initiatives focus on AI-based evaluation, intelligent shipping systems, alternative fuel capabilities, and international standardization. The results highlight the significance of adaptable, technology-driven, and industry-aligned competency-based education frameworks in equipping proficient and safety-oriented marine workers.

This study explores the strategic alignment of competency standards and curriculum innovation in maritime education to prepare a future-ready workforce. It highlights the integration of Competency-Based Education (CBE), emerging technologies, and global benchmarking to enhance training relevance and quality. Emphasis is placed on co-designing curricula through industry–academia collaboration, embedding ethics and sustainability in competency frameworks, and fostering a culture of lifelong learning. The discussion underscores the role of institutional capacity building, quality assurance, and global cooperation in ensuring excellence and adaptability. The study concludes that a human-centered, competence-based ecosystem is essential for sustaining innovation, global mobility, and environmental responsibility in maritime education.

This chapter analyzes the strategic execution of Competency-Based Education (CBE) in marine Education and Training (MET) institutions, highlighting its conformity with international standards and the changing requirements of the marine sector. This study examines how competence mapping, modular curriculum reform, and performance-based assessment might improve cadet preparedness and professional flexibility, utilizing international frameworks such as STCW norms and quality assurance systems. The document emphasizes institutional obstacles, including pedagogical reluctance, resource limits, and policy limitations, while delineating capacity-building solutions that incorporate digital facilitation, simulation-based learning, and industry engagement. The text posits that maintaining success in MET necessitates data-driven continuous enhancement, international credential recognition, and the establishment of intelligent adaptive learning ecosystems that can cultivate internationally competitive and future-ready maritime professionals.

Machine learning is revolutionizing maritime education by improving simulator realism, augmenting predictive safety systems, and facilitating individualized competency advancement. As navigation, engineering, and marine operations become progressively data-centric, maritime training must adapt by incorporating dynamic learning environments enhanced by sophisticated analytics. This study investigates the incorporation of machine learning in navigation instruction, simulation-based assessment, and safety management, emphasizing its ability to create dynamic situations, automate competency evaluation, and detect human-error tendencies. Ethical and practical obstacles, including infrastructure constraints, data governance, algorithmic equity, and instructor preparedness, are examined to guarantee ethical implementation. The results demonstrate that machine learning may markedly enhance training quality, safety results, and regulatory compliance, while emergent trends like AI copilots and MASS competences suggest new pathways for the advancement of the marine workforce.

Green shipping has become a decisive element in shaping the future of maritime education, particularly in regions like Indonesia where the sea defines both identity and economy. This chapter situates maritime transformation within the realities of climate change, technological disruption, and regional socio-economic pressures, arguing that Maritime Education and Training (MET) must no longer be limited to technical instruction. Instead, it should cultivate ecological awareness, adaptive skills, and a mindset oriented toward sustainability. The discussion draws on the Bugis-Makassar Pinisi tradition, a heritage of low-emission seafaring that demonstrates how indigenous practices can anticipate modern green principles. By proposing curriculum reforms that integrate environmental issues, innovative learning methods, and 21st-century competencies, the article frames green shipping education as a pathway to resilience. It concludes that empowering future seafarers through this approach is key to positioning Indonesia and Southeast Asia as leaders in sustainable maritime development.

This chapter explores the integration of economic literacy into maritime education as essential for developing professionals in the Blue Economy. It highlights the need for maritime education systems to balance technical skills with knowledge in economics, sustainability, and environmental policy. By focusing on cost-benefit analysis, resource efficiency, and long-term economic impacts, the chapter advocates for curriculum reforms that align with global sustainability goals, such as the UN SDGs. It suggests teaching methods like project-based learning, digital tools, and cross-sector partnerships to enhance economic competency, ultimately preparing students for leadership in a sustainable ocean economy.

This study examines the synchronization of global standards and regional collaboration in enhancing maritime education and training (MET). It examines how international frameworks, particularly those established by the IMO, ILO, and UNESCO, collaborate with regional organizations such as ASEAN

Preface

INTRODUCTION

The maritime industry is undergoing one of the most significant periods of transformation in its history. Driven by rapid advances in digital technologies, artificial intelligence, automation, sustainability initiatives, and global regulatory developments, maritime professionals are expected to possess far more than traditional technical expertise. Modern seafarers and maritime leaders must demonstrate digital literacy, ethical decision-making, intercultural competence, environmental stewardship, and the ability to adapt to an increasingly interconnected and technology-driven industry. Consequently, Maritime Education and Training (MET) institutions around the world are reevaluating longstanding educational models to prepare learners for careers that continue to evolve alongside technological innovation and global economic change. *Innovations in Maritime Education* was developed in response to these emerging challenges and opportunities, bringing together diverse scholarly perspectives that explore how maritime education can continue to evolve while maintaining its commitment to safety, professionalism, and excellence.

This volume presents a comprehensive examination of contemporary innovations influencing maritime education from multiple perspectives, including instructional design, competency-based learning, digital transformation, educational technology, artificial intelligence, sustainability, language education, curriculum development, ethics, and international collaboration. While technological advancement serves as a central theme throughout the book, the contributing authors consistently emphasize that innovation in maritime education must remain human-centered. Emerging technologies should enhance—not replace—the critical thinking, professional judgment, ethical responsibility, and experiential learning that have long defined effective maritime training. The chapters collectively demonstrate that successful educational innovation requires thoughtful integration of technology with sound pedagogical practice, institutional readiness, industry collaboration, and internationally recognized competency standards.

An important strength of this book lies in the diversity of its contributors and the breadth of topics represented. Researchers and educators from leading maritime institutions examine not only current educational practices but also future directions for Maritime Education and Training within a rapidly changing global environment. The volume addresses the implications of artificial intelligence, machine learning, virtual learning environments, mobile education, competency-based education, maritime English instruction, environmental literacy, climate resilience, economic education, cross-cultural communication, and global policy alignment. Together, these contributions reflect the increasingly interdisciplinary nature of maritime education, demonstrating that preparing future maritime professionals requires collaboration across educational, technological, environmental, and organizational domains.

As editors, we believe this collection offers timely insights for educators, researchers, administrators, policymakers, industry professionals, and graduate students seeking to understand the future direction of maritime education. Beyond presenting current research, the chapters encourage readers to critically consider how institutions can respond proactively to technological disruption while preserving the fundamental values of maritime professionalism, safety, ethics, and lifelong learning. We hope this volume serves not only as a scholarly reference but also as a catalyst for continued innovation, international collaboration, and evidence-based educational reform across the global maritime community.

OVERVIEW OF THE CHAPTERS

The chapters included in this volume collectively illustrate the breadth of innovation currently shaping Maritime Education and Training (MET). While each contribution examines a distinct aspect of maritime education, together they present a cohesive narrative demonstrating that the future of the profession depends upon integrating technological advancement, competency development, ethical leadership, sustainability, and international collaboration. The organization of this volume reflects these interconnected themes, highlighting both emerging educational practices and the broader transformation occurring across maritime institutions worldwide.

The opening chapters establish the foundation for understanding digital transformation within maritime education. Chapter 1 examines the growing influence of artificial intelligence and learning analytics in creating personalized educational experiences capable of supporting competency-based learning and predictive student success. Chapters 2 through 4 expand upon this discussion by exploring mobile learning, micro-credentialing, e-learning environments, and broader digital transformation strategies that increase educational accessibility, flexibility, and institutional resilience. Collectively, these chapters demonstrate how digital technologies are reshaping traditional instructional models while emphasizing the importance of maintaining pedagogical quality, faculty preparedness, and equitable access to learning resources.

Building upon this technological foundation, several chapters focus on curriculum modernization and competency-based education as essential components of preparing future maritime professionals. Chapter 5 discusses the integration of business and economic education into maritime curricula to better align graduates with evolving industry expectations. Chapters 6 through 8 examine the design and implementation of competency-based education frameworks, emphasizing performance assessment, curriculum innovation, institutional quality assurance, and alignment with international standards such as the STCW Convention. Chapter 21 further reinforces these principles by exploring competency-based training frameworks that combine simulation technologies, authentic assessment, lifelong learning, and global regulatory alignment to cultivate highly skilled and adaptable maritime professionals. Together, these chapters emphasize that curriculum reform must remain responsive to technological change while preserving the operational competencies fundamental to maritime safety and professional excellence.

Artificial intelligence emerges as another prominent theme throughout this collection. Chapters 9 through 11 examine the educational applications of machine learning and AI, demonstrating how intelligent systems can enhance navigation training, simulator performance, competency assessment, and personalized learning experiences. At the same time, these chapters carefully acknowledge the ethical responsibilities accompanying technological innovation, including issues surrounding transparency, fairness, privacy, accountability, and responsible governance. Rather than presenting AI as a replacement for educators or professional judgment, the contributors consistently advocate for human-centered approaches that ensure technological innovation strengthens educational quality while preserving ethical decision-making and professional integrity.

Communication, language proficiency, and learner development are explored through several complementary perspectives. Chapter 12 investigates technology-supported approaches to Maritime English instruction, demonstrating how digital learning environments can strengthen communication skills essential for international maritime operations. Chapters 18 through 20 examine intercultural competence, English language achievement, and officer trainees' attitudes toward online learning, highlighting the importance of communication, cultural awareness, learner motivation, and educational adaptability within increasingly diverse maritime workplaces. Collectively, these contributions recognize that successful maritime professionals require not only technical competence but also the communication and interpersonal skills necessary for effective collaboration within multinational crews.

Another significant theme throughout this volume centers on sustainability and environmental responsibility. Chapters 13 through 16 emphasize the integration of environmental literacy, climate resilience, green shipping, indigenous maritime knowledge, and Blue Economy principles into maritime education. These contributions demonstrate that environmental stewardship has become an essential educational objective rather than a supplementary consideration. By combining technological innovation with ecological awareness, ethical leadership, and sustainable economic development, the authors advocate for preparing future maritime professionals who are capable of addressing both operational challenges and the global environmental responsibilities facing the maritime sector.

The volume concludes by broadening its perspective to encompass international cooperation, educational policy, specialized disciplinary innovation, and emerging research directions. Chapter 17 explores the importance of aligning maritime education with international frameworks through regional collaboration and policy harmonization. Chapter 22 examines digital transformation within maritime architecture education, illustrating how technological innovation extends across specialized maritime disciplines. Finally, Chapter 23 provides a comprehensive bibliometric analysis of maritime education research, identifying major scholarly trends and future directions that continue to shape the evolution of Maritime Education and Training worldwide. Together, these concluding contributions reinforce the importance of evidence-based decision-making, global partnerships, and continuous innovation as maritime education responds to an increasingly complex and interconnected world.

CONCLUSION

The chapters presented in *Innovations in Maritime Education* collectively demonstrate that the future of Maritime Education and Training depends upon the ability of institutions to embrace innovation while remaining firmly grounded in the enduring principles of safety, professionalism, collaboration, and lifelong learning. Although the maritime industry continues to evolve through advances in artificial intelligence, digital technologies, automation, sustainability initiatives, and global policy development, the preparation of future maritime professionals remains fundamentally centered on people. Technology serves as an enabler of educational excellence, but it is the thoughtful integration of pedagogical innovation, ethical leadership, industry collaboration, and competency-based learning that will ultimately determine the success of future maritime education systems.

Throughout this volume, the contributing authors emphasize that meaningful educational transformation requires more than the adoption of new technologies. It demands institutional commitment to curriculum renewal, faculty development, international cooperation, continuous quality assurance, and the cultivation of adaptable learners capable of responding to an increasingly dynamic global maritime environment. The diversity of topics represented—from personalized learning and machine learning to environmental stewardship, cross-cultural competence, economic literacy, and competency-based education—reflects the interdisciplinary nature of modern maritime education and highlights the many dimensions that must work together to prepare future-ready professionals.

As editors, we hope this volume serves as both a valuable scholarly reference and a practical resource for educators, researchers, institutional leaders, policymakers, and maritime practitioners seeking to advance excellence in Maritime Education and Training. The ideas presented throughout these chapters are intended not only to document current innovations but also to inspire continued dialogue, collaborative research, and evidence-based educational reform across institutions and national boundaries. By sharing diverse perspectives and innovative practices, this collection contributes to the ongoing global conversation surrounding the future of maritime education and the preparation of highly competent, ethical, and resilient maritime professionals.

We extend our sincere appreciation to each of the contributing authors for sharing their expertise, research, and commitment to advancing maritime education. Their scholarly contributions have created a volume that reflects both the complexity of today's maritime landscape and the tremendous opportunities that lie ahead. We also thank the reviewers, editorial staff, and publishing team whose efforts made this collection possible. It is our hope that *Innovations in Maritime Education* will encourage continued innovation, strengthen international collaboration, and serve as a lasting resource that supports the advancement of maritime education for years to come.

Andi Asrifan
Universitas Negeri Makassar, Indonesia

Syahruddin Syahruddin
Universitas Negeri Makassar, Indonesia

Chapter 1
Reimagining Maritime Classrooms:
AI-Powered Learning Analytics and Personalized Education

Sarifuddin Sarifuddin
http://orcid.org/0000-0003-0348-7240
Politeknik Ilmu Pelayaran Makassar, Indonesia

Salman Faiz Muttaqin
http://orcid.org/0009-0001-7711-225X
Politeknik Ilmu Pelayaran Makassar, Indonesia

Tasdik Tona
Politeknik Ilmu Pelayaran Makassar, Indonesia

ABSTRACT

Artificial Intelligence (AI) is transforming Maritime Education and Training (MET) through data-driven personalization, intelligent tutoring, and predictive analytics. This study explores the evolution of maritime learning from traditional, standardized instruction to adaptive, competency-based systems powered by AI. It highlights the ethical, pedagogical, and infrastructural challenges accompanying digital transformation, including data privacy, automation bias, and institutional readiness. The analysis underscores the importance of designing human-centered, AI-integrated curricula and developing policy frameworks that balance innovation with accountability. By proposing a roadmap for human–AI co-learning ecosystems, the discussion envisions maritime institutions as dynamic environments that blend automation with experiential learning—ensuring the next generation of seafarers remain competent, ethical, and adaptable in an increasingly intelligent maritime world.

DOI: 10.4018/979-8-3373-6670-8.ch001

INTRODUCTION

1.1 The evolution of maritime education in the era of digital transformation

Maritime education has changed a lot since it started as traditional seamanship training. Now, it is a complex system of learning that uses technology to help students learn. Historically, maritime education was based on apprenticeship models that stressed learning navigation, mechanical operations, and seamanship skills through direct observation and practice. Classrooms and simulators were controlled environments that tried to mimic real-world maritime conditions, but the way they taught was mostly based on standard curricula and teacher-centered instruction. This model was good at teaching technical skills, but it didn't always allow for flexibility, adaptability to different situations, or responsiveness to the needs of each learner (Türkistanlı, 2023).

The start of the Fourth Industrial Revolution (Industry 4.0) has changed traditional maritime education in a big way. Artificial Intelligence (AI), the Internet of Things (IoT), cloud computing, and data analytics are some of the technologies that have changed how maritime knowledge is created, shared, and evaluated. The combination of digital navigation systems, electronic chart display and information systems (ECDIS), and smart simulation platforms has changed the way maritime education works by making it more data-driven. In this new ecosystem, learning outcomes are not just the result of how lessons are taught; they are also constantly shaped by real-time data collected from sensors, simulators, and digital learning platforms. As a result, the maritime classroom has changed into a hybrid and smart learning space where real and virtual worlds come together to support adaptive and experiential learning (Mke, 2024).

The digital transformation has also brought about the rise of AI-powered learning analytics as a key part of modern Maritime Education and Training (MET). With the help of advanced algorithms, teachers can now figure out how engaged students are, find areas where they could do better, and tailor their lessons to each student. This change from one-time tests to ongoing feedback loops is a big change in educational philosophy, moving from teaching-centered to learner-centered design. Moreover, AI-driven personalization facilitates the alignment of learning pathways with the International Convention on Standards of Training, Certification and Watchkeeping for Seafarers (STCW), guaranteeing that competency standards are dynamically correlated with individual advancement (Koshiry & Tony, 2025).

Along with new technologies, global maritime organizations like the International Maritime Organization (IMO) and the International Labour Organization (ILO) have stressed the importance of seafarers being able to use computers and learn new things throughout their lives. Their policies support adding simulation-based learning, e-assessment, and AI-supported decision-making to maritime courses. This shift is in response to the urgent need for flexible, tech-savvy sailors who can work in automated ship environments, manage autonomous systems, and make sense of complicated digital data streams while navigating and maintaining ships (Karimi et al., 2024).

But this change isn't easy. The digital divide between maritime institutions, different levels of infrastructure capacity, and a lack of digital pedagogy experts have all slowed down the sector's ability to adopt new technologies. Furthermore, although technology improves efficiency, it prompts concerns regarding the preservation of the traditional seamanship ethos—intuition, experience, and human judgment—that are crucial for maritime safety. Consequently, the advancement of maritime education should be regarded not as a substitution for human expertise but as an enhancement of it through intelligent tools (Koshiry & Tony, 2025).

In short, the time of digital transformation has changed maritime education into a flexible, data-driven, and learner-adaptive system. The combination of AI, learning analytics, and immersive technologies represents a major shift from mechanical training to intelligent education. This means that seafarers will be able to navigate not only the oceans but also the data. This change is a strategic shift toward maritime professionals who are ready for the future and can thrive in a world that is becoming more automated and connected (Türkistanlı, 2023; Karimi et al., 2024).

1.2 The emergence of Artificial Intelligence in learning and competency assessment

The integration of Artificial Intelligence (AI) into education represents a significant advancement in modern pedagogy, including Maritime Education and Training (MET) (Reyes, 2025). AI has become a transformative force in how knowledge is acquired, applied, and evaluated, particularly in the high-stakes maritime context (Chen et al., 2020). Traditionally, assessments in maritime education relied on summative evaluations such as examinations and simulator-based tests. These methods, while effective in certifying competencies, often overlook nuances in individual learning trajectories and adaptive decision-making skills essential for maritime professionals in dynamic settings (Sharma et al., 2022). AI facilitates a paradigm shift towards continuous, data-driven evaluation systems that align more closely with real-world maritime operations (Gardner et al., 2021).

In learning environments, AI algorithms enhance personalized learning by analyzing learners' behavior and performance across digital platforms (Sharma et al., 2022). Intelligent tutoring systems (ITS) and learning management systems (LMS) can identify struggling learners, recommend resources, and adjust simulation difficulties in real time (Reyes, 2025). This adaptive capability accelerates proficiency in core tasks before advancing to complex scenarios (Chen et al., 2020). AI's impact on competency assessment is notable; competency-based frameworks, such as the STCW Convention, require the demonstration of knowledge alongside operational proficiency (Gardner et al., 2021). AI analytics systems can continuously gather performance data, generating precise learner profiles to assess both technical skills and critical soft skills like teamwork and situational awareness (Gardner et al., 2021).

Moreover, AI supports predictive and prescriptive assessment models, which are crucial for identifying learning difficulties and recommending interventions proactively (Sharma et al., 2022). Natural language processing and machine vision technologies further enhance assessment processes, offering insights into competencies beyond traditional metrics (Gardner et al., 2021).

Despite these technological advancements, challenges related to data privacy, algorithmic bias, and reliance on automation exist (Gardner et al., 2021). Educators must ensure AI complements human expertise, shifting their role from evaluators to mentors who interpret AI-generated insights for holistic professional development (Sharma et al., 2022). Thus, the emergence of AI in learning and competency assessment signifies a critical move towards intelligent, evidence-based education in MET, enriching assessment practices while promoting continuous skill evolution.

1.3 Rationale for adopting AI-powered personalization in Maritime Education and Training (MET)

The rationale for integrating Artificial Intelligence (AI)-powered personalization into Maritime Education and Training (MET) is rooted in the increasing demand for adaptive, efficient, and competency-driven learning environments that reflect the rapidly digitizing maritime industry (Sijabat et al., 2024). Traditional maritime training models, which emphasize standardized curricula and fixed-time instruction, struggle to accommodate individual learning differences, diverse linguistic backgrounds, and varying digital literacy levels among cadets (Sihombing et al., 2024). As global shipping operations become more automated and data-centric, educational systems must adapt dynamically to each learner's profile while ensuring alignment with international standards, such as the STCW Convention and the competency frameworks established by the International Maritime Organization (IMO) (Sijabat et al., 2024).

AI-powered personalization directly addresses these challenges by customizing instructional content, pacing, and feedback according to individual cognitive patterns and performance data (Ala et al., 2024). Unlike conventional "one-size-fits-all" pedagogies, personalized AI systems analyze extensive data from simulators and e-learning platforms to create individualized learning pathways. This approach ensures, for instance, that a cadet with strong navigation skills but limited engineering knowledge receives targeted instruction that maximizes both efficiency and engagement (Sihombing et al., 2024).

Furthermore, research demonstrates that personalized learning environments enhance retention and operational readiness, which are critical in maritime training where safety and decision-making are paramount (Ala et al., 2024). AI can simulate high-risk scenarios and adjust difficulty in real-time based on learner performance, thereby improving procedural competence and nurturing essential qualities like resilience and critical thinking (Ala et al., 2024). These features support competency-based assessment by continuously monitoring progress across various dimensions—technical, cognitive, and behavioral—improving the fairness and accuracy of evaluations essential for global employability.

From an institutional perspective, adopting AI personalization enhances training efficiency and optimizes resources in maritime academies facing logistical constraints. AI-enabled platforms can automate routine feedback and offer analytics that facilitate educator decision-making, allowing instructors to focus on higher-order mentorship and engagement activities (Ala et al., 2024). Lastly, AI-powered personalization fosters lifelong learning, allowing seafarers to continuously update their skills to meet industry demands in an evolving technological landscape (Sihombing et al., 2024).

In summary, the adoption of AI-powered personalization in MET is not merely a technological enhancement but a strategic imperative. It aligns maritime education with adaptive learning principles, ensuring that every learner can develop into a competent, confident, and future-ready maritime professional (Sijabat et al., 2024).

FOUNDATIONS OF AI-DRIVEN LEARNING ANALYTICS

2.1 The concept and components of learning analytics in education

Learning analytics has emerged as a transformative innovation in education, reshaping how institutions understand, monitor, and enhance the learning process (Ouyang et al., 2023). Broadly defined, learning analytics involves the collection, measurement, analysis, and reporting of data related to learners and their contexts, with the aim of optimizing learning environments (Dawat, 2023). It integrates pedagogy, data science, and artificial intelligence (AI), providing educators with actionable insights that inform instructional design, student support, and curriculum improvement (Harrington & Sellberg, 2024). Essentially, learning analytics transforms raw educational data into meaningful intelligence, enabling personalized learning and evidence-based decision-making. Learning analytics comprises four interrelated components: data collection, data analysis, interpretation, and intervention (Talan & DEMIRBILEK, 2022). These stages form a continuous cycle that fuels adaptive learning ecosystems and ensures ongoing improvements in educational outcomes.

The first component, data collection, involves gathering learner-related data from diverse sources. In digital learning environments, these data points can include interaction logs, assessment results, and clickstream data from learning management systems (LMS) (Harrington & Sellberg, 2024). In the context of maritime education, this may include simulator performance data and navigation decision trails captured from electronic chart display and information systems (ECDIS). The reliability and richness of subsequent analyses depend on the quality and scope of data collection, making it a foundational step in any learning analytics framework.

The second component, data analysis, transforms raw information into interpretable patterns using statistical and computational methods (Dawat, 2023). AI algorithms, such as machine learning and deep learning models, play a pivotal role in detecting hidden correlations and predicting learner outcomes (Ouyang et al., 2023). Techniques like clustering can segment learners into performance groups, while regression models can forecast success probabilities (Pereira et al., 2024).

The third component, interpretation, links the analytical output with pedagogical relevance. Data visualizations, including dashboards and progress charts, make complex analytics accessible to instructors and learners (Harrington & Sellberg, 2024). For example, a maritime instructor may utilize dashboard analytics to ascertain whether students fully understand navigation safety procedures (Dawat, 2023). This interpretation phase ensures that analytics remain pedagogically relevant.

The final component, intervention, translates insights into action. Data-driven, targeted interventions can include personalized feedback and remedial tutorials (Dawat, 2023). AI systems often automate many of these responses, offering learners immediate support in maritime education and training (MET), such as prompting additional simulation exercises for cadets struggling with specific competencies (Ouyang et al., 2023).

Beyond these four components, ethical governance, data privacy, and institutional readiness are critical dimensions of any effective learning analytics framework. The absence of ethical safeguards can infringe on learner autonomy and privacy (Talan & DEMIRBILEK, 2022; Harrington & Sellberg, 2024). Transparency and accountability must underpin every analytic process.

2.2 Data sources and key metrics in maritime learning environments

The use of learning analytics in maritime education depends on a variety of data sources that show how cadets learn, interact, and do their jobs in both physical and digital training environments. Maritime learning environments are different from regular classrooms because they use a mix of theoretical lessons, simulator-based exercises, onboard practice, and digital tests. These complicated ecosystems produce a lot of data, which is a great base for AI-driven analytics to help people learn and improve their skills. To create effective AI-supported training and evaluation systems in Maritime Education and Training (MET), it's important to know what kinds of data are collected and what the most important metrics are.

1. Data from the simulator

Simulators are the most important part of maritime training because they let people practice navigation, engine operation, and emergency situations in a safe environment. They make high-resolution datasets that keep track of everything each learner does, such as control inputs, communication exchanges, reaction times, and following procedures. For example, bridge simulators keep track of how accurate the trajectory is, how to avoid collisions, and how well the rules for preventing collisions at sea (COLREGS) are followed. Engine room simulators also keep track of operational sequences, maintenance procedures, and choices about how to use energy. These data give teachers and AI systems detailed information about both technical and behavioral skills. Metrics like decision accuracy, response latency, procedural compliance rate, and error recovery efficiency are important signs that someone is ready to work in the real world on the water.

2. E-Learning Data and Learning Management System (LMS)

Digital learning platforms are becoming more and more important in MET because they host quizzes, assignments, discussion forums, and theoretical modules. The LMS is an important source of information because it records how students act online, how engaged they are, and how their performance is changing. AI algorithms can look at clickstream data, time spent on a task, how often people log in, and how many assessments are completed to figure out how motivated and persistent someone is. Teachers can use these analytics to see if students are getting tired or losing interest early on. Some common LMS-based metrics are participation frequency, quiz accuracy rate, content interaction time, and assessment improvement trajectory. All of these show how engaged a learner is and how well they are retaining what they learn.

3. Learning on the job and through experience Data

Maritime education doesn't just happen in classrooms and simulators; it also happens on board ships and in the field. Digital logbooks, wearable devices, and IoT-enabled sensors on training ships now record information about the environment, navigation choices, and interactions between team members. AI systems can use these real-time inputs to check on how aware people are of their surroundings, how clear their communication is, and how well they follow safety rules. To check how ready an operation is and how good a leader is, you need to look at things like incident response time, communication efficiency, and following Standard Operating Procedures (SOPs).

4. Analytics for Behavior and Cognition

New tools like eye-tracking devices, motion sensors, and biometric feedback systems give us useful information about how learners are feeling and thinking during stressful training. Eye-tracking data show how people pay attention to things while they are navigating, and biometric sensors measure stress and fatigue levels. These data sources enable AI to simulate cognitive load and anticipate possible declines in performance. Metrics such as attention stability, stress index, and decision confidence offer a comprehensive insight into learner behavior beyond mere technical proficiency.

5. Metrics for communication and working together

Maritime operations depend on tasks that require teamwork. Information from chat logs, voice communication systems, and collaborative simulation tasks can be used to measure leadership, teamwork, and interpersonal coordination. Natural Language Processing (NLP) tools can look at language patterns to see how clear, assertive, and in line with standard communication rules (like Standard Marine Communication Phrases) a message is. Metrics like message clarity score, response coherence, and coordination effectiveness show how well learners work together in maritime settings.

In summary, data sources in maritime learning environments include technical, cognitive, and behavioral aspects, providing a comprehensive perspective on learner performance. By using AI-powered learning analytics to look at these datasets, maritime schools can move toward evidence-based education, where competency assessment is always changing and tailored to each student. This data-driven approach makes sure that maritime workers are not only trained to follow the rules but also ready for the complicated, tech-heavy world of modern seafaring.

2.3 Predictive modeling and early-warning systems for student performance

Predictive modeling and early-warning systems are the most advanced uses of AI and learning analytics in modern Maritime Education and Training (MET). These technologies help teachers and administrators see academic risks coming, spot performance trends, and take action quickly to help students before they fail to meet competency standards. In the high-stakes world of maritime education, where safety, accuracy, and making decisions are the most important things, predictive analytics is a proactive tool that makes sure students are ready for both certification and real-world maritime operations.

The main idea behind predictive modeling is to use statistical and machine learning algorithms to look at both past and present data and find patterns that are linked to academic success or failure. AI systems can make predictions about each cadet by looking at a lot of data about them, such as their attendance, test scores, simulator logs, engagement frequency, and behavioral indicators. These scores give an idea of how likely it is that you will be able to learn certain skills or finish a course. Logistic regression, decision trees, random forests, and neural networks are all common methods for finding nonlinear patterns in educational data. Each has its own strengths. In MET settings, predictive models can identify cadets who may have difficulty with navigational accuracy, adherence to procedures, or communication under stress, enabling instructors to create customized remediation strategies.

A standard early-warning system (EWS) based on predictive analytics has three main parts: gathering data, finding risks, and taking action. During the data aggregation phase, inputs from different sources, like Learning Management Systems (LMS), simulators, attendance records, and online tests, are put together to make a full learner profile. During the risk identification stage, predictive algorithms look at this data and put students into risk groups like low, moderate, or high risk. During the intervention stage, the system lets teachers or academic advisors know that they need to take action, like giving one-on-one tutoring, suggesting extra modules, or giving students more practice with simulations.

For maritime schools, the most important thing about these systems is that they encourage proactive, data-driven teaching. Traditional maritime assessment methods frequently identify learning difficulties solely after summative evaluations, thereby restricting opportunities for remediation. On the other hand, predictive models give you real-time diagnostic information that lets you take steps to avoid failure long before it happens. For instance, an AI-powered system might notice that a cadet's engagement and simulator performance have been going down over several sessions. This would mean that the cadet is at risk of not meeting competency standards in radar navigation. Then, an instructor can step in early and give personalized help to fill in any gaps in understanding or skill execution.

Also, predictive modeling helps institutions run more smoothly and make sure the quality of their work. By putting together predictive data from different groups, administrators can find problems that affect the whole system, like misaligned curriculum, resource bottlenecks, or gaps in instruction. They can then change training programs to fix these issues. These analytics-driven insights improve the accountability and openness of maritime training institutions by following the quality standards set by the International Maritime Organization (IMO).

But using predictive analytics and early-warning systems also raises issues with data ethics, privacy, and how easy it is to understand the results. If the data quality is bad or the context is ignored, relying too much on algorithmic predictions could lead to bias or misclassification. So, human supervision is still very important. Instructors ought to regard predictive outcomes as instruments for decision support rather than as definitive judgments.

PERSONALIZATION AND ADAPTIVE LEARNING IN MARITIME CLASSROOMS

3.1 From traditional instruction to adaptive learning pathways

For decades, maritime education has adhered to a traditional, instructor-centered model characterized by uniform curricula, standardized assessments, and fixed instructional pacing (Bayotas, 2024). This conventional approach, while effective in transmitting foundational technical knowledge and ensuring compliance with international training standards such as the Standards of Training, Certification, and Watchkeeping for Seafarers (STCW), often overlooks the diversity of learners' cognitive abilities, prior experiences, and learning preferences (Göçen & AYDEMİR, 2020). In traditional maritime classrooms, all cadets are expected to progress at the same rate, regardless of individual readiness or performance variability, which can lead to disengagement among advanced learners and cognitive overload for struggling cadets (Ala et al., 2024).

The digital transformation of education, particularly through Artificial Intelligence (AI) and learning analytics, is catalyzing a paradigm shift toward adaptive learning pathways—a model that personalizes instruction to meet the unique needs and pace of each learner (Göçen & AYDEMİR, 2020). Adaptive learning replaces the static "one-size-fits-all" methodology with dynamic, data-driven systems that continually analyze learner performance and adjust content delivery, difficulty level, and feedback accordingly. This transformation aligns perfectly with the evolving demands of the maritime industry, where operational competence requires technical proficiency as well as situational judgment, decision-making, and adaptability in unpredictable maritime environments (Ala et al., 2024).

In adaptive learning frameworks, AI algorithms process real-time data from multiple sources—such as simulators, Learning Management Systems (LMS), and e-assessment platforms—to build individualized learner profiles (Ala et al., 2024). These profiles capture patterns of engagement and mastery levels, allowing the system to modify instructional trajectories based on each student's data. For instance, a cadet struggling with radar plotting might receive additional visual simulations or scaffolded exercises before advancing to advanced navigation scenarios, while a high-performing learner may face challenging, high-pressure simulations that test their leadership and multitasking skills (Ala et al., 2024).

The shift toward adaptive learning in maritime classrooms is further supported by intelligent tutoring systems (ITS) that emulate human instructors by providing immediate, context-sensitive feedback (Ala et al., 2024). These systems can monitor learner responses, diagnose misconceptions, and deliver corrective explanations at the moment of error. In practical maritime settings, such as engine room training or bridge management, AI-driven tutors can detect unsafe decisions and guide learners toward safer alternatives, reinforcing the necessary understanding of cause-and-effect dynamics in real-world operations (Ala et al., 2024).

Adaptive learning pathways also encourage self-regulated and lifelong learning, critical attributes for modern seafarers who need to continuously update their skills amid rapid technological advancements (Göçen & AYDEMİR, 2020). By offering personalized progress dashboards and competency tracking tools, learners can visualize their development, set goals, and take ownership of their learning journeys.

Despite its promise, the transition from traditional instruction to adaptive learning requires institutional readiness, including robust digital infrastructure, faculty training in data-informed pedagogy, and ethical governance concerning learner data (Ala et al., 2024). When implemented effectively, adaptive learning pathways can transform maritime classrooms into intelligent ecosystems that balance automation with essential human mentorship (Ala et al., 2024).

3.2 Intelligent tutoring systems and personalized feedback loops

Intelligent Tutoring Systems (ITS) are one of the most important uses of Artificial Intelligence (AI) in education. They completely change how Maritime Education and Training (MET) does instruction and assessment. Traditional maritime teaching methods, which include lectures led by teachers, standardized tests, and few chances to practice, often don't take into account how different students learn or give them timely feedback on their mistakes. ITS, on the other hand, allows for personalized, adaptive, and data-driven learning by simulating the role of a human tutor through constant interaction, analysis, and feedback generation. In the maritime setting, ITS acts as a digital co-instructor that can keep an eye on cadets' work, find their weaknesses, and give them personalized help right away.

An Intelligent Tutoring System usually has four main parts: the domain model, the student model, the tutoring model, and the user interface. The domain model tells you what specific skills and knowledge you need to learn, like how to use radar to find your way, handle cargo, or control an engine. The student model keeps an up-to-date profile of each learner, keeping track of their progress, mistakes, cognitive patterns, and how they respond. The tutoring model decides how the system teaches, including when to step in, what hints to give, and how to change the level of difficulty. The user interface makes it easy for the learner and the AI system to talk to each other. This architecture lets the ITS give each cadet the same level of attention as a human tutor while also being able to help large groups of cadets learn.

ITS applications are especially useful in maritime education when training is based on simulations. For example, an ITS built into a bridge simulator can keep an eye on navigational choices, check to see if safety rules are being followed, and give real-time, situation-specific advice. If a cadet makes a mistake during a collision avoidance scenario, the system can quickly point it out, explain the COLREGS rule that was broken, and suggest a different way to do things. The ITS can also track operational sequences and point out procedural mistakes in engine room simulations. This helps learners understand how their actions affect safety and technology. These personalized feedback loops change assessment from a one-time event that happens after an activity to a learning experience that happens all the time.

Personalized feedback is an important part of learning because it encourages thinking, fixing mistakes, and mastering new skills. AI-driven feedback systems in ITS do more than just give scores; they also look at why students got things wrong. The system can understand what learners write, how they talk to each other, or how they make decisions by using natural language processing (NLP) and pattern recognition. It can then give them feedback that is specific to their cognitive style. For instance, visual learners might get graphical explanations of how vessels move, while analytical learners might get data-driven reasons for each move. This responsiveness helps students understand concepts better and get more involved in their learning.

ITS also supports affective feedback loops by using behavioral and biometric cues to find out how people are feeling and what motivates them. If the system detects signs of confusion or fatigue, it can change the tone or speed of its feedback to keep the learning flow going. For example, it can offer encouragement, suggest breaks, or make tasks easier. This humanized interaction boosts learners' confidence and determination, especially in tough maritime simulations where being able to handle stress is a key part of being a good professional.

Using ITS and personalized feedback loops in MET also helps with quality assurance that can be scaled up. Institutions can gather anonymized performance data from different groups of students to find common learning problems and improve the curriculum based on that. But ethical issues, especially those about data privacy, openness, and the roles of teachers, need to be taken into account to make sure AI is used responsibly.

3.3 Case illustrations of AI-enhanced training simulators and e-assessment tools

Artificial Intelligence (AI) has become a transformative force in maritime education, reshaping how cadets are trained, assessed, and certified through advanced simulation and e-assessment technologies (Nyairo et al., 2025). The integration of AI into simulators and digital evaluation systems bridges the gap between theory and practice, creating immersive, data-driven, and adaptive learning experiences that closely mirror real-world maritime operations. Case illustrations from various maritime education and training (MET) contexts demonstrate how AI-enhanced systems foster individualized learning, operational accuracy, and safety awareness—key attributes for future-ready seafarers.

A prominent example is found in AI-integrated bridge simulators, increasingly used in leading maritime academies in Europe and Asia. These simulators employ machine learning algorithms to adapt navigational scenarios based on the learner's past performance (Atik, 2020). For instance, if a cadet consistently misjudges ship handling in high-traffic conditions, the AI dynamically modifies subsequent scenarios by introducing more complex collision avoidance tasks. Through continuous performance tracking, the system identifies recurring decision errors, provides real-time corrective prompts, and measures improvement across sessions. This feedback loop, powered by AI analytics, ensures that each cadet's progression follows a personalized trajectory, moving from basic control tasks to advanced multi-ship coordination exercises while adhering to the COLREGS (International Regulations for Preventing Collisions at Sea).

Similarly, AI-enhanced engine room simulators have revolutionized technical training by embedding predictive analytics and diagnostic feedback into operational exercises. These systems simulate machinery faults and emergency breakdowns that require immediate troubleshooting. The simulator records how cadets respond—capturing reaction time, procedural accuracy, and communication with team members. Based on these variables, the AI system evaluates competence in both technical execution and soft skills, such as leadership under pressure. Such intelligent feedback mechanisms enable instructors to assess readiness for real-life engine maintenance and crisis response with unprecedented granularity. Some maritime academies in Scandinavia and Japan have reported improved skill retention and reduced human error rates after adopting AI-supported engine simulators.

Another key innovation involves AI-based e-assessment tools that move beyond traditional written or multiple-choice testing. These platforms integrate natural language processing (NLP), computer vision, and learning analytics to evaluate cognitive and behavioral performance (Bello & Abdullah, 2021). For instance, during oral examinations, AI speech recognition systems analyze cadets' verbal responses for clarity, accuracy, and compliance with maritime communication protocols. NLP tools can detect linguistic markers of uncertainty, providing instructors with insights into a cadet's decision-making confidence. Additionally, computer vision tools analyze facial expressions, eye movements, and gestures during virtual teamwork assessments to gauge stress levels and collaborative engagement, factors often overlooked in conventional grading systems.

Furthermore, AI-driven assessment dashboards consolidate data from simulators, online learning management systems (LMS), and e-portfolios, generating comprehensive learner profiles. These dashboards visualize patterns in competency development, identify learning gaps, and recommend tailored interventions. For maritime institutions, such systems support continuous monitoring of training quality and compliance with IMO and STCW standards, offering data-backed evidence for accreditation and curriculum improvement (Nyairo et al., 2025).

CHALLENGES, ETHICS, AND PEDAGOGICAL IMPLICATIONS

4.1 Ethical considerations in data use and student privacy

As Artificial Intelligence (AI) and learning analytics become integral to Maritime Education and Training (MET), new ethical challenges emerge concerning data governance, transparency, and the protection of student privacy (Torrisi-Steele, 2025). The growing reliance on digital platforms, simulators, and AI-driven assessment tools has led to an unprecedented accumulation of learner data—from behavioral logs and biometric information to voice recordings and performance analytics. While these data offer valuable insights for improving instruction and competency evaluation, their use also raises critical ethical questions about ownership, consent, and fairness (Micheli et al., 2020). Addressing these issues is essential to ensuring that the integration of AI in maritime education aligns with human-centered and ethical principles.

The foremost ethical concern involves data privacy and informed consent. AI-based maritime learning systems continuously collect sensitive personal data such as biometric information (e.g., heart rate, eye movements), voice patterns, and real-time decision-making behaviors during simulator exercises (Balaji et al., 2025). Without clear consent mechanisms and transparent communication, learners may not fully understand how their data is being used, stored, or shared. Institutions must therefore develop explicit data policies that articulate the purpose, duration, and scope of data collection. Students should have the right to opt in or out, and their consent must be obtained in language that is clear and accessible (Torrisi-Steele, 2025). Ethical data practices also demand compliance with international regulations such as the General Data Protection Regulation (GDPR) or similar local frameworks governing digital data handling.

A second major concern relates to data ownership and access control. In AI-enhanced MET environments, the question of who owns and controls the generated data remains contentious. Is it the student who produces the data, the institution that collects it, or the software provider that processes it? Without clear ownership protocols, there is a risk of data misuse or exploitation by third parties, particularly commercial software vendors (Micheli et al., 2020). Establishing institutional data governance structures that define ownership boundaries and access permissions is therefore vital. Such frameworks should ensure that student data are used exclusively for educational improvement and competency verification, not for profit-driven or surveillance purposes (Micheli et al., 2020).

Another ethical challenge concerns algorithmic bias and fairness. AI systems trained on biased or incomplete datasets may produce unequal outcomes across diverse learner groups (Balaji et al., 2025). For instance, predictive models might inadvertently classify non-native English speakers or learners from underrepresented backgrounds as "at risk" due to linguistic or cultural differences rather than genuine performance deficiencies. To mitigate this, maritime educators must regularly audit algorithms for fairness, transparency, and inclusivity, incorporating human oversight in AI-based decision-making processes to ensure that data interpretations are contextualized and ethically sound (Balaji et al., 2025).

Data security is also a pressing concern. Given the sensitivity of maritime training data—especially those that involve safety protocols, communication logs, and performance metrics—cybersecurity measures must be prioritized. Encryption, anonymization, and secure cloud storage should be standard practices to prevent unauthorized access and data breaches. Regular audits and ethical reviews are necessary to maintain institutional accountability and protect the integrity of student information (Balaji et al., 2025).

Finally, educators must consider the pedagogical ethics of surveillance. While continuous monitoring enables precise feedback and early intervention, excessive data tracking may create anxiety or distrust among learners. Striking a balance between analytics and autonomy is critical; AI tools should empower learners rather than constrain them under constant observation (Balaji et al., 2025; Torrisi-Steele, 2025).

4.2 Pedagogical tensions between automation and experiential seamanship training

The growth of AI and automation in maritime education has made people both excited and scared. These technologies promise accuracy, speed, and personalized learning, but they also challenge the traditional way of teaching seamanship, which is based on human experience, intuition, and judgment gained through direct interaction with real maritime environments. This intersection between automation and experiential learning creates a profound pedagogical tension: how can maritime education embrace technological innovation without compromising the embodied, situational, and ethical dimensions that define professional seamanship?

Historically, experiential seamanship training has relied on apprenticeship and mentorship frameworks, facilitating knowledge transfer through observation, repetition, and situational decision-making at sea. Cadets learn to read environmental signals like wind, current, vessel motion, and human behavior by using their senses. These unspoken types of knowledge, which are often called "maritime intuition," are hard to write down or copy in digital simulations. As automation becomes more common in ship operations, thanks to autopilot systems, integrated navigation bridges, and autonomous vessel technologies, seafarers may become too dependent on AI systems and lose touch with basic manual skills and situational awareness.

In the classroom and simulator settings, this tension shows up in the way that AI-powered systems can both help and hurt learning. On the one hand, smart simulators offer adaptive scenarios, instant feedback, and data-driven assessments that make technical accuracy and decision-making speed much better. An AI system can, for instance, simulate dangerous situations like avoiding collisions in fog or machinery failure in heavy seas without putting cadets in danger. It can look at reaction times, how well procedures are followed, and how people communicate, giving detailed debriefs that go well beyond what human instructors can keep track of by hand. These features will definitely make learning more effective and easier to measure.

But this same automation makes it harder to develop experiential judgment and emotional skills. Real seamanship is more than just knowing how to do things technically; it also includes being able to control your emotions, make moral decisions, and stay strong in tough, high-pressure situations. AI systems can imitate stress but cannot completely emulate the sensory unpredictability and moral quandaries of the open sea. Cadets who learn mostly through automated systems may have a hard time applying what they've learned in real-life situations. The lack of variability in the real world may also make it harder to develop "practical wisdom," which is the ability to make decisions that are appropriate for the situation when standard procedures don't work.

There is also a conflict between teaching roles and the identity of the teacher. As AI systems take on more teaching tasks, like grading, giving feedback, and delivering content that adapts to each student's needs, the teacher's role as a mentor, moral guide, and interpreter of context may be diminished. Maritime instructors have always shown how to act professionally, be disciplined, and work as a team. These are all important parts of maritime culture and safety. Automation should be viewed as a means to enhance, rather than supplant, the experiential authority of the human instructor. To keep this relationship in balance, teachers need to plan their lessons carefully so that they use AI analytics along with reflective discussions, scenario-based debriefings, and hands-on fieldwork.

The cognitive-behavioral ramifications of automation constitute an additional pedagogical issue. Relying too much on AI-powered navigation and decision-support systems can make it harder to use your hands, think critically, and find mistakes—skills that are very important in emergencies or when a system fails. Because of this, MET institutions need to develop both technological skills and the ability to adapt to and make decisions about people. Combining digital simulation with hands-on learning on board is a promising way to keep this balance.

In conclusion, the tension between automation and experiential seamanship training is not a binary conflict but a call for pedagogical equilibrium. The future of maritime education is in human-AI collaboration, where automation makes things safer and more efficient, and experiential learning keeps the intuition, ethics, and resilience that are important for seafaring. Finding this balance makes sure that cadets not only learn how to use intelligent systems, but also stay smart operators who can confidently and wisely navigate both oceans and algorithms.

4.3 Barriers to institutional adoption: infrastructure, readiness, and digital literacy

The integration of Artificial Intelligence (AI), learning analytics, and adaptive technologies into Maritime Education and Training (MET) presents vast opportunities for innovation. However, successful adoption remains uneven across institutions due to structural, cultural, and human capacity constraints (Koo et al., 2024). Many maritime academies, particularly in developing regions, face persistent barriers related to infrastructure, institutional readiness, and digital literacy, which collectively hinder the full realization of AI's transformative potential. Understanding these challenges is essential for creating sustainable and equitable pathways toward digital transformation in maritime education.

The first major obstacle is technological infrastructure. Effective AI implementation requires robust digital ecosystems, including high-speed internet, powerful computing systems, cloud-based storage, and advanced simulation facilities (Ibrahim, 2024). Yet, many maritime institutions—especially those in low- and middle-income countries—continue to operate with outdated hardware, limited bandwidth, and unreliable power supply. AI-enhanced simulators, data analytics tools, and intelligent tutoring systems demand substantial processing power and real-time data transfer capabilities. Without sufficient infrastructure, even the best-designed AI platforms cannot function optimally. Moreover, the maintenance and upgrading of maritime simulators, servers, and cybersecurity systems impose significant financial burdens on institutions already constrained by limited budgets. Consequently, AI integration often remains superficial, restricted to pilot projects or demonstration modules rather than full-scale implementation.

The second barrier involves institutional readiness, encompassing organizational culture, leadership commitment, and policy alignment. Many maritime institutions still adhere to traditional pedagogical paradigms that prioritize instructor-led lectures and standardized training over innovation-driven learning (Wasson et al., 2024). Resistance to change—rooted in fears of job displacement, uncertainty about technology's pedagogical value, or lack of institutional incentives—slows this adoption. In some cases, administrative systems lack the strategic planning capacity to integrate AI within long-term institutional frameworks. The absence of coherent digital transformation policies, quality assurance mechanisms, and ethical guidelines further complicates implementation. Successful AI adoption requires not only technological capability but also organizational agility, where leadership promotes experimentation, cross-departmental collaboration, and continuous professional development for educators.

A third and equally critical challenge lies in digital literacy and human capacity. Effective use of AI tools depends on the technological competence of instructors, students, and administrative staff. Many maritime educators possess extensive sea experience and domain expertise but limited exposure to digital pedagogy or data analytics. This skill gap can result in underutilization or misuse of AI platforms. Similarly, students from varying socio-economic backgrounds may have unequal access to digital devices and online learning environments, thus creating layers of inequality within classrooms. Bridging this divide calls for systematic upskilling programs, digital literacy workshops, and mentorship initiatives that empower both faculty and cadets to confidently engage with AI technologies.

Furthermore, language and cultural barriers can impede AI adoption. Most AI-driven educational platforms are developed in English and designed for Western contexts, which may not align with local maritime communication norms or pedagogical practices. As such, localization and contextual adaptation are necessary to ensure relevance and inclusivity.

Finally, policy and regulatory frameworks often lag behind technological innovations. Without clear standards for data privacy, intellectual property, and AI ethics, maritime institutions may hesitate to implement large-scale digital systems due to potential legal and ethical risks. International collaboration and alignment with organizations such as the International Maritime Organization (IMO) and the International Labour Organization (ILO) are vital for developing standardized, globally recognized frameworks for AI integration in MET (Ibrahim, 2024).

FUTURE DIRECTIONS AND POLICY IMPLICATIONS

5.1 Designing competency-based, AI-driven maritime curricula

The future of Maritime Education and Training (MET) lies in reimagining curricula that seamlessly integrate Artificial Intelligence (AI) with competency-based education (CBE) frameworks. As the global maritime industry transitions toward digitalized and automated operations, traditional time-based and content-heavy curricula are no longer sufficient. The next generation of maritime professionals must possess not only technical skills but also digital literacy, adaptability, ethical awareness, and problem-solving abilities suited to complex, data-driven environments. Designing competency-based, AI-driven curricula thus represents both an educational innovation and a strategic necessity to align maritime training with the evolving demands of the global shipping sector.

Competency-based education focuses on measurable outcomes rather than time spent in training. In an AI-enhanced maritime curriculum, competencies are not static checklists but dynamic constructs shaped by real-time performance analytics and adaptive feedback. For example, instead of completing a fixed number of simulation hours, cadets advance upon demonstrating mastery in specific tasks such as collision avoidance, energy management, or emergency decision-making. AI systems embedded within simulators and e-learning platforms track learner performance across multiple indicators—response accuracy, decision efficiency, teamwork, and communication clarity—and generate data-driven competency profiles. These profiles enable personalized learning trajectories, ensuring that each cadet reaches the required skill threshold while progressing at an individualized pace.

The design of such curricula requires a modular and integrative structure. Core modules should address foundational maritime knowledge, while specialized modules incorporate AI-supported navigation systems, predictive maintenance, and cyber-security awareness. Each module must embed learning analytics and feedback loops, allowing continuous assessment and adaptive content delivery. For instance, an AI-driven bridge management module can adjust scenario complexity based on the learner's proficiency, while predictive analytics can identify areas requiring remediation before certification. This adaptive curriculum model supports the International Maritime Organization's (IMO) emphasis on evidence-based, outcome-oriented training aligned with the Standards of Training, Certification and Watchkeeping for Seafarers (STCW).

Moreover, AI-driven curricula enable interdisciplinary learning that bridges maritime operations, data science, and human factors engineering. Future maritime officers must interpret digital navigation data, analyze sensor outputs, and collaborate with automated systems—all of which demand cognitive flexibility and technological fluency. Integrating AI tools such as virtual reality (VR) simulators, digital twins, and machine learning-based assessment dashboards enhances both experiential and analytical dimensions of learning. These technologies promote deeper understanding of system interdependencies and foster situational judgment, critical for safe and sustainable maritime operations.

However, curriculum design must also address ethical and socio-technical dimensions of AI adoption. Courses should include components on digital ethics, data privacy, and human–AI collaboration to prepare seafarers for responsible technology use. Embedding these topics cultivates reflective practitioners who understand not only how to operate intelligent systems but also how to critically evaluate their implications for safety, equity, and accountability.

Institutional readiness is equally important. Faculty members must be equipped with pedagogical and technical competencies to design, implement, and evaluate AI-driven learning experiences. This may involve professional development programs, cross-institutional collaborations, and partnerships with maritime technology providers to ensure curricula remain current with industry innovations.

In conclusion, designing competency-based, AI-driven maritime curricula represents a paradigm shift from rigid, time-bound instruction to flexible, data-informed learning ecosystems. It ensures that maritime education evolves in tandem with technological transformation—producing professionals who are not merely compliant with global standards but capable of leading innovation at sea and ashore.

Through such forward-looking curricular frameworks, MET institutions can anchor maritime excellence in the intelligence, adaptability, and ethical awareness of the digital age.

5.2 Institutional and policy frameworks for AI integration in METs

The successful integration of Artificial Intelligence (AI) into Maritime Education and Training (MET) depends not only on technological readiness but also on robust institutional and policy frameworks that ensure ethical, sustainable, and equitable implementation. AI adoption in maritime education is inherently systemic—it reshapes governance, pedagogy, accreditation, and professional standards. Therefore, designing institutional and policy structures that align innovation with accountability is essential to ensure that AI enhances, rather than disrupts, the integrity of maritime training worldwide (Karimi et al., 2024).

At the institutional level, AI integration begins with visionary leadership and clear strategic direction. Maritime academies and training centers must embed AI within their long-term development plans, supported by policies that define objectives, standards, and evaluation mechanisms. Institutional frameworks should articulate a shared vision of "AI for maritime competency," emphasizing both digital innovation and human-centered values. Governance bodies—comprising administrators, educators, IT specialists, and maritime regulators—must coordinate the planning, deployment, and monitoring of AI systems to maintain alignment with global standards such as the International Maritime Organization (IMO)'s *Standards of Training, Certification and Watchkeeping (STCW)* (Meštrović et al., 2024).

A key component of institutional readiness is the establishment of AI ethics and data governance committees. These bodies oversee data collection, processing, and storage in compliance with privacy regulations, ensuring transparency and fairness in AI-driven learning analytics and assessment. They also safeguard against algorithmic bias and prevent misuse of learner data. Instructors and administrators should be trained in AI ethics, enabling them to make informed pedagogical and administrative decisions grounded in both technological understanding and professional integrity.

Policy frameworks at the national and international levels are equally crucial to standardize and guide AI implementation across the maritime sector. National maritime authorities, higher education ministries, and accreditation agencies must collaborate to develop policies that ensure AI-based educational tools meet rigorous quality assurance standards. This includes criteria for data security, interoperability, and algorithmic transparency. Policymakers should establish certification pathways for AI-assisted maritime courses and define guidelines for virtual and augmented simulation training so that competencies developed through AI-mediated platforms remain valid under international maritime conventions.

At the global governance level, international organizations such as the IMO, the International Labour Organization (ILO), and the International Association of Maritime Universities (IAMU) play pivotal roles in fostering transnational collaboration. They can facilitate the development of global benchmarks for AI literacy among seafarers, promote cross-border sharing of best practices, and create standardized evaluation rubrics for AI-supported training programs. Such frameworks ensure that seafarers trained in different parts of the world possess comparable digital competencies, supporting crew mobility and interoperability in the global maritime workforce.

Institutional and policy frameworks must also address capacity building and equity. Many institutions face gaps in infrastructure, funding, and human expertise. Policies should therefore encourage public–private partnerships, industry collaborations, and funding mechanisms to support digital transformation. Additionally, inclusivity must be prioritized—ensuring equal access to AI technologies for institutions in developing maritime nations through subsidized licenses, open-source learning tools, and regional knowledge-sharing initiatives.

In conclusion, effective institutional and policy frameworks for AI integration in METs require the convergence of visionary leadership, ethical governance, and international collaboration. When policies are grounded in transparency, inclusivity, and global standards, AI becomes not a disruptive force but a catalyst for educational excellence and operational safety. By aligning institutional strategies with coherent regulatory frameworks, maritime education can confidently navigate the digital era—equipping seafarers with the competencies, ethics, and adaptability needed for the intelligent ships and ports of the future.

5.3 Research gaps and the roadmap toward human-AI co-learning ecosystems

Despite the rapid advancement of Artificial Intelligence (AI) in Maritime Education and Training (MET), the integration of AI technologies into teaching, learning, and assessment remains in its formative stages. Numerous studies highlight the potential benefits of AI in simulation, adaptive learning, and data analytics; however, significant research gaps persist in understanding how these tools can be sustainably embedded into maritime pedagogy and institutional frameworks (Reyes, 2025). Addressing these gaps is essential to constructing a future-ready human–AI co-learning ecosystem—a collaborative model where technology enhances, rather than replaces, human expertise.

One major gap lies in the empirical validation of AI-assisted learning outcomes within maritime contexts. Existing research often focuses on the technical functionalities of AI tools, such as performance monitoring and navigation simulation. However, limited longitudinal studies examine how AI impacts learner cognition, critical thinking, and professional judgment in complex maritime scenarios. There is a pressing need for experimental and mixed-method research that evaluates the comparative effectiveness of AI-mediated learning against traditional or hybrid methods. Evidence-based research can help determine whether AI improves safety competence, decision-making accuracy, and retention of operational knowledge.

A second research gap concerns the psychological and human–machine interaction dimensions of AI integration. Maritime training emphasizes teamwork, leadership, and emotional regulation—skills that involve empathy and intuition, which are difficult for AI systems to replicate (Järvelä et al., 2023). Yet, little is known about how continuous interaction with intelligent systems affects learner motivation, autonomy, and confidence. Questions regarding "automation bias," where trainees may overtrust AI-generated feedback, remain underexplored. Future research should thus investigate how cadets negotiate agency and trust in human–AI learning environments, as well as how instructors can scaffold ethical engagement with automated systems.

Another critical gap exists in the institutional readiness and equity dimensions of AI adoption. Few studies examine the organizational transformation required for sustainable implementation, such as faculty digital upskilling and data governance policies. Comparative analyses across maritime institutions in different regions could reveal disparities in access, digital literacy, and technological infrastructure. Without addressing these inequities, AI adoption risks widening the global competence gap between developed and developing maritime nations (Reyes, 2025).

To bridge these gaps, a roadmap toward human–AI co-learning ecosystems is essential. Such a roadmap should begin with a multilevel research agenda integrating pedagogical innovation, technological design, and policy development. First, collaborative research networks among maritime universities, AI developers, and industry partners can foster the co-creation of AI tools tailored to the unique needs of

MET (Sharma et al., 2022). Second, establishing open data repositories and interoperability standards would allow cross-institutional learning analytics, promoting comparative research and best-practice sharing. Third, research should prioritize human-centered AI design, ensuring systems are transparent, explainable, and adaptable to different learner contexts.

At the pedagogical level, the roadmap envisions human–AI co-learning models where instructors and AI systems work synergistically. Instructors act as facilitators and ethical interpreters of AI feedback, while AI provides adaptive support and cognitive augmentation. This model encourages lifelong learning and reflective practice—qualities vital for operating in increasingly automated maritime environments.

CONCLUSION

The incorporation of Artificial Intelligence (AI) into Maritime Education and Training (MET) signifies a crucial evolution in the preparation of seafarers for the exigencies of a highly digitized and automated maritime sector. AI-driven tools, such as intelligent tutoring platforms, adaptive learning systems, predictive analytics, and e-assessment dashboards, are changing the way teachers teach. They are making learning more personalized, based on data, and focused on skills. This change means moving away from traditional teaching that focuses on memorization and uniformity and toward dynamic, learner-centered education that is based on constant feedback and performance analytics.

The conversation makes it clear that AI has a lot of potential to make learning more efficient, accurate, and accessible, but it needs to be adopted in a way that is ethical, well-prepared by institutions, and focused on people. Policies that make sure data security, fairness, and openness are needed to deal with the problems of infrastructure, digital literacy, and algorithmic bias. Also, maritime teachers need to find the right balance between automation and hands-on learning to keep the human judgment, intuition, and decision-making skills that are important for seamanship.

The future of maritime education will be based on people and AI working together, with technology being an intelligent partner instead of a replacement for human expertise. AI analytics can help competency-based curricula make sure that each student reaches mastery through personalized pathways. At the same time, policy frameworks and global cooperation can protect standardization and fairness.

In the end, the successful use of AI in MET depends not only on new technology but also on a shared commitment to education that is ethical, flexible, and open to everyone. By building ecosystems where people and AI can learn from each other, maritime schools can help future professionals who are not only good at their jobs but also able to think critically, act ethically, and bounce back from setbacks. These professionals will be able to navigate both the physical and digital aspects of the modern maritime world with confidence and wisdom.

REFERENCES

Ala, A., Hamidi, N., Yoniessa, S., Masito, F., & Muis, M. (2024). SIMULATION-BASED LEARNING IN MARITIME TRAINING: ENHANCING COMPETENCY AND PREPAREDNESS. *Meteor Stip Marunda*, *17*(1), 95–102. DOI: 10.36101/msm.v17i1.361

Atik, O. (2020). Eye tracking for assessment of situational awareness in bridge resource management training. *Journal of Eye Movement Research*, *12*(3). Advance online publication. DOI: 10.16910/jemr.12.3.7

Balaji, C., Rajeswari, G., Jain, H., Menaka, S., & Shukla, S. (2025). Understanding Data Privacy and Ethical Considerations in Learning Analytics., 579-606. DOI: 10.4018/979-8-3693-8593-7.ch034

Bayotas, M. (2024). Shifting from global maritime professional to global maritime citizen.. DOI: 10.5821/mt.13183

Bello, H., & Abdullah, N. (2021). Investigating the Influence of Quality Factors on User Satisfaction with Summative Computer-based Assessment. *Electronic Journal of e-Learning*, *19*(6), 490–503. DOI: 10.34190/ejel.19.6.2487

Chen, L., Chen, P., & Lin, Z. (2020). Artificial Intelligence in Education: A Review. *IEEE Access : Practical Innovations, Open Solutions*, *8*, 75264–75278. DOI: 10.1109/ACCESS.2020.2988510

Dawat, E. (2023). Advancing Education Through Data Analytics and Artificial Intelligence: A Comprehensive Literature Review. *International Journal of Research Publications*, *137*(1). Advance online publication. DOI: 10.47119/IJRP1001371120235686

Gardner, J., O'Leary, M., & Yuan, L. (2021). Artificial intelligence in educational assessment: 'Breakthrough? Or buncombe and ballyhoo?'. *Journal of Computer Assisted Learning*, *37*(5), 1207–1216. DOI: 10.1111/jcal.12577

Göçen, A., & Aydemir, F. (2020). Artificial Intelligence in Education and Schools. *Research on Education and Media*, *12*(1), 13–21. DOI: 10.2478/rem-2020-0003

Harrington, S., & Sellberg, C. (2024). User wants, needs and resistance in the postdigital university: prioritizing pedagogical concerns in learning analytics design. DOI: 10.21203/rs.3.rs-5561942/v1

Ibrahim, A. (2024). The influence of computerized simulation techniques on maritime security exercises: ISPS code. *Maritime Research and Technology*, *3*(1), 1. DOI: 10.21622/MRT.2024.03.1.747

Järvelä, S., Zhao, G., Heikkilä, J., Järvenoja, H., Mikkonen, K., & Kaleva, S. (2023). Hybrid Intelligence – Human-AI Co-Evolution and Learning in Multirealities (HI).. DOI: 10.3233/FAIA230107

Karimi, E., Smith, J., Billard, R., & Veitch, B. (2024). AI-based adaptive instructional systems for maritime safety training: A systematic literature review. *Discover Artificial Intelligence*, *4*(1), 51. Advance online publication. DOI: 10.1007/s44163-024-00153-0

Koo, K., Rødseth, Ø., Lislebø, G., & Ulvensøen, J. (2024). Harmonizing Maritime Innovation: Enhancing International and National Standardization in Intelligent Ship Transport Systems. *Journal of Physics: Conference Series*, *2867*(1), 012023. DOI: 10.1088/1742-6596/2867/1/012023

Koshiry, A., & Tony, M. (2025). Enabling smart education: An overview of innovations and challenges in modern learning. *International Journal of Innovative Research and Scientific Studies*, *8*(2), 3184–3200. DOI: 10.53894/ijirss.v8i2.5962

Meštrović, T., Pavić, I., Maljković, M., & Androjna, A. (2024). Challenges for the Education and Training of Seafarers in the Context of Autonomous Shipping: Bibliometric Analysis and Systematic Literature Review. *Applied Sciences (Basel, Switzerland)*, *14*(8), 3173. DOI: 10.3390/app14083173

Micheli, M., Ponti, M., Craglia, M., & Suman, A. (2020). Emerging models of data governance in the age of datafication. *Big Data & Society*, *7*(2), 2053951720948087. Advance online publication. DOI: 10.1177/2053951720948087

Mke, D. (2024). Assessment of Digital Competencies in South African Maritime Education and Training Institutions: A Study of Evaluation Methods for Future Seafarers. *SAJMET*, *3*, 103–120. DOI: 10.47348/SAJMET/2024/i1a8

Nyairo, F., Haavardtun, P., Lindroos, E., Munim, Z., Lampiola, J., Salokorpi, M., & Krabbel, H. (2025). Instructional Approaches for Simulator-Based Maritime. *Education + Training*, *1274*, 120–131. DOI: 10.1007/978-3-031-84170-5_11

Ouyang, F., Wu, M., Zheng, L., Zhang, L., & Jiao, P. (2023). Integration of artificial intelligence performance prediction and learning analytics to improve student learning in online engineering course. *International Journal of Educational Technology in Higher Education*, *20*(1), 4. Advance online publication. DOI: 10.1186/s41239-022-00372-4

Pereira, L., Ambrozio, A., Favarato, C., Brito, R., Nascimento, J., Souza, G., & Gonçalves, P. (2024). USO DE BIG DATA NA EDUCAÇÃO: COMO O ANALYTICS APOIA DECISÕES PEDAGÓGICAS. *LEV*, *15*(43), 8028–8039. DOI: 10.56238/levv15n43-029

Reyes, S. (2025). Status, Applications, and Prospects of AI in Maritime Education: Basis for Curriculum Planning. DOI: 10.21203/rs.3.rs-7827795/v1

Sharma, A., Undheim, P., & Nazir, S. (2022). Design and implementation of AI chatbot for COLREGs training. *Wmu Journal of Maritime Affairs*, *22*(1), 107–123. DOI: 10.1007/s13437-022-00284-0

Sihombing, D., Dwiyani, N., Martha, Y., Hutabarat, C., & Sutrisno, S. (2024). IMPACT OF INTERNATIONAL STANDARDS ON MARITIME EDUCATION: PERSPECTIVES OF JUNIOR CADETS. *Meteor Stip Marunda*, *17*(1), 7–15. DOI: 10.36101/msm.v17i1.357

Sijabat, P., Simanjuntak, M., Mudakir, M., Putrawan, B., & Lumingkewas, M. (2024). EMPOWERING LITERACY IN MARITIME EDUCATION: STRATEGIES AND PROFESSIONALISM ALIGNMENT. *Meteor Stip Marunda*, *17*(1), 42–50. DOI: 10.36101/msm.v17i1.359

Talan, T. and DEMIRBILEK, M. (2022). Bibliometric Analysis of Research on Learning Analytics Based on Web of Science Database. Informatics in Education. DOI: 10.15388/infedu.2023.02

Torrisi-Steele, G. (2025). AI and the Ethics of Student Data Privacy, 53-76. DOI: 10.4018/979-8-3373-2397-8.ch003

Türkistanlı, T. (2023). Advanced learning methods in maritime education and training: A bibliometric analysis on the digitalization of education and modern trends. *Computer Applications in Engineering Education*, *32*(1), e22690. Advance online publication. DOI: 10.1002/cae.22690

Wasson, B., Giannakos, M., Blikstad-Balas, M., Uppstad, P., Langford, M., & Bøhn, E. (2024). Implementing Learning Analytics in Norway. *Journal of Learning Analytics*, *11*(2), 268–280. DOI: 10.18608/jla.2024.8241

Chapter 2
Learning Beyond the Deck:
Mobile Learning and Micro-Credentialing Pathways for Lifelong Maritime Education

Chindy Adsaria Lembang
http://orcid.org/0009-0003-6680-5776
Politeknik Ilmu Pelayaran Makassar, Indonesia

Faisal Saransi
http://orcid.org/0000-0002-1505-8219
Politeknik Ilmu Pelayaran Makassar, Indonesia

Wardimansyah Ridwan
Universitas Negeri Makassar, Indonesia

ABSTRACT

This research examines the amalgamation of mobile learning and micro-credentialing as innovative approaches for continuous maritime education. It shows how digital technologies, modular learning, and competency-based frameworks can make the maritime industry more accessible, adaptable, and relevant to professionals. The conversation looks at the best practices, governance models, and policy directions from around the world that support learning ecosystems that are both sustainable and open to everyone. To improve workforce mobility and ongoing professional development, the focus is on digital infrastructure, collaboration among stakeholders, and interoperability between regions. The proposed framework envisions a globally connected maritime education system that promotes innovation, equity, and environmental responsibility, ensuring seafarers remain competent and future-ready in the era of digital and green transformation.

THE EVOLVING LANDSCAPE OF MARITIME EDUCATION IN THE DIGITAL ERA

1.1. Transformations in Maritime Learning Paradigms

As schools respond to the fast pace of technological, economic, and environmental change, the maritime education landscape has changed a lot. The emergence of digital and hybrid ecosystems is changing

DOI: 10.4018/979-8-3373-6670-8.ch002

traditional learning models that are based on classroom instruction and simulator training. The incorporation of digital tools has improved the effectiveness and security of maritime training procedures, offering students innovative approaches that connect theory and practice (Türkistanlı, 2023; Fernandes, 2025). To deal with the problems of global maritime operations, maritime academies, shipping companies, and regulatory bodies are using technology-enhanced learning more and more. Hybrid learning models now combine theory and practice through e-learning modules, immersive simulations, and onboard mobile applications. This has led to a shift in teaching methods from instructor-centered training to learner-centered, data-informed, and competency-based approaches (Diahyleva et al., 2025). This change gives seafarers the chance to keep growing professionally while also supporting the industry's push for more flexibility in meeting its needs. Kristiawan, 2025).

Globalization and digitalization have become pivotal forces influencing maritime education policies. As maritime trade grows and new technologies like automation, AI, and smart logistics change how ports and ships work, the maritime industry—one of the most internationalized sectors—needs workers who are good at more than just technical navigation and engineering (Purba & Simanjuntak, 2024;, (Pimiä et al., 2024; . The focus has shifted to interdisciplinary competence, which includes being good with technology, being aware of the environment, and being able to adapt to different cultures (Wang et al., 2023;, (Pimiä et al., 2024; . Sustainability has become a key part of learning design, showing that the industry is committed to the United Nations Sustainable Development Goals (SDGs) and the International Maritime Organization's (IMO) decarbonization goals. More and more, curricula are including topics like green shipping, energy efficiency, and environmental ethics (Pimiä et al., 2024;, Cahyadi et al., 2024). Consequently, maritime educators must cultivate seafarers who are both technically skilled and environmentally conscious (Belabyad et al., 2025; Kristiawan, 2025).

Digitalization has led to the creation of new rules for governance and quality assurance in the industry. Institutions are putting in place digital assessment systems and e-certification mechanisms that are in line with global standards like the Standards of Training, Certification, and Watchkeeping (STCW) Convention. These efforts make things more open, easy to track, and recognize people's skills across borders, which is very important in the digital age (Mataac et al., 2024). Aligning maritime education and training (MET) with global standards not only confirms the skills learned but also gives stakeholders peace of mind that quality will keep getting better (Mke, 2024). Partnerships between governments, businesses, and schools are becoming more and more important to encourage innovation and adapt to changes in the global labor market (Hendriawan et al., 2025).

The IMO's digitalization agenda and the larger idea of Industry 5.0 have changed what lifelong learning means for people who work in the maritime industry. Industry 5.0 stresses the need for educational systems that are ethical, sustainable, and focused on people (Belabyad et al., 2025; Diahyleva et al., 2025). It also stresses the synergy between human expertise and smart technologies. Lifelong learning has become necessary, with digital platforms and micro-learning pathways supporting ongoing cycles of upskilling, reskilling, and credentialing. The contemporary mariner is conceptualized not solely as a laborer but as a perpetual learner and a catalyst for innovation (Rahmawati et al., 2025). As maritime education progresses into the future, it must find a balance between technological efficiency and the preservation of human values. This will ensure that digital transformation enhances, rather than replaces, the professional identity, resilience, and global citizenship of the maritime workforce (Gray & Jónsson, 2022).

1.2 Drivers of Lifelong Maritime Learning

The maritime industry is going through a big change in technology, environmental responsibility, and the way people work. These factors are changing the skills that maritime professionals need and pushing the world toward lifelong learning. The period of fixed training cycles and static certification is being replaced by dynamic, ongoing professional development facilitated by digital and modular learning pathways (Jo et al., 2020; Humphries et al., 2022). In an industry where automation, artificial intelligence (AI), and sustainability are important, lifelong learning is now necessary to stay compliant, keep operations safe, and encourage adaptability (Arifin, 2023; Elhussieny et al., 2023). The International Maritime Organization (IMO) has recognized the need for seafarers to stay up-to-date as maritime technology changes quickly. This shift toward continuous education is in line with that. It stresses the importance of integrating training with real-world use (Kuncowati et al., 2022).

New skills in green shipping, AI navigation, and smart port management are at the heart of this change. The International Maritime Organization's (IMO) greenhouse gas (GHG) strategy is pushing the global maritime sector to reduce its carbon footprint. This means that maritime education and training (MET) needs to include environmental literacy and green technologies (Kuncowati et al., 2022; Elhussieny et al., 2023). Seafarers are now expected to know about low-emission propulsion systems, energy efficiency protocols, ballast water management, and ways to cut down on waste (Arifin, 2023;). At the same time, the growing use of AI-assisted navigation systems, predictive maintenance tools, and autonomous vessels shows that we need a new generation of professionals who are good with computers. Skills in data analytics, cybersecurity, and algorithmic decision-making are now as important as traditional seamanship skills (Jo et al., 2020; Humphries et al., 2022). At the same time, the growth of smart ports, which are made possible by IoT connectivity, blockchain logistics, and real-time monitoring, means that maritime officers and port managers need to work in integrated, data-driven environments. This makes the need for modern skills even more important (Arifin, 2023; Elhussieny et al., 2023).

This changing skill landscape has made it even more important for workers to keep learning and getting new certifications. The STCW Convention and other rules in the maritime industry require regular training and certification renewal, but modern trends in the industry go far beyond just following the rules. Global shipping companies and training providers are incorporating micro-credentialing systems and modular learning formats that allow seafarers to rapidly enhance specific skills in response to technological progress (Humphries et al., 2022; Темјановски et al., 2023). In a world where automation and environmental rules are always changing the way things work, workers need to keep learning to stay strong. The transition to lifelong learning signifies the industry's acknowledgment that maritime education should not be confined to pre-sea or early-career phases; it must develop to support professionals throughout their careers (Humphries et al., 2022; Main & Anderson, 2023).

The fact that seafarers are going from doing manual work to doing knowledge work shows how much things are changing. Seafarers today need to be able to think flexibly, solve problems, and work together online as part of their daily lives. Modern ships have turned into floating data centers, and maritime workers are spending more and more time keeping an eye on, understanding, and improving complex digital systems. Seafarers, as knowledge workers, must navigate both the physical seas and the extensive oceans of data and automation (Jo et al., 2020; Humphries et al., 2022). To embrace this new identity, you need to be curious, flexible, and willing to learn new things for the rest of your life. So, the maritime education system needs to keep changing to include flexible, technology-based models that help seafarers stay relevant, skilled, and competitive around the world as the world goes digital and green (Humphries et al., 2022; Темјановски et al., 2023).

1.3 Challenges and Opportunities in Digital Transition

The digital transformation of maritime education and training (MET) presents both significant challenges and promising opportunities. As institutions worldwide shift from traditional learning modes to digital ecosystems, disparities in accessibility, infrastructure, and policy readiness have become increasingly apparent. The maritime sector, characterized by its global workforce and diverse socioeconomic contexts, faces the complex task of ensuring that the benefits of digital learning are equitably distributed among seafarers, regardless of location, nationality, or institutional affiliation. The transition toward digitalization, while accelerating innovation, also demands careful navigation of equity, sustainability, and inclusivity concerns.

Accessibility remains one of the foremost challenges in maritime learning contexts. Many training institutions, particularly in developing and island nations, struggle with limited digital infrastructure, high connectivity costs, and inconsistent access to reliable internet—factors that hinder the effective delivery of online learning. Seafarers working in remote oceanic routes often experience connectivity disruptions, limiting their participation in synchronous virtual training. Moreover, digital inequality extends to learners' technological literacy: older or less tech-savvy seafarers may face barriers to engaging with digital platforms, while younger learners adapt more readily. Bridging these divides requires investments in low-bandwidth learning solutions, offline-capable mobile applications, and tailored digital literacy programs that ensure all learners can benefit from technology-enhanced education.

Institutional readiness and policy alignment represent another critical challenge. While leading maritime academies have integrated e-learning platforms, simulation technologies, and learning management systems (LMS), many others remain constrained by outdated curricula and rigid accreditation frameworks. Existing international regulations, including the Standards of Training, Certification and Watchkeeping (STCW) Convention, were not originally designed for digital or hybrid instruction. This creates policy gaps in areas such as virtual assessment, online certification, and cross-border recognition of digital credentials. To address these, institutions must collaborate with regulatory bodies, such as the International Maritime Organization (IMO) and regional maritime authorities, to develop governance structures that support digital transformation without compromising quality assurance. Faculty training and institutional digital strategies are also essential to ensure pedagogical coherence and sustainability.

Despite these challenges, the digital transition offers transformative opportunities for inclusive, flexible, and learner-centered maritime education. Online and mobile learning platforms extend the reach of maritime programs to seafarers who might otherwise be excluded due to geographic or occupational constraints. Modular learning, micro-credentialing, and adaptive learning analytics allow individualized pathways for skill development, aligning education with real-time industry needs. Virtual reality (VR), augmented reality (AR), and AI-powered simulators further enrich experiential learning while reducing operational costs and environmental impact. Digitalization also enables greater gender inclusivity and accessibility for underrepresented groups in maritime professions. Ultimately, the digital transition—if supported by equitable policies and robust infrastructure—can democratize maritime education, transforming it into a global, sustainable, and lifelong learning ecosystem that empowers every seafarer to thrive in the era of Industry 5.0.

MOBILE LEARNING AS A CATALYST FOR MARITIME KNOWLEDGE EXPANSION

2.1 Foundations of Mobile Learning (m-Learning)

Mobile learning (m-learning) has emerged as a transformative force in maritime education, offering flexible, accessible, and context-sensitive learning experiences that extend beyond the physical confines of classrooms and training simulators. Defined as the use of portable digital devices—such as smartphones, tablets, and wearable technologies—to facilitate anytime, anywhere learning, m-learning promotes continuous professional development across the global maritime workforce. Its defining principles—portability, personalization, and interactivity—make it particularly suitable for the unique learning environments faced by seafarers who operate across time zones and remote locations. Global best practices show that m-learning, when thoughtfully designed, enhances engagement, retention, and performance by placing learners at the center of the educational process.

International models of m-learning implementation in technical and vocational education have demonstrated its value in bridging the gap between theory and practice. In maritime contexts, where experiential learning and skill mastery are essential, m-learning provides an effective medium for integrating conceptual knowledge with operational competence. For instance, mobile applications can deliver interactive modules on ship safety, navigation, and emergency protocols, allowing seafarers to review procedures on demand. This aligns with the principles of just-in-time learning, enabling learners to access relevant content precisely when needed. Case studies from the European Maritime Safety Agency (EMSA) and the Maritime and Port Authority of Singapore (MPA) have illustrated how mobile learning platforms can complement simulator-based training, supporting continuous learning both onshore and at sea.

The pedagogical affordances of m-learning for maritime education are particularly noteworthy. Mobile devices can support multimodal learning through videos, infographics, interactive quizzes, and augmented reality (AR), thereby accommodating diverse learning styles. These tools allow learners to visualize complex ship systems, practice navigational decision-making, and simulate emergency responses without physical simulators. Furthermore, mobile platforms enable reflective learning and self-assessment, promoting metacognitive awareness among trainees. Collaborative applications also facilitate peer-to-peer knowledge sharing, mentoring, and discussion across dispersed maritime communities, creating virtual learning networks that strengthen professional identity and teamwork. The immediacy and interactivity of mobile learning foster a more engaging and learner-driven environment, encouraging autonomy and lifelong learning habits.

Integration of m-learning into blended and simulation-based maritime programs represents a strategic innovation. Rather than replacing traditional methods, mobile learning serves as a complementary layer that enhances flexibility and accessibility. Blended approaches combine formal instruction with digital engagement, allowing learners to reinforce classroom concepts through mobile exercises during voyages. In simulation-based programs, mobile platforms can be used for pre-simulation orientation, scenario debriefing, and performance tracking. Such integration promotes continuous competency development while addressing logistical challenges of maritime training schedules. Ultimately, m-learning embodies the spirit of modern maritime education—responsive, adaptive, and learner-centered—helping institutions and seafarers navigate the demands of an increasingly digital and interconnected world.

2.2 Designing Mobile Learning for Maritime Contexts

Mobile learning (m-learning) has become a game-changer in maritime education. It offers flexible, accessible, and context-sensitive learning experiences that go beyond traditional classrooms and training simulators. M-learning is the use of portable digital devices like smartphones, tablets, and wearable technologies to learn at any time and from any location. It also encourages ongoing professional development among the global maritime workforce. The key features of m-learning—portability, personalization, and interactivity—make it a great fit for seafarers, who often work in different time zones and faraway places Meštrović et al. (2024). Thoughtfully designed m-learning can improve engagement, retention, and performance by putting students at the center of the learning process.

International models of m-learning implementation in technical and vocational education illustrate its significant efficacy in reconciling theory with practice. In maritime contexts, where experiential learning and skill mastery are essential, m-learning effectively integrates conceptual knowledge with practical competence. For instance, mobile apps can offer interactive modules on ship safety, navigation, and emergency protocols, allowing seafarers to review procedures whenever they want. This method is in line with the ideas behind just-in-time learning, which lets students get to the information they need right when they need it (Ajayi & Udeh, 2024). Case studies from pertinent maritime agencies further demonstrate how mobile learning platforms can effectively enhance simulator-based training methods, thereby facilitating ongoing education both onshore and at sea.

The educational benefits of m-learning for maritime studies are especially noteworthy. Mobile devices can support multimodal learning by offering a variety of formats, such as videos, infographics, interactive quizzes, and augmented reality (AR). This makes it easier for people with different learning styles to learn. These tools help students see how complicated ship systems work, make decisions about navigation, and practice how to respond to emergencies without needing real-life simulators (Markopoulos et al., 2022). Mobile platforms also make it easier for trainees to learn by reflecting on their own work and assessing their own progress. Collaborative apps, on the other hand, make it easier for people in different maritime communities to share knowledge, mentor each other, and have discussions. This involvement builds virtual learning networks that improve professional identity and teamwork, making m-learning more immediate and interactive, which leads to a more engaged, learner-driven environment (Sudewo et al., 2025).

The incorporation of m-learning into blended and simulation-based maritime programs represents a strategic advancement. Mobile learning doesn't replace traditional methods; instead, it adds a layer that makes them more flexible and accessible. Blended approaches can mix formal teaching with digital interaction. For example, students can reinforce what they learned in class by doing mobile exercises while on a trip. Mobile platforms can help with pre-simulation orientation, scenario debriefing, and performance tracking in simulation-based programs. This helps with ongoing competency development and solves the logistical problems that come with maritime training schedules (Fabian-Perona, 2025). In the end, m-learning is the heart of modern maritime education. It is responsive, adaptable, and focused on the learner. It helps schools and sailors deal with the challenges of a world that is becoming more digital and connected.

2.3 Learner Engagement and Digital Competence

In maritime education, sustaining learner engagement and developing digital competence are crucial to ensuring that mobile learning (m-learning) initiatives achieve meaningful outcomes. Seafarers often operate in isolated environments with limited access to traditional learning support, making motivation and interactivity essential to sustaining participation and knowledge retention. To this end, mobile learning must go beyond content delivery—it must actively engage learners through interaction, gamification, feedback mechanisms, and authentic tasks that mirror real maritime challenges. When designed effectively, m-learning can transform passive learners into active participants who take ownership of their professional growth and continuously refine their competencies in an ever-evolving industry.

Strategies to enhance motivation and interactivity in mobile learning rely on personalization, relevance, and social engagement. Adaptive learning systems can analyze user performance and tailor content to individual needs, ensuring that seafarers receive material suited to their experience level and professional specialization. Gamification elements—such as badges, progress trackers, and leaderboards—have proven effective in increasing motivation by providing visible milestones of achievement. Peer collaboration through discussion forums or mobile-based teamwork tasks further enriches the learning experience, fostering a sense of community and professional solidarity across global maritime networks. Immediate feedback mechanisms, including interactive quizzes and performance dashboards, reinforce learning and sustain engagement even during long voyages where formal supervision may be limited.

Assessment through mobile-based tasks and reflective portfolios provides innovative ways to evaluate competence in maritime contexts. Mobile platforms enable formative assessment through scenario-based simulations, multimedia assignments, and digital logbooks that document learning progress. Seafarers can record short videos demonstrating technical skills, complete interactive navigation challenges, or submit digital reflections on safety practices. These authentic, performance-based assessments align closely with the practical nature of maritime work. Reflective portfolios, integrated into mobile applications, encourage learners to document experiences, analyze decision-making processes, and connect theory to practice. Such self-assessment fosters metacognition and critical thinking, essential qualities for adaptive performance in unpredictable maritime environments (Markopoulos et al., 2022).

Fostering digital literacy and autonomous learning skills is another core dimension of mobile learning for seafarers. Digital competence encompasses not only the ability to use technology effectively but also the capacity to evaluate, communicate, and create information ethically and securely. Training programs must therefore integrate digital literacy modules that address cybersecurity awareness, data management, and responsible digital communication. Encouraging self-directed learning enables seafarers to take initiative, identify skill gaps, and pursue targeted learning opportunities through online and mobile resources. This autonomy supports the principles of lifelong learning, empowering maritime professionals to stay current with evolving technologies, environmental regulations, and operational standards.

In essence, learner engagement and digital competence form the foundation of sustainable mobile maritime education. By blending interactive design, authentic assessment, and digital empowerment, m-learning cultivates a new generation of seafarers who are not only skilled navigators of the seas but also agile learners in the digital age.

MICRO-CREDENTIALING PATHWAYS IN MARITIME PROFESSIONAL DEVELOPMENT

3.1 Concept and Rationale of Micro-Credentials

Micro-credentialing has become a strategic innovation in maritime professional development, offering flexible, modular, and competency-based recognition of learning that meets the needs of the global maritime industry. Micro-credentials are short, focused certifications that show you have mastered certain skills or competencies. They work with traditional degrees and licenses to give you ways to keep learning new skills and improving your old ones (Abdullah & Ghazali, 2023). These credentials, which are usually given out through digital platforms, let students collect, stack, and share their achievements with different schools and employers. The maritime industry needs people to keep learning because technology is always changing, rules are always changing, and the need for sustainability is always changing (Lang, 2023).

Micro-credentials work within established standards and recognition systems to make sure they are credible and can be used in other places. They are built around clear learning goals, ways to grade students, and ways to make sure quality. In maritime education, it is important that these standards match up with international standards like the International Maritime Organization's (IMO) Standards of Training, Certification and Watchkeeping (STCW) Convention, which sets the rules for maritime training and certification around the world (Desmarchelier & Cary, 2022). The STCW establishes the minimum standards for seafarer competence. Micro-credentials, on the other hand, offer pathways for new skills in areas like autonomous vessel operations, digital navigation, cybersecurity, and green shipping (Orman et al., 2023). Additionally, aligning with regional frameworks makes maritime micro-credentials more portable around the world, making sure that they are recognized and valued across national borders (Reed, 2023).

Adding micro-credentials to maritime professional development frameworks makes institutions more flexible and gives learners more control over their own learning. Maritime academies and training centers have the option to modularize their curricula, providing short learning units that can be completed individually or accumulated for advanced certifications (Abdullah & Ghazali, 2023). This method lets seafarers move up in their careers without having to take time off from work, which is especially useful in an industry where working on the sea all the time makes it hard to get a full-time education. Micro-credentials are also good for employers because they make it easier to find the right people for the job by letting companies check specific skills and use their staff more effectively (Zou et al., 2023).

Micro-certifications are useful for more than just getting a job; they also help people move their skills around the world and build professional resilience in a maritime industry that is becoming more automated and focused on sustainability. Micro-credentials help seafarers quickly adapt to changes in technology and new rules. They also make it easier for people to move between different fields of work and improve the integration of formal, non-formal, and informal learning (Raj et al., 2024). As the maritime sector transitions towards a knowledge-based blue economy, micro-credentialing signifies not merely an educational innovation but a paradigm shift—fostering a culture of lifelong learning that equips seafarers to become adaptive, future-ready professionals capable of thriving in an interconnected global workforce (DIAB & ZHANG, 2023).

3.2 Implementation Frameworks for Maritime Institutions

To use micro-credentialing in maritime schools, there needs to be a complete framework that includes policy development, institutional partnerships, governance mechanisms, and technology integration. For maritime academies, training centers, and regulatory bodies, the use of micro-credentials is more than just a new way to teach; it is a change in the way education is structured to be more flexible and focused on the needs of the learner, in line with global standards for competency. For micro-credentialing programs to be successful in the long term, institutional policy must be the basis for them. This means that they must uphold academic integrity, industry relevance, and international recognition. To make this innovation permanent and make sure it has a long-term effect on maritime professional development, there must be clear governance structures, partnerships across sectors, and reliable assessment systems.

Institutional policy and governance frameworks are what make it possible to use micro-credentials effectively. Maritime schools need clear rules about the purpose, structure, and accreditation of micro-credentials in their academic systems. Policies should explain how micro-credentials fit in with or build on existing qualifications and how they fit in with the International Maritime Organization's (IMO) Standards of Training, Certification, and Watchkeeping (STCW) Convention. To make sure that rules are followed and that everything is the same, governance structures must include cooperation between curriculum developers, maritime authorities, industry representatives, and quality assurance bodies. Working with classification societies, shipping companies, and technology providers also helps institutions become stronger by making sure that what students learn is useful in the real world. Co-governance between academia and industry makes sure that micro-credentials stay up to date with new technologies in the maritime industry, like automation, artificial intelligence (AI), and environmental management systems (Abdullah & Ghazali, 2023).

To include micro-credentials in maritime training programs, you need to use a modular, outcome-based approach. You can break up traditional programs into smaller learning units, each of which stands for a separate set of skills that have been tested through strict testing. You can later combine these modules to meet the requirements for higher-level certifications, degrees, or professional licenses. For instance, as part of a larger certification program for sustainable shipping operations, a seafarer might get micro-credentials in digital navigation, cyber safety, and energy efficiency. This modularity lets learners tailor their educational path to fit their career goals and the way they work. Also, schools need to create flexible delivery models that include mobile learning, simulation-based practice, and online assessments to fit the unique schedules and working conditions of seafarers.

The micro-credentialing framework's technological and evaluative core consists of assessment, validation, and digital badge systems. Competency validation should use performance-based tests, simulations, peer evaluations, and digital portfolios to make sure that someone has mastered a skill. Digital badges that use blockchain technology are safe and can be verified as proof of achievement. This lets learners share their credentials with employers and regulatory bodies all over the world. These badges have metadata that includes information about the learning outcomes, the people who gave them out, and the dates they were validated. This makes sure that they are real and clear. By putting these kinds of systems into learning management platforms used by institutions, maritime academies can make dynamic ecosystems for ongoing professional development. In the end, a good implementation framework turns maritime institutions into flexible learning organizations. This gives seafarers the tools they need to keep learning throughout their lives and makes the industry more innovative, sustainable, and competitive on a global scale.

3.3 Global and Regional Best Practices

Numerous maritime education systems globally have effectively integrated micro-credentialing and modular learning into their strategies for modernizing professional development and promoting lifelong learning. Australia, Singapore, and the European Union (EU) show how policy alignment, new technologies, and quality assurance systems can all work together to make micro-credential adoption in maritime education and training (MET) last. These examples from around the world can help ASEAN maritime academies and training centers make their learning environments more flexible, help students find jobs, and get more international recognition.

Australia has been a world leader in adding micro-credentials to vocational and technical education, even in the maritime industry. The Australian Qualifications Framework (AQF) makes it easy to see how micro-credentials fit into formal qualification pathways. Maritime schools like the Australian Maritime College (AMC) now offer modular, stackable courses in maritime safety, logistics, and navigation technology. These courses let students gradually earn qualifications that meet industry standards. The Australian Maritime Safety Authority (AMSA) recognizes these micro-credentials, which are often co-designed with industry partners. This makes sure that academic training meets operational needs. Australia's success shows how important it is for national policies to be consistent and for businesses and schools to work together to keep micro-credential ecosystems going.

Singapore is another good example of micro-credentialing in maritime education because it has strong partnerships between businesses and schools and is ready for digital technology. The Maritime and Port Authority of Singapore (MPA) and the Singapore Maritime Academy (SMA) have led the way in creating digital learning pathways with short, competency-based training modules in areas like port automation, cybersecurity, and sustainable shipping. The Singapore Workforce Skills Qualifications (WSQ) framework, which combines micro-credentials with lifelong learning programs under SkillsFuture Singapore, verifies these modules. They are delivered through blended learning platforms. Singapore's model shows how important it is for the government and businesses to work together, have strong digital infrastructure, and promote a culture of lifelong learning with help from both the government and businesses.

The European Union has also helped the micro-credentialing movement move forward with its European Qualifications Framework (EQF) and European Maritime Safety Agency (EMSA). The European Quality Assurance in Vocational Education and Training (EQAVET) framework makes sure that micro-credentials from maritime training schools all over the EU are portable, work with each other, and are of high quality. SkillSea and MATES are two EU-funded projects that have improved regional cooperation models by adding micro-learning and digital credentials to maritime education. These projects focus on green and digital transitions.

These global practices show ASEAN maritime academies how important it is to make sure that regional frameworks, like the ASEAN Qualifications Reference Framework (AQRF), are in line with global standards. To stay relevant and grow, institutions need to work more closely with shipping companies, regulatory bodies, and technology providers. Accreditation agencies are just as important for protecting quality assurance. Accreditation organizations need to set clear rules for validating micro-credentials, giving out digital badges, and making sure that different institutions can work together. ASEAN maritime institutions can increase global trust, encourage workers to move around, and create strong learning ecosystems that prepare seafarers for the future of sustainable, technology-driven maritime operations by using clear, evidence-based evaluation systems.

INTEGRATING MOBILE LEARNING AND MICRO-CREDENTIALS FOR LIFELONG MARITIME EDUCATION

4.1 Pedagogical Synergies and Curriculum Design

Combining mobile learning and micro-credentials in maritime education is a big step toward lifelong learning systems that are flexible, personalized, and based on skills. Manousou and Galani (2025) say that these two approaches work together to give seafarers access to modular, context-aware learning whenever and wherever they want, while also giving them proof of their successes. This integration fundamentally redefines how maritime professionals acquire, demonstrate, and update their competencies, aligning education with the dynamic technological and regulatory realities of the global maritime industry. By carefully designing their curricula and using new technology, maritime schools can make interconnected ecosystems where mobile learning platforms offer micro-learning content that leads to stackable credentials that are recognized by the industry (Galić et al., 2020).

Mobile learning and micro-credentialing work well together because they both follow the same basic rules of being easy to use, modular, and giving students control over their own learning. Mobile delivery platforms are a good fit for modular micro-learning units, which are short, focused lessons on specific skills. This gives seafarers who have busy schedules more freedom (Темјановски et al., 2023). While on board or during port layovers, learners can take part in digital modules that last five to fifteen minutes and cover topics like safe navigation, energy-efficient vessel operations, or cybersecurity. Completing each module adds to a larger credential, which keeps learning focused on goals and builds on what you've already learned. This modularity also makes adaptive learning systems possible. In these systems, mobile apps look at how well a learner is doing and suggest content that is tailored to their needs to help them fill in skill gaps (Manousou & Galani, 2025). In short, combining mobile micro-learning with micro-credentialing makes sure that maritime education is both flexible and useful in the real world.

Competency-based and just-in-time training methods make this integrated model even more useful and relevant. Unlike traditional training, which follows set schedules, just-in-time learning lets seafarers access micro-modules exactly when they need to learn new skills, like how to fix engine problems or keep up with environmental compliance rules (Korhonen et al., 2020). Competency-based frameworks make sure that each micro-module meets measurable performance standards and international standards, like the STCW Convention from the International Maritime Organization (Galić et al., 2020). Mobile platforms that include assessment tools like scenario-based simulations, digital quizzes, and reflective logs make it possible to get feedback right away and show that you are competent. Instead of being a one-time event in the classroom, this model makes learning an ongoing process that happens at work.

Stackable credentials help people learn throughout their lives and give them a clear path to advancing their careers and getting professional recognition. You can collect and combine each micro-credential you earn through mobile learning into higher-level qualifications, creating a digital portfolio of verified achievements (Темјановски et al., 2023). For example, a certificate in Smart Maritime Operations could be made up of a number of micro-credentials in environmental compliance, AI navigation, and maritime communication. This kind of support not only makes people more likely to get jobs, but it also keeps them interested in their work. By connecting mobile access to credential-based recognition, maritime schools create a culture of lifelong learning that helps sailors stay flexible, skilled, and ready for the future in a world that is changing quickly because of technology, sustainability, and global connectivity (Yurzhenko et al., 2024).

4.2 Technological Infrastructure and Interoperability

For mobile learning and micro-credentialing to work well in maritime education, there needs to be strong technological infrastructure and interoperability frameworks. These systems make it possible for the global maritime workforce to learn without interruptions, share credentials safely, and have their qualifications recognized across borders. In an industry where people move around a lot, work with people from different countries, and follow rules from different countries, maritime learning platforms need to be technologically advanced, work with other systems, and be safe. Using Learning Management Systems (LMS), blockchain-based credentialing, and artificial intelligence (AI) analytics can make sure that digital learning environments are effective, open, and able to change to meet the needs of schools and businesses as they change (Galić et al., 2020).

Learning Management Systems (LMS) are the main part of digital maritime education. They host and manage mobile-based courses, tests, and credentialing data. Modern LMS platforms, like Moodle, Canvas, and custom maritime systems, make it easier for students who are spread out to take courses, keep track of their progress, and grade their work. Blockchain-enabled credentialing has become more and more important to improve the trust and traceability of certification. Blockchain technology makes it possible to keep a permanent record of learning achievements, which guarantees their authenticity and removes the risk of fake certifications. Seafarers can safely share their micro-credentials with employers, regulatory bodies, or port authorities all over the world without the need for middlemen thanks to decentralized verification. This openness is in line with international maritime standards and helps skills be recognized around the world, which makes it easier for workers to move around and follow the rules.

AI and learning analytics are changing the way maritime education is personalized. AI-powered maritime learning apps can change the content based on each learner's profile by looking at their performance data, engagement patterns, and preferred learning styles. This personalization makes sure that sailors get materials that are relevant to their situation. For example, they might get refresher modules on navigation safety before a trip or lessons in green port logistics that are specific to their job. Learning analytics also help teachers and schools find gaps in students' skills, predict how well they will do in school, and make changes to the curriculum on the spot. AI-powered recommendation engines can also find learning opportunities that are available right away, which helps create adaptive and data-driven professional learning pathways. So, AI and mobile learning together make an intelligent ecosystem that keeps changing to meet the needs of learners and the needs of the industry (Manousou & Galani, 2025).

But as digital learning in the maritime field gets better, there needs to be a balance between that and strong protections for privacy, data security, and interoperability. Seafarers' personal and performance data move between different systems and jurisdictions, so they must follow international data protection laws like the General Data Protection Regulation (GDPR). To keep information safe, it is important to use encryption, secure authentication, and access control protocols. Interoperability standards, like the Experience API (xAPI) and IMS Global Learning Consortium frameworks, also make it easier for different learning systems, institutions, and maritime authorities to share data. Getting global interoperability means that maritime credentials earned on one platform are automatically accepted in other countries. These technological building blocks work together to create the digital infrastructure that a connected, open, and future-ready maritime education system needs.

4.3 Stakeholder Collaboration and Industry Partnerships

For mobile learning and micro-credentialing to work well in maritime education, there needs to be a lot of cooperation and long-term partnerships between academia, industry, and regulatory bodies. The maritime industry is like a global ecosystem where education, rules, and jobs all depend on each other. Collaboration makes sure that new ways of teaching not only help students reach their academic goals, but also work in the real world and meet legal requirements. Maritime universities, businesses, and international organizations all work together to make a learning environment that encourages lifelong professional growth, workforce mobility, and digital transformation in the maritime industry.

Maritime universities and training centers are the main people who come up with new ways to teach, test, and design the curriculum. They give the academic rigor and research base needed to add mobile learning and micro-credentialing to competency-based education systems. Universities can give seafarers flexible ways to improve their skills that are based on real-world problems by adding micro-learning units to their existing maritime programs. Shipping companies, port authorities, and maritime service providers are all examples of industries that are important partners in making sure that educational materials stay up to date with new technologies and ways of doing business. Their input helps figure out what skills are needed for new fields like managing autonomous vessels, using AI to help with navigation, and following environmental rules. The International Maritime Organization (IMO), classification societies, and national maritime authorities are examples of regulatory bodies that make sure that conventions like the Standards of Training, Certification and Watchkeeping (STCW) are followed and recognized around the world.

Working with employers and seafarers to design learning pathways makes sure that mobile learning and micro-credentialing programs are based on real-life maritime situations. Collaborative curriculum development makes it possible to include real-time industry data, operational case studies, and shipboard experiences in digital learning materials. To make mobile learning apps easier to use, more accessible, and more useful, seafarers' feedback is very important. Jointly developed micro-credential programs can also quickly adapt to the changing needs of the workforce. This makes it possible to create short, stackable learning modules that are in line with new maritime technologies or environmental rules. This participatory approach makes learners feel like they own their learning and are involved in it, and it also builds trust between education providers and employers.

Frameworks for mutual recognition of micro-credentials are essential at the regional level for improving global employability and professional mobility. The ASEAN Qualifications Reference Framework (AQRF), the European Qualifications Framework (EQF), and the Asia-Pacific Economic Cooperation (APEC) Skills Recognition initiatives are examples of how regional cooperation can make micro-credential structures and validation processes the same across the board. These frameworks make sure that digital credentials earned in one country are accepted in others. This makes it easier for seafarers to move between different maritime sectors and regions. By working together on maritime education policies at the regional and global levels, schools can create a system that is consistent and works with other systems. This system will support lifelong learning, encourage new ideas, and create a more diverse and ready-to-work maritime workforce.

CHARTING THE FUTURE OF LIFELONG MARITIME LEARNING

5.1 Policy Directions and Governance Models

The future of lifelong maritime learning hinges on the formulation of cohesive policy frameworks and governance structures that integrate mobile learning and micro-credentialing into both national and international maritime strategies. As the industry experiences rapid technological, environmental, and regulatory changes, policy frameworks must adapt to maintain education systems that are responsive, inclusive, and forward-looking (Shkaruba & Marran, 2025). Incorporating adaptable digital learning and micro-credential pathways into national maritime policies can foster ongoing professional development, workforce resilience, and alignment with the overarching objectives of sustainable ocean governance.

Incorporating mobile learning and micro-credentialing into national maritime strategies is a smart way to respond to the global trend toward digitalization and decarbonization. Governments, maritime authorities, and higher education institutions must implement comprehensive strategies that prioritize lifelong learning as a fundamental component of maritime human capital development (Shkaruba & Marran, 2025). Policies should require that national maritime training standards include digital learning infrastructures and modular credentialing systems. For instance, adding micro-credential programs to competency-based frameworks that follow the International Maritime Organization's (IMO) Standards of Training, Certification, and Watchkeeping (STCW) Convention can make sure that they are recognized around the world and can be used in different places (Sudewo et al., 2025). Also, national maritime strategies should encourage universities, training centers, and industry stakeholders to work together to create innovation ecosystems that connect learning outcomes to new industry needs like smart shipping, green technologies, and artificial intelligence.

Regulatory and accreditation frameworks for ongoing education are very important for keeping quality, accountability, and international alignment. Accreditation bodies need to broaden their standards to encompass criteria tailored to digital and micro-credential programs, addressing elements such as learning outcomes, data integrity, and digital verification. Quality assurance agencies can implement adaptive monitoring systems that assess not only content but also technological performance and learner engagement (Cahyadi et al., 2024). The ASEAN Qualifications Reference Framework (AQRF) and the European Qualifications Framework (EQF) are two examples of initiatives that will help make maritime credentials recognized across borders by setting up interoperable accreditation standards in different regions. National regulatory agencies should also make it easier to renew and revalidate certifications by accepting verified micro-credentials as part of the requirements for ongoing professional development.

Incentive mechanisms are just as important for promoting innovation in institutions and helping faculty grow. Maritime schools need help with money and structure in order to invest in digital infrastructure, instructional design capacity, and research on technology-enhanced learning. To get people to try out mobile platforms and AI analytics, governments and businesses can give out grants, innovation funds, and public-private partnerships. To make teachers better at helping students learn for the rest of their lives, faculty development programs should focus on digital pedagogy, data literacy, and competency-based assessment. In the end, well-thought-out policies and governance models create an environment that not only encourages technological progress but also fosters a culture of lifelong learning, innovation, and working together across borders in the maritime education sector.

5.2 Sustainability and Inclusivity in Lifelong Learning

A maritime education system that looks to the future and encourages lifelong learning should be based on sustainability and inclusivity. As the global maritime industry moves toward digitalization and decarbonization, it is both morally and strategically important to make sure that all seafarers, no matter where they live, what gender they are, or how much money they have, have equal access to learning opportunities. In the maritime industry, lifelong learning should not only prepare workers for the demands of technology and operations, but it should also promote global citizenship, ethical awareness, and social responsibility. Institutions can make maritime education and training more accessible, welcoming, and sustainable by using mobile learning technologies and micro-credentialing frameworks.

One of the biggest problems in maritime education is making sure that seafarers in developing regions have equal access. A lot of maritime training schools in the Global South don't have enough infrastructure, bandwidth, or access to new technologies, which makes it hard for people to take part in digital learning. To get around these problems, mobile learning solutions need to be made for places with poor internet connections, with offline features and light content delivery systems. Governments, international organizations, and private tech companies can work together to help pay for access to digital tools and training materials. The ASEAN Qualifications Reference Framework (AQRF) and the Integrated Technical Cooperation Programme (ITCP) from the International Maritime Organization (IMO) are two examples of frameworks that can help ensure that seafarers in developing maritime economies have equal access to learning opportunities. Nations can stop the digital divide from becoming a new kind of job inequality at sea by making sure that their policies are open to everyone.

It is just as important for sustainability to include green skills, ethics, and global citizenship in digital maritime learning. To help fight climate change, the maritime industry needs seafarers who know a lot about the environment and act ethically. This includes decarbonization, energy efficiency, and waste management. Sustainability modules that stress green operations, taking care of the environment, and making responsible decisions should be part of all lifelong learning programs. Seafarers can learn about new practices like carbon accounting, circular shipping, and renewable marine energy through mobile-based micro-courses. In addition to teaching technical skills, these programs should also teach students about ethics and global citizenship. They should help students understand how environmental, social, and economic systems are all connected in global maritime operations.

Another important part of inclusive maritime education is using mobile devices to promote gender equality and cultural diversity. In the past, cultural norms, limited outreach, and strict training models have made it hard for women and other underrepresented groups to participate in maritime activities. Mobile learning platforms can help with these problems by giving students safe, flexible, and personalized learning spaces that they can access from anywhere. Digital platforms can also make more diverse voices heard by including case studies from different cultures, interfaces in different languages, and mentorship networks that welcome everyone. Maritime institutions can create a more diverse and resilient workforce by making sure that everyone has a fair chance to participate and be heard. In the end, sustainability and inclusivity in lifelong learning are not minor issues; they are at the heart of creating a maritime sector that is moral, environmentally friendly, and open to everyone.

5.3 Vision for a Connected and Competent Maritime Workforce

The goal of a connected and skilled maritime workforce is to create a globally recognized lifelong learning ecosystem that brings together education, technology, and industry with a shared goal of innovation, resilience, and sustainability. Seafarers and maritime professionals need to keep changing to meet new challenges in a world where automation, green transitions, and global interdependence are the norm. A connected learning ecosystem makes sure that knowledge flows easily across borders, fields, and institutions. Digital platforms and micro-credentialing frameworks give people the power to create their own learning paths. The goal is to create a maritime workforce that is not only skilled but also open-minded, ethical, and able to adapt to new situations.

The first step in creating such an ecosystem is to bring together the global and regional frameworks that govern maritime education and certification. To make systems for credential recognition that work with each other, international organizations like the International Maritime Organization (IMO), the International Labour Organization (ILO), and regional groups like ASEAN and the European Union need to work together. Using shared taxonomies and digital verification to standardize micro-credentials makes sure that seafarers' skills can be used and verified anywhere in the world. Artificial intelligence and data analytics can help digital learning platforms become the backbone of this ecosystem by keeping track of progress, finding skill gaps, and connecting learners with opportunities for more growth. Maritime schools also need to use open-access repositories and work together with other schools so that they can share resources, mentor students, and do research together. In this interconnected model, lifelong learning is both a right and a professional norm.

Maritime education should also be seen as a major source of new ideas, strength, and long-term success. Training schools can get seafarers ready to lead the industry's digital and green changes by using new technologies like virtual reality simulations, AI-assisted navigation tools, and environmental monitoring systems. Education is the link between new technology and moral behavior. It makes sure that new technologies are safe, efficient, and good for the environment. Also, lifelong learning makes the workforce more resilient by giving professionals the skills they need to adapt to global changes, whether they are economic, environmental, or technological. As maritime operations rely more and more on data, the ability to learn, forget, and relearn is becoming a key skill for sailors in the 21st century.

Finally, for digital transformation to create a culture of continuous improvement, everyone in the organization needs to be committed and change their way of thinking. Companies and maritime academies need to create spaces where learning never stops, is based on data, and is focused on new ideas. Digital transformation should be seen not as a way to improve technology, but as a way to change culture by valuing curiosity, collaboration, and inclusion. With this vision, the maritime industry can create a connected global workforce that is smart, moral, and ready for the future. This workforce will be based on knowledge, powered by technology, and guided by a shared commitment to sustainable oceans and global progress.

CONCLUSION

In an age of digital transformation and the need for sustainability, lifelong learning has become the most important idea in the maritime industry. Combining mobile learning with micro-credentialing is a revolutionary way to create a maritime workforce that is ready for the future—one that is flexible, skilled, and connected to the rest of the world. By combining modular, competency-based learning with mobile technologies, maritime education can go beyond geographical, institutional, and occupational barriers. This will make sure that seafarers keep learning and growing throughout their careers. These new ideas make it easier for everyone to get a good education and quickly adapt to changes in the industry caused by automation, green technologies, and changing international rules.

The creation of governance frameworks and partnerships that support quality, relevance, and fairness is a key part of this change. Universities, regulatory agencies, and industry stakeholders working together make sure that new ways of teaching stay in line with the International Maritime Organization's standards and the needs of the global job market. Setting up systems for accreditation and recognition that work across borders is just as important. These systems will help build trust, openness, and the ability for workers to move around the world. Institutions that incorporate these systems into national and regional strategies will be more adept at fostering resilient learning ecosystems.

In the end, the maritime education landscape is changing to a model that values adaptability, diversity, and long-term viability. Mobile learning lets people learn when they want and in a way that makes sense for them, while micro-credentials give learners the tools they need to create personalized, verifiable skill portfolios. These approaches work together to support a complete view of maritime human capital, one based on moral responsibility, digital skills, and caring for the environment. To move forward, we need to keep investing in infrastructure, faculty capacity, and new policies. The goal is clear: a connected and skilled maritime workforce that can confidently and purposefully navigate the complicated waters of globalization, technology, and sustainability.

REFERENCES

Abdullah, F. and Ghazali, N. (2023). Micro-credentials at higher education institutions: towards smooth sailing ahead., 118-126. https://doi.org/DOI: 10.2991/978-2-38476-196-8_11

Ajayi, F., & Udeh, C.Funmilayo Aribidesi AjayiChioma Ann Udeh. (2024). A comprehensive review of talent management strategies for seafarers: Challenges and opportunities. *International Journal of Science and Research Archive, 11*(2), 1116–1131. DOI: 10.30574/ijsra.2024.11.2.0560

Arifin, M. (2023). Application of internet of things (iot) and big data in the maritime industries: Ship allocation model. *International Journal of Marine Engineering Innovation and Research, 8*(1). Advance online publication. DOI: 10.12962/j25481479.v8i1.16405

Belabyad, M., Kontovas, C., Pyne, R., Shi, W., Li, N., Szwed, P., & Chang, C. (2025). *The human element in autonomous shipping: a study on skills and competency requirements.* Wmu Journal of Maritime Affairs., DOI: 10.1007/s13437-025-00366-9

Cahyadi, T., Ahmad, A., & Barasa, L. (2024). Integrating sustainability and digital advancements in maritime law education: Enhancing cadet preparedness. *IJLS, 1*(4), 217–228. DOI: 10.62951/ijls.v1i4.196

Cahyadi, T., Ahmad, A., & Barasa, L. (2024). Integrating sustainability and digital advancements in maritime law education: Enhancing cadet preparedness. *IJLS, 1*(4), 217–228. DOI: 10.62951/ijls.v1i4.196

Desmarchelier, R., & Cary, L. (2022). Toward just and equitable micro-credentials: An australian perspective. *International Journal of Educational Technology in Higher Education, 19*(1), 25. Advance online publication. DOI: 10.1186/s41239-022-00332-y

Diab, M., & Zhang, M.DIAB. (2023). Perceptions of industry professionals from diverse sectors on post-secondary micro-credentials on linkedin. *International Journal of Research in Education Humanities and Commerce, 04*(02), 63–115. DOI: 10.37602/IJREHC.2023.4211

Diahyleva, O., Kononova, O., Yurzhenko, A., & Svyryda, V. (2025). Development of professional competence of future specialists in the operation of shipboard technical systems and complexes using lms moodle. Scientific Bulletin of Mukachevo State University Series "Pedagogy and Psychology", 51-59. https://doi.org/DOI: 10.52534/msu-pp1.2025.51

Elhussieny, M., Arafat, O., & Kassar, A. (2023). The outcomes of applying smart green port concept in egyptian ports (case study: alexandria port). The International Archives of the Photogrammetry Remote Sensing and Spatial Information Sciences, XLVIII-1/W2-2023, 413-420. https://doi.org/DOI: 10.5194/isprs-archives-XLVIII-1-W2-2023-413-2023

Fabian-Perona, E. (2025). Maritime education and language as the acting link between bridge and engine room – a report. Educational Role of Language Journal, 2025-1(13), 64-67. https://doi.org/DOI: 10.36534/erlj.2025.01.07

Fernandes, R., & Rajan, S. S. (2025). E-learning and virtual simulations for advancing maritime engineering education. *Indian Journal of Information Sources and Services, 15*(3), 339–343. DOI: 10.51983/ijiss-2025.IJISS.15.3.38

Galić, S., Lušić, Z., & Stanivuk, T. (2020). E-learning in maritime affairs. *Journal of Naval Architecture and Marine Engineering*, *17*(1), 38–50. DOI: 10.3329/jname.v17i1.42203

Gray, H., & Jónsson, S. (2022). Lessons learnt: Digital transformation of processes led to a rethinking of how certificates of completion are issued. *AOE*, *1*(1), 87. DOI: 10.69554/UAKA9874

Hendriawan, A., Gautama, I., Siahaan, D., & Kurniawan, K. (2025). Analysis of the influence of factors on maritime cyber resilience on board with intervening maritime cyber security awareness. *Syntax Literate Jurnal Ilmiah Indonesia*, *10*(3), 2783–2794. DOI: 10.36418/syntax-literate.v10i3.56311

Humphries, F., Horne, R., Olsen, M., Dunbabin, M., & Tranter, K. (2022). Uncrewed autonomous marine vessels test the limits of maritime safety frameworks. *Wmu Journal of Maritime Affairs*, *22*(3), 317–344. DOI: 10.1007/s13437-022-00295-x

Jo, S., D'agostini, E., & Kang, J. (2020). From seafarers to e-farers: Maritime cadets' perceptions towards seafaring jobs in the industry 4.0. *Sustainability (Basel)*, *12*(19), 8077. DOI: 10.3390/su12198077

Korhonen, A., Ruhalahti, S., & Niinimäki, J. (2020). Vocational teachers' competences visible by open badges.. https://doi.org/DOI: 10.21125/inted.2020.0466

Kristiawan, D., & Marsudi, S. (2025). Sustainable maritime human resource development strategy in supporting the blue economy in indonesia. *International Journal of Materials in Engineering Applications*, *2*(2), 111–117. DOI: 10.30649/ijmea.v2i2.393

Kuncowati, K., Sholihah, Q., & Ciptadi, G. (2022). Handling waste on ships: a model based on safety and awareness. Logi – Scientific Journal on Transport and Logistics, 13(1), 222-232. https://doi.org/ DOI: 10.2478/logi-2022-0020

Lang, J. (2023). Workforce upskilling: Can universities meet the challenges of lifelong learning? *International Journal of Information and Learning Technology*, *40*(5), 388–400. DOI: 10.1108/IJILT-01-2023-0001

Main, P., & Anderson, S. (2023). Evidence for continuing professional development standards for regulated health practitioners in australia: A systematic review. *Human Resources for Health*, *21*(1), 23. Advance online publication. DOI: 10.1186/s12960-023-00803-x

Manousou, E., & Galani, M. (2025). Assessment and micro-credentials in distance learning for vet educators. *Ubiquity Proceedings*, *31*, 31. Advance online publication. DOI: 10.5334/uproc.199

Markopoulos, E., Nordholm, A., Iliadi, S., Markopoulos, P., Faraclas, J., & Luimula, M. (2022). A certification framework for virtual reality and metaverse training scenarios in the maritime and shipping industry... https://doi.org/DOI: 10.54941/ahfe1001505

Mataac, M., Manuel, M., & Pazaver, A. (2024). Interrogating the global application of e-certification of seafarers. *Digital Transformation and Society*, *4*(1), 21–38. DOI: 10.1108/DTS-03-2024-0023

Meštrović, T., Pavić, I., Maljković, M., & Androjna, A. (2024). Challenges for the education and training of seafarers in the context of autonomous shipping: Bibliometric analysis and systematic literature review. *Applied Sciences (Basel, Switzerland)*, *14*(8), 3173. DOI: 10.3390/app14083173

Mke, D. (2024). Assessment of digital competencies in south african maritime education and training institutions: A study of evaluation methods for future seafarers. *SAJMET, 3*, 103–120. DOI: 10.47348/SAJMET/2024/i1a8

Orman, R., Şimşek, E., & Çakır, M. (2023). Micro-credentials and reflections on higher education. *Higher Education Evaluation and Development, 17*(2), 96–112. DOI: 10.1108/HEED-08-2022-0028

Pimiä, A., Urponen, A., & Kolehmainen, A. (2024). Green horizons ahead: Navigating carbon neutrality in european transportation by sky and sea. *Economics and Culture, 21*(1), 149–158. DOI: 10.2478/jec-2024-0011

Purba, D., & Simanjuntak, M. (2024). Sustainable maritime education: Integrating environmental science for global competence. [Jurnal Pendidikan Biologi Indonesia]. *Jpbi, 10*(1), 310–319. DOI: 10.22219/jpbi.v10i1.32588

Rahmawati, M., Pitana, T., Handani, D., & Siswantoro, N. (2025). Utilization of ais data and ship simulator integration in maritime safety: A systematic literature review. *IOP Conference Series. Earth and Environmental Science, 1461*(1), 012049. DOI: 10.1088/1755-1315/1461/1/012049

Raj, R., Singh, A., Kumar, V., & Verma, P. (2024). Achieving professional qualifications using micro-credentials: A case of small packages and big challenges in higher education. *International Journal of Educational Management, 38*(4), 916–947. DOI: 10.1108/IJEM-01-2023-0028

Reed, A. (2023). Micro-credentials and the role of evidence: Increasing the potential for learner-centeredness, inclusivity and an expansive model of assessment and credentialing. *International Journal of Information and Learning Technology, 40*(5), 401–412. DOI: 10.1108/IJILT-12-2022-0228

Shkaruba, A., & Marran, C. (2025). Policies, strategies and regulations on microcredentials and lifelong learning: European and estonian framework. *Man and Environment Issues of Neoecology*, (43), 104–111. DOI: 10.26565/1992-4224-2025-43-08

Sudewo, G., Santoso, H., & Susanto, P. (2025). Strategic enhancement of maritime human resource quality: An integrated approach to assessment, talent management, and competency development. *International Research Journal of Innovations in Engineering and Technology, 09*(07), 131–140. DOI: 10.47001/IRJIET/2025.907015

Темјановски, Р., Chabukovski, V., Zlatkovski, D., & Todevski, D. (2023). The need, practice, and values of micro-credentials in the academic and business sector. *Journal of Economics, 8*(2), 75–86. DOI: 10.46763/JOE2382075t

Türkistanlı, T. (2023). Advanced learning methods in maritime education and training: A bibliometric analysis on the digitalization of education and modern trends. *Computer Applications in Engineering Education, 32*(1), e22690. Advance online publication. DOI: 10.1002/cae.22690

Wang, Q., Hu, Z., & Zhu, P. (2023). Using nuclear energy for maritime decarbonization and related environmental challenges: Existing regulatory shortcomings and improvements. *International Journal of Environmental Research and Public Health, 20*(4), 2993. DOI: 10.3390/ijerph20042993

Yurzhenko, A., Kononova, O., & Bevzenko, Y. (2024). Forming the environmental professional competence of future specialists in ship technical systems and complex operation. Scientific Bulletin of Mukachevo State University Series. *Pedagogy and Psychology*, *10*(4), 41–49. DOI: 10.52534/msu-pp4.2024.41

Zou, H., Ullah, A., Qazi, Z., Naeem, A., & Rehan, S. (2023). Impact of micro-credential learning on students' perceived employability: The mediating role of human capital. *International Journal of Educational Management*, *38*(4), 897–915. DOI: 10.1108/IJEM-01-2023-0002

Chapter 3
Sailing Into Digital Horizons:
Transforming Maritime Education Through E-Learning and Technological Innovation

I Ketut Patra
http://orcid.org/0000-0002-7716-0462
Universitas Muhammadiyah Palopo, Indonesia

Mas'ud Muhammadiah
Universitas Bosowa, Indonesia

R. Nasaruddin
Universitas Islam Makassar, Indonesia

ABSTRACT

This study explores the digital transformation of Maritime Education and Training (MET) through the integration of e-learning, simulation, and emerging technologies such as AI, VR, and IoT. It examines how digital platforms enhance accessibility, competence development, and global collaboration while addressing challenges in quality assurance, infrastructure, and faculty readiness. The discussion highlights the importance of ethical, sustainable, and human-centered approaches to technology adoption in maritime education. By aligning pedagogical innovation with international standards and lifelong learning principles, this work envisions a future-ready maritime ecosystem that fosters global partnerships, professional adaptability, and digital resilience.

NAVIGATING THE WAVES OF CHANGE: CONTEXT AND RATIONALE

1.1 The Evolution of Maritime Education in the Digital Era

Maritime Education and Training (MET) has long emphasized experiential learning, integrating theoretical instruction with practical sea-time experience to cultivate competence among cadets. This traditional framework, used by maritime academies globally, relies on classroom learning supplemented by simulator training and onboard apprenticeship opportunities (Tabora, 2023). Although effective in honing practical skills, this format has been hampered by technological limitations, high operational

DOI: 10.4018/979-8-3373-6670-8.ch003

costs, and geographical constraints that impact access to quality training resources (Chen & Almunawar, 2021) (Munawwaroh & Baharun, 2022).

As we entered the 21st century, rapid digital transformation has influenced all aspects of maritime education, particularly in how curricula are designed and delivered. The modernization of maritime education has become essential as digital navigation, automation, and smart port management increasingly dictate global trade and shipping practices (Barapatre et al., 2024). To address these shifts, organizations such as the International Maritime Organization (IMO) and the International Labour Organization (ILO) have underscored the importance of ongoing adaptation to technological advancements using frameworks like the Standards of Training, Certification and Watchkeeping (STCW). Countries such as Norway, Singapore, the Philippines, and the UK have embraced these changes by integrating advanced simulators and blended learning systems into their MET curricula (Holloway, 2024).

The emergence of cloud-based Learning Management Systems (LMS) has significantly altered educational paradigms, transforming how maritime professionals are equipped for future challenges. Such systems enhance access to educational materials and foster efficient tracking of students' progress while serving as platforms for collaborative learning (Chen & Almunawar, 2021). The COVID-19 pandemic acted as a catalyst for this digital transition, driving maritime institutions to swiftly adopt online platforms, remote simulations, and hybrid learning modalities (Sharma, 2024). This strategic pivot has illuminated pathways for increased inclusivity and cooperation across global MET programs, ultimately ensuring the continuity of education during unprecedented lockdowns (Chatterjee et al., 2023).

Today's maritime cadets must not only master core navigational and engineering skills but also navigate the complexities of digital literacy, data management, and collaborative problem-solving within digital environments (Febriana et al., 2025). Consequently, there has been a considerable shift from passive knowledge absorption to a more active, learner-centered engagement facilitated by digital tools, aligning educational processes with industry expectations (Simanjuntak, 2024; Vakaliuk, 2021). Furthermore, innovative technologies such as Virtual Reality (VR) and Augmented Reality (AR) are moving the boundary of experiential learning, allowing cadets to engage in advanced simulations beyond traditional classroom settings (Sikarwar et al., 2025).

The transformation of MET signifies more than mere technological advances; it encapsulates a paradigm shift in pedagogical approaches. The confluence of traditional seamanship training with digital competencies necessitates a re-evaluation of curriculum frameworks, teaching methodologies, and assessment practices (Srivastava, 2025; Оксенюк, 2023). By incorporating these digital innovations, MET institutions are not just responding to current global trends; they are charting a course toward a more connected, sustainable, and equipped future in maritime education (Venice et al., 2024).

1.2 Challenges and Opportunities in Maritime Digitalization

The digital transformation of Maritime Education and Training (MET) offers significant opportunities and considerable challenges for maritime institutions as they adopt e-learning, simulation technologies, and intelligent learning systems. However, many maritime schools, especially in developing areas, face big problems that make it hard for them to fully adopt digital technologies. Infrastructure, accessibility, and policy readiness problems make it hard for digital projects to get off the ground. Institutions face significant obstacles to the successful implementation of online learning platforms, including limited internet bandwidth and inadequate technological infrastructure (Mahundu, 2023; Iping, 2022). When students in coastal or remote island areas have unstable internet connections, they often have to stop and start during synchronous learning sessions and simulation tests. This has a big impact on their training results (Mahundu, 2023).

The costs of keeping advanced simulators, upgrading networks, and licensing digital platforms make these problems even worse. This difference in financial and technological resources means that maritime education is not as good in some parts of the world as it is in others (Mariatul, 2025). The human factor is also a big problem because many maritime instructors who were trained in traditional teaching methods may need a lot of extra training to be able to teach effectively in digital learning environments. To make the switch, you need to be able to teach online, create digital content, and use assessment systems that work in a virtual space. The absence of steady institutional backing could result in faculty burnout, resistance to change, or a deterioration in instructional quality, thereby impeding the digital transition (Muruga & Jamaludin, 2025).

Additionally, the historical focus on physical skills and in-person tests in maritime rules creates a regulatory gap that makes it harder to approve e-learning and virtual simulations (Setiawan & Kamil, 2021). This gap makes it hard to know if digitally mediated training is safe and effective, which shows how important it is for people all over the world to talk about how to set standards and rules for the future of digital maritime education (Setiawan et al., 2025). Despite these challenges, the digitalization of MET has the potential to bring about major changes by encouraging inclusion, innovation, and global connectivity. E-learning platforms cross borders, so maritime students can get high-quality instruction no matter where they are. Cloud-based simulators and virtual reality technologies make training more accessible to everyone, making sure that everyone has the same chance to learn new skills. This was not possible before at elite institutions (Tripathi, 2025).

Collaborative platforms also make it easier for people from different countries to work together. This lets cadets and instructors take part in cross-cultural exchanges and global learning communities. This connectivity improves the learning experience by giving students access to a wider range of information and points of view, which helps them become more skilled in a world that is becoming more interconnected (Ibrahim, 2021). Digitalization promotes adaptive and personalized learning pathways, as AI and analytics tools can track student progress, find areas where they need to improve, and give them feedback that is specific to their needs (Apriani et al., 2025). The strategic shift toward online and blended models also fits with goals for sustainability, since they use fewer resources and produce less carbon during training delivery (Siswanto et al., 2025).

In the end, the problems with MET's digital transformation are big and many, but the idea of making maritime education more open, ready for the future, and connected around the world is still very appealing. To make this happen, we need fair investments in infrastructure, policies that help people, and a focus on innovation that puts people first (Suh, 2020). Therefore, when combined with strategic initiatives and collaborative efforts, the digitalization of maritime education may lead to better learning experiences that better prepare the next generation of maritime professionals for the complexities of the global maritime landscape.

1.3 The Rationale for Digital Transformation in MET

The reason for adopting digital transformation in Maritime Education and Training (MET) is the urgent need to make sure that education systems keep up with how quickly technology is changing in the maritime industry. The shipping industry around the world is quickly moving toward automation, AI, and sustainable operations. This means that workers need to have advanced digital skills and the ability to learn new things. E-learning is not just another way to learn; it is a strategic necessity that makes sure that training is always available, flexible, and accessible from anywhere in the world, in line with the needs of Industry 5.0. In this context, maritime institutions must go beyond traditional teaching methods and use digital ecosystems that encourage collaboration between people and machines, making decisions based on data, and being able to adapt to changing conditions in maritime operations (Srivastava, 2025; Оксенюк, 2023).

E-learning is a strategic tool that helps MET come up with new ideas, include everyone, and make sure quality. The reliance on physical simulators and classroom instruction constrains scalability and adaptability, especially in a globally operating sector. Digital transformation lets maritime education offer ongoing learning through cloud-based platforms, mobile apps, and virtual simulators. These tools make it easier for cadets, seafarers, and lifelong learners to get the help they need, no matter where they are. They help people keep their skills up to date and learn new ones at different stages of their careers. E-learning also helps make learning outcomes more consistent, which means that trainees from different parts of the world can all meet the same international competency standards. By using multimedia resources, interactive modules, and analytics, maritime schools can make learning more personal while still meeting professional standards.

A key part of this change is that it fits with international standards, especially the International Maritime Organization's (IMO) Standards of Training, Certification, and Watchkeeping (STCW). The STCW Convention stresses education based on skills, ongoing professional growth, and the ability to adapt to new technologies. Digital tools like remote simulators, AI-assisted assessments, and online certification tracking help these goals by giving proof that skills have been learned and renewed. Digital record systems also make things more open and easier for regulators to keep an eye on, making sure that training results can be traced, checked, and are in line with international standards for maritime safety and quality.

The change also fits with the idea of Industry 5.0, which emphasizes how human intelligence, automation, and sustainability can work together. In this model, digital transformation in MET supports human-centered innovation, which means that technology enhances rather than replaces human knowledge. AI-enhanced learning analytics, augmented reality simulations, and smart credentialing systems create a connected world that values creativity, morality, and being aware of the environment. As maritime education adopts these technologies, it not only helps to train seafarers who are technically skilled, but also helps to develop global professionals who are flexible, ethical, and environmentally responsible and ready for the challenges of the modern maritime world.

ANCHORING E-LEARNING IN MARITIME PEDAGOGY

2.1 Pedagogical Foundations of Online Maritime Learning

The pedagogical underpinnings of online Maritime Education and Training (MET) are intricately connected to established educational theories, notably experiential learning, constructivism, and competency-based education. As MET moves toward digital and blended formats, it's important to understand these learning paradigms to make sure that maritime training is of high quality, real, and useful.

Experiential learning has traditionally been fundamental to maritime education, grounded in the belief that knowledge is best gained through practice, reflection, and evaluation. Kolb's experiential learning cycle explains this method, which fits well with the performance-based nature of seafaring. In this context, digital learning environments can improve this tradition by using tools like Virtual Reality (VR) and Augmented Reality (AR), which mimic real-world maritime operations. These technologies provide immersive and interactive experiences, facilitating authentic tasks within secure, reproducible digital environments, thereby fostering enhanced comprehension and skill acquisition among learners (Miyusov et al., 2022; Lee & Han, 2022). Research indicates that incorporating VR into training can improve student motivation and skills by providing realistic scenarios encountered at sea (Miyusov et al., 2022).

Constructivist learning theory, alongside experiential learning, exerts a substantial impact on online maritime education. Constructivism asserts that learners actively create knowledge through social interaction and problem-solving, rather than passively absorbing information (Sharma & Nazir, 2021). In e-learning environments, this is demonstrated by collaborative platforms, discussion forums, and virtual teamwork projects that promote peer interaction and collective learning experiences (Guo et al., 2021; Yousif, 2022). This interconnectedness is important in maritime work, where good communication and the ability to work as a team to solve problems are both very important. Digital technologies also improve situated learning by putting information in the context of maritime operations, which makes it more useful and relevant to real-life situations (Farsi et al., 2023).

Competency-Based Education (CBE), which puts more value on skills and performance outcomes than on traditional time-based teaching models, is just as important for the growth of maritime e-learning. CBE is very similar to the International Maritime Organization's (IMO) Standards of Training, Certification, and Watchkeeping (STCW). It calls for a mix of knowledge, skills, and judgment that is needed in operational settings. Digital platforms make CBE easier by using analytics and digital portfolios to keep track of and evaluate what students can do. Learning Management Systems (LMS) with simulation analytics create ongoing feedback loops that let learners move at their own pace while making sure they master important skills (Tusher et al., 2022; Schwaiger et al., 2024).

Blended and hybrid learning models have become the best ways to use these teaching methods in maritime education. Maritime schools find a good balance between flexibility and authenticity in learning by using both asynchronous and synchronous online instruction along with face-to-face simulator training. For example, cadets might first learn theoretical ideas online, then use them in virtual simulations, and finally improve their skills while being watched while they practice at sea. This integration not only improves access to and continuity of education, but it also supports lifelong learning by connecting the classroom and the workplace (Mladenović et al., 2021).

2.2 Curriculum Redesign for Digital Delivery

The redesign of maritime curricula for digital delivery signifies a pivotal advancement in the establishment of adaptive, flexible, and competency-based learning environments. As maritime education and training (MET) institutions move away from traditional classroom teaching and toward digital and blended learning, the curricula need to be redesigned to make the most of new technologies while still meeting the high standards of maritime competency. The change requires more than just putting existing course materials online; it requires a complete overhaul of syllabi, learning activities, and assessment methods to fit with the new ways that virtual simulations, cloud-based collaboration, and data-driven learning analytics work.

When teachers redesign syllabi for online and digital platforms, they should focus on learning outcomes that are based on experience and performance. Traditional maritime curricula, typically structured around theoretical lectures and static assessments, need to transform into dynamic modules that incorporate simulation-based exercises, interactive multimedia, and problem-solving tasks rooted in real-world maritime scenarios. Cadets can use virtual reality (VR) and augmented reality (AR) tools to practice their navigational, engineering, and safety skills in realistic digital environments. Digital twins and cloud-based simulators work in the same way as ships do, allowing students to do group exercises that are like real-world decision-making processes. Course structures must therefore facilitate both synchronous and asynchronous learning experiences, enabling learners to engage with flexibility while maintaining accountability for competency development through digital performance tracking and feedback mechanisms (Schwaiger et al., 2024).

The alignment of learning outcomes with the competence-based training standards established by the International Maritime Organization (IMO) in the Standards of Training, Certification and Watchkeeping (STCW) Convention is a key part of this change. Curriculum designers need to make sure that digital modules cover the necessary skills in navigation, marine engineering, safety management, and maritime communication while also teaching new digital literacy skills. There should be clear connections between each learning goal and observable performance indicators and assessment rubrics that can be checked through simulation logs, digital portfolios, or AI-assisted evaluations. Competency mapping makes sure that online learning is just as valid, reliable, and well-known in the industry as traditional training methods.

Also, redesigning the curriculum must include ways to give and get feedback and ongoing assessments that are supported by learning management systems (LMS). These platforms let teachers keep an eye on students' progress, see if they have learned what they need to know, and give them personalized help. The redesigned curriculum should teach more than just technical skills. It should also teach skills that are important for a globalized maritime workforce, such as problem-solving, making ethical decisions, working in teams, and communicating across cultures.

Digital curriculum redesign is not about making things more modern; it's about realigning them strategically. By aligning digital pedagogy with international maritime standards, institutions can establish a comprehensive framework that prepares seafarers to proficiently navigate both physical and digital oceans with competence, confidence, and ethical responsibility.

2.3 Instructional Design and Digital Content Development

Instructional design is the most important part of a successful digital transformation in Maritime Education and Training (MET). It connects technology and teaching, making sure that digital platforms are useful tools for developing skills instead of just places to store information. As MET schools adopt online and blended learning, the creation of digital content must reflect both the technical rigor of maritime training and the teaching methods that encourage participation, reflection, and skill mastery. Combining multimedia, interactivity, and scenario-based learning makes digital environments that are just as complicated as real-world maritime operations. This lets cadets learn by doing, analyzing, and solving problems in real-world situations.

Multimedia integration makes learning about the sea a multidimensional experience. Video tutorials, animations, digital charts, and interactive diagrams can make complicated engineering or navigation ideas easier to understand than just text. For example, 3D simulation videos of radar plotting or engine room operations give students a clear picture that helps them understand the concepts better. Students can change things like wind speed, cargo weight, or vessel position in interactive simulations. This encourages experiential learning through trial and error. Adding audio narration and subtitles also makes it easier for multilingual students to understand, which makes global maritime classrooms more welcoming. Also, embedding formative quizzes and systems for instant feedback helps reinforce learning by giving students ongoing assessments that are in line with competency standards (Guo et al., 2021; Yousif, 2022).

Scenario-based learning is another important part of good digital maritime instruction. Instructors can help students develop their critical thinking and decision-making skills by putting them in real-life problem-solving situations, like dealing with emergencies on board, navigating busy ports, or handling crew communication during crises. These virtual scenarios are very similar to the experiential learning principles that have been important in maritime education for a long time. They also take advantage of the safety and scalability of digital delivery. AI and adaptive learning systems make these environments even better by changing the difficulty of scenarios based on how well the learner does, which personalizes the training paths.

Alignment, interactivity, and real assessment are important parts of good maritime instructional design. The International Maritime Organization's (IMO) Standards of Training, Certification, and Watchkeeping (STCW) competencies should be used to clearly define and map learning outcomes. Each digital module should include cognitive, psychomotor, and affective goals that combine theory with practical skills and professional attitudes. Modular design makes things more flexible, so content can be quickly updated when technology or rules change. Also, working together with subject matter experts, instructional designers, and maritime professionals makes sure that the content is correct and that it makes sense from a teaching point of view.

Lastly, making digital content should put accessibility, usability, and compatibility across platforms first. Materials should be optimized for learning on both desktop and mobile devices, so that they can be accessed easily no matter where you are or how fast your internet connection is. By carefully planning their lessons, MET schools can create e-learning environments that are both technologically advanced and pedagogically rich. This will help future seafarers learn, adapt, and do well in a maritime world that is becoming more digital.

HARNESSING EMERGING TECHNOLOGIES FOR SMART LEARNING ENVIRONMENTS

3.1 Simulation and Virtual Reality in Maritime Training

Simulation and virtual reality (VR) technologies have fundamentally transformed Maritime Education and Training (MET) by providing immersive and risk-free environments that replicate real-world maritime operations with exceptional accuracy. The maritime industry has long recognized the significance of simulation as an essential educational instrument, given the intricacies of global navigation, engineering systems, and safety management. Recent improvements in digital technology, especially the coming together of virtual reality (VR), augmented reality (AR), and mixed reality (MR), have greatly increased the range and accuracy of simulation-based learning. These innovations allow maritime cadets and professionals to participate in highly realistic operational scenarios that formerly necessitated physical simulators or extensive sea-time practice, thereby bridging the gap between theory and practical application (Makransky & Klingenberg, 2022; Tusher et al., 2022).

VR and AR have changed how students learn and use important maritime principles in navigation training. Virtual bridge simulators let trainees steer digital ships across fake oceans. They can also face changing conditions like bad weather, heavy traffic, and emergencies. VR's immersive nature improves spatial awareness, decision-making skills, and procedural accuracy—skills that are essential for safe navigation in real-world maritime situations. Using AR improves these experiences by putting digital information on top of real-world equipment or navigational charts, making it possible to see important information like ship locations, headings, and radar signals in real time. This integration helps with situational awareness and operational accuracy while keeping training environments safe and efficient (Tusher et al., 2022).

The field of engineering education has also benefited from the use of virtual technologies. Digital twin technology makes it possible to make engine room simulators, which are virtual copies of ship machinery that let students explore, operate, and troubleshoot systems in a hands-on way. With these simulations, trainees can practice maintenance, figure out what's wrong with a system, and deal with emergencies without the risks that come with real operations. This method not only improves technical skills, but it also helps cadets learn how to solve problems and boosts their confidence, giving them the tools they need before they go to sea (Sousa et al., 2022).

When it comes to safety and being ready for an emergency, VR and AR are the best ways to learn by doing. Simulations for high-stakes situations, like fire-fighting drills, man-overboard recoveries, and collision avoidance exercises, put learners in situations where they have to make quick decisions and work together under pressure. These virtual drills are very helpful for getting people ready both behaviorally and cognitively, which is necessary for keeping the seas safe and handling crises well (Zhu et al., 2021; Lee, 2022).

The educational value of these advanced technologies goes beyond realism; it includes their ability to encourage reflective practice and ongoing evaluation. Using analytics dashboards, teachers can keep track of and analyze students' performance in great detail, which lets them give specific feedback and make evaluations based on performance. By incorporating VR and AR into their curriculum design, MET institutions can develop a new generation of maritime professionals who are not only proficient in digital technologies but also operationally skilled and adaptable in navigating complex maritime systems in an increasingly interconnected world (Laskey, 2022).

3.2 Artificial Intelligence and Learning Analytics

Artificial Intelligence (AI) and learning analytics are changing the way Maritime Education and Training (MET) works. They are making it possible to build adaptive, data-driven, and learner-centered ecosystems. By adding AI technologies to maritime learning platforms, schools can tailor lessons to each student, keep an eye on their progress in real time, and use behavioral data to guess what they will learn in the future. Unlike traditional teaching methods that use standard curricula and fixed tests, AI-driven methods give teachers the power to create flexible learning paths that fit each student's pace, needs, and skills. This is in line with the maritime industry's need for accuracy, safety, and ongoing skill development.

One of the most important things that adaptive AI systems can do is make personalized learning pathways.

E-learning platforms can use machine learning algorithms and intelligent tutoring systems to look at a learner's activity patterns, performance data, and engagement metrics to make personalized suggestions. For instance, if a cadet struggles with a navigation simulation, the AI system can automatically assign remedial modules, change the difficulty of the next exercises, or suggest specific practice scenarios. This level of customization makes sure that students learn at their own pace without lowering the standards for competency (Sousa et al., 2022). Adaptive AI also encourages motivation and self-control by giving learners immediate, contextual feedback. This helps them understand what they're good at and what they need to work on while keeping them interested through gamified and interactive settings.

In addition to personalization, data-driven assessment and predictive analytics are changing how maritime institutions measure learning outcomes and how well they are doing overall. Analytics dashboards in learning management systems (LMS) can record a lot of different metrics, such as how long students spend on simulations and how well they do on quizzes, as well as logs of collaborative activity and communication. By analyzing this data, predictive models can find students who are likely to do poorly or lose interest, which lets teachers step in early with focused help. AI can even check how accurate procedures are, how quickly decisions are made, and how well people are aware of their surroundings in simulation-based training by automatically recognizing and scoring performance. This makes sure that the evaluation is fair, open, and based on skills, which is important for meeting the requirements of the International Maritime Organization (IMO) and the Standards of Training, Certification, and Watchkeeping (STCW).

Also, analytics at the institutional level help make decisions based on facts about how to improve the curriculum, train teachers, and use resources. Aggregate data on learner outcomes can show where course design needs to be improved or where new skills are needed in the maritime workforce. So, AI and analytics are not only useful for teaching, but they are also useful for making decisions about how to run an institution (Tusher et al., 2022).

3.3 Mobile Learning and Cloud-Based Platforms

Mobile learning and cloud-based platforms have become important parts of modern Maritime Education and Training (MET). They make it possible for learning to happen all the time, in a flexible way, and from anywhere in the world. In an industry where people move around a lot and work in many different places, these technologies connect ship and shore, classroom and field, and teacher and student. Mobile learning, which is made possible by smartphones, tablets, and lightweight apps, lets seafarers and cadets access educational materials whenever and wherever they want. Cloud technologies, on the other hand, provide the infrastructure for collaborative learning, data storage, and performance tracking across different environments. They redefine maritime training as a flexible, on-demand process that keeps up with the changing nature of work in the maritime industry around the world.

Mobile access makes learning more flexible for maritime professionals, who can now work around the usual problems of time and place. Cadets who are on ships or working from afar can still use digital learning modules, join virtual classrooms, or watch simulation videos while they are at sea. Offline features and formats that don't require real-time communication make sure that connectivity problems don't get in the way of progress. Mobile platforms also encourage micro-learning, which are short, focused lessons that help people learn new things bit by bit. This model works best in maritime settings where learners only have a short amount of time to learn during duty cycles. Push notifications, progress tracking, and built-in chat features encourage active participation and real-time feedback from instructors, which keeps students motivated and accountable even when they are far apart.

Cloud-based collaboration makes mobile learning even better by letting people from different schools and fleets share access to course materials, tests, and performance records. Through centralized systems, teachers can quickly upload learning materials, keep track of students' progress, and give feedback. At the same time, students can work together on group projects or problem-solving exercises in real time (Sousa et al., 2022). Cloud integration also helps institutions work together by making it easier for maritime academies, shipping companies, and regulatory authorities to share data. Training records, certificates, and proof of competency can be stored and checked in secure cloud repositories. This makes it easier to follow the International Maritime Organization (IMO) and Standards of Training, Certification, and Watchkeeping (STCW) frameworks.

The combination of e-portfolios and micro-credentials for ongoing professional development is another game-changing idea. Digital portfolios let seafarers keep track of their learning, simulation results, and certification renewals over the course of their careers. These records can be moved and checked across borders when they are linked to cloud-based credentialing systems. Micro-credentials are digital badges that show you have certain skills, like "Bridge Resource Management" or "Environmental Compliance." They encourage lifelong learning and improving your skills in line with Industry 5.0 competencies.

NAVIGATING CHALLENGES AND ENSURING QUALITY IN E-MARITIME LEARNING

4.1 Digital Infrastructure and Accessibility Issues

The success of e-learning in Maritime Education and Training (MET) depends a lot on how strong its digital infrastructure is and how easy it is to find learning materials. Even though technology has come a long way, maritime institutions, especially in developing areas, still have a lot of problems with bandwidth, hardware availability, and connectivity. These problems make it harder to provide high-quality online instruction and make the differences between students from different geographic and socioeconomic backgrounds even worse. So, making sure that everyone has fair access to digital maritime education requires careful planning, money, and cooperation between governments, businesses, and schools.

Limited bandwidth and unreliable connections are still big problems for digital maritime education. Many maritime academies or training centers are located in coastal, island, and rural areas where high-resolution simulations, real-time navigation exercises, and virtual reality (VR) environments need fast internet speeds that are not always available. This lack of connection makes it hard for students to participate, makes it hard to fairly judge their work, and makes them less interested in learning (Amaglobeli et al. 2023; Hollimon et al. 2025). Also, the high cost of data and digital devices like computers, VR headsets, and simulators is another big problem for students and schools that don't have a lot of money (Henshaw, 2025). To deal with these problems, MET schools are using more and more lightweight mobile apps, offline learning modules, and hybrid delivery systems that mix digital and in-person training. Government initiatives that promote investment in national broadband expansion and shared digital infrastructure can ensure reliable access to maritime e-learning resources, thereby enhancing educational equity (Ahuja, 2023).

Equity and inclusion issues are still very important when it comes to digital transformation in maritime education. Digitalization can make existing inequalities even worse if not handled correctly. Vulnerable groups, such as students in remote areas, women pursuing maritime careers, and trainees with disabilities, may lack sufficient resources or support to engage in these educational settings (Miras et al., 2023). To reduce these risks, it is important that all digital maritime projects follow the rules of inclusive design. This entails the development of multilingual educational resources, the provision of adaptive technologies for students with disabilities, and the assurance of gender-sensitive representation in instructional materials. Furthermore, integrating digital literacy as a fundamental component of the curriculum can enable students to navigate online spaces with confidence and integrity (Piqueras et al., 2025; Saeed & Masters, 2021).

To fix the technical and accessibility problems, important people need to work together. Collaborations among maritime universities, shipping firms, and technology vendors can enable collective access to simulators, cloud resources, and Learning Management Systems (LMS) (Banerjee & Mete, 2024; Kumari & Madhavi, 2025). The maritime education sector can help close the digital divide and make e-learning a universal right instead of a privilege for a few by aligning investments and policies toward fair access. The goal of this change is to make sure that all sailors, no matter where they are, can get high-quality maritime training that uses technology (Eden et al., 2024).

4.2 Quality Assurance and Accreditation Mechanisms

Quality assurance and accreditation systems are very important for Maritime Education and Training (MET) to keep its credibility, safety, and international recognition. As more and more schools and businesses use e-learning and simulation-based methods, it becomes even more important to have strong frameworks that make sure they follow international and national standards. The International Maritime Organization (IMO) has strict rules for the skills, performance, and certification of maritime professionals through the Standards of Training, Certification and Watchkeeping for Seafarers (STCW) Convention. The International Labour Organization (ILO) and different national maritime authorities also make sure that policies are in place to protect the quality of training, fairness, and safety at work. In this global ecosystem, institutions must constantly change their policies, evaluation tools, and teaching methods to keep up with digital technologies while still following the rules.

According to the IMO, ILO, and national quality frameworks, e-learning and simulation-based programs must be as rigorous, valid, and effective as traditional instruction. Institutions must show that digital learning meets or exceeds the STCW Convention's performance standards, especially for training in navigation, engineering, and safety. To accomplish this, quality assurance units must incorporate digital learning audits, data verification protocols, and certification tracking into institutional governance. This means making sure that online materials, e-assessment systems, and simulation software are all checked, updated, and calibrated to match how things really work in the maritime world (Eden et al., 2024). Accreditation agencies now also stress evidence-based documentation, which means that schools must keep clear records of how well students are doing, how qualified their teachers are, and how well their systems are working.

At the same time, standards for evaluating online and simulation-based training are changing to keep up with the challenges of digital learning. Traditional assessments rely on direct observation by the instructor, while e-learning and simulation assessments rely on data generated by the system, interaction logs, and automated performance analytics. This requires the creation of new rubrics that assess cognitive, psychomotor, and affective competencies in virtual settings. For instance, VR-based tests can check how well people can make decisions under pressure, work as a team, and follow procedures. AI-enhanced analytics can find patterns in mistakes and give specific feedback. Quality assurance systems must also make sure that these technologies are dependable, fair, and available to all students.

To keep things fair and honest, more and more accreditation bodies are requiring triangulated evaluation systems that mix quantitative analytics with qualitative instructor judgment (Ahuja, 2023). Accountability is even stronger when there are regular external reviews, peer evaluations, and comparisons to the best practices in the world. In the end, MET institutions make sure that innovation doesn't put safety or competence at risk by making quality assurance and accreditation a part of every level of digital delivery. Instead, it strengthens the maritime education mission, which is to train seafarers who are recognized around the world, act ethically, and are skilled with technology so that they are ready for the challenges of a maritime world that is becoming more digital.

4.3 Faculty Development and Institutional Readiness

For digital transformation in Maritime Education and Training (MET) to work, faculty development and institutional readiness are very important. The quick use of e-learning, simulation, and artificial intelligence (AI) tools has changed the roles of maritime instructors from content providers to digital facilitators, learning designers, and mentors who use data to help students learn. To make this change happen, we need a complete plan to improve teachers' skills in digital pedagogy, instructional design, and technology-enhanced assessment. At the same time, we need to improve the infrastructure and governance of institutions to support long-term e-learning implementation. Even the best technologies could be used less than they should be or not at all if teachers and schools aren't ready for them.

To help teachers learn how to use technology in the classroom, they need to first understand how it changes the way people learn and teach. Maritime instructors, who have usually been trained to teach in person and supervise students in person, often need extra training in areas like designing online courses, using multimedia, navigating learning management systems (LMS), and leading virtual classes. Good faculty development programs should combine technical training with new ways of teaching, focusing on getting students involved, making interactive content, and using feedback strategies that change based on what the student does. For example, teachers need to learn how to use simulation analytics to grade students, use collaborative tools for virtual group projects, and run e-assessment platforms that follow the rules of competency-based education (CBE).

It is also important to help faculty members feel confident with technology and have a growth mindset. Institutions should promote peer mentoring, professional learning communities, and ongoing certification pathways that keep teachers up to date on new maritime technologies. Working with technology companies, maritime industries, and international training centers can help teachers learn about best practices and share knowledge across institutions. Also, recognizing and rewarding digital teaching innovation through institutional policies can encourage faculty to use and keep up with e-learning excellence (Banerjee & Mete, 2024).

Building institutional capacity and support systems is a good way to help faculty get ready for e-learning by setting up the organizational and technical foundations that are needed for it to work well. Institutions need to make strategic plans that cover infrastructure, governance, and quality control. This means putting money into strong LMS platforms, simulation labs, digital libraries, and cloud-based data systems to make sure that access is easy and performance can be tracked. Dedicated e-learning support teams made up of instructional designers, IT experts, and educational technologists are necessary to help teachers design courses, fix problems, and make them better all the time.

Institutional readiness also means that policies are in line and leaders are committed. Administrators need to include e-learning in their long-term plans, set aside money for it, and set clear standards for how to make and evaluate digital courses. Also, promoting a culture of innovation, collaboration, and responsibility makes sure that digitalization becomes a permanent and important part of the institution's identity. MET schools can turn digital problems into chances by giving teachers more power and making sure the whole system is ready. This will make learning environments that are strong, flexible, and ready for the future, while still meeting global standards of maritime excellence.

CHARTING THE FUTURE OF MARITIME EDUCATION

5.1 Toward Smart Maritime Ecosystems

Smart maritime ecosystems—digitally connected learning environments that use new technologies like the Internet of Things (IoT), blockchain, automation, and data-driven analytics—will change the future of Maritime Education and Training (MET) in a big way. These improvements are changing how people in the maritime industry learn, work together, and show off their skills in a field that is becoming more and more reliant on technology. Smart ecosystems are where maritime operations, digital innovation, and lifelong learning come together. They make it easy for institutions, fleets, and regulatory bodies to share knowledge and evaluate each other in real time (Emad & Kataria, 2022; Kitada, 2022).

The combination of IoT, blockchain, and automation is fundamentally changing how we learn about ships by making the difference between classroom simulations and real-life ship operations smaller. IoT-enabled devices and sensors can gather real-time information from shipboard systems, like engine performance, navigation status, and environmental conditions. This information can then be sent to maritime training platforms. Students can examine real-time operational data, participate in decision-making simulations, and acquire experiential knowledge without necessitating physical presence on a vessel (Kitada, 2022; Jo et al., 2020). This data integration not only makes learning more real, but it also makes people more aware of safety by connecting what they learn in theory to what they see in the real world (Pipchenko & Konon, 2023).

In addition, blockchain technology provides a safe and open way to do assessments, certifications, and credential checks. Digital certificates stored on blockchain networks make sure that seafarers' qualifications, simulation results, and professional accomplishments can't be changed and can be easily checked by employers and regulatory bodies. This new idea makes it easier for credentials to be recognized across borders and builds trust between institutions, which is in line with the International Maritime Organization's (IMO) goals for standardizing global training records (Kabashi & Snopçe, 2023; Bhavani, 2024). AI and machine learning (ML) can make assessment processes better by watching how students interact, finding patterns in their performance, and giving them personalized feedback. As a result, automation makes it easier and more accurate to assess competencies, making sure that tests measure real skills instead of just following the rules (Chae et al., 2021; Karimi et al., 2024).

In the context of smart maritime ecosystems, it is important to set up interconnected systems for global maritime knowledge networks. These kinds of networks help create a single digital community made up of institutions, shipping companies, research centers, and regulatory agencies. Using cloud-based platforms and Learning Management Systems (LMS), stakeholders can share research data, best practices, and simulation scenarios across borders. This encourages ongoing collaboration and new ideas. Through these networks, students and teachers from different countries can work together to create training modules, take part in joint virtual exercises, and access shared databases of maritime intelligence, which makes the whole learning experience better (Hadi, 2024; Nhleko, 2023).

Smart maritime ecosystems are more than just new technologies; they are a vision of collective intelligence and sustainability in the maritime industry. By connecting learning systems to real-time operational data, encouraging open credentialing, and encouraging global cooperation, maritime education can effectively deal with technological changes while making sure that the industry follows ethical, efficient, and environmentally friendly practices. As MET institutions embrace this evolution, they will not only prepare competent seafarers but also cultivate adaptable professionals capable of navigating the complexities of a digitized maritime future (Konon, 2022; Maşalacı, 2024).

5.2 Sustainability, Ethics, and Human-Centered Technology

As maritime education moves toward digital transformation, the combination of sustainability, ethics, and technology that puts people first becomes an important guide for new ideas. Automation, artificial intelligence (AI), and digital systems make things safer and more efficient, but they also bring up a lot of complicated moral, environmental, and social issues. The Maritime Education and Training (MET) program has to find a way to balance new technologies with environmental responsibility and the well-being of people. This means that new ideas should help make the sea safer, more dignified, and more sustainable. To achieve this balance, we need to change how we teach so that people and the planet are at the center of technological progress. This will create a new generation of sailors who are not only good with computers but also good with morals and the environment.

The maritime industry plays a key role in solving global sustainability problems, so we need to find a balance between innovation, environmental responsibility, and human welfare. As the shipping industry starts using smart navigation, autonomous ships, and energy-efficient technologies, maritime education needs to teach students how to use these systems safely. Training programs should include ideas about green shipping, cutting carbon emissions, and protecting marine life. They should also teach cadets to see digitalization as a way to protect the environment instead of a way to exploit it. For instance, virtual simulations can show how navigation choices affect the environment, giving students a chance to practice fuel-efficient routing or emergency responses that do the least amount of damage to the environment. IoT-enabled systems can also help students look at real-time emissions data and use environmentally friendly business practices.

Protecting people's well-being in a time of automation and digital control is just as important. People are still the most important part of safe and ethical maritime operations. MET institutions should stress how people and machines can work together and support technologies that add to, not replace, human expertise. Ethical digitalization means making systems that protect workers' privacy, dignity, and mental health. Courses should cover new topics like algorithmic bias, data protection, and how digital surveillance on board ships can affect mental health. By including these topics in training programs, maritime teachers help students become more aware of ethics while also teaching them how to do their jobs well.

Including ethical digital practices in maritime training makes sure that moral and professional responsibility guide technological progress. This means teaching people to be honest, open, and responsible when using AI, automation, and analytics. Scenario-based ethics training, case studies, and reflective assignments can assist learners in addressing dilemmas related to automation errors, environmental compliance, or data misuse. Institutions ought to implement ethical governance frameworks that oversee technology deployment, ensuring conformity with the International Maritime Organization (IMO), International Labour Organization (ILO), and United Nations Sustainable Development Goals (SDGs).

5.3 A Vision for Lifelong Learning and Global Collaboration

The maritime industry is global by nature, and the future of Maritime Education and Training (MET) depends on its ability to promote lifelong learning and work together with people from other countries. As technology moves faster, seafarers and other maritime professionals need to keep up with new rules, learn new skills, and connect with people all over the world who are learning. The old way of getting certified once and then having to retrain every now and then is no longer enough. Instead, lifelong learning, which is supported by cross-border e-learning partnerships and micro-credentials that are recognized around the world, has become the most important part of professional development that will last in the digital age.

International certification and cross-border e-learning partnerships can help make maritime education more consistent and of higher quality for students all over the world. Institutions can go beyond political and geographic boundaries thanks to digital platforms. This makes it possible for them to work together to teach courses, get joint certification, and share accreditation systems. For example, maritime academies in Europe, Asia, and Africa are working together more and more to offer online programs that are recognized by several national maritime authorities. These partnerships make it easier to transfer credits, make sure that the requirements of the International Maritime Organization (IMO) and the Standards of Training, Certification, and Watchkeeping (STCW) are met, and encourage the recognition of each other's qualifications. Cloud-based systems and blockchain-based credentialing make things even more clear. They let learners keep digital records of their training achievements that can be checked and accessed from anywhere in the world. This kind of cooperation between countries not only makes standardization stronger, but it also builds trust among maritime workers around the world, which helps them move up in their careers and move to new jobs.

It is just as important to train maritime professionals who are resilient, adaptable, and ready for the future so they can work in a digital and operational landscape that is always changing. In this case, lifelong learning goes beyond just technical skills to include things like digital literacy, moral judgment, leadership, and working with people from other cultures. As maritime operations become more reliant on automation, artificial intelligence (AI), and sustainable practices, training programs must cultivate individuals capable of merging human-centered decision-making with data-driven insights. AI and analytics can help adaptive learning technologies personalize professional development paths for seafarers by guiding them through ongoing opportunities to learn new skills and improve their current ones based on the needs of the industry at the time.

Collaboration between institutions is very important for keeping this vision alive. Shipping companies, maritime universities, and government agencies need to work together to create flexible learning paths that connect schools and businesses. International networks, like the International Association of Maritime Universities (IAMU) and regional maritime clusters, can help with joint research, shared simulations, and global competency frameworks.

CONCLUSION

The change in maritime education brought about by e-learning and new technologies is a major step forward in getting sailors ready for the challenges of a world that is becoming more digital. The maritime sector is moving quickly toward adaptive, data-driven, and learner-centered environments. This includes using simulation, virtual reality, and artificial intelligence, as well as mobile and cloud-based learning. Not only do these improvements make training better and more efficient, but they also make it more accessible and inclusive. This means that maritime professionals from all over the world can take part in ongoing, competency-based learning that meets international standards.

But technological progress needs to be based on strong moral, pedagogical, and institutional foundations. Ensuring quality assurance, accreditation, and faculty readiness is still the most important thing to do to keep the IMO and STCW frameworks in line with global standards. The move toward smart maritime ecosystems, which are based on IoT, blockchain, and automation, needs a comprehensive approach that balances new ideas with environmental sustainability, human welfare, and moral responsibility. Because of this, maritime institutions need to be both innovators and caretakers, leading the digital transition with honesty, openness, and a dedication to lifelong learning.

In the end, the future of maritime education depends on working together across borders, fields, and technologies. The maritime community can build a workforce that is not only technically skilled but also resilient, ethical, and globally minded by working together with other countries, using shared e-learning frameworks, and offering internationally recognized micro-credentials. By embracing digital transformation with a focus on people and the environment, maritime education will continue to be an important link between the past and the future. It will give seafarers the skills, flexibility, and vision they need to navigate the constantly changing tides of the global maritime industry.

REFERENCES

Оксенюк, І. (2023). Роль хмарних технологій у розвитку інформаційно-цифрової компетентності педагогів. *Перспективи Та Інновації Науки*, (12(30)). Advance online publication. DOI: 10.52058/2786-4952-2023-12(30)-407-417

Ahuja, V. (2023). Equity and access in digital education., 45-59. https://doi.org/DOI: 10.4018/979-8-3693-1826-3.ch005

Amaglobeli, D., Moszoro, M., & Oughton, E. (2023). Estimating digital infrastructure investment needs to achieve universal broadband. *IMF Working Paper*, *2023*(027), 1. DOI: 10.5089/9798400237768.001

Apriani, E., Arief, S., & Supriyadi, A. (2025). Sea tolls as indonesia's blue economy strategy. *IOP Conference Series. Earth and Environmental Science*, *1464*(1), 012001. DOI: 10.1088/1755-1315/1464/1/012001

Banerjee, S., & Mete, J. (2024). *Bridging the digital divide: strategies for empowering marginalized groups through technology in west bengal.* GIMRJ., DOI: 10.69758/GIMRJ2406IIV12P019

Barapatre, O., Sultan, L., Agrawal, M., Sahu, N., & Patel, S. (2024). A review on e-learning based on cloud computing. *International Journal of Research Publication and Reviews*, *5*(1), 371–376. DOI: 10.55248/gengpi.5.0124.0109

Bhavani, K. (2024). Academic credentials issuance and validation system using blockchain. *Interantional Journal of Scientific Research in Engineering and Management*, *08*(03), 1–5. DOI: 10.55041/IJSREM29435

Chae, C., Kim, D., & Lee, H. (2021). A study on the analysis of the effects of passenger ship abandonment training using vr. *Applied Sciences (Basel, Switzerland)*, *11*(13), 5919. DOI: 10.3390/app11135919

Chatterjee, P., Bose, R., Banerjee, S., & Roy, S. (2023). Enhancing data security of cloud based lms. *Wireless Personal Communications*, *130*(2), 1123–1139. DOI: 10.1007/s11277-023-10323-5 PMID: 37168441

Chen, C. and Almunawar, M. (2021). Cloud learning management system in higher education., 1564-1586. https://doi.org/DOI: 10.4018/978-1-7998-5339-8.ch076

Eden, C., Chisom, O., & Adeniyi, I. (2024). Harnessing technology integration in education: strategies for enhancing learning outcomes and equity. World Journal of Advanced Engineering Technology and Sciences, 11(2), 001-008. https://doi.org/DOI: 10.30574/wjaets.2024.11.2.0071

Emad, G. and Kataria, A. (2022). Challenges of simulation training for future engineering seafarers - a qualitative case study.. https://doi.org/DOI: 10.54941/ahfe1002501

Farsi, G., Yusof, A., Rusli, M., & AlSinani, M. (2023). The current perceptions about instructional tools in educational towards adoption of virtual reality among undergraduate students. *International Journal of Interactive Mobile Technologies (Ijim)*, *17*(08), 169–180. DOI: 10.3991/ijim.v17i08.36935

Febriana, W., Sumadewa, I., Anggriani, R., & Zahrah, Z. (2025). Analysis of the effectiveness of cloud-based operations management in digital smes. *Journal of Metals*, *3*(2), 222–235. DOI: 10.61277/jmet.v3i2.198

Guo, X., Guo, Y., & Liu, Y. (2021). The development of extended reality in education: Inspiration from the research literature. *Sustainability (Basel)*, *13*(24), 13776. DOI: 10.3390/su132413776

Hadi, N. (2024). An exploratory review of maritime education and training through collaborative innovation ecosystems: A case for south africa. *SAJMET*, *3*, 15–30. DOI: 10.47348/SAJMET/2024/i1a2

Henshaw, C. (2025). Multimedia learning and udl in uk higher education. *Journal of Advanced Research in Education*, *4*(2), 27–33. DOI: 10.56397/JARE.2025.03.03

Hollimon, L., Taylor, K., Fiegenbaum, R., Carrasco, M., Arruza, L., Chung, D., & Seixas, A. (2025). Redefining and solving the digital divide and exclusion to improve healthcare: Going beyond access to include availability, adequacy, acceptability, and affordability. *Frontiers in Digital Health*, *7*, 1508686. Advance online publication. DOI: 10.3389/fdgth.2025.1508686 PMID: 40330871

Holloway, S. (2024). The impact of cloud-based information systems on collaboration and productivity in remote teams. https://doi.org/DOI: 10.20944/preprints202412.0958.v1

Ibrahim, A. (2021). E-services in sudan during the covid-19 pandemic as a model: A case study of university of bahri-sudan. *Journal of Governance and Public Policy*, *8*(2). Advance online publication. DOI: 10.18196/jgpp.v8i2.11422

Iping, B. (2022). Implications of implementing education and learning in higher education institutions post covid-19: Overview of challenges and strategic policies. *Unes Law Review*, *4*(4), 469–478. DOI: 10.31933/unesrev.v4i4.272

Jo, S., D'agostini, E., & Kang, J. (2020). From seafarers to e-farers: Maritime cadets' perceptions towards seafaring jobs in the industry 4.0. *Sustainability (Basel)*, *12*(19), 8077. DOI: 10.3390/su12198077

Kabashi, F. and Snopçe, H. (2023). Implementation of elliptic curve digital signatures in blockchain for management of certificates in higher education. J Eng App Sci Technol, 1-6. https://doi.org/DOI: 10.47363/JEAST/2023(5)166

Karimi, E., Smith, J., Billard, R., & Veitch, B. (2024). Ai-based adaptive instructional systems for maritime safety training: A systematic literature review. *Discover Artificial Intelligence*, *4*(1), 51. Advance online publication. DOI: 10.1007/s44163-024-00153-0

Kitada, M. (2022). Forward thinking for leading excellence in maritime education and training. *SAJMET*, *1*(1), 71–78. DOI: 10.47348/SAJMET/2022/i1a8

Konon, N. (2022). Prospects for modern maritime education and training practices in terms of distance learning. *Shipping & Navigation*, *33*(1), 54–66. DOI: 10.31653/2306-5761.33.2022.54-66

Kumari, S. and Madhavi, K. (2025). Understanding the evolution of outcome-based education in the age of digital transformation., 12-38. DOI: 10.71443/9789349552685-01

Laskey, L. (2022). Space games: evaluating game-based virtual reality in higher education.. https://doi.org/DOI: 10.5821/conference-9788419184405.057

Lee, H., & Han, J. (2022). Development and evaluation of a virtual reality mechanical ventilation education program for nursing students. *BMC Medical Education*, *22*(1), 775. Advance online publication. DOI: 10.1186/s12909-022-03834-5 PMID: 36357886

Lee, J. (2022). Implementation and evaluation of a virtual reality simulation: Intravenous injection training system. *International Journal of Environmental Research and Public Health*, *19*(9), 5439. DOI: 10.3390/ijerph19095439 PMID: 35564835

Mahundu, F. (2023). Challenges of e-learning during the covid-19 lockdown: A survey of undergraduate students at mwalimu nyerere memorial academy, tanzania. *International Journal of Research Publication and Reviews*, *4*(8), 2668–2674. DOI: 10.55248/gengpi.4.823.51636

Makransky, G., & Klingenberg, S. (2022). Virtual reality enhances safety training in the maritime industry: An organizational training experiment with a non-weird sample. *Journal of Computer Assisted Learning*, *38*(4), 1127–1140. DOI: 10.1111/jcal.12670

Mariatul, M. (2025). Manajemen pendidikan di indonesia dalam menghadapi era digital: Kajian literatur atas strategi dan tantangan. *Khatulistiwa Jurnal Pendidikan Dan Sosial Humaniora*, *5*(1), 93–103. DOI: 10.55606/khatulistiwa.v5i1.5704

Maşalacı, B. (2024). Mobbing exposed by deck cadets at onboard training during the internship period. *Transportation Research Record: Journal of the Transportation Research Board*, *2679*(3), 229–243. DOI: 10.1177/03611981241275540

Miras, S., Bañuls, M., Trigueros, I., & Guillén, C. (2023). Implications of the digital divide: A systematic review of its impact in the educational field. *Journal of Technology and Science Education*, *13*(3), 936. DOI: 10.3926/jotse.2249

Miyusov, M., Nikolaieva, L., & Smolets, V. (2022). Future perspectives of immersive learning in maritime education and training. *Transactions on Maritime Science*, *11*(2). Advance online publication. DOI: 10.7225/toms.v11.n02.014

Mladenović, R., Matvijenko, V., Šubarić, L., & Mladenović, K. (2021). Augmented reality as e-learning tool for intraoral examination and dental charting during covid-19 era. *Journal of Dental Education*, *86*(S1), 862–864. DOI: 10.1002/jdd.12780 PMID: 34420217

Munawwaroh, I. and Baharun, H. (2022). Analysis of the effectiveness of cloud-based learning management systems (lms) in university. ijit, 1(2), 48-57. https://doi.org/DOI: 10.33650/ijit.v1i2.9317

Muruga, K. and Jamaludin, K. (2025). Challenges in the application of digital gamification approaches in teaching and learning at primary schools. International Journal of Research and Innovation in Social Science, 6629-6640. https://doi.org/DOI: 10.47772/IJRISS.2025.903SEDU0488

Nhleko, Y. (2023). Challenges in international convention on the standards of training, certification and watchkeeping compliance: A case study of the south african maritime education and training system. *SAJMET*, *2*(1), 121–131. DOI: 10.47348/SAJMET/2023/i1a8

Pipchenko, O., & Konon, N. (2023). Improvement of marine professional training methods through the involvement of modern technologies. *Shipping & Navigation*, *35*(1), 128–142. DOI: 10.31653/2306-5761.35.2023.128-142

Piqueras, R., González-García, R., Ponce, R., & Plaza, J. (2025). Digital divides in older people: Assessment of digital competencies and proposals for meaningful inclusion. *European Journal of Investigation in Health, Psychology and Education*, *15*(10), 196. DOI: 10.3390/ejihpe15100196 PMID: 41149147

Saeed, S., & Masters, R. (2021). Disparities in health care and the digital divide. *Current Psychiatry Reports*, *23*(9), 61. Advance online publication. DOI: 10.1007/s11920-021-01274-4 PMID: 34297202

Schwaiger, M., Krajnčan, M., Vukovič, M., Jenko, M., & Doz, D. (2024). Educators' opinions about vr/ar/xr: An exploratory study. *Education and Information Technologies*, *29*(18), 24861–24880. DOI: 10.1007/s10639-024-12808-7

Setiawan, A., Suharto, D., & Haryanti, R. (2025). Implementation of the web-based maritime security data integration policy at tanjung uban port. *Ganaya Jurnal Ilmu Sosial Dan Humaniora*, *8*(2), 165–175. DOI: 10.37329/ganaya.v8i2.4040

Setiawan, R., & Kamil, M. (2021). National policy on china one belt-one road (obor) initiative towards indonesia as global maritime nexus. *Jurnal Sosial Politik*, *7*(1), 77–88. DOI: 10.22219/sospol.v7i1.15141

Sharma, A., & Nazir, S. (2021). Assessing the technology self-efficacy of maritime instructors: An explorative study. *Education Sciences*, *11*(7), 342. DOI: 10.3390/educsci11070342

Sharma, R. (2024). Transformative horizons in education: Navigating challenges, embracing innovations, and shaping global landscapes. *IJCE*, *1*(1), 1–3. DOI: 10.47852/bonviewIJCE42022702

Sikarwar, P., Tiwari, A., Joshi, R., & Agrawal, J. (2025). Cloud computing in education: a revolution in learning management systems. Innovare Journal of Education, 10-17. https://doi.org/DOI: 10.22159/ijoe.2025v13i5.54161

Simanjuntak, M.Marudut Bernadtua Simanjuntak. (2024). Towards enhancing linguistic proficiency in maritime education: A study of cadets' perspectives at the maritime institute jakarta. *Bima*, *2*(1), 61–72. DOI: 10.61132/bima.v2i1.543

Siswanto, S., Subiyantoro, H., & Ratnasih, C. (2025). Factors affecting the performance of sea transportation and port infrastructure development and its implications for the economic growth of the maritime sector in indonesia. *Nawala Education*, *2*(2), 17–25. DOI: 10.62872/2fzb1d82

Sousa, C., Hwang, J., Cabrera-Perez, R., Fernandez, A., Misawa, A., Newhook, K., & Lu, A. (2022). Active video games in fully immersive virtual reality elicit moderate-to-vigorous physical activity and improve cognitive performance in sedentary college students. *Journal of Sport and Health Science*, *11*(2), 164–171. DOI: 10.1016/j.jshs.2021.05.002 PMID: 34004390

Srivastava, M. (2025). A research on: E-learning management system. *Interantional Journal of Scientific Research in Engineering and Management*, *09*(05), 1–9. DOI: 10.55041/IJSREM48040

Suh, S. (2020). Diagnosis tool development & verification on readiness of asean higher-ed. institution. J Field-based Lesson stud., 1(2), 155-190. https://doi.org/DOI: 10.22768/JFLS.2020.1.2.155

Tabora, B. (2023). Aligning the ship engine cadets' skills to the 21st century. *International Journal of Multidisciplinary Applied Business and Education Research*, *4*(7), 2277–2295. DOI: 10.11594/ijmaber.04.07.11

Tripathi, M. (2025). Adopting hybrid wireless network architectures to support autonomous maritime vehicle operations. *Journal of Wireless Mobile Networks, Ubiquitous Computing and Dependable Applications*, *16*(2), 95–104. DOI: 10.58346/JOWUA.2025.I2.006

Tusher, H., Nazir, S., Mallam, S., & Munim, Z. (2022). Artificial neural network (ann) for performance assessment in virtual reality (vr) simulators: from surgical to maritime training., 0334-0338. https://doi.org/DOI: 10.1109/IEEM55944.2022.9989816

Vakaliuk, T. (2021). Structural model of a cloud-based learning environment for bachelors in software engineering. *Educational Technology Quarterly*, *2021*(2), 257–273. DOI: 10.55056/etq.17

Venice, J., Vettriselvan, R., Rajesh, D., Suresh, N., & Abirami, P. (2024). Enabling personalized learning and adaptive systems through strategic management., 49-72. https://doi.org/DOI: 10.4018/979-8-3693-6705-6.ch003

Yousif, M. (2022). Vr/ar environment for training students on engineering applications and concepts. Artificial Intelligence & Robotics Development Journal, 173-186. https://doi.org/DOI: 10.52098/airdj.202254

Zhu, S., Sui, Y., Shen, Y., Zhu, Y., Ali, N., Guo, C., & Wang, T. (2021). Effects of virtual reality intervention on cognition and motor function in older adults with mild cognitive impairment or dementia: A systematic review and meta-analysis. *Frontiers in Aging Neuroscience*, *13*, 586999. Advance online publication. DOI: 10.3389/fnagi.2021.586999 PMID: 34025384

Chapter 4

Sailing Into the Digital Era: E-Learning Strategies and Digital Transformation in Maritime Education

Subehana Rachman
http://orcid.org/0009-0007-3523-5837
Politeknik Ilmu Pelayaran Makassar, Indonesia

Meti Kendek
http://orcid.org/0000-0002-2936-4196
Politeknik Ilmu Pelayaran Makassar, Indonesia

Haerani Asri
http://orcid.org/0009-0001-2300-2573
Politeknik Ilmu Pelayaran Makassar, Indonesia

Oktavera Sulistiana
http://orcid.org/0000-0002-3405-5953
Politeknik Ilmu Pelayaran Makassar, Indonesia

Nurwahidah Hidah
Politeknik Ilmu Pelayaran Makassar, Indonesia

Ade Chandra
http://orcid.org/0009-0003-6549-7169
Politeknik Ilmu Pelayaran Makassar, Indonesia

ABSTRACT

This chapter critically examines the strategic significance of e-learning and digital transformation in Maritime Education and Training (MET), highlighting the impact of technological innovation on pedagogical models, institutional structures, and global competency standards. This analysis utilizes current research to explore the amalgamation of mixed, flipped, and entirely online learning environments facilitated by LMS platforms, simulation technologies, AI-driven feedback mechanisms, and VR-based experiential learning. The research assesses institutional preparedness, faculty digital proficiency, and quality assurance frameworks in accordance with STCW and ISO/IEC standards. Critical obstacles, such as infrastructure inequities, user opposition, and ethical issues pertaining to data protection and cyber-ethics, are thoroughly examined. The report contends that sustainable digital transformation necessitates comprehensive policy formulation, inclusive digital ecosystems, and international collaboration to develop a resilient, future-ready maritime workforce.

DOI: 10.4018/979-8-3373-6670-8.ch004

INTRODUCTION

1.1 From Traditional Classrooms to Digital Bridges

The transition from traditional classrooms to digital learning environments has significantly influenced maritime education, paralleling broader educational trends. Historically, maritime pedagogy relied heavily on in-person instruction, emphasizing hands-on training crucial for navigating and operating vessels. However, over recent decades, there has been a marked evolution from purely physical learning environments toward hybrid models that integrate digital platforms and resources. The uptake of blended learning, which combines conventional face-to-face instruction with online elements, has become especially pertinent. Studies indicate that this hybrid approach has become increasingly favored due to its flexibility and ability to cater to diverse learning styles (Abubakar et al., 2022; Müller, 2022).

Several drivers have accelerated the shift toward digital learning in maritime education. One of the most significant factors has been globalization, which demands that educational institutions adapt to increasingly international labor markets. The industry requires maritime professionals to engage with cutting-edge technology and be adaptable in their training methods. The integration of digital tools allows for synchronous and asynchronous learning, providing educators with opportunities to reach students worldwide, offering greater content accessibility, and accommodating different learning preferences (Atwa et al., 2022; Alshammary & Alhalafawy, 2023). As noted by Abdelfattah et al., the increase in e-learning adoption is facilitated by platforms that can connect learners across various geographical locations, which is particularly transformative for maritime education that relies on industry-standard practices (Abdelfattah et al., 2023).

Another critical driver of digital adoption has been the COVID-19 pandemic, which necessitated a rapid shift to online learning across educational sectors, including maritime training. The pandemic acted as both a catalyst and an accelerator for already emerging trends toward digital education. Evidence indicates that during this period, educational institutions adopted new technologies swiftly to continue delivering educational content effectively, often switching to what has been referred to as "emergency remote teaching" (Varma & Jafri, 2020; Christabel & Prawira, 2023). Many institutions, including those in maritime education, began utilizing a range of digital platforms, enabling the delivery of lectures through video conferencing tools and fostering interactive learning environments (Mbugi et al., 2022; Elsalem et al., 2021). This abrupt transition prompted a recognition of the importance of robust technological infrastructure and instructional design in ensuring instructional quality and student engagement in digital settings (Hermanto & Srimulyani, 2021; Christabel & Prawira, 2023).

Amid these shifts, studies have shown that student preferences have evolved. Many learners express favorable attitudes toward blended and online learning, likely due to the newfound flexibility in scheduling and access to diverse resources (Atwa et al., 2022; Mudenda et al., 2023). This is particularly relevant in maritime education, where real-time simulations and practical exercises can be enriched through blended learning models, helping students not only gain theoretical knowledge but also apply it in simulation environments that reflect real-world scenarios of maritime operations (Mbugi et al., 2022; Xing & Saghaian, 2022). Consequently, the future of maritime education lies in effectively harnessing digital transformation to build bridges that encompass both traditional and modern pedagogical paradigms, ensuring that sea professionals are equipped for the complexities of global maritime challenges.

1.2 Understanding Digital Transformation in Maritime Contexts

Digital transformation within the sphere of Maritime Education and Training (MET) denotes a comprehensive and systematic evolution of instructional methodologies and institutional operations, utilizing advanced digital technologies to enhance learning outcomes and organizational efficiency. In the context of MET, digital transformation involves not merely the adoption of digital tools but a fundamental rethinking of educational frameworks, curricula, and pedagogies to prepare maritime professionals for the complexities of modern maritime environments. This conceptualization aligns with definitions provided in broader higher education contexts, emphasizing that effective digital transformation incorporates strategic implementation that extends beyond mere technological upgrades (Alenezi, 2021).

The interplay between technology, pedagogy, and institutional change is pivotal in driving the successful digital transformation of maritime education. The integration of technology into pedagogical practices has the potential to augment teaching effectiveness by facilitating interactive and personalized learning experiences. These experiences are essential for engaging students in a digital-native generation who benefit from a learning environment that combines traditional methods with innovative digital tools, such as simulations and virtual reality (Oliveira & Souza, 2021; Adarkwah & Huang, 2023). These tools allow learners to practice navigational and operational skills in realistic environments, improving their preparedness for real-world challenges.

Institutional change is equally crucial in the transition to digitally enhanced maritime education. Educational institutions must cultivate a culture of adaptability and continuous improvement to respond effectively to the rapid advancements in technology and shifting industry demands. Leadership plays an instrumental role in this regard; transformational leadership can foster an environment conducive to innovation and experimentation with new pedagogical models and digital technologies (Tiwow et al., 2023; Niţă & Gu u, 2023). Such leadership encourages collaboration among faculty members, allowing their collective insights to shape a cohesive strategy for implementing these technological solutions within the maritime curriculum.

Moreover, digital transformation necessitates significant investments in infrastructure and faculty development to ensure that educators are well-equipped to navigate the emerging digital landscape. Effective professional development programs are essential in acclimating educators to new instructional strategies and digital tools (Kumar et al., 2022). As the maritime industry increasingly embraces digitalization—evidenced by the adoption of automation and data-driven decision-making—so too must educational institutions evolve to meet these expectations. Institutions are finding that the successful integration of technology into MET hinges on understanding the pedagogical implications of digital tools and adapting organizational structures to support these changes (Trevisan et al., 2023).

Ultimately, the future of MET lies in a synergistic approach that recognizes the dynamic interconnections between technology, pedagogy, and institutional strategy. As maritime education continues to transition into the digital era, embracing this holistic understanding of digital transformation will be critical for developing competent maritime professionals capable of meeting industry demands while fostering safety and environmental sustainability (Kuzminska et al., 2023). By implementing a strategic vision that prioritizes continuous adaptation and innovation, the maritime education sector will be well-positioned to navigate the challenges and opportunities presented by digital transformation.

1.3 The Strategic Importance Of E-Learning In The Maritime Sector

The strategic importance of e-learning in the maritime sector is underscored by its ability to enhance accessibility, flexibility, and resilience in maritime learning environments. The integration of online and blended learning frameworks stands out as a transformative approach that significantly broadens the reach of educational opportunities. Traditionally, maritime education and training (MET) has been limited by geographical constraints, expensive infrastructure, and the availability of practical training facilities. However, e-learning mechanisms dismantle these barriers, allowing learners from remote or underserved regions to access quality maritime education Sulistyono et al., 2024). This broad access ensures that aspiring maritime professionals can engage with the curriculum, participate in simulations, and collaborate with peers or instructors, regardless of their location.

Furthermore, the flexibility inherent in e-learning enables maritime students to tailor their educational experiences according to their unique needs and schedules. Those balancing work commitments, for instance, can engage with learning materials at their convenience, subsequently enhancing their capacity to absorb and apply knowledge effectively. This flexible approach not only fosters a more inclusive educational environment but also helps to build resilience among learners by allowing them to adapt their studies to dynamic professional landscapes, which is especially pertinent in the maritime industry, where operational demands are often unpredictable (Kim et al., 2023).

Moreover, the shift towards e-learning and blended learning models addresses the global competency gaps evident in the maritime workforce. The maritime sector is facing significant challenges regarding skill shortages and insufficient training to meet evolving industry standards and technological advancements (Kim et al., 2023). By implementing e-learning strategies, educational institutions can offer targeted training that is responsive to the competencies required by modern maritime operations. These online modules can incorporate relevant updates in safety regulations, environmental protocols, and technology usage that align with the International Convention on Standards of Training, Certification, and Watchkeeping for Seafarers (STCW) framework (Kim et al., 2023).

Research has shown that blended learning models, which combine face-to-face and online components, are particularly effective in enhancing educational outcomes. Studies reveal that learners favor the dual approach, as it fosters better engagement and retention of information compared to traditional pedagogical methodologies (Mojarad et al., 2023; Nong et al., 2023). This pedagogical efficacy is instrumental for addressing the urgent need for maritime professionals who are not only adequately trained but also versatile and equipped to manage complex challenges in their roles.

Additionally, the impetus for adopting e-learning within MET reflects a strategic response to external pressures such as the COVID-19 pandemic. The necessity to pivot swiftly to online learning forced many educational institutions to innovate, leading to the rapid development of digital resources and adaptive teaching strategies that can now be leveraged for ongoing and future training (Mafara & Haki, 2023). Through e-learning, maritime education can continue to provide essential training and development opportunities, thus maintaining the flow of skilled personnel into the industry while also ensuring high standards of safety and operational excellence (Mafara & Haki, 2023).

FRAMEWORKS AND MODELS OF E-LEARNING IN MARITIME EDUCATION

2.1 Pedagogical Models for Digital Maritime Learning

The implementation of effective e-learning programs in Maritime Education and Training (MET) must be underpinned by robust pedagogical models that embrace foundational learning theories. In this respect, constructivism, connectivism, and experiential learning principles play vital roles in shaping efficient digital learning experiences. Constructivist theory posits that learners build their understanding through experiences and reflections, advocating for educational practices that encourage active engagement and collaborative knowledge construction Galić et al., 2020). This model is particularly beneficial in MET, as students can learn to apply maritime principles actively through virtual simulations and collaborative projects that reflect real-world scenarios (Федорова & Bobrysheva, 2021).

Connectivism, as another significant educational theory, highlights the role of social and technological networks in learning. It recognizes that in a digital age, knowledge is distributed across various nodes and that learners must be adept at navigating these networks to synthesize information meaningfully (Fabian-Perona, 2025). In MET, this can involve utilizing online forums, collaborative platforms, and digital resources to create a learning ecosystem where students—whether in traditional or remote settings—connect with instructors and peers, perpetuating a continuous flow of ideas and problem-solving experiences (Sharma & Nazir, 2021).

Experiential learning theory emphasizes the fundamental role of experience in the learning process. In maritime contexts, where practical skills are paramount, integrating experiential learning through virtual labs and scenario-based training environments offers students opportunities to engage actively in the learning process. For instance, engaging students in simulated maritime operations allows for hands-on practice while developing critical skills such as decision-making and teamwork, which are essential for effective maritime professionals (Diahyleva et al., 2025).

In the framework of MET, various instructional models, namely blended, flipped, and fully online learning, enhance pedagogical practices. Blended learning combines both face-to-face and online teaching components, providing a structured environment that allows for initial traditional instruction followed by deeper exploration through digital means. This method has been recognized for its efficacy in improving learning outcomes while catering to diverse student needs (Youhasan et al., 2022). Studies have indicated that blended learning approaches can enhance student engagement and performance in maritime education, aligning tightly with the dynamic demands of the maritime industry (Федорова & Bobrysheva, 2021).

The flipped classroom model further enhances the accessibility of learning materials, allowing students to learn foundational concepts through online lectures or resources before engaging in more intensive, application-oriented activities in class. This student-centered learning approach shifts the focus from teacher-led instruction to student engagement, encouraging learners to take ownership of their educational journey (al., 2023). For maritime students, this means they can come to class more prepared and apply their knowledge in real-time simulations or collaborative problem-solving settings (Tan et al., 2022).

Finally, fully online learning frameworks provide a complete digital learning environment that eliminates geographical constraints, enabling institutions to reach a wider audience of maritime learners. Research demonstrates that this model has been indispensable for maintaining continuity in education during disruptions such as the COVID-19 pandemic (Sharma & Nazir, 2021). By leveraging online platforms effectively, educational institutions can ensure that essential maritime training continues uninterrupted, preparing students for their roles within an increasingly complex and global maritime environment (Sharma & Nazir, 2021).

2.2 Technology Integration and Learning Management Systems (LMS)

The adoption of Learning Management Systems (LMS) in Maritime Education and Training (MET) represents a significant advancement in how educational institutions deliver content and engage with students. Platforms such as Moodle, Blackboard, and Google Classroom have become widely implemented, providing structured environments for course management, content delivery, and student assessments. The versatility of LMS platforms contributes to their importance in maritime education by facilitating collaborative learning and offering resources such as video lectures, interactive simulations, and access to a variety of digital maritime tools (Sharma & Nazir, 2021). This accessibility is particularly critical in a field where practical training often faces logistical challenges.

LMS not only streamlines administrative processes but also fosters engagement through integrated assessments that can accommodate diverse learning styles. For maritime instructors, utilizing these platforms supports a more organized and efficient approach to student feedback and progress tracking (Sharma & Nazir, 2021). However, successful integration requires that instructors possess a degree of technological self-efficacy, which influences their ability to effectively employ these digital tools in pedagogical practices (Sharma & Nazir, 2021). This transformation is imperative, as the maritime field often necessitates the engagement of learners in dynamic, interactive learning experiences that traditional classroom settings may fail to provide.

In addition to LMS, technology integration in MET heavily relies on simulation software, virtual reality (VR), and artificial intelligence (AI)-based feedback systems. Simulation software serves as a cornerstone of practical training in maritime education by reproducing real-world maritime scenarios that can be experienced virtually, significantly enhancing students' skill development and decision-making capabilities (Ala et al., 2024). Tools such as ship bridge simulators allow learners to engage in realistic navigational challenges, practice crisis management, and refine their technical abilities without the risks associated with live maritime operations (D'Augusta et al., 2025; Lvov & Popova, 2020).

VR technology is particularly impactful in maritime training; it creates immersive environments that replicate on-board experiences, dramatically improving students' situational awareness and fostering the development of critical thinking and problem-solving skills by placing them in scenarios where they must make quick, informed decisions (D'Augusta et al., 2025; Xue et al., 2024). Furthermore, AI-based feedback systems can assess student performance in real-time, providing personalized insights that enhance learning outcomes. By analyzing learners' interactions and progress, these AI technologies can identify areas for improvement and suggest tailored resources or instructional strategies (Sharma et al., 2022).

The fusion of these technologies—LMS, simulation software, VR, and AI—creates a robust framework for MET, enabling institutions to deliver efficient and effective education that meets the evolving demands of the maritime industry. The increased reliance on technology not only prepares students for their immediate learning needs but also instills adaptability in a rapidly changing technological landscape. As reflected in current literature, the integration of these educational technologies is becoming critical for producing competent maritime professionals capable of navigating the complexities of an increasingly digitized shipping and logistics environment (Ala et al., 2024; Buthelezi & Wyk, 2020; Rylander, 2022).

2.3 E-Learning Standards and Quality Assurance

The establishment of e-learning standards and quality assurance frameworks is crucial in maintaining the integrity and efficacy of Maritime Education and Training (MET). Benchmarking frameworks such as the International Maritime Organization's Standards of Training, Certification, and Watchkeeping (STCW) are vital in ensuring that digital training adheres to established international benchmarks. STCW outlines guidelines for the quality assurance of education and training services and sets benchmarks for the organization of e-learning programs, focusing on elements such as curriculum design, learning environments, and outcomes. Adoption of such standards in MET ensures that training programs are aligned with international competencies and regulatory requirements, thereby enhancing the credibility and recognition of maritime qualifications.

STCW compliance is particularly pertinent in the maritime industry, which demands rigorous training standards due to safety and navigation responsibilities associated with sea operations. Compliance with STCW guidelines not only ensures the competency of seafarers but also aligns maritime training programs with global expectations, thereby fostering trust among stakeholders in the shipping industry. By adhering to these standards, maritime educational institutions affirm their commitment to delivering quality training, which is crucial for enhancing the employability and preparedness of graduates in a competitive global workforce.

Quality assurance in online maritime training entails ensuring consistency, assessment validity, and various accreditation processes. One significant dimension of quality assurance is the assessment of both formative and summative evaluation criteria in e-learning programs. Formative assessments provide ongoing feedback to learners, while summative assessments evaluate the overall learning outcomes and competencies achieved upon completion of the course. In this respect, assessments must be designed and implemented accurately, ensuring that they reflect the intended learning objectives and outcomes specified by regulatory bodies such as STCW.

Furthermore, institutions must ensure that their e-learning assessments are validated through accreditation processes that recognize their adherence to established standards. Accreditation, particularly from a recognized maritime authority or educational body, guarantees the program's adherence to quality benchmarks and reinforces stakeholders' confidence in graduates' competencies. Quality assurance frameworks, such as those recommended by the European Standards and Guidelines (ESG), offer robust mechanisms to monitor and evaluate e-learning practices, ensuring they meet educational standards.

In the maritime sector, where practical skills and theoretical knowledge must converge, the development of rigorous quality assurance measures will support continuous evaluation and improvement of e-learning strategies, directly impacting learner outcomes and competency achievements. This is especially critical when ensuring that online learning environments facilitate meaningful engagement, effective skill transfer, and a comprehensive understanding of maritime safety and operational best practices.

DIGITAL TRANSFORMATION STRATEGIES FOR MET INSTITUTIONS

3.1 Institutional Readiness And Strategic Planning

The digital transformation of Maritime Education and Training (MET) institutions relies significantly on institutional readiness and strategic planning, which are essential for navigating the complexities introduced by technology. Leadership plays a pivotal role in this transition, as effective change management hinges on the vision and direction set by educational leaders. Leaders in MET institutions must foster a culture of innovation and adaptability to address the challenges posed by digital integration while ensuring that staff and stakeholders buy into the transformation process (Laila et al., 2025). This involves not only articulating a clear digital strategy but also ensuring that all members of the institution understand their roles in its implementation. Strong leadership encourages open communication, promotes professional development, and creates an environment where feedback is valued, enabling the institution to adapt quickly to the evolving technological landscape.

As part of fostering institutional readiness, MET institutions must build their capacity and enhance their digital infrastructure. This means investing in technologies that support digital learning, such as Learning Management Systems (LMS) like Moodle or Blackboard. These platforms facilitate course management, engagement, and assessment while allowing instructors to tailor learning experiences to meet students' individual needs (Luo, 2024). Furthermore, creating robust digital infrastructure encompasses not only the technological tools but also the necessary technical support to ensure effective usage (Varhata et al., 2025). For instance, institutions must provide training sessions for both faculty and students to enhance digital literacy and promote the effective use of these technologies in educational settings.

Moreover, MET institutions can benefit from aligning their strategic planning processes with established quality frameworks, such as the ISO/IEC 40180 standards. These frameworks provide guidelines for ensuring the credibility and quality of e-learning programs, which is essential for meeting international competencies and expectations related to maritime training (Shraim, 2020). Participation in accreditation processes also strengthens institutional capacity, affirming compliance with quality assurance standards and enhancing stakeholder confidence in the program's effectiveness (Shraim, 2020).

In developing a comprehensive digital transformation strategy, MET institutions should consider partnerships and collaborations with stakeholders in academia, industry, and government. Such collaborations can provide access to additional funding, expertise, and resources that further support the infrastructure needed for effective e-learning programs. Additionally, fostering relationships with technology providers can yield beneficial insights into emerging tools and best practices that can enhance the educational experience.

3.2 Curriculum Redesign and Digital Content Development

The shift towards e-learning in Maritime Education and Training (MET) necessitates a comprehensive curriculum redesign that integrates innovative educational approaches, such as e-learning modules, micro-credentials, and competency-based frameworks. Integrating e-learning modules into the MET curriculum enables institutions to offer modular courses, allowing students to engage with content flexibly and progressively. Micro-credentialing represents a strategic response to the demand for targeted skill development, offering learners a pathway to build specific competencies recognized by employers. This approach is particularly beneficial in rapidly evolving fields like maritime operations, where the ability to adapt to new technologies and standards is critical.

Competency-based education (CBE) focuses on the mastery of specific skills and knowledge rather than traditional time-based learning models. For MET, adopting a competency-based approach allows institutions to deliver customized educational experiences that address individual learners' needs and align with industry standards. As a result, students can progress at their own pace, ensuring that they acquire the necessary competencies for future maritime roles. Furthermore, this approach fosters a culture of continuous learning, essential for professionals in an industry characterized by technological advancements and regulatory changes.

As part of the curriculum redesign, it is imperative to design interactive, multimedia-rich, and simulation-based learning resources tailored to the maritime context. The integration of multimedia elements—such as videos, animations, and interactive diagrams—enhances student engagement and facilitates deeper learning by catering to various learning styles. This is particularly vital in MET, where complex concepts related to navigation, safety protocols, and maritime law may benefit from visual representations and real-world applications.

Simulation-based learning, in particular, plays a crucial role in MET, as it allows students to practice skills in realistic scenarios without the dangers associated with live operations. Technologies such as virtual simulations and augmented reality can recreate maritime environments where students can experiment, make decisions, and receive immediate feedback. Research indicates that simulation-based training significantly improves decision-making skills and situational awareness, both of which are critical for success in maritime careers. These interactive learning experiences not only enhance skill acquisition but also contribute to building confidence in students as they prepare for real-world challenges.

Moreover, the development of digital content must be aligned with quality assurance frameworks that emphasize maintaining high standards in online education. Ensuring that these learning resources are consistently evaluated and refined will help institutions deliver effective educational experiences and uphold their reputation within the maritime sector.

3.3 Faculty Empowerment and Digital Pedagogical Skills

Empowering maritime instructors with the necessary skills for online delivery and digital assessment is fundamental for adapting to the digital era of education. As maritime education and training (MET) institutions increasingly shift towards blended and fully online learning environments, it becomes essential to upskill instructors in various pedagogical and technological competencies. Training programs must focus on enhancing instructors' capabilities to deliver engaging online content and effectively utilize digital assessment tools. Research indicates that ongoing professional development is a key factor in improving educators' confidence and competence in employing digital technologies, facilitating their ability to create interactive and meaningful learning experiences for students (Karmin et al., 2025).

Upskilling programs can cover various areas critical for effective online education, including how to design and deliver engaging e-learning modules, assess student performance in a digital context, and utilize data analytics to inform instructional decisions. Digital assessment tools, which can range from online quizzes to sophisticated learning analytics systems, enable instructors to obtain timely feedback on student progress and performance, allowing for improvements in instruction and learner engagement (Tripathi, 2025). However, successful implementation requires that educators are comfortable using these tools, making empowerment through training initiatives an indispensable component of any digital transformation strategy in MET.

In addition to technical training, cultivating a culture of digital literacy and adaptability among faculty members is paramount. This involves fostering an environment where instructors are encouraged to experiment with new technologies and instructional methodologies, thereby promoting a culture of innovation within the institution (Nazaruddin, 2025). A commitment to continuous learning enables faculty to stay updated on emerging trends in maritime education and technology, such as simulation-based training and artificial intelligence in assessment, which can significantly enhance the educational experience.

Leadership must play an active role in this transformation by providing support and resources, encouraging a mindset shift towards innovation and adaptability. By modeling adaptive behaviors and celebrating successes in the integration of digital tools, institutional leaders can inspire faculty to embrace these changes as opportunities rather than disruptions (Aquino, 2025). In this context, an empowered faculty equipped with digital pedagogical skills not only enhances the quality of education provided to students but also ensures institutions remain competitive in a rapidly evolving educational landscape.

Moreover, there is a need for institutional policies that underpin the digital empowerment of instructors by allocating resources for technology training. Establishing clear frameworks for professional development tailored to the specific demands of maritime education can facilitate the smooth transition and integration of digital tools in teaching practices (Mariyono & Mistar, 2025). Continuous monitoring and evaluation of faculty training programs will further ensure they meet the evolving needs of educators, helping to address any gaps in knowledge or skill that may emerge as technology continues to evolve.

CHALLENGES AND ETHICAL CONSIDERATIONS IN DIGITAL MARITIME LEARNING

4.1 Barriers to E-Learning Implementation

The implementation of e-learning in Maritime Education and Training (MET) is fraught with various challenges that can hinder its success, particularly in developing contexts. One of the primary barriers is inadequate technical infrastructure and connectivity. In many regions, particularly in developing countries, institutions struggle with unreliable internet access and insufficient technological resources necessary for effective online learning. This lack of infrastructure limits the ability of educators to deliver quality content and affects students' access to critical learning materials and interactive platforms (Yurzhenko et al., 2023). Research shows that the digital divide exacerbates educational inequalities, leaving those without reliable internet or technological devices at a significant disadvantage (Kononova et al., 2024). To facilitate a successful digital transformation in MET, institutions must prioritize investments in infrastructure and ensure access to stable internet connectivity.

User resistance is another significant barrier to successful e-learning implementation. Educators and students accustomed to traditional teaching methods may be hesitant to embrace new technologies and pedagogical approaches. This resistance can stem from various factors, including fear of change, lack of training, and doubts about the effectiveness of e-learning compared to conventional methods. Instructors may feel inadequately prepared to transition to digital delivery and assess student performance effectively within an online framework, leading to diminished confidence and reluctance to adopt these transformative strategies (Sulistyono et al., 2024). To overcome this barrier, institutions should implement comprehensive training programs that focus not only on technical skills but also highlight the benefits and effectiveness of e-learning as a valuable educational tool.

Institutional and cultural challenges further complicate the adoption of digital pedagogies in MET. Some institutions may lack a strategic vision for digital transformation or the requisite leadership to drive such initiatives. An organization's culture can also impact the willingness of faculty members to adopt innovative teaching practices, as entrenched traditional methods can create an environment resistant to change (Cabaron, 2023). Institutions must establish an inclusive culture that values innovation and recognizes the importance of digital competencies. By promoting a culture of collaboration and encouraging open dialogue about the transition to digital pedagogies, institutions can enhance faculty engagement and foster a more supportive environment for technological adoption within the education framework (Prasetyo et al., 2023).

Furthermore, addressing the specific cultural aspects of maritime education and training is crucial. In many maritime academies, traditional teaching practices may dominate, creating a reluctance to integrate new methodologies. This cultural inertia can contribute to misconceptions about e-learning being less rigorous or effective than in-person instruction. Educational stakeholders should actively work to dismantle these misconceptions through awareness campaigns and data-driven presentations that showcase successful e-learning implementations and their outcomes (Pipchenko & Kovtunenko, 2020).

4.2 Student Engagement and Digital Inclusion

In the context of Maritime Education and Training (MET), addressing barriers to student engagement and ensuring digital inclusion is paramount for fostering an equitable learning environment. One significant challenge faced by institutions is digital fatigue, which can detract from the motivation of both students and faculty. The sudden transition to online learning due to external pressures, such as the COVID-19 pandemic, has led to a reliance on screens and digital interactions, which can be exhausting for learners (Swaminathan et al., 2021). As a result, strategies need to be implemented to combat digital fatigue. These strategies could include incorporating synchronous and asynchronous learning modalities, allowing students to alternate between more engaging, interactive sessions and self-paced study time, thereby reducing the burden of constant online engagement (Selivanova et al., 2023).

Additionally, motivation can be closely linked to equitable access to learning technologies. Significant disparities exist between different socio-economic groups regarding access to essential digital tools and reliable internet connectivity, leading to exacerbated educational inequities. For instance, students from lower socio-economic backgrounds may lack the necessary devices or broadband access, hindering their ability to participate fully in digital learning experiences (Ehimuan et al., 2024; Nasrati et al., 2024). Institutions must prioritize providing resources and support to ensure that all students can engage with the learning materials. This may involve investment in technology lending programs or partnerships with local organizations to improve connectivity within their communities (Eden et al., 2024).

One effective way to promote equitable access is to adopt inclusive digital participation strategies that take into consideration the diverse socio-economic backgrounds of students. Institutions can implement policies that support the provision of technological resources, such as subsidized internet access or the loaning of devices to students. Additionally, by promoting digital literacy programs that target underrepresented groups, institutions can enhance students' confidence and competence in using digital tools effectively (Tahmasebi, 2023). By doing so, it becomes possible to create a more inclusive educational setting where all students feel empowered to engage with digital learning.

Moreover, curriculum redesign efforts should emphasize the integration of culturally relevant materials and diverse perspectives to enrich the learning experience for all students (Eden et al., 2024). For instance, incorporating case studies, examples, and practices from various maritime cultures can make content more relatable and engaging, fostering a sense of belonging and motivation among learners. Engaging students in dialogue about their experiences and perspectives can further enrich the learning environment and enhance retention (Eden et al., 2024).

Finally, fostering a sense of community among students is crucial for engagement in an increasingly digital world. MET institutions can implement collaborative projects, peer-assisted learning, and community-building activities within online environments to facilitate connections among students and reduce feelings of isolation, which may arise in purely online settings. Such initiatives will not only support student engagement but also enhance the overall learning experience.

4.3 Ethical, Legal, and Data Privacy Concerns

In the landscape of digital learning, the ethical, legal, and data privacy concerns associated with Maritime Education and Training (MET) institutions are of paramount importance. As organizations increasingly adopt technology to enhance educational outcomes, they must also navigate the complexities of data security, intellectual property, and maritime cyber-ethics. Ensuring that sensitive student information and intellectual outputs are adequately protected from breaches and unauthorized access is a critical responsibility for educators and administrators alike (Abubakar et al., 2022). The rise of cyber threats in the maritime sector necessitates robust security protocols and policies to safeguard educational data, particularly in an environment where personal and organizational information must be shared online (Müller, 2022).

Furthermore, intellectual property rights can become a controversial subject in digital contexts. Clear guidelines need to be established concerning the ownership and use of digital content created by educators and students. Protecting intellectual property rights is essential not only for fostering creativity and innovation but also for maintaining trust within the educational environment (Atwa et al., 2022). Institutions are urged to develop frameworks for the ethical use and sharing of learning resources, ensuring that all parties are aware of their rights and responsibilities regarding copyright and attribution in digital spaces.

Maritime cyber-ethics represents another critical dimension of this discussion. The maritime domain faces unique challenges, including the integration of technology not only in training but also in operational practices. As cyber-physical systems become more commonplace on vessels, a robust ethical framework must be established to govern how data is collected, analyzed, and leveraged in educational and operational contexts (Alshammary & Alhalafawy, 2023). Adopting ethical standards helps to mitigate the risks of cyber exploitation and fosters a culture of responsibility among maritime professionals. By aligning with existing ethical guidelines, MET institutions can ensure that their graduates are equipped to handle cybersecurity challenges with integrity.

In light of these concerns, establishing governance frameworks that promote responsible digital transformation is imperative. These frameworks should encompass guidelines for data privacy, cybersecurity policies, and intellectual property management specific to the educational context. Institutional policies need to be designed in collaboration with legal experts to guarantee compliance with local and international laws while creating standards that support ethical decision-making within educational contexts (Abdelfattah et al., 2023).

Moreover, engaging faculty and students in discussions around ethical practices will facilitate a deeper understanding of the implications of digital technologies in maritime education. Training sessions that address issues related to data security, intellectual property, and digital citizenship can empower stakeholders to contribute positively to the ethical culture of their institutions (Varma & Jafri, 2020). By prioritizing education on these topics, MET institutions not only enhance the ethical conduct of their community but also prepare students for challenges they may face in the maritime sector.

FUTURE DIRECTIONS AND GLOBAL IMPLICATIONS

5.1 Emerging Technologies and Smart Learning Ecosystems

The integration of emerging technologies such as Artificial Intelligence (AI), Extended Reality (XR), and the Internet of Things (IoT) into maritime e-learning represents a significant advancement in the creation of smart learning ecosystems. These technologies are revolutionizing how maritime education is delivered, enhancing engagement and effectiveness while facilitating personalized learning experiences for students. The increasing adoption of AI in educational settings offers the potential for intelligent tutoring systems that can adapt to individual learning styles and needs, allowing for a more personalized approach to skill development (Mahmadov, 2025). AI-driven systems can analyze learner behavior, assess performance, and provide customized feedback, effectively promoting active engagement and assisting educators in optimizing instructional strategies (Mahmadov, 2025).

Extended Reality, encompassing both Virtual Reality (VR) and Augmented Reality (AR), offers immersive training experiences that are particularly beneficial for maritime education. Simulation-based learning in VR environments enables students to practice navigation, ship handling, and emergency response scenarios in a safe and controlled setting (Shafik, 2025). This experiential learning not only deepens understanding but also boosts retention by allowing learners to engage in hands-on training that reflects real-world applications (Abir et al., 2023). The incorporation of AR can enhance the understanding of complex maritime systems by overlaying digital information onto physical environments, enabling real-time interaction with virtual elements (Shaikhanova et al., 2025).

The Internet of Things (IoT) further augments the potential of maritime education by facilitating data collection and connectivity among various educational tools and platforms. IoT devices can track student engagement and performance, providing educators with valuable insights into learning patterns and outcomes. This real-time data can inform adjustments to instructional methods and content, ensuring that educational processes remain responsive to the needs of students. As these technologies converge, they contribute to the development of smart learning ecosystems that are flexible, connected, and student-centered (Bibri & Jagatheesaperumal, 2023).

In addition to enhancing traditional educational structures, these technologies facilitate the emergence of intelligent tutoring systems that personalize learning paths based on individual progress and needs. By leveraging big data analytics, these systems can identify knowledge gaps and recommend tailored learning resources, thus supporting students in achieving their competencies. Such data-driven personalization not only enhances the learning experience but also promotes student autonomy and self-directed learning (Behl & Zhang, 2023).

In a global context, the implications of these developments are profound, as the adoption of such technologies can contribute to the democratization of maritime education. By making high-quality, interactive learning experiences accessible to diverse populations, these technologies can bridge educational gaps and prepare a qualified workforce ready to tackle the challenges of a rapidly evolving maritime industry (Tirumalamba, 2025).

5.2 Global Collaboration and Digital Maritime Networks

Global collaboration among maritime institutions, industries, and international bodies is crucial for fostering advancements in Maritime Education and Training (MET) through digital maritime networks.

Such partnerships create opportunities for sharing resources, expertise, and best practices that can facilitate the integration of technology in maritime education. Collaborative efforts can include joint curricula development, faculty exchanges, research initiatives, and the creation of global learning platforms that promote innovation and enhance training outcomes across institutions. This cooperative framework enriches the educational environment and ensures that maritime training is consistent with global standards, thereby improving the transparency and quality of education in diverse geographical contexts.

Strengthening partnerships among educational institutions, industry stakeholders, and regulatory bodies can lead to a more integrated and responsive maritime education system. For example, collaboration with shipping companies and maritime authorities can provide valuable insights into industry demands, allowing curricula to be tailored to the evolving needs of the workforce. This alignment enhances employability for graduates and ensures that they are well-prepared to face real-world challenges within the maritime sector.

Another key aspect of global collaboration is the establishment of knowledge-sharing networks that facilitate interoperability among various MET platforms. By promoting data exchange and collaboration across global e-learning environments, institutions can leverage shared resources and tools, enhancing the educational experiences of students worldwide. In this context, standardizing digital curricula and assessment practices can foster increased consistency in training, enabling maritime professionals to operate seamlessly across borders. Effective knowledge sharing can lead to improved access to learning materials and innovative teaching methods, enriching the overall educational experience.

Interoperability can also support the development of comprehensive competency frameworks recognized internationally, ensuring that the qualifications obtained by maritime students are valued globally. This is particularly important in an increasingly interconnected maritime industry, where the ability to work alongside international partners demands a common understanding of competencies and standards. The implementation of such frameworks depends on the collaborative efforts of maritime institutions and competent authorities to ensure alignment with international regulatory standards.

In addition to the technological aspect, global collaboration in maritime education can lead to a shared commitment to addressing social and environmental challenges within the industry. Collaborative initiatives aimed at sustainability, maritime safety, and addressing global issues, such as climate change, can create a collective impact that extends beyond individual institutions. By working together, maritime educators and industry experts can co-create solutions, share insights, and develop innovative practices to prepare students for a future where environmental and social responsibility become increasingly critical in maritime operations.

5.3 Navigating the Digital Horizon

As maritime education and training (MET) institutions transition into the digital age, synthesizing strategies for sustainable digital transformation emerges as a critical imperative. To successfully navigate this transformation, institutions must consider a holistic approach that integrates technology, curriculum redesign, faculty development, and student engagement. Sustainable digital transformation involves leveraging emerging technologies, such as Artificial Intelligence (AI), Extended Reality (XR), and the Internet of Things (IoT), to enrich learning experiences while addressing the specific needs of the maritime industry.

Partnerships among maritime institutions, industries, and international bodies can further strengthen these strategies. Collaborating with industry stakeholders can provide valuable insights into labor market requirements and emerging maritime technologies, thereby aligning curricula effectively with workforce needs. Establishing frameworks for mutual recognition of qualifications and competencies across borders can enhance global mobility and create a seamless transition for maritime professionals. Furthermore, international partnerships can contribute to the development of shared resources and best practices, creating a collaborative learning ecosystem that fosters innovation in pedagogy and technology adoption.

The vision for a resilient, inclusive, and technology-empowered maritime education system emphasizes the importance of equitable access to digital learning opportunities. Institutions should prioritize initiatives that address socio-economic disparities, ensuring all students have access to the necessary tools and resources to thrive in a digital learning environment. This can be achieved by implementing scholarship programs, technology lending initiatives, and community partnerships to enable underrepresented students to engage meaningfully with maritime education.

Moreover, as maritime education transitions into a more technology-infused landscape, a commitment to ethical practices and data privacy will be essential. Institutions must establish governance frameworks that guide the responsible use of technology and data within educational contexts, promoting transparency, security, and ethical decision-making. By fostering a culture of digital ethics, educators can instill in students a sense of responsibility towards maritime operations and data usage, preparing them to navigate the complexities of an increasingly interconnected world.

Additionally, the utilization of intelligent tutoring systems powered by AI can enhance personalized learning paths, tailoring educational experiences to meet individual needs. As educational technologies evolve, fostering a culture of innovation within educational institutions becomes critical to ensure sustained engagement and positive learning outcomes. This can be accomplished through continuous professional development for educators, focusing on building digital competencies and pedagogical skills that emphasize collaboration and adaptability.

CONCLUSION

In conclusion, the transformation of Maritime Education and Training (MET) through digital integration presents both profound opportunities and significant challenges. The incorporation of emerging technologies, such as Artificial Intelligence (AI), Extended Reality (XR), and the Internet of Things (IoT), fosters an environment where learning is more immersive, personalized, and aligned with industry demands. The vision for a robust maritime education system encompasses not only technological advancements but also the creation of sustainable frameworks that ensure equitable access to resources, thereby fostering inclusivity among diverse student populations.

To navigate this digital horizon successfully, MET institutions need to synthesize effective strategies that promote collaboration among educational entities, industries, and regulatory bodies. This includes building partnerships that facilitate knowledge sharing, standardization, and alignment with global competencies, ensuring that graduates are well-prepared to meet the complexities of a rapidly evolving maritime landscape. Moreover, the emphasis on creating open, interoperable platforms for global cooperation allows for shared resources and practices that enhance educational quality and accessibility.

The ethical implications of digital transformation within education also warrant significant attention. Institutions must address the concerns surrounding data privacy, intellectual property, and cyber-ethics to build a responsible and secure digital learning environment. As technology continues to advance, a commitment to ethical practices ensures that future maritime professionals are not only technologically adept but also equipped with the social and ethical frameworks necessary for responsible decision-making.

Ultimately, the future of MET lies in its ability to embrace and adapt to digital innovations while ensuring that education remains resilient, inclusive, and task-oriented. By cultivating a technology-empowered educational ecosystem, MET institutions can effectively prepare a new generation of maritime professionals capable of navigating the vast challenges and opportunities that lie ahead in the global maritime industry. Through these efforts, MET can remain at the forefront of fostering sustainable practices and driving positive changes in maritime operations worldwide.

REFERENCES

Abdelfattah, F., Alawi, A., Dahleez, K., & El-Saleh, A. (2023). Reviewing the critical challenges that influence the adoption of the e-learning system in higher educational institutions in the era of the covid-19 pandemic. *Online Information Review*, *47*(7), 1225–1247. DOI: 10.1108/OIR-02-2022-0085

Abir, M., Chowdhury, M., & Jang, Y. (2023). Software-defined uav networks for 6g systems: Requirements, opportunities, emerging techniques, challenges, and research directions. *IEEE Open Journal of the Communications Society*, *4*, 2487–2547. DOI: 10.1109/OJCOMS.2023.3323200

Abubakar, A., Kabara, M., & Enriquez, A. (2022). Face-to-face, online, or hybrid learning in post covid-19 recovery? scrutinizing Nigerian students' preferences. *Journal of Educational Management and Instruction (Jemin)*, *2*(2), 63–74. DOI: 10.22515/jemin.v2i2.5026

Adarkwah, M., & Huang, R. (2023). Technology addiction, abduction and adoption in higher education: Bird's eye view of the ict4ad policy in ghana 20 years on. *British Journal of Educational Technology*, *54*(6), 1484–1504. DOI: 10.1111/bjet.13352

Ala, A., Hamidi, N., Yoniessa, S., Masito, F., & Muis, M. (2024). Simulation-based learning in maritime training: Enhancing competency and preparedness. *Meteor Stip Marunda*, *17*(1), 95–102. DOI: 10.36101/msm.v17i1.361

Alenezi, M. (2021). Deep dive into digital transformation in higher education institutions. *Education Sciences*, *11*(12), 770. DOI: 10.3390/educsci11120770

Alshammary, F., & Alhalafawy, W. (2023). Digital platforms and the improvement of learning outcomes: Evidence extracted from meta-analysis. *Sustainability (Basel)*, *15*(2), 1305. DOI: 10.3390/su15021305

Aquino, J. (2025). Best practices of high performing higher education institutions in thephilippines towards the development of harmonized quality-assured instructional leadership framework. *Frontiers in Education*, *10*, 1663289. Advance online publication. DOI: 10.3389/feduc.2025.1663289

Atwa, H., Shehata, M., Ansari, A., Kumar, A., Jaradat, A., Ahmed, J., & Salem, A. (2022). Online, face-to-face, or blended learning? faculty and medical students' perceptions during the covid-19 pandemic: A mixed-method study. *Frontiers in Medicine*, *9*, 791352. Advance online publication. DOI: 10.3389/fmed.2022.791352

Behl, A., & Zhang, Z. (2023). Guest editorial: role of technology in e-commerce: bright and the dark side. *South Asian Journal of Business Studies*, *12*(3), 317–320. DOI: 10.1108/SAJBS-08-2023-460

Bibri, S., & Jagatheesaperumal, S. (2023). Harnessing the potential of the metaverse and artificial intelligence for the internet of city things: Cost-effective xreality and synergistic aiot technologies. *Smart Cities*, *6*(5), 2397–2429. DOI: 10.3390/smartcities6050109

Buthelezi, L., & Wyk, J. (2020). The use of an online learning management system by postgraduate nursing students at a selected higher educational institution in kwazulu-natal, south africa. *African Journal of Health Professions Education*, *12*(4), 211. DOI: 10.7196/AJHPE.2020.v12i4.1391

Cabaron, R. (2023). Enhancing the digital competence of maritime education faculty in the philippines using digcomp 2.0 framework. *International Journal of Multidisciplinary Applied Business and Education Research*, *4*(4), 1096–1101. DOI: 10.11594/ijmaber.04.04.06

Christabel, H. and Prawira, I. (2023). Practical study of digital learning and virtual laboratory in post-pandemic era. E3s Web of Conferences, 388, 04012. DOI: 10.1051/e3sconf/202338804012

D'Augusta, V., Gazzaneo, L., Longo, F., Manfredi, K., Nicoletti, L., Padovano, A., … & Talarico, S. (2025). Advancing maritime training through a vr-enhanced ship bridge simulator: a preliminary usability analysis.. DOI: 10.3233/PMST250101

Diahyleva, O., Kononova, O., Yurzhenko, A., & Svyryda, V. (2025). Development of professional competence of future specialists in the operation of shipboard technical systems and complexes using lms moodle. Scientific Bulletin of Mukachevo State University Series "Pedagogy and Psychology", 51-59. DOI: 10.52534/msu-pp1.2025.51

Eden, C., Chisom, O., & Adeniyi, I. (2024). Harnessing technology integration in education: strategies for enhancing learning outcomes and equity. World Journal of Advanced Engineering Technology and Sciences, 11(2), 001-008. DOI: 10.30574/wjaets.2024.11.2.0071

Eden, C., Chisom, O., & Adeniyi, I.Chima Abimbola EdenOnyebuchi Nneamaka ChisomIdowu Sulaimon Adeniyi. (2024). Promoting digital literacy and social equity in education: Lessons from successful initiatives. *International Journal of Management & Entrepreneurship Research*, *6*(3), 687–696. DOI: 10.51594/ijmer.v6i3.880

Ehimuan, B., Anyanwu, A., Olorunsogo, T., Akindote, O., Abrahams, T., & Reis, O. (2024). Digital inclusion initiatives: Bridging the connectivity gap in africa and the usa – a review. *International Journal of Science and Research Archive*, *11*(1), 488–501. DOI: 10.30574/ijsra.2024.11.1.0061

Elsalem, L., Al-Azzam, N., Jum'ah, A., & Obeidat, N. (2021). Remote e-exams during covid-19 pandemic: A cross-sectional study of students' preferences and academic dishonesty in faculties of medical sciences. *Annals of Medicine and Surgery (London)*, *62*, 326–333. DOI: 10.1016/j.amsu.2021.01.054

Fabian-Perona, E. (2025). Maritime education and language as the acting link between bridge and engine room – a report. Educational Role of Language Journal, 2025-1(13), 64-67. DOI: 10.36534/erlj.2025.01.07

Galić, S., Lušić, Z., & Stanivuk, T. (2020). E-learning in maritime affairs. *Journal of Naval Architecture and Marine Engineering*, *17*(1), 38–50. DOI: 10.3329/jname.v17i1.42203

Hermanto, Y., & Srimulyani, V. (2021). The challenges of online learning during the covid-19 pandemic. *Jurnal Pendidikan Dan Pengajaran*, *54*(1), 46. DOI: 10.23887/jpp.v54i1.29703

Karmin, K., Rosani, M., & Pahlawan, P. (2025). Strategic management and digital literacy: Enhancing teacher pedagogical competence in the digital era. *Journal of Social Work and Science Education*, *6*(3), 1305–1318. DOI: 10.52690/jswse.v6i3.1272

Kim, J., Lee, C., Jeong, M., Cho, E., & Lee, Y. (2023). Identifying optimal approaches for sustainable maritime education and training: Addressing technological, environmental, and epidemiological challenges. *Sustainability (Basel)*, *15*(10), 8092. DOI: 10.3390/su15108092

Kononova, O., Diahyleva, O., & Yurzhenko, A. (2024). Interactive module "environment protection" of maritime english course on lms moodle for future ship engineers. *Georgian Maritime Scientific Journal*, *2*(1). Advance online publication. DOI: 10.70791/gmsj.2.2024.8015

Kumar, S., Ritzhaupt, A., & Pedro, N. (2022). Development and validation of the online instructor support survey (oiss). *Online Learning : the Official Journal of the Online Learning Consortium*, *26*(1). Advance online publication. DOI: 10.24059/olj.v26i1.2622

Kuzminska, O., Морзе, Н., & Osadchyi, V. (2023). Digitization of learning environment of higher education institutions: Conceptual foundations and practical cases. *Journal of Physics: Conference Series*, *2611*(1), 012024. DOI: 10.1088/1742-6596/2611/1/012024

Laila, D., Izzatul, R., & Miftah, M. (2025). Transformasi digital di dunia pendidikan: Implementasi dan dampak teknologi pembelajaran. *J. Sci. Tech. Alpha*, *1*(2), 37–41. DOI: 10.70716/alpha.v1i2.172

Luo, H. (2024). Exploration and research on the construction of vocational english curriculum in china under the context of digital transformation., 1(3), 116-121. DOI: 10.62517/jhve.202416319

Lvov, M. and Popova, H. (2020). Simulation technologies of virtual reality usage in the training of future ship navigators.. DOI: 10.31812/123456789/3758

Mafara, M., & Haki, A. (2023). Imperatives of online learning in tertiary institutions during covid-19 pandemic. *MIMJRI*, *1*(1). Advance online publication. DOI: 10.59479/jiaheri.v1i001.10

Mahmadov, Y. (2025). Transforming education through digital learning: Embracing the new era of learning. *International Journal of Education and Digital Learning (Ijedl)*, *3*(4), 157–166. DOI: 10.47353/ijedl.v3i4.258

Mariyono, D., & Mistar, J. (2025). Digital education strategies in anaesthesiology: a systematic review and swot analysis. DOI: 10.21203/rs.3.rs-7476309/v1

Mbugi, E., Hawkins, C., Hirschhorn, L., Kaaya, S., Christian, E., Anaeli, A., Balandya, E., Moshiro, C., & Drane, D. (2022). Using evidence-based pedagogical approaches to pivot from in-person to online training in a d43 program during the covid-19 pandemic. *The American Journal of Tropical Medicine and Hygiene*, *107*(4), 948–955. DOI: 10.4269/ajtmh.22-0150

Mojarad, F., Hesamzadeh, A., & Yaghoubi, T. (2023). Exploring challenges and facilitators to e-learning based education of nursing students during covid-19 pandemic: A qualitative study. *BMC Nursing*, *22*(1), 278. Advance online publication. DOI: 10.1186/s12912-023-01430-6

Mudenda, S., Daka, V., Mufwambi, W., Matafwali, S., Chabalenge, B., Skosana, P., Mfune, R. L., Kasanga, M., Okonji, O. C., Mayoka, G., Kampamba, M., Hikaambo, C. N., Mukosha, M., Kanaan, M. H. G., Zikalala-Mabope, L. A., Sinkamba, G., Okoro, R. N., Chulu, M., Godman, B., & Fadare, J. (2023). Student's perspectives, satisfaction and experiences with online and classroom learning during the covid-19 pandemic: Findings and implications on blended learning. *SAGE Open Medicine*, *11*, 20503121231218904. Advance online publication. DOI: 10.1177/20503121231218904

Müller, M. (2022). Significance of hybrid learning model during covid-19 pandemic at higher education institution. *European Journal of Teacher Education*, *4*(2), 70–80. DOI: 10.33422/ejte.v4i2.818

Nasrati, S., Khalil, D., Ahmadi, L., & Quraishi, T. (2024). Digital empowerment of women: The role of the internet in an online university setting. *Soc. Econ. Hum. Aspects Town. Ind.*, *2*(3), 467–476. DOI: 10.59535/sehati.v2i3.326

Nazaruddin, M. (2025). Rethinking arts education in the digital era: a narrative review. harmonia, 3(2), 81-94. DOI: 10.61978/harmonia.v3i2.898

Niţă, V., & Gu u, I. (2023). The role of leadership and digital transformation in higher education students' work engagement. *International Journal of Environmental Research and Public Health*, *20*(6), 5124. DOI: 10.3390/ijerph20065124

Nong, W., Ye, J., Chen, P., & Lee, Y. (2023). A study on the blended learning effects on students majoring in preschool education in the post-pandemic era: An example of a research-method course in a chinese university. *Frontiers in Psychology*, *13*, 962707. Advance online publication. DOI: 10.3389/fpsyg.2022.962707

Oliveira, K., & Souza, R. (2021). *Digital transformation towards education 4.0*. Informatics in Education., DOI: 10.15388/infedu.2022.13

Pipchenko, O., & Kovtunenko, D. (2020). A suggestion of an application of blended learning in met through a harmonized stcw model. *Transnav the International Journal on Marine Navigation and Safety of Sea Transportation*, *14*(3), 545–548. DOI: 10.12716/1001.14.03.04

Prasetyo, K., Ansori, A., & Suseto, B. (2023). Maritime defense strategy education as an effort of the indonesian government in maintaining maritime security. *International Journal of Asian Education*, *4*(1), 58–67. DOI: 10.46966/ijae.v4i1.325

Rylander, S. (2022). Maritime simulator training: eye-trackers to improve training experience.. DOI: 10.54941/ahfe100724

Selivanova, M., Frolova, O., Maksimova, M., Этуев, Х., & Александрова, Л. (2023). Experience in implementing the project «digital workshop of the educator». *Citise*, *35*(1). Advance online publication. DOI: 10.15350/2409-7616.2023.1.07

Shafik, W. (2025). The rise of online learning and its impact on education., 39-76. DOI: 10.4018/979-8-3373-2257-5.ch002

Shaikhanova, A., Iklassova, K., Uvaliyeva, I., Kyrgyshbaeva, R., & Myrzakhanov, K. (2025). Analytical review of the digital technologies usage in education. *Bulletin of Shakarim University Technical Sciences*, (1(17)), 21–30. DOI: 10.53360/2788-7995-2025-1(17)-3

Sharma, A., & Nazir, S. (2021). Assessing the technology self-efficacy of maritime instructors: An explorative study. *Education Sciences*, *11*(7), 342. DOI: 10.3390/educsci11070342

Sharma, A., & Nazir, S. (2021). Assessing the technology self-efficacy of maritime instructors: An explorative study. *Education Sciences*, *11*(7), 342. DOI: 10.3390/educsci11070342

Sharma, A., Undheim, P., & Nazir, S. (2022). Design and implementation of ai chatbot for colregs training. *Wmu Journal of Maritime Affairs*, *22*(1), 107–123. DOI: 10.1007/s13437-022-00284-0

Shraim, K. (2020). Quality standards in online education: The iso/iec 40180 framework. *International Journal of Emerging Technologies in Learning*, *15*(19), 22. DOI: 10.3991/ijet.v15i19.15065

Sulistyono, N., Suparji, S., Wiyanto, T., Suhartini, R., & Ilham, I. (2024). Understanding maritime subjects in vocational high schools through online learning. *Nawala Education*, *1*(5), 1–13. DOI: 10.62872/dvfypx37

Sulistyono, N., Suparji, S., Wiyanto, T., Suhartini, R., & Ilham, I. (2024). Understanding maritime subjects in vocational high schools through online learning. *Nawala Education*, *1*(5), 1–13. DOI: 10.62872/dvfypx37

Swaminathan, N., Govindharaj, P., Jagadeesh, N., & Ravichandran, L. (2021). Evaluating the effectiveness of an online faculty development programme for nurse educators about remote teaching during covid-19. *Journal of Taibah University Medical Sciences*, *16*(2), 268–273. DOI: 10.1016/j.jtumed.2020.11.003

Tahmasebi, F. (2023). The digital divide: a qualitative study of technology access in rural communities. aitechbesosci, 1(2), 33-39. DOI: 10.61838/kman.aitech.1.2.6

Tan, C., Zakuan, N., & Aziz, M. (2022). Recent trends of blended learning and flipped classroom in malaysia. *Arab World English Journal*, (2), 290–301. DOI: 10.24093/awej/covid2.19

Tirumalamba, K. (2025). The digital learning revolution: Prospects, challenges, and the future of online education. *IJEMMASSS*, *07*(01(II)), 102–106. DOI: 10.62823/IJEMMASSS/7.1(II).7276

Tiwow, G., Batmetan, J., Sumual, T., & Sumual, S. (2023). Human resources management in trouble time: Strategy to increase organization agility for digital transformation in university. *IJITE*, *2*(4), 99–112. DOI: 10.62711/ijite.v2i4.166

Trevisan, L., Eustachio, J., Galleli, B., Filho, W., & Pedrozo, E. (2023). Digital transformation towards sustainability in higher education: State-of-the-art and future research insights. *Environment, Development and Sustainability*, *26*(2), 2789–2810. DOI: 10.1007/s10668-022-02874-7

Tripathi, S. (2025). A role of technology integration in improvizing pedagogical skills of prospective teachers to meet the challenges of 21st century. Stallion Journal for Multidisciplinary Associated Research Studies, 6-11. DOI: 10.55544/sjmars.icmri.2

Varhata, O., Udodova, O., Арделян, O., Apalat, H., & Vykhrystiuk, A. (2025). Advancing higher education through technology and innovation. *Multidisciplinary Reviews*, *9*(1), 2026037. DOI: 10.31893/multirev.2026037

Varma, A., & Jafri, M. (2020). Covid-19 responsive teaching of undergraduate architecture programs in india: Learnings for post-pandemic education. *Archnet-IJAR*, *15*(1), 189–202. DOI: 10.1108/ARCH-10-2020-0234

Xing, X., & Saghaian, S. (2022). Learning outcomes of a hybrid online virtual classroom and in-person traditional classroom during the covid-19 pandemic. *Sustainability (Basel)*, *14*(9), 5263. DOI: 10.3390/su14095263

Xue, H., Røds, J., Haugseggen, Ø., Christensen, A., Batalden, B., & Gudmestad, O. (2024). A study on the effects of rapid training method related to ship handling in decision-making skills under stressful situations. *Journal of Navigation*, *77*(3), 395–414. DOI: 10.1017/S0373463324000213

Youhasan, P., Henning, M., Chen, Y., & Lyndon, M. (2022). Developing and evaluating an educational web-based tool for health professions education: The flipped classroom navigator. *BMC Medical Education*, *22*(1), 594. Advance online publication. DOI: 10.1186/s12909-022-03647-6

Yurzhenko, A., Diahyleva, O., & Kononova, O. (2023). An overview of maritime english teaching and its principles, with a focus on practical applications and best practices online. *Освітній Вимір*, *9*, 45–58. DOI: 10.31812/ed.641

Chapter 5

Maritime Business and Economic Education: Aligning Curricula With Global Industry Needs

Andi Annisa Sulolipu
http://orcid.org/0009-0007-8212-577X
Universitas Negeri Makassar, Indonesia

Muhammad Ihsan Said Ahmad
Universitas Negeri Makassar, Indonesia

Vivit Rosmayanti
http://orcid.org/0000-0002-3648-9878
Universitas Negeri Makassar, Indonesia

Andi Tenri Ampa
Universitas Negeri Makassar, Indonesia

St. Wijdanah Ram
http://orcid.org/0009-0005-1890-5355
Universitas Negeri Makassar, Indonesia

ABSTRACT

The maritime industry, handling over 80% of global trade, faces rapid changes due to digitalization, automation, and sustainability pressures. However, many maritime education systems focus primarily on technical skills, neglecting the integration of business, management, and economic knowledge. This chapter discusses the need for curriculum reform in maritime education to align with the evolving global maritime industry. It highlights the importance of interdisciplinary skills like logistics analytics, environmental economics, and digital trade management. The chapter also proposes strategies such as integrating sustainability, interdisciplinary learning, and simulation technologies to prepare students for the challenges and opportunities of the modern maritime economy.

DOI: 10.4018/979-8-3373-6670-8.ch005

1. INTRODUCTION

1.1 Background of the Study

The maritime industry is a fundamental component of the global economy, enabling almost 80% of world trade by volume (Nguyen et al., 2022). This significant dependence on sea transport underscores its crucial role in facilitating global economic integration. The industry supports the uninterrupted movement of goods across continents, connecting markets, resources, and production networks. However, despite its importance, the sector is undergoing rapid transformation driven by digitalization, automation, and sustainability pressures (Chan et al., 2025; Lau et al., 2024)

Recent studies highlight that technologies such as artificial intelligence (AI), big data, and the Internet of Things (IoT) are reshaping maritime operations by improving efficiency, safety, and decision-making processes. At the same time, environmental regulations and decarbonization targets introduced by international bodies are pushing the industry toward greener practices (Xiao et al., 2024). These transformations are not only technological but also economic and organizational in nature, requiring a workforce that is both technically competent and economically literate.

Despite the growing body of literature addressing digital transformation and sustainability in the maritime sector, there remains limited integration of these dimensions within maritime business and economic education frameworks. Previous studies (Yuen et al., 2022). primarily focus on competency identification without critically examining how curricula align with evolving industry requirements. Therefore, this chapter addresses this gap by proposing a structured alignment between global industry needs and maritime education systems.

1.2 Rationale

1.2.1 The gap between maritime business education and evolving global industry needs.

The marine sector is swiftly transforming, propelled by technology innovations, environmental sustainability initiatives, and changing global trade patterns. Nonetheless, a considerable disparity persists between contemporary marine business education and the evolving demands of the industry (Kilpi et al., 2021). The maritime sector is rapidly evolving; however, maritime education systems have not fully kept pace with these changes. Traditional curricula remain heavily focused on technical competencies such as navigation and ship operations, with limited emphasis on business, economic, and digital competencies (Jeon & Jung, 2023; Lopes et al., 2025). This mismatch creates a gap between graduate capabilities and industry expectations.

In addition, the increasing complexity of global supply chains, sustainability demands, and digital trade systems requires professionals who can integrate technical knowledge with economic reasoning and strategic thinking (Caesar, 2023; Yuen et al., 2022). Without curriculum reform, graduates may struggle to adapt to real-world maritime challenges, particularly in areas such as green shipping finance, digital logistics, and global market analysi (Bogusławski et al., 2022).

1.2.2 Necessity to align maritime curricula with competencies demanded by the globalized maritime economy (e.g., digital trade, supply chain management, environmental economics, and green shipping finance).

In the age of globalisation, the marine economy is increasingly intertwined with many industries, such as digital trade, logistics, environmental economics, and sustainability. Maritime business education must adapt to this transformation, integrating courses with the capabilities required by the contemporary globalised maritime economy. As trade patterns increasingly digitise, the capacity to manage supply chains in real-time, utilise big data, and comprehend the economics of global logistics is essential. Maritime workers must be adept at utilising new tools and technology that facilitate efficient, cost-effective, and transparent trade, with supply chain management increasingly being a crucial element in maritime business education (Fagerholt et al., 2023; Lau et al., 2024).

Furthermore, as the business encounters increasing demand to mitigate its environmental footprint, comprehending the economics of sustainability and the intricacies of green shipping finance is imperative. This encompasses expertise in alternative fuels, initiatives for emission reduction, and the financial frameworks that facilitate sustainable shipping practices. The necessity of including environmental economics into the maritime business curriculum is more imperative, as industry experts must reconcile economic objectives with environmental responsibilities (Gavalas, 2025; Olaniyi et al., 2024).

Moreover, nascent trends in digital commerce and automation are revolutionising the operations of global maritime trade. The emergence of digital platforms, blockchain technologies, and automated logistics necessitates that marine professionals possess not just knowledge of conventional trade processes but also expertise in digital tools and platforms that improve transparency, security, and efficiency in global shipping. To maintain competitiveness, educational institutions must modify their curricula to prepare students to confront challenges directly, providing them with the knowledge and skills essential for fostering innovation in maritime business practices and navigating the intricacies of the global maritime economy (Phewa, 2021).

1.3 Objectives

This chapter aims to critically analyze the present condition of marine business and economic education and evaluate its alignment with the changing requirements of the global maritime industry. This study examines existing curriculum at academic institutions to assess how effectively marine business education meets the competences demanded by a swiftly evolving global economy. The maritime sector is progressively influenced by technology innovations, environmental laws, and the incorporation of digital and sustainable methodologies. Therefore, it is crucial to ascertain if existing educational frameworks sufficiently equip students for these emerging issues (Jafari et al., 2020).

A primary purpose is to discern the discrepancies between academic curricula and the demands of the maritime industry. Traditional maritime education has mostly emphasized technical abilities like navigation and ship management; however, there is an increasing acknowledgment of the necessity for professionals possessing a more comprehensive skill set that encompasses business acumen, economic literacy, and a profound awareness of global trade dynamics. This chapter will examine if contemporary academic programs equip students with the requisite understanding in supply chain management, environmental economics, digital trade, and green shipping financing. The study aims to elucidate the areas requiring enhancements and innovations in education to align with industry demands by identifying these gaps (Kilpi et al., 2021).

Finally, the chapter seeks to present a curriculum alignment structure that incorporates essential global industry trends, sustainability factors, and economic competencies. The framework will offer pragmatic recommendations for educational institutions to modify their curricula to more effectively prepare students with the skills required to succeed in the global maritime economy. This framework will integrate contemporary trends in digitization, sustainability, and economics to enhance maritime business education, equipping graduates to address present and future industry difficulties effectively (Gavalas, 2025).

This chapter aims to critically analyze the alignment between maritime business and economic education and the evolving demands of the global maritime industry. Specifically, it seeks to: 1. Identify gaps between existing curricula and industry needs. 2. Evaluate the extent to which current programs address digitalization, sustainability, and economic competencies. 3. Propose a curriculum alignment framework integrating global industry trends.

2. CONCEPTUAL AND THEORETICAL FRAMEWORK

2.1 The Global Maritime Industry Landscape

2.1.1 Overview of maritime sectors: shipping, ports, logistics, marine finance, and blue economy enterprises.

The maritime industry consists of interconnected sectors including shipping, ports, logistics, marine finance, and the blue economy (Gardin et al., 2023; Sumaila et al., 2021). While these sectors collectively support global trade, they are increasingly influenced by emerging challenges such as automation, decarbonization, digital supply chains, and geopolitical uncertainty. Shipping is fundamental to the marine business, facilitating the transportation of the majority of global goods. This industry encompasses the operation of cargo vessels, tankers, container ships, and bulk carriers that transport commodities including oil, coal, grain, and manufactured goods worldwide. Shipping businesses and fleet operators, regulated by international entities such as the International Maritime Organization (IMO), facilitate seamless trade while complying with safety, environmental, and operational regulations (Hendriksen, 2020).

Ports are essential infrastructural centers where vessels berth to load and discharge cargo. Port operations encompass the administration of container terminals, bulk handling facilities, and warehouses, rendering them essential contributors to the efficacy of global supply chains. As global trade volumes expand, numerous ports are progressively implementing automation and digital technology to improve operational efficiency, mitigate congestion, and decrease operating costs, thereby ensuring the swift and secure transfer of commodities from vessels to land (Jahangard et al., 2025).

Logistics include the strategizing, execution, and regulation of the transportation of products from the place of origin to the ultimate destination. In the maritime sector, logistics converges with shipping and port operations. It encompasses the coordination of transportation, warehousing, and inventory management to guarantee that products are delivered to consumers or businesses promptly and economically. The logistics sector is essential for optimizing international trade, minimizing transit durations, and improving the competitiveness of firms dependent on global supply chains

(Ohakwe & Wu, 2025). Marine finance supports the financial elements of the maritime sector, supplying the necessary funds for the building, operation, and maintenance of vessels, ports, and maritime infrastructure. It include the funding of maritime insurance, investments in innovative technologies, and the creation of financial instruments to promote sustainable behaviors.

The blue economy has arisen as a crucial sector alongside traditional marine sectors, emphasizing the sustainable utilization of ocean resources for economic growth, innovation, and employment generation. This encompasses sectors including offshore energy, marine biotechnology, and sustainable fisheries, all of which advance the economic and environmental objectives of global maritime development. Collectively, these industries provide the foundation of the maritime industry, influencing the trajectory of global trade and economic development (Pace et al., 2022; Sun et al., 2024; Veríssimo et al., 2021).

These trends not only reshape operational practices but also redefine workforce expectations, creating a mismatch between traditional education models and emerging industry needs. For example, digital supply chains require data-driven decision-making skills, while decarbonization demands knowledge of environmental economics and sustainable finance.

2.1.2 Emerging challenges: automation, decarbonization, digital supply chains, and geopolitical trade shifts.

The global maritime industry is entering a period of accelerated transformation marked by several emerging challenges that are reshaping how maritime operations, logistics networks, and international trade systems function. One of the most significant challenges is **automation**, which is rapidly changing vessel operations, port activities, and logistics processes. The introduction of autonomous ships, automated cranes, AI-based navigation systems, and robotics in port operations is improving efficiency and safety but also demanding a workforce with advanced digital and technical competencies. Maritime professionals are now required to manage automated systems, analyze complex data, and integrate digital technologies into daily operations (Jeon & Lee, 2025).

A parallel challenge is decarbonization, driven by increasingly stringent environmental regulations and global climate commitments. The International Maritime Organization (IMO) has set ambitious targets to reduce greenhouse gas emissions from ships, pushing the industry toward cleaner fuels such as LNG, methanol, hydrogen, and ammonia, as well as energy-efficient technologies. This transition requires not only technological innovation but also economic expertise to assess investment feasibility, fuel cost structures, and long-term sustainability strategies (Jamasb & Sornn-Friese, 2024).

The rise of digital supply chains is another defining challenge. Digital platforms, blockchain, IoT devices, and predictive analytics are revolutionizing cargo tracking, documentation, and supply chain visibility. These technologies enhance transparency and resilience, yet they also require maritime professionals who understand digital trade systems, cyber risks, and data-driven decision-making. Finally, geopolitical trade shifts including trade wars, regional conflicts, shifting alliances, and supply chain realignments—are reshaping global shipping routes and logistics hubs. These shifts influence freight rates, port competitiveness, and shipping demand patterns. As a result, maritime professionals must combine economic literacy with geopolitical awareness to navigate uncertainty and maintain strategic resilience in global trade networks (Dawar & Bai, 2024; Ferrarini et al., 2025).

In addition to digital and economic competencies, maritime professionals must develop capabilities in risk management and cybersecurity. The increasing reliance on digital platforms exposes maritime systems to cyber threats, making cybersecurity awareness a critical component of maritime education.

Furthermore, global disruptions such as pandemics and geopolitical conflicts highlight the importance of resilience and crisis management skills.

2.2 Maritime Business and Economic Education

Maritime business studies is an interdisciplinary field that blends economic, commercial, operational, and legal perspectives to address the unique challenges of the global maritime industry. This field covers a broad range of topics, including shipping management, port operations, logistics, marine finance, maritime law, and global trade dynamics (Pallis et al., 2023). The primary aim of maritime business studies is to equip students with the knowledge and skills necessary to navigate the complexities of international trade, global supply chains, and the regulatory frameworks that govern maritime operations. By combining economics, management, and law, this field prepares professionals to manage the operational, financial, and strategic aspects of maritime enterprises (Jiang, 2021).

The scope of maritime business studies is extensive, covering essential areas such as shipping company operations, port management, and logistics. Additionally, students learn about marine insurance, trade regulations, and the economics behind international shipping routes and services. With a growing focus on sustainability and digital transformation, maritime business education also addresses contemporary challenges such as green shipping practices, environmental economics, and the impact of new technologies like automation and big data on the industry. This broad scope ensures that graduates are equipped with the interdisciplinary skills required to respond to both traditional and emerging challenges in the maritime sector (Prousaloglou et al., 2025).

The integration of economics into maritime education helps students understand the financial aspects of maritime business, such as cost management, pricing strategies, and the economic impact of shipping. Management education is equally vital, providing students with the skills to lead maritime organizations effectively. Topics such as organizational behavior, logistics management, and strategic decision-making are key components of maritime business curricula. Students learn how to manage resources, teams, and operations in a globalized maritime environment, preparing them for leadership roles in shipping companies, ports, and other maritime-related enterprises (Guntoro & Simanjuntak, 2024).

Furthermore, maritime education increasingly incorporates policy and technology. Understanding maritime law and regulatory frameworks, including international conventions and environmental policies, is essential for navigating the legal landscape of global shipping. Technological advancements, including automation, AI, and blockchain, are reshaping the maritime industry, and integrating these technologies into education ensures that graduates are prepared to implement innovative solutions in their future careers. By blending economics, management, policy, and technology, maritime education offers a comprehensive approach that prepares students to thrive in the rapidly evolving global maritime economy (Theotokas et al., 2024).

2.3 Theoretical Basis

Theoretical frameworks are essential in structuring maritime business education to align with the demands of a changing global industry. Human Capital Theory underscores the need of investing in education and training to improve labor productivity. This idea posits that providing marine professionals with specific knowledge and skills enhances their value in the industry, hence improving both individual and organizational performance. The increasing complexity of the maritime business, driven by technical breakthroughs and environmental restrictions, necessitates investment in human capital to sustain a competitive advantage. The Curriculum Alignment Theory reinforces the significance of education by ensuring that learning outcomes correspond with industrial competencies. As global trade dynamics and marine technology evolve, it is essential to match maritime curricula with developing trends and industry requirements to adequately prepare students for future difficulties. This theory promotes an educational framework that aligns with contemporary advancements in digital commerce, sustainability, and environmentally friendly shipping practices, guaranteeing that students obtain competencies relevant to practical marine operations (Alop, 2021; Autsadee et al., 2024).

The notion of Lifelong Learning and Competency-Based Education (CBE) is essential for the continuous advancement of marine professionals. The maritime industry's dynamic nature necessitates lifelong learning, which promotes ongoing skill enhancement throughout a professional's career, allowing adaptation to emerging technology, laws, and market changes. CBE emphasizes the mastery of specific competencies over the mere completion of coursework, guaranteeing that professionals possess high proficiency in the actual abilities demanded by the industry. Integrating these frameworks enables maritime education to develop a resilient and adaptive workforce capable of handling the complexity of the global maritime sector (Pazaver & Kitada, 2025).

3. MAPPING GLOBAL INDUSTRY NEEDS

3.1 Competencies Required in the Modern Maritime Sector

The contemporary maritime industry necessitates a varied array of skills to tackle the changing difficulties of international commerce, sustainability, and technological progress. Business management and financial literacy are essential, since marine professionals must oversee intricate operations, optimize resources, and make strategic financial decisions to guarantee profitability and growth. Effective logistics analytics is essential for managing global supply chains, enhancing efficiency, and adapting to fluctuating market conditions. The growing reliance on data in shipping and port operations enables organizations to examine and interpret logistical data, thereby optimizing routes, minimizing costs, and improving operational efficiency (Fagerholt et al., 2023; Rao, 2025).

Environmental economics has become increasingly vital in the maritime sector, especially as restrictions concerning emissions, carbon footprints, and sustainable practices intensify. Comprehending the economic ramifications of environmental legislation, including carbon pricing and green shipping incentives, is essential for professionals responsible for executing sustainable practices in the maritime industry. Data-driven decision-making is a crucial competency, as technology breakthroughs in automation, artificial intelligence, and big data yield significant insights that can guide operational, financial, and strategic choices (Aerts & Mathys, 2024).

Furthermore, cross-cultural communication is becoming essential, as the marine industry operates globally, involving professionals across diverse areas, cultures, and regulatory frameworks. Digital literacy is essential as the sector adopts digital platforms, automation, and remote monitoring technology. Ultimately, sustainability-focused leadership is essential for steering marine enterprises towards ecologically responsible practices while achieving commercial success, rendering leadership skills centered on sustainability a vital capability in the contemporary maritime workforce. (Dewan & Godina, 2023).

3.2 Global Standards and Frameworks

The global marine industry functions within a well delineated regulatory framework, influenced by norms and standards set by the International marine Organization (IMO). (Casaca & Loja, 2021) The International marine Organization (IMO), a specialized institution of the United Nations, is tasked with formulating binding international standards that guarantee the safety, security, and environmental efficacy of the marine industry. Essential conventions, including the International Convention for the Safety of Life at Sea (SOLAS), the International Convention for the Prevention of Pollution from Ships (MARPOL), and the International Convention on Standards of Training, Certification, and Watchkeeping for Seafarers (STCW), establish the protocols for maritime safety, pollution mitigation, and crew training. These agreements are crucial to global shipping operations, guaranteeing that vessels conform to safety requirements, comply with environmental legislation, and get internationally recognized certifications, so fostering a safer and more sustainable marine industry (Knapp & Franses, 2022; Xu et al., 2023).

The UN Sustainable Development Goals (SDGs) and Environmental, Social, and Governance (ESG) principles have progressively impacted the marine industry, promoting a transition to more sustainable practices. The Sustainable Development Goals, especially Goal 14, which emphasizes the conservation and sustainable utilization of oceans, seas, and marine resources, strongly correlate with maritime business practices. The industry is incorporating ESG concepts to mitigate environmental effects, enhance social responsibility, and improve governance processes. This encompasses the use of greener technology, the reduction of carbon emissions, the promotion of labor rights, and the assurance of transparent corporate governance. Integrating these concepts enables marine enterprises to fulfill stakeholder expectations, adhere to rules, and promote long-term sustainability in a competitive market (Diniz et al., 2024; Tsatsaronis et al., 2024).

Collaborating with premier maritime education institutions, such the World Maritime University and the Singapore Maritime Academy, is essential for advancing the future of maritime education. These colleges lead in offering advanced maritime business programs that incorporate contemporary industry trends, IMO standards, and sustainability practices. By studying these global leaders, maritime education systems may modify and synchronize curricula with the shifting requirements of the maritime industry, ensuring that graduates possess the essential skills to excel in a rapidly growing sector (Olaniyi et al., 2024).

3.3 Industry Expectations and Future Workforce Trends

The marine sector is seeing a substantial shift towards environmentally sustainable and technologically advanced shipping, propelled by regulatory mandates and innovations. In response to the escalating global emphasis on sustainability, shipping companies are implementing environmentally friendly measures to decrease their carbon footprint, reduce emissions, and adhere to international environmental regulations established by the IMO. The sector is progressively allocating resources towards alternative fuels, energy-efficient vessel designs, and sustainable technology, including wind-assisted propulsion and hybrid power systems. Innovative shipping technology, such as autonomous vessels and digital navigation systems, are increasingly being adopted, enhancing operating efficiency and minimizing environmental effect (Kondratenko et al., 2025; Werner et al., 2023).

Automation, artificial intelligence, and digital platforms are transforming maritime commercial processes. Automation is optimizing multiple facets of the sector, encompassing cargo handling and vessel management, so enhancing efficiency and reducing costs. Artificial intelligence (AI) is utilized for predictive maintenance, route optimization, and decision-making, hence improving the efficiency of ships and port operations. Digital technologies, like blockchain and real-time data analytics, are revolutionizing supply chain management by enhancing transparency, bolstering security, and facilitating more intelligent operations. These technologies enhance operational performance and equip maritime enterprises with the means to more effectively address market demands (Surucu-Balci et al., 2023).

As the business progresses, there is an increasing demand for hybrid professionals with both technical and economic expertise. Modern maritime operations necessitate professionals proficient in shipping and logistics, as well as possessing a robust comprehension of company administration, finance, and sustainability. Hybrid professionals will be essential in advancing the business, enabling enterprises to stay competitive while addressing the issues of sustainable shipping, technological advancements, and global economic changes (Chua et al., 2024).

4. CURRICULUM ANALYSIS

4.1 Review of Existing Maritime Business and Economics Curricula

Upon examining the current maritime business and economics curricula at prominent universities, a distinct pattern is evident in both topic scope and instructional focus. Academic programs, such as the Piri Reis University MA in marine Business and Economics, encompass essential courses such business analytics, supply chain management, marine economics, cost analysis in maritime logistics, and subjects pertaining to maritime markets, policy, and finance. The undergraduate Bachelor's in Economics of Maritime Business, Logistics, and Transport at the University of Genoa equips students to oversee enterprises in the shipping, port, and logistics industries, emphasizing economic, legal, and mathematical aspects (Ambrosino & Sciomachen, 2021; Cariou et al., 2015; Parola et al., 2020).

Programs like the MSc in Maritime Economics & Logistics at Erasmus University Rotterdam focus on the integration of shipping, ports, terminal management, and logistics with economics, statistics, and management science. Recurring topic elements in these programs encompass shipping management (including liner, bulk, and offshore sectors), port economics and terminal operations, maritime insurance and risk management, as well as logistics and supply chain analytics. The Antwerp Management School's Masterclass in Maritime Economics & Business includes modules on shipping business economics, investment and finance, market dynamics, and technological innovation in shipping. This signifies that education institutions continuously emphasize essential commercial and economic skills pertinent to conventional marine trade and infrastructure (DíazDíaz et al., 2020; Jiang, 2021).

However, there are discernible limitations in the extent to which these curriculum address contemporary industrial demands. Although numerous programs increasingly emphasize digital transformation, alternative fuels, and ESG factors, many curricula still devote insufficient time to subjects such as advanced digital trade platforms, big data analytics in logistics, sustainable finance (green shipping finance), and policy innovation in maritime regulation. For instance, while Piri Reis University's curriculum includes business analytics and supply chain management, the incorporation of emerging subjects such as digitalization, autonomous shipping, or environmental governance seems to be more peripheral. In conclusion, although the fundamental business, economics, and logistics material is adequately addressed, existing curricula may not completely correspond with the rapid developments in the maritime industry, particularly with digital, environmental, and policy-innovation dimensions (İnal et al., 2021; Yuen et al., 2022).

4.2 Industry-Academia Disconnect

The disconnection between industry and academics in marine business education is a considerable difficulty, mainly due to the incongruence between academic learning goals and practical industry applications. (Kataria et al., 2024; Lau et al., 2021) Although maritime education programs impart essential knowledge in shipping management, port economics, and logistics, they frequently fail to adequately prepare graduates for the intricate and dynamic realities of the global marine business. Academic programs often emphasize theoretical frameworks and conventional operational methodologies, whereas the industry is progressively influenced by digital transformation, automation, sustainability, and sophisticated financial strategies. Consequently, students may graduate possessing robust technical knowledge yet lacking the competencies required to address the evolving issues of contemporary marine commerce, such as managing digital supply chains or executing green shipping finance (Barus & Simanjuntak, 2023; Simmons & McLean, 2020).

A further issue exacerbating this divergence is the inadequate involvement of industry players in the curriculum development process. Academic institutions and marine enterprises frequently function in isolation, exhibiting minimal cooperation in the formulation of curriculum that align with the industry's changing requirements. Industry experts, possessing superior insight into market trends, technical advancements, and regulatory changes, ought to have a more prominent role in the development of academic curricula. Their findings could facilitate the alignment of graduates' skills, tools, and knowledge with industry demands, so enhancing the transition from education to employment (Lin, 2025; Popli & Singh, 2024).

Moreover, obsolete evaluation frameworks in maritime business education do not reflect the complexities of the global maritime sector. Conventional assessment techniques, including examinations and written tasks, may insufficiently represent the problem-solving, critical-thinking, and digital competencies demanded by the industry. As the global maritime environment grows increasingly intricate and data-centric, evaluation methodologies must advance to integrate practical, real-time simulations, case studies, and industry-specific initiatives. This alteration in assessment would more effectively equip students for the obstacles they will encounter in their jobs and reconcile the disparity between academic education and industrial standards (Alsmadi et al., 2024; Ghosh & Francia, 2021).

5. CURRICULUM ALIGNMENT STRATEGIES

5.1 Integrating Global Competencies into Learning Outcomes

To address these gaps, maritime curricula must integrate digital economy concepts, sustainability, and innovation management. Equal emphasis should be placed on sustainability economics and green financing mechanisms, as these are critical for long-term industry viability. With the swift integration of digital technologies in the marine sector, educational programs must equip students with an awareness of how innovations like blockchain, big data, artificial intelligence (AI), and automation are revolutionizing logistics, shipping, and port administration. Incorporating these subjects into fundamental courses, such as shipping operations and logistics management, will enhance students' preparedness to utilize the digital technologies propelling business progress (Ferrarini et al., 2025). Sustainability must be a fundamental focus in maritime education, tackling the sector's environmental challenges. This encompasses subjects such as sustainable shipping technologies, alternative fuels, initiatives for emission reduction, and the economic implications of environmental legislation, including the decarbonization objectives set by the International Maritime Organization (IMO). Integrating innovation management will enhance students' capabilities to lead and manage technological transformation, providing them with the skills necessary to advance sustainability initiatives and improve operations in a swiftly changing industry (Narula et al., 2021).

Additionally, interdisciplinary learning approaches should be adopted to combine economics, technology, and environmental policy. The marine industry is confronting intricate issues that necessitate a comprehensive comprehension of the economic ramifications of global trade, technical progress, and environmental restrictions. Integrating marine economics with technology enables students to understand how economic factors influence the adoption of new technologies and how digital tools can enhance operations and minimize expenses. These modules may encompass case studies about the financial feasibility of green technology, the influence of digital supply chains on cost efficiency, and the function of automation in port operations. By integrating these disciplines, students acquire a more holistic understanding of the intersection between economics and technology within the maritime sector, empowering them to make educated career decisions. (Bogusławski et al., 2022; Zou et al., 2025).

Moreover, integrating marine economics with environmental policy is essential for tackling the increasing focus on sustainability within the maritime industry. As international commerce proliferates, the maritime sector must reconcile economic advancement with ecological stewardship. Incorporating environmental policy into maritime economics curricula will enhance students' comprehension of the economic implications of international rules such as the IMO's sulfur cap, carbon pricing, and emissions reduction methods. This integration will enable students to examine how maritime enterprises can adhere to these laws while sustaining profitability. By comprehending the financial and environmental concerns, graduates will be adept at making strategic decisions that promote sustainable company practices (Simanjuntak, 2023).

Ultimately, creating these interdisciplinary curricula equips students to address the complex difficulties confronting the maritime sector. The integration of technology, economic analysis, and policy comprehension will render graduates more versatile and proficient in addressing the swiftly evolving requirements of the maritime sector. As global shipping evolves, experts must exhibit technical expertise and strategic thinking to incorporate new technologies, adhere to environmental requirements, and foster innovation. By providing these thorough, multidisciplinary educational experiences, schools may guarantee that their graduates possess the necessary skills to guide the sector towards a more sustainable and technologically advanced future (Hitt et al., 2025; Otto et al., 2023).

5.2 Industry Collaboration and Work-Based Learning

Stronger partnerships between academia and industry are essential. Internship programs, certifications, and simulation-based learning can enhance practical skills and improve graduate employability. Enhancing collaborations with shipping businesses, port authorities, and marine logistics firms is crucial for maintaining the relevance and currency of academic programs in relation to industry trends (Lopes et al., 2025; Rauf et al., 2023). These collaborations provide students direct access to contemporary advancements in shipping operations, logistics management, and port operations, allowing them to acquire insights into the challenges and possibilities encountered by industry experts. Through collaboration with these pivotal stakeholders, universities and training institutions can align their curricula with real-world demands, ensuring that students are acquainted with contemporary practices, technologies, and advances in the maritime industry. This collaboration can enhance information transfer between academia and industry, enabling both sectors to remain at the forefront of developing trends like as digitization, sustainability, and automation in maritime operations (Aerts & Mathys, 2024).

The integration of internship programs, professional certifications, and experiential learning opportunities significantly improves students' preparedness for the workforce. Internships enable students to implement theoretical information acquired in the classroom in practical, hands-on contexts, so acquiring valuable experience in shipping, port management, marine logistics, and other maritime industries. This practical experience enhances their technical abilities while also refining their problem-solving, communication, and collaboration skills. Moreover, professional certifications from industry organizations, such as the International Maritime Organization (IMO) or The Institute of Chartered Shipbrokers (ICS), furnish students with esteemed qualifications that augment their employability and professional credibility. These qualifications conform to industry standards, guaranteeing that students are adequately equipped to fulfill employer expectations in the nautical sector (Mojafi, 2023; Phanphichit & Bartusevičienė, 2024).

Furthermore, experiential learning opportunities, including simulation-based training and collaborative projects with industry partners, provide students the opportunity to engage with real-world difficulties. These chances may encompass activities such as enhancing port operations, overseeing logistics networks, or formulating sustainability initiatives in shipping. By incorporating these experiential learning opportunities, academic institutions may furnish students with the practical skills and industry expertise necessary to thrive in the maritime business sector. These partnerships and educational experiences connect academia with the workforce, guaranteeing that graduates are prepared to make meaningful contributions to the marine sector from the outset (Bogusławski et al., 2022).

5.3 Pedagogical Innovation

Adoption of simulation-based learning, project-based learning (PjBL), and problem-solving approaches represents an innovative strategy to enhance the practical application of theoretical knowledge in maritime business education. Simulation-based learning, in particular, allows students to engage in realistic, risk-free environments where they can simulate the operation of ships, manage port activities, or oversee logistics networks (Jamil & Bhuiyan, 2021; Nyairo et al., 2025). These simulations replicate real-world scenarios, such as managing a fleet under fluctuating market conditions or responding to logistical disruptions, giving students hands-on experience with decision-making processes and operational challenges. This approach not only reinforces theoretical knowledge but also helps students develop critical thinking, strategic planning, and crisis management skills, all of which are essential in the. Simulation-based learning, in particular, allows students to engage in realistic, risk-free environments where they can simulate the operation of ships, manage port activities, or oversee logistics networks (Jamil & Bhuiyan, 2021; Nyairo et al., 2025). These simulations replicate real-world scenarios, such as managing a fleet under fluctuating market conditions or responding to logistical disruptions, giving students hands-on experience with decision-making processes and operational challenges. This approach not only reinforces theoretical knowledge but also helps students develop critical thinking, strategic planning, and crisis management skills, all of which are essential in the dynamic maritime industry (Abeysiriwardhane, 2020; Nurfaida Tasni, Andi Syukriani, 2025).

Project-based learning (PjBL) further enhances student engagement by involving them in long-term, industry-relevant projects. This approach places students in the role of industry professionals, where they are required to tackle real-world maritime challenges. For instance, students could collaborate on projects to design a green shipping solution, optimize port logistics, or develop a new business model for a shipping company. PjBL fosters teamwork, innovation, and leadership, as students work in groups to solve complex problems. It also encourages interdisciplinary collaboration, allowing students to integrate knowledge from different fields such as economics, environmental policy, and maritime technology. By working on real-world projects, students gain valuable experience that directly aligns with the expectations of the maritime business sector, making them more job-ready upon graduation (Eid et al., 2023; Xin-rong et al., 2024).

Incorporating AI, big data analytics, and business intelligence (BI) tools in classroom activities is becoming increasingly crucial as the maritime industry embraces digital transformation. These technologies provide students with the tools necessary to analyze and interpret vast amounts of data, a skill that is vital in today's data-driven maritime operations. For instance, AI can be used to optimize shipping routes, forecast demand, and automate logistics processes, while big data analytics enables the examination of complex data sets to improve decision-making. Integrating these technologies into maritime curricula helps students develop a comprehensive understanding of how digital tools can be applied to enhance efficiency, reduce costs, and improve sustainability in the maritime sector. Using BI tools, students can analyze shipping trends, financial data, and operational performance, helping them make informed decisions in real-world scenarios. By incorporating AI, big data, and BI into classroom activities, students gain a competitive edge, making them highly valuable to employers who are seeking professionals proficient in the latest technological innovations (Olsen & Dupin-Bryant, 2012; Tsai, 2024).

Together, these learning strategies simulation-based learning, project-based learning, problem-solving approaches, and the integration of digital tools ensure that students are equipped not only with theoretical knowledge but also with the practical, hands-on experience and technical expertise needed to excel in the rapidly evolving maritime business environment. These strategies bridge the gap between academia and industry, providing students with the skills necessary to address current challenges and drive future innovation in the maritime sector (Lopes et al., 2025).

6. CONCLUSION

This chapter highlights the urgent need to align maritime business and economic education with global industry demands. While current curricula provide a strong foundation, they require significant enhancement to address digital transformation, sustainability, and economic complexity. Essential findings indicate that the incorporation of digital economy principles, sustainability frameworks, and innovation management into core curricula, alongside the adoption of interdisciplinary learning, can provide students with a thorough comprehension of the intricate dynamics of the marine industry. The integration of real-world applications via simulation-based learning, project-based learning, and practical industry partnerships guarantees that students possess both theoretical knowledge and the practical skills necessary to adapt to the evolving marine environment.

The ramifications for curriculum designers, educators, and legislators are substantial. Curriculum planners must collaborate with industry stakeholders to ensure that academic programs align with the most critical developments in marine business, such as digital transformation, sustainable shipping, and the incorporation of AI and big data analytics. Educators ought to integrate real-world case studies, simulations, and industry-driven projects to connect classroom learning with industry requirements. Policymakers should advocate for the incorporation of global competences, including economic literacy and technical fluency, into maritime education by promoting policies that facilitate collaboration between academic institutions and industry leaders. By matching educational strategies with industry requirements, authorities can ensure that maritime education stays pertinent and that graduates are prepared to contribute to the sector's growth and sustainability.

Future curriculum development should focus on producing hybrid professionals who are technologically skilled, economically literate, and globally aware. By integrating industry collaboration, interdisciplinary learning, and competency-based approaches, maritime education can better prepare graduates for the challenges of the modern maritime industry.

REFERENCES

Abeysiriwardhane, A. (2020). Learning and Learning-to-Learn by Doing: An Experiential Learning Approach for Integrating Human Factors into Maritime Design Education. *Maritime Technology and Research, 3*(1). Advance online publication. DOI: 10.33175/mtr.2021.241912

Aerts, G., & Mathys, G. (2024). Discovering Trends in the Digitalization of Shipping: An Exploratory Study into Trends Using Natural Language Processing. *Journal of Marine Science and Engineering, 12*(4), 618. DOI: 10.3390/jmse12040618

Alop, A. (2021). Smart Shipping Needs Smart Maritime Education and Training. In *Springer eBooks* (pp. 131–142). Springer Nature., DOI: 10.1007/978-3-030-64088-0_12

Alsmadi, H., Kandasamy, G., Al Kafri, A. S., & Zahirah, K. F. (2024). Empowering computing students through multidisciplinary project based learning (PBL): Creating meaningful differences in the real world. *Social Sciences & Humanities Open, 10*, 101180. DOI: 10.1016/j.ssaho.2024.101180

Ambrosino, D., & Sciomachen, A. (2021). Impact of Externalities on the Design and Management of Multimodal Logistic Networks. *Sustainability (Basel), 13*(9), 5080. DOI: 10.3390/su13095080

Autsadee, Y., Jeevan, J., Salleh, N. H. M., & Othman, M. R. (2024). Digital wind of changes: Navigating competitiveness in the maritime sector through the transformation in human resource development. *Maritime Business Review, 9*(3), 204–228. DOI: 10.1108/MABR-11-2023-0079

Barus, I. R. G., & Simanjuntak, M. B. (2023). Integrating Environmental Education into Maritime English Curriculum for Vocational Learners: Challenges and Opportunities. *BIO Web of Conferences, 79*, 8001. DOI: 10.1051/bioconf/20237908001

Bogusławski, K., Gil, M., Nasur, J., & Wróbel, K. (2022). Implications of autonomous shipping for maritime education and training: The cadet's perspective. *Maritime Economics & Logistics, 24*(2), 327–343. DOI: 10.1057/s41278-022-00217-x

Caesar, L. D. (2023). Emerging Dynamics of Training, Recruiting and Retaining a Sustainable Maritime Workforce: A Skill Resilience Framework. *Sustainability (Basel), 16*(1), 239. DOI: 10.3390/su16010239

Cariou, P., Ferrari, C., & Parola, F. (2015). Strategies in maritime and port logistics. *Maritime Economics & Logistics, 17*(1), 1–8. DOI: 10.1057/mel.2014.30

Chan, J. P., Pazouki, K., Norman, R., & Golightly, D. (2025). Investigating the Impact of Seafarer Training in the Autonomous Shipping Era. *Journal of Marine Science and Engineering, 13*(4), 818. DOI: 10.3390/jmse13040818

Chua, C., Li, X., Tan, K. H., & Yuen, K. F. (2024). Building sustainable performance in the maritime industry via digital resources and innovation. *Transport Policy, 149*, 282–299. DOI: 10.1016/j.tranpol.2024.02.014

Dawar, A., & Bai, Y. (2024). Impact of Geopolitical Risk on the Maritime Supply Chain: A Regional Analysis of the Effects on Global Trade. *International Journal of Supply Chain Management, 13*(3), 42–53. DOI: 10.59160/ijscm.v13i3.6245

Dewan, M. H., & Godina, R. (2023). An overview of seafarers' engagement and training on energy efficient operation of ships. *Marine Policy*, *160*, 105980. DOI: 10.1016/j.marpol.2023.105980

Diniz, N. V., Cunha, D. R., de Santana Porte, M., Pereira, N. N., & Oliveira, C. B. M. (2024). Sustainable Practices in Brazilian Ports: Aligning with SDGs 9, 13, and 14. *Revista de Gestão Social e Ambiental*, *18*(11), e09744. Advance online publication. DOI: 10.24857/rgsa.v18n11-096

Eid, J., Aanerud, M., & Enberg, K. (2023). Teaching sustainability at the high sea: The "One Ocean Expedition.". *Sustainability Science*, *19*(1), 347–359. DOI: 10.1007/s11625-023-01419-9

Fagerholt, K., Heilig, L., Lalla-Ruiz, E., Meisel, F., & Wang, S. (2023). Data-driven optimization and analytics for maritime logistics. *Flexible Services and Manufacturing Journal*, *35*(1), 1–4. DOI: 10.1007/s10696-023-09487-w

Ferrarini, L., Filippopoulos, I., & Lajic, Z. (2025). Digital Transformation in the Shipping Industry: A Network-Based Bibliometric Analysis. *Journal of Marine Science and Engineering*, *13*(5), 894. DOI: 10.3390/jmse13050894

Gardin, F., Jespersen, K., Güntzer, E., de Bar, M., & Hjorth-Falsted, T. (2023). Unlocking the Potential of Ocean-related Data to Develop Insightful Blue Metrics for Financial Institutions : Key Highlights from the Making Oceans Count Initiative. In *Research Portal Denmark*. Technical University of Denmark. https://local.forskningsportal.dk/local/dki-cgi/ws/cris-link?src=cbs&id=cbs-31052f47-3b94-4416-b218-1c16e63592c9&ti=Unlocking the Potential of Ocean-related Data to Develop Insightful Blue Metrics for Financial Institutions %3A Key Highlights from the Making Oceans Count Initiative

Gavalas, D. (2025). Green finance frameworks for sustainable shipping industry and blue economy: A review. In *Maritime Technology and Research* (Vol. 7, Issue 3). Chiang Mai University. DOI: 10.33175/mtr.2025.277132

Ghosh, T., & Francia, G. A.III. (2021). Assessing Competencies Using Scenario-Based Learning in Cybersecurity. *Journal of Cybersecurity and Privacy*, *1*(4), 539–552. DOI: 10.3390/jcp1040027

Guntoro, R. H., & Simanjuntak, P. D. (2024). Integration of Ship Machinery Maintenance and Control Systems in Maritime Education: Enhancing Industry Readiness. [JBFE]. *Journal Of Business Finance and Economics*, *5*(1), 409–419. DOI: 10.32585/jbfe.v5i1.5687

Hendriksen, C. (2020). Inside the Blue Box : Explaining Industry Influence in the International Maritime Organization. *Research Portal Denmark*, 286. https://local.forskningsportal.dk/local/dki-cgi/ws/cris-link?src=cbs&id=cbs-adca015e-a3ee-4de3-9038-ca6cf84e7374&ti=Inside the Blue Box %3A Explaining Industry Influence in the International Maritime Organization

Hitt, S. J., Seminara, P., Binding, T., & Hairstans, R. (2025). Developing sustainability competencies through extra-curricular interdisciplinary challenges. *European Journal of Engineering Education*, •••, 1–19. DOI: 10.1080/03043797.2025.2481965

İnal, Ö. B., Dere, Ç., Zincir, B., & Deniz, C. (2021). Hybrid propulsion and alternative fuels education in the course of decarbonised shipping. *Australian Journal of Maritime and Ocean Affairs*, *14*(2), 97–113. DOI: 10.1080/18366503.2021.1940475

Jafari, H., Lista, A., Siekapen, M. M., Ghaffari-Bohlouli, P., Nie, L., Alimoradi, H., & Shavandi, A. (2020). Fish Collagen: Extraction, Characterization, and Applications for Biomaterials Engineering. In *Polymers* (Vol. 12, Issue 10, p. 2230). Multidisciplinary Digital Publishing Institute. DOI: 10.3390/polym12102230

Jahangard, M., Xie, Y., & Feng, Y. (2025). Leveraging machine learning and optimization models for enhanced seaport efficiency. *Maritime Economics & Logistics*, *27*(4), 710–751. Advance online publication. DOI: 10.1057/s41278-024-00309-w

Jamasb, T., & Sornn-Friese, H. (2024). Regulatory Economics and the Future of Ports as Energy Hubs. *Research Portal Denmark*, 34–42. https://local.forskningsportal.dk/local/dki-cgi/ws/cris-link?src=cbs&id=cbs-9a3f2b03-6270-4b1c-8c90-51bb39dcd2ae&ti=Regulatory Economics and the Future of Ports as Energy Hubs

Jamil, M. G., & Bhuiyan, Z. (2021). Deep learning elements in maritime simulation programmes: A pedagogical exploration of learner experiences. *International Journal of Educational Technology in Higher Education*, *18*(1), 18. Advance online publication. DOI: 10.1186/s41239-021-00255-0

Jeon, T.-Y., & Jung, B.-G. (2023). A Study of PI Controller Tuning Methods by IMC Guide for a Ship Central Cooling System as a MISO System. *Preprints.Org*. DOI: 10.20944/preprints202309.1594.v1

Jeon, T.-Y., & Lee, Y.-C. (2025). Energy Saving in Ship Central Cooling Systems: IMC-Tuned PID with Feedforward Control. *Journal of Marine Science and Engineering*, *13*(3), 510. DOI: 10.3390/jmse13030510

Jiang, L. (2021). Shuo Ma: Economics of maritime business (1st Edition): Routledge, London, 2020, pp. 470. ISBN: 9781138999657. *WMU Journal of Maritime Affairs, 20*(3), 401–403. DOI: 10.1007/s13437-021-00246-y

Kilpi, V., Solakivi, T., & Kiiski, T. (2021). Maritime sector at verge of change: Learning and competence needs in Finnish maritime cluster. *WMU Journal of Maritime Affairs*, *20*(1), 63–79. DOI: 10.1007/s13437-021-00228-0

Knapp, S., & Franses, P. H. (2022). Empirical analysis of the effectiveness of the legislative framework in the maritime industry. *Marine Policy*, *147*, 105401. DOI: 10.1016/j.marpol.2022.105401

Kondratenko, A. A., Zhang, M., Tavakoli, S., Altarriba, E., & Hirdaris, S. (2025). Existing technologies and scientific advancements to decarbonize shipping by retrofitting. *Renewable & Sustainable Energy Reviews*, *212*, 115430. DOI: 10.1016/j.rser.2025.115430

Lau, Y., Chen, Q., Poo, M. C., Ng, A. K. Y., & Ying, C. C. (2024). Maritime transport resilience: A systematic literature review on the current state of the art, research agenda and future research directions. *Ocean and Coastal Management*, *251*, 107086. DOI: 10.1016/j.ocecoaman.2024.107086

Lin, Z. (2025). The Impact of Trade Openness on Income Inequality: A Theoretical and Empirical Review. *International Journal of Economics Business and Management Research*, *9*(5), 28–39. DOI: 10.51505/IJEBMR.2025.9502

Lopes, L. S., Nabais, J. L., Pinto, C. J., Caldeirinha, V., & Pinho, T. (2025). Essential Competencies in Maritime and Port Logistics: A Study on the Current Needs of the Sector. *Sustainability (Basel)*, *17*(6), 2378. DOI: 10.3390/su17062378

Mojafi, T. A. (2023). Maritime education and training – responding to the changing role of the seafarer. *South African Journal of Maritime Education and Training*, *2*(1), 97–120. DOI: 10.47348/SAJMET/2023/i1a7

Narula, S., Puppala, H., Kumar, A., Frederico, G. F., Dwivedy, M., Prakash, S., & Talwar, V. (2021). Applicability of industry 4.0 technologies in the adoption of global reporting initiative standards for achieving sustainability. *Journal of Cleaner Production*, *305*, 127141. Advance online publication. DOI: 10.1016/j.jclepro.2021.127141

Nguyen, T.-T., Tran, D. T., Duc, T. T. H., & Thai, V. V. (2022). Managing disruptions in the maritime industry – a systematic literature review. *Maritime Business Review*, *8*(2), 170–190. DOI: 10.1108/MABR-09-2021-0072

Nyairo, F., Haavardtun, P., Lindroos, E., Munim, Z. H., Lampiola, J., Salokorpi, M., & Krabbel, H. (2025). Instructional Approaches for Simulator-Based Maritime Education and Training. In *Lecture notes in networks and systems* (pp. 120–131). Springer International Publishing., DOI: 10.1007/978-3-031-84170-5_11

Ohakwe, C. R., & Wu, J. (2025). The Impact of Macroeconomic Indicators on Logistics Performance: A Comparative Analysis Using Simulated Scenarios. *Sustainable Futures : An Applied Journal of Technology, Environment and Society*, *100567*, 100567. Advance online publication. DOI: 10.1016/j.sftr.2025.100567

Olaniyi, E. O., Solarte-Vásquez, M. C., & Inkinen, T. (2024). Smart regulations in maritime governance: Efficacy, gaps, and stakeholder perspectives. *Marine Pollution Bulletin*, *202*, 116341. DOI: 10.1016/j.marpolbul.2024.116341

Olsen, D., & Dupin-Bryant, P. A. (2012). Combining Business Intelligence And Stock Market Data: A Primer For Data Analytics And Business Intelligence. [JABR]. *Journal of Applied Business Research*, *29*(1), 139. DOI: 10.19030/jabr.v29i1.7562

Otto, S., Bertel, L. B., Guerra, A., Chen, J., Lavi, R., Bertel, L. B., & Lindsay, E. (2023). Engineering Students' Perceptions of Digital Competences in a PBL Environment. *Research Portal Denmark*, 118–123. https://local.forskningsportal.dk/local/dki-cgi/ws/cris-link?src=aau&id=aau-cdcc785d-5a26-4794-97d8-4ba737811d3f&ti=Engineering Students 19 Perceptions of Digital Competences in a PBL Environment

Pace, L. A., Saritas, O., & Deidun, A. (2022). Exploring future research and innovation directions for a sustainable blue economy. *Marine Policy*, *148*, 105433. DOI: 10.1016/j.marpol.2022.105433

Pallis, A. A., Kladaki, P., & Notteboom, T. (2023). Port economics, management and policy studies (2009–2020): A bibliometric analysis. *WMU Journal of Maritime Affairs*, *23*(2), 217–255. DOI: 10.1007/s13437-023-00325-2

Parola, F., Satta, G., Buratti, N., & Vitellaro, F. (2020). Digital technologies and business opportunities for logistics centres in maritime supply chains. *Maritime Policy & Management*, *48*(4), 461–477. DOI: 10.1080/03088839.2020.1802784

Pazaver, A., & Kitada, M. (2025). Integrating twenty-first century skills into STCW competences: Implications for maritime education and training. *WMU Journal of Maritime Affairs*, *24*(3), 397–418. DOI: 10.1007/s13437-025-00368-7

Phanphichit, T., & Bartusevičienė, I. (2024). Perspectives of stakeholders on onboard training: A thematic analysis of qualitative interviews. *Journal of International Maritime Safety Environmental Affairs and Shipping*, *8*(4), 2408698. Advance online publication. DOI: 10.1080/25725084.2024.2408698

Phewa, N. C. (2021). Maritime Education and Training (MET) Curriculum Challenges in the Twenty-First Century. In *Springer eBooks* (pp. 163–171). Springer Nature. DOI: 10.1007/978-3-030-64088-0_15

Popli, N. K., & Singh, R. (2024). Enhancing academic outcomes through industry collaboration: Our experience with integrating real-world projects into engineering courses. *Discover Education*, *3*(1), 217. Advance online publication. DOI: 10.1007/s44217-024-00300-w

Prousaloglou, P., Kyriakopoulou-Roussou, M.-C., Stavroulakis, P. J., Tsioumas, V., & Papadimitriou, S. (2025). Artificial intelligence in the service of sustainable shipping. *Journal of Ocean Engineering and Marine Energy*, *11*(3), 621–653. DOI: 10.1007/s40722-025-00390-0

Rao, P. (2025). Multimodal AI Analytics: Converging data streams for predictive logistics flow optimization. *World Journal of Advanced Research and Reviews*, *26*(1), 3537–3544. DOI: 10.30574/wjarr.2025.26.1.1438

Rauf, U. A. A., Aziz, N. I., Zulkarnaini, N. A. S., Deli, M. M., Asha'ari, M. J., Jamil, A. H., & Abdullah, S. I. N. W. (2023). Strengthening the University-Maritime Industry Collaborations (UMICs): Technology Issues. [JAETS]. *Journal of Applied Engineering and Technological Science*, *5*(1), 515–530. DOI: 10.37385/jaets.v5i1.3211

Simanjuntak, M. B. (2023). Enhancing Environmental Awareness and Sustainable Communication Skills in Maritime Education. *BIO Web of Conferences, 79*, 1002. DOI: 10.1051/bioconf/20237901002

Simmons, E. S., & McLean, G. (2020). Understanding the paradigm shift in maritime education. *Worldwide Hospitality and Tourism Themes*, *12*(1), 90–97. DOI: 10.1108/WHATT-10-2019-0062

Sumaila, U. R., Walsh, M., Hoareau, K., Cox, A. D., Teh, L., Abdallah, P. R., Akpalu, W., Anna, Z., Benzaken, D., Crona, B., Fitzgerald, T., Heaps, L., Issifu, I., Karousakis, K., Lange, G., Leland, A., Miller, D., Sack, K., Shahnaz, D., . . . Zhang, J. (2021). Financing a sustainable ocean economy. In *Nature Communications* (Vol. 12, Issue 1). Nature Portfolio. DOI: 10.1038/s41467-021-23168-y

Sun, S., Zhang, Z., & Tan, M. (2024). Financial Mechanism for Sustainable Development of the Marine Economy with Respect to Technology, Digitalization, and Low Carbonization. *Water (Basel)*, *16*(19), 2841. DOI: 10.3390/w16192841

Surucu-Balci, E., Iris, Ç., & Balcı, G. (2023). Digital information in maritime supply chains with blockchain and cloud platforms: Supply chain capabilities, barriers, and research opportunities. *Technological Forecasting and Social Change*, *198*, 122978. DOI: 10.1016/j.techfore.2023.122978

Theotokas, I., Lagoudis, I. N., & Raftopoulou, K. (2024). Challenges of maritime human resource management for the transition to shipping digitalization. *Journal of Shipping and Trade*, *9*(1), 6. Advance online publication. DOI: 10.1186/s41072-024-00165-0

Tsai, Y. (2024). Empowering students through active learning in educational big data analytics. *Smart Learning Environments*, *11*(1), 14. Advance online publication. DOI: 10.1186/s40561-024-00300-1

Tsatsaronis, M., Syriopoulos, T., Karamperidis, S., Boura, G., & Dimopoulos, A. (2024). Quality assessment of ESG reporting among listed maritime companies. *Maritime Economics & Logistics*, *26*(4), 592–611. DOI: 10.1057/s41278-024-00299-9

Veríssimo, N. V. P., Mussagy, C. U., Oshiro, A. A., Mendonça, C. M. N., Santos-Ebinuma, V. C., Pessoa, A., de Souza Oliveira, R. P., & Pereira, J. F. B. (2021). From green to blue economy: Marine biorefineries for a sustainable ocean-based economy. *Green Chemistry*, *23*(23), 9377–9400. DOI: 10.1039/D1GC03191K

Werner, S., Papanikolaou, A., Werner, S., Fagergren, C., Dessen, L., Kuttenkeuler, J., Santén, V., & Steinbach, C. (2023). The ORCELLE Project – Towards Wind-Powered Ships for Deep Sea Cargo Transport. *SNAME Maritime Convention*. DOI: 10.5957/SMC-2023-089

Xiao, G., Wang, Y., Wu, R., Li, J., & Cai, Z. (2024). Sustainable Maritime Transport: A Review of Intelligent Shipping Technology and Green Port Construction Applications. In *Journal of Marine Science and Engineering* (Vol. 12, Issue 10, p. 1728). Multidisciplinary Digital Publishing Institute. DOI: 10.3390/jmse12101728

Xin-rong, H., Yang, D., Wang, K., Tong, J., & Han, T. T. (2024). Impact of Student Backgrounds on the Outcomes of Maritime Postgraduate Professional Education. *Transport Policy*, *159*, 392–404. Advance online publication. DOI: 10.1016/j.tranpol.2024.10.020

Xu, M., Ma, X., Zhao, Y., & Qiao, W. (2023). A Systematic Literature Review of Maritime Transportation Safety Management. *Journal of Marine Science and Engineering*, *11*(12), 2311. DOI: 10.3390/jmse11122311

Yuen, K. F., Tan, L., & Loh, H. S. (2022). Core Competencies for Maritime Business Educators in the Digital Era. *Frontiers in Psychology*, *13*, 915980. Advance online publication. DOI: 10.3389/fpsyg.2022.915980

Zou, Y., Xiao, G., Li, Q., & Biancardo, S. A. (2025). Intelligent Maritime Shipping: A Bibliometric Analysis of Internet Technologies and Automated Port Infrastructure Applications. *Journal of Marine Science and Engineering*, *13*(5), 979. DOI: 10.3390/jmse13050979

Chapter 6
Designing Competency-Based Education Frameworks for Maritime Training Institutions:
Principles and Practices

Andi Asrifan
http://orcid.org/0000-0002-9934-6129
Universitas Negeri Makassar, Indonesia

Sajed S. Ingilan
http://orcid.org/0000-0002-4466-2028
University of Southeastern Philippines, Philippines

ABSTRACT

This study investigates the execution of Competency-Based Education (CBE) at maritime training institutions by evaluating the identification, structuring, delivery, and assessment of competencies to satisfy current industry requirements. It emphasizes the amalgamation of occupational analysis, performance metrics, simulation-based pedagogy, and ongoing evaluation to improve learners' operational preparedness. The discourse examines quality assurance tools, including tracer studies, audit cycles, and industry input, as well as institutional difficulties such as resource constraints, instructor readiness, and technical deficiencies. Future initiatives focus on AI-based evaluation, intelligent shipping systems, alternative fuel capabilities, and international standardization. The results highlight the significance of adaptable, technology-driven, and industry-aligned competency-based education frameworks in equipping proficient and safety-oriented marine workers.

DOI: 10.4018/979-8-3373-6670-8.ch006

INTRODUCTION TO COMPETENCY-BASED EDUCATION (CBE) IN MARITIME CONTEXTS

1.1 The Evolution of Maritime Education and Training (MET)

Maritime Education and Training (MET) has had a substantial evolution over the last fifty years, shifting from conventional time-based teaching methods to more organized, outcome-focused competency frameworks. Historically, MET systems were predicated on the premise that adequate exposure to classroom education, practical experience, and simulator activities would inherently result in professional preparedness. This paradigm prioritized fixed training hours, seniority, and adherence to procedures over demonstrated mastery (Harrington et al., 2025; Longridge et al., 2001). Although effective in its era, the swift advancement of maritime operations—propelled by innovations in vessel technology, automation, environmental regulations, and globalized shipping—exposed deficiencies in time-based methodologies, especially in ensuring that cadets and officers consistently attained the competencies necessary for safe and efficient ship operations.

The transition to an outcome-oriented framework commenced significantly with the implementation of the International Maritime Organization (IMO) requirements of Training, Certification and Watchkeeping (STCW) Convention in 1978, which set forth universal minimum requirements for maritime qualifications. The 1995 and 2010 Manila Amendments expedited the transition to Competency-Based Education (CBE). The adjustments highlighted quantifiable learning outcomes, practical skill assessment, and quality assurance protocols within MET institutions (Vujičić et al., 2020). The emphasis broadened from theoretical knowledge to encompass visible performance metrics, evidence-based evaluations, and ongoing validation of proficiency, both throughout training and throughout marine careers. Consequently, MET providers globally were necessitated to implement structured competency frameworks that correspond with industry requirements, safety management protocols, and the operational complexities of advanced ship systems.

Simultaneously, technological advancements transformed the domain of marine education. The implementation of full-mission simulators, ECDIS training platforms, VR- and AR-enhanced simulations, and AI-assisted navigation tools enabled cadets to engage in realistic operational scenarios that were previously unattainable in conventional classrooms (Magsino et al., 2023). These technologies facilitated the transition from rote learning to immersive, scenario-based training that prioritizes learners in the competency development process. Cadets must now exhibit proficiency in essential competencies, including situational awareness, decision-making, bridge resource management, safety compliance, and emergency response, rather than simply amassing sea-time hours.

The shift to Competency-Based Education (CBE) signifies wider trends in professional education that prioritize adaptability, individualization, and demonstrable learning outcomes. Competency-based MET frameworks facilitate varied learning speeds, previous educational experiences, and personalized routes to certification. This method enhances cooperation among maritime academies, ship operators, classification societies, and regulatory authorities, guaranteeing that training results are consistent with the advancing practices and technological standards of the industry (Kim et al., 2023; Simanjuntak et al., 2024). The transition of MET to a competency-driven approach signifies a fundamental dedication to cultivating maritime professionals who are not only aware but also demonstrably competent, adaptive, and proficient in navigating the difficulties of contemporary global shipping.

1.2 Core Principles of Competency-Based Education

Competency-Based Education (CBE) signifies a transformative approach in the preparation of maritime professionals for the escalating complexities of global shipping demands. In contrast to conventional methods that prioritize time spent in classrooms or on board, Competency-Based Education (CBE) emphasizes learners' capacity to exhibit mastery of specific abilities directly linked to real-world jobs, safety-critical operations, and regulatory mandates. This educational approach is grounded in four fundamental principles: mastery learning, observable performance, flexible pacing, and continuous assessment, which collectively influence the structure, delivery, and evaluation of learning in Maritime Education and Training (MET) institutions (Baldevarona et al., 2024).

Mastery learning is fundamental to the CBE paradigm. This method assesses progress based on the learner's ability to fulfill specific performance standards rather than the length of teaching (Vasquez et al., 2021). MET systems implementing mastery learning necessitate that cadets regularly practice skills—such as maneuvering functions, safety protocols, or bridge resource management—until they attain a certain level of proficiency. This guarantees that every student attains operational readiness, minimizing discrepancies in skill levels among prospective officers. Mastery learning fosters profound comprehension, as learners interact with material via intentional practice and obtain specific feedback designed to bridge performance discrepancies.

The principle of observable performance, closely associated with mastery, underscores the significance of demonstrable and measurable actions over mere abstract knowledge. Observable performance guarantees that cadets can use theoretical concepts in genuine marine situations, whether via simulated exercises, aboard training, or performance assignments evaluated by trained instructors (Sevilla & Arceño, 2017). Competency frameworks often encompass behavioral indicators and observable criteria that direct both instruction and evaluation. A capability like "maintaining situational awareness on the bridge" encompasses quantifiable components such as observing environmental conditions, analyzing instrument data, and collaborating with the bridge team.

Competency-Based Education (CBE) facilitates mastery and performance demonstration through flexible pacing, enabling learners to progress at varying rates according on their readiness and prior experience (Vasquez et al., 2021). This adaptability caters to the many backgrounds of maritime trainees, encompassing individuals with prior sea experience, industrial exposure, or significant technical proficiency. Flexible pace alleviates stress for cadets, as individuals needing additional time to attain proficiency are not disadvantaged by inflexible course timelines. Conversely, learning routes are tailored to the individual, facilitating individualized growth while upholding stringent standards.

Ultimately, continuous assessment guarantees that the progression of competency is tracked by persistent, formative evaluations instead of depending exclusively on high-stakes tests. Continuous assessment encompasses performance checklists, simulation-based evaluations, reflective journals, digital portfolios, peer assessments, and teacher feedback (Goldhamer et al., 2022). This method enables educators to detect learning deficiencies promptly and provide focused assistance, so guaranteeing steady advancement towards proficiency. In the marine domain, ongoing evaluation bolsters the credibility of certification and improves safety by guaranteeing that each cadet continually fulfills international competency standards.

1.3 Relevance of CBE for Maritime Training Institutions

Competency-Based Education (CBE) has gained significance for Maritime Training Institutions (MTIs) as they adapt to changing legislative mandates, swift technology progress, and increased demands for safety and operational excellence (Kim et al., 2023; Park et al., 2024). The marine industry, more than several other professions, necessitates individuals who can exhibit persistent, verified proficiency in intricate, high-risk settings. CBE provides an educational framework that complies with the Standards of Training, Certification and Watchkeeping (STCW) Convention, industry requirements, digitalization trends, and the safety-critical aspects of maritime operations.

The primary justification for implementing CBE in MTIs is its conformity with the STCW Convention and its subsequent revisions. The STCW delineates comprehensive competency standards for officers and ratings, highlighting the requisite knowledge, abilities, and attitudes essential for the safe operation of vessels (Karahalil et al., 2024). These competencies are intended to be quantifiable and discernible—principles that align strongly with the tenets of CBE. By organizing curriculum around competency units, performance criteria, and evidence requirements, MTIs may guarantee adherence to international regulatory standards while improving transparency and uniformity in certification procedures. This alignment is essential for preserving global acknowledgment of qualifications and facilitating smooth crew mobility within international maritime labor markets.

CBE not only adheres to regulatory compliance but also efficiently addresses industry expectations for highly skilled, adaptive, and operationally prepared seafarers. Contemporary vessels increasingly depend on integrated navigation systems, modern propulsion technologies, automated equipment, and ecologically sustainable technology (Grimett, 2023). Shipping firms today anticipate that cadets possess the ability to navigate intricate operating situations, mitigate hazards, and demonstrate robust decision-making capabilities. CBE enables MTIs to design learning experiences that replicate real-world problems, guarantee task proficiency, and develop competencies such as situational awareness, collaboration, and problem-solving—crucial for contemporary maritime operations.

The significance of CBE is further amplified by the digitalization of maritime training and vessel operations. The emergence of e-navigation, intelligent vessels, Internet of Things (IoT) applications, and digital logbooks has transformed the competencies necessary for maritime workers. MTIs incorporating CBE can utilize digital tools—such as full-mission simulators, AR/VR systems, AI-driven assessment platforms, and remote learning technologies—to facilitate experiential, learner-centered training (Yuen et al., 2022). These digital advancements provide more dependable competency assessment, instantaneous feedback, and ongoing skill enhancement.

The safety-critical duties associated with maritime occupations highlight the significance of CBE. Miscalculations in navigation, cargo management, or emergency protocols can result in disastrous outcomes. Competency-Based Education (CBE) guarantees that each learner attains a requisite level of proficiency prior to progression, hence minimizing performance variability and enhancing the overall safety culture in the maritime sector. By implementing thorough evaluations and organized competence frameworks, MTIs may cultivate people that are not only qualified but also adept at navigating the hazards and complexities of global seafaring (Ajayi & Udeh, 2024).

THEORETICAL AND REGULATORY FOUNDATIONS OF MARITIME COMPETENCIES

2.1 International Frameworks and Standards

The establishment of comprehensive competency frameworks in marine Education and Training (MET) is fundamentally based on internationally acknowledged legislative instruments and quality standards that dictate the training, certification, and deployment of seafarers within the global marine sector. Four principal frameworks—the IMO Standards of Training, Certification and Watchkeeping (STCW) Code, IMO Model Courses, the ILO Maritime Labour Convention (MLC) 2006, and ISO 9001 quality management systems—constitute essential pillars for competency assurance and institutional governance in Maritime Education and Training (MET) (Tusher et al., 2021). Collectively, these criteria guarantee that training programs conform to international benchmarks for safety, professionalism, and operational dependability.

The IMO STCW Code constitutes the preeminent regulatory framework governing marine skills globally. Initially enacted in 1978 and later amended in 1995 and 2010, the STCW delineates specific skill standards for officers and ratings in deck, engine, and electro-technical positions (Bouzón et al., 2023). These abilities are articulated through knowledge, skills, and attitudes, supplemented by performance requirements and requisite documentation. The STCW establishes basic training standards, delineates evaluation procedures, specifies simulator needs, and outlines quality assurance measures. By organizing curriculum according to STCW competence tables, MET institutions guarantee that their graduates fulfill internationally acknowledged standards and preserve the global transferability of their qualifications.

The IMO Model Courses complement the STCW Code by converting regulatory mandates into practical instructional guidelines. These model courses offer uniform syllabi, pedagogical methodologies, assessment tasks, and learning outcomes that assist MET institutions in consistently implementing training programs across various country contexts (Rouvrais et al., 2019). Despite lacking legal enforceability, IMO Model Courses function as authoritative resources for curriculum developers, educators, and evaluators aiming to synchronize their programs with global best practices. They additionally facilitate the harmonization of competencies, thereby diminishing disparities in training quality among nations.

The ILO Maritime Labour Convention (MLC) 2006, also referred to as the "seafarers' bill of rights," enhances competence governance by setting standards for aboard working and living circumstances (Politakis, 2013). The MLC does not expressly dictate training curriculum but emphasizes the necessity for skilled, well trained seafarers via regulations concerning occupational safety, health protection, social services, and employment circumstances. MET institutions include MLC principles into their competency frameworks to guarantee that graduates comprehend their rights, responsibilities, and duties in upholding safe and humane conditions aboard ships.

Ultimately, ISO 9001 is essential for guaranteeing institutional quality and fostering continual development inside MET enterprises. By implementing ISO 9001-compliant quality management systems, MET institutions can institutionalize procedures for curriculum development, assessment validation, instructor qualification, and stakeholder input (Rais et al., 2021). This reinforces adherence to STCW quality standards and improves openness, accountability, and uniformity in training execution. These worldwide frameworks collectively create a thorough regulatory foundation for marine competency-based education.

2.2 National Policies and Accreditation Requirements

National rules and accreditation standards significantly influence the competency frameworks employed by Maritime Education and Training (MET) institutes in Indonesia. These policies guarantee that maritime training conforms to both international standards, such as the IMO STCW Convention, and the national objectives for workforce development, digital transformation, and the advancement of higher education quality. Principal regulatory mechanisms comprise the Non-Convention Vessel Standard (NCVS), the Indonesian National Qualification Framework (KKNI), the Electronic-Based Government System (SPBE) requirement, and accreditation standards implemented by BAN-PT and LAMEMBA (Andriani, 2021). Collectively, these frameworks establish a thorough basis for competency verification within marine programs.

The NCVS (Non-Conventional Vessel Standard), promulgated by the Indonesian Ministry of Transportation, delineates the technical and operational competency prerequisites for seafarers aboard vessels exempt from the STCW Convention (Junus et al., 2024). This standard is especially pertinent to Indonesia, where a significant proportion of domestic maritime operations entails non-convention vessels, including fishing boats, passenger ships, and small cargo carriers. The NCVS delineates competency units, training hours, certification processes, and safety-related credentials specifically designed for national maritime conditions. MET institutions must synchronize their training programs with NCVS standards to guarantee that graduates are adequately trained to function safely within Indonesia's varied marine sectors.

The KKNI (*Kerangka Kualifikasi Nasional Indonesia*) establishes a nationwide standard for educational certification levels, encompassing outcomes-based criteria for knowledge, skills, and professional accountability. Maritime programs at vocational, undergraduate, and postgraduate levels must connect their learning outcomes with KKNI levels to guarantee vertical coherence, transparency, and comparability among institutions (Ahid & Chamid, 2021). KKNI strengthens the tenets of Competency-Based Education by mandating explicit delineation of learning outcomes, performance indicators, and assessment criteria that embody the professional competencies anticipated in the marine sector.

Simultaneously, the government's initiative for digital transformation via the SPBE (Sistem Pemerintahan Berbasis Elektronik) policy promotes MET institutions to include digital technologies in curriculum management, competency assessment, and instructional delivery (Magsino et al., 2023). This encompasses the utilization of digital learning platforms, electronic assessment systems, and data-informed quality assurance instruments. SPBE facilitates more effective governance and improves transparency in the reporting of training results and institutional performance.

The accreditation criteria mandated by BAN-PT for academic programs and LAMEMBA for vocational and professional programs enhance competency assurance in maritime education (Sevilla & Arceño, 2017). These entities assess universities based on curricular pertinence, attainment of learning outcomes, integrity of assessments, faculty credentials, and involvement of stakeholders. Adherence to accreditation standards guarantees that marine programs uphold national reputation and consistently enhance their offerings based on industry input and regulatory changes. These national regulations collectively create a strong regulatory framework that facilitates the implementation, quality assurance, and ongoing improvement of competency-based maritime education in Indonesia.

2.3 Educational Theories Supporting CBE in MET

Competency-Based Education (CBE) in Maritime Education and Training (MET) is based on various significant educational ideas that influence the teaching and assessment of knowledge, skills, and professional dispositions. Theories such as constructivism, contextual learning, experiential learning, and performance-based assessment jointly underpin the construction of training settings that correspond with authentic marine contexts (Sellberg et al., 2018). Their incorporation into MET guarantees that cadets not only gain theoretical knowledge but also effectively apply their learning in intricate operational environments on ships, in simulators, and within maritime businesses.

Constructivism serves as the philosophical basis for learner-centered, competency-based methodologies (Magsino et al., 2023). Constructivism is founded on the principle that learners acquire knowledge via active engagement, prioritizing meaning-making, reflection, and problem-solving over passive information absorption. In maritime training, constructivist methodologies manifest in activities like bridge simulators, collaborative voyage planning, and resolving engine room malfunctions. These educational experiences necessitate that cadets utilize past knowledge, analyze new information, evaluate hypotheses, and formulate solutions. Constructivism fosters the cultivation of critical thinking and decision-making abilities, which are vital for watchkeeping, navigation, and safety management.

Situated learning, which asserts that learning is most successful in authentic circumstances, is closely connected. Maritime competences cannot be entirely cultivated by theoretical instruction; they arise from immersion in environments that replicate the challenges and limitations of real ship operations (Harrington et al., 2025). Situated learning is implemented in MET via aboard training, realistic simulation situations, and role-based activities that mirror the social and operational dynamics of maritime work. Through participation in activities like collision-avoidance maneuvers, port entrance simulations, or emergency drills, learners assimilate the implicit knowledge, collaborative standards, and situational awareness necessary for practical execution.

Experiential learning, sometimes linked to Kolb, enhances competency-based education by fostering a cycle of action, reflection, conceptualization, and application. Maritime training institutes utilize experiential learning via laboratory exercises, simulator operations, and required sea-time, allowing cadets to acquire direct experience with shipboard systems, weather conditions, and navigational obstacles (Sibali et al., 2026). Reflection reports, debriefing sessions, and supervisor assessments assist cadets in transforming experience into proficiency. This theory emphasizes the significance of experiential learning in developing operational preparedness and self-assurance.

Ultimately, performance-based assessment directly corresponds with the emphasis of Competency-Based Education (CBE) on exhibited proficiency. Instead of depending exclusively on written tests, MET programs employ evaluations that necessitate students to execute activities under genuine settings, showcasing their competence in navigation, machinery operation, communication, or emergency reaction (Manuel, 2017). Instruments such as checklists, rubrics, OSCE-style exams, and simulator evaluations guarantee that competency is assessed objectively and uniformly. Performance-based assessment guarantees that certification accurately represents practical vocational competence rather than mere theoretical knowledge. Collectively, these educational ideas establish a unified framework that enhances the efficacy and credibility of competency-based maritime training.

DESIGNING COMPETENCY FRAMEWORKS FOR MARITIME PROGRAMS

3.1 Identifying and Mapping Maritime Competencies

The development of competency frameworks for maritime programs commences with the methodical identification and mapping of the competencies necessary for particular maritime jobs. This approach guarantees that the curriculum corresponds with the actual demands of maritime operations, regulatory standards, and industry expectations. The initial phase involves a comprehensive occupational analysis that scrutinizes the activities, responsibilities, and work environments of maritime professions, including deck officers, marine engineers, electro-technical officers, and ratings. Occupational analysis offers a comprehensive understanding of the situational aspects affecting performance, such as ship type, voyage conditions, technological complexity, and safety standards (Massami & Manyasi, 2021). It elucidates the cognitive, technical, and interpersonal competencies required for effective work performance.

The analysis of occupations leads to the creation of task inventories that enumerate and classify all critical tasks executed inside a maritime position. The tasks may encompass voyage planning, watch-keeping, engine maintenance, cargo handling, emergency response, communication protocols, pollution prevention, and operation of integrated bridge or engine-room systems (Dewan & Godina, 2023). Every task is evaluated based on its frequency, significance, complexity, and necessary circumstances. High-risk activities, including collision avoidance, firefighting, and equipment fault detection, are prioritized due to the potential for catastrophic outcomes resulting from failures in these domains. Task inventories ensure that training programs emphasize essential competencies and give adequate time and resources to areas where mistakes are unacceptable. Upon identification, tasks are categorized into competency categories that represent the multifaceted character of maritime performance. The predominant paradigm classifies competencies into knowledge, skills, and attitudes (KSA) (Kuzu & Taç, 2025).

a. **Knowledge** encompasses theoretical and procedural understanding, such as COLREGs, meteorology, ship stability, engine thermodynamics, and safety regulations.
b. **Skills** refer to technical and cognitive abilities required to perform tasks, including maneuvering vessels, interpreting navigational instruments, using communication equipment, conducting inspections, and solving engineering problems.
c. **Attitudes** involve behavioral and interpersonal attributes such as teamwork, leadership, cultural awareness, situational awareness, discipline, and safety-oriented mindset.

These domains collectively ensure that competency frameworks reflect not only technical proficiency but also the human element of maritime work. Effective seafaring depends heavily on decision-making, emotional regulation, adaptability, and ethical conduct—factors that have contributed to many maritime accidents when neglected. By mapping competencies across KSA domains, curriculum designers ensure comprehensive development of learners and alignment with the broader objectives of the STCW Convention, ILO MLC standards, and industry safety management systems.

3.2 Developing Competency Standards and Performance Indicators

Upon identifying competencies, the subsequent step is to convert them into competency standards that explicitly delineate anticipated performance levels. Competency standards delineate the operational criteria for defining "competence" within a marine framework (Kour et al., 2025; Sarı et al., 2025). They delineate not just the knowledge or actions required of learners but also the expected level of performance under specified situations. These standards provide uniformity, clarity, and responsibility in marine training and evaluation.

A fundamental element of competency standards is the incorporation of behavioral descriptors, which delineate observable activities that signify mastery of a competency. The ability "Maintain a safe navigational watch" may encompass descriptors such as "continuously monitors radar, AIS, and visual indicators," "identifies potential collision hazards," and "executes prompt corrective measures in accordance with COLREGs Rule 8." (Sharif et al., 2025). Behavioral descriptors transform abstract competencies into quantifiable activities that educators can assess consistently. They also instruct students by elucidating the characteristics of good performance in actual operational contexts.

A fundamental component is the design of proficiency levels that distinguish between basic, intermediate, and advanced performance goals. These levels may reflect the competence tables of STCW or institutional norms (Escallada et al., 2025). Proficiency levels enable programs to structure learning across several semesters, ensuring that cadets initially acquire foundational knowledge before advancing to intricate, multi-task competencies. For example, introductory levels may prioritize equipment familiarization, whereas advanced levels concentrate on decision-making under duress, leadership in emergencies, or the management of multi-system failures.

Competency development must match with institutional and industry Key Performance Indicators (KPIs). Key Performance Indicators (KPIs) guarantee that competency requirements align with overarching corporate objectives, including safety performance, operational efficiency, regulatory compliance, and graduate employability (Kes et al., 2025). In maritime training institutes, key performance indicators (KPIs) may encompass a reduction in training accidents, enhanced simulator assessment scores, elevated certification pass rates, or favorable evaluations from shipping businesses employing graduates. Connecting competencies to KPIs guarantees that training results immediately enhance institutional performance and meet industry requirements. To guarantee accurate evaluation, each competency must encompass explicitly stated proof criteria. Evidence can be classified into categories (Tisoy, 2025):

a. **Direct evidence** – performance in simulators, practical demonstrations, onboard evaluations, and OSCE-style assessments;
b. **Indirect evidence** – written tests, oral examinations, assignments, and reflection journals demonstrating cognitive understanding;
c. **Supplementary evidence** – supervisor reports during sea-time, digital portfolios, logbooks, and peer assessments.

Evidence requirements outline the conditions under which competence must be demonstrated (e.g., weather simulation settings, ship type, emergency context), the criteria for judgment, and the minimum acceptable performance. This strengthens the validity, reliability, and fairness of assessment processes. When competency standards incorporate behavioral descriptors, performance levels, KPI alignment, and evidence requirements, maritime programs achieve consistency in assessment and ensure that graduates possess not just theoretical knowledge but demonstrable operational competence.

3.3 Constructing Curriculum Structures Based on Competencies

Converting competency standards into an operational curriculum necessitates meticulous design of course frameworks, learning trajectories, and instructional sequences. Competency-based curriculum are structured around explicit learning outcomes, cohesive learning experiences, and a methodical advancement from fundamental knowledge to sophisticated maritime operations (Boonadir et al., 2020). The objective is to guarantee the systematic advancement of abilities throughout the program's duration.

A fundamental strategy is course clustering, wherein linked competencies are organized into cohesive sections or modules. Navigation competencies may be categorized under courses such as Terrestrial Navigation, Electronic Navigation Systems, and Ship Maneuvering. Engineering programs may consolidate competencies in Marine Engineering Science, Machinery Operation, Maintenance Management, and Safety Engineering (Andersen et al., 2012). Course clustering facilitates the efficient structuring of information, reduces redundancy, and guarantees that learning experiences are systematically structured. It also facilitates interdisciplinary integration, such as merging meteorology with bridge operations or incorporating electrical expertise with engine-room diagnostics.

Learning outcomes mapping is a fundamental instrument for curriculum development, connecting each course to the distinct competencies and performance metrics it cultivates. Curriculum designers establish a competency-course matrix to guarantee that each competency is covered and evaluated in one or more courses (Okojie et al., 2022). This mitigates discrepancies, redundancies, or misalignments between training results and regulatory standards. Mapping learning outcomes elucidates the function of each course within the broader training framework, aiding instructors and students in comprehending how specific learning elements contribute to overall nautical proficiency.

The curriculum must include intentional scaffolding, allowing learners to grow from fundamental concepts to sophisticated, integrative skills. Scaffolding guarantees that preliminary courses establish the cognitive and technical groundwork essential for the intricate difficulties faced subsequently in the program (Masava et al., 2022). Fundamental studies in physics and mathematics facilitate subsequent comprehension of ship stability and engineering systems. Introductory communication classes equip cadets for advanced bridge team management training. Simulations may initially concentrate on equipment familiarization, subsequently progressing to comprehensive bridge operations under demanding conditions such as heavy traffic, limited visibility, or system malfunctions. Scaffolding consequently fosters learners' confidence, mitigates cognitive overload, and improves long-term memory.

Competency-based maritime curricula must delineate explicit progression pathways that facilitate learners' advancement throughout the program (Latifah et al., 2026). These paths delineate the sequence of courses, needed prerequisites, and integrated assessments that signify critical transitions in competency development. Progression tracks incorporate sea-time prerequisites, enabling students to implement classroom knowledge in actual maritime settings. Efficient paths encompass milestone evaluations, gateway competencies (such as preparedness for sea-time), and capstone experiences that synthesize various performance dimensions. These components guarantee that graduates are both intellectually equipped and operationally prepared for the duties associated with shipboard positions.

The integration of course clustering, learning objectives mapping, scaffolding, and organized progression routes establishes a comprehensive curricular framework based on skills. This design guarantees that maritime training programs are cohesive, systematically structured, linked with international and national standards, and capable of generating professionals who fulfill the intricate requirements of contemporary marine operations.

IMPLEMENTING CBE THROUGH PEDAGOGY, SIMULATION, AND ASSESSMENT

4.1 Instructional Strategies for Competency Development

Implementing Competency-Based Education (CBE) in Maritime Education and Training (MET) necessitates instructional methodologies that prioritize active learning, contextual comprehension, and the presentation of practical skills. Conventional lecture-based methods are inadequate for equipping mariners to operate advanced boats, handle crises, and navigate fluctuating situations. MET institutions must implement learner-centered pedagogies aimed at developing both technical and non-technical skills. Three principal methodologies—problem-based learning (PBL), scenario-based learning, and blended/AI-enhanced instruction—provide effective avenues for promoting competency development (Varma & Malik, 2023).

Problem-based learning (PBL) centers learners in the educational process by involving them in intricate, genuine problems that reflect actual nautical challenges (Germo et al., 2024). In PBL, students collectively examine problems such as route planning in limited sight, detecting engine performance difficulties, or addressing crew communication failures. These challenges necessitate the use of diverse expertise, analytical reasoning, and collaboration—skills vital for operational success. Project-Based Learning (PBL) augments metacognition by prompting learners to recognize knowledge deficiencies, autonomously pursue information, and substantiate conclusions with evidence. In marine situations, PBL enhances situational awareness, risk assessment, and leadership skills, which are essential qualities in the STCW Code.

Scenario-based learning enhances PBL concepts by engaging students in organized operational scenarios that replicate authentic maritime circumstances (Khan, 2020). Scenarios may encompass collision avoidance in crowded waterways, engine failure during navigation, cargo contamination during loading, or emergency reaction to an onboard fire. These scenarios are structured with explicit learning objectives and quantifiable performance standards, facilitating learners in acquiring procedural proficiency and decision-making abilities in regulated settings. Scenario-based learning improves learners' comprehension of cause-and-effect dynamics, promotes adaptive reasoning, and strengthens adherence to safety regulations. Debriefing sessions following each scenario promote reflective learning, enabling students to transform experience into profound conceptual comprehension.

The third instructional technique, blended and AI-enhanced instruction, utilizes digital technology to augment maritime training. Blended learning combines online modules, asynchronous assignments, and in-person instruction, providing flexibility and individualized pacing—essential features of Competency-Based Education (CBE) (Ochavillo, 2020). Digital learning platforms may encompass e-navigation simulations, interactive COLREGs modules, cloud-based engineering laboratories, or virtual mentorship sessions.

AI-enhanced instruction advances by integrating intelligent tutoring tools, adaptive learning platforms, and analytics-driven performance feedback. Artificial intelligence can monitor learner advancement, detect deficiencies, suggest specific educational resources, and provide customized practice assignments (Ciaschi & Barone, 2025). For example, AI systems can replicate meteorological conditions or provide dynamic collision scenarios that adapt according to the learner's choices. These technologies facilitate ongoing skill enhancement and guarantee that learners have prompt, actionable feedback consistent with competency criteria.

PBL, scenario-based learning, and AI-enhanced training collectively constitute a pedagogical environment that fosters mastery, engagement, and preparedness for real-world challenges. By incorporating these methodologies into maritime curricula, schools can establish educational settings that mirror the intricacies of contemporary ship operations while conforming to CBE principles.

4.2 Use of Simulators and Onboard Training for Skill Mastery

Simulation-based training is fundamental to the implementation of Competency-Based Education in marine education. The intricacy and hazards associated with maritime operations—ranging from navigation in congested waters to resolving engine malfunctions—demand secure, regulated settings where trainees can repetitively hone their abilities until proficiency is attained (Alshareef & Alghanmi, 2024). The amalgamation of bridge and engine simulations, VR/AR systems, e-navigation tools, and onboard training creates a holistic framework for cultivating operational competencies.

Bridge simulators emulate the visual, aural, and operational environments of a vessel's nautical bridge. They integrate authentic representations of maritime conditions, traffic volume, port access, meteorological phenomena, and navigational obstacles (Sibali et al., 2026). Students engage in activities like collision avoidance, navigation, anchoring, route planning, and bridge team coordination. Advanced simulators enable teachers to design stress-inducing scenarios, such as equipment malfunctions or emergencies, facilitating students' development of resilience and effective decision-making skills. Bridge simulators also improve non-technical competencies, such as collaboration, situational awareness, and communication—frequently identified as fundamental factors in marine incidents.

Engine-room simulators offer significant advantages for cadets in marine engineering schools. These simulators emulate propulsion systems, auxiliary machinery, electrical networks, fuel systems, and automated control interfaces (Li et al., 2025). Students execute activities include diagnosing mechanical malfunctions, monitoring engine efficiency, controlling load allocation, and conducting maintenance operations. Realistic fault simulations enable students to hone problem-solving skills under duress without jeopardizing actual apparatus. Engine simulators facilitate the evaluation of procedural adherence, safety protocols, and system integration expertise.

In addition to conventional simulators, Virtual Reality (VR) and Augmented Reality (AR) technologies are progressively integrated into marine training. Virtual reality immerses trainees in three-dimensional environments that replicate engine rooms, cargo holds, lifeboat stations, or dangerous areas (Morsy et al., 2025). This technology improves spatial awareness, knowledge of ship layout, and comprehension of emergency protocols. Augmented Reality (AR) superimposes digital information onto physical locations, enabling cadets to visualize system components, examine machinery, or adhere to sequential maintenance protocols. These technologies enhance psychomotor learning, decrease training expenses, and provide scalable alternatives for schools without full-mission simulators.

The incorporation of e-navigation technologies in training guarantees that cadets are equipped for the digital operations that are becoming increasingly prevalent on contemporary boats. Instruments including Electronic Chart Display and Information Systems (ECDIS), automatic identification systems (AIS), radar, GNSS receivers, and voyage planning software offer learners the chance to engage with digital navigation technologies (Lee et al., 2025). These tools enable trainees to experience analyzing sensor data, planning secure routes, and responding to electronic notifications—skills vital for contemporary watchkeeping.

Notwithstanding the advancement of simulation technology, onboard training is important for skill mastering. Sea-time offers practical experience in vessel operations, environmental factors, crew interactions, and unforeseen obstacles (Cordeiro et al., 2025). Cadets acquire the ability to amalgamate theoretical knowledge with practical tasks, including mooring operations, cargo handling, engine-room watchkeeping, and emergency exercises. The integration of onboard training with competency frameworks guarantees alignment between classroom instruction and practical sea-time experiences. Supervisors employ organized logbooks, assignment completion records, and performance checklists to assess pupils' competencies during sea-time.

The integration of simulation and onboard training creates an effective dual-training system: simulators provide secure environments for repetitive practice, whereas shipboard experience confirms competencies in genuine working conditions. This integrated strategy fosters proficiency, improves operational preparedness, and reinforces the tenets of Competency-Based Education in maritime training.

4.3 Competency Assessment Methods in Maritime Training

Assessment is fundamental to Competency-Based Education, serving as the means by which competency is validated, recorded, and recognized. Maritime training assessments must accurately represent ship operations and furnish credible proof of learners' ability to accomplish tasks safely and effectively. An effective assessment system integrates skills demonstration, performance checklists, digital portfolios, psychomotor rubrics, and OSCE-style evaluations to guarantee a thorough evaluation of competence (Videlia et al., 2025).

The demonstration of skills is the most straightforward method of evaluating marine ability. In this approach, learners execute tasks in authentic or simulated settings while being monitored by qualified evaluators (Cordeiro et al., 2025). Examples encompass performing a Williamson turn, identifying a mechanical malfunction, doing a safety inspection, or addressing a fire emergency. The skills demonstration evaluates both technical and non-technical competencies, including communication, collaboration, and decision-making. Its adherence to CBE principles guarantees that learners are evaluated based on their capabilities rather than the duration of their study.

Performance checklists furnish assessors with systematic instruments to appraise observed behaviors and procedural procedures during skills presentations. Checklists provide consistency and objectivity by delineating particular criteria necessary for successful performance (Sheptian et al., 2025). A checklist for "Preparing the ECDIS for departure" may encompass tasks such as validating chart availability, updating ENC data, adjusting safety contours, and inspecting alarm settings. Checklists diminish subjectivity, enhance transparency, and provide formative input.

Students develop digital portfolios to record cumulative learning and report on professional development. These portfolios comprise diverse evidence, including simulator performance reports, video recordings of evaluations, reflective journals, sea-time logs, completed assignments, and diplomas from online modules (Omer et al., 2025). Digital portfolios offer a comprehensive perspective on learner progression over time and function as an essential instrument for self-regulation and educator feedback. They also correspond with SPBE and digital transformation objectives in maritime education.

Psychomotor rubrics offer comprehensive criteria for evaluating the quality of physical task execution. These rubrics assess criteria like precision, coordination, timeliness, safety protocols, and compliance with procedures (Bonvicini et al., 2025). In marine settings, psychomotor criteria are essential for evaluating tasks like as handling engine-room controls, utilizing firefighting equipment, launching lifeboats, or maneuvering vessels. Rubrics delineate proficiency levels, allowing evaluators to monitor learner advancement and confirm preparedness for practical applications.

Ultimately, OSCE-style (Objective Structured Clinical Examination) evaluations—derived from medical education—provide an effective approach for evaluating marine competencies across various stations. In marine OSCEs, participants rotate through stations that simulate various operational activities, including oil spill response, distress call management, electrical problem resolution, and CPR execution (Düzenli et al., 2025). Every station has defined scenarios, time constraints, and evaluation criteria. OSCEs improve reliability by enabling several evaluators to examine a diverse array of competencies in one assessment session.

Collectively, these evaluation techniques constitute a comprehensive and cohesive competency validation framework. They guarantee that learners possess not only information but also the ability to apply their abilities consistently across diverse conditions. Through the implementation of multi-modal evaluation methodologies, MET schools reinforce their dedication to cultivating safe, competent, and industry-prepared maritime workers.

QUALITY ASSURANCE, CHALLENGES, AND FUTURE DIRECTIONS

5.1 Monitoring and Evaluating CBE Effectiveness

Ensuring the efficacy of Competency-Based Education (CBE) in Maritime Education and Training (MET) necessitates a systematic and continuous approach to quality assurance (Nguyen et al., 2025). The assessment of CBE outcomes must be thorough, multifaceted, and attuned to industry requirements, as maritime competences are closely associated with safety, regulatory adherence, and operating efficiency. Four essential mechanisms—Continuous Quality Improvement (CQI), tracer studies, audit cycles, and industry feedback loops—collectively sustain the integrity and ongoing advancement of marine competency frameworks.

Continuous Quality Improvement (CQI) is fundamental to quality assurance in Competency-Based Education (CBE). CQI underscores continuous, data-informed enhancement of teaching methodologies, evaluation procedures, and curricular frameworks (Nguyen et al., 2025). For MET institutions, Continuous Quality Improvement (CQI) may encompass regular assessments of competency standards, analysis of student performance metrics, evaluation of simulator utilization, and reflection on assessment results. Instructor meetings, moderation sessions, and student feedback activities facilitate the identification of deficiencies in learning experiences and assure compliance with the growing STCW and NCVS standards. CQI frameworks frequently employ Plan–Do–Check–Act (PDCA) cycles to guarantee that enhancements are methodically executed and recorded. By integrating Continuous Quality Improvement approaches, MET institutions sustain training relevance, augment instructional efficacy, and strengthen a culture of accountability.

Tracer studies are crucial for comprehending the enduring effects of marine training programs. These studies monitor graduates' employment paths, professional efficacy, and perceived readiness for maritime responsibilities (Cruz, 2026). Information from shipping businesses, crewing agencies, and port authorities provide insight into the effectiveness of graduates in using their skills in practical settings. Tracer studies also reveal developing skill deficiencies in domains such as digital navigation, integrated bridge systems, vessel automation, and cargo handling technologies. This information enables MET institutions to amend courses and enhance competency frameworks to more accurately represent operational realities. Tracer studies provide as a conduit between training institutions and the maritime labor market, guaranteeing that educational achievements correspond with industry standards.

Audit cycles provide an essential element of competency-based education quality assurance. Internal audits analyze adherence to institutional policies, evaluation standards, and accreditation criteria, whereas external audits—performed by maritime authorities, classification societies, or accreditation bodies—confirm conformity with national and international regulations. Audits evaluate assessment protocols, simulator accreditation, teacher credentials, curriculum development, and quality management frameworks (Wang et al., 2025). Compliance with STCW quality standards necessitates the documentation of assessment validation, simulator approvals, and instructor competency records. Regular audits assist institutions in recognizing non-compliance risks and executing corrective measures, hence preserving the integrity of maritime certifications.

Ultimately, industry feedback mechanisms guarantee that maritime training stays congruent with technical and operational changes in the global shipping business. Frequent interactions with shipowners, crewing management, maritime pilot associations, engine supervisors, and port authorities yield significant insights regarding evolving competency requirements (Sulistiana et al., 2025). Advisory boards, stakeholder meetings, and collaborative training programs enable MET institutions to modify training content to address emerging concerns, including cyber threats, LNG and alternative fuel operations, autonomous navigation technology, and environmental compliance. Industry feedback bolsters the pertinence of CBE programs and improves the employability of graduates.

Collectively, Continuous Quality Improvement procedures, tracer studies, audit cycles, and industry feedback mechanisms establish a dynamic quality assurance framework. They guarantee that CBE implementation in maritime training is adaptive, uniform, and in accordance with regulatory standards and changing global marine circumstances.

5.2 Institutional and Operational Challenges in CBE Adoption

Although CBE possesses transformational potential for maritime training, its implementation faces various institutional and practical constraints. These problems may impede the efficacy of CBE if not handled strategically. Primary challenges encompass restricted resources, instructor preparedness, technology deficiencies, corporate culture, and regulatory compliance mandates, all of which affect the sustainability and efficacy of competency-based systems (Oroszi, 2020).

A significant difficulty is the scarcity of resources. Implementing Competency-Based Education necessitates significant investment in comprehensive mission simulators, engine-room simulators, virtual and augmented reality systems, digital learning platforms, and evaluation technologies. Numerous MET institutions, especially in poor areas, face financial limitations that hinder their capacity to upgrade educational facilities (Magsino et al., 2023). Furthermore, the upkeep of simulators necessitates continuous calibration, software enhancements, and professional assistance. Sea-time training also entails logistical expenses related to obtaining berths for cadets. Resource constraints may result in inconsistent execution of CBE, with certain competencies being developed through high-quality simulations while others depend solely on theoretical instruction.

The preparedness of instructors presents an additional considerable challenge. Competency-based instruction necessitates that educators shift from conventional lecture-based teaching to facilitation, coaching, and performance assessment (Aikat, 2024). Numerous marine teachers have extensive technical expertise yet may be deficient in pedagogical methodologies, such problem-based learning, scenario facilitation, or competency-based assessment. Enhancing instructors' pedagogical and assessment competencies necessitates organized professional development programs, mentorship frameworks, and certification procedures. In the absence of instructor preparedness, even meticulously crafted CBE frameworks falter in realizing their intended objectives.

Technological disparities also hinder CBE implementation. Dependable digital infrastructure is crucial for blended learning, e-navigation training, and digital portfolio management (Bingham et al., 2021). In areas with restricted connectivity or insufficient digital infrastructure, institutions may struggle to properly execute AI-enhanced instruction, data-driven evaluation, or cloud-based competency monitoring. Technological discrepancies result in inequitable learning experiences and hinder institutional adherence to contemporary marine training standards.

The organizational culture of institutions profoundly impacts the efficacy of CBE implementation. Competency-Based Education necessitates cooperation among educators, evaluators, administrators, and industry stakeholders. Institutions must adopt openness, ongoing enhancement, and evidence-informed decision-making (Açıkgöz & Babadoğan, 2021). Resistance to change, frequently arising from entrenched marine traditions, can impede the implementation of novel educational approaches or evaluation systems. Some professors may choose traditional lecture models instead of interactive, learner-centered methodologies, despite regulatory criteria prioritizing performance-based learning.

Ultimately, regulatory compliance constitutes both an opportunity and a challenge. Adherence to STCW, NCVS, KKNI, and accrediting criteria necessitates rigorous documentation, validation of assessment instruments, certification of simulators, and compliance with quality management systems (Wegner, 2024). The administrative requirements of regulatory compliance might inundate institutions that lack specialized quality assurance departments or proficient staff. Noncompliance with regulatory standards jeopardizes accreditation, raises safety issues, and undermines confidence. Confronting these difficulties necessitates strategic planning, investment in capacity development, collaboration with industry, and definitive institutional leadership. Institutions must prioritize sustainable implementation techniques that account for present limitations and future requirements.

5.3 Future Trends in Maritime Competency Development

As marine operations progress, the development of competencies must align with increasing technical, environmental, and regulatory trends. Future developments in maritime CBE will be influenced by advancements including AI-driven assessments, smart-ship technology, green shipping capabilities, and the global harmonization of standards (Peng et al., 2023). These trends indicate a transition towards more technologically integrated, environmentally sustainable, and globally coordinated marine training systems.

AI-driven assessment signifies a revolutionary advancement in marine training. Artificial intelligence can evaluate student performance data, discern error patterns, forecast learning challenges, and produce tailored training suggestions (Karimi et al., 2024). Within simulated environments, AI can monitor ocular movements, response times, decision-making sequences, and compliance with safety protocols—yielding detailed performance insights that beyond conventional evaluation methods. AI may develop adaptive situations that escalate in complexity as learners exhibit enhanced proficiency. These features improve assessment reliability and enable instructors to concentrate on advanced instruction instead of manual scoring.

The emergence of smart-ship technologies, alongside AI evaluation, is transforming the skills necessary for contemporary sailors. Intelligent vessels incorporate sophisticated sensor systems, autonomous navigation technologies, predictive maintenance algorithms, and cyber-secure communication networks (Grimett, 2023). Mariners must now comprehend data analytics, cyber risk management, human-machine interface operations, and remote troubleshooting. CBE frameworks must include these growing skill sets to ensure that graduates can function in progressively automated maritime situations. Training institutions must enhance simulation systems, amend curricula, and engage with industry stakeholders to incorporate smart-ship technologies into training programs.

A significant factor impacting the advancement of maritime expertise is the worldwide transition to environmentally sustainable shipping practices. Climate change policies, decarbonization activities, and new IMO rules necessitate that sailors have skills in alternative fuels (including LNG, hydrogen, ammonia, and methanol), energy-efficient operations, emissions monitoring, and waste management (Dewan et al., 2024). Green shipping competencies encompass knowledge of ballast water treatment, efficiency management systems (SEEMP), and carbon intensity indicators. CBE models must integrate these competencies into navigation, engineering, and cargo management curricula. Institutions must invest in simulators and laboratories that represent developing energy systems and environmental technologies.

The initiative for global harmonization of marine competency requirements is anticipated to escalate. As maritime labor becomes progressively globalized, the uniformity of training outcomes across nations becomes increasingly essential. Harmonization initiatives will necessitate enhanced alignment of national qualification frameworks, increased utilization of digital certificates, and heightened dependence on international audits. Global harmonization enhances seafarer mobility, mitigates disparities in training quality, and bolsters the safety and efficiency of international shipping.

CONCLUSION

Competency-Based Education (CBE) establishes a transformational basis for enhancing the quality and relevance of maritime training amid rapid technological advancement, regulatory growth, and increased safety demands. The discussions highlight that cultivating a proficient maritime workforce necessitates a comprehensive and systematic strategy, commencing with the meticulous identification and mapping of occupational competencies and extending to the formulation of quantifiable performance standards, evidence-based instructional methodologies, simulation-enhanced learning environments, and stringent assessment frameworks. This integrated framework enables maritime training institutes to ensure that learners acquire both technical understanding and the critical non-technical abilities for safe and effective operations.

The execution of CBE further illustrates the significance of ongoing quality enhancement, underpinned by tracer studies, audit cycles, and proactive collaboration with industry partners.

These tools allow institutions to assess training efficacy, adapt to changing operational requirements, and ensure compliance with national and international standards. Simultaneously, numerous challenges persist. Resource limitations, instructor preparedness deficiencies, technical limitations, and the intricacies of regulatory compliance underscore the necessity for strategic planning, ongoing investment, and capacity-building efforts.

Future worldwide trends indicate a vibrant trajectory for the advancement of maritime competencies. AI-driven evaluations, intelligent maritime operations, alternative fuel technologies, and sustainability mandates will transform the competences required of seafarers. These advancements necessitate adaptive, progressive training methods designed to equip graduates for the growing digital, automated, and ecologically sustainable maritime operations.

CBE offers a robust foundation for developing a highly competent, adaptive, and safety-conscious maritime workforce. By incorporating strong educational principles, innovative technologies, and rigorous quality assurance measures, maritime education providers may markedly improve the preparedness and professional competence of future seafarers.

REFERENCES

Açıkgöz, T., & Babadoğan, C. (2021). COMPETENCY-BASED EDUCATION: THEORY AND PRACTICE. *Psycho-Educational Research Reviews*. DOI: 10.52963/PERR_Biruni_V10.N3.06

Ahid, N., & Chamid, N. (2021). Implementation of Indonesian National Qualification Framework Based Curriculum in Higher Islamic Education. *Deleted Journal*, *7*(1), 109–122. DOI: 10.15575/jpi.v7i1.12425

Aikat, A. (2024). Navigating the transition: Implementing competency-based medical education in medical curriculum in India. *Asian Journal of Medical Sciences*, *15*(6), 145–150. DOI: 10.71152/ajms.v15i6.532

Ajayi, F. A., & Udeh, C. A. (2024). A comprehensive review of talent management strategies for seafarers: Challenges and opportunities [Review of A comprehensive review of talent management strategies for seafarers: Challenges and opportunities]. *International Journal of Science and Research Archive*, *11*(2), 1116–1131. DOI: 10.30574/ijsra.2024.11.2.0560

Alshareef, M., & Alghanmi, A. F. (2024). Optimizing Maritime Energy Efficiency: A Machine Learning Approach Using Deep Reinforcement Learning for EEXI and CII Compliance. *Sustainability (Basel)*, *16*(23), 10534. DOI: 10.3390/su162310534

Andersen, I. M. V., Nielsen, U. D., & Lützen, M. (2012). The Maritime Engineering Education : Meeting Industry Demands. *Research Portal Denmark*. https://local.forskningsportal.dk/local/dki-cgi/ws/cris-link?src=dtu&id=dtu-8048e1db-a7cc-46e0-86e1-e317636ed397&ti=The%20Maritime%20Engineering%20Education%20%3A%20Meeting%20Industry%20Demands

Andriani, D. (2021). A critical review of the labor competitiveness as human capital in Indonesia [Review of *A critical review of the labor competitiveness as human capital in Indonesia*]. *International Journal of Research in Business and Social Science (2147-4478)*, *10*(5), 52. Ümit Hacıoğlu. DOI: 10.20525/ijrbs.v10i5.1303

Baldevarona, G. B., Miguel, A. S., Bentulan, E., Cerbito, A. F., & Cerbito, A. F. (2024). Exploring the Interplay of Authentic Assessment and Instructor Competencies in Enhancing Industry Readiness in Maritime Education. *APJAET - Journal Ay Asia Pacific Journal of Advanced Education and Technology*, *3*(3). DOI: 10.54476/apjaet/91820

Bingham, A. J., Adams, M., & Stewart, R. (2021). Competency-Based Education: Examining Educators' Experiences. *The Qualitative Report*. Advance online publication. DOI: 10.46743/2160-3715/2021.4383

Bonvicini, A., Cangelosi, D., Ingargiola, R., Marchese, A. J., & Previti, G. (2025). Digital Twin Approach for Ship Energy Management. In *Progress in marine science and technology*. IOS Press., DOI: 10.3233/PMST250138

Boonadir, N., Ishak, R., Yusof, H., & Lamakasauk, A. F. (2020). Theories of Maritime Education and Training (MET) in Improving Maritime Sector in Malaysia. *Open Journal of Business and Management*, *8*(3), 1193–1200. DOI: 10.4236/ojbm.2020.83076

Bouzón, R., Antón-Sancho, Á., Amado-Sánchez, Y., & Vergara, D. (2023). Relevance of Communicative, Team Effectiveness, and Long-Range Planning Skills in Vessel Crewmembers. *International Journal of Instruction*, *16*(2), 965–984. DOI: 10.29333/iji.2023.16251a

Ciaschi, M., & Barone, M. (2025). Examining the Increasing Use of Artificial Intelligence in Education, A step Closer to Personalized Learning. *Annals of Computer Science and Information Systems*, *44*, 9–14. DOI: 10.15439/2025F7856

Cordeiro, A., Ferreira, Y., Leite, R., Almeida, L., Catapan, M., Siqueira, A., Silva, T., & Winkler, I. (2025). Immersive technologies for evaluating industrial safety training in high-risk environments: A review on opportunities and challenges. *Frontiers in Virtual Reality*, *6*, 1726058. Advance online publication. DOI: 10.3389/frvir.2025.1726058

Cruz, V. P. D. (2026). CHARTING OPTIMUM EMPLOYMENT PROSPECTS FOR COLLEGE OF MARITIME EDUCATION STUDENTS AND GRADUATES. *Sprin Journal of Arts Humanities and Social Sciences*, *4*(11), 8–13. DOI: 10.55559/sjahss.v4i11.601

Dewan, M. H., & Godina, R. (2023). An overview of seafarers' engagement and training on energy efficient operation of ships. *Marine Policy*, *160*, 105980. DOI: 10.1016/j.marpol.2023.105980

Dewan, M. H., Mustafi, M. A. A., Matos, F., & Godina, R. (2024). Exploring seafarers' knowledge, understanding, and proficiency in SEEMP: A strategic training framework for enhancing seafarers' competence in energy-efficient ship operations. *Heliyon*, *10*(17), e36505. Advance online publication. DOI: 10.1016/j.heliyon.2024.e36505

Düzenli, E., Kayışoğlu, G., Bolat, P., Arslan, Ö., Bolat, F., & Dzneladze, T. (2025). MAR-LSD project: Embedding learning station design to transform maritime education and training. *WMU Journal of Maritime Affairs*, *24*(3), 381–396. DOI: 10.1007/s13437-025-00369-6

Escallada, O., Lasa, G., Mazmela, M., Carrubba, D. L., Bosani, E., Dacal-Nieto, Á., & García, M. (2025). Exploring operator responses to augmented reality training: Insights from the SELFEX platform case study. *Frontiers of Computer Science*, *7*, 1507439. Advance online publication. DOI: 10.3389/fcomp.2025.1507439

Germo, R., Tan, V., & Casaáare, A. F. (2024). Effectiveness of Problem-based Learning (PBL) on Maritime Courses in a Blended Learning Modality. *TransNav the International Journal on Marine Navigation and Safety of Sea Transportation*, *18*(3), 649–655. DOI: 10.12716/1001.18.03.19

Goldhamer, M. E. J., Martínez-Lage, M., Black-Schaffer, W. S., Huang, J. T., Co, J. P. T., Weinstein, D. F., & Pusic, M. (2022). Reimagining the Clinical Competency Committee to Enhance Education and Prepare for Competency-Based Time-Variable Advancement. *Journal of General Internal Medicine*, *37*(9), 2280–2290. DOI: 10.1007/s11606-022-07515-3

Grimett, L. (2023). Understanding the Plight and Challenges Facing South African Seafarers. *American Journal of Industrial and Business Management*, *13*(6), 532–567. DOI: 10.4236/ajibm.2023.136033

Harrington, S., Sellberg, C., & Lindwall, O. (2025). Crafting congruence: Towards systematic scenario design in maritime simulator training and assessment. *WMU Journal of Maritime Affairs*, *24*(2), 157–178. DOI: 10.1007/s13437-024-00356-3

Junus, A. D. P., Tjiptoherijanto, P., Sobari, N., & Subroto, A. (2024). Indonesian seafarers in global job competition: Developing global work competencies in increasing end-user acceptance. *Uncertain Supply Chain Management*, *12*(2), 815–828. DOI: 10.5267/j.uscm.2024.1.005

Karahalil, M., Lützhöft, M., & Scanlan, J. (2024). *Factors impacting curricula in maritime simulator-based education*. WMU Journal of Maritime Affairs., DOI: 10.1007/s13437-024-00351-8

Karimi, E., Smith, J., Billard, R., & Veitch, B. (2024). AI-based adaptive instructional systems for maritime safety training: A systematic literature review. *Discover Artificial Intelligence*, *4*(1), 51. Advance online publication. DOI: 10.1007/s44163-024-00153-0

Kes, L., van Wesel, F., Saunders-Smits, G., & Specht, M. (2025). Defining Valid Criteria for Transversal Competency Assessment in Vocational Education and Training for Aircraft Maintenance using the Delphi Method. *Research Square (Research Square)*. DOI: 10.21203/rs.3.rs-7675244/v1

Khan, U. A. (2020). Developing critical thinking in student seafarers: An exploratory study. *Journal of Applied Learning & Teaching*, *3*(Sp. Iss. 1), 40–50. Advance online publication. DOI: 10.37074/jalt.2020.3.s1.15

Kim, J.-K., Lee, C.-H., Jeong, M., Cho, E., & Lee, Y.-G. (2023). Identifying Optimal Approaches for Sustainable Maritime Education and Training: Addressing Technological, Environmental, and Epidemiological Challenges. *Sustainability (Basel)*, *15*(10), 8092. DOI: 10.3390/su15108092

Kour, M., Taneja, S., & Özen, E. (2025). Demystifying the Connection between Corporate Board Structure and Financial Performance in Maritime Firms. *Transactions on Maritime Science*, *14*(1). Advance online publication. DOI: 10.7225/toms.v14.n01.w07

Kuzu, A. C., & Taç, U. (2025). AHP-Based Evaluation of Core Non-Technical Skills for Seafarers in Maritime Operations. *Turkish Journal of Maritime and Marine Sciences*, *11*(3), 216–228. DOI: 10.52998/trjmms.1703538

Latifah, H., Rozak, A., & Zuhdi, M. (2026). DESAIN KURIKULUM BERBASIS CAPAIAN (OUTCOME-BASED CURRICULUM): DARI TUJUAN HINGGA IMPLEMENTASI EFEKTIF. *MANAJERIAL Jurnal Inovasi Manajemen Dan Supervisi Pendidikan*, *6*(1), 34–44. DOI: 10.51878/manajerial.v6i1.8677

Lee, H., Park, K., & Bae, H. (2025). Knowledge transfer Q-learning for vessel route planning using automatic identification system-derived expert trajectories. *Maritime Transport Research*, *9*, 100142. DOI: 10.1016/j.martra.2025.100142

Li, F., Sun, Y., Tang, X., Yuan, C., Yin, H., & Luo, W. (2025). Review on the development and challenges of clean energy sources for ships. *Renewable & Sustainable Energy Reviews*, *225*, 116181. DOI: 10.1016/j.rser.2025.116181

Longridge, T. M., Bürki-Cohen, J., Go, T. H., & Kendra, A. (2001). *SIMULATOR FIDELITY CONSIDERATIONS FOR TRAINING AND EVALUATION OF TODAY'S AIRLINE PILOTS*. https://rosap.ntl.bts.gov/view/dot/9963/dot_9963_DS1.pdf

Magsino, R. G., Paraggua, V. Q., Mobo, F. D., Acuavera, R. C., Villavicencio, L. D., Pasa, G. C., & Guiang, S. L. A. (2023). Students' Onboard Experiences: Basis for Improved Shipboard Training Program Policy. *International Journal of English Literature and Social Sciences*, *8*(2), 259. DOI: 10.22161/ijels.82.38

Manuel, M. E. (2017). Vocational and academic approaches to maritime education and training (MET): Trends, challenges and opportunities. *WMU Journal of Maritime Affairs*, *16*(3), 473–483. DOI: 10.1007/s13437-017-0130-3

Masava, B., Nyoni, C. N., & Botma, Y. (2022). Scaffolding in Health Sciences Education Programmes: An Integrative Review [Review of *Scaffolding in Health Sciences Education Programmes: An Integrative Review*]. *Medical Science Educator, 33*(1), 255. Springer Science+Business Media. DOI: 10.1007/s40670-022-01691-x

Massami, E. P., & Manyasi, M. M. (2021). Analysis of determinants of work performance for seafarers based on fuzzy Electre model. *Journal of Shipping and Trade*, *6*(1), 7. Advance online publication. DOI: 10.1186/s41072-021-00088-0

Morsy, A. M., Aziz, M., & Awad, M. H. (2025). COMPARATIVE STUDY FOR TRAINING USING VIRTUAL REALITY SIMULATING AND CONVENTIONAL FIREFIGHTING. *The International Maritime Transport and Logistic Journal, 14*(0), 516. DOI: 10.21622/MARLOG.2025.14.1.91

Nguyen, S., Gadel, M., Wang, K., Li, J., Zhang, X., Siang-Ching, K., Fu, X., & Qin, Z. (2025). Maritime decarbonization through machine learning: A critical systematic review of fuel and power prediction models. *Cleaner Logistics and Supply Chain, 14*, 100210. DOI: 10.1016/j.clscn.2025.100210

Ochavillo, G. S. (2020). A Paradigm Shift of Learning in Maritime Education amidst COVID-19 Pandemic. *International Journal of Higher Education*, *9*(6), 164. DOI: 10.5430/ijhe.v9n6p164

Okojie, M. U., Baştaş, M., & Miralay, F. (2022). Using Curriculum Mapping as a Tool to Match Student Learning Outcomes and Social Studies Curricula. *Frontiers in Psychology*, *13*, 850264. DOI: 10.3389/fpsyg.2022.850264

Omer, A., Vadivelu, J., & Wh, H. (2025). Early perceptions of portfolios in an outcome-based curriculum. *BMC Medical Education*, *25*(1), 1204. Advance online publication. DOI: 10.1186/s12909-025-07583-z

Oroszi, T. (2020). Competency-Based Education. *Creative Education*, *11*(11), 2467–2476. DOI: 10.4236/ce.2020.1111181

Park, S., Lee, H., & Kim, D. (2024). Regulatory compliance and operational efficiency in maritime transport: Strategies and insights. *Transport Policy*, *155*, 161–177. DOI: 10.1016/j.tranpol.2024.06.024

Peng, F., Sun, Y., Chen, Z., & Gao, J. (2023). An Improved Apriori Algorithm for Association Rule Mining in Employability Analysis. *Tehnicki Vjesnik - Technical Gazette, 30*(5). DOI: 10.17559/TV-20230327000481

Politakis, G. P. (2013). Bringing the human element to the forefront: The ILO's Maritime Labour Convention, 2006 ready to sail. *Aegean Review of the Law of the Sea and Maritime Law*, *2*(1-2), 37–51. DOI: 10.1007/s12180-013-0024-y

Rais, R. N. B., Rashid, M., Zakria, M., Hussain, S., Qadir, J., & Imran, M. A. (2021). Employing Industrial Quality Management Systems for Quality Assurance in Outcome-Based Engineering Education: A Review [Review of *Employing Industrial Quality Management Systems for Quality Assurance in Outcome-Based Engineering Education: A Review*]. *Education Sciences, 11*(2), 45. Multidisciplinary Digital Publishing Institute. DOI: 10.3390/educsci11020045

Rouvrais, S., Alnasser, M., Jordan, K., Stewart, M., Lebris, S. G., Joder, A., Agredano, M., & Camacho, M. del M. S., Tudela, L., Bardon, P., Chelin, N., Diaz, A., Gallée, F., Ghaffari, S., Jacovetti, G., Lannuzel, A., Marschal, N., Retif, H., Serrec, S., … Dunn, S. (2019). Innovative D-Skills Training Models for Higher and Vocational Education & Training Students. *HAL (Le Centre Pour La Communication Scientifique Directe)*. https://hal.science/hal-03727540

Sarı, N. V., Egar, N., & Purwosaputro, S. (2025). IMPLEMENTASI PROGRAM SMK PUSAT KEUNGGULAN PADA KONSENTRASI NAUTIKA KAPAL PENANGKAP IKAN. *SOCIAL Jurnal Inovasi Pendidikan IPS*, *5*(1), 62–72. DOI: 10.51878/social.v5i1.4572

Sellberg, C., Lindmark, O., & Rystedt, H. (2018). Learning to navigate: The centrality of instructions and assessments for developing students' professional competencies in simulator-based training. *WMU Journal of Maritime Affairs*, *17*(2), 249–265. DOI: 10.1007/s13437-018-0139-2

Sevilla, G. S., & Arceño, R. (2017). Structured Shipboard Training Program and Performance of Maritime Cadets. *International Journal of English Literature and Social Sciences*, *2*(4), 90–110. DOI: 10.24001/ijels.2.4.12

Sharif, N., Rönnqvist, M., Cordeau, J., Audy, J., & Warya, G. (2025). Multi-objective maritime vessel routing with safety considerations. *International Transactions in Operational Research*, itor.70117. Advance online publication. DOI: 10.1111/itor.70117

Sheptian, R., Sarifah, I., & Riyadi, R. (2025). CLASSICAL TEST THEORY ANALYSIS USING ANATES: A STUDY OF MATHEMATICS READINESS TEST FOR ELEMENTARY SCHOOL STUDENTS. *SCIENCE Jurnal Inovasi Pendidikan Matematika Dan IPA*, *5*(1), 20–29. DOI: 10.51878/science.v5i1.3863

Sibali, A., Kurniawaty, K., Amran, A., & Yusriadi, Y. (2026). Maritime cadet experiences with bridge simulators in terrestrial navigation education. *Frontiers in Education*, *11*, 1691292. Advance online publication. DOI: 10.3389/feduc.2026.1691292

Simanjuntak, M. B., Rafli, Z., & Utami, S. R. (2024). Enhancing maritime education for ocean sustainability: A multidisciplinary approach. *BIO Web of Conferences, 106*, 2006. DOI: 10.1051/bioconf/202410602006

Sulistiana, O., Rachman, T., Jinca, M. Y., & Ali, M. S. S. (2025). Competency and Certification Gaps Among Traditional Shipping Seafarers in South Sulawesi, Indonesia. *Future Transportation*, *5*(4), 139. DOI: 10.3390/futuretransp5040139

Tisoy, R. I. (2025). Competencies of Maritime Students in Professional Courses: A Study at a Philippine University in the Context of Joint CHED-MARINA Memorandum Circular. *Journal of Education Learning and Management*, *2*(2), 344–352. DOI: 10.69739/jelm.v2i2.1133

Tusher, H. M., Sharma, A., Nazir, S., & Munim, Z. H. (2021). Exploring the Current Practices and Future Needs of Marine Engineering Education in Bangladesh. *Journal of Marine Science and Engineering*, *9*(10), 1085. DOI: 10.3390/jmse9101085

Varma, C., & Malik, S. B. (2023). TVET in the 21st Century: A Focus on Innovative Teaching and Competency Indicators. In *Technical and vocational education and training*. Springer International Publishing., DOI: 10.5772/intechopen.112516

Vasquez, J. A., Marcotte, K., & Gruppen, L. D. (2021). The parallel evolution of competency-based education in medical and higher education. *The Journal of Competency-Based Education*, *6*(2), e1234. Advance online publication. DOI: 10.1002/cbe2.1234

Videlia, B., Mulyono, M., & Waluya, S. B. (2025). ANALISIS KOMPARATIF KERANGKA KURIKULUM VICTORIA F-10 DAN KURIKULUM MERDEKA: IMPLIKASI TERHADAP PENGEMBANGAN KURIKULUM NASIONAL INDONESIA. *MANAJERIAL Jurnal Inovasi Manajemen Dan Supervisi Pendidikan*, *5*(4), 1241–1251. DOI: 10.51878/manajerial.v5i4.7672

Vujičić, S., Hasanspahić, N., Gundić, A., & Hrdalo, N. (2020). Assessment for Ensuring Adequately Qualified Instructors in Maritime Education and Training Institutions. *Athens Journal of Sciences*, *7*(2), 115–126. DOI: 10.30958/ajs.7-2-4

Wang, K., Liang, H., Liu, X., Li, Z., Jing, Z., Chi, Y., Ma, R., Cao, J., & Huang, L. (2025). Investigations and applications of carbon control technology: The roadmap to zero-carbon shipping. *Ocean Engineering*, *339*, 121898. DOI: 10.1016/j.oceaneng.2025.121898

Wegner, D. C. (2024). Safety Training and Certification Standards for Offshore Engineers: A Global Review. *International Journal of Multidisciplinary Research and Growth Evaluation*, *5*(2), 1142–1154. DOI: 10.54660/.IJMRGE.2024.5.2.1142-1154

Yuen, K. F., Tan, L., & Loh, H. S. (2022). Core Competencies for Maritime Business Educators in the Digital Era. *Frontiers in Psychology*, *13*, 915980. Advance online publication. DOI: 10.3389/fpsyg.2022.915980

ADDITIONAL READING

Baldevarona, G. B., Miguel, A. S., Bentulan, E., Cerbito, A. F., & Cerbito, A. F. (2024). Exploring the interplay of authentic assessment and instructor competencies in enhancing industry readiness in maritime education. *Asia Pacific Journal of Advanced Education and Technology*, *3*(3). Advance online publication. DOI: 10.54476/apjaet/91820

Germo, R., Tan, V., & Casañare, A. F. (2024). Effectiveness of problem-based learning (PBL) on maritime courses in a blended learning modality. TransNav. *International Journal on Marine Navigation and Safety of Sea Transportation*, *18*(3), 649–656. DOI: 10.12716/1001.18.03.19

Harrington, S., Sellberg, C., & Lindwall, O. (2025). Crafting congruence: Towards systematic scenario design in maritime simulator training and assessment. *WMU Journal of Maritime Affairs*, *24*(2), 157–178. DOI: 10.1007/s13437-024-00356-3

Karahalil, M., Lützhöft, M., & Scanlan, J. (2024). *Factors impacting curricula in maritime simulator-based education*. WMU Journal of Maritime Affairs., DOI: 10.1007/s13437-024-00351-8

Karimi, E., Smith, J., Billard, R., & Veitch, B. (2024). AI-based adaptive instructional systems for maritime safety training: A systematic literature review. *Discover Artificial Intelligence*, *4*(1), 51. Advance online publication. DOI: 10.1007/s44163-024-00153-0

Kim, J.-K., Lee, C.-H., Jeong, M., Cho, E., & Lee, Y.-G. (2023). Identifying optimal approaches for sustainable maritime education and training: Addressing technological, environmental, and epidemiological challenges. *Sustainability (Basel)*, *15*(10), 8092. DOI: 10.3390/su15108092

Lee, H., Park, K., & Bae, H. (2025). Knowledge transfer Q-learning for vessel route planning using automatic identification system-derived expert trajectories. *Maritime Transport Research*, *9*, 100142. DOI: 10.1016/j.martra.2025.100142

Sellberg, C., Lindmark, O., & Rystedt, H. (2018). Learning to navigate: The centrality of instructions and assessments for developing students' professional competencies in simulator-based training. *WMU Journal of Maritime Affairs*, *17*(2), 249–265. DOI: 10.1007/s13437-018-0139-2

Simanjuntak, M. B., Rafli, Z., & Utami, S. R. (2024). Enhancing maritime education for ocean sustainability: A multidisciplinary approach. BIO Web of Conferences, 106, 02006. DOI: 10.1051/bioconf/202410602006

Tusher, H. M., Sharma, A., Nazir, S., & Munim, Z. H. (2021). Exploring the current practices and future needs of marine engineering education in Bangladesh. *Journal of Marine Science and Engineering*, *9*(10), 1085. DOI: 10.3390/jmse9101085

KEY TERMS AND DEFINITIONS

Bridge Resource Management (BRM): A systematic approach to teamwork, communication, leadership, and decision-making on a ship's bridge to ensure safe and efficient vessel operations.

Competency-Based Education (CBE): An educational approach that emphasizes the achievement and demonstration of clearly defined competencies, skills, and learning outcomes rather than time-based instruction.

Continuous Quality Improvement (CQI): An ongoing process of evaluating and enhancing educational programs, assessment systems, and institutional practices to ensure consistent quality and effectiveness.

Experiential Learning: A learning process in which knowledge and skills are developed through direct experience, reflection, application, and practical engagement in authentic contexts.

Maritime Education and Training (MET): A structured system of academic, technical, and professional preparation designed to develop competent maritime personnel for shipboard and maritime industry operations.

Performance-Based Assessment: An evaluation method that measures learners' competencies through the demonstration of practical tasks, operational procedures, and real-world problem-solving activities.

Simulation-Based Training: An instructional method that uses realistic simulators and virtual environments to replicate maritime operations for skill development, decision-making practice, and safety training.

Situational Awareness: The ability to perceive, interpret, and anticipate operational conditions and environmental changes in order to make safe and effective maritime decisions.

Standards of Training, Certification and Watchkeeping (STCW): An international regulatory framework established by the International Maritime Organization (IMO) that defines minimum competency standards for seafarers worldwide.

Virtual Reality (VR) Maritime Training: An immersive digital training environment that enables maritime learners to practice operational procedures, emergency response, and technical skills within simulated shipboard settings.

Chapter 7
Sailing Toward Excellence: Aligning Competency Standards and Curriculum Innovation in Maritime Education

Albertha Lolo Tandung
http://orcid.org/0000-0002-0046-1726
Politeknik Pelayaran Barombong, Indonesia

Obet Lumalan Bijang
Politeknik Pelayaran Barombong, Indonesia

Nenny Nenny
Politeknik Pelayaran Barombong, Indonesia

Inriani Inriani
Institut Teknologi Pendidikan dan Bisnis Qanaáh Sidenreng Rappang, Indonesia

ABSTRACT

This study explores the strategic alignment of competency standards and curriculum innovation in maritime education to prepare a future-ready workforce. It highlights the integration of Competency-Based Education (CBE), emerging technologies, and global benchmarking to enhance training relevance and quality. Emphasis is placed on co-designing curricula through industry–academia collaboration, embedding ethics and sustainability in competency frameworks, and fostering a culture of lifelong learning. The discussion underscores the role of institutional capacity building, quality assurance, and global cooperation in ensuring excellence and adaptability. The study concludes that a human-centered, competence-based ecosystem is essential for sustaining innovation, global mobility, and environmental responsibility in maritime education.

DOI: 10.4018/979-8-3373-6670-8.ch007

NAVIGATING CHANGE IN MARITIME EDUCATION

1.1 The Evolving Landscape of Maritime Training and Global Competence

The maritime sector is currently experiencing a substantial transformation propelled by swift technological progress, escalating global economic interdependence, and shifting requirements for safety and sustainability. In the past, maritime training models focused on operational efficiency and technical expertise. Now, they are being changed to meet global competency standards and embrace digital innovation (Simmons & McLean, 2020). Maritime education institutions (METs) must combine traditional seamanship skills with a curriculum that looks to the future and focuses on automation, data analytics, green shipping initiatives, and skills that are centered on people. This change is in line with the International Maritime Organization's (IMO) recognition of the need to develop a workforce that is globally competent and can work responsibly and sustainably in a variety of maritime settings (Sharma et al., 2022).

In maritime education, the term "global competence" now means more than just navigation and engineering. It now includes important skills like intercultural communication, taking care of the environment, and being able to use technology that are needed to handle the complexities of maritime operations, such as managing autonomous vessels and smart ports (Simmons & McLean, 2020). As a result, seafarers need to quickly learn how to use new technologies and follow new rules, which means that maritime training needs to change. This change means that we need to move away from a mostly procedural education model and toward one that encourages critical thinking, making moral choices, and being aware of global issues. These are all things that are becoming more important in higher education systems (Sharma, 2024).

The globalization of maritime operations makes it even more important for countries to agree on what skills are needed and how to recognize those skills in each other. The International Maritime Organization's (IMO) Standards of Training, Certification, and Watchkeeping (STCW) Convention is the basis for this global competence alignment. However, there are still many problems to solve because of differences between regions and institutions. Advanced economies quickly adopt digital simulations and blended learning frameworks, but developing regions often fall behind because they don't have enough resources or up-to-date curricula (Marsudi, 2023). To fix these differences, we need to use a variety of methods, such as using new technologies, making changes to the curriculum, working together more closely with all stakeholders, and making sure that policies are in line with each other (Sijabat & Simanjuntak, 2023).

The maritime workforce also needs a more complete set of skills that includes sustainability and resilience. As the industry works hard to cut down on carbon emissions and move toward a blue economy, maritime workers need to know how to deal with environmental problems. This includes knowing a lot about international environmental laws, promoting a culture of safety, and supporting Sustainable Development Goals (SDGs) like SDG 4 (Quality Education), SDG 8 (Decent Work and Economic Growth), and SDG 13 (Climate Action) (Simmons & McLean, 2020).

Ultimately, redefining excellence in maritime training requires a shift that values not only technical skills but also moral leadership, the ability to adapt, and the ability to work with people from different cultures. METs must go beyond the usual compliance-based educational systems to make learning environments that change the way people learn and prepare seafarers for lifelong learning and leadership roles in a global industry that is always changing. By strategically realigning competency standards and implementing innovative curricular reforms, METs can prepare the next generation of maritime professionals with the skills needed to navigate the complexities of the maritime sector in the future (Marsudi, 2023; Sharma, 2024).

1.2 Challenges of Traditional Curriculum Models in Meeting Industry Demands

Historically, maritime education has focused on rote learning, procedural training, and standardized classroom instruction that meets regulatory requirements instead of developing well-rounded skills. This method has made seafarers who are good at their jobs, but it is not meeting the changing needs of the modern maritime industry. The traditional "input-based" curriculum, which is based on hours of instruction, set syllabi, and theoretical tests, often doesn't prepare students for the unpredictable, technology-driven, and globally connected maritime world of the twenty-first century.

One big problem with traditional models is that they are inflexible and don't adapt quickly to change. Maritime curricula usually follow national rules, which change more slowly than new ideas in the industry. Many training centers are having trouble keeping up with changes in maritime operations brought about by automation, artificial intelligence, and digital navigation systems. As a result, there is a growing gap between what students learn in the classroom and what they actually do on board. This means that graduates are not ready for new technologies like electronic chart display systems (ECDIS), predictive maintenance tools, and smart ship communication networks. This delay makes it harder for students to be ready for work and makes the institution less relevant in the competitive field of maritime education.

Another problem is that there is too much focus on technical and operational skills and not enough on soft skills, critical thinking, and moral judgment. More and more, the industry needs professionals who can work with people from different cultures, solve complicated logistical problems, and adapt to environmentally friendly maritime practices. Traditional models, on the other hand, tend to separate learning into different areas, with little overlap between leadership, communication, or environmental literacy. As a result, graduates may have strong technical skills but not the interpersonal and adaptive skills needed for working with people from different fields and countries.

Also, traditional maritime education assessment systems often put more emphasis on remembering facts and following rules than on performance-based evaluation. Written tests and simulator exercises that only show fixed situations make it hard for students to show how well they can solve problems in real life. Competency-based assessment frameworks, which measure learners based on observable results and job performance, are still not used enough. This gap between how assessments are done and what is expected of people on the job makes it harder to move from the classroom to the ship.

These problems are made worse by limitations on institutions and infrastructure. Many Maritime Education and Training institutions (METs), especially in developing areas, don't have easy access to the latest simulation technologies, qualified teachers, or programs for ongoing professional development. There aren't enough strong connections between academics and business people, which makes it harder to work together on curriculum design, internships, and applied research projects that could make the work more useful. To meet the complex, interdisciplinary, and technology-driven needs of the maritime industry, traditional curriculum models in maritime education need to change. The way forward is to use learning frameworks that are flexible, focused on results, and in line with the needs of the industry. These frameworks should include digital innovation, soft skills, and principles of sustainability. Only by making these kinds of changes can maritime education systems turn out skilled, moral, and future-ready seafarers who can handle global problems with ease.

1.3 The Call for Innovation and Standard Alignment in the Era of Digitalization

The rapid digitalization of the maritime industry has completely changed the skills that modern sailors need and the standards that Maritime Education and Training (MET) schools must meet. As automation, smart ships, and interconnected maritime systems become more common, innovation and compliance with international standards have become necessary for success in this changing environment (Kim et al., 2023; Belabyad et al., 2025). The maritime industry's digital transformation is now the most important thing to do to keep the industry safe, sustainable, and competitive on a global scale. This change means that schools and universities need to not only use new technologies, but also completely rethink how they teach, how they grade students, and how their cultures work in order to meet new global standards for competency (Fabian-Perona, 2025; Belabyad et al., 2025).

Innovation in maritime education encompasses both technological and pedagogical aspects. The use of simulation-based learning, virtual and augmented reality (VR/AR), artificial intelligence (AI), and digital twins is changing the way maritime training environments work. These kinds of tools make it easier for cadets to learn by doing things that are very similar to what they would do in real life on the water. This improves their ability to assess risks, make decisions, and be aware of their surroundings (Makransky & Klingenberg, 2022; Kim et al., 2021; Ala et al., 2024). However, implementing these new technologies will require a lot of money to be spent on improving infrastructure and training teachers so that they can effectively teach these new skills. Furthermore, MET institutions must ensure that the integration of digital tools is consistent with international standards, notably the International Maritime Organization's (IMO) Standards of Training, Certification, and Watchkeeping (STCW) Convention, to preserve global recognition and interoperability (Johnson, 2020; Belabyad et al., 2025; Vujičić et al., 2020).

From an educational point of view, making maritime education digital means moving from teacher-centered methods to learner-centered, competency-based education (CBE). According to the outcomes-based educational principles that are being pushed for in global reforms (Nyairo et al., 2025), the focus should shift from “time spent in training” to “competence demonstrated through performance.” This learner-centered approach encourages active participation in building knowledge through problem-solving, teamwork, and reflective practice. It uses data-driven learning analytics to tailor training paths to each learner and keep track of their progress. This kind of personalized growth fits with the IMO's goal of having adaptable and strong maritime professionals (Fabian-Perona, 2025; Konon, 2022).

It is just as important to make sure that educational standards are in line with global standards for this change to happen. Different national maritime curricula and accreditation systems often make it hard to recognize and certify skills consistently. Aligning institutional curricula with international standards is necessary to make sure that seafarers can move around the world and to build trust in their skills (Belabyad et al., 2025; Vujičić et al., 2020). Collaborative networks among MET institutions, regulatory bodies, and industry partners can promote the joint development of unified standards that address practical maritime challenges, sustainability concerns, and technological innovations (Doucouré, 2024; Cahyadi et al., 2024).

FRAMEWORKS OF COMPETENCE: GLOBAL AND REGIONAL PERSPECTIVES

2.1 International Maritime Organization (IMO) Standards and the STCW Convention

The International Maritime Organization (IMO) is the main global body that sets and enforces rules for safety, security, and environmental protection at sea. The Standards of Training, Certification, and Watchkeeping for Seafarers (STCW) Convention, which was first adopted in 1978 and changed in 1995 and 2010 (the Manila Amendments), is one of the most important frameworks for improving maritime skills around the world. The STCW Convention establishes the minimum global standards for training, certification, and watchkeeping. This guarantees that all seafarers, regardless of their nationality or the institution they work for, meet the same professional and operational standards. This framework supports not only the technical skills of maritime workers, but also their ethical, safety, and human performance skills that are needed for global shipping operations.

The STCW framework sets standards for skills at different levels of the hierarchy, such as officers, ratings, and masters. These skills include navigation, engineering, cargo handling, maritime law, and managing people. It stresses the importance of combining theoretical and practical learning, such as classroom instruction, simulator training, and real-world experience. This all-encompassing method makes sure that maritime workers have not only the procedural knowledge they need, but also the judgment, decision-making, and leadership skills they need to handle complicated shipboard situations. The Convention requires that certification be revalidated on a regular basis. This reinforces the idea of continuous competence and lifelong learning, which is becoming more and more important as technology and rules change (Doucouré, 2024).

The IMO's role in governance goes beyond setting standards. It also makes sure that countries follow the rules by using the White List system, which lists countries whose training and certification systems are in line with STCW rules. This global standard helps seafarers' qualifications be recognized by other countries, which makes it easier for workers to move around and find work in other countries. Nonetheless, differences persist in the quality and enforcement of training programs across member states. Some developing maritime countries have trouble because their institutions aren't strong enough, their training facilities are out of date, and their academic programs don't always match what employers want. These gaps show that we need to keep working together on technical issues, building our skills, and making sure that policies are the same all over the world in order to get fair competence outcomes.

The 2010 Manila Amendments made the STCW framework even more up-to-date by adding new skills in modern communication systems, electronic navigation, and leadership and management. These changes show how the industry is moving toward automation and digitalization, which shows how the IMO is keeping up with changes in the maritime world. The Convention now also stresses safety culture, managing fatigue, and being responsible for the environment. This makes maritime education more in line with the bigger goals of sustainable development and being a good global citizen.

In short, the IMO and its STCW Convention set a standard for global maritime competence that strikes a balance between following the rules and coming up with new ways to teach. As the maritime industry moves toward smart shipping, eco-friendly operations, and self-driving navigation, it is still very important that STCW keeps changing. Because of this, maritime education and training institutions must not see these standards as fixed rules, but as flexible frameworks that encourage new ideas in the curriculum, collaboration across borders, and the development of seafarers who are ready for the future and can work anywhere in the world.

2.2 Regional and National Qualification Frameworks for Seafarer Competence

The International Maritime Organization (IMO) and the Standards of Training, Certification, and Watchkeeping for Seafarers (STCW) Convention set the global standard for maritime competence. Regional and national qualification frameworks are just as important for putting these standards into context and making them work. These frameworks are flexible tools that turn international rules into policies, curricula, and assessment systems that are more relevant to the needs of local industries, the readiness of technology, and the cultural context. By making sure that educational outcomes are in line with both global standards and national goals, they make sure that seafarers can compete in the international job market while also helping to grow the maritime industry in their own country.

In a lot of places, qualification frameworks are part of bigger education and training systems that focus on competency-based and outcome-based methods. The European Qualifications Framework (EQF), for instance, encourages a standard structure across member states so that maritime qualifications can be recognized by all and workers in the European maritime industry can move around more easily. The ASEAN Qualifications Reference Framework (AQRF) is another example of a regional platform that brings together skills and makes sure that seafarers trained in Southeast Asia meet the same standards as those trained in other parts of the world. These frameworks are important for filling in policy gaps, encouraging cooperation between Maritime Education and Training institutions (METs), and improving cross-border employability in a maritime economy that is becoming more globalized.

Countries use these frameworks in their education and regulatory systems to create different levels of advancement for seafarers. For example, in Indonesia, the Kerangka Kualifikasi Nasional Indonesia (KKNI) makes sure that maritime education is in line with national occupational standards. This makes sure that academic programs, certification levels, and professional advancement all make sense. This framework combines learning in school, at work, and in the industry. It encourages a well-rounded approach that values both hard skills and soft skills like communication, teamwork, and leadership. Similar programs in the Philippines, India, and China show how different countries use the STCW standards while also taking into account local maritime customs, languages, and government systems (Belabyad et al., 2025).

Even with these improvements, it is still hard to get full alignment at the regional and national levels. Inconsistencies in quality assurance and certification recognition are often caused by differences in how policies are interpreted, how assessments are done, and how well institutions can handle them. Some countries don't have easy access to modern simulation technologies, or their teachers aren't trained well enough to teach competency-based education well. These differences can make it harder for people to move around in the workforce and get recognized around the world, which is especially true for developing maritime nations that want to compete in the global labor market.

To deal with these problems, governments, maritime administrations, industry stakeholders, and schools need to work together for a long time. Regional networks, like the ASEAN Maritime Education and Training Council and the European Maritime Safety Agency (EMSA), can make it easier to set standards, work together to create new courses, and review each other's work. Regional and national qualification frameworks can be powerful tools for excellence because they build trust and recognition between people. This helps seafarers confidently, competently, and globally navigate the complexities of modern maritime operations.

2.3 Bridging Global Competence Standards with Local Educational Contexts

One of the most important and difficult problems in maritime education today is how to connect global maritime competence standards with local educational settings. International frameworks like the Standards of Training, Certification, and Watchkeeping for Seafarers (STCW) Convention set universal standards for safety and professional competence. However, for these standards to work, they need to be adapted to fit the needs of each country, organization, and social and economic priorities. So, maritime education and training institutions (METs) need to find a balance between meeting international rules and regulations and meeting the needs, cultures, and infrastructures of their local maritime sectors.

Global competence standards stress the importance of consistency, interoperability, and being able to move around the world. The maritime landscape, on the other hand, is very different in different parts of the world because of things like different types of industries, access to technology, and worker expectations. For example, advanced maritime nations often work in high-tech settings that have advanced simulators, digital navigation systems, and strong research partnerships. On the other hand, developing maritime countries might use traditional teaching methods, have few digital resources, and have curricula that are tailored to their own needs. These differences show that we need flexible educational models that support global competence outcomes while also taking into account the differences in how teaching is done and the resources that are available.

Localization of global standards means adding international requirements to national qualification frameworks, institutional curricula, and teaching methods. This process requires more than just turning rules into policies; it also requires turning them into ways of teaching, learning, and testing. For instance, incorporating IMO's competence tables into competency-based curricula necessitates meticulous alignment of learning outcomes, instructional activities, and assessment tasks to guarantee compliance while preserving cultural and contextual relevance. To keep up with global standards, you can use local maritime traditions, ways of communicating, and work ethics to get students more involved and help them build their professional identity.

Furthermore, connecting these levels of standards necessitates strong cooperation among stakeholders, including governments, maritime administrations, educational institutions, and industry participants. Joint curriculum design, internship partnerships, and faculty exchange programs can help knowledge flow and make sure that global standards are followed correctly in local ecosystems. Digital learning platforms and simulation-based environments also help level the playing field by letting schools with limited physical infrastructure offer high-quality training that meets international standards.

This bridging process should not be seen as just a way to comply, but as a chance to come up with new ideas and build a sense of self. By putting global standards in context, local METs can build unique strengths based on their knowledge of the area, their awareness of the environment, and their ability to adapt to different cultures. These are all qualities that are becoming more important in a globalized maritime workforce. This synergy makes sure that seafarers are not only skilled in global waters but also in their own waters, able to handle both international waters and the specific problems that come with working in their own region. In short, bringing together global and local points of view makes maritime education a dynamic, open-minded, and future-ready business that values both excellence and diversity.

CURRICULUM INNOVATION FOR THE FUTURE MARITIME WORKFORCE

3.1 Integrating Competency-Based Education (CBE) into Maritime Curricula

Adding Competency-Based Education (CBE) to maritime curricula is a big change from the old way of teaching, which was based on time and focused on performance, mastery, and real-world application. In the maritime industry, where safety, accuracy, and professional responsibility are very important, CBE gives graduates a structured way to make sure they have the skills that meet international standards like the Standards of Training, Certification, and Watchkeeping for Seafarers (STCW) Convention. This change focuses on not only what students learn, but also how well they can use their knowledge, skills, and attitudes in real-life maritime situations.

CBE changes maritime education by changing the way courses are taught to focus on measurable learning goals and job standards. CBE doesn't just look at seat time, grades, or theoretical tests to see if someone has mastered something. It also looks at how well they do in simulated and real-life situations. Each learning module is built around a set of clearly defined skills that include technical knowledge, the ability to solve problems, and the ability to make moral decisions. For example, a navigation class would not only test students' knowledge of chart plotting, but it would also require them to show that they can make good navigational decisions in real time using electronic chart display systems (ECDIS) or bridge simulators. This method closes the gap between what students learn in school and what they do in their jobs, making sure that graduates are ready to work right away (Sharma & Nazir, 2021).

CBE is also in line with global trends toward lifelong learning and skill development that can change over time. As smart shipping technologies, automation, and artificial intelligence (AI) change how ships work, seafarers need to keep learning new skills to stay useful. CBE makes this flexibility possible by allowing modular and stackable learning paths. This lets seafarers learn new skills or improve their current ones through micro-credentials or competency units that can be added up to formal qualifications. This flexibility is especially helpful in meeting the needs of the industry for specialized roles in areas like cybersecurity, sustainability management, and digital navigation systems.

To make CBE work, schools need to change their rules, update their curricula, retrain their teachers, and come up with new ways to test students. Teachers need to stop being people who just give information and start being people who help students learn and check their skills. They should guide each student through their own learning path. Assessment methods need to change to include performance-based rubrics, reflective portfolios, and scenario-driven simulations that look at both technical and behavioral skills as a whole. Also, it is important for MET institutions, maritime authorities, and industry partners to work together to make sure that competency frameworks reflect real operational needs and the best practices around the world.

Even though there are clear benefits, there are still problems with fully implementing CBE, especially in places where resources are limited. It takes a lot of money and teamwork to create standardized assessment tools, improve simulators, and make sure that evaluations are the same at all schools. Still, adding CBE to maritime curricula is an important step toward creating a maritime workforce that is globally competent, safety-conscious, and driven by innovation. Maritime education institutions can produce professionals who are not only qualified but also capable, adaptable, and prepared to lead in the evolving landscape of global shipping by making competency the basis of learning.

3.2 Infusing Emerging Technologies: Simulation, AI, and Smart Learning Environments

The use of new technologies like simulation, artificial intelligence (AI), and smart learning environments is changing the way maritime education is done. As the maritime industry goes through a digital transformation brought on by automation, smart shipping, and the Internet of Things (IoT), Maritime Education and Training (MET) institutions must use new technologies that make learning more real, efficient, and open to everyone. In the context of global maritime operations, these technologies not only bring things up to date, but they also change the way competence is developed, tested, and maintained (Bačnar et al., 2025).

For a long time, simulation technologies have been an important part of maritime training. However, recent improvements in high-fidelity and immersive systems have made them much more useful for teaching. Bridge simulators, engine room simulators, and full-mission simulation systems can now accurately recreate complicated operational settings. Learners can practice navigating busy ports, dealing with changing weather, and handling emergencies without putting anyone's life or property at risk. Experiential learning like this helps people make decisions, work together, and be aware of their surroundings, which are all important parts of being a good sailor, as the Standards of Training, Certification, and Watchkeeping for Seafarers (STCW) Convention Kim et al. (2021) says. Virtual and augmented reality (VR/AR) take this ability even further by offering cheap and portable options that bring real-life training experiences into classrooms and remote learning environments (Sharma & Nazir, 2021).

Artificial intelligence (AI) makes maritime education better by allowing for personalized and adaptive learning. Analytics powered by AI can keep track of how well students are doing, find areas where they need to improve, and give them personalized feedback. Intelligent tutoring systems mimic mentoring by helping cadets work through difficult problems and giving them feedback in real time. AI also helps with predictive assessment and competency forecasting, which lets schools better match their training to the changing needs of the industry (Karimi et al., 2024; Riyanto et al., 2025). AI tools help with more than just teaching. They also help with improving ship operations, safety analysis, and maintenance prediction. These are all areas of knowledge that need to be added to the maritime curriculum to make sure the next generation of workers is ready (Reyes, 2025).

Digital connectivity and cloud-based platforms make smart learning environments possible. They are the next big thing in maritime education. Learning management systems (LMS) work with simulation databases, virtual classrooms, and tools for real-time communication to make a complete system for developing skills. These spaces make it possible to work together from afar, get feedback all the time, and connect to global maritime knowledge networks. The merging of AI, simulation, and smart platforms encourages lifelong learning, which means that seafarers can keep learning new skills no matter where they are (Simmons & McLean, 2020).

But using these technologies requires careful compliance with both national rules and global standards for competence. For technological innovation to support, not replace, pedagogical integrity, schools must spend money on infrastructure, faculty digital literacy, and quality assurance systems. When used correctly, new technologies can not only make maritime education more modern, but they can also help create a generation of maritime professionals who are digitally savvy, ethically responsible, and globally competent, ready to handle the challenges of Industry 5.0 and the blue economy (Umanets et al., 2024).

3.3 Embedding Soft Skills, Ethics, and Sustainability in Competency Frameworks

In today's complicated and interconnected maritime industry, seafarers need to be good at more than just their technical skills. They also need to be good at soft skills, ethical reasoning, and being aware of sustainability. Sijabat et al. (2024). As automation and digitalization change how things work at sea, being able to communicate clearly, make moral choices, and be responsible toward people and the planet is becoming more and more important for people. Putting soft skills, ethics, and sustainability into maritime competency frameworks makes sure that education and training create professionals who are not only technically skilled but also morally sound and aware of the environment. These professionals will be able to handle the changing demands of global maritime work (Simanjuntak et al., 2023).

Soft skills like communication, leadership, teamwork, adaptability, and intercultural competence are very important for shipboard operations because crews are usually made up of people from many different countries and are organized in a hierarchy (Simanjuntak et al., 2023). Safety and operational efficiency are directly affected by the ability to work together under stress, handle conflict, and keep lines of communication open across language and cultural barriers. But traditional maritime education models have often put more emphasis on technical training, which doesn't leave much room for the systematic development of these interpersonal skills. Maritime Education and Training (MET) institutions can prepare seafarers to confidently navigate complex social environments by incorporating soft skills training into competency-based curricula (Purba & Simanjuntak, 2024). Role-playing exercises, simulation-based communication tasks, and reflective practice modules can strengthen these competencies as quantifiable and evaluable results (Castellanos et al., 2020).

It is just as important to include ethics in maritime competency frameworks. Ethical competence includes following professional standards, treating people with respect, and being responsible for your choices. As AI-assisted navigation, autonomous vessels, and digital surveillance systems become more common, it is more important than ever to make moral decisions that protect safety, fairness, and openness (Cho & Costa, 2024). Incorporating maritime ethics into training prompts cadets to contemplate matters such as adherence to international conventions, equitable treatment of seafarers, and environmental stewardship (Concina & Frate, 2023; Sigua et al., 2023). Case-based learning and discussions of ethical dilemmas can help future officers develop their moral reasoning and critical thinking skills. This will help them internalize the values of honesty, fairness, and professional duty.

In the age of the blue and green economies, sustainability has become a key skill. According to the International Maritime Organization's (IMO) decarbonization strategy and the United Nations Sustainable Development Goals (SDGs) (Ghoneim et al., 2023; Ibáñez et al., 2020), maritime professionals are now expected to help reduce carbon emissions, manage waste, and protect the oceans. Including sustainability literacy in training programs makes sure that future seafarers know how their actions affect the environment and society and can take part in sustainable operations (Wang et al., 2025).

By including soft skills, ethics, and sustainability in maritime competency frameworks, MET schools can help students become well-rounded professionals who can lead with empathy, responsibility, and foresight (Martín-Sánchez et al., 2022). This human-centered approach changes maritime education from a system based on following rules to one that promotes global citizenship, ethical leadership, and sustainable maritime development—three important traits for the future workforce that will have to deal with a lot of change (Cuevas-Cancino et al., 2024).

ALIGNING INSTITUTIONAL PRACTICE WITH COMPETENCY STANDARDS

4.1 Co-Designing Curricula through Industry–Academia Collaboration

Working together with businesses and schools to design curricula is now an important way to make sure that maritime education is relevant, responsive, and of high quality. The maritime industry changes quickly because of things like digitalization, automation, environmental regulations, and changes in the job market. To keep up, Maritime Education and Training (MET) schools need to close the long-standing gap between what they teach in class and how they do their jobs. Collaborative curriculum design helps make sure that what students learn, how they learn it, and what skills they need match the real needs of the maritime workforce. This synergy changes traditional education models into flexible, competency-based systems that give graduates both theoretical knowledge and hands-on experience.

Shipping companies, port authorities, classification societies, and maritime administrations are all part of the maritime sector. They are a great source of practical knowledge and operational insight. When businesses help design the curriculum, MET programs stay up-to-date with current practices, rules, and technological advances. For example, getting feedback from shipping companies and maritime logistics companies can help schools add new modules on electronic navigation, predictive maintenance, and green shipping. By working together to create learning outcomes, case studies, and assessment criteria, industry partners help keep the training real and useful for getting a job.

From an academic point of view, working together helps turn global standards, like the Standards of Training, Certification, and Watchkeeping for Seafarers (STCW) Convention, into learning frameworks that make sense in the real world. Faculty members are very important for figuring out what regulatory competencies mean and how they fit with teaching methods. They make sure that the curricula not only meet all the rules, but also encourage critical thinking, moral reasoning, and learning for life. Academic knowledge in instructional design, assessment theory, and educational technology goes well with the business side of things, which leads to balanced curricula that cover both the technical and the human aspects of maritime competence.

Advisory boards, curriculum review committees, joint research projects, and internship programs are all ways to make collaboration work better. Setting up ongoing conversations between academia and industry makes it easier for feedback loops to keep curricula up to date and looking ahead. Partnerships can also include co-teaching arrangements, in which professionals from the industry give guest lectures or lead exercises based on simulators. This gives students a more realistic view of what they are learning. Collaborative ventures can also create innovation ecosystems where universities and maritime organizations work together to find new ways to solve problems like decarbonization, cybersecurity, and autonomous ship operation (Wang et al., 2025).

But for collaboration to last, institutions need to be committed, trust each other, and have structured governance. If not dealt with through clear agreements and shared goals, problems like differing priorities, confidentiality issues, and resource imbalances can make it harder for people to work together. Successful models show that when academia and industry work together to create curricula, they end up with a strong competency framework that keeps up with changes in the maritime world.

4.2 Assessment, Certification, and Quality Assurance Mechanisms

A credible and competency-based maritime education system is built on assessment, certification, and quality assurance mechanisms. In a field where safety, reliability, and professional competence have a direct impact on human life and the environment, it is essential that training outcomes meet strict standards (Sihombing et al., 2024; Meštrović et al., 2023). These mechanisms ensure that Maritime Education and Training (MET) institutions produce graduates whose skills and knowledge meet the global standards set by the Standards of Training, Certification, and Watchkeeping for Seafarers (STCW) Convention and related International Maritime Organization (IMO) frameworks.

Assessment in maritime education transcends conventional examinations to include performance-based and outcomes-oriented evaluations (Kumar & Rajini, 2024). Competency-Based Education (CBE) necessitates that students exhibit proficiency in designated skills within authentic operational contexts. Students can use what they learned in class in real-life maritime situations through simulation-based assessments, onboard practicums, and scenario-driven evaluations. For instance, bridge simulator exercises evaluate navigation and decision-making abilities under time constraints and fluctuating weather conditions, whereas engine room simulations examine mechanical troubleshooting and adherence to safety regulations (Sijabat et al., 2024; Ala et al., 2024). These tests not only check for technical skills but also for important soft skills like leadership, teamwork, and situational awareness, which are all important for a modern seafarer (Mudakir et al., 2024).

In competency-based systems, certification is an official way to show that someone has met a certain level of competence. The International Maritime Organization (IMO) oversees national maritime authorities that give out certificates of competency (CoC) after standardized tests and sea-time requirements are met. Certification processes must be open, fair, and verifiable, so that every credential shows real mastery instead of just following the rules (Kuncowati et al., 2022). The IMO's White List system helps build trust around the world by listing countries whose certification systems follow STCW rules. However, the integrity of certification relies significantly on institutional accountability, uniform evaluation criteria, and the deterrence of malpractice or fraudulent credentials—challenges that persist in certain areas (Sellberg & Sharma, 2024).

Quality assurance mechanisms give the training and certification processes a way to make sure that these standards are met. Institutions can keep an eye on how well they are meeting national and international standards with the help of external audits, accreditation visits, and internal evaluation systems (Lee et al., 2021). The European Maritime Safety Agency (EMSA) and regional groups in ASEAN and other blocs check to make sure that training facilities, curriculum implementation, and instructor qualifications are all up to par (Atik, 2020). Continuous improvement cycles in institutions, which include planning, implementation, evaluation, and feedback, make sure that programs keep up with changes in technology and rules (Sharma & Nazir, 2021).

Digitalization also opens up new ways to ensure quality, such as learning analytics, e-portfolios, and blockchain-based credential verification. These new ideas make things more clear and easy to follow, which cuts down on the work for administrators and makes sure that qualifications are real. In the end, good assessment, certification, and quality assurance systems give seafarers credibility and the ability to move around the world, which builds trust among regulators, employers, and the general public (Fabian-Perona, 2025; Meštrović et al., 2023). MET institutions help make the maritime profession safer, more ethical, and ready for the future by keeping high standards. This will help the industry deal with the challenges of a more complicated world.

4.3 Faculty Development and Institutional Capacity Building for CBE Implementation

The effective execution of Competency-Based Education (CBE) in maritime institutions is fundamentally reliant on faculty development and the enhancement of institutional capacity. CBE focuses on outcomes that are centered on the learner and mastery of performance. To be successful, teachers need to be technically skilled, good at teaching, able to use technology, and in line with global competency frameworks. Institutions must also create organizational structures, resources, and cultures that encourage innovation, teamwork, and ongoing improvement. Without strategic investment in human and institutional capacity, even the most well-designed competency frameworks risk remaining theoretical rather than transformative.

The main reason for adopting CBE is to help teachers grow. In Maritime Education and Training (MET), traditional teaching methods have often been based on delivering content and making sure students follow the rules. In a CBE model, on the other hand, teachers are facilitators, mentors, and judges of competence. This change requires teachers to learn new skills, like how to create modules based on outcomes, give real assessments, and give feedback that helps students learn. Because of this, workshops on instructional design, simulation pedagogy, and digital learning integration should be part of ongoing professional development programs. In addition, teachers need to learn how to use technology-enhanced tools like learning management systems (LMS), virtual simulators, and e-assessment platforms that make personalized and data-driven learning possible (Meštrović et al., 2023).

It is just as important to teach faculty how to assess students. When you evaluate someone's competence, you look at more than just how well they do their job. You also look at how they make decisions, how they act morally, and how well they work with others. Faculty must be able to create performance rubrics, carry out standardized evaluations, and stay objective in high-stakes tests like simulator-based tests or onboard practicums. Peer mentoring and exchange programs with professionals in the field can help faculty see things from different angles, making sure that what they teach in class is in line with what happens in the real world of maritime operations.

Institutional capacity building is the systemic basis for long-term CBE implementation, in addition to individual training. Institutions need to set up clear rules for how they will run things, set aside money for digital and simulation infrastructure, and create quality assurance systems that follow international standards like the STCW Convention. Institutional leaders should also create an environment that encourages new ideas and working together. This means encouraging research across disciplines, partnerships with businesses, and faculty involvement in global maritime education networks. Setting up centers of excellence or professional development units within METs can make it easier for faculty to improve their skills and make sure that training programs can be used in the future and on a larger scale.

Capacity building also includes help with policies and administrative systems. Transparent evaluation processes, acknowledgment of teaching excellence, and incentives for innovation encourage faculty to adopt CBE methodologies. Working with international groups like the European Maritime Safety Agency (EMSA), the International Maritime Organization (IMO), and regional groups makes sure that local practices are still useful around the world.

CHARTING THE COURSE TOWARD EXCELLENCE

5.1 Global Benchmarking and Continuous Curriculum Renewal

To achieve excellence and long-term success in maritime education, it is important to use global benchmarks and keep the curriculum up to date. In an industry that is changing quickly because of digital transformation, environmental concerns, and changes in global trade, Maritime Education and Training (MET) institutions need to make sure that their programs stay up-to-date, look to the future, and follow international best practices. Benchmarking is a structured way to compare the performance of institutions, the content of their curricula, and the results of their students with global standards like the Standards of Training, Certification, and Watchkeeping for Seafarers (STCW) Convention. Continuous renewal, on the other hand, makes sure that institutions are ready for changes in technology and regulations. These processes work together to create a feedback loop that keeps quality, competitiveness, and innovation going in the maritime education ecosystem.

By comparing their programs to world-class models, maritime institutions can find their strengths, weaknesses, and chances for improvement through global benchmarking. This process looks at the curriculum, assessment, and competency frameworks of top MET schools around the world, like those in Norway, Japan, the Netherlands, and Singapore. Their programs are often seen as the best in the world. Benchmarking also means working with international accreditation bodies and being a part of global maritime education networks. Institutions can adopt new teaching methods, digital learning tools, and practices that are good for the environment through peer reviews, faculty exchanges, and collaborative research. Benchmarking enhances global trust and mobility by ensuring compliance with established standards, which promotes mutual recognition of qualifications and improves graduates' employability in the international maritime labor market.

But benchmarking isn't something you do once; it's a process of learning, thinking, and changing that goes on all the time. The maritime industry changes quickly because automation, artificial intelligence (AI), and environmental regulations are always changing the way things need to be done. So, updating the curriculum all the time becomes a necessary part of running the school instead of something that happens every so often. To keep up with new technologies, changes in the law, and feedback from the industry, MET curricula must be reviewed on a regular basis. Updating course material on topics like smart navigation, green shipping, cybersecurity, and maritime leadership keeps training up to date and focused on the future.

Stakeholders, such as academia, industry, regulators, and seafarers, must also work together to update the curriculum. Institutions can make sure that changes to the curriculum are based on evidence and real-world situations by setting up curriculum advisory boards that include shipping companies, port authorities, and alumni. Digital tools like learning analytics and feedback dashboards can give you real-time information about how well students are doing and how relevant their skills are, which can help you improve the curriculum even more.

5.2 Building a Culture of Innovation, Adaptability, and Lifelong Learning

For Maritime Education and Training (MET) schools to get seafarers ready for a global industry that is becoming more complex and technology-driven, they need to create a culture of innovation, flexibility, and lifelong learning. Digitalization, automation, the need for sustainability, and the growth of the blue economy are all changing the maritime industry in big ways. To do well in these changing times, people who work in the maritime industry need to be open to learning new things, be creative, and be strong. As a result, MET institutions need to go beyond traditional training models that are based on compliance and create learning environments that value curiosity, experimentation, and adaptability as important professional skills. Sanli (2024).

Innovation is what drives progress in maritime education. To make innovation a part of an institution's culture, you have to rethink how knowledge is made, shared, and used. This means using flexible learning paths, bringing in simulation and artificial intelligence (AI) technologies, and encouraging collaboration between different fields. Digital twins, augmented reality (AR), and virtual reality (VR) are some examples of how learners can practice real-life shipboard situations and problem-solving tasks (Panaite et al., 2024). Innovation also includes new ways of teaching, like flipped classrooms, problem-based learning, and competency-based micro-credentials, that make the learning process more personal and fit with what people need in the real world (Galindo et al., 2024). Faculty are key to creating this culture by being creative, asking tough questions, and working with students and industry partners to come up with new ways to teach (Iucu & Car i , 2025).

Adaptability is just as important, and it's a skill that is becoming more and more important in an industry that is always changing because of new rules, technology, and environmental factors. Maritime professionals need more than just static knowledge; they also need skills that can be used in other situations so they can deal with new problems. MET institutions can help students become more adaptable by using scenario-based learning, exposing them to knowledge from different fields, and giving them tests that require them to make decisions and improvise when they don't know what to do. Integrating AI and analytics-driven adaptive learning systems customizes educational experiences for each learner, facilitating individualized advancement and mastery of competencies (Sharma et al., 2022). Institutionalizing adaptability necessitates agile management frameworks that facilitate prompt and strategic curriculum revisions, policy alterations, and partnership cultivation (Surono & Jusuf, 2025).

Finally, encouraging lifelong learning is essential for maintaining professional excellence. In a time when technologies change faster than regulatory frameworks, the old model of one-time qualification is no longer enough. MET institutions must encourage ongoing professional development via modular learning, online courses, and stackable credentials (Coelho, 2025; Fabian-Perona, 2025). Working with shipping companies, classification societies, and maritime administrations can help people learn throughout their careers in a structured way. Lifelong learning ought to be regarded as a professional ethos—an enduring dedication to development, introspection, and excellence that transcends formal education (Fang & Xu, 2025).

5.3 Vision for a Future-Ready, Competence-Based Maritime Education Ecosystem

A future-ready, competence-based maritime education ecosystem sees a framework that is connected to the rest of the world, uses cutting-edge technology, and puts people first to help train the next generation of maritime professionals. In this imagined system, learning doesn't just happen in classrooms or simulators. It also happens in digital, adaptive, and collaborative settings that are more like how things really work in the 21st century maritime world. The focus is on overall competence, which includes technical skill, moral judgment, awareness of sustainability, and a commitment to lifelong learning. This vision puts Maritime Education and Training (MET) schools at the center of innovation, where they can adapt to changes in the global industry and meet international standards.

Competency-based learning, which is based on measurable outcomes that show how well someone is doing in the real world, is at the heart of this ecosystem. The Standards of Training, Certification, and Watchkeeping for Seafarers (STCW) Convention is still the most important reference, but it needs to be more flexible, adaptable, and tech-enabled in the future. MET institutions will be able to tailor learning paths and give real-time feedback on skill development thanks to data analytics, AI-powered learning systems, and immersive simulations. These kinds of systems can test not only technical skills but also critical thinking, working with others, and making moral decisions. These are all skills that are becoming more and more important in maritime environments that are autonomous and connected to the internet.

A maritime education system that is ready for the future also includes working together with people from all over the world and being open to everyone. MET institutions, maritime administrations, and industry partners need to work together more across borders so that everyone can recognize each other's skills, do research together, and let students and faculty move around. The ASEAN Qualifications Reference Framework (AQRF) and the European Qualifications Framework (EQF) are examples of regional frameworks that show how transnational alignment can work. This makes it easier for seafarers around the world to move up in their careers. It is also important to make sure that everyone has equal access to high-quality training, no matter where they live, what gender they are, or how much money they have. Digital and remote learning platforms can help make maritime education more accessible to everyone, including people who don't have access to it now, and they can also give more people around the world a chance to participate.

The vision also stresses that competence includes sustainability, ethics, and human resilience. The maritime industry's move toward decarbonization, green energy, and taking care of the environment means that all levels of training need to include lessons on sustainability and moral reasoning. Future-ready METs should develop leaders who not only follow environmental rules but also actively promote responsible practices that support the UN's Sustainable Development Goals (SDGs), especially SDG 4 (Quality Education), SDG 8 (Decent Work), and SDG 13 (Climate Action).

CONCLUSION

The path to excellence in maritime education is based on combining competency-based frameworks, constant innovation, and working together to make decisions. As the maritime industry moves toward a future that is more digital, sustainable, and connected across borders, Maritime Education and Training (MET) institutions need to change from systems that focus on compliance to ones that focus on transformative learning. Aligning curricula with international standards like the Standards of Training, Certification, and Watchkeeping for Seafarers (STCW) Convention makes them relevant around the world. Regional and national frameworks, on the other hand, make these standards fit with the needs of the area. This dual alignment creates an education system that works the same way around the world and can be changed to fit local needs.

Competency-Based Education (CBE) is at the center of this change. It offers a structured way to focus on performance, mastery, and moral judgment. The use of new technologies like simulation, artificial intelligence (AI), and smart learning platforms makes maritime training more realistic and easier to access. It also helps to connect what you learn in school with what you do in the real world. At the same time, including soft skills, ethics, and sustainability in competency frameworks makes sure that seafarers are not only technically skilled professionals, but also responsible global citizens who can lead with integrity and purpose.

REFERENCES

Ala, A., Hamidi, N., Yoniessa, S., Masito, F., & Muis, M. (2024). Simulation-based learning in maritime training: Enhancing competency and preparedness. *Meteor Stip Marunda*, *17*(1), 95–102. DOI: 10.36101/msm.v17i1.361

Atik, O. (2020). Eye tracking for assessment of situational awareness in bridge resource management training. *Journal of Eye Movement Research*, *12*(3). Advance online publication. DOI: 10.16910/jemr.12.3.7 PMID: 33828730

Bačnar, D., Barić, D., & Ogrizović, D. (2025). Charting the future of maritime education and training: A technology-acceptance-model-based pilot study on students' behavioural intention to use a fully immersive vr engine room simulator. *Applied System Innovation*, *8*(3), 84. DOI: 10.3390/asi8030084

Belabyad, M., Kontovas, C., Pyne, R., Shi, W., Li, N., Szwed, P., & Chang, C. (2025). *The human element in autonomous shipping: a study on skills and competency requirements*. Wmu Journal of Maritime Affairs., DOI: 10.1007/s13437-025-00366-9

Cahyadi, T., Ahmad, A., & Barasa, L. (2024). Integrating sustainability and digital advancements in maritime law education: Enhancing cadet preparedness. *IJLS*, *1*(4), 217–228. DOI: 10.62951/ijls.v1i4.196

Castellanos, P., Queiruga-Dios, A., Encinas, A., & Acosta, L. (2020). Environmental education in environmental engineering: Analysis of the situation in colombia and latin america. *Sustainability (Basel)*, *12*(18), 7239. DOI: 10.3390/su12187239

Cho, C., & Costa, E. (2024). Sustainability accounting education: Challenges and outlook. *International Journal of Sustainability in Higher Education*, *25*(7), 1412–1425. DOI: 10.1108/IJSHE-02-2024-0152

Coelho, C. (2025). Acreditación adaptativa y descentralizada: Integrando microcredenciales, sistemas cibernéticos y blockchain en el marco de los ods 4 y 9. *Educational Regent Multidisciplinary Journal*, *2*(4), 1–12. DOI: 10.63969/ay6amv07

Concina, E., & Frate, S. (2023). Assessing university students' beliefs and attitudes towards sustainability and sustainable development: A systematic review. *Trends in Higher Education*, *2*(4), 705–717. DOI: 10.3390/higheredu2040041

Cuevas-Cancino, M., Peña-Becerril, M., Mondragon-Estrada, E., & Camacho-Zúñiga, C. (2024). Incorporating vertical collaboration to address sustainable development goals: The monarch route project. *Frontiers in Education*, *9*, 1246889. Advance online publication. DOI: 10.3389/feduc.2024.1246889

Doucouré, M. (2024). Decarbonisation in shipping and maritime innovation call for readiness in maritime education and skills training in south africa. *SAJMET*, *3*, 31–38. DOI: 10.47348/SAJMET/2024/i1a3

Fabian-Perona, E. (2025). Maritime education and language as the acting link between bridge and engine room – a report. Educational Role of Language Journal, 2025-1(13), 64-67. https://doi.org/DOI: 10.36534/erlj.2025.01.07

Fabian-Perona, E. (2025). Maritime education and language as the acting link between bridge and engine room – a report. Educational Role of Language Journal, 2025-1(13), 64-67. https://doi.org/DOI: 10.36534/erlj.2025.01.07

Fabian-Perona, E. (2025). Maritime education and language as the acting link between bridge and engine room – a report. Educational Role of Language Journal, 2025-1(13), 64-67. https://doi.org/DOI: 10.36534/erlj.2025.01.07

Fang, R., & Xu, W. (2025). Obe-based micro-credentials and their role in bridging the gap between university education and job market demands in china. *Research and Advances in Education*, *4*(3), 26–34. DOI: 10.56397/RAE.2025.03.04

Galindo, M., Fennelly-Atkinson, R., Franklin, K., & Luna, C. (2024). The role of micro-credentials in lifelong learning and development: empowering learners, empowering organizations.. https://doi.org/DOI: 10.51388/20.500.12265/225

Ghoneim, N., Colak, A., & Amer, A. (2023). Exploring the regulatory framework of maritime decarbonization to achieve imo ghg emission targets. *Port-Said Engineering Research Journal*, *27*(1), 8–14. DOI: 10.21608/pserj.2023.209426.1234

Ibáñez, M., Cid, I., Muñoz, L., & Claros, F. (2020). Environmental education, an essential instrument to implement the sustainable development goals in the university context. *Sustainability (Basel)*, *12*(19), 7883. DOI: 10.3390/su12197883

Iucu, O. and Car i , A. (2025). Competency profiles in administrative sciences. an analysis of the students' perceptions and possible curricular reshapes through micro-credentials. Transylvanian Review of Administrative Sciences, (74 E), 5-29. https://doi.org/DOI: 10.24193/tras.74E.1

Johnson, E. (2020). Exploring the effects of technology and innovation on changing market requirements and the evolving maritime curriculum. *Worldwide Hospitality and Tourism Themes*, *12*(1), 69–79. DOI: 10.1108/WHATT-10-2019-0065

Karimi, E., Smith, J., Billard, R., & Veitch, B. (2024). Ai-based adaptive instructional systems for maritime safety training: A systematic literature review. *Discover Artificial Intelligence*, *4*(1), 51. Advance online publication. DOI: 10.1007/s44163-024-00153-0

Kim, J., Lee, C., Jeong, M., Cho, E., & Lee, Y. (2023). Identifying optimal approaches for sustainable maritime education and training: Addressing technological, environmental, and epidemiological challenges. *Sustainability (Basel)*, *15*(10), 8092. DOI: 10.3390/su15108092

Kim, T., Sharma, A., Bustgaard, M., Gyldensten, W., Nymoen, O., Tusher, H., & Nazir, S. (2021). The continuum of simulator-based maritime training and education. *Wmu Journal of Maritime Affairs*, *20*(2), 135–150. DOI: 10.1007/s13437-021-00242-2

Konon, N. (2022). Prospects for modern maritime education and training practices in terms of distance learning. *Shipping & Navigation*, *33*(1), 54–66. DOI: 10.31653/2306-5761.33.2022.54-66

Kumar, N. and Rajini, G. (2024). Reimaging maritime education and training using latest technologies. Salud Ciencia Y Tecnología - Serie De Conferencias, 3, 895. https://doi.org/DOI: 10.56294/sctconf2024895

Kuncowati, K., Sholihah, Q., & Ciptadi, G. (2022). Handling waste on ships: a model based on safety and awareness. Logi – Scientific Journal on Transport and Logistics, 13(1), 222-232. https://doi.org/DOI: 10.2478/logi-2022-0020

Lee, J., Dhesi, S., Phillips, I., Jeong, M., & Lee, C. (2021). Korean maritime cadets' onboard training environment survey. *Sustainability (Basel)*, *13*(8), 4161. DOI: 10.3390/su13084161

Makransky, G., & Klingenberg, S. (2022). Virtual reality enhances safety training in the maritime industry: An organizational training experiment with a non-weird sample. *Journal of Computer Assisted Learning*, *38*(4), 1127–1140. DOI: 10.1111/jcal.12670

Marsudi, S. (2023). Development of a shipping higher education curriculum that is responsive to the challenges of industry 4.0. Maritime Park Journal of Maritime Technology and Society, 99-105. https://doi.org/DOI: 10.62012/mp.v2i3.28267

Martín-Sánchez, A., González-Gómez, D., & Jeong, J. (2022). Service learning as an education for sustainable development (esd) teaching strategy: Design, implementation, and evaluation in a stem university course. *Sustainability (Basel)*, *14*(12), 6965. DOI: 10.3390/su14126965

Meštrović, T., Pavić, I., Androjna, A., & Maljković, M. (2023). Challenges for seafarers education and training in the context of autonomous ships development. Časopis Pomorskog Fakulteta Kotor - Journal of Maritime Sciences, 24(2), 31-42. https://doi.org/DOI: 10.56080/jms231103

Mudakir, M., Jogo, B., Krismawati, I., Pambudiyatno, N., & Santoso, A. (2024). Pedagogical approaches in maritime cadet teaching: Enhancing learning outcomes. *Meteor Stip Marunda*, *17*(1), 25–33. DOI: 10.36101/msm.v17i1.360

Nyairo, F., Haavardtun, P., Lindroos, E., Munim, Z., Lampiola, J., Salokorpi, M., … & Krabbel, H. (2025). Instructional approaches for simulator-based maritime education and training., 120-131. https://doi.org/DOI: 10.1007/978-3-031-84170-5_11

Panaite, F., Leba, M., & Ionică, A. (2024). Assessing cnn architectures for estimating correct posture in cruise machinists. Eng—advances in Engineering, 5(3), 1785-1803. DOI: 10.3390/eng5030094

Purba, D., & Simanjuntak, M. (2024). Sustainable maritime education: Integrating environmental science for global competence. [Jurnal Pendidikan Biologi Indonesia]. *Jpbi*, *10*(1), 310–319. DOI: 10.22219/jpbi.v10i1.32588

Reyes, S. (2025). Status, applications, and prospects of ai in maritime education: basis for curriculum planning. https://doi.org/DOI: 10.21203/rs.3.rs-7827795/v1

Riyanto, R., Tampubolon, B., & Herawati, S. (2025). Transforming maritime education through a competency-based framework for marine engineering technicians. *Research and Development in Education (Raden)*, *5*(1), 593–604. DOI: 10.22219/raden.v5i1.39399

Sanli, E. (2024). Motor learning theory can benefit seafarers. *Journal of Navigation*, *77*(3), 415–426. DOI: 10.1017/S0373463324000328

Sellberg, C., & Sharma, A. (2024). The automation of feedback in collaborative learning: a design ethnography of maritime simulation. https://doi.org/DOI: 10.21203/rs.3.rs-3993280/v1

Sharma, A., & Nazir, S. (2021). Assessing the technology self-efficacy of maritime instructors: An explorative study. *Education Sciences*, *11*(7), 342. DOI: 10.3390/educsci11070342

Sharma, A., Undheim, P., & Nazir, S. (2022). Design and implementation of ai chatbot for colregs training. *Wmu Journal of Maritime Affairs*, *22*(1), 107–123. DOI: 10.1007/s13437-022-00284-0

Sharma, R. (2024). Transformative horizons in education: Navigating challenges, embracing innovations, and shaping global landscapes. *IJCE*, *1*(1), 1–3. DOI: 10.47852/bonviewIJCE42022702

Sigua, R., Mesa, M., & Contreras, Y. (2023). Teachers' ideas and educational experiences regarding urban environmental sustainability in bogotá, colombia. *Sustainability (Basel)*, *15*(15), 11882. DOI: 10.3390/su151511882

Sihombing, D., Dwiyani, N., Martha, Y., Hutabarat, C., & Sutrisno, S. (2024). Impact of international standards on maritime education: Perspectives of junior cadets. *Meteor Stip Marunda*, *17*(1), 7–15. DOI: 10.36101/msm.v17i1.357

Sijabat, P., Simanjuntak, M., Mudakir, M., Putrawan, B., & Lumingkewas, M. (2024). Empowering literacy in maritime education: Strategies and professionalism alignment. *Meteor Stip Marunda*, *17*(1), 42–50. DOI: 10.36101/msm.v17i1.359

Sijabat, P., & Simanjuntak, M.Panderaja Soritua SijabatMarudut Bernadtua Simanjuntak. (2023). Mapping competencies: A profound analysis of semester 1 cadets at a premier maritime institute. *Semantik*, *2*(1), 100–112. DOI: 10.61132/semantik.v2i1.199

Simanjuntak, M., Zuriyati, Z., Utami, S., Rahmat, A., & Setiadi, S. (2023). Fostering intercultural understanding and environmental consciousness in maritime education. Bio Web of Conferences, 79, 06004. https://doi.org/DOI: 10.1051/bioconf/20237906004

Simmons, E., & McLean, G. (2020). Understanding the paradigm shift in maritime education. *Worldwide Hospitality and Tourism Themes*, *12*(1), 90–97. DOI: 10.1108/WHATT-10-2019-0062

Surono, S., & Jusuf, H. (2025). Future-proofing graduates: A dynamic micro-credential quality management system in higher education to ensure self-learning ability, innovation capacity, and career growth. *Edunity Kajian Ilmu Sosial Dan Pendidikan*, *4*(3), 143–152. DOI: 10.57096/edunity.v4i3.385

Umanets, V., Shakhina, I., & Rozputnia, B. (2024). Training future computer science teachers to use artificial intelligence technologies in the educational process. *Modern Information Technologies and Innovation Methodologies of Education in Professional Training Methodology Theory Experience Problems*, (72), 162–169. DOI: 10.31652/2412-1142-2024-72-162-170

Vujičić, S., Hasanspahić, N., Gundić, A., & Hrdalo, N. (2020). Assessment for ensuring adequately qualified instructors in maritime education and training institutions. *Athens Journal of Sciences*, *7*(2), 115–126. DOI: 10.30958/ajs.7-2-4

Wang, L., Jia, Y., He, J., Li, H., & Huang, Z. (2025). Developing green design competencies in engineering undergraduates. *Engineering Reports*, *7*(8), e70343. Advance online publication. DOI: 10.1002/eng2.70343

Chapter 8
Navigating Excellence:
Implementing Competency-Based Education Models in Maritime Training Institutions (METs)

Adrianta Sahar
http://orcid.org/0009-0003-9795-4395
Politeknik Ilmu Pelayaran Makassar, Indonesia

Sumiati Putri Natalia
Institut Agama Kristen Negeri Toraja, Indonesia

Wahyuniar Wahyuniar
Universitas Musamus, Indonesia

Amriani Amriani
Universitas Muhammadiyah Palopo, Indonesia

ABSTRACT

This chapter analyzes the strategic execution of Competency-Based Education (CBE) in marine Education and Training (MET) institutions, highlighting its conformity with international standards and the changing requirements of the marine sector. This study examines how competence mapping, modular curriculum reform, and performance-based assessment might improve cadet preparedness and professional flexibility, utilizing international frameworks such as STCW norms and quality assurance systems. The document emphasizes institutional obstacles, including pedagogical reluctance, resource limits, and policy limitations, while delineating capacity-building solutions that incorporate digital facilitation, simulation-based learning, and industry engagement. The text posits that maintaining success in MET necessitates data-driven continuous enhancement, international credential recognition, and the establishment of intelligent adaptive learning ecosystems that can cultivate internationally competitive and future-ready maritime professionals.

DOI: 10.4018/979-8-3373-6670-8.ch008

1. INTRODUCTION

1.1 The Global Shift Toward Competency-Based Education (Cbe)

The evolution of maritime education from knowledge-based systems to performance-driven models reflects a broader recognition of the necessity for competencies that directly align with industry demands. Traditionally, maritime training has relied heavily on theoretical instruction that emphasized knowledge acquisition without sufficient emphasis on practical skills applicable in real-world scenarios. This shift to competency-based education (CBE) reflects the growing imperative to ensure that graduates are not only knowledgeable but are also competent in performing tasks related to their professional roles within the maritime industry. The adoption of frameworks such as the International Convention on Standards of Training, Certification, and Watchkeeping for Seafarers (STCW) has played a pivotal role in this transformation, promoting a performance-oriented approach to training (Bayotas, 2024). The manifestation of CBE in maritime training suggests a reassessment of pedagogical strategies that prioritize the integration of hands-on experiences, thereby facilitating mastery in skills that are critical for operational success.

Moreover, international trends increasingly advocate for educational outcomes that highlight mastery and industry relevance. Educational frameworks are now being developed that ensure both the learning objectives and competency requirements are meticulously aligned with real-world practices in the maritime sector. For instance, studies emphasize the importance of aligning curricula with industry standards that reflect current technological advancements and emerging sectoral needs, such as those posed by artificial intelligence and sustainability initiatives (Riyanto et al., 2025). As maritime operations evolve with innovative technologies, educational institutions must reassess their training strategies to cultivate competencies that equip future maritime professionals with the requisite skills to thrive in a changing landscape (Riyanto et al., 2025).

Stakeholders within the maritime community, including employers, educators, and accrediting bodies, are focusing on employing competency-based metrics to evaluate student readiness. For example, feedback mechanisms from graduates highlight the effectiveness of integrated training programs, which blend classroom instruction with onboard training, in enhancing job performance and employability (Salvador, 2024). By emphasizing this dual approach, maritime education can provide a comprehensive framework that ensures students not only gain theoretical knowledge but also demonstrate the application of their competencies in real maritime environments.

Furthermore, the current shift towards CBE is indicative of a larger global movement towards skills-based education across various disciplines. Maritime institutions are beginning to adopt pedagogical reforms that not only address immediate industry needs but also prepare graduates with the adaptive skills necessary for lifelong learning and professional growth in a dynamically evolving industry (Ahmmed, 2021). This alignment with global educational standards, such as those advocated by the European Qualifications Framework (EQF), serves to enhance the overall quality of maritime education and ensures recognition of qualifications across borders (Abidin et al., 2021).

1.2 Defining Competency in Maritime Contexts

In maritime education, "competence" is a multidimensional construct encompassing a blend of technical, cognitive, and affective domains, each playing a critical role in shaping the capabilities of maritime professionals. The technical domain refers to the practical skills necessary for performing specific tasks, such as operating navigational equipment or managing onboard safety protocols (Ala et al., 2024). The cognitive domain encompasses the knowledge and comprehension required to make informed decisions, understand complex maritime regulations, and solve problems encountered at sea (Lee et al., 2021). Lastly, the affective domain pertains to the interpersonal skills and attitudes necessary for effective teamwork, communication, and ethical behavior in high-stakes maritime environments (Ala et al., 2024). This tripartite framework illustrates the necessity for maritime training programs to focus on developing a holistic competence that prepares individuals for the complexities of modern maritime operations.

Operationalization of competencies in maritime contexts is primarily guided by the International Convention on Standards of Training, Certification, and Watchkeeping for Seafarers (STCW), which sets forth the minimum competencies required for seafarers under international law Kristiyono et al., 2023). The STCW provides a robust framework that operationalizes the previously discussed multidimensional competencies by specifying not only the knowledge and skills required but also the methodologies by which these competencies should be demonstrated and assessed. These guidelines are supplemented by the International Maritime Organization (IMO), which promotes continuous alignment of training curricula with emerging operational standards and technological advancements (Kristiyono et al., 2023). The STCW covers diverse competencies relevant to different roles within maritime operations, ensuring that personnel are adequately prepared to navigate the challenges they may encounter while at sea.

For instance, under the revised Manila Amendments to the STCW, there is an increased emphasis on non-technical skills, such as leadership, teamwork, and crisis management, reflecting the acknowledgment that effective maritime operations hinge on both technical proficiency and soft skills (Hosny & Mohamed, 2024). Additionally, as the maritime industry adapts to advancements such as autonomous vessel operations, the competencies defined by the STCW and corresponding guidelines have begun to evolve to incorporate the complexities introduced by new technologies (Kim, 2024). This ongoing evolution underscores the need for maritime education institutions to continually reassess and update their programs to meet international standards and industry needs.

Moreover, research indicates that a significant majority of maritime cadets perceive their training programs as aligning well with STCW standards, showcasing the relevance of the competencies they develop during their education (Sihombing et al., 2024). This perception suggests that MET institutions are increasingly successful in bridging the gap between theoretical knowledge and practical application, thus preparing students to face the operational realities of the maritime workforce (Gundić et al., 2020). However, it is crucial for these institutions to remain vigilant and proactive in updating their curricula to reflect the rapid pace of change within the maritime sector and to address gaps in both training and assessment methodologies (Edar et al., 2024; Kristiyono et al., 2023).

1.3 The Rationale for Implementing CBE in METs

Implementing Competency-Based Education (CBE) in Maritime Education and Training (MET) is critical for addressing the existing skill gaps and employability challenges faced by graduates. The maritime industry is experiencing a transformative shift, driven by advancements in technology, changes in regulatory frameworks, and heightened safety standards. There is a notable disconnect between the skills possessed by newly graduated seafarers and the competencies required by employers, leading to significant concern regarding employability rates among maritime professionals (Belabyad et al., 2025). Moreover, incidents related to human error in maritime operations underscore the urgency of addressing these gaps; research has shown that enhancing fundamental competencies is essential for ensuring safety and operational efficiency (Hickethier & Yang, 2023). A CBE framework provides a structured approach to equipping students with both technical and soft skills necessary to navigate complex maritime environments, enabling them to meet and exceed industry expectations.

In addition to addressing skill gaps, aligning maritime education with the evolving demands of Industry 5.0 is of strategic importance. The maritime sector is increasingly influenced by technological advancements such as automation, artificial intelligence (AI), and the Internet of Things (IoT) (Bencio, 2025). By embracing CBE, MET institutions can refine their curricula to incorporate these innovations, preparing students for careers in a rapidly changing labor market where adaptability and continuous learning are paramount Riyanto et al., 2025). Implementing a curriculum that combines technical knowledge with competencies in digital literacy and critical thinking can significantly enhance the employability prospects of maritime graduates (Paramasivam et al., 2025).

Furthermore, the maritime industry's proximity to global trade and logistics necessitates a skill set that is not only comprehensive but also adaptable to various contexts. As the demand for Maritime Autonomous Surface Ships (MASS) increases, educational institutions must ensure that their programs integrate specific competencies related to the operation and management of these vessels (Belabyad et al., 2025; Riyanto et al., 2025). The existing STCW guidelines provide a baseline for competency requirements, indicating the need for continuous refinement of MET curricula to keep pace with technological developments (Kristiyono et al., 2023).

Additionally, evidence suggests that CBE frameworks support a more authentic learning experience through simulation-based training, effectively connecting theoretical knowledge with real-world situations, thereby enhancing readiness for the maritime workforce (Ala et al., 2024). Stakeholder feedback has indicated a positive correlation between CBE implementations and improved graduate performance in the field, further emphasizing the need for MET institutions to adopt this educational model (Riyanto et al., 2025).

2. FOUNDATIONAL FRAMEWORKS AND THEORETICAL UNDERPINNINGS

2.1 Principles and Pedagogical Foundations of CBE

Competency-Based Education (CBE) stands as a pivotal paradigm within the current educational landscape, particularly in the context of Maritime Education and Training (MET). Its principles, characterized by learner-centeredness, flexibility, and mastery learning, serve as foundational elements that distinguish it from traditional educational models.

The learner-centeredness feature of CBE places the student at the core of the educational experience. This approach encourages active engagement, critical thinking, and personal ownership of learning outcomes. In CBE, learners progress through their training at their own pace, allowing for varied paces and depth of understanding according to individual needs and learning styles Schio & Reis (2024). Such personalization fosters a richer, more inclusive educational environment, facilitating the development of robust competencies that align with industry requirements.

Flexibility is another key attribute of CBE, which allows educational institutions to adapt curricula to reflect real-world applications and emerging industry trends. This adaptability is particularly significant in the maritime sector as it experiences rapid technological changes, such as the integration of automation and digital navigation tools (Toit, 2022). Such flexibility ensures that prospective seafarers acquire the most relevant skills and knowledge in a constantly evolving industry, thus enhancing their employability.

Mastery learning, the third key feature, revolves around the principle of ensuring that students achieve a thorough understanding of a subject before moving forward. This contrasts sharply with traditional educational practices, where time constraints often dictate learning outcomes rather than the mastery of competencies (Kayyali, 2024). In CBE, the emphasis on mastery means that a student must demonstrate the required skills and knowledge to a predetermined standard, often measured through assessments that reflect practical, real-life scenarios (Krakhecke et al., 2025). This principle not only increases competency but also builds confidence in learners, ensuring they are better prepared for the demands of the maritime workforce.

In comparison, traditional time-based instructional models often rely on predetermined curricula that emphasize the completion of coursework over actual competency. In these models, expectations are set based on time spent in a classroom rather than the demonstration of skills and knowledge (Qizi, 2024). This can lead to graduates who may have completed the program but lack the sufficient practical skills necessary for the profession. For example, a maritime cadet might pass their theoretical examinations yet still struggle with applying that knowledge during practical training or in real-world maritime operations.

Furthermore, while traditional models often prioritize uniformity in educational delivery, they can miss addressing the diverse learning needs and paces of individual students. Such a lack of engagement can result in disengagement and lower motivation levels among learners, ultimately affecting their performance and readiness for industry demands.

2.2 International Policy and Standardization Frameworks

In the realm of maritime education, the adoption and implementation of international policies and standardization frameworks are crucial for ensuring the quality and relevance of training programs. Key frameworks, including the International Maritime Organization's Standards of Training, Certification, and Watchkeeping (IMO-STCW) and various regional accreditation systems such as those found in ASEAN and the European Union, provide a comprehensive foundation for enhancing educational practices in maritime training institutions.

The IMO-STCW laid the groundwork for maritime training standards globally by setting minimum competencies for seafarers to ensure safety and efficiency at sea. By establishing benchmarks for knowledge, skills, and attitudes, the STCW framework facilitates harmonization of maritime training across different countries, thereby fostering a more competent global maritime workforce. The emphasis on aligning training with international standards helps institutions provide graduates who are adequately prepared to meet the operational demands of the maritime industry, as well as to address the increasing complexities associated with contemporary maritime operations.

In addition to the STCW, ISO 9001 establishes principles for quality management systems, advocating for continuous improvement and customer satisfaction. This standard enhances the effectiveness and efficiency of maritime education and training (MET) programs by fostering a culture of systematic evaluation and enhancement of educational practices. Institutions that adopt ISO 9001 can enhance their operational and educational workflows, ensuring that they meet both industry and learner expectations. Integrating ISO guidelines with the STCW framework creates an environment conducive to high-quality educational delivery, ultimately preparing cadets for the challenges they will face in the maritime sector.

Regional accreditation systems, such as those within ASEAN and the EU, further contribute to the standardization of maritime education. In the ASEAN region, efforts are underway to establish a unified higher education framework that recognizes and compares qualifications across member countries. This system enhances mobility and employability for graduates across Southeast Asia, ensuring that maritime programs adhere to a set of common standards. Similarly, the European Union's Bologna Process aims to create a European Higher Education Area by promoting comparability, compatibility, and quality assurance across member states. This regional integration supports the exchange of best practices and mutual recognition of qualifications, greatly benefiting maritime training institutions.

Benchmarking best practices from world-leading maritime academies serves as an essential tool for continual improvement. Institutions like the United States Merchant Marine Academy and the World Maritime University exemplify best practices in blending academic rigor with practical training. These academies often engage in international collaborations, facilitating knowledge exchange and the sharing of innovative educational methodologies. By studying and adopting the successful strategies of these institutions, MET programs can enhance their curricula, teaching methods, and assessment processes.

2.3 Competency Mapping and Learning Outcome Design

Effective competency mapping and the design of measurable learning outcomes are paramount in maritime education to ensure that training aligns with industry standards and prepares future professionals for their roles. The objective of these processes is to systematically translate occupational standards into specific, assessable learning outcomes that reflect the skills and knowledge needed in the maritime field.

Translating occupational standards into measurable learning outcomes involves a rigorous analysis of the competencies required in various maritime roles. This process begins with identifying the essential tasks outlined by international standards, such as those established by the International Maritime Organization (IMO) and the Standards of Training, Certification, and Watchkeeping for Seafarers (STCW) (Sihombing et al., 2024). According to these guidelines, each competency must be clearly defined and relevant to the operational context in which students will eventually work. For instance, outcomes might include not only theoretical knowledge but demonstrable skills in navigation, safety protocol management, and crisis response, which can be measured through practical assessments and direct observations (Ramdev & Bhandari, 2025). By focusing on learning outcomes that are specific, observable, and tied to real-world applications, educators can ensure that students develop the requisite competencies for successful careers in the industry.

A crucial methodology for achieving these measurable outcomes is the DACUM (Developing A Curriculum) approach. DACUM involves a structured workshop setting where panels of experts from the maritime industry collaboratively define the key tasks and competencies associated with a particular occupation. This method ensures that curriculum development is rooted in current industry demands and best practices (Yu et al., 2025). Task analysis within DACUM helps educators break down the competencies into individual elements that can be taught and assessed, conveniently linking theoretical knowledge with practical skills. By employing this approach, institutions can ensure that the curricula are contemporary and relevant, directly addressing the evolving landscape of the maritime workforce.

The integration of DACUM with competency mapping facilitates the creation of a transparent framework that informs instructors and students alike about the skills needed for various maritime careers. As emerging technologies and practices rescale the skills required in the maritime sector, continuous updates to the competency maps become essential. Recent studies illustrate how maritime educational programs that employ

DACUM not only align their learning outcomes with international standards but also enhance students' preparedness for employment by reflecting real-time industry needs (Sihombing et al., 2024; Yu et al., 2025).

Furthermore, learning outcomes based on competency mapping must also consider the feedback mechanisms necessary for continuous improvement. Incorporating programmatic assessments, which include multiple low-stakes evaluations over time, helps gauge student progress while informing instructional adjustments. This long-term tracking aligns with best practices in Competency-Based Education (CBE), ensuring that students meet the developed competencies effectively.

3. INSTITUTIONAL STRATEGIES FOR EFFECTIVE IMPLEMENTATION

3.1 Curriculum Redesign and Modularization

The effective implementation of Competency-Based Education (CBE) in Maritime Education and Training (MET) necessitates a strategic approach to curriculum redesign and modularization. This process involves closely integrating performance criteria, behavioral indicators, and robust assessment rubrics, alongside the design of modular, micro-credentialed learning pathways that foster flexible certification.

Integrating performance criteria and behavioral indicators into the curriculum design is critical for aligning educational outcomes with industry standards. Performance criteria delineate specific tasks and competencies students must achieve, while behavioral indicators provide actionable benchmarks for assessing students' application of knowledge and skills in real-world scenarios (Sijabat et al., 2024). In maritime training, competencies related to ship navigation or emergency response can be clearly defined and assessed through practical simulations. Document analysis, including course syllabi and instructional materials, can reveal how effectively these elements are currently integrated and highlight areas for improvement (Sijabat et al., 2024). Utilizing a comprehensive framework that incorporates these performance and behavioral standards ensures that students develop both the theoretical understanding and practical skills necessary for successful employment in the maritime industry.

Assessment rubrics serve as essential tools in this context by providing clear, objective criteria that facilitate the evaluation of student performance (Lim et al., 2023). These rubrics guide instructors in assessing students' competencies and clarify expectations for learners, enhancing their understanding of what is required for successful completion. By emphasizing formative assessments throughout the learning process, educators can track progress more effectively and adjust teaching strategies, thereby fostering an environment conducive to mastery learning (Nemakhavhani, 2024).

In parallel to integrating performance metrics, the design of modular, micro-credentialed learning pathways plays a crucial role in enhancing flexibility and accessibility in maritime training. Modularization allows students to progress through the curriculum at their own pace, earning micro-credentials for individual competencies as they master them. This approach accommodates diverse learning styles and schedules and aligns with the current trend towards lifelong learning within the maritime sector (Anand & Lall, 2022).

Micro-credentialing offers various advantages, such as allowing students to demonstrate their qualifications for specific skills or tasks tangibly, enhancing their employability prospects. For instance, a student may accumulate micro-credentials in areas such as safety management or advanced navigation before completing a full program, enabling them to enter the workforce sooner or advance more rapidly.

This modular approach also benefits employers, who gain a clearer understanding of potential employees' qualifications based on the competencies they have mastered through short, targeted learning experiences.

3.2 Faculty Capacity Building and Professional Development

The successful implementation of Competency-Based Education (CBE) in Maritime Education and Training (MET) institutions is heavily reliant on the capacity and professional development of faculty members. As the maritime industry rapidly evolves with the integration of new technologies and pedagogical methods, it is essential to equip educators with the necessary skills and knowledge to facilitate effective learning experiences. This can be achieved through comprehensive training in competency-based pedagogy and digital facilitation, as well as the establishment of strong communities of practice and mentoring systems among instructors.

Training maritime educators in competency-based pedagogy is fundamental to fostering a learner-centered environment. Competency-based approaches emphasize clear articulation of expected outcomes, active learning, and the experiential application of skills (Harahap et al., 2025). This educational philosophy invites instructors to shift from traditional teaching methods focused on content delivery to those that facilitate student engagement and practical application of knowledge. Recent research highlights that maritime educators must familiarize themselves with innovative teaching strategies, such as computer-based training (CBT) and flipped classroom models, to enhance learning outcomes and adapt to the digital landscape (Lapesigue, 2024; Ray & Guha, 2025). Professional development programs tailored to these pedagogical methods should include workshops, peer-training sessions, and access to online resources, ensuring educators remain knowledgeable about current best practices.

Furthermore, as digital technology continues to transform the educational landscape, maritime instructors must also develop strong skills in digital facilitation. Enhancing digital literacy among faculty aligns teaching strategies with contemporary pedagogical practices and ensures that they are capable of effectively integrating technology into their classrooms (Nyairo et al., 2025). Research advocates that targeted faculty training sessions on emerging technologies and best practices will improve teaching methodologies and enhance student engagement and learning satisfaction (Lapesigue, 2024). Offering continuous learning opportunities, such as online courses or webinars, will help instructors build confidence in their ability to use digital tools effectively.

Building communities of practice (CoP) among faculty members is another strategic approach to enhancing professional development in MET institutions. Communities of practice foster collaborative learning environments, where instructors can share experiences, discuss challenges, and develop solutions collectively (Rivera et al., 2025). Coordinating regular meetings, professional learning communities, and collaborative project-based initiatives can promote a culture of continuous improvement and peer support. Within these CoP, experienced educators can serve as mentors for less experienced instructors, providing guidance and sharing insights on effective practices in competency-based education.

Mentoring systems further enrich faculty development by pairing experienced instructors with newcomers. Such mentorship programs can facilitate knowledge transfer and skill building while promoting a cohesive educational approach (Saifudin et al., 2025). These systems should focus not only on pedagogical practices but also on navigating the evolving maritime industry and its associated competencies. Reports indicate that structured mentorship helps new instructors adapt more quickly to their roles and contributes to higher retention rates (Cahyadi et al., 2024).

3.3 Industry Partnerships and Experiential Learning Integration

Incorporating industry partnerships and experiential learning into Maritime Education and Training (MET) is vital for aligning educational outcomes with real-world demands. These partnerships enhance curriculum relevance and provide students with practical experiences that are crucial for effective learning. By integrating industry perspectives into educational frameworks, MET institutions can foster a robust learning environment that prepares graduates to meet the evolving demands of the maritime sector.

One of the primary benefits of establishing partnerships with industry stakeholders is the integration of experiential learning opportunities into the curriculum. Experiential learning, as defined by Kolb (Waddell, 2021). This pedagogical approach facilitates active engagement, enabling students to apply theoretical knowledge in practical settings, which has been shown to enhance understanding and retention of information (Ho et al., 2022). Through collaborations with maritime industry partners, educational institutions can provide students with hands-on experiences that closely simulate real-world situations, such as voyages, ship operations, and port management (Barreto & Silveira, 2024). For example, internship programs or work-integrated learning placements allow students to immerse themselves in an industry environment, enabling them to gain valuable skills and insights directly relevant to their future careers.

Moreover, experiential learning opportunities enhance student employability by developing the soft skills required in professional settings, such as teamwork, communication, and problem-solving abilities (Dipitso, 2021). Engaging with industry peers during internships and training programs allows students to cultivate a professional network, enhancing their prospects upon graduation. MET curricula must incorporate structured feedback mechanisms from industry partners to ensure that the skills taught remain aligned with the current and anticipated needs of the maritime labor market (Speier-Pero & Schoenherr, 2020). This feedback loop between academia and industry enriches the educational experience, ensuring that training is dynamically responsive to emerging trends in the maritime sector.

The establishment of communities of practice (CoP) among industry partners and educators further enriches the learning environment. These communities enable knowledge sharing, collaboration, and mentorship, leading to the continuous improvement of both teaching practices and industry standards (Iskandarova & Ford, 2024). For instance, a structured CoP can facilitate workshops, seminars, and joint research initiatives that engage both educators and industry professionals in discussions about best practices, pedagogical strategies, and technological advancements in the field (Nawagi & Raman, 2023). This collaborative approach can also inform curriculum updates and innovations, ensuring students are equipped with cutting-edge skills that meet the modern demands of the maritime job market (Kang et al., 2022).

In addition, partnerships should focus on designing immersive, project-based learning experiences that simulate real-life scenarios within the maritime industry. These projects can involve problem-solving tasks that require students to collaborate with industry practitioners, fostering an environment of authentic learning (Ajayi & Udeh, 2024). By engaging in multidisciplinary projects that address actual challenges faced by maritime organizations, students can develop critical analytical and innovative skills that are directly applicable in the workplace. Such initiatives not only benefit the students but also provide value to industry partners, who can derive insights or solutions from the academic projects.

Another important aspect of industry partnerships is the incorporation of mentorship programs where professionals guide students throughout their educational journey. This mentoring can offer students tailored career advice, insights into industry trends, and practical guidance on navigating career paths within the maritime sector (O'Connor et al., 2023). Mentorship builds strong ties between the academic and professional realms, further bridging the gap between theory and practice.

The integration of industry partnerships with experiential learning represents a transformative approach to maritime education. As highlighted in various studies, these collaborations provide meaningful learning experiences that foster student engagement and enhance overall competency (Napier & Wada, 2024; Li et al., 2023). Moreover, they ensure that educational programs are reflective of, and responsive to, industry needs, thus preparing students not only to enter the workforce but also to thrive within it.

4. CHALLENGES, QUALITY ASSURANCE, AND CONTINUOUS IMPROVEMENT

4.1 Institutional Barriers and Change Management

The implementation of Competency-Based Education (CBE) within Maritime Education and Training (MET) institutions is accompanied by several significant institutional barriers and challenges related to change management. These barriers primarily manifest as resistance to pedagogical innovation, resource constraints, and policy rigidity, all of which can impede the effective transformation of education practices within maritime training programs.

Resistance to pedagogical innovation is common in educational institutions, particularly in traditional disciplines such as maritime training, where established practices have been in place for decades. Faculty members may cling to familiar methods of teaching, valuing the time-honored approaches over newer pedagogical innovations. This inertia stems from fears of obsolescence, inadequate training in CBE methodologies, and concerns about fundamentally shifting their instructional strategies. Such resistance can delay the adoption of innovative teaching practices that integrate experiential learning opportunities, project-based work, and real-world problem-solving as core components of the curriculum. Furthermore, this reluctance can contribute to underinvestment in professional development programs tailored to introduce faculty to new pedagogical frameworks (Rizqi & Syafika, 2024).

Resource constraints significantly hinder the effective implementation of CBE in MET. Many institutions face financial challenges that limit their ability to invest in the necessary training, technology, or infrastructure required for a successful transition to competency-based frameworks. These constraints can affect the ability to develop new curricula, create effective assessment instruments, and integrate cutting-edge technology into teaching and learning processes. Insufficient resources can also lead to inadequate support for ongoing professional development and collaboration opportunities, thereby restricting faculty engagement in innovative teaching and assessment practices (Khasanah et al., 2025). Addressing these resource challenges requires commitment from institutional leadership to prioritize funding and allocate resources effectively.

Policy rigidity is another critical barrier to implementing CBE in maritime programs. Existing policies may be inflexible or outdated, insufficiently accommodating the dynamic nature of the maritime industry and its workforce demands. Regulatory frameworks governing maritime education may impose stringent compliance requirements that prioritize traditional time-based learning outcomes over mastery and competency metrics (Fitrihana & Nurdiyanto, 2023). Consequently, institutions find themselves constrained by bureaucratic processes that limit their capacity for timely curriculum adjustments and innovative program development.

Overcoming these institutional barriers necessitates strong leadership and strategic planning to navigate the transformation towards CBE effectively. Leaders must play an essential role in articulating a clear vision for change, fostering a culture of innovation, and actively supporting professional development initiatives. By encouraging open dialogue among faculty, administrators, and industry stakeholders, leadership can facilitate collaborative decision-making that addresses resistance and promotes buy-in from all stakeholders (Yeri & Baylon, 2025).

Strategic planning should include the establishment of clear objectives and metrics for transition, harnessing stakeholder input to design initiatives that align with both institutional goals and industry needs. To support a successful shift to CBE, institutions should initiate comprehensive training programs for faculty that focus on pedagogical innovations and effective change management practices. Leadership also must cultivate an environment that encourages risk-taking and experimentation in teaching methodologies, addressing potential challenges with resilience and adaptability.

4.2 Assessment and Evaluation of Competence

Effective assessment and evaluation of competence in Maritime Education and Training (MET) are essential for ensuring that graduates are adequately equipped for the demands of the maritime industry. To achieve this, institutions must employ diverse techniques, such as performance-based assessment, rubrics, evidence portfolios, simulations, peer reviews, and reflective journals. Each of these methods contributes to a holistic evaluation of student competence.

Performance-based assessment is a vital strategy that centers on students demonstrating their abilities through practical tasks rather than traditional examinations. In the maritime context, performance assessments can include simulations of real-world maritime scenarios, where students must apply their knowledge and skills in navigation, safety management, or ship operations. This method allows instructors to observe the application of theoretical learning in action and aligns closely with the competencies outlined in international frameworks like the STCW (Standards of Training, Certification and Watchkeeping for Seafarers) (Curto-Reverte et al., 2025). Clearly defined rubrics accompany these assessments, providing objective criteria for evaluation that specify expectations for student performance (Abeysiriwardhane, 2020). Rubrics help educators assess specific aspects of competence, including technical skills, teamwork, problem-solving, and communication, ensuring comprehensive feedback that facilitates student growth.

Furthermore, evidence portfolios serve as a systematic way for students to document and showcase their learning journey. These portfolios can include a variety of artifacts, such as completed assignments, project reports, performance evaluations from internships or training programs, and reflective pieces that demonstrate critical thinking and growth. By compiling a range of evidence, students create a comprehensive picture of their competencies, making it easier for potential employers and educators to assess their readiness for the maritime profession. Portfolios not only encourage students to take ownership of their learning but also facilitate a continuous reflection process that fosters self-assessment and personal development (Mqukuse & Mvunge, 2025).

In addition to traditional performance assessments and portfolios, incorporating simulations into the assessment process provides an engaging and insightful avenue to evaluate student competence. Simulations can range from computer-based navigation exercises to full-scale ship operation scenarios, enabling learners to experience the complexities and dynamics of maritime operations in a controlled environment. These experiential assessments promote active learning and require students to think critically, make decisions, and adapt under pressure. Importantly, simulations emphasize the importance of human factors in maritime safety, which are critical for cultivating highly competent professionals (Hosny & Mohamed, 2024).

Peer review processes can further enhance the evaluation of students' competencies. By engaging in peer evaluations, students can critically assess each other's performance, fostering collaborative learning environments where constructive feedback is instrumental. This approach not only develops critical observation and analytical skills but also encourages accountability and improvement among students (Simanjuntak et al., 2025). Furthermore, integrating reflective journals into the assessment framework allows students to articulate their thoughts on learning experiences, helping them recognize their strengths and areas for growth (VanLeeuwen et al., 2020). Reflective practice encourages self-awareness, which is essential for personal and professional development in the maritime field.

4.3 Quality Assurance and Accreditation Mechanisms

Quality assurance and accreditation mechanisms play a crucial role in the effective implementation of Competency-Based Education (CBE) within Maritime Education and Training (MET). These mechanisms ensure the validity and reliability of educational programs by employing internal and external audits for competence validation, alongside continuous improvement processes aligned with established standards such as ISO and IMO.

Internal and external audits serve as a fundamental strategy for validating competence and maintaining educational quality. Internal audits are conducted within institutions to evaluate the effectiveness of their quality assurance processes. These audits typically assess curricula, teaching methodologies, and student outcomes against set performance criteria and standards (Ahmmed, 2021). By systematically reviewing these elements, institutions can identify strengths and weaknesses, thereby facilitating necessary improvements to ensure that learners achieve the competences expected by the industry.

External audits are performed by independent accrediting bodies that assess educational programs against national and international standards, such as those established by the International Maritime Organization (IMO). These organizations evaluate the effectiveness of MET programs based on criteria that reflect current industry needs and trends (Abidin et al., 2021). The incorporation of such audits ensures transparency and accountability in educational practices, thereby enhancing stakeholder confidence in the quality of maritime training institutions. Continuous engagement with accrediting bodies also helps institutions stay abreast of best practices and innovations within the maritime field, ensuring curricula remain relevant and effective.

Moreover, implementing a continuous improvement loop is vital for fostering educational excellence. Aligning these improvement processes with ISO (International Organization for Standardization) standards and IMO guidelines can significantly enhance the quality of maritime education (A. et al., 2025). The ISO framework emphasizes the importance of systematic evaluation and ongoing refinements, promoting a cycle where feedback from audits informs policy adjustments, curricular updates, and teaching enhancements. This approach encourages institutions to set measurable objectives, implement changes, assess outcomes, and repeat the cycle to reinforce quality and relevance over time.

Responding to insights gained through audits enables MET institutions to build a culture of quality that permeates every aspect of their operations. Establishing mechanisms for ongoing faculty development, student feedback, and stakeholder engagement ensures that institutions foster an environment committed to continuous learning and improvement (Abidin et al., 2021). As institutional leaders prioritize accountability, they cultivate a climate where quality assurance becomes intrinsic to educational practices, empowering faculty and students alike to strive for excellence.

5. FUTURE DIRECTIONS AND GLOBAL IMPLICATIONS

5.1 Toward Smart and Adaptive Maritime Learning Ecosystems

The future of Maritime Education and Training (MET) is increasingly characterized by the integration of smart and adaptive learning ecosystems, enabled by advancements in artificial intelligence (AI), analytics, and immersive technologies. These innovations promise to personalize learning experiences, optimize learner competence trajectories, and fundamentally transform educational practices within the maritime sector.

Integrating AI and analytics into MET curricula allows for personalized learning experiences tailored to individual student needs and capabilities. AI-based adaptive learning systems can analyze student performance in real-time, providing feedback and adjusting instructional content based on learners' progress (Kamalov et al., 2023). Such systems facilitate the creation of customized educational pathways, allowing students to engage with materials and activities that best suit their learning styles and paces. For instance, AI can recommend supplementary resources for students who struggle with specific competencies, thereby supporting mastery at an individualized level (Água et al., 2020). Furthermore, immersive technologies, such as virtual reality (VR), enhance these personalized experiences by simulating real-world maritime environments where learners can practice skills in a safe, controlled setting (Mughal et al., 2025). As highlighted in the literature, VR can significantly improve skill acquisition, providing interactive learning experiences that foster not only knowledge retention but also practical application (Mughal et al., 2025).

In addition to AI and immersive technologies, the utilization of learning analytics systems plays a critical role in creating adaptive maritime learning ecosystems. Learning analytics involves the collection, analysis, and interpretation of data generated by students during their learning processes. This data can provide insights into student engagement, learning outcomes, and areas where learners may require additional support, thus informing instructional strategies (Ifenthaler & Yau, 2020). By harnessing this information, educators and program managers can make data-informed decisions to optimize learner competence trajectories, ensuring that students progress effectively through the curriculum and meet the competencies set forth by industry standards (Lee et al., 2023). This approach fosters a proactive learning environment in which educational institutions can anticipate and address challenges before they impact student success.

Moreover, continuous improvement loops that leverage data from learning analytics contribute to the ongoing refinement of educational programs. This iterative process enables MET institutions to regularly assess the effectiveness of their training methodologies and ensure responsiveness to the changing demands of the maritime industry (Mulenga & Shilongo, 2024). By integrating feedback mechanisms into the learning ecosystem, institutions can adapt their curricula and pedagogical practices to meet emerging trends and expectations within the maritime sector.

5.2 Global Collaboration and Mutual Recognition of Competence

As the maritime industry continues to evolve in a globalized environment, fostering cross-border credentialing and enhancing the mutual recognition of competence among maritime professionals has become imperative. These initiatives not only facilitate workforce mobility but also contribute to the establishment of regional frameworks that promote shared excellence in maritime education and training.

Cross-border credentialing is crucial in enabling maritime workforce mobility, allowing professionals to demonstrate their qualifications and competencies across different jurisdictions. With varying regulations and requirements governing maritime operations in different countries, a standardized and transparent credentialing system can simplify the transition for professionals seeking employment or training opportunities abroad (Jain, 2025). The growing need for effective credential verification has led to increasing interest in innovative solutions, such as blockchain technology, which can ensure secure and reliable verification of qualifications (Jain, 2025). By establishing universally recognized credentialing systems, educational institutions and industry stakeholders can facilitate smoother transitions for maritime professionals, thereby meeting the challenges posed by an increasingly interconnected world.

Mutual recognition of competence is essential to ensure that maritime professionals possess the necessary qualifications regardless of their country of origin. This recognition is particularly important in the context of international conventions, such as the STCW (Standards of Training, Certification, and Watchkeeping for Seafarers), which establishes globally applicable standards for training, certification, and watchkeeping (Setiawan, 2024). By aligning national policies with international standards, countries can streamline credential recognition processes and enhance the mobility of their maritime workforce across borders. This alignment promotes not only the skills development of individual professionals but also ensures that countries can more easily meet their maritime industry demands as they adopt best practices from other jurisdictions (Guricci & Seniwati, 2024).

Regional cooperation is another critical component in fostering shared maritime excellence frameworks. Initiatives like ASEAN's collaboration on maritime education and training highlight the importance of establishing a cohesive approach to competency standards across Southeast Asia (Agastia, 2021). By working together, member states can share best practices, resources, and experiences, ultimately leading to the development of comprehensive frameworks that support the training and certification of maritime professionals. Such regional collaborations can address common challenges faced by member nations, such as piracy, illegal fishing, and environmental protection, and create synergies that enhance maritime security and sustainability throughout the region (Daihani, 2025).

Moreover, coordinating regional efforts in capacity building and knowledge transfer can accelerate the progression toward excellence in maritime education. For instance, sharing curricular elements, training resources, and faculty development opportunities among partner institutions can significantly improve educational outcomes and professional readiness. Cooperative research initiatives can further promote innovation within the maritime sector, combining expertise to address shared challenges and leverage technological advancements effectively (Yu & Wang, 2025; Dallara & Grasso, 2022).

CONCLUSION

Sustaining a culture of excellence within Maritime Education and Training (MET) institutions requires a comprehensive synthesis of key strategies for the effective adoption of Competency-Based Education

(CBE). By integrating innovative practices with adaptive learning environments, MET institutions can ensure that they meet the current demands of the maritime industry while preparing their graduates for future challenges.

One essential strategy for sustaining excellence involves fostering a robust framework for continuous professional development among faculty members. This includes providing training in new pedagogical approaches, such as the integration of technology and immersive learning experiences, which are crucial in a rapidly evolving educational landscape (Sihombing et al., 2024). Encouraging educators to embrace innovative teaching methods and maintain relevant qualifications ensures high-quality instruction that responds to industry needs.

Moreover, establishing strong industry partnerships is critical in creating opportunities for practical learning experiences and facilitating mutual recognition of competencies across borders. Collaborative initiatives with industry stakeholders enhance curriculum relevance and provide students with internships and real-world training opportunities. These partnerships bridge theoretical learning and practical application, fostering graduates who are workforce-ready and adaptable to the maritime industry's dynamic demands (Ahmmed, 2021). Student participation in continuous feedback loops with industry partners can drive curriculum improvements, keeping educational offerings aligned with industry best practices.

The integration of advanced technologies such as AI and analytics presents a significant opportunity for MET institutions to personalize learning pathways. Utilizing data-informed decision-making to track learner progress and optimize training outcomes is essential for addressing learner disparities and enhancing overall competence trajectories (Selvakumar et al., 2024; Díaz-Parra et al., 2025). As educational approaches shift toward smart, adaptive learning environments, MET institutions must prioritize flexibility and responsiveness in their methodologies. By leveraging these technologies, institutions can create more interactive and engaging educational experiences that foster a deeper understanding of maritime competencies (Okunade, 2024).

Furthermore, embracing a culture of quality assurance through ongoing evaluations and accredited frameworks is vital for maintaining high standards within MET programs. Establishing robust internal and external review processes allows institutions to continually assess the effectiveness of their instructional approaches. Aligning these efforts with international standards, such as those established by the International Maritime Organization (IMO) and the Standards of Training, Certification, and Watchkeeping for Seafarers (STCW), enhances institutional credibility and ensures that graduates are equipped with the necessary skills to excel in the maritime workforce (Adel, 2024).

Looking forward, the vision for resilient and future-ready maritime education institutions hinges on adaptability, innovation, and collaboration. By focusing on cultivating a forward-thinking culture that embraces change and prioritizes student competency, MET institutions can become leaders in maritime education. Such institutions will produce highly qualified maritime professionals capable of addressing existing challenges while also contributing to the advancement of the maritime sector on a global scale (Delgado et al., 2023; Rubi & Sharma, 2024).

In conclusion, sustaining a culture of excellence in MET involves synthesizing key strategies, investing in continuous improvement, leveraging technology, and fostering collaborative industry partnerships. As maritime education evolves, embracing these principles will ensure that institutions remain resilient and responsive, effectively preparing graduates for a complex and multifaceted maritime industry.

REFERENCES

A., A., K, A., & W, O. (2025). Effects of audit service quality on internal auditors' performance in tertiary institutions in oyo state. IJMSBAR. DOI: 10.70382/caijmsbar.v8i7.021

Abeysiriwardhane, A. (2020). Learning and learning-to-learn by doing: An experiential learning approach for integrating human factors into maritime design education. *Maritime Technology and Research, 3*(1). Advance online publication. DOI: 10.33175/mtr.2021.241912

Abidin, S., Bahari, S., Ibrahim, A., Ghazali, A., Ahmad, M., Mujir, M., & Amin, M. (2021). Analysing the malaysian higher education training offer for furniture design and woodworking industry 4.0 as an input towards joint curriculum validation protocol. *Asia Pacific Journal of Educators and Education, 36*(1), 1–24. DOI: 10.21315/apjee2021.36.1.1

Adel, A. (2024). The convergence of intelligent tutoring, robotics, and iot in smart education for the transition from industry 4.0 to 5.0. *Smart Cities, 7*(1), 325–369. DOI: 10.3390/smartcities7010014

Agastia, I. (2021). Maritime security cooperation within the asean institutional framework: A gradual shift towards practical cooperation. [Journal of Asean Studies]. *Jas, 9*(1). Advance online publication. DOI: 10.21512/jas.v9i1.6919

Água, P., Frias, A., Carrasqueira, M., & Daniel, J. (2020). Future of maritime education and training. *Pomorstvo, 34*(2), 345–353. DOI: 10.31217/p.34.2.15

Ahmmed, R. (2021). A framework for maritime english language planning in bangladeshi maritime education and training institutes. *SN Social Sciences, 1*(7), 168. Advance online publication. DOI: 10.1007/s43545-021-00188-5

Ajayi, F., & Udeh, C. (2024). Review of workforce upskilling initiatives for emerging technologies in it. *International Journal of Management & Entrepreneurship Research, 6*(4), 1119–1137. DOI: 10.51594/ijmer.v6i4.1003

Ala, A., Hamidi, N., Yoniessa, S., Masito, F., & Muis, M. (2024). Simulation-based learning in maritime training: Enhancing competency and preparedness. *Meteor Stip Marunda, 17*(1), 95–102. DOI: 10.36101/msm.v17i1.361

Anand, K. and Lall, M. (2022). Delhi's education revolution.. DOI: 10.14324/111.9781800081383

Barreto, N. and Silveira, C. (2024). Optimal strategies for implementing multidisciplinary and trans disciplinary education in management programs: insights from goan colleges. International Journal of Research -Granthaalayah, 12(9). DOI: 10.29121/granthaalayah.v12.i9.2024.5794

Bayotas, M. (2024). Shifting from global maritime professional to global maritime citizen.. DOI: 10.5821/mt.13183

Belabyad, M., Kontovas, C., Pyne, R., Shi, W., Li, N., Szwed, P., & Chang, C. (2025). *The human element in autonomous shipping: a study on skills and competency requirements*. Wmu Journal of Maritime Affairs., DOI: 10.1007/s13437-025-00366-9

Bencio, J. (2025). Awareness of deck faculty on current maritime technology and industry trends and perceived appropriateness of the bachelor of science in marine transportation curriculum: A basis for curriculum enhancement. *Apcore Online Journal, 1*(1), 191–199. DOI: 10.65232/pdy6j953

Cahyadi, T., Ahmad, A., & Barasa, L. (2024). Integrating sustainability and digital advancements in maritime law education: Enhancing cadet preparedness. *IJLS, 1*(4), 217–228. DOI: 10.62951/ijls.v1i4.196

Curto-Reverte, A., Carré, M., Rius, H., & Martí, C. (2025). The role of work-integrated learning in the european higher education area: A systematic review. *Review of Education, 13*(3), e70114. Advance online publication. DOI: 10.1002/rev3.70114

Daihani, D. (2025). Geo-maritime resilience in the indo-pacific: Strategic insights from the jakarta geopolitical forum viii/2024. *JGF, 8*(1), 109–115. DOI: 10.55960/jgf.v8i1.281

Dallara, A. and Grasso, D. (2022). Analysis of new sustainable mobility solutions for maritime passengers transport.. DOI: 10.30687/978-88-6969-617-6/002

Delgado, S., Panganiban, N., & Robles, K. (2023). The role of ai-powered analytics in building a human-centered smart campus. ijss, 1(3), 135-143. DOI: 10.63876/ijss.v1i3.81

Díaz-Parra, O., Ruíz-Vanoye, J., Marroquín-Gutiérrez, F., Salgado-Ramírez, J., Ramos-Fernández, J., Xicoténcatl-Pérez, J., … & Trejo-Macotela, F. (2025). Fundamentals of smart education., 1-18. DOI: 10.4018/979-8-3693-7793-2.ch001

Dipitso, P. (2021). Work-integrated learning for mining engineering training and the employability nexus in traditional research universities. Journal of Comparative & International Higher Education, 12(6S1). DOI: 10.32674/jcihe.v12i6S1.2192

Edar, A., Tongco, A., Arizalita, B., Baldomar, L., Leon, N., Manlimos, J., & Parami, M. (2024). Teaching strategies in simulator-based courses: Basis for faculty development program. *Jpair Institutional Research, 22*(1), 112–129. DOI: 10.7719/irj.v22i1.885

Fitrihana, N., & Nurdiyanto, H. (2023). Improving student competence through informatics-based vocational education. *International Journal of Artificial Intelligence Research, 7*(2), 226. DOI: 10.29099/ijair.v7i2.1180

Gundić, A., Vujčić, S., Maglić, L., & Ivanišević, D. (2020). Methods for demonstrating a competence and criteria for evaluating a competence in stcw convention. *Pomorstvo, 34*(2), 245–251. DOI: 10.31217/p.34.2.5

Guricci, M. and Seniwati, S. (2024). Strategi keamanan maritim di asia tenggara: kerjasama diplomasi maritim di asean. konsensus, 1(6), 130-139. DOI: 10.62383/konsensus.v1i6.474

Harahap, D., Sumarsih, S., & Husein, R. (2025). Computer-based training (cbt) as interactive learning media for english maritime course in maritime education and training (met). *Forum for Linguistic Studies, 7*(9). Advance online publication. DOI: 10.30564/fls.v7i9.10204

Hickethier, A., & Yang, C. (2023). An analysis of causes related to human factors in maritime accidents. *International Journal of Maritime Engineering, 165*(A2), 125–134. DOI: 10.5750/ijme.v165iA2.1193

Ho, S., Hsu, Y., Lai, C., Chen, F., & Yang, M. (2022). Applying game-based experiential learning to comprehensive sustainable development-based education. *Sustainability (Basel), 14*(3), 1172. DOI: 10.3390/su14031172

Hosny, M., & Mohamed, E. (2024). Ranking seafarers' duties towards unmanned and autonomous ships in prospective of stcw. *Ain Journal En, 1*(47). Advance online publication. DOI: 10.59660/47113

Ifenthaler, D., & Yau, J. (2020). Utilising learning analytics to support study success in higher education: A systematic review. *Educational Technology Research and Development, 68*(4), 1961–1990. DOI: 10.1007/s11423-020-09788-z

Iskandarova, S., & Ford, K. (2024). A case study for experiential teaching and learning. *Journal of Effective Teaching in Higher Education, 7*(1), 3–27. DOI: 10.36021/jethe.v7i1.358

Jain, S. (2025). Blockchain for transparent university credential verification. *Scientific Journal of Artificial Intelligence and Blockchain Technologies, 2*(2). Advance online publication. DOI: 10.63345/sjaibt.v2.i2.105

Kamalov, F., Calonge, D., & Gurrib, I. (2023). New era of artificial intelligence in education: Towards a sustainable multifaceted revolution. *Sustainability (Basel), 15*(16), 12451. DOI: 10.3390/su151612451

Kang, J., Roestel, N., & Girouard, A. (2022). Experiential learning to teach user experience in higher education in past 20 years: A scoping review. *Frontiers of Computer Science, 4*, 812907. Advance online publication. DOI: 10.3389/fcomp.2022.812907

Kayyali, M. (2024). Defining micro-credentials., 219-246. DOI: 10.4018/979-8-3693-6915-9.ch009

Khasanah, U., Trisnawati, S., & Falaah, M. (2025). Stakeholder synergy in realizing muhammadiyah vocational high school as a center of excellence based on muhammadiyah values. *Eduprof Islamic Education Journal, 7*(1), 86–101. DOI: 10.47453/eduprof.v7i1.351

Kim, J. (2024). A fundamental study of the sustainable key competencies for remote operators of maritime autonomous surface ships. *Sustainability (Basel), 16*(12), 4875. DOI: 10.3390/su16124875

Krakhecke, E., Voss, D., & Leite, M. (2025). "dura lex sed lex": direito, justiça social e pedagogia jurídica. Relacult - Revista Latino-Americana De Estudos Em Cultura E Sociedade, 11. DOI: 10.23899/c338xm18

Kristiyono, A., Wardoyo, D., & Roesminingsih, M. (2023). Four factors influencing the implementation of the 2010 manila amendment standards of training certification and watchkeeping (stcw) policy. *International Journal of Social Science and Human Research, 06*(07). Advance online publication. DOI: 10.47191/ijsshr/v6-i7-39

Lapesigue, J. (2024). Digital literacy and technical competence: Assessing the competence and performance of senior high school physical education teachers in online distance learning. *IJODeL, 10*(1). Advance online publication. DOI: 10.58887/ijodel.v10i1.273

Lee, A., Koh, E., & Looi, C. (2023). Ai in education and learning analytics in singapore: an overview of key projects and initiatives. Information and Technology in Education and Learning, 3(1), Inv-p001-Inv-p001. DOI: 10.12937/itel.3.1.Inv.p001

Lee, J., Dhesi, S., Phillips, I., Jeong, M., & Lee, C. (2021). Korean maritime cadets' onboard training environment survey. *Sustainability (Basel), 13*(8), 4161. DOI: 10.3390/su13084161

Li, M., Ling, G., & Turnbull, K. (2023). Deeper student-teacher partnership in 5 steps. *Ascilite Publications, 477-481*, 477–481. Advance online publication. DOI: 10.14742/apubs.2023.496

Lim, J., Ong, S., Ng, C., Chan, K., Wu, S., So, W., Tey, G. J. C., Lam, Y. X., Gao, N. L. X., Lim, Y. X., Tay, R. Y. K., Leong, I. T. Y., Rahman, N. D. A., Chiam, M., Lim, C., Phua, G. L. G., Murugam, V., Ong, E. K., & Krishna, L. (2023). A systematic scoping review of reflective writing in medical education. *BMC Medical Education, 23*(1), 12. Advance online publication. DOI: 10.1186/s12909-022-03924-4 PMID: 36624494

Mqukuse, B., & Mvunge, N. (2025). Enhancing social work education through e-portfolios: pedagogical practices and praxis at the university of fort hare. European Conference on E-Learning, 24(1), 289-296. DOI: 10.34190/ecel.24.1.4228

Mughal, Z., Gupta, K., & Fruhstorfer, B. (2025). Otolaryngology education in medical training: A literature review of current practice, challenges, and future directions. *The Annals of Otology, Rhinology, and Laryngology, 134*(10), 783–791. DOI: 10.1177/00034894251343373 PMID: 40458060

Mulenga, R., & Shilongo, H. (2024). Hybrid and blended learning models: Innovations, challenges, and future directions in education. *Acta Pedagogia Asiana, 4*(1), 1–13. DOI: 10.53623/apga.v4i1.495

Napier, P., & Wada, T. (2024). Bridging the skills gap: The design education landscape with ai and experiential learning. *Design Management Journal, 19*(1), 19–30. DOI: 10.1111/dmj.12094

Nawagi, F., & Raman, A. (2023). The importance of in-country african instructors in international experiential training programs; a qualitative case study from the university of minnesota. *BMC Medical Education, 23*(1), 145. Advance online publication. DOI: 10.1186/s12909-023-04129-z PMID: 36869302

Nemakhavhani, R. (2024). Enhancing student engagement through problem-based learning: A case of the built environment. *ICER, 1*(1), 238–245. DOI: 10.34190/icer.1.1.3053

Nyairo, F., Haavardtun, P., Lindroos, E., Munim, Z., Lampiola, J., Salokorpi, M., … & Krabbel, H. (2025). Instructional approaches for simulator-based maritime education and training., 120-131. DOI: 10.1007/978-3-031-84170-5_11

O'Connor, E., Marcogliese, E., Anis, H., Faye, G., Flynn, A., Hayman, E., & Stambouli, J. (2023). Adapting experiential learning in times of uncertainty: Challenges, strategies, and recommendations moving forward. *Engaged Scholar Journal Community-Engaged Research Teaching and Learning, 8*(4), 49–56. DOI: 10.15402/esj.v8i4.70793

Okunade, A. (2024). The role of artificial intelligence in teaching of science education in secondary schools in nigeria. *European Journal of Computer Science and Information Technology, 12*(1), 57–67. DOI: 10.37745/ejcsit2013/vol12n15767

Paramasivam., T., Mustapha, R., Vejaratnam, N., & James, S. (2025). The role of artificial intelligence in the industrial revolution 4.0 era and talent development through malaysian technical and vocational education and training (tvet) programmes. International Journal of Research and Innovation in Social Science, IX(IIIS), 5559-5567. DOI: 10.47772/IJRISS.2025.903SEDU0404

Qizi, I. (2024). Theoretical foundations of the study of phraseological units. *International Journal of Literature and Languages*, *4*(1), 26–29. DOI: 10.37547/ijll/Volume04Issue01-06

Ramdev, R., & Bhandari, D. (2025). Analyzing the role of competency based education in nep 2020 and its potential benefits & challenges. *IJARCMSS*, *08*(03(I)), 231–238. DOI: 10.62823/IJARCMSS/8.3(I).8030

Ray, S., & Guha, D. (2025). Integration of flipped classroom model in teacher education programme. *Sprin Journal of Arts Humanities and Social Sciences*, *4*(7), 9–14. DOI: 10.55559/sjahss.v4i7.517

Rivera, M., Calleja, L., Gómez, S., Malaran, D., Olivero, S., & Saim, T. (2025). Perceived occupational hazard preparation among third year marine transportation students of aims. *OL-IJMOS*, *2*(1), 22–31. DOI: 10.62718/vmca.ol-ijmos.2.1.SC-1024-011

Riyanto, R., Kuntadi, C., Barasa, L., Krismawati, I., Martha, Y., & Simanjuntak, M. (2025). Competency and sustainability integration in enhancing maritime vocational training for deck officers. *Digital Innovation*, *2*(1), 143–159. DOI: 10.61132/digitalinnovation.v2i1.181

Riyanto, R., Tampubolon, B., & Herawati, S. (2025). Transforming maritime education through a competency-based framework for marine engineering technicians. *Research and Development in Education (Raden)*, *5*(1), 593–604. DOI: 10.22219/raden.v5i1.39399

Rizqi, P., & Syafika, W. (2024). Strengthening professional learning communities through policy and institutional support in diverse educational contexts. *Education*, *2*(3), 141–156. DOI: 10.61194/education.v2i3.587

Rubi, K. and Sharma, P. (2024). Teacher professional development in the digital age., 533-556. DOI: 10.4018/979-8-3693-7723-9.ch030

Saifudin, I., Palapa, A., Sutopo, F., Teriyanti, T., & Alamsyah, J. (2025). Enhancing maritime vocational training in naval engine operations: A study in north sulawesi. *Diajar Jurnal Pendidikan Dan Pembelajaran*, *4*(2), 291–299. DOI: 10.54259/diajar.v4i2.4254

Salvador, N. (2024). Evaluating mol-magsaysay maritime academy's educational program: performance of first graduates and stakeholders' feedback. Apjaet - Journal Ay Asia Pacific Journal of Advanced Education and Technology, 3(3). DOI: 10.54476/apjaet/32701

Schio, C., & Reis, P. (2024). Design of a pedagogical model to foster ocean citizenship in basic education. *Sustainability (Basel)*, *16*(3), 967. DOI: 10.3390/su16030967

Selvakumar, P., Sakthiradha, M., Jeeva, C., Mujrai, P., Satyanarayana, P., & Singh, D. (2024). Global perspectives on smart education and sustainable development., 253-272. DOI: 10.4018/979-8-3693-7723-9.ch015

Setiawan, A. (2024). Indonesia's maritime diplomacy under joko widodo administration: Advancing the global maritime fulcrum vision. *Jurnal Indonesia Sosial Sains, 5*(12), 3221–3228. DOI: 10.59141/jiss.v5i12.1519

Sihombing, D., Dwiyani, N., Martha, Y., Hutabarat, C., & Sutrisno, S. (2024). Impact of international standards on maritime education: Perspectives of junior cadets. *Meteor Stip Marunda, 17*(1), 7–15. DOI: 10.36101/msm.v17i1.357

Sijabat, P., Simanjuntak, M., Mudakir, M., Putrawan, B., & Lumingkewas, M. (2024). Empowering literacy in maritime education: Strategies and professionalism alignment. *Meteor Stip Marunda, 17*(1), 42–50. DOI: 10.36101/msm.v17i1.359

Simanjuntak, M., Rafli, Z., Utami, S., Winarno, W., & Barasa, L. (2025). Sustainable maritime literacy: Navigating education for eco-conscious professionals. *Transactions on Maritime Science, 14*(1). Advance online publication. DOI: 10.7225/toms.v14.n01.024

Speier-Pero, C., & Schoenherr, T. (2020). Creating impactful student learning in a business analytics program through leveraging scholar-practitioner engagement. *Decision Sciences Journal of Innovative Education, 18*(1), 59–89. DOI: 10.1111/dsji.12198

Toit, A. (2022). Critiquing playful project-based learning as pedagogy for entrepreneurship education.. DOI: 10.5772/intechopen.100509

VanLeeuwen, C., Veletsianos, G., Belikov, O., & Johnson, N. (2020). Institutional perspectives on faculty development for digital education in canada. *Canadian Journal of Learning and Technology, 46*(2). Advance online publication. DOI: 10.21432/cjlt27944

Waddell, J. (2021). Bridging the theory/practice divide: experiential learning for a critical, people-centred economy.. DOI: 10.32920/ryerson.14669076

Yeri, M., & Baylon, J. (2025). Project based learning: Strengthening technical vocational education for quality learning and workforce readiness. *PEMJ, 46*(1), 1–14. DOI: 10.70838/pemj.460101

Yu, M., & Wang, L. (2025). China's cross-border maritime data flow governance: Progress, challenges, and prospects. *Frontiers in Marine Science, 12*, 1600050. Advance online publication. DOI: 10.3389/fmars.2025.1600050

Yu, Y., Lee, C., & Ahn, Y. (2025). Developing a competency-based transition education framework for marine superintendents: A dacum-integrated approach in the context of eco-digital maritime transformation. *Sustainability (Basel), 17*(14), 6455. DOI: 10.3390/su17146455

KEY TERMS AND DEFINITIONS

Competency-Based: Education (CBE): An educational approach that emphasizes the achievement and demonstration of measurable competencies, skills, and learning outcomes rather than time-based instructional completion.

Competency Mapping: A systematic process of identifying, organizing, and aligning required skills, knowledge, and professional attributes with occupational standards and learning outcomes.

Experiential Learning: A learning approach in which learners acquire knowledge and skills through direct experience, active participation, reflection, and real-world application.

Learning Analytics: The collection, analysis, and interpretation of learner data to monitor progress, improve instructional strategies, and enhance educational decision-making.

Maritime Education and Training (MET): A specialized system of education and professional preparation designed to develop competent maritime personnel in accordance with international industry standards.

Micro-Credentialing: A certification approach that recognizes the achievement of specific competencies or skills through short, focused, and competency-oriented learning experiences.

Performance-Based Assessment: An evaluation method that measures learners' competencies through authentic tasks, practical demonstrations, simulations, and real-world problem-solving activities.

Simulation-Based Training: An instructional strategy that utilizes realistic simulations and virtual environments to replicate maritime operations for competency development and decision-making practice.

Standards of Training, Certification and Watchkeeping (STCW): An international framework established by the International Maritime Organization (IMO) that defines minimum competency standards for seafarers worldwide.

Work-Integrated Learning (WIL): An educational approach that combines academic learning with practical workplace experiences to strengthen professional competence and employability.

Chapter 9
Machine Learning in Maritime Education:
Transforming Navigation, Simulation, and Safety Training

Andi Asrifan
http://orcid.org/0000-0002-9934-6129
Universitas Negeri Makassar, Indonesia

Sajed S. Ingilan
http://orcid.org/0000-0002-4466-2028
University of Southeastern Philippines, Philippines

ABSTRACT

Machine learning is revolutionizing maritime education by improving simulator realism, augmenting predictive safety systems, and facilitating individualized competency advancement. As navigation, engineering, and marine operations become progressively data-centric, maritime training must adapt by incorporating dynamic learning environments enhanced by sophisticated analytics. This study investigates the incorporation of machine learning in navigation instruction, simulation-based assessment, and safety management, emphasizing its ability to create dynamic situations, automate competency evaluation, and detect human-error tendencies. Ethical and practical obstacles, including infrastructure constraints, data governance, algorithmic equity, and instructor preparedness, are examined to guarantee ethical implementation. The results demonstrate that machine learning may markedly enhance training quality, safety results, and regulatory compliance, while emergent trends like AI copilots and MASS competences suggest new pathways for the advancement of the marine workforce.

INTRODUCTION TO MACHINE LEARNING IN MARITIME EDUCATION

1.1 The Digitalization of Maritime Training Ecosystems

The marine industry is seeing one of the most profound technical revolutions in its history. Swift progress in automation, digital connection, and intelligent systems has transformed vessel operations

DOI: 10.4018/979-8-3373-6670-8.ch009

and the training of marine personnel (Chan et al., 2025; Kim et al., 2023). Traditionally, maritime training depended significantly on didactic teaching, instructor-led demonstrations, and manually operated simulators. These methods facilitated foundational skill development but frequently lacked real-time adaptation, tailored learning assistance, and the analytical capacity to assess individual performance discrepancies. As warships progressively adopt integrated navigation systems, intelligent sensors, and decision-support tools, maritime training institutions must transition from traditional pedagogical models to data-driven and technologically enhanced environments.

The transition from conventional teaching to digital, data-centric training arose due to increasing operational complexity at sea. Mariners today engage with progressively automated bridge and engine systems that necessitate enhanced situational awareness and technological proficiency. Digitalization facilitates the amalgamation of extensive datasets, including voyage data recorder (VDR) records, Automatic Identification System (AIS) data, engine health metrics, and simulator logs (Li et al., 2024). These records provide diagnostic analytics that uncover performance trends, risk behaviors, and educational requirements. Instructors can transition from subjective assessment to evidence-based evaluation, while cadets gain from feedback rooted in quantifiable performance metrics. Consequently, the transition to digitalization not only modernizes educational practices but also significantly improves training quality, safety culture, and operational preparedness.

Multiple fundamental factors propel this digital transition. Automation in marine operations requires a crew proficient in managing intelligent ship systems, evaluating machine-generated data, and adapting to swiftly evolving navigational conditions. The International Maritime Organization (IMO) has set global standards that prioritize competency, safety, and human-technology interaction, positioning digital proficiency as central to maritime education. Moreover, the labor landscape of the industry is transforming. Emerging generations in the maritime profession anticipate digitally augmented learning settings, simulation-intensive experiences, and AI-assisted practical activities (Theotokas et al., 2024). Workforce technological expectations correspond with institutional responsibilities to equip cadets for progressively hybrid digital-physical environments.

The digital change in marine training mirrors wider worldwide initiatives. The IMO's e-Navigation and MASS programs underscore the necessity for integrated information systems, decision-support technology, and standardized training protocols that encompass digital proficiency (Li & Wang, 2025). The Standards of Training, Certification, and Watchkeeping for Seafarers (STCW) serve as the regulatory foundation for competency development. While STCW has traditionally focused on conventional maritime abilities, recent amendments prioritize digital navigation, cyber awareness, and safety management in intricate systems—domains where intelligent technologies and machine learning (ML) can substantially improve competency development.

Simultaneously, Industry 5.0 principles underscore the importance of human-technology collaboration, resilience, and sustainability within industrial systems. Maritime education must consequently develop a workforce that not only operates technology but collaborates with intelligent systems to enhance safety, efficiency, and environmental stewardship (Lin et al., 2024). Machine learning-driven maritime education strongly matches with this paradigm by facilitating adaptive simulations, individualized learning, predictive safety analytics, and real-time performance diagnostics.

1.2 Fundamentals of Machine Learning for Maritime Applications

Machine learning lets artificial intelligence learn from data, detect patterns, and make judgments without human interaction (Kretschmann, 2020). Essential ML types benefit maritime education navigation, simulations, and safety programs. Labelled datasets train predictive models in supervised learning, the major machine learning method. Supervised learning can detect navigational hazards, estimate vessel trajectories, and assess cadet performance in marine simulations. A simulator record-trained model can spot risky maneuvers or inadequate situational awareness (Munim et al., 2025). Unlabeled datasets reveal hidden patterns using unsupervised learning. Clustering can classify cadet performance profiles, detect odd AIS vessel behavior, or find engine performance anomalies. These insights assist teachers and operators recognize emerging hazards and training needs that people may miss.

The third kind of marine training, reinforcement learning (RL), is increasing. In simulated environments, reinforcement learning agents learn optimal actions by trial and error, like marine learning. Reinforcement learning-driven simulators can alter the environment, introduce hazards, or increase scenario complexity based on student behaviour (Armon et al., 2023). This capacity follows competency-based training best practices of gradual challenges, experiential learning, and performance evaluation. Reinforcement Learning enhances bridge simulators, navigation, and autonomous vessel development.

Many machine learning architectures enhance maritime apps. Visual navigation systems, radar overlays, and collision avoidance technologies use CNNs to distinguish objects. LSTM RNNs can predict vessel trajectories, meteorological trends, and engineering system problems using sequential data (Marlantes et al., 2024). Real-time decision-support systems and adaptive training simulations use reinforcement learning agents.

Machine learning's marine training success depends on data quality and accessibility. Many maritime databases improve training and evaluation. AIS data on vessel positions, movements, and contacts prevents collisions and studies navigational patterns (Felski et al., 2015). Bridge and engine room sensors monitor vessel, ambient, and equipment health. Cadet actions, decision timelines, control inputs, and scenario results are recorded in training simulator logs. Machine learning assessment systems that autonomously assess situational awareness, communication, and emergency response need these records.

Machine learning models marine behavior and training needs using several data sources. Advanced simulators, integrated learning management systems, and AI-enhanced instructional frameworks are helping training institutions collect data for machine learning-driven diagnostics, competence mapping, and predictive analytics (Munim et al., 2025).

1.3 Rationale for Integrating Machine Learning in Maritime Education

Machine learning in maritime education is driven by rising competency requirements in navigation, engineering, safety, and operations. Modern ships have complex control systems, automated decision-support, and multiple information displays that require digital capabilities (Bonvicini et al., 2025). Cadets must study conventional seamanship, machine-generated insights, automated systems, and intelligent technology collaboration. Machine learning-enhanced training environments provide personalized learning paths, rapid feedback, and adaptive teaching experiences that mimic real-world complexity.

Simulation-based learning shows machine learning's potential to improve marine training. Instructor discretion, which can vary, is crucial to traditional simulator evaluations. By analyzing high-resolution performance data and identifying competency accomplishment patterns, machine learning-driven analytics enable objectivity (Winkler-Schwartz et al., 2019; Xu, 2024). In collaborative exercises, machine learning models can identify procrastinated decision-making, incorrect helm inputs, inadequate navigational indication monitoring, and poor communication. These insights allow instructors to give targeted feedback and help cadets improve. Adaptive simulators using machine learning algorithms can automatically modify scenario complexity, provide novel obstacles, or replicate infrequent high-risk situations, enhancing training breadth and authenticity beyond manual instructor-generated content.

Machine learning reduces skill gaps caused by student backgrounds, learning preferences, and technological proficiency. Customized training routes let cadets grow at their own pace while receiving performance-specific education. Advanced learners may engage in more complex environments that build decision-making resilience, while novice cadets may get simpler scenarios, guided prompts, or prolonged practice sessions. Competency-based maritime education emphasizes measurable, verifiable STCW competencies over predefined hours (Ala et al., 2024).

Machine learning is used to improve safety culture. Predictive analytics can identify navigational risks, engine failures, and emergency response deficiencies. Timely identification helps preventive training and reduces human error, a major cause of maritime accidents (Passarella et al., 2024). Machine learning models can uncover deficiencies including poor lookout procedures, bridge teamwork, and equipment performance monitoring, allowing enterprises to design risk-mitigation training programs.

Machine learning coincides with industrial changes like autonomous vessels, e-Navigation, and global movements toward AI-assisted decision-making. As marine operations move toward hybrid human-machine collaboration, training institutions must ensure seafarers can work with sophisticated technologies. Cadets learn to use artificial intelligence, assess predictive data, and ethically and securely manage emerging technologies using machine learning-enhanced maritime education (Sharma et al., 2022).

MACHINE LEARNING FOR NAVIGATION TRAINING

2.1 Intelligent Decision Support for Navigational Planning

Modern maritime planning relies on machine learning to evaluate information, assess threats, and make urgent decisions (Lee et al., 2025). Officers must integrate charts, radar, ARPA, AIS, weather reports, and visual observations while maintaining situational awareness in rapidly changing sea conditions for conventional navigation. Intelligent decision-support systems that can evaluate large data sets and provide predictive insights are in high demand due to the complexity of maritime operations, congested traffic routes, and unpredictable weather. Machine learning-based nautical planning improves voyage precision, efficiency, and safety.

Route optimization and weather routing use it extensively. Machine learning algorithms use previous trip data, meteorological conditions, sea-state factors, and vessel performance indicators to recommend routes that balance safety, fuel efficiency, environmental standards, and operational schedules. Traditional weather routing systems use deterministic algorithms, but machine learning-enhanced models can detect nonlinear trends, use prior trip data, and adjust suggestions in real time (Zis et al., 2020). Using wind patterns, ocean currents, and wave heights, neural networks can predict delays or increased fuel use. In simulated environments, reinforcement learning systems can use dynamic feedback to choose routes that maximize safety and efficiency. They are especially useful in complex ecosystems like the North Atlantic, Southeast Asian archipelagos, and polar regions, where conditions change quickly and unpredictably.

In addition to route planning, machine learning improves collision prevention and hazard recognition. COLREGS, radar ARPA systems, and officer judgment have been used for collision avoidance, but machine learning introduces prediction models that surpass sensor data. Using AIS traffic patterns, vessel behavioral histories, and environmental data, machine learning systems can forecast collision scenarios minutes or hours before traditional technology can. SVMs, LSTM networks, and gradient-boosting models can forecast vessel trajectories, assess risk, and identify anomalous movements that may indicate dangers (Yang et al., 2023). These predictive skills allow authorities to anticipate situations, make appropriate modifications, and maintain safer maritime standards, especially in crowded waterways like the Singapore Strait and Bosphorus.

Additionally, machine learning-supported hazard detection systems can identify threats that humans may miss (Matveev, 2025). Anomaly vessel velocities, erratic motions, proximity infringements, and sensor abnormalities may indicate malfunctioning equipment. Over time, machine learning algorithms learn from prior incident reports and near-misses, improving risk assessment. These systems are being integrated into bridge consoles and navigational decision-support platforms for early warning and risk management. Machine learning works seamlessly with ECDIS, e-Navigation, and intelligent ship systems. ECDIS is the main navigational interface on modern warships, and machine learning-enhanced modules add predictive overlays, hazard alerts, and automated route recommendations (Bonvicini et al., 2025).

2.2 Prediction and Analytics for Navigational Performance

Predictive analytics has emerged as a fundamental component of machine learning applications in maritime navigation. Precise forecasting of vessel behavior, traffic dynamics, and potential hazards improves situational awareness and facilitates decision-making during intricate operations (Ma et al., 2025). Machine learning algorithms are especially adept at navigating due to maritime environments producing huge volumes of continuous, sequential, and multidimensional data necessitating sophisticated analytical methods.

The utilization of machine learning for predicting vessel behavior is crucial for ensuring safe and efficient navigation in congested or restricted seas. Models such LSTM neural networks, random forests, and Bayesian forecasting systems use AIS data, past maneuvers, hydrodynamic properties, and environmental factors to estimate future vessel trajectories. These forecasts assist seafarers in discerning the intents of nearby vessels, alleviating potential confrontations, and ensuring adherence to COLREGS (Spadon et al., 2024). During navigation, maneuvering in constricted channels, or approaching congested ports, trajectory prediction technologies furnish commanders with essential insights about vessel interactions that may otherwise be ambiguous. Additionally, machine learning-based traffic pattern analysis detects developing congestion, atypical navigation patterns, or departures from normal traffic flows. These findings can assist port authorities, ship operators, and training institutions in formulating risk-mitigation strategies and improving navigational training.

The creation of early-warning systems for navigational hazards represents another significant use of machine learning analytics. Conventional alert systems often depend on threshold-based triggers; however, machine learning techniques utilize contextual information and acquired behavior to enhance precision and minimize false alerts (Wahab et al., 2025). Early-warning systems can identify concerns including grounding possibilities, CPA/TCPA infringements, adverse weather conditions, or closeness to navigational hazards. Machine learning models analyze sensor data, environmental predictions, vessel behavior, and traffic information to assess danger levels and issue alerts prior to severe circumstances arising. This predictive sensitivity improves situational awareness on the bridge, particularly amid high workload, inclement weather, or diminished visibility.

Machine learning significantly contributes to the analysis and assessment of cadet performance in navigation instruction. Simulation environments produce comprehensive datasets that document decisions, control inputs, ocular motions, communication patterns, and scenario results (Munim et al., 2025). Machine learning-driven performance analytics convert these records into significant insights that indicate navigational proficiency, decision-making efficacy, and compliance with safety regulations. Classification algorithms can classify cadet activities as ideal, acceptable, or hazardous, facilitating objective evaluations in accordance with competency criteria. Pattern recognition models detect persistent performance deficiencies, including delayed helm adjustments, inadequate surveillance of radar and ECDIS, and suboptimal foresight of vessel motions. These insights enable instructors to deliver evidence-based feedback and assist cadets in cultivating more robust decision-making processes.

Performance analytics facilitate scenario reconstruction, allowing teachers to examine decision points, reaction timelines, and failures in situational awareness. Over time, educational institutions can utilize aggregated machine learning information to enhance curriculum design, modify simulation complexity, and synchronize evaluation criteria with industry requirements (Naji et al., 2025). Integrating the predictive capabilities of machine learning with comprehensive behavioral analysis enhances navigational performance training, making it more resilient, individualized, and congruent with actual operational requirements.

2.3 Personalized ML-driven Learning in Navigation Simulators

Machine learning facilitates a novel generation of adaptive, tailored training systems that cater to individual cadet requirements and performance trajectories (Karimi et al., 2024). Navigation simulators have traditionally been employed to mimic actual vessel operations; however, machine learning enhances their educational efficacy by adaptively modifying learning tasks, difficulty levels, and instructional feedback in accordance with the learner's progressing proficiency.

Adaptive learning pathways facilitated by machine learning utilize data from multiple simulator sessions to construct personalized performance profiles. These profiles delineate the cadet's strengths, limitations, learning velocity, mistake patterns, and decision-making inclinations. Machine learning algorithms group analogous performance traits and suggest specific training modules—such as collision-avoidance drills, radar analysis, or maneuvering practice in adverse environmental situations (Wild et al., 2025). Reinforcement learning agents integrated within simulators can dynamically adjust scenario settings, presenting novel traffic patterns, weather adversities, or equipment malfunctions to align with the cadet's proficiency level. This personalized method corresponds with competency-based education models, wherein the advancement of proficiency—rather than the duration of engagement—is the principal criterion for success.

Real-time feedback, facilitated by machine learning analytics, improves the timeliness and accuracy of training interventions. Cadets receive immediate alarms and diagnostic insights during simulation exercises, rather than depending exclusively on post-scenario debriefings (Fountoulakis, 2024). Instances encompass alerts on inadequate lookout procedures, procrastinated decision-making in collision-avoidance scenarios, overdependence on autopilot systems, or erroneous interpretation of radar/ARPA data. By emphasizing particular performance deficiencies as they arise, ML feedback enhances cadet awareness, decreases training duration, and expedites skill acquisition. Instructors benefit from automatic feedback systems that highlight faults needing correction and identify cadets wanting more tutoring or remedial practice.

To enhance adaptive learning and real-time feedback, machine learning-enabled dashboard platforms furnish instructors with extensive insights regarding cadet performance. Dashboards amalgamate simulator logs, behavioral analytics, performance measurements, and visuals that elucidate trends, risk behaviors, and advancement towards competency objectives. Instructors can oversee compliance with COLREGS, assess situational awareness metrics, and analyze enhancements in decision-making during many training sessions (Gleeson et al., 2024). These dashboards promote equitable, evidence-based evaluations in accordance with STCW competency descriptors, minimizing subjectivity and enhancing consistency in assessment results.

Dashboard systems facilitate longitudinal monitoring, allowing instructors to assess the progression of cadet competencies over time. A learner who initially has difficulties with cross-track error management or maintaining safe distances when overtaking may exhibit gradual enhancement as machine learning-driven recommendations optimize their learning path (Rehm et al., 2024). Training institutions may utilize aggregated dashboard data to discern prevalent deficiencies within cohorts, enhance instructional methodologies, and synchronize training programs with evolving industry demands.

MACHINE LEARNING IN MARITIME SIMULATION AND ASSESSMENT

3.1 Enhancing Simulator Realism through ML Models

Simulation-based training has emerged as a fundamental component of maritime education, providing cadets with opportunities to rehearse intricate navigational and operational duties in regulated, risk-free settings. The emergence of machine learning (ML) markedly improves the accuracy, flexibility, and responsiveness of these simulation systems (Alshareef & Alghanmi, 2024). Conventional simulators depend on pre-established situations, static hydrodynamic models, and modifications created by instructors. Machine learning incorporates an intelligence layer, allowing simulators to emulate real-world complexity, create dynamic settings, and adaptively respond to cadet behaviors. These improvements provide more genuine training experiences that more effectively equip sailors for the swiftly changing maritime operations.

A major advancement facilitated by machine learning is the development of data-driven scenarios derived from actual travels. Historical AIS recordings, engine logs, sensor data, meteorological observations, and near-miss reports constitute comprehensive datasets that encapsulate genuine operating issues. Machine learning algorithms examine these statistics to discern standard traffic patterns, high-risk interactions, port arrival intricacies, and environmental factors such as wind variations or tide influences (Rawson et al., 2021). These insights enable simulation systems to generate scenarios that reflect actual operational requirements, rather than depending exclusively on instructor-generated situations. The training situations presented to cadets simulate real-world conditions—congested rivers, erratic vessel movements, and heavy nighttime traffic—thereby enhancing situational awareness, decision-making capabilities, and operational preparedness.

Machine learning also improves hydrodynamic modeling, which conventionally relies on mathematical approximations to characterize vessel behavior under various conditions. While these models are beneficial, they frequently oversimplify the nonlinear interactions among hull shapes, propellers, environmental factors, and engine dynamics. Machine learning systems can derive insights from vast datasets produced by sea trials, ship logs, computational fluid dynamics (CFD) simulations, and sensor feedback to yield more accurate hydrodynamic predictions. Neural networks and regression-based machine learning models can more accurately simulate vessel reactions to helm inputs, wind forces, and currents than solely physics-based models. This results in more authentic maneuvering simulations, allowing cadets to encounter the intricate behavior of vessels under conditions like shallow water effects, bank suction, or difficult berthing maneuvers (Mansuy et al., 2023).

Reinforcement learning (RL) enhances simulation realism by facilitating dynamic and adaptive reactions during training activities. In contrast to static algorithms, reinforcement learning agents acquire knowledge through iterative interactions with a simulated environment, optimizing their actions to attain peak performance according to reward frameworks. In marine simulation, reinforcement learning agents can function as intelligent vessels, erratic traffic participants, or environmental entities (Waltz & Okhrin, 2023). A virtual vessel managed by a reinforcement learning agent may modify its speed, trajectory, and collision-avoidance tactics in response to cadet movements, thereby establishing a more authentic traffic scenario. RL-enhanced simulations enable cadets to practice maneuvering around dynamic, autonomous creatures that mimic actual boats instead of predetermined behaviors.

3.2 Intelligent Assessment in Simulation-Based Training

Machine learning is transforming evaluation procedures in marine simulation training through the implementation of automated, data-driven techniques that improve objectivity, accuracy, and fairness. Historically, simulation assessment has depended significantly on teacher judgment, which, while valuable, can fluctuate based on individual competence, observational constraints, and subjective interpretation (Schwengel et al., 2024). Machine learning provides systematic analytical tools that measure cadet performance across intricate behaviors, uncover latent patterns, and produce competency-based evaluations in accordance with regulatory and institutional norms.

The use of machine learning classifiers for automated scoring represents a pivotal advancement in simulation assessment. Classification methods, including random forests, support vector machines, and neural networks, are trained on expert-validated datasets comprising labeled instances of optimal, acceptable, and poor performance. Upon concluding simulation situations, ML models evaluate cadets' actions—rudder maneuvers, throttle modifications, CPA/TCPA compliance, communication records, and adherence to COLREGS—against established performance criteria. The system is capable of autonomously evaluating abilities including situational awareness, decision-making accuracy, prioritization, teamwork on the bridge, and emergency reaction. Automated scoring diminishes evaluator bias, improves uniformity, and delivers prompt feedback to cadets based on measurable criteria (Wahdiana et al., 2025).

Machine learning-driven behavioral analytics offer profound insights into the decision-making processes of cadets during simulation training. Rather than concentrating exclusively on outcomes, ML models analyze micro-level behaviors including decision cycles, response time metrics, radar scanning patterns, and information prioritization. Decision cycle analysis examines how cadets identify cues, process information, and perform maneuvers under different levels of pressure (Qu et al., 2022). Time-to-response indicators assess the speed at which cadets identify dangers or react to evolving road conditions. Machine learning algorithms also examine spatial behavior, including cross-track error patterns and proximity management, to uncover practices that may lead to risky navigation. By identifying these behavioral patterns, instructors acquire a more thorough grasp of cadet competencies and areas necessitating focused interventions.

Situational awareness (SA)—a crucial skill in maritime navigation—can also be evaluated using machine learning techniques. Analysis of eye-tracking data, radar/ECDIS interaction logs, and attention-distribution patterns might yield inferences regarding situational awareness levels. Machine learning systems can identify when a cadet's focus neglects essential knowledge sources or when cognitive overload results in mistakes (Avetisyan, 2024). These results feed training approaches that enhance cue identification, attention management, and information integration during operational stress.

Competency dashboards epitomize the integration of ML-driven assessment technologies, providing educators and administrators with a detailed, visual representation of cadet performance. Dashboards amalgamate evaluation scores, behavioral metrics, risk indicators, and trend analyses from various simulation sessions (Albaladejo-González et al., 2021). In competence-based education (CBE) settings, dashboards correlate performance data with established competency standards, allowing institutions to monitor cadet advancement towards regulatory and programmatic learning objectives. Dashboards can exhibit heatmaps illustrating performance strengths, longitudinal advancements, and competency deficiencies in navigation, communication, safety management, and teamwork. These visualizations bolster evidence-based assessments, enable tailored rehabilitation efforts, and improve transparency in evaluation practices.

3.3 VR/AR and ML Integration for Immersive Maritime Training

Virtual reality (VR) and augmented reality (AR) are revolutionizing maritime training by facilitating immersive, interactive settings in which cadets may perform tasks that are challenging, dangerous, or unfeasible to recreate in traditional simulators (Simanjuntak et al., 2024). Machine learning enhances the instructional efficacy of VR/AR through intelligent object recognition, risk assessment, adaptive feedback mechanisms, and customized learning trajectories. This integration aligns maritime training with authentic operating situations while ensuring safety and instructional oversight.

Machine learning-enhanced object detection is essential in virtual and augmented reality maritime instruction. Vision-based machine learning algorithms, especially convolutional neural networks (CNNs), are capable of identifying and categorizing objects like buoys, vessels, engine components, mooring equipment, and safety risks (Hasan et al., 2025). In augmented reality environments, object recognition enables automatic digital overlays to manifest when cadets observe particular components, such as illuminating fault signs on an engine panel or displaying safety protocols when a cadet inspects firefighting apparatus. In virtual reality settings, machine learning techniques guarantee that simulated objects respond consistently and accurately to cadet interactions. An ML system can identify when cadets improperly manipulate tools during engine-room repair drills or inaccurately assess distances during mooring operations.

Risk identification in VR/AR settings is enhanced by machine learning algorithms that can identify risky behaviors, poor postures, incorrect job sequencing, or insufficient safety compliance. In a fire-fighting exercise, machine learning may identify when cadets approach flames from hazardous angles, improperly utilize equipment, or neglect communication protocols (Kim et al., 2024). In engine-room simulations, machine learning can detect improper lockout-tagout protocols, unsafe equipment handling, or neglect in monitoring system signs. This data-driven risk assessment fosters a safety-oriented mentality and facilitates real-time corrective education.

Machine learning-driven interactive feedback loops facilitate adaptable, responsive, and learner-centered training. When a cadet commits an error—such as neglecting to detect a leak during an engine-room examination or employing an incorrect grip when throwing a heaving line—the system can promptly offer recommendations, promote appropriate conduct, or modify scenario settings to enhance comprehension (Scorgie et al., 2023). Reinforcement learning agents integrated into VR/AR systems can adjust scenario complexity according to cadet performance, elevating challenge levels for advanced learners or offering supplementary hints and structured guidance for novices. These strategies augment engagement, expedite skill gain, and facilitate mastery learning.

Machine learning-enhanced virtual reality and augmented reality systems have exhibited significant applications across several marine training disciplines. In firefighting, the integration of virtual reality and machine learning allows cadets to train in hose management, fire suppression, decision-making in smoky environments, and emergency collaboration without encountering actual dangers (Scorgie et al., 2023). Machine learning examines flame propagation patterns, cadet maneuvers, and extinguishing methodologies to customize training feedback. In engine-room operations, cadets can engage in diagnosing mechanical faults, performing safety checks, and adhering to procedural checklists. Machine learning models identify deviations from established protocols, highlight high-risk behaviors, and create personalized enhancement strategies.

The integration of VR/AR with ML provides significant training advantages in mooring safety. Mooring activities include considerable hazards owing to snap-back zones, substantial loads, and swift environmental fluctuations. VR/AR simulations enable cadets to refine skills in rope handling, winch operation, communication protocols, and hazard identification within highly realistic settings (Abro et al., 2025). Machine learning algorithms monitor movement patterns, spatial awareness, and communication efficacy to evaluate whether cadets identify hazardous zones or respond suitably to unforeseen incidents, such as line tension breakdowns.

MACHINE LEARNING FOR MARITIME SAFETY AND RISK MANAGEMENT

4.1 Predictive Safety Systems

Safety is fundamental to marine operations, and the incorporation of machine learning (ML) into vessel safety systems is transforming the detection, prevention, and management of risks. The maritime industry has always depended on scheduled inspections, manual evaluations, and reactive strategies to sustain vessel integrity (Simion et al., 2024). Contemporary warships provide substantial digital data via integrated sensors, engine monitoring systems, electrical panels, and navigational instruments. Machine learning utilizes these datasets to develop predictive safety models that detect anomalies, anticipate breakdowns, and offer early warnings well in advance of significant problems. Consequently, safety management shifts from a reactive to a proactive framework, markedly diminishing the probability of operational failures and human fatalities.

Predictive maintenance signifies a significant enhancement in maritime safety. Conventional maintenance schedules, determined by set intervals, frequently result in superfluous inspections or, more critically, neglected system faults. Machine learning-based predictive maintenance systems examine sensor data from engines, generators, electrical circuits, and auxiliary machinery to identify small deviations that signify deterioration or impending failure. Neural networks, regression models, and anomaly-detection algorithms can discern patterns including elevated vibration levels, atypical temperature increases, reduced lubrication efficacy, or alterations in fuel injection timing (Tharun et al., 2025). These indicators enable engineers to implement targeted interventions prior to small difficulties escalating into catastrophic failures. In electrical systems, machine learning can identify insulation failures, harmonic distortions, overloaded circuits, or sporadic defects that conventional monitoring may overlook. This predictive capability improves the dependability of propulsion, steering, and power systems—essential elements that directly affect vessel safety.

Fault detection and anomaly recognition encompass not only machinery integrity but also the wider activities of the vessel. Machine learning algorithms can evaluate navigational metrics, fuel consumption trends, rudder angles, helm inputs, and gyrocompass data to identify operational anomalies. Anomalies may signify system failures, cyber attacks, sensor deviations, or human operating mistakes. Unsupervised learning models are particularly adept at this task since they may detect anomalies in normal behavior without the necessity of labeled fault data (Shaikh et al., 2025). Through the ongoing analysis of operational trends, machine learning systems can identify the initial indicators of hazardous vessel behavior, such atypical turning patterns, delayed throttle responses, or unpredictable speed variations. These insights assist bridge officers in making informed corrective decisions while allowing shore-based monitoring centers to uphold oversight of fleet-wide safety.

A significant contribution of machine learning in predictive safety systems is the early identification of safety infractions and patterns of human error. Human error continues to be a predominant factor in marine mishaps, especially in navigation, cargo management, and engine-room procedures. Machine learning algorithms can evaluate performance data, communication records, and operational metrics to discern behaviors linked to heightened risk (Passarella et al., 2024). A system may identify instances when officers consistently disregard lookout duties, neglect to uphold safe CPA/TCPA distances, or contravene bridge collaboration protocols. In engine rooms, machine learning models can detect irregularities such as irregular monitoring of gauge readings, incorrect startup sequences, or noncompliance with lockout-tagout procedures. Timely identification enables organizations to implement focused training, remedial coaching, or policy reinforcement.

4.2 Human Factors and ML-based Behavioral Analysis

Human factors significantly influence marine safety. Despite the growing automation of boats, the performance, situational awareness, and decision-making of crew members continue to be important for safe operations. Machine learning provides robust instruments for assessing human behavior, detecting danger patterns, and guiding training interventions that mitigate cognitive and operational constraints (Aderamo et al., 2024). Through the analysis of behavioral data in navigation, engineering, and communication contexts, machine learning facilitates a sophisticated comprehension of the impact of human variables on safety outcomes.

Fatigue detection is a significant application of machine learning in the investigation of human factors. Fatigue diminishes cognitive performance, impairs reaction times, and elevates error rates—factors that can lead to disastrous outcomes in critical marine settings. Machine learning algorithms can evaluate biometric data, eye-tracking patterns, watchkeeping schedules, micro-sleep indications, heart rate variability, and facial signals to assess fatigue levels (Cui et al., 2025). Computer vision algorithms identify drooping eyelids, head nodding patterns, or diminished blink frequency, whereas time-series models examine physiological data for indicators of cognitive decline. These machine learning-based tiredness monitoring systems can provide alerts to watch officers, modify duty allocation, or inform supervisors when intervention is necessary. By detecting exhaustion promptly, these devices facilitate adherence to rest-hour rules and improve operational alertness.

Workload monitoring constitutes a crucial aspect of machine learning-based human-factor analysis. Maritime operations sometimes entail phases of significant cognitive strain, such navigating crowded waterways, managing emergencies, or overseeing several information systems. Machine learning methods evaluate interaction patterns with navigational devices, communication records, the frequency of control modifications, and sensor-monitoring activities to assess workload levels. Elevated workload may result in delayed reactions, diminished instrument scanning, or excessive dependence on automation (Roques et al., 2025). By identifying workload disparities, ML technologies facilitate the execution of techniques such as task reallocation, augmented reality overlays, or decision-support functions that assist in sustaining safe performance standards.

Machine learning greatly aids in the analysis of behavioral patterns in Bridge Resource Management (BRM) and Engine Room Resource Management (ERM). BRM and ERM prioritize collaboration, communication, situational awareness, and collective decision-making—skills essential for safety although frequently challenging to assess objectively (Hayes et al., 2020). Machine learning algorithms can evaluate communication intelligibility, timeliness, coordination efficiency, and compliance with protocols by analyzing audio recordings, speech patterns, control inputs, and task sequences. Behavioral pattern recognition models categorize activities as ideal, poor, or hazardous, enabling organizations to pinpoint deficiencies in teamwork, leadership, or coordination. These insights enhance BRM/ERM training programs and fortify collaborative safety practices.

Evaluating communication, coordination, and compliance behaviors is crucial for comprehending the impact of human interactions on safety outcomes. Machine learning algorithms can assess voice commands, facilitate conversations, radio communications, and team interactions to determine the effectiveness of information sharing, clarity of decision transmission, and adherence to protocols (Brutschi et al., 2024). Natural language processing (NLP) facilitates the automated analysis of communication sentiment, clarity, urgency, and conformity with operational standards. For compliance monitoring, machine learning algorithms identify deviations from regular operating procedures, overlooked communication checks, or inadequate handovers. These insights offer a comprehensive understanding of human performance, facilitating tailored interventions that enhance safety behaviors at both individual and collective levels.

4.3 Safety Drills and Emergency Preparedness Supported by ML

Emergency readiness is essential in maritime operations, where severe disasters like fires, collisions, flooding, and machinery failures can quickly intensify. Machine learning improves emergency training by automated assessment, intelligent tutoring, and the creation of scenarios that replicate infrequent, high-risk situations rarely experienced in conventional drills (Pretolesi et al., 2024). These capabilities enhance crew preparedness, augment decision-making, and foster a more robust safety culture.

The automated assessment of emergency response drills represents a significant advancement in machine learning. Conventional assessments rely significantly on instructor observation, which may fail to detect nuanced performance indications such as hesitation, job sequencing, communication quality, or response speed. Machine learning algorithms evaluate video footage, audio recordings, sensor data, and simulator logs to determine the efficacy of crew members in hazard recognition, procedural execution, and coordination during emergencies. Metrics for time-to-response, decision correctness, adherence to emergency checklists, and collaborative behaviors are assessed quantitatively (Morian et al., 2023). Machine learning can identify instances when crew members overlook indications such as smoke alarms, misinterpret situational data, or neglect to execute critical actions like isolating electrical sources during fire emergencies. Automated evaluation guarantees impartiality, uniformity, and comprehensive feedback that facilitates ongoing enhancement.

Machine learning-driven intelligent tutoring systems offer tailored assistance during emergency decision-making simulations. These systems evaluate learner behavior, detect misconceptions or procedural inaccuracies, and provide customized recommendations that reinforce appropriate actions. Intelligent tutoring customizes teaching material according to the learner's performance level, progressively presenting increasingly intricate scenarios as competence increases (Skinner et al., 2018). A cadet encountering difficulties with smoke management in firefighting drills may be provided with supplementary targeted assignments, corrective feedback, or visual cues. Intelligent tutoring enhances learning by delivering prompt, practical insights that reinforce procedural memory and situational awareness in high-pressure situations.

The simulation of infrequent, high-stakes occurrences represents another significant leap facilitated by machine learning. Numerous emergency scenarios—such as engine-room explosions, flooding from collisions, steering malfunctions, or chemical fires—are perilous or unfeasible to simulate via live exercises. Machine learning systems evaluate historical accident data, near-miss reports, and environmental factors to create realistic emergency scenarios that reflect real-world complications. Reinforcement learning agents can emulate the dynamics of fire propagation, flood advancement, or equipment malfunction in response to the trainee's activities (Kwegyir-Afful et al., 2021). These adaptive scenarios instruct individuals in managing unforeseen, rapidly shifting catastrophes, fostering resilience and confidence in high-pressure situations.

VR/AR emergency simulations augmented by machine learning significantly improve readiness by immersing crew members in realistic settings to practice spatial awareness, hazard identification, evacuation protocols, and collaboration (Wu et al., 2024). Machine learning models monitor their efficacy, identify hazardous decisions, and encourage appropriate actions via real-time feedback. This facilitates trainees' internalization of safety protocols more efficiently than conventional classroom education.

IMPLEMENTATION CHALLENGES, ETHICAL CONSIDERATIONS, AND FUTURE DIRECTIONS

5.1 Institutional and Operational Barriers

Machine learning (ML) can revolutionize maritime education by improving simulation accuracy, facilitating competency-based training, and enhancing safety results. The deployment of ML-driven systems poses many institutional and operational problems (Joseph & Uzondu, 2024). Maritime academies, shipping firms, and regulatory authorities must confront these obstacles to guarantee the proper integration, operational sustainability, and pedagogical alignment of ML technologies with professional training objectives.

A major obstacle is the inadequacy of institutional infrastructure and the substantial expense associated with the adoption of modern technologies. Machine learning-driven simulators, high-performance computer systems, virtual and augmented reality platforms, and integrated sensor networks necessitate a resilient digital infrastructure, reliable internet connectivity, and specialized hardware (Koukaras et al., 2025). Numerous maritime training institutes, particularly in poor nations, encounter challenges in acquiring such technologies owing to constrained finances, competing institutional agendas, or inadequate maintenance capabilities. Despite the availability of complex simulators, their integration with machine learning models necessitates technical proficiency, software updates, and ongoing calibration—elements that might burden institutional resources. Moreover, the operating expenses associated with data storage, cloud computing, cybersecurity measures, and machine learning system licensing further hinder mainstream use.

Instructor preparedness and deficiencies in digital literacy are a significant obstacle. ML-enhanced technologies redefine the instructor's role from conventional lecturer to data interpreter, simulation analyst, and competency evaluator. Numerous educators lack familiarity with machine learning topics, including algorithmic decision-making, reinforcement learning behaviors, and predictive analytics. In the absence of focused professional development, educators may be reluctant to depend on machine learning-generated insights or may find it challenging to accurately evaluate algorithmic results (Li, 2024). This reluctance may constrain the educational efficacy of ML technologies and diminish their integration into routine training practices. Furthermore, educators may experience a sense of being inundated by additional duties associated with analyzing dashboards, verifying machine learning-generated evaluations, and incorporating intelligent feedback into pedagogical approaches. Establishing a technologically proficient faculty is thus crucial for the successful incorporation of machine learning.

The availability and interoperability of data further complicate implementation. Machine learning systems need on extensive datasets, including simulator logs, engine sensors, AIS recordings, and training evaluations, to develop precise models. Numerous marine organizations lack regular data gathering methodologies, leading to fragmented or inadequate datasets that constrain machine learning accuracy. Proprietary simulation platforms may utilize closed data formats or impose access restrictions, hindering easy integration with machine learning frameworks (Wang et al., 2025). Interoperability issues emerge when integrating machine learning technologies with legacy systems, such outdated simulators, independent navigation devices, or incompatible Learning Management Systems (LMS). Institutional data governance standards, cybersecurity mandates, and legal limitations may further impede the dissemination of sensitive operational or navigational data necessary for model building.

Regulatory factors introduce an extra dimension of complication. Maritime training and evaluation must adhere to STCW standards, flag-state rules, IMO guidelines, and institutional accreditation criteria. Regulatory regimes have not yet comprehensively addressed the incorporation of machine learning systems in training, particularly with automated evaluation, predictive analytics, and intelligent tutoring (Nguyen et al., 2025). Ambiguity regarding the validity of ML-generated assessments for certification may deter institutions from implementing such systems. Moreover, the maritime sector must evaluate how machine learning aids in adherence to the ISM Code, risk management protocols, and auditing standards.

5.2 Ethical, Legal, and Pedagogical Considerations

As machine learning becomes more integrated into maritime education, it is crucial to consider the ethical, legal, and pedagogical ramifications of intelligent training systems. Machine learning-driven platforms present novel problems including privacy, fairness, prejudice, interpretability, and instructional integrity (Antonio et al., 2024). These issues must be addressed proactively to uphold trust, safeguard cadets' rights, and guarantee that ML augments rather than supplants human-centered maritime education.

Data privacy is a significant ethical concern. Machine learning systems necessitate the aggregation of comprehensive personal data, including performance measurements, voice recordings, physiological markers, communication patterns, simulator actions, and behavioral analytics. In the absence of robust data governance structures, such information may be susceptible to misuse, unlawful access, or breaches (Lim et al., 2023). Maritime institutions must adhere to national data protection regulations and implement policies to provide secure data storage, encryption, anonymization, and restricted access. Furthermore, cadets must be clearly informed of the utilization of their data, the individuals authorized to access it, and the duration of its storage.

Equity, clarity, and responsibility hold equal significance. Machine learning algorithms may unintentionally inject bias into evaluations or training recommendations. An ML classifier trained on data from highly experienced officers may inaccurately assess beginner cadets as underperforming, despite their performance conforming to anticipated learning stages (Kostyszyn et al., 2024). An algorithm trained on restricted datasets may impose excessively restrictive thresholds that penalize cadets with varying learning styles, communication patterns, or cultural backgrounds. Bias detection systems, algorithmic audits, and different training datasets are crucial for ensuring fairness in evaluation processes.

Transparency is essential for sustaining confidence. Cadets and instructors must comprehend the decision-making processes of ML systems, the generation of performance evaluations, and the assumptions that underpin prediction models (Khan et al., 2024). Opaque systems devoid of interpretability may erode trust in machine learning evaluations. Consequently, maritime training institutions must to emphasize explainable AI (XAI) principles that enable users to comprehend the rationale behind machine learning suggestions and detect possible inaccuracies.

Accountability must be properly delineated. While machine learning can aid in performance evaluation and suggest training modifications, instructors and institutions must maintain final accountability for assessment decisions (Webb et al., 2020). Completely delegating judgments to machine learning systems presents legal issues, particularly in certification or disciplinary scenarios. Maintaining human oversight—the "human-in-the-loop" principle—is crucial for preserving educational integrity and adhering to regulatory standards. Educators must authenticate ML-generated insights, situate them inside comprehensive competency frameworks, and utilize them to guide—not determine—educational choices.

From a pedagogical perspective, machine learning should augment rather than supplant human mentorship. Maritime education relies significantly on experiential learning, instructor discretion, and cooperative problem-solving. Excessive dependence on ML techniques may jeopardize these vital human attributes (Sellberg & Sharma, 2024).

5.3 Future Trends in ML-driven Maritime Education

Machine learning will persist in transforming maritime education, presenting novel opportunities for adaptive learning, sophisticated simulation, safety improvement, and competency advancement. Emerging trends suggest that machine learning will assume a more pivotal role in equipping the maritime workforce for the technological changes taking place in global shipping (Aljahdali et al., 2025).

A significant trend is the advent of AI copilots for navigation training and real-time guidance. As vessels implement more sophisticated decision-support systems, training will include intelligent copilots who aid cadets during simulation exercises by offering navigational guidance, hazard alerts, route optimization recommendations, and feedback on decision-making (Smith et al., 2020). AI copilots serve as virtual mentors, assisting cadets with intricate responsibilities including collision avoidance, berthing operations, and emergency response. These solutions will facilitate autonomous vessel operations, allowing cadets to develop crucial human–machine collaboration skills for future marine environments.

A significant development is to the cultivation of competences for Maritime Autonomous Surface Ships (MASS). Autonomous and semi-autonomous vessels will necessitate staff proficient in autonomous control systems, remote monitoring, algorithmic decision-making, and cyber-physical interactions (Luchenko et al., 2023). Machine learning-based training systems will replicate autonomous vessel behaviors, remote control problems, and AI-driven navigation patterns. Training programs will focus on abilities such overseeing autonomous navigation systems, controlling algorithmic risks, understanding predictive analytics, and addressing technological problems in autonomous settings. MASS-related competencies will be essential to maritime education as global shipping evolves towards increased automation.

The global standardization of machine learning-enhanced marine education constitutes a third developing trend. Regulatory authorities, accreditation entities, and marine institutions must formulate explicit standards for the incorporation of machine learning in training, evaluation, and certification (Giannopoulos et al., 2024). These standards may encompass the validation of machine learning-based evaluations, the application of predictive analytics in safety training, stipulations for explainable artificial intelligence, and rules for safeguarding data privacy and transparency. International harmonization would guarantee that cadets educated using ML-enhanced systems achieve uniform competency criteria across regions, facilitating global mobility and enhancing maritime safety.

Machine learning will also enable the creation of hybrid training environments that incorporate simulators, internet platforms, virtual reality/augmented reality technology, and onboard training modules. These ecosystems will facilitate integrated learning experiences by merging data-driven insights with practical skill development (Zahid et al., 2025). Machine learning algorithms will customize educational pathways, enhance training sequences, and perpetually revise training materials in accordance with changing industry requirements.

In the future, ML-driven maritime education will prioritize human-centric approaches over just technology-centric ones. Intelligent systems will assist instructors in their roles as facilitators, decision-makers, and mentors, while providing cadets with tailored, adaptive learning experiences (Sellberg & Sharma, 2024). This harmonious amalgamation of machine learning and human expertise will characterize the forthcoming future of maritime education—one that is data-driven, competency-oriented, technologically sophisticated, yet anchored in human discernment and marine heritage.

CONCLUSION

Machine learning is transforming maritime education by facilitating more flexible, data-driven, and competency-based training environments. As navigational systems, shipboard operations, and safety management processes become more digitalized, maritime professionals must cultivate novel types of situational awareness, technical proficiency, and decision-making skills that surpass conventional training methods. Machine learning-driven intelligent systems facilitate this shift by improving simulator realism, providing predictive safety measures, and customizing learning trajectories according to individual performance patterns.

Machine learning enhances performance assessment accuracy, facilitates the effective detection of risk behaviors, and bolsters preparedness for normal and emergency operations across navigation training, simulation environments, and safety management. Machine learning-driven analytics enhance impartiality in evaluation procedures, facilitate continuous development, and assist institutions in aligning their programs with competency-based frameworks and regulatory requirements. The amalgamation of VR/AR with advanced analytics enhances immersive learning, providing authentic experiences that augment technical proficiency and strengthen safety measures.

Notwithstanding these prospects, problems in implementation endure, encompassing infrastructure deficiencies, faculty preparedness disparities, data governance issues, and the ethical oversight of algorithmic decision-making. Institutions must implement strategic methodologies that harmonize technological innovation with human knowledge, guaranteeing that machine learning enhances rather than supplants instructor judgment and professional mentorship. The establishment of legislative clarity and ethical principles for data protection, algorithmic fairness, and accountability is equally crucial.

In the future, machine learning will persist as a pivotal element of nautical instruction. Emerging developments, like AI copilots, autonomous ship capabilities, and globally standardized ML-supported protocols, will influence the future of maritime workforce growth. Through meticulous planning, accountable governance, and continuous investment, machine learning may foster a safer, more resilient, and technologically adept maritime industry.

REFERENCES

Abro, G.-E.-M., Zahid, F., Ali, S. S. A., & Aromoye, I. A. (2025). Exploring the Potential Benefits and Overcoming the Constraints of Virtual and Augmented Reality in Operator Training. *Transportation Research Procedia*, *84*, 625–632. DOI: 10.1016/j.trpro.2025.03.117

Aderamo, A. T., Olisakwe, H. C., Adebayo, Y. A., & Esiri, A. E.Adeoye Taofik AderamoHenry Chukwuemeka OlisakweYetunde Adenike AdebayoAndrew Emuobosa Esiri. (2024). AI-Driven HSE management systems for risk mitigation in the oil and gas industry. *Comprehensive Research and Reviews in Engineering and Technology*, *2*(1), 1. DOI: 10.57219/crret.2024.2.1.0059

Ala, A., Hamidi, N., Yoniessa, S., Masito, F., & Muis, M. A. (2024). SIMULATION-BASED LEARNING IN MARITIME TRAINING: ENHANCING COMPETENCY AND PREPAREDNESS. *Meteor STIP Marunda*, *17*(1), 95–102. DOI: 10.36101/msm.v17i1.361

Albaladejo-González, M., Strukova, S., Ruipérez-Valiente, J. A., & Mármol, F. G. (2021). Exploring the Affordances of Multimodal Data to Improve Cybersecurity Training with Cyber Range Environments. In *Colección Jornadas y congresos*. https://doi.org/DOI: 10.18239/jornadas_2021.34.52

Aljahdali, B. M., Alsubhi, Y., Alghanmi, A. F., Sulaimani, H. T., & Samman, A. E. (2025). An Innovation Machine Learning Approach for Ship Fuel-Consumption Prediction Under Climate-Change Scenarios and IMO Standards. *Journal of Marine Science and Engineering*, *13*(4), 805. DOI: 10.3390/jmse13040805

Alshareef, M., & Alghanmi, A. F. (2024). Optimizing Maritime Energy Efficiency: A Machine Learning Approach Using Deep Reinforcement Learning for EEXI and CII Compliance. *Sustainability (Basel)*, *16*(23), 10534. DOI: 10.3390/su162310534

Antonio, G. P., Alfonso, C. M., & Enrique, N. J. (2024). Tourism and ICTs: Advances in Data Science, Artificial Intelligence and Sustainability. In *Springer proceedings in business and economics*. Springer International Publishing., DOI: 10.1007/978-3-031-52607-7

Armon, B., Chris, D., & Joseph, C. (2023). Optimizing Naval Movement Using Deep Reinforcement Learning. In *Calhoun: The Naval Postgraduate School Institutional Archive (Naval Postgraduate School)*. Naval Postgraduate School. https://hdl.handle.net/10945/72426

Avetisyan, L. (2024). Building a Situation Awareness Framework for Communicating Among Road Users in Mixed Automated and Manual Traffic Environments. *Deep Blue (University of Michigan)*. https://doi.org/DOI: 10.7302/23549

Bonvicini, A., Cangelosi, D., Ingargiola, R., Marchese, A. J., & Previti, G. (2025). Digital Twin Approach for Ship Energy Management. In *Progress in marine science and technology*. IOS Press., DOI: 10.3233/PMST250138

Brutschi, R., Wang, R., Kolbe, M., Weiss, K. E., Lohmeyer, Q., & Meboldt, M. (2024). Speech recognition technology for assessing team debriefing communication and interaction patterns: An algorithmic toolkit for healthcare simulation educators. *Advances in Simulation (London, England)*, *9*(1), 42. DOI: 10.1186/s41077-024-00315-1

Chan, J. P., Pazouki, K., Norman, R., & Golightly, D. (2025). Investigating the Impact of Seafarer Training in the Autonomous Shipping Era. *Journal of Marine Science and Engineering, 13*(4), 818. DOI: 10.3390/jmse13040818

Cui, M.-X., He, K., Wang, F., & Paik, J.-K. (2025). Human Digital Healthcare Engineering for Enhancing the Health and Well-Being of Seafarers and Offshore Workers: A Comprehensive Review [Review of *Human Digital Healthcare Engineering for Enhancing the Health and Well-Being of Seafarers and Offshore Workers: A Comprehensive Review*]. *Systems, 13*(5), 335. Multidisciplinary Digital Publishing Institute. https://doi.org/DOI: 10.3390/systems13050335

Felski, A., Jaskólski, K., & Banyś, P. (2015). Comprehensive Assessment of Automatic Identification System (AIS) Data Application to Anti-collision Manoeuvring. *Journal of Navigation, 68*(4), 697–717. DOI: 10.1017/S0373463314000897

Fountoulakis, M.Dr. Michail St. Fountoulakis. (2024). Optimizing Police and Military Academy Training: Implementing a Tiered Education Program through Comprehensive Cadet Assessments. *International Journal of Scientific Research in Science and Technology, 11*(3), 705–721. DOI: 10.32628/IJSRST2411346

Giannopoulos, A., Gkonis, P. K., Bithas, P. S., Νομικός, N., Kalafatelis, A., & Trakadas, P. (2024). Federated Learning for Maritime Environments: Use Cases, Experimental Results, and Open Issues. *Journal of Marine Science and Engineering, 12*(6), 1034. DOI: 10.3390/jmse12061034

Gleeson, J., Dunbabin, M., & Ford, J. (2024). COLREG Scenario classification and Compliance Evaluation with temporal and multi-vessel awareness for collision avoidance systems. *Ocean Engineering, 313*, 119552. DOI: 10.1016/j.oceaneng.2024.119552

Hasan, S. M. R., Islam, M., Awal, Z. I., & Hossain, K. A. (2025). Prediction and optimization of efficient ship design particulars through advanced machine learning approaches. *Ocean Engineering, 341*, 122572. DOI: 10.1016/j.oceaneng.2025.122572

Hayes, P., Bearman, C., Butler, P. C., & Owen, C. (2020). Non-technical skills for emergency incident management teams: A literature review [Review of *Non-technical skills for emergency incident management teams: A literature review*]. *Journal of Contingencies and Crisis Management, 29*(2), 185. Wiley. https://doi.org/DOI: 10.1111/1468-5973.12341

Joseph, O. B., & Uzondu, N. C.Olatunbosun Bartholomew JosephNwankwo Charles Uzondu. (2024). Integrating AI and Machine Learning in STEM education: Challenges and opportunities. *Computer Science & IT Research Journal, 5*(8), 1732–1750. DOI: 10.51594/csitrj.v5i8.1379

Karimi, E., Smith, J., Billard, R., & Veitch, B. (2024). AI-based adaptive instructional systems for maritime safety training: A systematic literature review. *Discover Artificial Intelligence, 4*(1), 51. Advance online publication. DOI: 10.1007/s44163-024-00153-0

Khan, U. A., Kauttonen, J., Aunimo, L., & Alamäki, A. (2024). A System to Ensure Information Trustworthiness in Artificial Intelligence Enhanced Higher Education. *Journal of Information Technology Education, 23*, 13. DOI: 10.28945/5295

Kim, B., An, E.-J., Kim, S.-H., Preethaa, K. R. S., Lee, D., & Lukacs, R. R. (2024). SRGAN-enhanced unsafe operation detection and classification of heavy construction machinery using cascade learning. *Artificial Intelligence Review*, *57*(8), 206. Advance online publication. DOI: 10.1007/s10462-024-10839-7

Kim, J.-K., Lee, C.-H., Jeong, M., Cho, E., & Lee, Y.-G. (2023). Identifying Optimal Approaches for Sustainable Maritime Education and Training: Addressing Technological, Environmental, and Epidemiological Challenges. *Sustainability (Basel)*, *15*(10), 8092. DOI: 10.3390/su15108092

Kostyszyn, K., Wiedemann, C., Bermejo, R. M., Paige, A. J., Kalb-DellaRatta, K., & Brennan, S. (2024). A Computational Decision-Tree Approach to Inform Post-Conviction Intake Decisions. *The Wrongful Conviction Law Review*, *5*(1), 80–102. DOI: 10.29173/wclawr110

Koukaras, C., Hatzikraniotis, E., Mitsiaki, M., Koukaras, P., Tjortjis, C., & Stavrinides, S. G. (2025). Revolutionising Educational Management with AI and Wireless Networks: A Framework for Smart Resource Allocation and Decision-Making. *Applied Sciences (Basel, Switzerland)*, *15*(10), 5293. DOI: 10.3390/app15105293

Kretschmann, L. (2020). Leading indicators and maritime safety: Predicting future risk with a machine learning approach. *Journal of Shipping and Trade*, *5*(1), 19. Advance online publication. DOI: 10.1186/s41072-020-00071-1

Kwegyir-Afful, E., Hassan, T. O., & Kantola, J. (2021). Simulation-based assessments of fire emergency preparedness and response in virtual reality. *International Journal of Occupational Safety and Ergonomics*, *28*(2), 1316–1330. DOI: 10.1080/10803548.2021.1891395

Lee, H., Park, K., & Bae, H. (2025). Knowledge transfer Q-learning for vessel route planning using automatic identification system-derived expert trajectories. *Maritime Transport Research*, *9*, 100142. DOI: 10.1016/j.martra.2025.100142

Li, J., Dong, W., Yan, X., Liang, S., & Lv, C. (2024). A study on digital literacy and influencing factors among Chinese seafarers. *Scientific Reports*, *14*(1), 29574. DOI: 10.1038/s41598-024-81069-8

Li, J., & Wang, Z. (2025). Navigating digital transformation: Assessing the digital literacy of Chinese seafarers. *Information Research*, *30*(3), 370–389. DOI: 10.47989/ir30357587

Li, W. (2024). Understanding Learners and the Interplay Between Metacognitive Judgements of Learning and AI-Generated Explanations. *Deep Blue (University of Michigan)*. https://doi.org/DOI: 10.7302/23945

Lim, T., Gottipati, S., & Cheong, M. L. F. (2023). Artificial Intelligence in Today's Education Landscape: Understanding and Managing Ethical Issues for Educational Assessment. *Research Square (Research Square)*. https://doi.org/DOI: 10.21203/rs.3.rs-2696273/v1

Lin, S., Du, B., He, Z. Y., & Zhang, Z. (2024). Research on the Construction of Education System for Maritime Technology in the Context of Intelligent Ships. In *Atlantis Highlights in Computer Sciences/ Atlantis highlights in computer sciences* (p. 640). Atlantis Press., DOI: 10.2991/978-94-6463-502-7_67

Luchenko, D., Georgiievskyi, I., & Bielikova, M. (2023). Challenges and Developments in the Public Administration of Autonomous Shipping. *Lex Portus*, *9*(1). Advance online publication. DOI: 10.26886/2524-101X.9.1.2023.2

Ma, Q., Lian, Z., Du, X., Jiang, Y., BahooToroody, A., & Zhang, M. (2025). A deep learning method to predict ship short-term trajectory for proactive maritime traffic management. *Reliability Engineering & System Safety*, *265*, 111542. DOI: 10.1016/j.ress.2025.111542

Mansuy, M., Candries, M., Eloot, K., Page, S., Adams, R., Thorel, X., & Decroix, G. (2023). Optimized Turning Basin Design for Inland Waterways. *Journal of Waterway, Port, Coastal, and Ocean Engineering*, *149*(4), 04023008. Advance online publication. DOI: 10.1061/JWPED5.WWENG-1978

Marlantes, K. E., Bandyk, P. J., & Maki, K. J. (2024). Predicting ship responses in different seaways using a generalizable force correcting machine learning method. *Ocean Engineering*, *312*, 119110. DOI: 10.1016/j.oceaneng.2024.119110

Matveev, A. S. (2025). Artificial Intelligence in Maritime Fleet Management: Enhancing Operational Efficiency and Cost Reduction. *The American Journal of Engineering And Technology*, *7*(3), 133–140. DOI: 10.37547/tajet/Volume07Issue03-13

Morian, H., Härgestam, M., Hultin, M., Jönsson, H., Jönsson, K., Amorøe, T. N., & Creutzfeldt, J. (2023). Reliability and validity testing of team emergency assessment measure in a distributed team context. *Frontiers in Psychology*, *14*, 1110306. DOI: 10.3389/fpsyg.2023.1110306

Munim, Z. H., Kjeldsberg, F., Bustgaard, M., Bhagat, S., Haavardtun, P., Kim, T.-E., Lindroos, E., Thorvaldsen, H., Nyairo, F., & Lampiola, J. (2025). Predictive Performance Assessment in Simulation Training using Machine Learning. *International Journal of Artificial Intelligence in Education*, *35*(4), 2154–2184. DOI: 10.1007/s40593-025-00464-y

Naji, G. M. A., Sugathan, S. K., & Kalid, K. S. (2025). Integrating AI-Powered Mobile Immersive Technology for HSE Induction in an Oil and Gas Facility. A Conceptual Review. *Journal of Ecohumanism*, *4*(1). Advance online publication. DOI: 10.62754/joe.v4i1.6365

Nguyen, S., Gadel, M., Wang, K., Li, J., Zhang, X., Siang-Ching, K., Fu, X., & Qin, Z. (2025). Maritime decarbonization through machine learning: A critical systematic review of fuel and power prediction models. *Cleaner Logistics and Supply Chain*, *14*, 100210. DOI: 10.1016/j.clscn.2025.100210

Passarella, R., Safitri, A. I., Husni, N. L., Widyastuti, R., & Veny, H. (2024). Classification Models for Assessing the Severity of Marine Accidents Based on Machine Learning. *International Journal of Safety and Security Engineering*, *14*(4), 1213–1221. DOI: 10.18280/ijsse.140418

Pretolesi, D., Zechner, O., Guirao, D. G., Schrom-Feiertag, H., & Tscheligi, M. (2024). AI-Supported XR Training: Personalizing Medical First Responder Training. In *Smart innovation, systems and technologies* (p. 343). Springer Nature. https://doi.org/DOI: 10.1007/978-981-99-9018-4_25

Qu, J., Guo, H., Wang, W., Dang, S., & Liu, H. (2022). A Study on the Intuitive Design of Target Search Tasks under Time and Information Pressure. *Brain Sciences*, *12*(11), 1464. DOI: 10.3390/brainsci12111464

Rawson, A., Brito, M., & Sabeur, Z. (2021). Spatial Modeling of Maritime Risk Using Machine Learning. *Risk Analysis*, *42*(10), 2291–2311. DOI: 10.1111/risa.13866

Rehm, J., Reshodko, I., Børresen, S. Z., & Gundersen, O. E. (2024). The Virtual Driving Instructor: Multi-Agent System Collaborating via Knowledge Graph for Scalable Driver Education. *Proceedings of the AAAI Conference on Artificial Intelligence*, *38*(21), 22806–22814. DOI: 10.1609/aaai.v38i21.30315

Roques, A., Serpollet, D. K., Nicolaï, A., Buffat, S., James, Y., Vayatis, N., Bargiotas, I., & Vidal, P. (2025). Continuous Assessment of Mental Workload During Complex Human–Machine Interaction: Inferring Cognitive State from Signals External to the Operator. *Sensors (Basel)*, *25*(12), 3624. DOI: 10.3390/s25123624

Schwengel, D. A., Villagrán, I., Miller, G. T., Miranda, C., & Toy, S. (2024). Multimodal Assessment in Clinical Simulations: A Guide for Moving Towards Precision Education. *Medical Science Educator*, *35*(2), 1025–1034. DOI: 10.1007/s40670-024-02221-7

Scorgie, D. G., Feng, Z., Paes, D., Parisi, F., Yiu, T. W., & Lovreglio, R. (2023). Virtual reality for safety training: A systematic literature review and meta-analysis. *Safety Science*, *171*, 106372. DOI: 10.1016/j.ssci.2023.106372

Sellberg, C., & Sharma, A. (2024). Toward multimodal learning analytics in simulation-based collaborative learning: A design ethnography of maritime training. *International Journal of Computer-Supported Collaborative Learning*. Advance online publication. DOI: 10.1007/s11412-024-09435-2

Shaikh, F., Ahmed, B. S., & Swerin, A. (2025). Unsupervised detection of faults in industrial pumps from multivariate time series. *Machine Learning with Applications*, *22*, 100784. DOI: 10.1016/j.mlwa.2025.100784

Sharma, A., Undheim, P. E., & Nazir, S. (2022). Design and implementation of AI chatbot for COLREGs training. *WMU Journal of Maritime Affairs*, *22*(1), 107–123. DOI: 10.1007/s13437-022-00284-0

Simanjuntak, M. B., Rafli, Z., & Utami, S. R. (2024). Enhancing maritime education for ocean sustainability: A multidisciplinary approach. *BIO Web of Conferences, 106*, 2006. https://doi.org/DOI: 10.1051/bioconf/202410602006

Simion, D., Postolache, F., Fleacă, B., & Fleacă, E. (2024). AI-Driven Predictive Maintenance in Modern Maritime Transport—Enhancing Operational Efficiency and Reliability. *Applied Sciences (Basel, Switzerland)*, *14*(20), 9439. DOI: 10.3390/app14209439

Skinner, A., Diller, D., Kumar, R., Cannon-Bowers, J. A., Smith, R., Tanaka, A., Julian, D., & Perez, R. S. (2018). Development and application of a multi-modal task analysis to support intelligent tutoring of complex skills. *International Journal of STEM Education*, *5*(1), 14. Advance online publication. DOI: 10.1186/s40594-018-0108-5

Smith, J., Yazdanpanah, F., Thistle, R., Musharraf, M., & Veitch, B. (2020). Capturing Expert Knowledge to Inform Decision Support Technology for Marine Operations. *Journal of Marine Science and Engineering*, *8*(9), 689. DOI: 10.3390/jmse8090689

Spadon, G., Kumar, J., Eden, D., van Berkel, J., Foster, T., Soares, A., Fablet, R., Matwin, S., & Pelot, R. (2024). Multi-path long-term vessel trajectories forecasting with probabilistic feature fusion for problem shifting. *Ocean Engineering*, *312*, 119138. DOI: 10.1016/j.oceaneng.2024.119138

Tharun, A., Abrar, S. M., Ugashri, R., Boro, L. S. S. M., Sarma, K., Aziz, M., Jeneeth, T. S., & Sridharan, N. V. (2025). AI-DRIVEN EVOLUTION IN SOLID-PROPELLANT ROCKETRY: A HISTORICAL AND TECHNOLOGICAL PERSPECTIVE. *International Journal of Aerospace Engineering*, *3*(1), 1–18. DOI: 10.34218/IJASE_03_01_001

Theotokas, I., Lagoudis, I. N., & Raftopoulou, K. (2024). Challenges of maritime human resource management for the transition to shipping digitalization. *Journal of Shipping and Trade*, *9*(1), 6. Advance online publication. DOI: 10.1186/s41072-024-00165-0

Wahab, M. Y., Shazali, S. T. S., Mohamed, N. H., & Abdullah, A. R. A. (2025). Comprehensive structured analysis of machine learning in safety models. *International Journal of Advances in Applied Sciences*, *14*(3), 627. DOI: 10.11591/ijaas.v14.i3.pp627-638

Wahdiana, D., Ekohariadi, E., & Suhartini, R. (2025). The application of on training monitoring digital model for effectiveness maritime cadets on board training activities. *Edelweiss Applied Science and Technology*, *9*(9), 386–405. DOI: 10.55214/2576-8484.v9i9.9807

Waltz, M., & Okhrin, O. (2023). Spatial–temporal recurrent reinforcement learning for autonomous ships. *Neural Networks*, *165*, 634–653. DOI: 10.1016/j.neunet.2023.06.015

Wang, S., Wang, R., Ren, F., Chen, M., & Yan, R. (2025). A privacy-preserving federated transfer learning with ship mapping (FTL-SM) framework for accurate ship energy efficiency prediction. *Advanced Engineering Informatics*, *68*, 103569. DOI: 10.1016/j.aei.2025.103569

Webb, M., Fluck, A., Magenheim, J., Malyn-Smith, J., Waters, J., Deschênes, M., & Zagami, J. (2020). Machine learning for human learners: Opportunities, issues, tensions and threats. *Educational Technology Research and Development*, *69*(4), 2109–2130. DOI: 10.1007/s11423-020-09858-2

Wild, G., Nanyonga, A., Iqbal, A., Bano, S., Somerville, A., & Pollock, L. (2025). Lightweight and mobile artificial intelligence and immersive technologies in aviation [Review of *Lightweight and mobile artificial intelligence and immersive technologies in aviation*]. *Visual Computing for Industry Biomedicine and Art, 8*(1). Springer Nature. https://doi.org/DOI: 10.1186/s42492-025-00203-z

Winkler-Schwartz, A., Yilmaz, R., Mirchi, N., Bissonnette, V., Ledwos, N., Siyar, S., Azarnoush, H., Karlık, B., & Maestro, R. F. D. (2019). Machine Learning Identification of Surgical and Operative Factors Associated With Surgical Expertise in Virtual Reality Simulation. *JAMA Network Open*, *2*(8), e198363. Advance online publication. DOI: 10.1001/jamanetworkopen.2019.8363

Wu, H., Nie, R., Zeng, X., Cheng, C., Pan, J., Han, D., & Hosamo, H. (2024). Review of advanced emergency evacuation procedures in hospital buildings: Comprehensive analysis and insights. *Frontiers in Built Environment*, *10*, 1381813. Advance online publication. DOI: 10.3389/fbuil.2024.1381813

Xu, R., Cao, S., Kearns, S. K., Niechwiej-Szwedo, E., & Irving, E. L. (2024). Computational Cognitive Modeling of Pilot Performance in Pre-flight and Take-off Procedures. *Journal of Aviation/Aerospace Education Research*, *33*(4). Advance online publication. DOI: 10.58940/2329-258X.2026

Yang, S., Dai, P., Hua, Y., Tang, Q., Rui, M., & Lai, W. (2023). *3C Tecnología_Glosas de Innovación Aplicadas a La Pyme, 12*(1). https://doi.org/DOI: 10.17993/3ctecno.2023.v12n1e43

Zahid, A., Ferraro, A., Petrillo, A., & Felice, F. D. (2025). Exploring the Role of Digital Twin and Industrial Metaverse Technologies in Enhancing Occupational Health and Safety in Manufacturing. *Applied Sciences (Basel, Switzerland)*, *15*(15), 8268. DOI: 10.3390/app15158268

Zis, T., Psaraftis, H. N., & Ding, L. (2020). Ship weather routing: A taxonomy and survey. *Ocean Engineering*, *213*, 107697. DOI: 10.1016/j.oceaneng.2020.107697

ADDITIONAL READING

Ala, A., Hamidi, N., Yoniessa, S., Masito, F., & Muis, M. A. (2024). Simulation-based learning in maritime training: Enhancing competency and preparedness. *Meteor STIP Marunda*, *17*(1), 95–104. DOI: 10.36101/msm.v17i1.361

Chan, J. P., Pazouki, K., Norman, R., & Golightly, D. (2025). Investigating the impact of seafarer training in the autonomous shipping era. *Journal of Marine Science and Engineering*, *13*(4), 818. DOI: 10.3390/jmse13040818

Giannopoulos, A., Gkonis, P. K., Bithas, P. S., Kalafatelis, A., & Trakadas, P. (2024). Federated learning for maritime environments: Use cases, experimental results, and open issues. *Journal of Marine Science and Engineering*, *12*(6), 1034. DOI: 10.3390/jmse12061034

Karimi, E., Smith, J., Billard, R., & Veitch, B. (2024). AI-based adaptive instructional systems for maritime safety training: A systematic literature review. *Discover Artificial Intelligence*, *4*(1), 51. Advance online publication. DOI: 10.1007/s44163-024-00153-0

Lee, H., Park, K., & Bae, H. (2025). Knowledge transfer Q-learning for vessel route planning using automatic identification system-derived expert trajectories. *Maritime Transport Research*, *9*, 100142. DOI: 10.1016/j.martra.2025.100142

Passarella, R., Safitri, A. I., Husni, N. L., Widyastuti, R., & Veny, H. (2024). Classification models for assessing the severity of marine accidents based on machine learning. *International Journal of Safety and Security Engineering*, *14*(4), 1213–1223. DOI: 10.18280/ijsse.140418

KEY TERMS AND DEFINITIONS

Adaptive Learning Systems: Adaptive educational systems that modify instructional content, difficulty levels, and feedback according on learners' performance, progress, and specific competency requirements.

Artificial Intelligence (AI): A subdivision of computer science dedicated to creating computers that can execute activities usually necessitating human intelligence, such as decision-making, forecasting, and pattern recognition.

Competency-Based Maritime Education: A pedagogical method in maritime training that prioritizes quantifiable abilities, exhibited competencies, and performance results over time-based learning completion.

Machine Learning (ML): A branch of artificial intelligence that allows systems to learn from data, recognize patterns, and enhance decision-making processes autonomously, without explicit programming.

Maritime Simulation Training: An instructional approach enhanced by technology that simulates authentic marine operations and navigational situations within regulated virtual settings for educational and safety objectives.

Predictive Safety Analytics: A data-centric methodology employing machine learning algorithms to detect potential operational risks, predict equipment malfunctions, and improve maritime safety management proactively.

Reinforcement Learning: A machine learning method wherein an intelligent agent acquires optimal actions through ongoing contact with an environment, utilizing incentives and punishments as feedback mechanisms.

Situational Awareness: The capacity of maritime workers to assess environmental circumstances, analyze operational data, and foresee future changes to facilitate safe and effective decision-making.

Virtual Reality (VR) Maritime Training: A comprehensive digital training platform that allows cadets and marine professionals to rehearse operational protocols, emergency responses, and navigational tasks in authentic simulated environments.

Voyage Data Recorder (VDR): An onboard electronic system that persistently documents navigational, operational, and communication data for the purposes of accident investigation, performance analysis, and training assessment.

Chapter 10
Human Values at Sea:
Ethical Frameworks for AI-Driven Maritime Learning and Evaluation Systems

Egbert Edward Djajasasana
http://orcid.org/0009-0005-8268-5887
Politeknik Ilmu Pelayaran Makassar, Indonesia

Rusman Rusman
Politeknik Ilmu Pelayaran Makassar, Indonesia

Aprianto Aprianto
Politeknik Ilmu Pelayaran Makassar, Indonesia

Ni Ajeng Ratih Tuningrat
Politeknik Ilmu Pelayaran Makassar, Indonesia

ABSTRACT

The increasing incorporation of Artificial Intelligence (AI) into maritime education and training alters the comprehension and application of competence, ethics, and responsibility. This study examines the formulation of ethical frameworks that govern AI-driven learning and assessment in global maritime settings. It stresses human-centered design, data governance, openness, and moral responsibility as the most important parts of responsible innovation. The conversation talks about the need for fairness, inclusivity, and sustainability in AI-assisted maritime education from philosophical, institutional, and cross-cultural points of view. In the end, it calls for a vision of global ethical cooperation and lifelong moral education at sea, making sure that technological progress respects human dignity and professional integrity in a world where ships are becoming more automated.

DOI: 10.4018/979-8-3373-6670-8.ch010

HUMAN VALUES IN THE AGE OF AI AND MARITIME EDUCATION

1.1 The Human Dimension of AI Integration

To understand the complicated dynamics of this integration, we need to look at both the benefits and the moral problems that AI faces in maritime learning. In a good way, AI can make MET Ala et al. (2024) and Sundaram & Karimi (2023) more accurate, efficient, and tailored to each person. On the other hand, worries about relying too much on algorithms and the possible loss of moral agency among students and teachers need to be addressed (Ibrahim, 2024; Jiang & Zheng, 2020). The ethical concerns are mostly about making sure that these kinds of technologies make human moral reasoning better instead of worse. So, moving toward a model that combines human intuition with machine logic is important for making better decisions (Tomilin et al., 2023; Horbowska, 2024).

In the past, maritime training has been based on a human-centered approach that includes mentorship, apprenticeship, and hands-on learning experiences at sea. Prior to the advent of digital technologies, proficiency was predominantly exhibited through practical experiences and collaborative learning settings, supported by a culture of ethical discipline (Engtrø, 2022). The emergence of simulation technologies in the late twentieth century marked a transformation, facilitating more regulated training environments for essential domains such as navigation and crisis management (Kim et al., 2021; Fabian-Perona, 2025). This evolution persists with the advancement of AI-driven methodologies that provide customized educational trajectories while conforming to International Maritime Organization (IMO) standards (Sijabat et al., 2024; Ala et al., 2024). It is crucial that the equilibrium between human supervision and algorithmic efficiency in training programs precludes a solely data-driven educational methodology that neglects vital human attributes such as empathy and moral discernment (Rahmawati et al., 2025; Eklund et al., 2020).

As maritime education becomes more focused on data, important questions about fairness, openness, and responsibility in AI-driven tests come up. The core of human judgment—rooted in empathy, contextual understanding, and ethical reasoning—must remain integral to evaluative processes. This equilibrium is essential for the formulation of ethical frameworks for AI systems (Saxena & Bajotra, 2024; Renganayagalu et al., 2021). Maritime educators must act as both teachers and moral guardians, making sure that new technologies used in training raise the profession's ethical standards instead of lowering them.

1.2 Defining Core Human Values in Maritime Contexts

Human values are the moral compass that maritime professionals use to make decisions, act, and think about ethics. In the fast-changing world of AI-driven maritime learning, these values are even more important. They make sure that technological progress doesn't hurt the moral standards that have always been part of the seafaring profession. Safety, responsibility, honesty, and social justice are some of the most important values. Together, they make up the moral foundations of maritime education and practice. Safety is the most important thing in all maritime operations. It goes beyond just following the rules; it means protecting human life, the environment, and the health and safety of everyone. AI-enabled systems can make things safer by using predictive analytics and automation, but they need to be built and used in ways that support, not undermine, the human vigilance and moral duty that are important parts of maritime culture (Kim et al., 2021).

Responsibility goes beyond personal accountability to include duties to institutions and groups. In maritime education, it means using data responsibly, making decisions based on morals, and being open about AI-based evaluations. As automation grows, responsibility must be carefully spread out so that people are still in charge and seafarers know what intelligent systems can and can't do. Integrity, on the other hand, means being honest, professional, and morally consistent. In AI-mediated learning environments, integrity necessitates the prevention of bias, manipulation, or dishonesty in algorithmic evaluations, as well as the assurance that human evaluators maintain fairness and transparency in the interpretation of AI-generated outcomes (Tomilin et al., 2023; Horbowska, 2024).

Social justice is just as important. It means that everyone should have equal access to AI-enhanced learning opportunities, no matter where they live, what gender they are, or how much money they have. Maritime education must reject technological elitism, guaranteeing inclusivity for seafarers from developing regions and marginalized communities. Putting social justice into AI-powered training platforms encourages diversity, equal opportunity, and moral fairness—values that are important for creating a morally sound and globally competent maritime workforce.

In addition to these structural values, human connection is still the most important part of maritime education. Digital learning spaces must actively promote empathy, respect for other cultures, and the well-being of seafarers. Empathy helps people from different backgrounds and learning groups understand each other better, especially in a field where teams are made up of people from many different cultures and people move around the world. Respecting other cultures means that AI systems and digital teaching methods take into account the values, languages, and customs of different maritime cultures. This prevents cultural bias in content design or evaluation algorithms. In the digital age, it is important to put the health and well-being of seafarers first. Technology cannot replace the sense of belonging, purpose, and care that keeps morale high at sea (Horbowska, 2024).

In the end, defining and protecting these core values in AI-mediated maritime learning is not just the right thing to do; it is also necessary for long-lasting, human-centered innovation. By incorporating ethical principles into both design and practice, maritime education can successfully adapt to the digital age while remaining true to its fundamental mission: to develop seafarers who are not only skilled and adaptable but also compassionate, just, and acutely aware of their collective responsibility to humanity and the oceans.

1.3 AI, Automation, and Ethical Paradoxes at Sea

The incorporation of Artificial Intelligence (AI) and automation into maritime education and training has resulted in significant transformations—improving efficiency, predictive capabilities, and data-informed decision-making. However, these improvements also create moral dilemmas that go against long-held maritime values like responsibility, human judgment, and fairness. As ships, simulators, and training systems become more and more autonomous, the question of who is morally and operationally responsible when intelligent systems make mistakes comes up. The main ethical issue here is finding the right balance between being efficient and being responsible. AI improves navigation, performance evaluation, and safety management, but it also takes away some of our ability to make decisions, which could make it harder to tell who is morally responsible for what when sailing.

AI-driven decision-making promises never-before-seen accuracy in judging how skilled seafarers are by using real-time analytics, tracking their behavior, and automatic certification systems. But if you rely too much on data-driven evaluation, you might turn human learning into numbers and miss the subtleties and moral aspects of being a professional in the maritime industry. Ethical gatekeepers of maritime training used to be teachers and testers, but now they share power with algorithms that may not be clear or sensitive to different cultures. The problem of who is responsible gets worse when AI systems make mistakes, like misclassifying performance, misinterpreting intent, or giving biased advice. Who should be held responsible: the people who trained the system, the organizations that used it, or the AI developers who made the algorithms? These questions show how automation can both help and hurt people, making it an ethical paradox of shared responsibility (Tomilin et al., 2023; Horbowska, 2024).

The automation of evaluation and competency certification makes the ethical landscape even more complicated. More and more, maritime training schools use AI tools to standardize tests, check skills, and give out credentials. Even though these systems make things more efficient and fair, they also risk separating evaluation from the human context in which seafaring skills are learned. Data analytics alone cannot fully capture a seafarer's decision-making under stress, moral integrity, or teamwork ethics. When AI-generated assessments are used as the final word on someone's competence, it can lead to ethical dilemmas, especially if the trainees don't know the system's rules or biases. Without clear communication and human supervision, automated certification processes could hurt trust, lower professional dignity, and create a culture of relying on technology instead of moral judgment.

To deal with these contradictions, maritime education needs to reaffirm human-centered ethics as the basis for AI integration. Accountability must remain clear, and human teachers and testers must be moral anchors in decision-making loops. When designing AI systems, ethical frameworks should be used to make sure they are explainable, inclusive, and in line with maritime values like fairness, honesty, and respect for life. By putting these protections in place, the maritime community can make sure that automation enhances—not replaces—the moral duty that defines its profession, keeping the human conscience as the ultimate guide for a technologically advanced but morally sound maritime future.

NAVIGATING ETHICAL THEORIES AND FRAMEWORKS IN MARITIME AI SYSTEMS

2.1 Philosophical Foundations of Maritime Ethics

Long-standing moral traditions in the maritime profession stress duty, responsibility, and respect for human life at sea. As Artificial Intelligence (AI) becomes an important part of maritime learning and operations, these long-lasting moral principles become even more important. Comprehending the philosophical foundations of maritime ethics—specifically deontological, utilitarian, and virtue ethics—establishes a framework for assessing the role of technology in upholding human and institutional values in the age of automation. Each viewpoint provides unique yet synergistic insights into the ethical obligations of seafarers, educators, and policymakers operating within AI-assisted contexts (Jadaan et al., 2024).

From a deontological standpoint, maritime ethics focuses on moral obligation and the observance of universal principles, irrespective of consequences. For centuries, seafarers have been governed by codes of conduct that stress their duty to safety, honesty, and following maritime rules like the International Convention on Standards of Training, Certification, and Watchkeeping for Seafarers (STCW) (Sharma et al., 2022). Deontological ethics says that technology should follow these moral rules instead of making them. When automated systems suggest actions or evaluations, human actors must ensure that those decisions adhere to ethical obligations, prioritizing life, integrity, and fairness over algorithmic efficiency. Duty-oriented reasoning makes sure that AI is still a tool for doing the right thing, not a replacement for it.

Utilitarian ethics judges actions by what happens as a result, with the goal of maximizing overall well-being and minimizing harm. In the maritime context, utilitarianism endorses AI innovations that improve safety, efficiency, and global connectivity (Jadaan et al., 2024). Predictive analytics, automated navigation, and intelligent evaluation systems can stop accidents, make better use of resources, and help people learn better. But if you only look at the practical side of things, you might end up making morally questionable decisions, like putting profit or efficiency ahead of people's health or the environment. Thus, maritime educators and regulators must guarantee that the quest for collective advantage does not eclipse the ethical duty to safeguard individual dignity and human rights at sea (Jadaan et al., 2024).

Virtue ethics, on the other hand, puts more value on moral and character excellence than on rules or results. It calls for the development of virtues like courage, temperance, honesty, and kindness—traits that make up the perfect seafarer and maritime teacher. In AI-enhanced settings, virtue ethics emphasizes that ethical conduct is derived from developed moral discernment rather than algorithmic programming (Madancian & Hamed, 2025). A virtuous professional employs AI judiciously, informed by empathy and caution, guaranteeing that technology fosters moral development rather than undermining it.

In conclusion, these philosophical frameworks together create a maritime culture that is strong in morals. Deontological duty protects moral values, utilitarian reasoning finds the best way to do things for everyone, and virtue ethics helps people develop good moral character. Together, they lay the groundwork for moral responsibility and ethical decision-making in AI-assisted maritime learning and operations. This makes sure that technology upholds human values while keeping the spirit of honesty and professionalism alive at sea.

2.2 AI Ethics Frameworks in Education and Training

As AI becomes more common in schools and other educational settings, global organizations have created detailed ethical guidelines to make sure that new technologies are in line with human rights, fairness, and moral responsibility. In the maritime education and training (MET) sector, these frameworks are very important for making sure that AI systems are fair, open, and responsible. Ulnicane et al. (2020). The European Union (EU), the Institute of Electrical and Electronics Engineers (IEEE), the United Nations Educational, Scientific and Cultural Organization (UNESCO), and the International Maritime Organization (IMO) are all international groups that have set rules that are coming together to form a global agreement on how to govern AI responsibly (Dragomir, 2025). Applying these principles to the maritime sector guarantees that automation improves education and assessment while preserving the dignity, safety, and ethical responsibilities inherent in maritime professions (Reyes, 2025).

The EU Ethical Guidelines for Trustworthy AI list seven main ideas: human agency and oversight, technical robustness, privacy, transparency, diversity, societal well-being, and accountability (Dragomir, 2025). These principles are very important for maritime training, where AI can help with decision-making but people must still be in charge. The guidelines stress explainability, which means that seafarers and teachers should know how AI systems come to conclusions, especially when it comes to testing and certification (Ravi et al., 2022). Transparent algorithms in maritime simulation and e-learning platforms stop evaluations that aren't clear and make learners trust technology even more.

The IEEE's Ethically Aligned Design framework builds on this idea by making ethics a part of the design process. It promotes "values-driven innovation," which means that systems should be built with respect for human rights, cultural differences, and professional standards (Eyinade et al., 2025). This idea is especially important for MET schools that are using AI-based competency tests or predictive analytics. Including ethical reflection in the design and implementation stages makes sure that maritime technologies help create learning environments that are open to everyone and don't favor certain regions, languages, or socioeconomic groups (Sharma, 2025).

The 2021 UNESCO Recommendation on the Ethics of Artificial Intelligence builds on this by stressing fairness, inclusion, and sustainability in AI use in schools (Reyes, 2025). This means that maritime teachers need to make sure that everyone has equal access to digital tools, keep student data safe, and be open about how algorithms make decisions. The framework from UNESCO also stresses the need to build teachers' skills so they can understand, audit, and use AI technologies in a moral way in classrooms and simulators (Ignjatović, 2024).

At the same time, the IMO, which is the global authority on maritime safety and training, can put these universal principles into the context of seafaring standards. Aligning AI ethics with STCW conventions makes sure that automation adds to human skills instead of taking them away (Folorunso et al., 2024). Institutions can maintain moral integrity and promote innovation by incorporating fairness, transparency, and accountability into AI-driven maritime systems. In the end, these global ethical frameworks work together to lead the maritime industry toward a digital transformation that puts people first. In this transformation, technology enhances rather than undermines the moral and professional values that protect life, learning, and work at sea.

2.3 Toward a Maritime-Specific Ethical Model

Global AI ethics frameworks are useful, but the maritime industry needs a model that is based on its own unique operational risks, multicultural workforce, and regulatory challenges. Maritime education and training (MET) are different from most other professional learning environments because they require students to make high-risk decisions, work with people from other countries, and follow strict safety rules. So, an ethical model for AI integration in this field needs to bring together human-centered design, risk ethics, and maritime professional codes into a single framework that protects both moral responsibility and technological progress (Reyes, 2025).

The main idea behind this method is human-centered design. The needs, values, and limitations of sailors and teachers should be the main focus when creating AI-powered maritime learning systems. The model doesn't put technology in charge of making decisions. Instead, it encourages participatory co-design, where teachers, cadets, regulators, and engineers all help shape AI tools. This kind of inclusiveness makes sure that ethical values like fairness, respect, and cultural sensitivity are built into the project from the start and throughout its use. A human-centered model also needs AI that is easy to understand and explain, so that seafarers can trust it and understand how it works instead of seeing it as an unknown authority.

It is just as important to include risk ethics. AI-based decisions can have effects on life, the environment, and property, and maritime environments are naturally dangerous. Risk ethics says that we should actively find, reduce, and talk about any uncertainties related to AI. For example, predictive algorithms that check for navigation errors or judge how well a simulator works must have ways for humans to check them to avoid being too sure of machine outputs. Ethical risk management goes beyond just making sure that AI systems are technically reliable. It also includes moral foresight, which means making sure that AI systems are used responsibly when things are uncertain (Folorunso et al., 2024).

A maritime-specific ethical model can use long-standing professional codes of conduct, like those set out by the International Maritime Organization (IMO) and national maritime academies, as a starting point. These codes stress honesty, safety, professionalism, and helping others. Including them in AI governance makes sure that traditional maritime values and new digital practices stay connected.

To put this synthesis into action, the chapter suggests a "Ethical Compass" model for AI-based maritime learning and testing. This model has four connected parts: (1) Human Agency, which says that human judgment is the most important thing; (2) Transparency, which makes sure that AI processes are clear and can be checked; (3) Accountability, which says that developers, educators, and institutions all share responsibility; and (4) Justice, which says that everyone should have equal access and outcomes. The compass metaphor captures the seafaring ethos of navigation and direction—reminding educators, engineers, and policymakers that ethical decision-making, like navigation, requires constant adjustment amid dynamic conditions. This Ethical Compass can help maritime education find a way for AI to make people better at their jobs, protect their moral integrity, and guide the industry toward a future where technology makes people more professional at sea but still keeps their morals in check.

THE ETHICS OF LEARNING ANALYTICS AND AUTOMATED ASSESSMENT

3.1 AI-Enhanced Learning Evaluation Systems

The use of Artificial Intelligence (AI) in learning evaluation systems has changed how maritime schools check for competence, track performance, and give students the green light to go to sea. Maritime academies can use machine learning and data analytics to gather and analyze a lot of information from simulators, online platforms, and training modules to see how well students are doing in terms of their cognitive, technical, and behavioral skills. Rao et al. (2025). These systems promise efficiency, accuracy, and real-time feedback, which will make maritime assessments more reliable than they have been in the past, when they were based on human observation and judgment (Tariq, 2025). However, beneath this technological progress exists a convoluted ethical landscape wherein bias, opacity, and accountability present substantial obstacles to fairness and integrity in AI-assisted evaluation.

AI-enhanced evaluation systems use machine learning algorithms to keep an eye on how well students are doing in many areas (Alshebani et al., 2023). In maritime settings, these may encompass navigational decision-making, situational awareness, teamwork, and crisis response, all evaluated through simulation data and digital interaction logs. Predictive analytics can find gaps in learning, tailor training to each person, and suggest flexible paths that follow the Standards of Training, Certification, and Watchkeeping for Seafarers (STCW) (Abisoye, 2024). Data-driven evaluation, on the other hand, makes things more objective, but it also runs the risk of turning competence into numbers that don't have any context. Maritime skills are inherently contextual and ethical, necessitating judgment, accountability, and empathy—qualities that are challenging to quantify through algorithms (Saeed et al., 2024).

When bias gets into algorithmic grading, it creates ethical risks. Imbalanced data sets, cultural differences in how people learn, or differences in gender and language in training data can all lead to bias (Raaj, 2025). For instance, an algorithm that mostly learns how to navigate in the West might not understand how cadets from other areas make decisions. If these systems aren't carefully checked, they could keep inequality going and make AI-driven tests less trustworthy. Additionally, opacity, commonly known as the "black box" issue, exacerbates these risks. When students and teachers don't understand how AI comes to its conclusions, trust breaks down, and the evaluation process becomes less credible

(Щербан, 2022). For maritime education institutions, it is morally necessary to be open about how algorithms are designed, where data comes from, and how decisions are made.

Accountability makes the moral landscape even more complicated. If an AI system misclassifies competence or fails to detect a critical error, who is responsible—the educator, the developer, or the institution that uses it? Maritime ethics says that accountability must always be focused on people (Tariq, 2021). Teachers and testers must still have the final say on how to interpret AI-generated results. This is to make sure that moral reasoning works with algorithmic accuracy (Raaj, 2025).

To promote ethical resilience, AI-enhanced maritime evaluation must implement human-in-the-loop models, wherein instructors supervise, authenticate, and contextualize algorithmic results (Garima & Jain, 2025). Regular bias audits, transparency reports, and participatory feedback mechanisms can help keep things fair and open to everyone (Motz et al., 2022). Ultimately, AI should enhance—not supplant—the ethical and pedagogical discernment that characterizes maritime education. When used correctly, AI evaluation systems can help make maritime learning more fair, safe, and competent. They can also help shape the future of maritime learning by promoting both technological excellence and moral responsibility.

3.2 Data Governance and Privacy at Sea

In this age of AI-driven maritime learning and performance evaluation, privacy and data governance have become major ethical issues. The digitization of training, certification, and onboard operations has produced vast amounts of personal and professional data, including simulator performance logs, biometric readings, learning analytics, and behavioral assessments. When used properly, these data streams can make things safer, better for learning, and help people make decisions based on facts. But without strong ethical guidelines, the same data can be used for spying, discrimination, or other wrong purposes. So, protecting the privacy and dignity of maritime students and workers is an important part of using AI in an ethical way (Motz et al., 2022).

Personal learning data and records of seafarer performance must be treated as private information, with rules about consent, privacy, and proportionality. More and more, maritime schools are using AI to gather detailed information about how cadets steer virtual ships, deal with emergencies, and work together in team simulations. These kinds of analytics can help teachers see how students are doing and how they are improving their skills, but they also put students at risk of being judged unfairly and profiled. If performance data is not properly anonymized or protected, it could be used to decide who can get a job, get a promotion, or face disciplinary action. This raises ethical questions about fairness, data ownership, and informed consent. Because of this, the maritime education sector needs to use clear data management rules that explain what data is collected, how it is used, and who can see it. Learners and seafarers must have the right to review, change, or delete their data. This will bring maritime practices in line with international data protection standards like the EU's General Data Protection Regulation (GDPR).

Another level of difficulty comes from maritime data sovereignty and compliance across borders. Because seafaring is a global activity, data often crosses borders where privacy laws and ethical standards are different. A cadet's training data that was collected in Indonesia, stored on a European server, and analyzed by a company in Singapore may be subject to different rules and regulations. This movement of data across borders needs clear rules that protect both national sovereignty and international cooperation. Maritime organizations need to make ethical data-sharing agreements that follow cultural norms, protect against abuse, and follow regional rules like the ASEAN Digital Data Governance or the IMO cybersecurity guidelines (Raaj, 2025).

As AI systems become more dependent on cloud-based infrastructure and global databases, maritime organizations must also make sure they can handle cyber threats and manage risks in an ethical way. Unauthorized access to performance records or data breaches can have serious effects on safety, reputation, and human rights. To lessen these risks, data governance should be a part of the ethics codes of institutions, with a focus on accountability, openness, and fairness. In the end, responsible data governance at sea is not only a technical requirement but also a moral duty. This means that the search for digital efficiency should not hurt trust, dignity, or justice for people who live, work, and learn in the world's oceans.

3.3 Human Oversight and Moral Agency

As Artificial Intelligence (AI) becomes more common in maritime education and training, it becomes more and more important for people to be in charge and make moral decisions. Automation improves the accuracy and scalability of assessments, but it can't replace the moral judgment, empathy, and situational awareness that make human decision-making unique. AI must be a tool that helps, not replaces, human authority in the high-stakes world of maritime operations, where ethical, safety, and professional consequences are huge. Because of this, instructors, examiners, and maritime authorities are the ethical gatekeepers in AI decision loops. They make sure that the results of algorithms stay in line with human values, institutional integrity, and international maritime standards (Abisoye, 2024).

Instructors and examiners do more than just watch over technical work. They serve as moral interpreters of AI-generated data, converting algorithmic suggestions into evaluations that take the situation into account. An AI system might flag a trainee's poor performance based on navigation simulator metrics, but a human instructor can put these results in context by realizing that stress, language barriers, or equipment problems may have affected behavior. This kind of interpretive intervention keeps things fair and stops judgments that are based on machines and not on real people. Instructors are also very important in teaching cadets about AI literacy. They help them understand how automated systems work, what their limits are, and how to ask questions about algorithmic decisions in a responsible way. By being both assessors and mentors, teachers help future seafarers become more aware of ethics and learn how to think critically.

Likewise, maritime authorities and regulatory bodies have a moral duty to keep an eye on things. As AI becomes more important for certification and performance monitoring, regulators need to set ethical standards for algorithmic transparency, explainability, and accountability. The International Maritime Organization (IMO) and national maritime administrations can make sure that all AI-assisted evaluations have a human-in-the-loop mechanism. This means that human assessors must check the final decisions, especially those that affect certification or career advancement. This makes sure that moral responsibility can still be traced and that seafarers still believe in the fairness of institutions (Tariq, 2025).

One of the most important ethical issues in AI-assisted maritime learning is avoiding "automation bias," which is the tendency to trust machine-generated outputs too much. When people think that algorithms are always right or fair, they may stop thinking critically and taking moral responsibility. The answer is to promote participatory ethics, where people and machines make decisions together through open dialogue. Human-in-the-loop models exemplify this philosophy by guaranteeing ongoing human evaluation throughout all phases of AI implementation—design, operation, assessment, and modification.

In the end, keeping moral agency in maritime education means keeping the human conscience as the final judge of what is right and wrong. AI can handle data, but only people can tell what's right and wrong when things aren't clear. Maritime institutions make sure that technology enhances, not lessens, the moral responsibility and professional honor that have always guided those who work on the seas by putting oversight, reflection, and empathy into AI systems.

INSTITUTIONAL AND GLOBAL DIMENSIONS OF ETHICAL AI IN MARITIME EDUCATION

4.1 Governance and Policy Structures

To safely use Artificial Intelligence (AI) in maritime education and training (MET), there needs to be strong governance and policy structures that make sure of ethical accountability, institutional transparency, and international alignment. As AI technologies become more important to learning management systems, simulation platforms, and assessment tools, maritime schools need to set up governance systems that protect integrity while allowing for new ideas (Reyes, 2021). Policies that work must protect against the ethical risks of automation, such as bias, lack of transparency, and privacy violations, while also encouraging consistency in standards and practices around the world (Dragomir, 2025). Governance in this context transcends mere administration; it constitutes a moral framework aimed at maintaining equity, security, and professionalism throughout the maritime education ecosystem (Kim et al., 2021).

Ethics boards and AI oversight committees are very important for making decisions at the institutional level. These groups, which include teachers, technologists, lawyers, and ethicists, are in charge of checking the design, use, and monitoring of AI-powered tools used in maritime training (Folorunso et al., 2024). Some of their jobs are to check the fairness of algorithms, make sure they follow privacy laws, and keep the human-in-the-loop principle in place during assessments. Ethical review protocols ought to be institutionalized in conjunction with accreditation procedures, mandating that AI-based systems undergo regular audits to ensure transparency, explainability, and cultural sensitivity (Khakpaki & Sepehri, 2025). This governance model makes sure that AI programs not only meet technical and educational goals, but also follow ethical standards that reflect the values of people who work in the maritime industry (Sharma et al., 2022).

Accreditation bodies and maritime regulators take this system of governance to the next level. The International Maritime Organization's (IMO) Standards of Training, Certification, and Watchkeeping for Seafarers (STCW) convention is still the best way to make sure that training centers keep their skills, safety, and moral standards. AI technologies are changing how tests and certifications are done, so it's important to follow STCW principles (Ahmmed, 2021). AI governance in MET must embody the same strictness and responsibility that are the basis for safety rules at sea. For instance, recognized maritime authorities should give AI-assisted simulators and evaluation platforms their stamp of approval. This would prove that they are not only technically sound but also morally sound. In collaboration with international organizations, national maritime administrations can create ethical AI guidelines that align with the IMO's overarching goal of safe, secure, and sustainable shipping (Hastuti & Syafruddin, 2023).

Also, policies that are in line with new AI governance standards, like those set by the IEEE, UNESCO, and the European Union, can help maritime institutions gain more credibility around the world (Dragomir, 2025). Including ideas like fairness, accountability, and openness in national and institutional policies makes sure that systems can work together and that people in different countries can recognize each other.

Governance structures must also be ready for problems that could come up in the future, like training autonomous vessels, certifying them from afar, and managing data across borders (Badhan et al., 2024).

4.2 Ethical Leadership and Professional Development

The quick use of Artificial Intelligence (AI) in maritime education and training (MET) means that everyone involved needs to be ready technically and also need to learn how to be an ethical leader and grow professionally. As maritime institutions undergo digital transformation, educators, assessors, and technologists must develop into ethical leaders adept at managing the moral intricacies associated with automation, data analytics, and algorithmic evaluation. In this case, ethical leadership goes beyond following the rules. It means being proactive about moral reflection, inclusivity, and human-centered innovation that protects the integrity of maritime learning (Badhan et al., 2024).

The key to this change is getting teachers and other professionals to be more aware of ethics. Maritime teachers and examiners are moral authorities who shape the moral values of future sailors. They need to know not only how AI tools work, but also what they mean for the bigger picture—how algorithms affect grading, how data is gathered and understood, and how bias can creep into systems that seem to be fair. Educators can learn how to spot ethical risks and handle situations that involve fairness, privacy, or accountability through institutional training programs, workshops, and conversations between people from different fields. In the same way, technologists and software developers who work for maritime institutions need to learn about ethical design principles. They should work closely with teachers to make sure that AI systems are in line with maritime values like safety, honesty, and respect for human life. When everyone involved has the same moral vision, it creates a culture of trust and openness that makes both the institution and the students more confident.

To keep this culture going, people need to keep getting ethical training. You can't learn ethical competence in just one lesson; you have to keep learning, thinking, and changing. Maritime institutions ought to integrate ethics education into professional development frameworks, guaranteeing that every innovation—be it in simulation technology, data analytics, or automated assessment—is scrutinized through an ethical perspective. Scenario-based learning, reflective journals, and peer dialogue can assist educators in critically evaluating real-world instances of AI failures, data misuse, or automation bias. These reflective practices build ethical resilience, which helps professionals see moral problems coming before they turn into crises (Maheswari, 2025).

At the top, administrators and policymakers need to show how to run an ethical government by making decisions that are clear and holding people accountable. Leaders send the message that ethical competence is just as important as technical skill by including ethics in institutional policies, promotion criteria, and performance evaluations. So, ethical leadership is always a journey of awareness, reflection, and responsibility—it's a living practice that changes as technology does. In AI-driven maritime institutions, such leadership ensures that innovation is guided not solely by efficiency or profit, but by the enduring moral compass of the maritime profession: safeguarding human dignity, fostering fairness, and promoting the greater good at sea and ashore.

4.3 Cross-Cultural and Global Justice Perspectives

The incorporation of Artificial Intelligence (AI) into maritime education and training (MET) occurs within a highly globalized framework, linking seafarers, educators, and institutions from various cultural, economic, and political contexts. When AI-powered systems change the way we learn, get certified, and move up in our careers, issues of inequality, inclusivity, and cultural diversity become very important ethical issues. So, the promise of technological progress must be balanced with the goal of global justice. This means that digital transformation should help all regions equally, not make the gaps between the Global North and South even bigger. Ethical AI in maritime education must embody the diversity of human experiences, languages, and values inherent in the global maritime community (Dragomir, 2025).

To fight inequality and make sure everyone is included, we need to recognize that the world's maritime academies don't all have the same amount of technology and resources. Institutions in developing countries often have problems like slow internet connections, old simulators, and not enough money to adopt AI. The growth of AI could make the gaps between rich and poor countries even bigger, giving more power to well-funded schools in the Global North and leaving seafarers from less-developed maritime areas behind. To fight this, ethical maritime frameworks need to include ideas of accessibility and inclusiveness. This means that AI tools should be made to work well in a variety of situations and at different levels of technological maturity. Low-bandwidth learning platforms, multilingual interfaces, and culturally responsive algorithms can all help make sure that everyone can participate fairly. This way, all seafarers can benefit from AI-enhanced training, no matter where they are or how much money they have (Reyes, 2021).

Another important part of ethical maritime education is cultural diversity. AI systems used in maritime training must take into account that seafaring crews are some of the most diverse professional groups in the world. Cultural biases built into data or algorithmic design can unintentionally favor some behavioral norms over others. For example, different cultures have different ways of talking to each other, different levels of leadership, and different ideas about risk. However, AI-based tests often don't take these differences into account. By using different data sets, creating content that includes everyone, and getting feedback from everyone, we can make sure that AI respects the human side of seafaring instead of making it all the same.

Cooperation between the North and the South is very important for raising global ethical standards for AI in seafarer training. Developed maritime nations have the technological know-how, while developing regions offer useful information about the cultural and operational realities of the situation. Collaborative policy networks that connect maritime organizations from the IMO, ASEAN, the EU, and Africa can help people work together to make ethical guidelines that work in all parts of the world. Partnerships like these should focus on building skills, sharing research, and making technology available to everyone, which will encourage fairness and learning from each other. In the end, an ethically sound and globally inclusive AI ecosystem in maritime education depends on solidarity. This means bringing people together through shared responsibility, respect for diversity, and a shared commitment to justice on the world's oceans.

STEERING TOWARD AN ETHICALLY INTELLIGENT MARITIME FUTURE

5.1 Designing Ethical-by-Design AI Systems

As AI becomes more common in maritime education, training, and testing, the focus shifts from just using it to designing it in a way that reflects human values, fairness, and responsibility. The idea of "ethical-by-design" stresses that ethics shouldn't be an afterthought; they should be built into the very beginning of technological development. In maritime settings, where safety, human welfare, and environmental stewardship are of utmost importance, this design philosophy guarantees that AI reinforces rather than undermines the ethical principles of the profession (Karnavas et al., 2025). Ethical-by-design AI is a moral commitment that brings together teachers, developers, policymakers, and sailors to work together to find solutions that fit their values.

Integrating value-sensitive design (VSD) into AI development is essential to this effort. VSD directly includes moral, social, and cultural factors in the design and use of AI systems. In maritime education and training, this entails developing AI tools that honor seafarers' autonomy, protect privacy, and guarantee equity in evaluation and certification procedures (Karimi et al., 2024). For instance, if an AI system is in charge of judging someone's navigational skills, it should give explanations that both teachers and students can understand. This kind of explainability not only builds trust, but it also makes it easier for people to keep an eye on things and do regular ethical audits (D'Augusta et al., 2025). Furthermore, the choices made by these systems should be able to be traced, so that people can be held accountable and mistakes can be fixed. This openness turns AI from a black box into a partner that works with people to improve their judgment (Yorulmaz & Buyukozturk, 2025).

The ethical design process necessitates the active involvement of maritime stakeholders in the collaborative formulation of ethical guidelines. If technologists are the only ones who shape AI development in schools, it can't be ethically sound. It needs to reflect the values and experiences of people who work and train at sea. Collaborative workshops, multi-stakeholder consultations, and cross-sector partnerships can help make sure that important ethical principles like safety, fairness, inclusivity, and human dignity are included in AI design projects from the start (Nhleko, 2023). Maritime educators, regulators, unions, and students should all help decide what AI should and shouldn't do and what the limits of automation in training and tests should be.

Also, adopting ethical-by-design practices makes maritime institutions leaders in moral innovation, making sure that their digital transformations are based on ethical foresight rather than just new technology. Ethical-by-design AI combines technical accuracy with human values to make maritime learning spaces more open, welcoming, and trustworthy. In the end, it changes AI from just a tool for making things more efficient into a moral compass that guides the maritime industry toward a future where technology enhances human wisdom, protects dignity, and strengthens the moral duties that come with every voyage at sea.

5.2 Sustainability, Human Dignity, and Environmental Responsibility

In the age of Artificial Intelligence (AI), maritime education must change in a way that is consistent with the values of sustainability, human dignity, and environmental responsibility. As the maritime industry goes through both digital and environmental changes at the same time, it is not only desirable but also necessary to include ethical AI in the framework of green shipping, safety, and sustainable operations. The oceans, which belong to all of us, need a technological future that balances new ideas with caring for the environment and fairness for all (Yorulmaz & Buyukozturk, 2025). So, maritime AI needs to work in a moral ecosystem where technological intelligence works with ecological wisdom and human compassion.

To make ethical AI work with green shipping and sustainability, we need to rethink how digital technologies can help maritime operations have less of an effect on the environment. AI systems that can improve fuel efficiency, predict when equipment needs to be serviced, and keep an eye on emissions are directly helping to decarbonize and reach the goals of the International Maritime Organization's (IMO) Green Shipping Strategy. In maritime education and training (MET), learners can use simulation tools and AI-driven analytics to learn how to navigate and manage logistics in a way that is good for the environment. Ethical AI design makes sure that these technologies raise awareness about the environment instead of putting profit or speed ahead of safety for the environment. Also, algorithmic decision-making in route planning, cargo handling, and energy management needs to be clear, able to be checked, and follow international environmental laws. By incorporating sustainability metrics and ethical reasoning into AI systems, maritime institutions develop seafarers who possess not only digital proficiency but also environmental awareness and moral responsibility for the ocean's well-being (Karimi et al., 2024).

But protecting human dignity in technology-based maritime work is an important part of sustainability. As automation changes how people work, ethical frameworks need to make sure that seafarers' roles, rights, and identities are still respected. AI can take over tasks that are the same over and over, but it should never make people feel less important or take away their pride in their work. So, maritime education should put more emphasis on teaching empathy, teamwork, and moral decision-making along with technical skills. Ethical AI tools should help people stay healthy by spotting fatigue, keeping an eye on safety conditions, and stopping exploitation, but they shouldn't go too far and invade people's privacy. To protect human dignity, we must protect agency. This means that workers should be active participants in the technological transition instead of passive subjects of algorithmic control.

In the end, environmental responsibility and human ethics must come together to form a complete maritime ethos. Institutions that use AI in a responsible way can help bring about a change where sustainability is not just a policy goal but a way of life. AI can be a force for stewardship when it brings together environmental awareness, social justice, and digital integrity. This will create a maritime future that respects both the planet and the people who depend on it.

5.3 Vision for Global Ethical Collaboration

The maritime world is global by nature, with its operations, workforce, and learning systems going beyond national borders. As AI becomes more important in education, training, and government in the field, it is necessary to work toward an ethically unified but culturally diverse framework. For maritime learning and operations to thrive in the future, countries, organizations, and businesses must work together to set the moral direction for the development and use of AI. Such collaboration must extend beyond policy alignment to foster shared values of trust, inclusivity, and sustainability across the world's oceans.

Making global partnerships for responsible maritime AI is a key step toward this goal. Ethical issues, such as data governance and algorithmic bias, affect people all over the world and need to be dealt with in a coordinated way. The International Maritime Organization (IMO), the International Labour Organization (ILO), and regional groups like ASEAN and the European Maritime Safety Agency (EMSA) can all help make this cooperation happen. These partnerships can help set and keep up-to-date shared ethical standards for using AI in training, certification, and operations. A global maritime AI ethics charter, created by educators, policymakers, industry leaders, and seafarer unions working together, could be a moral guide that makes sure that technological progress never puts safety, human dignity, or the environment at risk (Yorulmaz & Buyukozturk, 2025).

These frameworks would also encourage the sharing of open data, clear algorithmic auditing, and training programs that cross borders. This would make AI-driven maritime education available to both developed and developing countries.

It is just as important to foster a culture of moral resilience and lifelong ethical literacy at sea. As automation changes the roles of seafarers, ethical reasoning needs to become a part of maritime education that is always changing and growing. Lifelong ethical literacy gives seafarers, teachers, and administrators the tools they need to question, adapt, and act responsibly in the face of quick changes in technology and morals. Ethics should be a central part of all training modules at institutions, from navigation and engineering to leadership and communication. Seafarers can learn to think critically and have moral courage in difficult situations involving AI and automation through scenario-based learning, ethical simulation exercises, and intercultural dialogue (Karimi et al., 2024).

Moral resilience also helps maritime workers stay strong when they aren't sure what to do about ethical issues, like when data is misused, automation goes wrong, or there are conflicts between caring for the environment and making money. To build this resilience, institutions need to have cultures that support ethical discussion and reflection instead of punishment. In the end, a maritime community that is connected around the world and shares a sense of moral responsibility will protect not only the integrity of technology but also the bond between people and the sea that has lasted for centuries. Maritime education can lead the world to a morally intelligent future by promoting cooperation, openness, and compassion. In this future, technology and morality will work together in harmony on every horizon.

CONCLUSION

The integration of Artificial Intelligence (AI) into maritime education and training represents both a transformative opportunity and a profound ethical responsibility. As learning environments become increasingly data-driven and automated, the essence of maritime professionalism—rooted in duty, safety, and human dignity—must remain the guiding compass of innovation. The discussions across this work underscore that technology alone cannot ensure competence or moral integrity; it is the conscious design, governance, and ethical stewardship of AI that determine whether progress serves humanity or undermines it.

Building an ethically intelligent maritime ecosystem requires a multi-dimensional approach. At the institutional level, ethical governance structures, continuous professional development, and transparent evaluation systems ensure that AI applications remain accountable to human oversight. Globally, cooperation among maritime organizations, educators, and policymakers is essential to establish unified standards that reflect fairness, inclusivity, and environmental sustainability. By aligning ethical frameworks with the International Maritime Organization (IMO) conventions and emerging global AI governance principles, the sector can maintain coherence while respecting regional and cultural diversity.

Equally vital is nurturing human-centered leadership and lifelong ethical literacy. Seafarers, educators, and technologists must be equipped not only with digital competence but also with the moral resilience to navigate complex decisions in AI-mediated contexts. Through participatory ethics, explainable AI design, and the preservation of moral agency, the maritime community can ensure that automation strengthens rather than diminishes human judgment and compassion.

In essence, the ethical future of maritime education depends on harmonizing intelligence—both artificial and human—with responsibility. By embedding human values, transparency, and justice into every layer of AI development and deployment, the maritime sector can chart a sustainable and humane course forward, where technology advances not in isolation from ethics, but in faithful service to life, safety, and the shared stewardship of the oceans.

REFERENCES

Abisoye, A. (2024). Creating a conceptual framework for ai-powered stem education analytics to enhance student learning outcomes. *IJFMR, 5*(1), 157–167. DOI: 10.54660/.IJFMR.2024.5.1.157-167

Ahmmed, R. (2021). A framework for maritime english language planning in bangladeshi maritime education and training institutes. *SN Social Sciences, 1*(7), 168. Advance online publication. DOI: 10.1007/s43545-021-00188-5

Ala, A., Hamidi, N., Yoniessa, S., Masito, F., & Muis, M. (2024). Simulation-based learning in maritime training: Enhancing competency and preparedness. *Meteor Stip Marunda, 17*(1), 95–102. DOI: 10.36101/msm.v17i1.361

Alshebani, M., Alanazi, M., Alanazi, A., Almotlaq, M., ALdawsari, F. M., Almeshari, A. M., & Nofal, A. R. (2023). Application of artificial intelligence in paramedic education: current scenario and future perspective: a narrative review. *The Journal of Medicine Law & Public Health, 4*(1), 299–306. DOI: 10.52609/jmlph.v4i1.98

Badhan, I., Hasnain, M., Rahman, M., Chowdhury, I., & Sayem, M. (2024). Strategic deployment of advance surveillance ecosystems: An analytical study on mitigating unauthorized u.s. border entry. *International Journal of Systems and Society, 3*(4), 82–94. DOI: 10.63544/ijss.v3i4.105

D'Augusta, V., Gazzaneo, L., Longo, F., Manfredi, K., Nicoletti, L., Padovano, A., … & Talarico, S. (2025). Advancing maritime training through a vr-enhanced ship bridge simulator: a preliminary usability analysis.. DOI: 10.3233/PMST250101

Dragomir, A. (2025). The role of the european union in shaping an ethical and legal framework for artificial intelligence (ai) in education. *SDGS, 6*, e035. DOI: 10.37497/sdgs.v6istudies.35

Eklund, R., Sellberg, C., & Osvalder, A. (2020). From tacit knowledge to visual expertise: eye-tracking support in maritime education and training., 269-275. DOI: 10.1007/978-3-030-50896-8_39

Engtrø, E. (2022). A discussion on the implementation of the polar code and the stcw convention's training requirements for ice navigation in polar waters. *Journal of Transportation Security, 15*(1-2), 41–67. DOI: 10.1007/s12198-021-00241-7

Eyinade, W., Ezeilo, O., & Ogundeji, I. (2025). Navigating the complexities of ethical ai and algorithmic accountability in modern technological practices. *Computer Science & It Research Journal, 6*(6), 371–381. DOI: 10.51594/csitrj.v6i6.1962

Fabian-Perona, E. (2025). Maritime education and language as the acting link between bridge and engine room – a report. Educational Role of Language Journal, 2025-1(13), 64-67. DOI: 10.36534/erlj.2025.01.07

Folorunso, A., Olanipekun, K., Adewumi, T., & Samuel, B. (2024). A policy framework on ai usage in developing countries and its impact. *Global Journal of Engineering and Technology Advances, 21*(1), 154–166. DOI: 10.30574/gjeta.2024.21.1.0192

Garima, M. and Jain, D. (2025). Artificial intelligence and its impact on higher education. Journal Global Values, XVI(SI), 56-64. DOI: 10.31995/jgv.2025.v16iSI7.009

Hastuti, R., & Syafruddin, S. (2023). Ethical considerations in the age of artificial intelligence: Balancing innovation and social values. *West Science Social and Humanities Studies*, *1*(02), 76–87. DOI: 10.58812/wsshs.v1i02.191

Horbowska, J. (2024). Ethical competencies in machine learning from a communicational perspective in educational process. Kwartalnik Naukowy Fides Et Ratio, 58(2), 38-45. DOI: 10.34766/fetr.v58i2.1277

Ibrahim, A. (2024). The influence of computerized simulation techniques on maritime security exercises: Isps code. *Maritime Research and Technology*, *3*(1), 1. DOI: 10.21622/MRT.2024.03.1.747

Ignjatović, G. (2024). Ai technologies in education: Regulatory frameworks at the international, regional and national level. *Zbornik Radova Pravnog Fakulteta Nis*, *63*(103), 235–260. DOI: 10.5937/zrpfn1-55374

Jadaan, O., Zaidi, H., Faress, M., & Jabas, A. (2024). Ethics in ai and computation in automated decision-making., 397-424. DOI: 10.4018/979-8-3693-6230-3.ch012

Jiang, Y., & Zheng, K. (2020). The single-shore-station-based position estimation method of an automatic identification system. *Sensors (Basel)*, *20*(6), 1590. DOI: 10.3390/s20061590 PMID: 32178367

Karimi, E., Smith, J., Billard, R., & Veitch, B. (2024). Ai-based adaptive instructional systems for maritime safety training: A systematic literature review. *Discover Artificial Intelligence*, *4*(1), 51. Advance online publication. DOI: 10.1007/s44163-024-00153-0

Karnavas, S., Peteinatos, I., Kyriazis, A., & Barbounaki, S. (2025). Using fuzzy multi-criteria decision-making as a human-centered ai approach to adopting new technologies in maritime education in greece. *Information (Basel)*, *16*(4), 283. DOI: 10.3390/info16040283

Khakpaki, A., & Sepehri, H. (2025). "artificial intelligence in medical education: a narrative review of challenges, ethical implications, and practical solutions" (preprint). DOI: 10.2196/preprints.72581

Kim, T., Sharma, A., Bustgaard, M., Gyldensten, W., Nymoen, O., Tusher, H., & Nazir, S. (2021). The continuum of simulator-based maritime training and education. *Wmu Journal of Maritime Affairs*, *20*(2), 135–150. DOI: 10.1007/s13437-021-00242-2

Madancian, M., & Hamed, T. (2025). Ethical theories, governance models, and strategic frameworks for responsible ai adoption and organizational success. *Frontiers in Artificial Intelligence*, *8*, 1619029. Advance online publication. DOI: 10.3389/frai.2025.1619029 PMID: 40741285

Maheswari, A. (2025). Beyond algorithms: A g.e.n.d.e.r. ai framework for advancing workplace equity in automation. *IJGRIT*, *03*(02(II)), 51–59. DOI: 10.62823/IJGRIT/03.2(II).7624

Motz, B., Quick, J., Brooks, C., Bergner, Y., Gray, G., Lang, C., & Marmolejo-Ramos, F. (2022). A lak of direction: misalignment between the goals of learning analytics and its research scholarship. DOI: 10.35542/osf.io/bzahw

Nhleko, Y. (2023). Challenges in international convention on the standards of training, certification and watchkeeping compliance: A case study of the south african maritime education and training system. *SAJMET*, *2*(1), 121–131. DOI: 10.47348/SAJMET/2023/i1a8

Raaj, J. (2025). Ai-powered learning: Revolutionizing student assessment. *International Journal of Research and Innovation in Applied Science*, *X*(V), 583–587. DOI: 10.51584/IJRIAS.2025.100500052

Rahmawati, M., Pitana, T., Handani, D., & Siswantoro, N. (2025). Utilization of ais data and ship simulator integration in maritime safety: A systematic literature review. *IOP Conference Series. Earth and Environmental Science*, *1461*(1), 012049. DOI: 10.1088/1755-1315/1461/1/012049

Ramoni, R. and Manuel, P. (2020). Ethics of artificial intelligence.. DOI: 10.1093/oso/9780190905033.001.0001

Rao, T., Santhoshi, N., & Anusha, G. (2025). Smart learning platforms., 299-332. DOI: 10.4018/979-8-3373-2185-1.ch011

Ravi, N., Chaturvedi, P., Huerta, E., Liu, Z., Chard, R., Scourtas, A., Schmidt, K. J., Chard, K., Blaiszik, B., & Foster, I. (2022). Fair principles for ai models with a practical application for accelerated high energy diffraction microscopy. *Scientific Data*, *9*(1), 657. Advance online publication. DOI: 10.1038/s41597-022-01712-9 PMID: 36357431

Renganayagalu, S., Mallam, S., & Nazir, S. (2021). Effectiveness of vr head mounted displays in professional training: A systematic review. *Technology Knowledge and Learning*, *26*(4), 999–1041. DOI: 10.1007/s10758-020-09489-9

Reyes, S. (2025). Status, applications, and prospects of ai in maritime education: basis for curriculum planning. DOI: 10.21203/rs.3.rs-7827795/v1

Saeed, M., Saeed, R., Ahmed, Z., Gaid, A., & Mokhtar, R. (2024). Ai technologies in engineering education., 61-87. DOI: 10.4018/979-8-3693-2728-9.ch003

Saxena, M., & Bajotra, V. (2024). Potential of artificial intelligence in education and ethical issues. *Far Western J. Educ.*, *1*(1), 1–18. DOI: 10.3126/fwje.v1i1.68773

Sharma, A., & Nazir, S. (2021). Assessing the technology self-efficacy of maritime instructors: An explorative study. *Education Sciences*, *11*(7), 342. DOI: 10.3390/educsci11070342

Sharma, A., Undheim, P., & Nazir, S. (2022). Design and implementation of ai chatbot for colregs training. *Wmu Journal of Maritime Affairs*, *22*(1), 107–123. DOI: 10.1007/s13437-022-00284-0

Sharma, R. (2025). Corporate governance and ai ethics: A strategic framework for ethical decision-making in business. *Journal of Information Systems Engineering & Management*, *10*(30s), 61–69. DOI: 10.52783/jisem.v10i30s.4775

Sijabat, P., Simanjuntak, M., Mudakir, M., Putrawan, B., & Lumingkewas, M. (2024). Empowering literacy in maritime education: Strategies and professionalism alignment. *Meteor Stip Marunda*, *17*(1), 42–50. DOI: 10.36101/msm.v17i1.359

Sundaram, A., & Karimi, I. (2023). Sustainability analysis of an lng bunkering protocol. *ACS Sustainable Chemistry & Engineering*, *11*(37), 13584–13593. DOI: 10.1021/acssuschemeng.3c02914

Tariq, M. (2025). Ai-powered assessment platforms., 117-146. DOI: 10.4018/979-8-3373-2130-1.ch004

Tomilin, A., Tomilina, S., & Panikina, S. (2023). On diagnosing the level of students' knowledge in special (conventional) disciplines. SHS Web of Conferences, 164, 00058. DOI: 10.1051/shsconf/202316400058

Ulnicane, I., Knight, W., Leach, T., Stahl, B., & Wanjiku, W. (2020). Framing governance for a contested emerging technology:insights from ai policy. *Policy and Society*, *40*(2), 158–177. DOI: 10.1080/14494035.2020.1855800

Yorulmaz, M., & Buyukozturk, G. (2025). Evaluation of ship simulator effectiveness and suitability by maritime instructors. *Information Technologies and Learning Tools*, *106*(2), 58–75. DOI: 10.33407/itlt.v106i2.5828

Chapter 11
Navigating Ethics:
Responsible Use of Artificial Intelligence in Maritime Education and Assessment

Raja Aditya Pramana Putra
http://orcid.org/0009-0007-7398-6316
Politeknik Ilmu Pelayaran Makassar, Indonesia

Annisa Rahmah
Politeknik Ilmu Pelayaran Makassar, Indonesia

Nurul Hatifah
Politeknik Ilmu Pelayaran Makassar, Indonesia

ABSTRACT

The increasing use of Artificial Intelligence (AI) in Maritime Education and Training (MET) brings about transformative opportunities as well as intricate ethical dilemmas. This study examines the principles of AI ethics in maritime education, emphasizing data privacy, equity, intellectual property, and human-machine collaboration in evaluation. It shows how important institutional governance, following the law, and getting stakeholders involved are for responsible AI integration. The discussion suggests a plan for making the maritime education system more ethically strong by focusing on ethical literacy, sustainability, and human dignity. By making sure that innovation is morally responsible, maritime institutions can make sure that AI improves both professional skills and global citizenship in the digital age.

UNDERSTANDING AI ETHICS IN MARITIME EDUCATION

1.1 The Rise of AI in Maritime Training and Assessment

Artificial Intelligence (AI) has quickly become a game-changer in Maritime Education and Training (MET), changing the way seafarers learn, show, and prove their skills. Worldwide, maritime academies are using AI-powered tools to improve learning through simulations, automate testing, and make lessons more personalized. AI is changing the way we teach and run things in Maritime Education. This is in line with the International Maritime Organization's (IMO) focus on digitalization and competency-based

DOI: 10.4018/979-8-3373-6670-8.ch011

education (Chen et al., 2020). Examples include smart navigational simulators, adaptive e-learning platforms, and predictive analytics in safety management. This integration makes training more effective and helps modernize maritime practices. However, the rapid adoption of these technologies raises complicated ethical questions about how open, responsible, and human oversight should be in educational and evaluative processes. This means that their use must be done with care (Kronivets et al., 2024; Kiran, 2025).

AI technologies are being used more and more in simulations that closely resemble real-world maritime conditions. Algorithmic evaluation is used by intelligent simulators to look at how students make decisions, how quickly they respond, and how aware they are of their surroundings (Bao, 2024; Basnawi & Koshak, 2024). These systems promise to be fair and efficient, but they might unintentionally reinforce hidden biases in data sets or algorithms, which raises important ethical questions. For example, automated scoring systems might not take into account important human factors that are important for maritime competence, like how well you handle stress, how well you work with others, or how well you make moral decisions (Basnawi & Koshak, 2024). So, the ethical problem is how to find a balance between the accuracy of technology and the overall evaluation of human performance. In the same way, AI-based proctoring tools keep an eye on students' behavior during digital tests by using facial recognition and motion tracking. This raises concerns about privacy, surveillance, and consent (Kronivets et al., 2024; Kiran, 2025).

AI makes adaptive learning paths possible in maritime e-learning, which lets trainees move forward at their own pace based on their strengths and weaknesses. AI-based learning analytics give teachers real-time information about how engaged and successful their students are (Li & Wong, 2023). But these analytics also raise moral issues about who owns and keeps private the huge amounts of personal learning data that are created and how it is used for business or institutional decision-making. Kiran, 2025. Also, the fact that not all maritime institutions have equal access to advanced AI technologies, especially in developing areas, could make educational gaps worse. This would create an ethical divide between technologically advanced and resource-constrained academies (Bao, 2024; Munir et al., 2022).

In the end, adding AI to maritime education needs more than just excitement about technology; it needs ethical navigation. Responsible implementation must prioritize human-centric principles, protect fairness, and guarantee accountability in algorithmic decision-making (Chen et al., 2020; Kiran, 2025). The maritime sector's long-standing culture of discipline and responsibility provides a strong moral foundation for addressing these challenges. As AI continues to shape the evolution of MET, ethical reflection becomes a central topic of discussion instead of a side issue. This is important for creating trustworthy and skilled seafarers for the digital age (Munir et al., 2022; Narayanan et al., 2023).

1.2 Foundations of AI Ethics: Principles and Frameworks

The moral basis for using AI in maritime education is based on philosophical ideas and global governance frameworks that set standards for how technology should be used responsibly. As maritime institutions increasingly utilize AI for simulation, assessment, and data-driven decision-making, ethical frameworks such as deontology, consequentialism, and virtue ethics provide essential perspectives for evaluating the morality of these systems. Deontological ethics stresses duty and following the rules, and it tells teachers and developers to make sure that AI programs follow professional standards, privacy laws, and human rights obligations (Bao, 2024; Munir et al., 2022).. From this perspective, actions—like gathering trainee data or automating assessments—should be evaluated not by their results but by their adherence to learners' autonomy and dignity.

Consequentialism, on the other hand, looks at the results of decisions to see if they are ethical. In this sense, ethical AI must maximize benefits like safety, fairness, and competence while minimizing harm or bias. Virtue ethics, in contrast, underscores the moral integrity of individuals and institutions involved in the design and implementation of AI, prioritizing virtues such as honesty, empathy, and prudence to ensure that technology benefits humanity rather than supplanting it.

Based on these moral traditions, global and regional groups have come up with plans for how to make ethical AI governance work in practice. The International Maritime Organization (IMO) mainly works on safety and competency standards, but it also supports digital transformation that is based on principles of human-centeredness and sustainability. The United Nations Educational, Scientific and Cultural Organization (UNESCO) put out the Recommendation on the Ethics of Artificial Intelligence (2021), which says that human rights, inclusivity, and accountability should be the main ethical principles for using AI in education. The European Union's AI Act also uses a risk-based regulatory model, putting AI systems into groups based on how much harm they could do and setting strict safety and transparency standards for high-stakes areas like education and certification. ASEAN frameworks, on the other hand, call for AI ethics that are flexible enough to work in different parts of the region and take into account local situations, cultural differences, and differences in development. They also encourage policymakers, industry, and academia to work together (Li & Wong, 2023).

To use these frameworks in maritime education, AI governance needs to be based on people and openness. Human-centered design makes sure that technology enhances, not replaces, human knowledge. This strengthens the teacher's role as a moral guide and critical evaluator. For AI systems used in training and testing to be transparent, they must be able to be explained, traced, and checked. Teachers, students, and maritime regulators need to know how algorithms make decisions so that they can be held accountable and trusted. Participatory mechanisms are also part of ethical AI governance. In these, different groups of people, such as teachers, seafarers, software developers, and regulators, work together to make rules about data protection, reducing bias, and fair assessment (Chen et al., 2020).

In short, a strong ethical base for maritime AI must combine philosophical integrity with institutional responsibility. The maritime education sector can make sure that new technologies help achieve the ultimate goal of training competent, responsible, and morally aware maritime professionals by including moral reasoning, global standards, and human-centered values at every step of AI design and deployment.

1.3 Maritime Education in the Digital Era

The digital transformation of maritime education signifies a significant transition from conventional seamanship based on experiential learning to a technologically advanced ecosystem influenced by algorithms, data analytics, and automation. In the past, maritime training focused on teaching people how to use their hands, be aware of their surroundings, and learn from mentors on ships or in simulators run by teachers. In the digital age, AI-powered tools are changing these methods by simulating complicated engineering and navigation situations, keeping track of performance automatically, and tailoring instruction to each student (Li & Wong, 2023). This change means that maritime institutions need to find a delicate balance between keeping the spirit of seamanship and using digital technologies to improve accuracy, efficiency, and scalability (Li & Wong, 2023). Finding this balance makes sure that human judgment, empathy, and moral reasoning stay at the heart of seafaring skills, even as machines take over more and more tasks. Automation and algorithmic learning systems have added new levels to how people learn and get certified. Competence assessment is no longer limited to human observation; it now encompasses algorithmic evaluation utilizing extensive datasets of learner performance. These kinds of systems make things more objective and consistent, but they also make it harder for people to pick up on subtleties and make decisions based on the situation. For instance, an AI model that looks at navigation mistakes might not take into account environmental stressors or how people work together that affect performance outcomes. The ethical concern arises from excessive dependence on algorithmic decisions that may unintentionally undermine critical human skills, including leadership, moral reasoning, and adaptive thinking. Also, using automation in certification, like AI-generated performance summaries or predictive readiness scores, raises questions about who is responsible when automated systems get competence wrong. Maritime teachers and regulators need to make sure that digital validation works with, not instead of, human evaluation. This will keep things fair, open, and professiona (Chen et al., 2020)l. The role of the teacher is also changing a lot in this new digital world. Instructors are no longer the only ones who pass on knowledge; they are now facilitators who help human learners and smart systems work together. They need to understand what algorithmic outputs mean, put data-driven feedback in context, and teach students how to use AI tools in a moral way. As AI literacy becomes an important part of maritime training, teachers are expected to teach digital ethics, focusing on how to use automation responsibly, protect data privacy, and make sure everyone has fair access to technology. In addition to teaching students how to use AI-enabled systems, teachers are also responsible for teaching them when and why to question them. This reflective stance enhances professional judgment and ethical resilience—attributes essential for maritime safety and leadership.

ETHICAL DIMENSIONS IN AI-DRIVEN LEARNING ENVIRONMENTS

2.1 Data Privacy and Surveillance Concerns

As AI becomes more common in maritime education, there has been more collection and analysis of learners' biometric, performance, and behavioral data. Contemporary simulators and e-learning platforms now monitor gaze direction, facial expressions, vocal tone, reaction time, and decision-making patterns to assess competence and safety awareness (Virdi et al., 2022; Ibokette et al., 2024). These datasets provide valuable insights for personalized learning and predictive assessment; however, they also present ethical dilemmas concerning privacy, consent, and data protection (Fachola et al., 2023; Zhang et al., 2024). To use this kind of sensitive information in an ethical way, there needs to be a system that respects people's rights while also using the data to improve education (Tanaka & Tezuka, 2021). Maritime institutions must implement rigorous ethical and legal protections to guarantee that AI-driven analytics serve as instruments of empowerment rather than surveillance (Fachola et al., 2023; Filipiak et al., 2020). The ethical dilemma emerges when data collection transcends the line between performance assessment and invasive surveillance. AI-enabled sensors in maritime simulators watch what students do, from how they navigate to how stressed they are, making a digital record of each student (Virdi et al., 2022; Ibokette et al., 2024). This data can be misused for non-educational purposes, like making decisions about discipline or profiling students for administrative purposes (Seyedan & Mafakheri, 2020). Too much monitoring breaks down the trust between teachers and students, creating a climate of surveillance instead of mentorship. Also, constant tracking could change how learners behave; when trainees know they are being watched, their responses in simulation environments could change, making competency assessments less accurate (Ibokette et al., 2024). So, to keep integrity in maritime learning, it's important to find a balance between technological ability and moral restraint. Another ethical issue is informed consent and data anonymization in AI-driven analytics. Students often take part in online training programs without knowing what data is being collected, how long it will be kept, or who can see it (Fachola et al., 2023; Zhang et al., 2024). For informed consent, there needs to be clear communication about the types of data, why they are being used, the risks involved, and the right to withdraw. Maritime institutions ought to formulate explicit consent protocols in accordance with international data protection standards, including the General Data Protection Regulation (GDPR) (Fachola et al., 2023). Anonymization is just as important: before data can be looked at or shared, any identifying information must be taken out so that people can't be identified again (Nguyen et al., 2022). It is the responsibility of both AI developers and maritime educators to make sure that data handling processes are clear, can be checked, and follow ethical standards (Gray et al., 2021; Zhang et al., 2024). In the end, keeping privacy safe in AI-driven maritime education is not just a technical issue; it is also a moral duty. Ethical data governance protects learners' freedom, trust, and dignity, which are important values in the maritime profession's ethical culture (Cruz et al., 2023; Filipiak et al., 2020). Maritime schools can use AI's benefits while still respecting human rights and professional ethics in a digital learning environment by following privacy-by-design principles and raising awareness among teachers and students (Hlongwa, 2022; Molina et al., 2024).

2.2 Bias, Fairness, and Transparency in AI Systems

As maritime education and training rely more and more on artificial intelligence (AI), there are more and more complicated ethical issues about bias, fairness, and transparency. When AI-based tools for testing and making decisions become the main way to judge a seafarer's skills, these systems often reflect the data and design choices that went into making them. Algorithmic bias can happen when training datasets aren't representative, when labels are wrong, or when developers make assumptions without realizing it. In the context of maritime education, this kind of bias could lead to unfair grades, performance evaluations in simulations, or candidate selection, which would hurt the credibility of Maritime Education and Training (MET) institutions (Gray et al., 2021; Zhang et al., 2024). To protect both ethical integrity and institutional accountability, it is important to make sure that these systems are fair and open. Algorithmic bias occurs when AI systems consistently favor or disadvantage specific individuals or groups based on irrelevant characteristics such as gender, nationality, language proficiency, or educational background. For example, speech recognition tools built into communication simulators may not work as well for cadets whose first language is different from the main language data used to train AI, which could lead to unfair competency scores. Facial-recognition-based proctoring systems may also misidentify or flag students of certain ethnicities because their datasets are not balanced. These kinds of events show that bias in AI is not just a technical problem; it is also an ethical problem that affects fairness, inclusiveness, and equal opportunity in maritime learning. To fix these biases, we need to take action on many levels, from designing algorithms that are fair to setting up systems for ongoing monitoring and auditing. For MET institutions to be fair, they need to use AI frameworks that can be explained and checked. Explainability makes sure that people can understand and check the reasons behind AI-made choices. This helps teachers and students understand how grades or performance ratings are determined. This openness builds trust and makes it easier to find possible systemic mistakes. Auditable AI means that independent experts or institutional committees regularly and in a structured way check to make sure that it follows ethical standards and rules. Educators can use algorithmic audits and fairness dashboards to find differences in outcomes between demographic groups. These tools can also help create a culture of accountability and constant improvement (Molina et al., 2024). A number of MET institutions have started looking into ways to find and reduce bias. For instance, European maritime academies and technology providers have worked together on projects that have brought in "ethical AI audits" to check how fair navigation simulation data is. In Southeast Asia, regional training centers supported by ASEAN have incorporated localized datasets into machine learning systems to better reflect diverse maritime conditions and learner backgrounds. These practices show that taking steps to reduce bias ahead of time—by using a variety of data sources, involving users in system design, and having ethical oversight—can make a big difference in reducing unfairness and building trust excellence (Jones et al., 2022; Visanich, 2025).

2.3 Intellectual Property and Authorship in AI-Assisted Learning

The incorporation of Artificial Intelligence (AI) into maritime education has profoundly altered the creation and dissemination of instructional materials, simulations, and evaluations. Smart systems now help teachers by making lesson plans, quizzes, and detailed performance reports (Mugambiwa, 2024; Draxler et al., 2023). But this new technology brings up important questions about who owns and authors intellectual property (IP) in AI-assisted learning. When an AI system makes or helps make educational materials, it's important to know who owns the rights: the developer, the teacher using the tool, or the school itself (Nyaboke, 2024). Maritime Education and Training (MET) institutions must address these inquiries to guarantee that innovation is consistent with ethical and legal standards, especially as AI transitions into a creative collaborator rather than merely a technical tool (Mahingoda, 2024). It is hard to say who owns AI-generated training materials and tests because AI systems don't have legal personhood or moral agency. In many places, the person or group that designed, trained, or directed the AI system is usually given credit for the intellectual property of its outputs (Nyaboke, 2024). In maritime settings, an instructor utilizing AI to generate navigation case studies or simulation tasks is typically acknowledged as the author, contingent upon their retention of creative control and oversight (Toresano et al., 2024). But when teachers use AI-generated materials too much without checking or putting them in context, it raises ethical issues (Mahingoda, 2024). This dependence may jeopardize the integrity of maritime pedagogy, possibly endangering safety-critical precision (Mugambiwa, 2024). Moreover, the use of proprietary AI tools may result in shared or contested ownership by software providers, creating uncertainty regarding data rights and content reuse within institutions (Karimi et al., 2024). The ethical limits on AI co-authorship in academic and professional work are just as important. AI can help with writing, analyzing data, or making visualizations, but it can't take on responsibility, intent, or accountability, which are all important parts of authorship (Battineni et al., 2023). International editorial standards, including those established by the Committee on Publication Ethics (COPE) and UNESCO, assert that AI should not be recognized as an author in publications or official documents (Saxena & Bajotra, 2024). Instead, it must be clearly stated in the acknowledgments or methodology sections that it was used. In maritime research, ethical co-authorship requires that human authors maintain intellectual responsibility for the validity, originality, and ethical integrity of their work, even when AI has significantly contributed to its creation (Adeleye, 2024). To uphold these principles, institutional policies regarding AI utilization in research and instructional design are becoming increasingly critical. MET institutions need to make clear rules about how AI can be used in content creation, data analysis, assessment design, and publication (Karimi et al., 2024). These rules must cover recognizing authorship, protecting data, stopping plagiarism, and keeping academic integrity (Nyaboke, 2024). Additionally, faculty and students ought to be educated in AI ethics and digital authorship to cultivate a culture of responsible innovation (Mahingoda, 2024).

RESPONSIBLE ASSESSMENT: INTEGRITY AND ACCOUNTABILITY IN THE AGE OF AI

3.1 Academic Integrity and AI-Augmented Evaluation

The integration of Artificial Intelligence (AI) into maritime education has revolutionized assessment methodologies, presenting both avenues for innovation and obstacles to academic integrity. AI-driven systems can grade homework, judge how well a student does on a simulation, and even guess how well they will do in the future (Reyes, 2025). But these improvements also come with new ethical problems, like plagiarism, impersonation, and abusing AI (Wilstic, 2025). Students can use generative AI tools to write essays, reports, or solutions. This makes it hard to tell the difference between work that was done by hand and work that was done by a machine. Moreover, online assessment platforms are susceptible to impersonation, as biometric recognition or facial verification can be undermined by deepfake technologies (Saxena & Bajotra, 2024). In simulation-based maritime training, unethical data manipulation or AI-assisted cheating during performance evaluations can compromise certification validity, thereby jeopardizing maritime safety and professional standards (Adams et al., 2022).

To tackle these issues, teachers need to use ethical assessment designs that combine AI's analytical skills with human judgment. Instead of just using automated scoring or detection tools, maritime schools should think about using hybrid models that combine algorithmic evaluation with expert oversight (Park et al., 2022). Human evaluators offer contextual comprehension, elucidating subtleties in performance, collaborative dynamics, and ethical decision-making that AI cannot completely comprehend (Susilo & Aritonang, 2023). On the other hand, AI is objective, efficient, and data-driven, which helps to cut down on human bias in traditional grading. AI can help teachers by spotting patterns or outliers in simulator data that show how well a student is doing. Teachers can then look at these trends in the context of the student's overall training. This balanced approach makes sure that tests are both high-tech and morally sound (Alanazi, 2025).

Also, the design of ethical assessments must put a premium on openness, fairness, and responsibility. Students should be told how AI tools are used to grade or keep an eye on their work, as well as how the data is looked at and how decisions are made. This kind of openness builds trust and encourages responsible participation (Hastuti & Syafruddin, 2023). In addition, teachers must be professionally responsible for all AI-assisted evaluations and check the results of the algorithms before giving grades or certificates. The "human-in-the-loop" principle of decision-making, which means that people are still in charge, should be the basis for all AI-integrated assessment processes in Maritime Education and Training (MET) (Wilstic, 2025).

It is just as important to set up moral guidelines for AI-based proctoring and evaluation. To avoid crossing moral lines, AI surveillance systems that look for suspicious behavior during online tests need to be properly controlled. Institutions ought to implement proctoring practices that uphold privacy and dignity while guaranteeing fairness (Gunder et al., 2023). Ongoing monitoring should concentrate on critical observations, ensuring that data is securely stored and anonymized (Kronivets et al., 2024). International organizations like the International Maritime Organization (IMO) and UNESCO's principles for ethical AI can help maritime institutions a lot (Song et al., 2023).

To protect academic integrity in the age of AI, we need more than just knowledge of technology; we need a set of moral rules. By incorporating transparency, human accountability, and respect for learner autonomy into AI-enhanced assessment systems, maritime education can uphold fairness and trust, ensuring that technological innovation fortifies rather than compromises professional ethics and competency validation (Sharma et al., 2022; Mandinach & Abrams, 2022).

3.2 Human–Machine Collaboration in Competency Testing

As Artificial Intelligence (AI) continues to change Maritime Education and Training (MET), competency testing is more and more based on a mix of human and machine work. Automated evaluation tools can look at performance data, find mistakes, and give instant feedback, which makes things more efficient and consistent. But if we let machines do all the judging, we risk losing the human aspects of judgment, context, and ethics that are so important to being a professional mariner. So, for competency testing to work well, it needs to find a balance between automation and human oversight. This means that technology should enhance, not replace, human judgment. This partnership is a key point where digital innovation and moral responsibility meet. The accuracy of the assessment depends on both machine accuracy and human ethical control.

There are clear benefits to using automation for performance evaluation. AI systems can handle a lot of simulator data, keep track of behavioral metrics, and find learning gaps that people might miss. Machine learning models can find mistakes people make when they are trying to navigate or guess how well they will do in the future based on past simulation data. However, without careful human oversight, these systems might misinterpret actions that need to be understood in context, like making moral choices in emergencies or differences in communication across cultures. These nuances are essential to maritime proficiency yet remain challenging for AI to quantify objectively. So, human oversight serves as an ethical safeguard by making sure that algorithmic results are in line with professional standards and that final decisions are based on both data accuracy and human values.

In this model of collaboration, teachers and examiners act as ethical judges who mediate between evaluations based on algorithms and evaluations based on people. Their job goes beyond just checking the technology; they also have to make sure that every AI-assisted decision is fair, accountable, and respectful of the different types of learners. Teachers need to think critically about the results of algorithms: Does the AI tool assess competence fairly among genders, linguistic backgrounds, or learning styles? Does it make biases in the training data stronger or ignore soft skills like working together and making moral decisions? By being morally aware, teachers protect the moral authority of maritime education and encourage responsible use of AI technologies.

For AI grading systems to be fair and accountable, there must be openness at every step of the assessment process. Students should know how AI helps with grading, what data is looked at, and how the results are checked (Gunder et al., 2023). Institutions need to set up clear rules for who is responsible for checking AI-generated results. This way, qualified human assessors will always be responsible for certifying the results. In AI-supported MET assessments, regular audits, bias testing, and explainability reports should be the norm. Also, ethical frameworks like UNESCO's 2021 Recommendation on the Ethics of AI and the IMO's STCW Convention standards are useful guides for making sure that AI-assisted testing is fair and competent by global standards.

3.3 Accreditation and Quality Assurance in AI-Based Assessment

The incorporation of Artificial Intelligence (AI) into assessment systems in Maritime Education and Training (MET) requires a reevaluation of accreditation and quality assurance frameworks. As AI technologies automate evaluation, grading, and certification processes, ethical considerations must take center stage in the accreditation of AI-supported programs. Accreditation, which used to focus on things like the curriculum, the qualifications of the teachers, and the facilities, now needs to include things like algorithmic design, data integrity, transparency, and fairness. Ethical accreditation makes sure that new technologies don't violate the basic principles of accountability, human dignity, and professional competence that define the maritime field (Gunder et al., 2023).

When giving AI-driven programs accreditation, ethical issues come up that have to do with transparency, accountability, and human oversight. Accreditation bodies must make sure that AI systems used for training and testing follow clear ethical rules, such as explainability, bias mitigation, and data privacy. For example, an AI-based grading system that looks at how well students did in simulations should give a clear reason for each decision so that teachers can check and understand the results. Accreditation cannot effectively assess the reliability or fairness of automated systems without such transparency. Furthermore, institutions pursuing accreditation must exhibit that AI applications are developed and implemented responsibly, underpinned by policies governing data management, learner consent, and algorithmic accountability. AI must not only work correctly, but it must also be in line with human values and help all types of students learn in a fair way.

The International Maritime Organization (IMO) and regional bodies are very important for making sure that AI-integrated MET systems follow the rules. The International Maritime Organization (IMO) sets the global standard for maritime safety and competency. Its Standards of Training, Certification, and Watchkeeping for Seafarers (STCW) framework already stresses training and evaluation that focuses on people. The IMO can build on this foundation by adding AI ethics principles like fairness, inclusiveness, and explainability to its rules for digital and simulation-based tests. Likewise, maritime authorities and accreditation councils in ASEAN, the EU, and the Middle East are working together more and more to set ethical standards for AI governance in education. These organizations make sure that AI tools used for testing not only work well technically, but also follow moral and legal rules, such as protecting data and getting consent.

For ethical quality assurance to work, there also needs to be constant monitoring and the creation of audit trails to check that algorithms are reliable. AI systems are different from traditional assessment tools because they change over time through machine learning. This means that their behavior and outputs can change. This evolution necessitates continuous assessment instead of a singular accreditation. Institutions need to do regular audits to find any bias, system drift, or mistakes in AI grading and decision-making. During accreditation reviews, detailed audit trails should show the whole life cycle of AI systems, from data collection to output generation. This will make the process more open and easy to follow.

The trustworthiness of AI-based assessment in maritime education depends on ethical governance that is backed by global cooperation and constant supervision.

INSTITUTIONAL POLICIES AND GOVERNANCE FOR ETHICAL AI INTEGRATION

4.1 Developing Ethical Codes and Institutional Frameworks

The incorporation of Artificial Intelligence (AI) into Maritime Education and Training (MET) demands the immediate formulation of ethical standards and governance structures to ensure its responsible application. AI opens up new ways to be creative in simulation, testing, and making administrative decisions. However, it also raises difficult moral questions about fairness, responsibility, and human rights. Mthuli and Singh (2024), Islam (2024). Creating detailed institutional ethics charters is necessary to deal with these problems in the best way possible. These kinds of charters should spell out shared values like fairness, openness, human-centered design, and professional integrity that will guide AI-driven educational activities (Sharma et al., 2022). By incorporating these ethical considerations into institutional governance, maritime academies can guarantee that technological progress aligns with their educational objectives and complies with international standards set by entities like the International Maritime Organization (IMO) (Meštrović et al., 2024).

An institutional ethics charter for AI education should be both a set of rules and a list of values. It must set standards for acceptable AI use, set limits on how data can be used, and explain how to deal with ethical problems that come up when automation is used. An organization, for example, could say that AI systems used for performance reviews must have human oversight, protect data privacy, and be checked for ethical issues on a regular basis. This kind of charter also makes the institution more accountable to students, faculty, and the public by making it clear that AI should work with, not replace, human expertise (Kim et al., 2021). In practice, these ethics charters are in line with international guidelines like UNESCO's Recommendation on the Ethics of Artificial Intelligence (2021), which stresses the importance of accountability, sustainability, and inclusivity in education (Islam, 2024).

Ethical governance also depends a lot on giving faculty and staff training on how to use AI responsibly. Many ethical breaches in AI implementation happen not because people want to do wrong, but because they don't understand or aren't good with technology. So, training programs need to give teachers and administrators the skills they need to spot possible ethical risks, critically evaluate the results of algorithms, and always follow the rules of the school. Some ideas for initiatives are workshops on how to handle data ethically, how to find bias in simulations, and how to make sure that AI-driven tests are fair (Awosanya et al., 2024). Continuous professional development is essential to ensure that all staff members are proficient in utilizing AI technologies while comprehending their ethical implications. This emphasis on ethical literacy turns teachers into moral guides who can help students use technology in a responsible way (Kim et al., 2021).

4.2 Legal and Regulatory Considerations

You can't talk about the moral use of AI in Maritime Education and Training (MET) without also talking about the laws and rules that protect data, hold people accountable, and encourage international cooperation. As AI systems have more and more of an impact on how students are tested, watched, and certified, it is important for maritime institutions to make sure they follow all the rules and regulations.

Legal governance gives ethical AI adoption a solid structure by making sure that new ideas stay within the limits of fairness, openness, and human rights (Prasetyo et al., 2023)..

Following data protection laws and international agreements is a key part of this discussion. AI-based assessment systems often use huge amounts of data that contain private information like biometric identifiers, behavioral analytics, and performance metrics. You have to follow national data protection laws and global rules like the European Union's General Data Protection Regulation (GDPR) when you collect, process, and store this data. The GDPR stresses informed consent, limiting the use of data, and minimizing the amount of data collected. In maritime contexts, compliance also includes international agreements made by the International Maritime Organization (IMO) and the International Labour Organization (ILO), which protect seafarers' rights to privacy, dignity, and fair treatment. Institutions that work across borders, especially those that run joint maritime training programs, have to deal with different data protection laws while making sure that students' rights are always protected, no matter where they are.

A major problem is figuring out who is responsible and liable for decisions made by AI. When AI systems are used to help with performance evaluations or certification results, it gets harder to figure out who is legally responsible for mistakes or bias. If an AI algorithm incorrectly assesses a candidate's competence or produces erroneous data, should the responsibility lie with the software developer, the institution implementing the system, or the individual instructor supervising its application? Legal experts say that the principle of human-in-command must always hold: qualified human assessors and institutional authorities should always be the ones who are ultimately responsible. Because of this, MET institutions need to set up clear chains of accountability and keep records of how AI systems are built, tested, and monitored. Liability frameworks should also require algorithms to be open and clear, so that decisions can be checked and explained in legal or accreditation settings (Qadhi et al., 2024).

Also, as digitalization changes how people learn about sailing around the world, efforts to make maritime AI governance more ethical are growing at the national and international levels. The IMO is working with regional groups like ASEAN and the European Maritime Safety Agency (EMSA) to look into policy frameworks that include AI ethics in current competency standards. These efforts call for regulatory harmonization, which means that the ethical and technical standards for using AI in training and certification should be the same around the world. National maritime authorities are starting to add AI governance clauses to their accreditation and quality assurance protocols.

4.3 Stakeholder Engagement and Participatory Governance

To ethically include AI in Maritime Education and Training (MET), there needs to be a dedicated effort that includes all important stakeholders in governance that is open and participatory. For AI-driven projects to work, everyone involved—teachers, sailors, regulators, technologists, and industry leaders—needs to take responsibility and be involved (Buhmann & Fieseler, 2022; Deroncele-Acosta et al., 2024). Multi-stakeholder models make sure that ethical choices take into account a wide range of points of view, which helps to close the gaps between making policies, developing new technologies, and putting them into action. Maritime organizations that use participatory governance encourage accountability and build trust in AI systems that are meant to improve competence, safety, and sustainability (Hastuti & Syafruddin, 2023).

In a governance framework with many stakeholders, each one brings their own skills and moral insights. Teachers have a lot of experience and knowledge about how AI affects learning and testing. Seafarers give real-world feedback on how AI tools affect safety culture, skill development, and fairness at work

(Feng et al., 2024). Regulators make sure that institutions follow the rules and follow moral codes. It is the job of technologists and AI developers to make sure that fairness, openness, and inclusivity are built into the design of algorithms. When these groups work together, maritime education systems can become more ethically strong, finding the right balance between new ideas and basic human values like trust, dignity, and responsibility (Muzumdar et al., 2025).

The cultivation of ethical literacy through continuous dialogue and collaboration is fundamental to participatory governance. Ethical literacy gives everyone the tools they need to think critically about AI technologies, question their results, and understand how they affect society as a whole. Maritime academies can make this literacy a part of their programs by holding workshops, public consultations, and cross-sector dialogues that deal with new problems like data privacy and algorithmic bias (Thakur & Sharma, 2024). Open dialogue creates a culture of openness where people can talk about their worries about fairness or accountability and work together to fix them. Involving seafarers and learners in these discussions also makes sure that ethical frameworks are based on real-life experiences and not just on administrative or technological points of view. This method changes AI governance from a top-down order to a collaborative ethical practice based on respect and understanding for all (Kumar et al., 2023).

Furthermore, partnerships between institutions are important for building trust and openness in AI governance. Maritime universities, government agencies, industry groups, and tech companies can work together to set ethical standards for using AI in training and testing. For example, creating joint ethics committees or regional research networks can help maritime institutions share best practices, do audits, and make rules for using AI responsibly (Güneş & Kaban, 2025). When stakeholders work together to design, test, and review AI systems, trust grows. This makes sure that governance stays open and consistent in different situations (Reyes, 2025).

CHARTING THE FUTURE: BUILDING AN ETHICAL AND SUSTAINABLE AI CULTURE

5.1 Ethical Literacy and Lifelong Learning for Seafarers

In this time of digital change, teaching seafarers how to be morally literate is just as important as teaching them how to navigate, build things, or stay safe. The maritime profession, historically grounded in principles of responsibility and integrity, now confronts novel ethical challenges influenced by Artificial Intelligence (AI), automation, and data-driven systems (Du & Xi, 2023). To guarantee that future mariners function as proficient professionals and principled digital citizens, maritime education must integrate ethics instruction directly into training programs. Ethical literacy enables learners to comprehend the functionality of AI and to critically evaluate its societal, environmental, and professional ramifications, thereby cultivating a generation of mariners equipped to make responsible decisions in intricate, technology-mediated contexts (Куцак, 2025).

To include ethics education in maritime curricula, we need to go beyond just teaching technical skills. Instead of treating ethics as a separate subject, it should be included in lessons on navigation, engineering, logistics, and communication. For instance, when using a simulator for training, talking about moral dilemmas like making decisions when automation fails or when algorithmic alerts are biased can help students think more deeply about moral issues (Eden et al., 2024). Case studies on data privacy, AI-driven decision systems, and environmental compliance promote ethical awareness in actual maritime operations. Institutions can amplify this impact by integrating ethics education with global standards, including UNESCO's Recommendation on the Ethics of Artificial Intelligence (2021) and the International Maritime Organization's (IMO) human-centered learning principles, thereby ensuring that seafarers cultivate a moral compass in conjunction with technical proficiency (Tariq & Sergio, 2024).

The changing digital world means that people need to keep learning about AI and how to use it responsibly even after they leave school. As ships become more automated and depend on smart systems, maritime workers need to keep learning to stay up-to-date on both technology and ethics. Maritime universities and professional groups may support lifelong learning programs that include online micro-credentials, modular AI awareness courses, and certification schemes that focus on ethics (Ogunsakin, 2024). These programs should focus on how to handle data responsibly, how to make algorithms clear, and how to make ethical choices in automated settings. Maritime education strengthens resilience, adaptability, and reflective judgment by making ethical learning a part of everyday life. These are all important traits for leadership in a fast-changing, AI-enhanced maritime sector (Zou, 2025).

As part of ethical literacy, it is just as important to teach values of global citizenship and sustainability. Seafarers work in many different countries and cultures, making them the first line of defense in promoting environmental responsibility and understanding between cultures. Teaching global citizenship along with AI ethics helps people understand how digital technologies affect climate change, ocean health, and fair access to maritime opportunities. So, ethical AI literacy is linked to the bigger goal of sustainable maritime development, which is to get sailors to be responsible stewards of both technology and the environment (Regula, 2025).

5.2 Emerging Frontiers: Green AI, Sustainability, and Human Dignity

The future of Artificial Intelligence (AI) in Maritime Education and Training (MET) is inextricably linked to the worldwide quest for sustainability, environmental stewardship, and human dignity. As the maritime industry goes through a digital transformation, more and more people are realizing that new ideas must be responsible, long-lasting, and based on ethics. In this case, "green AI" is a new idea that focuses on making and using AI technologies that have the least impact on the environment and the most benefit for society. So, maritime institutions have two problems to solve: they need to improve AI technologies that make ship operations cleaner, safer, and more efficient, and they also need to make sure that these technologies follow the moral values of fairness, inclusion, and respect for human life (Davids et al., 2025).

Responsible innovation for AI that is energy-efficient and good for the environment means making and using technologies that use less energy and resources. AI can help maritime operations reduce greenhouse gas emissions by making fuel use, route planning, and cargo management more efficient. But the algorithms that run these systems also use energy because they have to process a lot of data and train models. Green AI projects call for computer systems that use less energy, easier ways to share data, and evaluations of the entire life cycle of technology systems. MET institutions need to rethink their digital infrastructure, switch to data centers that run on renewable energy, and teach sailors about the environmental costs of using technology. In maritime education, ethical AI design should put sustainability first, not just in the results but also in the steps that lead to new ideas. This means that digital progress should be in line with the International Maritime Organization's (IMO) goals for decarbonization and the United Nations' (UN) Sustainable Development Goals (SDGs).

The ethical consequences of AI in climate monitoring and ship operations are equally important. AI technologies are being used more and more to keep an eye on ocean ecosystems, forecast unusual weather, and make sure that ships follow environmental rules. These systems make things safer and more sustainable, but they also make people wonder who owns the data, how open it is, and who is responsible for it. For example, predictive AI models used to make decisions about the environment must be able to be explained and checked so that people can verify and justify the actions taken by machines. Ethical use of climate-related AI tools also means respecting the maritime knowledge systems of local and indigenous people and combining digital insights with human experience. In this way, AI shouldn't take the place of human judgment; instead, it should make it better in the name of responsible maritime governance.

Lastly, it's important to promote human dignity and social justice during the technological transformation to make sure that everyone gets a fair share of the benefits of AI. Automation and digitalization can take over some maritime jobs, which hurts workers in developing areas more than others. So, ethical governance needs to fix these unfair situations by offering retraining programs, fair job transitions, and access to digital tools for everyone.

5.3 Vision for an Ethically-Driven Maritime Future

The incorporation of Artificial Intelligence (AI) into Maritime Education and Training (MET) entails significant technological opportunities and a substantial ethical obligation. As maritime institutions deal with the difficulties of automation, digital learning, and data governance, they need a long-term plan that is based on ethics and humanity. An ethically-driven maritime future sees a global learning ecosystem where new ideas are based on fairness, openness, inclusion, and responsibility. To make sure that AI helps people move forward without hurting the values that define the maritime profession—discipline, integrity, and respect for life at sea—there needs to be ethical leadership, strong institutions, and cooperation between countries.

A thorough plan for ethical leadership and governance in MET must start with the understanding that technology alone cannot ensure fairness or quality. Maritime leaders, such as rectors, deans, policymakers, and training directors, need to set an example of ethical behavior by making moral reasoning a part of how institutions make decisions. This means making sure that AI ethics policies are clear, that assessments and accreditations are open, and that people are still in charge of automated systems. Digital ethics and governance modules should be a part of leadership training to help administrators make tough choices about how to use data, hold algorithms accountable, and be more inclusive. Ethical leadership also means giving teachers and sailors the power to help build responsible AI ecosystems, where technology decisions are made together instead of being forced on people. Such participatory governance makes sure that new ideas fit with the goals of the organization and the global maritime standards set by the International Maritime Organization (IMO).

Another important part of this vision is making institutions more resilient and holding people morally accountable in the age of AI. As AI systems change quickly, maritime organizations need to stay flexible without losing their moral compass. This means creating flexible governance frameworks that can deal with new risks, like bias, data breaches, or the wrong use of automation, through constant monitoring and ethical review. Moral accountability goes beyond just following the rules; it means that organizations must take responsibility for the effects their technology choices have on people. Transparent reporting, regular audits of AI systems, and open communication with learners and stakeholders all help to build trust in institutions. Resilient institutions not only adapt to changes in technology, but they also protect human values as the guiding force behind progress.

CONCLUSION

The quick use of Artificial Intelligence (AI) in Maritime Education and Training (MET) is both a technological advance and an ethical necessity. As maritime institutions implement AI for simulation, evaluation, and decision-making, the industry must traverse intricate ethical terrains concerning data privacy, algorithmic equity, transparency, and responsibility. The main point of this conversation is clear: new technologies must always be based on human values. Ethics should not be seen as an optional part of the equation; they are the basis for trust, competence, and safety around the world.

For AI to be used responsibly in maritime settings, there needs to be a system that balances automation with human oversight and includes ethical reflection at every step of learning and governance. As ethical stewards, teachers and schools have a big job to make sure that AI improves, not hurts, honesty, fairness, and inclusion. Including ethics in schoolwork, accreditation systems, and institutional policies not only makes professionals more responsible but it also makes future seafarers more morally strong. Legal and regulatory frameworks must also change to protect human rights and make sure that international standards are followed while also promoting fairness and openness across regions.

Shared responsibility is what will make AI in maritime education ethical in the future. Stakeholders, including educators, regulators, technologists, and learners, need to keep talking to each other to promote participatory governance and ethical literacy. Such cooperation makes sure that maritime AI stays in line with the values of fairness, sustainability, and respect for life at sea.

REFERENCES

Adams, C., Pente, P., Lemermeyer, G., Turville, J., & Rockwell, G. (2022). Artificial intelligence and teachers' new ethical obligations. *International Journal of Information Ethics*, *31*(1). Advance online publication. DOI: 10.29173/irie483

Adeleye, I. (2024). The impact of artificial intelligence on design: Enhancing creativity and efficiency. *JEAS*, *3*(1), 1–14. DOI: 10.70560/vvsfej12

Alanazi, A. (2025). Assessing clinicians' legal concerns and the need for a regulatory framework for ai in healthcare: A mixed-methods study. *Healthcare (Basel)*, *13*(13), 1487. DOI: 10.3390/healthcare13131487

Awosanya, O., Harris, A., Creecy, A., Qiao, X., Toepp, A., McCune, T., Kacena, M. A., & Ozanne, M. (2024). The utility of ai in writing a scientific review article on the impacts of covid-19 on musculoskeletal health. *Current Osteoporosis Reports*, *22*(1), 146–151. DOI: 10.1007/s11914-023-00855-x

Bao, H. (2024). Learning evaluation method based on artificial intelligence technology and its application in education. jes, 20(3s), 1833-1842. DOI: 10.52783/jes.1722

Basnawi, A., & Koshak, A. (2024). Application of artificial intelligence in advanced training and education of emergency medicine doctors: A narrative review. *Emergency Care and Medicine*, *1*(3), 247–259. DOI: 10.3390/ecm1030026

Battineni, G., Chintalapudi, N., Ricci, G., Ruocco, C., & Amenta, F. (2023). Exploring the integration of artificial intelligence (ai) and augmented reality (ar) in maritime medicine: a narrative literature review (preprint). DOI: 10.2196/preprints.53870

Buhmann, A., & Fieseler, C. (2022). Deep learning meets deep democracy: Deliberative governance and responsible innovation in artificial intelligence. *Business Ethics Quarterly*, *33*(1), 146–179. DOI: 10.1017/beq.2021.42

Chen, L., Chen, P., & Lin, Z. (2020). Artificial intelligence in education: A review. *IEEE Access : Practical Innovations, Open Solutions*, *8*, 75264–75278. DOI: 10.1109/ACCESS.2020.2988510

Cruz, M., Teixeira, E., Mafra, S., & Figueiredo, F. (2023). A multi-faceted approach to maritime security: federated learning, computer vision, and iot in edge computing.. DOI: 10.14209/sbrt.2023.1570923804

Davids, A., Camarero-Figuerola, M., & Camacho, M. (2025). Navigating the challenges and opportunities of artificial intelligence in educational leadership: A scoping review. *Review of Education*, *13*(2), e70101. Advance online publication. DOI: 10.1002/rev3.70101

Deroncele-Acosta, Á., Bellido-Valdiviezo, O., Trujillo, M., Palacios-Núñez, M., Rueda-Garcés, H., & Brito-Garcías, J. (2024). Ten essential pillars in artificial intelligence for university science education: A scoping review. *SAGE Open*, *14*(3), 21582440241272016. Advance online publication. DOI: 10.1177/21582440241272016

Draxler, F., Werner, A., Lehmann, F., Hoppe, M., Schmidt, A., Buschek, D., . . . Welsch, R. (2023). The ai ghostwriter effect: users do not perceive ownership of ai-generated text but self-declare as authors. / arxiv.2303.03283DOI: 10.48550

Du, X., & Xi, W. (2023). Play by design: Developing artificial intelligence literacy through game-based learning. *Journal of Computer Science Research*, *5*(4), 1–12. DOI: 10.30564/jcsr.v5i4.5999

Eden, C., Chisom, O., & Adeniyi, I. (2024). Integrating ai in education: opportunities, challenges, and ethical considerations. Magna Scientia Advanced Research and Reviews, 10(2), 006-013. DOI: 10.30574/msarr.2024.10.2.0039

Fachola, C., Tornaria, A., Bermolen, P., Capdehourat, G., Etcheverry, L., & Fariello, M. (2023). Federated learning for education data analytics. DOI: 10.20944/preprints202301.0092.v1

Feng, Q., Harte, M., Carey, B., Alqarni, A., Monteiro, L., Freitas, M., & Albuquerque, R. (2024). The risks of artificial intelligence: A narrative review and ethical reflection from an oral medicine group. *Oral Diseases*, *31*(2), 348–353. DOI: 10.1111/odi.15100

Filipiak, D., Węcel, K., Stróżyna, M., Michalak, M., & Abramowicz, W. (2020). Extracting maritime traffic networks from ais data using evolutionary algorithm. *Business & Information Systems Engineering*, *62*(5), 435–450. DOI: 10.1007/s12599-020-00661-0

Gray, G., Schalk, A., Rooney, P., & Lang, C. (2021). A stakeholder informed professional development framework to support engagement with learning analytics., 237-247. DOI: 10.1145/3448139.3448162

Gunder, A., Casino, V., Vito, M., & Dickson, R. (2023). *Empowering ai: recontextualizing our pedagogical impact through supportive uses of machine learning*. Ubiquity Proceedings., DOI: 10.5334/uproc.81

Güneş, A., & Kaban, A. (2025). A delphi study on ethical challenges and ensuring academic integrity regarding ai research in higher education. *Higher Education Quarterly*, *79*(4), e70057. Advance online publication. DOI: 10.1111/hequ.70057

Hastuti, R., & Syafruddin, S. (2023). Ethical considerations in the age of artificial intelligence: Balancing innovation and social values. *West Science Social and Humanities Studies*, *1*(02), 76–87. DOI: 10.58812/wsshs.v1i02.191

Hastuti, R., & Syafruddin, S. (2023). Ethical considerations in the age of artificial intelligence: Balancing innovation and social values. *West Science Social and Humanities Studies*, *1*(02), 76–87. DOI: 10.58812/wsshs.v1i02.191

Hlongwa, L. (2022). Artificial intelligence and big data in the maritime silk road initiative: The road towards sea power 2.0. *Scientia Militaria South African Journal of Military Studies*, *49*(2). Advance online publication. DOI: 10.5787/49-2-1329

Ibokette, A., Ogundare, T., Anyebe, A., Alao, F., Odeh, I., & Okafor, F. (2024). Mitigating maritime cybersecurity risks using ai-based intrusion detection systems and network automation during extreme environmental conditions. *International Journal of Scientific Research and Modern Technol*, *3*(10), 65–91. DOI: 10.38124/ijsrmt.v3i10.73

Islam, M. (2024). Maritime security in a technological era: addressing challenges in balancing technology and ethics. Mersin University Journal of Maritime Faculty, 6(1), 1-16. DOI: 10.47512/meujmaf.1418239

Jones, K., Nurse, J., & Li, S. (2022). Are you robert or roberta? deceiving online authorship attribution models using neural text generators. *Proceedings of the International Aaai Conference on Web and Social Media*, 16, 429-440. DOI: 10.1609/icwsm.v16i1.19304

Karimi, E., Smith, J., Billard, R., & Veitch, B. (2024). Ai-based adaptive instructional systems for maritime safety training: A systematic literature review. *Discover Artificial Intelligence*, *4*(1), 51. Advance online publication. DOI: 10.1007/s44163-024-00153-0

Kim, T., Sharma, A., Bustgaard, M., Gyldensten, W., Nymoen, O., Tusher, H., & Nazir, S. (2021). The continuum of simulator-based maritime training and education. *Wmu Journal of Maritime Affairs*, *20*(2), 135–150. DOI: 10.1007/s13437-021-00242-2

Kiran, A. (2025). Applications and impacts of ai tools in education.. DOI: 10.47716/978-93-92090-38-7

Kronivets, T., Yakovenko, O., Tymoshenko, Y., & Ilnytskyi, M. (2024). Dimensions of legal and moral use of artificial intelligence in education. *Rev. Artif. Intell. Educ*, *5*, e025. DOI: 10.37497/rev.artif.intell.educ.v5i00.25

Kronivets, T., Yakovenko, O., Tymoshenko, Y., & Ilnytskyi, M. (2024). Dimensions of legal and moral use of artificial intelligence in education. *Rev. Artif. Intell. Educ*, *5*, e025. DOI: 10.37497/rev.artif.intell.educ.v5i00.25

Kumar, A., Singh, N., Israel, M., Gupta, E., & Sharma, A. (2023). Intelligence and its impact on society. Journal Global Values, XIV(S.Issue), 132-140. DOI: 10.31995/jgv.2023.v14iS3.016

Li, K., & Wong, B. (2023). Artificial intelligence in personalised learning: A bibliometric analysis. *Interactive Technology and Smart Education*, *20*(3), 422–445. DOI: 10.1108/ITSE-01-2023-0007

Mahingoda, C. (2024). Challenges and frontiers in intellectual property rights amidst the rise of artificial intelligence. *Sliit Journal of Humanities and Sciences*, *4*(2), 1–16. DOI: 10.4038/sjhs.v4i2.55

Mandinach, E. and Abrams, L. (2022). Data literacy and learning analytics., 196-204. DOI: 10.18608/hla22.019

Meštrović, T., Pavić, I., Maljković, M., & Androjna, A. (2024). Challenges for the education and training of seafarers in the context of autonomous shipping: Bibliometric analysis and systematic literature review. *Applied Sciences (Basel, Switzerland)*, *14*(8), 3173. DOI: 10.3390/app14083173

Molina, M., Suárez, Y., & Valdés-Mosquera, D. (2024). Smart, green, and sustainable: Unveiling technological trajectories in maritime port operations. *IEEE Access : Practical Innovations, Open Solutions*, *12*, 47713–47723. DOI: 10.1109/ACCESS.2024.3376431

Mthuli, S., & Singh, N. (2024). State-led maritime governance, education and training nexus in south africa. *ECMLG*, *20*(1), 401–407. DOI: 10.34190/ecmlg.20.1.2950

Mugambiwa, S. (2024). Reaping the rewards with minimal toil: Evaluating the polemics of artificial intelligence in academia and the future of academic writing. *Edelweiss Applied Science and Technology*, *8*(6), 3535–3541. DOI: 10.55214/25768484.v8i6.2752

Munir, H., Vogel, B., & Jacobsson, A. (2022). Artificial intelligence and machine learning approaches in digital education: A systematic revision. *Information (Basel)*, *13*(4), 203. DOI: 10.3390/info13040203

Muzumdar, P., Muley, A., Singh, K., & Cheemalapati, S. (2025). Ethical ai in the healthcare sector: Investigating key drivers of adoption through the multi-dimensional ethical ai adoption model (meaam). *Asian Journal of Medicine and Health*, *23*(5), 95–115. DOI: 10.9734/ajmah/2025/v23i51228

Narayanan, S., Rajprasath, R., Durairaj, E., & Das, A. (2023). Artificial intelligence revolutionizing the field of medical education. *Cureus*. Advance online publication. DOI: 10.7759/cureus.49604

Nguyen, D., Pham, Q., Pathirana, P., Ding, M., Seneviratne, A., Lin, Z., Dobre, O., & Hwang, W. (2022). Federated learning for smart healthcare: A survey. *ACM Computing Surveys*, *55*(3), 1–37. DOI: 10.1145/3501296

Nyaboke, Y. (2024). Intellectual property rights in the era of artificial intelligence. *Journal of Modern Law and Policy*, *4*(2), 57–72. DOI: 10.47941/jmlp.2162

Ogunsakin, I. (2024). Unlocking the potential of artificial intellignce. *International Journal on Research in Stem Education*, *6*(2), 37–49. DOI: 10.33830/ijrse.v6i2.1698

Park, J., Tiefenbach, J., & Demetriades, A. (2022). The role of artificial intelligence in surgical simulation. *Frontiers in Medical Technology*, *4*, 1076755. Advance online publication. DOI: 10.3389/fmedt.2022.1076755

Prasetyo, K., Ansori, A., & Suseto, B. (2023). Maritime defense strategy education as an effort of the indonesian government in maintaining maritime security. *International Journal of Asian Education*, *4*(1), 58–67. DOI: 10.46966/ijae.v4i1.325

Qadhi, S., Alduais, A., Chaaban, Y., & Khraisheh, M. (2024). Generative ai, research ethics, and higher education research: Insights from a scientometric analysis. *Information (Basel)*, *15*(6), 325. DOI: 10.3390/info15060325

Regula, K. (2025). Ai and cybersecurity., 299-318. DOI: 10.4018/979-8-3373-1142-5.ch015

Reyes, S. (2025). Status, applications, and prospects of ai in maritime education: basis for curriculum planning. DOI: 10.21203/rs.3.rs-7827795/v1

Reyes, S. (2025). Status, applications, and prospects of ai in maritime education: basis for curriculum planning. DOI: 10.21203/rs.3.rs-7827795/v1

Saxena, M., & Bajotra, V. (2024). Potential of artificial intelligence in education and ethical issues. *Far Western J. Educ.*, *1*(1), 1–18. DOI: 10.3126/fwje.v1i1.68773

Seyedan, M., & Mafakheri, F. (2020). Predictive big data analytics for supply chain demand forecasting: Methods, applications, and research opportunities. *Journal of Big Data*, *7*(1), 53. Advance online publication. DOI: 10.1186/s40537-020-00329-2

Sharma, A., Undheim, P., & Nazir, S. (2022). Design and implementation of ai chatbot for colregs training. *Wmu Journal of Maritime Affairs*, *22*(1), 107–123. DOI: 10.1007/s13437-022-00284-0

Sharma, A., Undheim, P., & Nazir, S. (2022). Design and implementation of ai chatbot for colregs training. *Wmu Journal of Maritime Affairs*, *22*(1), 107–123. DOI: 10.1007/s13437-022-00284-0

Song, M., Moon, J., & Jang, A. (2023). Text network analysis of research topics and trends on simulations using virtual patients in nursing education. *Computers, Informatics, Nursing*, *41*(9), 639–646. DOI: 10.1097/CIN.0000000000000993

Susilo, T., & Aritonang, S. (2023). Optimizing the potential of artificial intelligence in education management for era 5.0. *Al-Fikrah Jurnal Manajemen Pendidikan*, *11*(2), 219. DOI: 10.31958/jaf.v11i2.10371

Tanaka, M., & Tezuka, S. (2021). A scoping review of alternative methods of delivering ethics education in nursing. *Nursing Open*, *9*(6), 2572–2585. DOI: 10.1002/nop2.987

Tariq, M. and Sergio, R. (2024). Nurturing digital citizenship in society 5.0 through ai and computational intelligence education., 59-84. DOI: 10.4018/979-8-3693-4326-5.ch003

Thakur, N., & Sharma, A. (2024). Ethical considerations in ai-driven financial decision making. *JMPP*, *15*(3), 41–57. DOI: 10.47914/jmpp.2024.v15i3.003

Toresano, C., Castells, M., & Altés, C. (2024). Conceptualization of the era of autonomous shipping within maritime education and training framework.. DOI: 10.5821/mt.12808

Virdi, S., Liu, Y., & Zhang, D. (2022). Eeg-based stress recognition in competency assessment using maritime navigation simulator.. DOI: 10.54941/ahfe1002504

Visanich, V. (2025). Artificial intelligence and art: Functions and frictions in the contemporary artworld. *Journal of Cultural Management and Cultural Policy*, *11*(2), 163–175. DOI: 10.1177/27018466251369008

Wilstic, D. (2025). Ai in education: leveraging artificial intelligence to combat academic malpractice in higher education. DOI: 10.21203/rs.3.rs-7094161/v1

Zhang, D., Chu, X., Liu, C., He, Z., Zhang, P., & Wu, W. (2024). A review on motion prediction for intelligent ship navigation. *Journal of Marine Science and Engineering*, *12*(1), 107. DOI: 10.3390/jmse12010107

Zou, Q., & Xu, T. (2025). Challenges and opportunities for primary education in the age of artificial intelligence. *Contemporary Education Frontiers*, *3*(6), 79–86. DOI: 10.18063/CEF.v3i6.702

Chapter 12
Technology-Supported Maritime English Learning:
Empowering Seafarers' Communication Skills for the Digital Ocean

Vivit Rosmayanti
http://orcid.org/0000-0002-3648-9878
Universitas Negeri Makassar, Indonesia

St. Wijdanah Ram
http://orcid.org/0009-0005-1890-5355
Universitas Negeri Makassar, Indonesia

Agussalim Djirong
Universitas Negeri Makassar, Indonesia

Suryadi Ishak
Universitas Negeri Makassar, Indonesia

Andi Annisa Sulolipu
http://orcid.org/0009-0007-8212-577X
Universitas Negeri Makassar, Indonesia

Fathullah Wajdi
Universitas Negeri Makassar, Indonesia

ABSTRACT

This chapter looks at how technology-enhanced learning is being used in Maritime English education as the maritime industry goes through a digital transformation brought on by automation, AI, the Internet of Things, and better communication systems. It examines how digital tools and innovative teaching methods can help individuals improve their communication skills in line with international maritime standards, such as the STCW Convention and the IMO Model Course 3.17. The chapter proposes a Technology-Supported Maritime English Learning (TSMEL) framework that includes immersive learning design, adaptive assessment, digital collaboration, and sustainability alignment. This framework is based on ideas from English for Specific Purposes (ESP) and Technology-Enhanced Language Learning (TELL). It emphasizes the effectiveness of virtual reality simulations, AI-driven tutoring, and mobile-assisted learning as strategies for genuine, skill-oriented education.

1. INTRODUCTION

Maritime English, a specialized branch of the English language, has become an essential aspect of international maritime communication. The significance arises from English functioning as the lingua

DOI: 10.4018/979-8-3373-6670-8.ch012

franca within an industry marked by a diverse range of cultures and languages. The International Convention on Standards of Training, Certification and Watchkeeping for Seafarers (STCW) stresses the importance of Maritime English for safety, compliance, and smooth operations on ships, especially in multicultural settings where clear communication is key (Fabian-Perona, 2025; Litikova, 2021). Knowing how to speak Maritime English is not just a skill; it is an important part of maritime safety and operational efficiency (Ahmmed, 2021).

Technology is making big changes in the modern maritime industry. Smart shipping, e-Navigation, and the Internet of Things (IoT) are all becoming more common on ships. This has changed the way sailors communicate. Automation and autonomous systems are becoming more common, which makes operations more complicated and requires a good understanding of digital communication platforms (Popoola et al., 2024; Meštrović et al., 2024). With ships using artificial intelligence (AI) and processing data in real time, the need for good communication in a technologically advanced maritime environment has grown even more, making it even more important to be able to speak Maritime English (Sharma et al., 2022).

Even with these improvements, there is still a big difference between traditional language teaching and the changing needs of maritime communication in the digital ocean. Traditional maritime education often emphasizes the grammar and structure of the English language; however, contemporary seafaring necessitates practical communicative competencies that include both linguistic proficiency and technological literacy (Abila et al., 2023). This misalignment is a problem because seafarers need to be good at both English and using digital tools and technologies that are important to modern maritime operations (Ajayi & Udeh, 2024). As we rely more and more on high-tech solutions, it's important to teach languages in a way that fits with these new realities instead of using old methods.

There are many important reasons to use technology in Maritime English learning. As digital literacy becomes necessary for safe and effective maritime operation, teaching methods must change to include simulation, interactive learning environments, and digital tools that are similar to how things work in the real world (Die & You, 2024). Technological advancements can improve cadets' engagement and understanding, as research shows that students are more motivated and satisfied when they learn in environments that use technology (Rosedi, 2021). So, using technology can help people talk to each other and create a generation of sailors who are ready for the challenges of the maritime industry of the future.

The structure of this chapter is designed to systematically investigate these themes, commencing with an overview of the essential function of Maritime English, an analysis of the changing communication requirements in the digital maritime domain, and a critique of the current pedagogical methodologies. The following sections will go into more detail about how technology is changing the way Maritime English is taught and look at case studies that show the best ways to use technology in maritime education. By focusing on these important points, the chapter will add to the larger conversation about how to improve seafarers' communication skills, which will make the maritime industry safer and more efficient.

2. THEORETICAL FOUNDATIONS

2.1 English for Specific Purposes (ESP) and Maritime English

Maritime English is an important part of English for Specific Purposes (ESP) because it meets the specific communication needs of people who work in the maritime industry. This specialized form of

English is necessary for seafarers to communicate clearly and safely, and it is also important for navigation and teamwork in a variety of maritime situations. In the ESP framework, Maritime English includes the specialized language skills needed in different maritime situations, such as working on ships, dealing with port authorities, organizing logistics, and working with crews from other countries. Consequently, it addresses unique linguistic functions and vocabulary pertinent to maritime tasks, ensuring clarity and efficiency in communication vital for safe and successful maritime operations (Saridaki, 2023; Bojović, 2024).

To communicate effectively in Maritime English, seafarers need to learn certain skills that are very important to them. These competencies encompass more than linguistic proficiency; they include specialized skills in safety communication, navigation instructions, and collaboration within multicultural teams (Fabian-Perona, 2025; SIRBU, 2023). The ability to clearly explain emergency procedures or give clear directions can have a big impact on what happens in critical situations at sea. The complexities of teamwork on ships require sailors to be proficient in both technical jargon and everyday conversational skills, which creates a collaborative environment that is necessary for success (Tymofyeyeva & Konstantynova, 2021).

To improve the framework for teaching Maritime English, the International Maritime Organization (IMO) has set standards for education and operations. The IMO Model Course 3.17 is a guide for teachers of Maritime English. It lists the important topics and skills that must be covered in training programs in order to meet the Standards of Training, Certification, and Watchkeeping (STCW) requirements. The STCW stresses how important it is for maritime workers to be able to communicate well. This means that schools need to teach both the technical and language skills that are needed for safe and effective communication (Die & You, 2024; Batu et al., 2021). The relationship between established protocols in the STCW and the educational framework underscores the importance of incorporating Maritime English instruction into comprehensive maritime education, guaranteeing that trainees possess not only linguistic proficiency but also the capability to navigate practical maritime challenges (Diahyleva et al., 2023).

2.2 Technology-Enhanced Language Learning (TELL) Framework

The incorporation of Information and Communication Technology (ICT) into English for Specific Purposes (ESP) contexts, especially in Maritime English education, signifies a revolutionary change in teaching methods. Using modern technology makes language learning environments more interesting, interactive, and useful. Different ICT tools, like mobile learning apps, platforms powered by Artificial Intelligence (AI), and online collaborative resources, make learning a lot better for students. These technologies offer customized solutions specifically designed to meet the communication needs of maritime professionals (Garba, 2025; Ramli et al., 2025).

There are many ways to look at the theoretical basis of Technology-Enhanced Language Learning (TELL), such as constructivism, blended learning, and multimodal communication. Constructivism asserts that knowledge is developed through interaction and engagement with the environment, aligning with the experiential characteristics of maritime training. In this context, digital tools facilitate simulation-based learning and genuine communication tasks that promote active learner engagement (Zhou et al., 2023). Blended learning, which combines traditional face-to-face instruction with online learning, offers flexibility and expands access to educational resources, thus catering to various learning needs and preferences (Yin et al., 2022; Holiver et al., 2020). Multimodal communication illustrates the necessity for learners to participate through diverse channels, utilizing text, audio, video, and interactive content, thereby accommodating different learning styles and improving understanding (Ullah et al., 2024).

Artificial intelligence (AI) has become an important part of maritime training, offering many uses that make the learning process better. Smart chatbots, voice assistants, and adaptive learning platforms can make learning more personal by giving students personalized feedback and letting them practice speaking in real time (Losi et al., 2024; Obari et al., 2022). These tools not only improve language skills but also simulate real-life maritime situations that sailors are likely to face, closing the gap between theory and practice (Liashenko et al., 2025). Additionally, the integration of mobile learning initiatives enables learners to study while on the move, ensuring that language acquisition is both convenient and compatible with their demanding maritime schedules (Wang & Erdenebold, 2025).

Simulation technologies are also very important for maritime training because they give people realistic experiences that make them think critically and communicate well under pressure. These simulations can recreate emergencies or navigation difficulties that require proficiency in Maritime English, thereby guaranteeing that trainees are sufficiently equipped for the realities of their profession (Ramli et al., 2025; Rybina et al., 2025). The significance of mobile-assisted language learning (MALL) and other ICT methodologies is further substantiated by their recorded improvement of student motivation and engagement, which are critical components in effective language acquisition across various learning environments (Zhou et al., 2023).

3. THE DIGITAL TRANSFORMATION OF MARITIME COMMUNICATION

The maritime sector's digital transformation is a major change brought about by new technologies that completely change how people talk to each other and do business. e-Navigation, smart ports, and digital ship logs are some of the most important parts of this change. According to Usluer (2024), e-navigation is the integration of digital systems that use data from different sources to make navigation safer and more efficient by creating an interconnected operational environment. Smart ports have changed port logistics by making cargo handling and asset management more efficient. They have advanced technologies like Internet of Things (IoT) devices and advanced data processing systems. Digital ship logs make it possible to record and report a ship's status and activities in real time. This greatly increases transparency and accountability by using automated systems that cut down on the need for paper-based records (Durana et al., 2025).

These technological advances will have a big effect on language and communication skills. As more and more sailors use digital tools for navigation and communication at work, they need to improve their language skills, which should include both technical vocabulary and good online communication. For technological integration to work, we need to move away from traditional communication skills and toward a new way of thinking where digital literacy is very important. Seafarers must navigate complex interfaces and communicate effectively with automated systems, which means that both spoken and written communication must be clearer and more precise. Moreover, effective communication in multicultural teams underscores intercultural competence, facilitating productive engagement among seafarers from varied backgrounds (Demirel, 2020; Narayanan et al., 2023).

The emergence of new literacy requirements in the maritime sector aligns with the evolving skills essential for effective functioning in a digitalized setting. Digital literacy is more than just knowing how to use technology; it also includes knowing how to use digital tools, how to send and receive data, and how to critically evaluate digital information that is found during operations (Li, 2025). Moreover, the capacity to convey data efficiently and collaboratively in real-time improves situational awareness on vessels and promotes safer maritime operations, while intercultural competence is essential due to the growing diversity of crews and passengers (Baylon & Santos, 2025).

The idea of the "Digital Seafarer" is starting to take shape in this technological world. This term describes sailors who not only know how to do things the old-fashioned way, but also have advanced digital skills that help them do well in fully automated and connected environments. The Digital Seafarer can combine traditional maritime knowledge with new tech tools and platforms. This shows a bigger trend toward having professionals with many skills in maritime operations (Hosny & Mohamed, 2024; Taylor et al., 2023). This idea has a big effect on education. Maritime training programs need to change their curricula to include full training in digital tools, data analytics, and soft skills needed for working and communicating well with others in high-pressure, tech-heavy situations.

4. TECHNOLOGY-SUPPORTED APPROACHES TO MARITIME ENGLISH LEARNING

4.1 Simulation-Based and VR Learning

Simulation-based learning and virtual reality (VR) have become important tools in maritime English education. They give students real-world language practice that is very similar to what they would do in real life. Bridge simulators, which replicate the working conditions of a ship's bridge, allow trainees to face realistic navigation problems while talking to crew members. This immersive context not only facilitates the acquisition of technical skills but also augments essential language competencies pertinent to maritime vocabulary and situational speaking under duress, thereby enhancing seafarers' proficiency in Maritime English (Makransky & Petersen, 2021; Kim et al., 2021).

Bridge simulators and virtual reality are important for maritime training because they can make learning fun and safe. Trainees can work on their communication skills and navigation skills without the risks that come with real maritime operations. For instance, a maritime training school that uses cutting-edge simulation technologies can set up different emergency situations, like an engine failure or bad weather, that require trainees to work together and communicate well to come up with quick fixes (Kim et al., 2021). This hands-on practice not only helps students learn words that are specific to maritime situations, but it also helps them become better at working together, leading, and being aware of their surroundings.

Many studies have shown that training in technology-mediated communication works well in the maritime industry. Research indicates substantial enhancements in students' verbal communication abilities when immersed in VR environments specifically designed for Maritime English. A study examining the incorporation of VR in language acquisition underscored its beneficial effects on students' fluency and communicative proficiency, noting increased engagement and motivation as participants interacted with scenarios that simulated real-life communication contexts in a maritime setting (Journal, 2024; Raman et al., 2023). Learners can gain more confidence in their language skills by putting them in simulated situations that require quick and interactive responses.

By using both simulation and VR technologies, teachers can create curriculum modules that focus on language skills while also covering other areas of maritime operations. For instance, bridge simulator training programs teach not only technical terms but also how to stay safe, follow navigational commands, and work well with others in stressful situations. Lou (2025) says that these kinds of simulations let trainees work together to practice realistic situations, which helps them learn Maritime English while dealing with both language and operational problems.

Furthermore, the application of VR in maritime English training transcends mere language acquisition; it enhances intercultural communication by presenting learners with varied viewpoints within the maritime sector, which is essential in the contemporary globalized workforce. Trainees can participate in virtual exchanges that showcase diverse communication styles, facilitating the development of intercultural competencies vital for effective functioning in multicultural settings (Sellberg et al., 2024).

4.2 AI and Adaptive Learning Tools

The incorporation of artificial intelligence (AI) and adaptive learning tools into Maritime English education signifies a substantial progression in meeting the distinct linguistic and communicative needs of seafarers. AI-based tools like chatbots, speech recognition systems, and pronunciation feedback systems make learning more fun and give students personalized help as they learn the ins and outs of Maritime English. These technologies let students practice their language skills in a way that is both interactive and realistic, and they get feedback right away, which is important for learning the subtleties of maritime communication (Sari & Sari, 2022).

Chatbots are like conversation partners for learners, letting them practice talking in different maritime situations. Chatbots help people learn how to speak and respond to situations by simulating real-life interactions, like working with port authorities or responding to emergencies. AI-driven speech recognition technology makes this process even better by letting students get real-time feedback on how they pronounce words and their intonation. These quick corrections give students the chance to improve their speaking skills, which makes them more confident when they speak English on board. These AI tools can also be set up to understand maritime-specific vocabulary and jargon, which makes sure that learners are practicing language that is relevant to their work environment (Nurdin et al., 2023).

Adaptive learning tools make the experience of learning Maritime English even more personal. These systems can change the curriculum paths for each student based on their strengths, weaknesses, and learning styles by looking at their performance data. This guarantees that students interact with material that is most pertinent to their individual requirements, thereby improving their proficiency in Maritime English over time (Batu et al., 2021). If a student has trouble with maritime vocabulary related to navigation, for instance, the adaptive learning tool will change the difficulty and focus of the assignments, giving them extra resources and exercises to help them improve their language skills. This personalized approach not only makes learning more effective, but it also fits the specific needs of maritime training, where being good at English is directly related to safety and effectiveness in the field (Anggraini et al., 2020).

The focus on personalized learning paths in Maritime English training takes into account the wide range of backgrounds and English skills that learners have. The International Maritime Organization (IMO) says that future seafarers must be able to communicate clearly, so personalized learning is important to make sure that all trainees can reach the required competency levels (Budiman & Ganap, 2024). Studies show that adaptive learning environments can help students stay interested and remember what they learn, which can help them get used to maritime education (Shi & Fan, 2021).

4.3 Mobile and Blended Learning Environments

Mobile learning and blended learning environments are important parts of modernizing Maritime English education. They offer more freedom and access than traditional methods do. The rise of mobile learning apps has made it easier for sailors to practice their vocabulary. Mobile-based vocabulary practice enables learners to interact with customized content that addresses their particular maritime requirements, promoting language acquisition through microlearning modules crafted for concise learning experiences (Yurzhenko et al., 2022). These modules can have games, quizzes, flashcards, and audio exercises that help students learn maritime vocabulary and communication skills in a fun way. This lets them practice on their own, often when they want and at their own pace.

These mobile learning apps also help people learn important communication skills by giving them content that is relevant to their lives. By using realistic scenarios that mimic everyday maritime operations, learners can practice language skills that are useful in their jobs, which will help them be better prepared for real-life situations on board. For example, an app might put cadets in situations where they have to use the right Maritime English words and phrases to respond to different emergencies. Research shows that adding gamification features to these apps can make users even more interested and motivated, which can lead to better learning results (Yurzhenko et al., 2022).

Blended instruction, which combines online and in-person learning, is a good way to teach Maritime English. This method combines traditional classroom teaching with technology-enhanced learning. This lets students learn theoretical concepts online and then use those skills in real-world maritime situations. A maritime cadet learning about navigation theory online could also take part in practical sessions with ship simulators or bridge training exercises at the same time. This would help them understand the language used in navigation tasks better (D'Augusta et al., 2025; Wibowo et al., 2025). This two-pronged approach not only promotes deeper learning, but it also makes sure that training is useful and relevant to the real problems that sailors face at sea.

Blended learning also supports different learning styles, which is helpful for students with different backgrounds and skills. It gives learners the freedom to access resources whenever and wherever they want, which is very important for seafarers who may not always have access to schools and other educational facilities. Cadets can keep practicing their language skills while they are traveling or on duty by using mobile devices. This makes learning easier and more flexible for them (Huang, 2025).

To sum up, combining mobile learning with blended learning environments is a revolutionary way to teach Maritime English. Maritime training programs can get seafarers ready for the communication needs of the modern maritime industry by using mobile apps to help them learn new words and blended instruction to help them improve their language skills. This combination of technology and teaching methods makes sure that cadets are not only good at Maritime English but also able to handle the challenges of a maritime environment that is becoming more digital (Hafita et al., 2024; Simanjuntak, 2023).

4.4 Digital Assessment and Competency Evaluation

Digital assessment and competency evaluation in Maritime English education have experienced substantial changes due to technological advancements and the incorporation of artificial intelligence (AI) tools. Automated speaking tests and digital performance tracking are very important for measuring language skills in a more fair and effective way. AI-powered platforms can listen to cadets' spoken responses and give them instant feedback on their pronunciation, fluency, and the use of maritime terms during simulations or recorded conversations. These kinds of tests help students figure out what they're good at and what they need to work on, so they can focus on those areas without having to wait for grades (Wang, 2024; Ulfa, 2023).

These automated systems make the assessment process easier and give you information about how well you communicate and what styles work best. AI tools can give information about common mistakes or misunderstandings by looking at how a learner talks in simulated maritime situations. This is important in maritime operations where safety compliance depends on clear and accurate communication. This information can also improve the curriculum by helping teachers deal with problems that many students have and change how they teach to fit those problems (Akbarani, 2024).

Digital performance tracking is also a big part of competency evaluation, along with automated speaking tests. By keeping track of test scores and progress over time, teachers can see how students' language skills and overall ability to do maritime tasks are getting better. This method is in line with the idea of continuous learning, which is important in an industry that is always changing because of new technologies and rules. Digital assessments produce reports that give students and teachers clear metrics to track progress over time, which helps them plan their professional growth (Yurzhenko et al., 2025; Sudewo et al., 2025).

Feedback loops for making sure communication is accurate and following safety rules are another important part of digital assessment in maritime education. Real-time corrections and suggestions during practice create a culture of constant improvement. This is made possible by mechanisms for immediate feedback. For instance, during simulated emergencies, immediate feedback can be provided regarding communication with crew members or shore-side authorities, highlighting the accuracy of language usage and compliance with safety protocols (Idham et al., 2024; Diahyleva et al., 2025). This ongoing feedback helps cadets improve their language skills by putting them into practice, which helps them understand the terms and procedures they need to know for their jobs.

The use of digital assessment methods fits with the skills that maritime regulators and groups, like the International Maritime Organization (IMO), say are important. These skills include being able to communicate well in situations where safety is at stake. By using technology to regularly test skills, teachers can make sure that cadets are not only good at languages but also have the skills they need to handle the challenges of communication in their future maritime careers (Ганношина & Levchenko, 2024).

In conclusion, digital assessment and competency evaluation tools are transformative elements in Maritime English education. Maritime training programs can improve the effectiveness and relevance of language education by using automated assessments and detailed performance tracking. This will prepare seafarers to meet the communication needs of a digitalized maritime environment and make sure they follow safety rules (Moorhouse et al., 2023; Li, 2025).

5. PEDAGOGICAL MODEL FOR TECHNOLOGY-SUPPORTED MARITIME ENGLISH

To meet the changing communication needs of the maritime industry, it is important to create a teaching model for technology-supported Maritime English education. This model combines new ways of teaching with the technology improvements that seafarers need to learn the language well. The suggested framework for incorporating Information and Communication Technology (ICT) into Maritime English instruction seeks to establish a dynamic learning environment that prioritizes adaptability, engagement, and customized educational experiences (Danelova & Astaduryan, 2023; Simanjuntak et al., 2024).

The first step in this framework is to add different ICT tools to the Maritime English curriculum. These tools could include video conferencing platforms, mobile apps, and artificial intelligence (AI) tools. These tools let cadets learn interactively, giving them a safe place to practice their language skills online. For example, using virtual reality (VR) technologies as simulations can put students in real-life maritime situations, which can help them improve their language skills and their understanding of navigation and communication protocols. This is very similar to the International Maritime Organization's (IMO) communication standards, which stress the importance of seafarers having good language skills to make things safer and more efficient at sea (Simanjuntak et al., 2024). Following these standards, the pedagogical model makes sure that cadets learn the specific communication skills they need for their jobs.

Additionally, the participation of educators, maritime educational institutions, and industry stakeholders is essential for the effective execution of this pedagogical model. Teachers are key to making sure that students have learning experiences that make good use of these tech tools. As part of their professional development, they should learn how to use ICT tools and how to meet the different learning needs of cadets. To make this happen, schools and other organizations need to provide the right tools for integrating technology, like reliable internet access and the right software. Finally, working with people in the industry is very important to make sure that the curriculum is in line with current maritime practices and what employers want. Ongoing feedback from industry partners can help make changes and improvements to the curriculum, making sure that the training stays useful and up-to-date (Arif et al., 2023; Ahmmed, 2021).

A technology-enhanced lesson plan in this framework might include a blended learning module that teaches how to communicate in an emergency on board. The first part of this module would be online, where the teacher would use video conferencing tools to teach maritime emergency vocabulary and communication protocols. After that, the cadets would take part in a VR simulation that puts them in an emergency, like an engine failure or a man-overboard situation, where they have to talk to the crew and shore authorities in Maritime English. The session would end with a time for students to think about what they learned and talk about it with their instructors and AI-powered assessment tools. This is when they would get feedback on how well they communicated (Швецова et al., 2021; Diahyleva et al., 2025). This structured but flexible approach not only improves language skills but also helps people think critically and work together, which are both important for managing crises in maritime operations.

To sum up, the suggested teaching model shows how important it is to use ICT in Maritime English lessons and make sure they meet industry standards. By fostering collaborative roles among educators, institutions, and industry stakeholders, this model aims to create a robust framework for preparing future seafarers equipped to navigate the communication challenges of a digital maritime environment (Tolba et al., 2024).

6. CHALLENGES AND CONSIDERATIONS

There are many problems and things to think about when it comes to using technology in Maritime English education. These problems must be solved to make sure that all students learn effectively and fairly. To use technology to support learning effectively, maritime schools must deal with technical, infrastructure, and teaching problems.

6.1. Problems with technology and infrastructure

Many maritime organizations, especially in developing areas, have big gaps in their technology and infrastructure. Limited access to reliable internet, a lack of technological resources, and old hardware make it hard to use digital learning tools effectively. Sihombing et al. (2024). For instance, institutions may have trouble offering online courses or accessing the vast resources available on the internet if they don't have the right servers and networking capabilities. Also, because technology is changing so quickly, institutions need to keep their software and hardware up to date all the time to stay relevant. This necessitates a financial commitment that may not be accessible in all maritime educational institutions (Ahmmed, 2021).

6.2. The Digital Divide Among Sailors

The digital divide is a big problem in maritime education. Seafarers from developed countries generally possess superior access to advanced training resources and opportunities for the enhancement of their Maritime English skills in comparison to their counterparts in developing regions. This difference can lead to a big skills gap, which makes it hard for professionals from less privileged backgrounds to compete in the global maritime labor market (Barus et al., 2024). Institutions in developing regions frequently lack the financial resources to acquire the latest training technologies or employ qualified instructors skilled in advanced pedagogical techniques, resulting in an inequitable educational environment.

6.3. Concerns about ethics and privacy

As AI and other digital tools become more integrated, there are more ethical and privacy concerns. As maritime schools start using AI-assisted tools for learning and testing, people are worried about data security and the possibility of sensitive information being used in the wrong way. For example, schools must be very careful when collecting personal information from students to protect their privacy and follow the law. The use of AI-generated assessments has ethical implications because biases in these systems can affect how well a learner is judged, which could hurt their job prospects (Gadalla, 2022). Because data-driven decision-making is so important, it's important to be open about how these tools work and the algorithms that power them.

6.4. Ongoing Professional Development for Teachers

To deal with the problems that come with using technology to teach Maritime English, teachers need to be very committed to ongoing professional development. Teachers often need to keep learning to stay up to date on new technologies and teaching methods. Their ability to use technology in the classroom is important for making learning fun and meaningful for cadets and helping them improve their communication skills (Bayotas, 2024; Vujičić et al., 2020). As maritime training changes to keep up with new technologies, paying for instructors' professional development makes sure they stay skilled and sure of themselves when teaching.

7. CONCLUSION

The incorporation of technology into Maritime English education has yielded considerable progress while simultaneously introducing challenges that necessitate comprehension and resolution. The use of Information and Communication Technology (ICT) in maritime training settings not only makes language learning easier, but it also shows how important it is to train sailors to be good communicators in a globalized world.

Key insights show that when technology is carefully added to maritime education, it can help seafarers become more competent by giving them new ways to practice their language skills, get feedback in real time, and create personalized learning paths. Using tools like virtual simulations, mobile apps, and adaptive learning platforms makes teaching more interesting and relevant to how things work in the maritime industry. By improving language learning in these ways, seafarers are better able to deal with the communication problems that are specific to their field. This makes them more useful members of a multicultural maritime workforce (Kumi–Yeboah et al., 2023).

Furthermore, equipping seafarers as globally competent communicators involves more than just being able to speak the language. It means developing intercultural competence and digital literacy, which are important skills for a job that involves working with people from different cultures and countries. As the maritime industry keeps using new technologies, it is very important to have workers who are not only good at languages but also good with computers. Institutions must take the initiative to make sure that their training programs help people learn these skills. This will create seafarers who can work safely and well in a digital world that crosses borders (Martínez & Sancho, 2020; Houpert et al., 2023).

Maritime English education needs to be sustainable, open to everyone, and able to adapt to new technologies in the future. This includes making it easier for maritime institutions and seafarers, especially in developing areas, to get modern educational tools and closing the digital divide that still exists between them. To close this gap, educational leaders, policymakers, and industry stakeholders must work together to create support systems that make sure all teachers have equal access to digital resources and ongoing chances to improve their skills (Joshi, 2024; Amirova et al., 2023).

To sum up, creating a strong pedagogy for technology-supported Maritime English education is not just an improvement on what we already do; it is a crucial need that will shape the future of maritime operations. We prepare seafarers to do well in an interconnected and increasingly digital maritime industry by teaching them how to communicate with people from all over the world in a way that is fair and long-lasting. It is clear what we need to do: we need to work together to keep up with new technologies and make sure that all seafarers have the chance to do well in their important jobs on the world's oceans (Kurent & Avsec, 2023).

REFERENCES

Abila, S., Kitada, M., Malecosio, S.Jr, Tang, L., & Subong-Espina, R. (2023). Empowering seafarers as agents of their mental health: The role of information and communication technology in seafarers' well-being. *Inquiry : a Journal of Medical Care Organization, Provision and Financing*, *60*, 00469580231162752. Advance online publication. DOI: 10.1177/00469580231162752

Ahmmed, R. (2021). A framework for maritime english language planning in bangladeshi maritime education and training institutes. *SN Social Sciences*, *1*(7), 168. Advance online publication. DOI: 10.1007/s43545-021-00188-5

Ajayi, F. and Udeh, C. (2024). Review of crew resilience and mental health practices in the marine industry: pathways to improvement. Magna Scientia Advanced Biology and Pharmacy, 11(2), 033-049. https://doi.org/DOI: 10.30574/msabp.2024.11.2.0021

Akbarani, R. (2024). Use of artificial intelligence in english language teaching. *International Journal of English Learning and Applied Linguistics (Ijelal)*, *4*(1), 14–23. DOI: 10.21111/ijelal.v4i1.10756

Amirova, A., Nurumov, K., Kaša, R., Akhmetzhanova, A., & Kuzekova, A. (2023). The impact of the digital divide on synchronous online teaching in kazakhstan during covid-19 school closures. *Frontiers in Education*, *7*, 1083651. Advance online publication. DOI: 10.3389/feduc.2022.1083651

Anggraini, L., Ernis, E., & Jelenska, J. (2020). Students' perceptions towards ideal maritime english teacher. *Biormatika Jurnal Ilmiah Fakultas Keguruan Dan Ilmu Pendidikan*, *6*(02), 29–35. DOI: 10.35569/biormatika.v6i02.796

Arif, T., Armiwati, A., & Handayani, R. (2023). The use of ict for english language learning: A mixed-method study of efl university students. [Indonesian Journal of English Language Teaching and Applied Linguistics]. *Ijeltal*, *8*(2), 199. DOI: 10.21093/ijeltal.v8i2.1554

Barus, I., Simanjuntak, R., Siahaan, R., Toko, G., & Resmayasari, I. (2024). Cultural and linguistic challenges in global maritime education (navigating english usage). *Meteor Stip Marunda*, *17*(1), 121–130. DOI: 10.36101/msm.v17i1.358

Batu, P., Bewafa, S., & Cahyaningrum, W. (2021). Online resourcing in maritime english teaching: The teachers' challenges. *Prosiding Politeknik Ilmu Pelayaran Makassar*, *1*(4), 209–213. DOI: 10.48192/prc.v1i4.341

Batu, P., Priadi, A., & Cahyaningrum, W. (2021). Accessible learning sources: A need analysis on maritime english learning apps. *Transactions on Maritime Science*, *10*(2), 520–525. DOI: 10.7225/toms.v10.n02.020

Baylon, A., & Santos, V. (2025). Innovative leadership in aligning seafarers' skills and policy in this era of emerging technologies: Implications for a regional strategic policy and training framework towards success in a dynamic world. *Journal of Marine Technology and Environment*, (2), 19–29. DOI: 10.53464/JMTE.02.2025.02

Bayotas, M. (2024). Shifting from global maritime professional to global maritime citizen.. https://doi.org/DOI: 10.5821/mt.13183

Bojović, M. (2024). Communicative language ability in maritime english: concept, significance, and assessment. Časopis Pomorskog Fakulteta Kotor - Journal of Maritime Sciences, 25(1), 34-51. https://doi.org/DOI: 10.56080/jms240503

Budiman, J. and Ganap, N. (2024). Investigating students motivation as autonomous learners in english language acquisition: a study on politeknik pelayaran sulawesi utara. Edumaspul - Jurnal Pendidikan, 8(1), 361-377. https://doi.org/DOI: 10.33487/edumaspul.v8i1.7655

D'Augusta, V., Gazzaneo, L., Longo, F., Manfredi, K., Nicoletti, L., Padovano, A., … & Talarico, S. (2025). Advancing maritime training through a vr-enhanced ship bridge simulator: a preliminary usability analysis.. https://doi.org/DOI: 10.3233/PMST250101

Danelova, G., & Astaduryan, A. (2023). Applying information and communication technology in the teaching of foreign language to maritime cadets. SHS Web of Conferences, 164, 00078. https://doi.org/DOI: 10.1051/shsconf/202316400078

Demirel, E. (2020). Maritime education and training in the digital era. *Universal Journal of Educational Research*, *8*(9), 4129–4142. DOI: 10.13189/ujer.2020.080939

Diahyleva, O., Yurzhenko, A., & Kononova, O. (2023). Design of flipped classroom lesson in educational electronic environment of maritime higher education institutions. Scientific Bulletin of Mukachevo State University Series. *Pedagogy and Psychology*, *9*(3), 45–53. DOI: 10.52534/msu-pp3.2023.45

Diahyleva, O., Yurzhenko, A., & Kononova, O. (2025). Exploring the effectiveness of online learning tools and technologies while teaching maritime english to future ship engineers. *Cte Workshop Proceedings*, 12, 350-362. https://doi.org/DOI: 10.55056/cte.711

Die, W. and You, Z. (2024). Research on teaching and reform of maritime english listening and conversation course based on imo maritime english demonstration course., 1(4), 164-171. https://doi.org/DOI: 10.62517/jhve.202416423

Durana, C., Balga, I., Bernardo, J., Cardano, L., Maniapao, K., & Pracambo, K. (2025). The impact of digitalization in enhancing maritime safety of cruise ships. *OL-IJMOS*, *3*(1), 48–56. DOI: 10.62718/vmca.ol-ijmos.3.1.SC-1024-015

Fabian-Perona, E. (2025). Maritime education and language as the acting link between bridge and engine room – a report. Educational Role of Language Journal, 2025-1(13), 64-67. https://doi.org/DOI: 10.36534/erlj.2025.01.07

Gadalla, H. (2022). Investigating proactive measures towards met development with respect to 4ir. *Maritime Research and Technology*, *1*(2), 46. DOI: 10.21622/mrt.2022.01.2.046

Garba, A.AMINATU GARBA. (2025). The role of ict i n english language and pedagogy. *Nigerian Journal of Technical Education*, *24*(2), 141–161. DOI: 10.63996/njte.v24i2.41

Hafita, Y., Sumarta, R., Riyanto, B., & Sulistiono, A. (2024). A comprehensive needs analysis of maritime english for ship machinery students. *Exposure Jurnal Pendidikan Bahasa Inggris*, *13*(2), 554–569. DOI: 10.26618/exposure.v13i2.15389

Holiver, N., Kurbatova, T., & Bondar, I. (2020). Blended learning for sustainable education: moodle-based english for specific purposes teaching at kryvyi rih national university. E3s Web of Conferences, 166, 10006. https://doi.org/DOI: 10.1051/e3sconf/202016610006

Hosny, M., & Mohamed, E. (2024). Ranking seafarers' duties towards unmanned and autonomous ships in prospective of stcw. *Ain Journal En*, *1*(47). Advance online publication. DOI: 10.59660/47113

Houpert, R., Almont, T., Mésenge, C., Kleinebreil, L., Forlini, L., Magnone, B., Leroux, V., Vestris, M., Montabord, C., Carmenate, J., Galán, Y., Rubio, M. C., Enriquez, R., Burte, C., Gatimel, N., Bujan, L., Kara, N., Edwige, O., Huyghe, É., & Véronique-Baudin, J. (2023). International cooperation and the challenge of internet accessibility in caribbean territories: Example of a collaborative platform between the university hospital of martinique and ramón gonzález coro hospital in cuba, through the french prph-3 program. *BMC Medical Education*, *23*(1), 352. Advance online publication. DOI: 10.1186/s12909-023-04321-1

Huang, X. (2025). Research on the innovation of maritime english teaching mode in the big data environment. *IJESD*, *2*(1), 26–28. DOI: 10.54097/1kndgz71

Idham, A., Rauf, W., & Rajab, A. (2024). Navigating the transformative impact of artificial intelligence on english language teaching: Exploring challenges and opportunities. *JES*, *4*(1), 8–14. DOI: 10.56185/jes.v4i1.620

Joshi, D. (2024). Impact of online learning platforms on student engagement in india. *International Journal of Online and Distance Learning*, *5*(1), 1–13. DOI: 10.47604/ijodl.2436

Journal, A. (2024). Exploring the impact of vr integration on esl leaners' english verbal communication skills: a case study in a malaysian high school. https://doi.org/DOI: 10.31235/osf.io/857f2

Kim, T., Sharma, A., Bustgaard, M., Gyldensten, W., Nymoen, O., Tusher, H., & Nazir, S. (2021). The continuum of simulator-based maritime training and education. *Wmu Journal of Maritime Affairs*, *20*(2), 135–150. DOI: 10.1007/s13437-021-00242-2

Kumi–Yeboah, A., Kim, Y., & Armah, Y. (2023). Strategies for overcoming the digital divide during thecovid-19 pandemic in higher education institutions in ghana. *British Journal of Educational Technology*, *54*(6), 1441–1462. DOI: 10.1111/bjet.13356

Kurent, B., & Avsec, S. (2023). Systems thinking skills and the ict self-concept in preschool teachers for sustainable curriculum transformation. *Sustainability (Basel)*, *15*(20), 15131. DOI: 10.3390/su152015131

Li, J., & Wang, Z. (2025). Navigating digital transformation: Assessing the digital literacy of chinese seafarers. *Information Research*, *30*(3), 370–389. DOI: 10.47989/ir30357587

Liashenko, I., Chepeliuk, N., & Rumiantseva, O. (2025). Enhancing esp for stem students: Ai tools and their effects on language and content learning. *Fìlologìčnì Traktati*, *17*(1), 284–293. DOI: 10.21272/Ftrk.2025.17(1)-25

Litikova, H. (2021). Linguistic peculiars of discourse in multilingual maritime crew. *Humanities Science Current Issues*, *7*(35), 82–88. DOI: 10.24919/2308-4863/35-7-14

Losi, R., Putra, E., Ali, N., & Dewi, A. (2024). Using artificial intelligence (ai) to improve efl students' writing skill. *International Journal of English and Applied Linguistics (Ijeal)*, *4*(1), 62–70. DOI: 10.47709/ijeal.v4i1.3694

Lou, Y. (2025). The impact of virtual reality environments on english language acquisition: Innovative immersive learning technologies for communication skills development. *Journal of Computational Methods in Sciences and Engineering*, *25*(5), 4616–4632. DOI: 10.1177/14727978251337950

Makransky, G., & Petersen, G. (2021). The cognitive affective model of immersive learning (camil): A theoretical research-based model of learning in immersive virtual reality. *Educational Psychology Review*, *33*(3), 937–958. DOI: 10.1007/s10648-020-09586-2

Martínez, J., & Sancho, A. (2020). Interactions between virtual spaces and schools: A collective case study. *Future Internet*, *12*(12), 217. DOI: 10.3390/fi12120217

Meštrović, T., Pavić, I., Maljković, M., & Androjna, A. (2024). Challenges for the education and training of seafarers in the context of autonomous shipping: Bibliometric analysis and systematic literature review. *Applied Sciences (Basel, Switzerland)*, *14*(8), 3173. DOI: 10.3390/app14083173

Moorhouse, B., Wong, K., & Li, L. (2023). Teaching with technology in the post-pandemic digital age: Technological normalisation and ai-induced disruptions. *RELC Journal*, *54*(2), 311–320. DOI: 10.1177/00336882231176929

Narayanan, S., Emad, G., & Fei, J. (2023). Theorizing seafarers' participation and learning in an evolving maritime workplace: An activity theory perspective. *Wmu Journal of Maritime Affairs*, *22*(2), 165–180. DOI: 10.1007/s13437-023-00311-8

Nurdin, M., Rosiana, E., & Rahman, M. (2023). Investigating maritime cadets' difficulties in english speaking at nusantara maritime academy banjarmasin. *Pena Jangkar*, *2*(2), 1–10. DOI: 10.54315/penajangkar.v2i2.51

Obari, H., Lambacher, S., & Kikuchi, H. (2022). Exploring the impact of ai on efl teaching in japan., 101-125. https://doi.org/DOI: 10.29140/9781914291012-6

Popoola, O., Akinsanya, M., Nzeako, G., Chukwurah, E., & Okeke, C. (2024). The impact of automation on maritime workforce management: A conceptual framework. *International Journal of Management & Entrepreneurship Research*, *6*(5), 1467–1488. DOI: 10.51594/ijmer.v6i5.1095

Raman, K., Hashim, H., & Ismail, H. (2023). Enhancing english verbal communication skills through virtual reality: A study on engagement, motivation, and autonomy among english as a second language learners. *International Journal of Learning Teaching and Educational Research*, *22*(12), 237–261. DOI: 10.26803/ijlter.22.12.12

Ramli, R., Fansury, A., & Rosmayanti, V. (2025). Technological tools in efl class. *Klasikal Journal of Education Language Teaching and Science*, *7*(1), 390–406. DOI: 10.52208/klasikal.v7i1.1313

Rosedi, S. (2021). Evaluating students' level of motivation in learning maritime english during the movement control order (mco) period: Preliminary findings on online distance learning of an stcw course. *Journal of Research Policy & Practice of Teachers & Teacher Education, 11*(2), 139–151. DOI: 10.37134/jrpptte.vol11.2.10.2021

Rybina, N., Koshil, N., & Hyryla, O. (2025). Artificial intelligence and translation in english language teaching: Opportunities and challenges. *Медична Освіта*, (2), 87–91. DOI: 10.11603/m.2414-5998.2025.2.15494

Sari, L., & Sari, R. (2022). Lecturers' challenges and strategies in teaching maritime english online to students with low english proficiency. *Register Journal, 15*(2), 222–244. DOI: 10.18326/rgt.v15i2.222-244

Saridaki, E. (2023). The necessity of maritime english for the shipping industry. Journal of Academic Social Resources, 8(Cilt 8 Sayı 45), 1908-1913. https://doi.org/DOI: 10.29228/ASRJOURNAL.67256

Sellberg, C., Nordenström, E., & Säljö, R. (2024). The development of visual expertise in a virtual environment: A case of maritime pilots in training. *Frontline Learning Research, 12*(1), 16–33. DOI: 10.14786/flr.v12i1.1217

Sharma, A., Undheim, P., & Nazir, S. (2022). Design and implementation of ai chatbot for colregs training. *Wmu Journal of Maritime Affairs, 22*(1), 107–123. DOI: 10.1007/s13437-022-00284-0

Shi, J., & Fan, L. (2021). Investigating teachers' and students' perceptions of online english learning in a maritime context in china. *SAGE Open, 11*(3), 21582440211040800. Advance online publication. DOI: 10.1177/21582440211040800

Sihombing, D., Dwiyani, N., Martha, Y., Hutabarat, C., & Sutrisno, S. (2024). Impact of international standards on maritime education: Perspectives of junior cadets. *Meteor Stip Marunda, 17*(1), 7–15. DOI: 10.36101/msm.v17i1.357

Simanjuntak, M. (2023). Enhancing environmental awareness and sustainable communication skills in maritime education. Bio Web of Conferences, 79, 01002. https://doi.org/DOI: 10.1051/bioconf/20237901002

Simanjuntak, M., Sijabat, P., Barasa, L., Malau, A., & Mudakir, M. (2024). Exploring english literacy and communication needs among new cadets in maritime education. *Edukatif Jurnal Ilmu Pendidikan, 6*(1), 996–1003. DOI: 10.31004/edukatif.v6i1.6026

Sirbu, A.SIRBU. (2023). Communication skills in engineering higher education with a focus on maritime english in met. *Scientific Bulletin of Naval Academy, XXVI*(1), 100–106. DOI: 10.21279/1454-864X-23-I1-012

Sudewo, G., Santoso, H., & Susanto, P. (2025). Strategic enhancement of maritime human resource quality: An integrated approach to assessment, talent management, and competency development. *International Research Journal of Innovations in Engineering and Technology, 09*(07), 131–140. DOI: 10.47001/IRJIET/2025.907015

Taylor, N., Bekker, A., & Kruger, K. (2023). Mariner 4.0: Integrating seafarers into a maritime 4.0 environment. *International Journal of Maritime Engineering, 164*(A4), 373–384. DOI: 10.5750/ijme.v164iA4.773

Tolba, R., Elarif, T., Taha, Z., & Hammady, R. (2024). Interactive augmented reality system for learning phonetics using artificial intelligence. *IEEE Access : Practical Innovations, Open Solutions*, *12*, 78219–78231. DOI: 10.1109/ACCESS.2024.3406494

Tymofyeyeva, O., & Konstantynova, T. (2021). The strategies of collaborative learning in maritime english. *Humanities Science Current Issues*, *3*(37), 219–225. DOI: 10.24919/2308-4863/37-3-34

Ulfa, K. (2023). The transformative power of artificial intelligence (ai) to elevate english language learning. *Majalah Ilmiah Methoda*, *13*(3), 307–313. DOI: 10.46880/methoda.Vol13No3.pp307-313

Ullah, H., Anwar, S., & Khan, S. (2024). Enhancing english language acquisition through chatgpt: Use of technology acceptance model in linguistics. *Journal of English Language Literature and Education*, *6*(4), 119–145. DOI: 10.54692/jelle.2024.0604262

Usluer, H. (2024). Understanding of the maritime future mentality; safe e-navigation and safe maritime surface communication. Turkish Journal of Maritime and Marine Sciences, 10(Özel Sayı: 1), 1-18. https://doi.org/DOI: 10.52998/trjmms.1519901

Vujičić, S., Hasanspahić, N., Gundić, A., & Hrdalo, N. (2020). Assessment for ensuring adequately qualified instructors in maritime education and training institutions. *Athens Journal of Sciences*, *7*(2), 115–126. DOI: 10.30958/ajs.7-2-4

Wang, Q. (2024). Ai-driven autonomous interactive english learning language tutoring system. *Journal of Computational Methods in Sciences and Engineering*, *25*(2), 1155–1166. DOI: 10.1177/14727978241296719

Wang, S., & Erdenebold, T. (2025). Integrating generative ai into project-based esp learning: A fashion design case in chinese vocational education. *JEVE*, *5*(4), 1–8. DOI: 10.63650/jeve.v5i4.67

Wibowo, A., Gupron, A., & Dewi, R. (2025). Integrating teaching factory method in esp maritime english: Cadets' perceptions and implications for maritime training. *Script Journal Journal of Linguistic and English Teaching*, *10*(1), 46–67. DOI: 10.24903/sj.v10i1.1998

Yin, H., Khan, S., Alharbi, A., & Nazir, S. (2022). Assessing english teaching linguistic and artificial intelligence for efficient learning using analytical hierarchy process and technique for order of preference by similarity to ideal solution. *Journal of Software (Malden, MA)*, *36*(2), e2462. Advance online publication. DOI: 10.1002/smr.2462

Yurzhenko, A., Bevzenko, J., & Kononova, O. (2022). Creation of a distance communication channel with gamification elements., 226-240. https://doi.org/DOI: 10.4018/978-1-6684-4287-6.ch012

Yurzhenko, A., Kononova, O., & Diahyleva, O. (2025). The use of the callan method in maritime english teaching. *Educational Challenges*, *30*(2). Advance online publication. DOI: 10.34142/2709-7986.2025.30.2.10

Zhou, Q., Hashim, H., & Sulaiman, N. (2023). A systemic review (2014–2023) on the mobile-assisted blended learning for english as a foreign language education with a focus on empirical studies. *International Journal of Interactive Mobile Technologies (Ijim)*, *17*(24), 153–172. DOI: 10.3991/ijim.v17i24.42019

KEY TERMS AND DEFINITIONS

Adaptive Learning: A technology-based instructional approach that adjusts content, pace, and learning activities to match a learner's needs, performance, and progress.

Artificial Intelligence: Computer-based technology that can simulate human-like functions, such as feedback, speech analysis, and personalized support, to improve Maritime English learning.

Blended Learning: An instructional model that combines face-to-face teaching with online learning activities to create a more flexible and effective learning experience.

Digital Literacy: The ability to use digital tools, interpret digital information, and communicate effectively in technology-rich maritime environments.

Digital Seafarer: A maritime professional who combines traditional seafaring competence with digital skills needed to operate and communicate in modern, technology-driven settings.

Maritime English: A specialized form of English used in the maritime industry for safe, clear, and efficient communication during navigation, operations, and teamwork.

Simulation-Based Learning: A learning approach that uses realistic training scenarios and digital simulations to help learners practice language and operational skills in safe, controlled environments.

Technology-Enhanced Language Learning: A framework for language instruction that uses digital tools and platforms to make learning more interactive, personalized, and relevant to real-world communication needs.

Virtual Reality: An immersive digital environment that allows learners to experience realistic maritime situations for practicing communication, decision-making, and language use.

Chapter 13
Greening the Waves:
Integrating Environmental Education and Climate-Resilient Training in Maritime Education

Agus Salim
http://orcid.org/0009-0000-9381-5388
Politeknik Ilmu Pelayaran Makassar, Indonesia

ABSTRACT

This study explores the integration of environmental education and climate-resilient training within Maritime Education and Training (MET) institutions to prepare future seafarers for sustainable and adaptive operations. It examines pedagogical innovations such as simulation, digital learning, and community engagement alongside institutional frameworks for green governance, accreditation, and global collaboration. Emphasis is placed on developing environmental competencies, ethical awareness, and lifelong learning pathways that align with international sustainability standards. The discussion highlights how MET institutions serve as catalysts for eco-innovation and policy transformation, fostering a new generation of maritime professionals committed to environmental stewardship and global climate resilience.

NAVIGATING THE GREEN TRANSITION IN MARITIME EDUCATION

1.1 The Global Imperative for Sustainable Seas

The maritime industry is becoming an important part of the global sustainability agenda because it plays a big role in international trade, which depends on shipping to move almost 90% of goods. This heavy reliance has a big impact on the environment, causing a lot of problems like greenhouse gas (GHG) emissions, marine pollution, and ecosystem degradation (Werkmeister et al., 2023). The shipping industry is responsible for about 2.9% of all CO_2 emissions, which has a big effect on the climate and the health of ocean systems (Fan et al., 2024). Climate change and maritime activities work together to make

DOI: 10.4018/979-8-3373-6670-8.ch013

coastal areas more vulnerable. This raises risks like rising sea levels and more extreme weather events, which can disrupt maritime operations and put seafaring communities in danger (Hananto et al., 2025).

Due to these problems, it is now not only necessary but also strategically important to include environmental education and climate-resilient training in maritime curricula (Islam, 2024). Research highlights the necessity of improving environmental literacy among maritime professionals, thereby preparing future seafarers to effectively address sustainability challenges (Simanjuntak et al., 2023). Maritime education is increasingly acknowledged as a potential driver for cultivating ecological literacy, environmental ethics, and systems-oriented problem-solving skills (Fan et al., 2024; Roy et al., 2025).

The maritime sector encounters numerous environmental challenges, such as air pollution resulting from ship emissions of sulfur oxides (SOx) and nitrogen oxides (NOx), the introduction of invasive species via ballast water discharges, and the inadequate disposal of waste materials produced by vessels (Werkmeister et al., 2023; Roy et al., 2025). Oil spills, microplastic pollution, and noise pollution from underwater sources make these problems worse and hurt the health of the ocean as a whole. The international regulatory framework shows how important it is to deal with these issues quickly. For example, the International Maritime Organization (IMO) created the MARPOL Convention, which sets rules for ship pollution and tries to lessen the environmental impact of the maritime industry (Fan et al., 2024; İnal, 2024). To fully comply with these rules, businesses need to do more than just follow the law; they also need to promote new ideas and environmentally friendly practices in the industry (Moshiul et al., 2021).

The IMO has been a key player in setting and enforcing global environmental standards at the governance level. This is especially true for its efforts to cut GHG emissions from ships, as described in the 2018 Initial Strategy on the Reduction of GHG Emissions (Moshiul et al., 2021). This strategy aims to cut total annual GHG emissions by at least 50% by 2050 compared to 2008 levels. This aligns with broader global climate goals, such as the Paris Agreement (Tran et al., 2021; Moshiul et al., 2021). The rise in regulatory requirements underscores the necessity of integrating the United Nations Sustainable Development Goals (SDGs) into maritime education (Roy et al., 2025). SDG 13 (Climate Action) and SDG 14 (Life Below Water) are two examples of frameworks that schools should use to teach students about sustainability in maritime practices (Moshiul et al., 2021).

In conclusion, the convergence of policy, education, and practice constitutes a fundamental element for the maritime sector's green transition—an evolution necessitating the development of professionals skilled in managing the intricacies of sustainability and technology-driven challenges within maritime operations. This transition relies heavily on educational reforms that prepare future maritime leaders with the knowledge and skills essential to advocate for sustainability throughout their careers (Islam, 2024; Hsu et al., 2024).

1.2 Evolving Paradigms in Environmental Education

The framework of environmental education in maritime settings has experienced considerable change, transitioning from a predominantly passive awareness approach to one defined by active, transformative engagement. Sustainability topics have historically been peripheral, frequently regarded as ancillary to fundamental maritime disciplines such as navigation and engineering (Reddy, 2021). But now the profession knows that being ecologically competent is important for doing a good job, staying safe, and following rules that are getting stricter all the time (Morales et al., 2025). This transition from "knowing" to "doing" demands a comprehensive pedagogical reform, wherein prospective mariners must not only comprehend environmental issues but also implement sustainability principles in essential domains such as decision-making, voyage planning, maintenance procedures, and crisis management (Sibarani et al., 2025).

So, environmental education is becoming an immersive and cross-disciplinary framework that influences the behavior, values, and sense of duty of maritime professionals. This movement is influenced by global educational reforms, especially the Education for Sustainable Development (ESD) model promoted by UNESCO. This model encourages learning and problem-solving through participation, which are skills that modern maritime professionals need (Hallinger & Nguyen, 2020). In Maritime Education and Training (MET) institutions, this methodology has been implemented through experiential learning modules, allowing students to address authentic environmental issues, including oil spill response and fuel efficiency enhancement (Sibarani et al., 2025). These types of educational systems push students to think critically about how their actions affect the environment and come up with new projects that fit with the International Maritime Organization's (IMO) plan to cut down on carbon emissions (Morales et al., 2025).

A key part of this change in education is teaching people how to be environmentally literate. This includes being able to understand ecological systems, evaluate human impacts, and act responsibly to protect marine environments. For seafarers, this transcends mere awareness; it requires proficiency in the interconnections between maritime operations and ecological systems, comprehension of climate change's impact on ocean currents, recognition of pollution pathways, and implementation of environmentally sustainable operational practices (Zhen et al., 2020; ŞEREN & GÜL, 2022). For people to be able to read and write like this, they need to learn about oceanography, environmental law, and green engineering all at once (Butler, 2022).

It is also important to encourage systems thinking in maritime education. This method teaches sailors to see maritime operations as parts of bigger ecological and socio-economic networks (Badarnah, 2025). Professionals can use systems thinking to predict how their choices will affect ecosystems and communities in a chain reaction. For example, decisions about how to handle ballast water affect biodiversity around the world, and choices about energy use have a direct effect on carbon footprints (Supangat et al., 2025). MET institutions can develop seafarers who are system-aware problem solvers by using reflective inquiry, digital simulations, and group projects. These seafarers will be able to include environmental, technical, and ethical factors into their work (Tusher et al., 2021).

The changing ideas about environmental education in maritime settings call for a complete teaching method that connects knowing something with being responsible. The next generation of seafarers must go beyond simply following the rules and make sustainability a core part of their professional identity. They must be able to navigate the oceans with the skill, conscience, and commitment needed to make the future greener (Morales et al., 2025; Hallinger & Nguyen, 2020).

1.3 The Role of Maritime Education and Training (MET) Institutions

Maritime Education and Training (MET) institutions hold a strategic and moral responsibility in steering the shipping industry toward sustainability and climate resilience. As the custodians of seafarer knowledge, skills, and ethics, MET institutions serve as the bridge between international environmental mandates and practical maritime operations. The integration of sustainability into their missions, curricula, and institutional culture ensures that environmental responsibility becomes embedded in the professional identity of future maritime personnel. Rather than treating sustainability as a separate discipline, progressive METs are reframing it as a cross-cutting principle that informs leadership, engineering, navigation, and management decisions.

Embedding sustainability into institutional missions begins with a philosophical reorientation. Maritime academies and training centers are increasingly revising their vision statements to emphasize "green seamanship," "eco-efficient operations," and "climate-smart maritime education." This shift is supported by curriculum reform that aligns teaching and assessment practices with environmental performance standards. For example, navigation courses now incorporate modules on energy-efficient routing and emission reduction strategies, while marine engineering programs integrate green propulsion technologies and waste management systems. Similarly, ethics and leadership classes highlight the moral dimensions of environmental decision-making at sea. Through simulation training, case studies, and project-based learning, students are encouraged to translate sustainable theories into operational practice—transforming sustainability from a policy requirement into an applied maritime competency.

Institutional embedding also extends to campus operations and research initiatives. Green campus programs—covering energy conservation, waste recycling, and digitalization—allow METs to serve as living laboratories for sustainability. Research centers are being established to explore decarbonization, ocean renewable energy, and biodiversity conservation, thereby linking academic inquiry with industry transformation. Collaboration with maritime companies ensures that these innovations respond to real-world needs while fostering a culture of shared responsibility between education and industry.

Aligning MET goals with the **United Nations Sustainable Development Goals (SDGs)** reinforces this mission. In particular, **SDG 13 (Climate Action)** urges METs to integrate climate science, mitigation, and adaptation strategies into their teaching and research agendas. This involves preparing seafarers to understand the impact of extreme weather, carbon management, and emergency preparedness in changing oceanic conditions. Meanwhile, **SDG 14 (Life Below Water)** calls for active engagement in protecting marine ecosystems, reducing pollution, and promoting responsible resource use. MET institutions can operationalize these goals through fieldwork, coastal restoration programs, and partnerships with marine conservation organizations.

By aligning curricula, governance, and community outreach with these global goals, METs become agents of transformation within the broader maritime ecosystem. They not only produce technically competent graduates but also cultivate climate-conscious professionals equipped to champion sustainable seas. In doing so, MET institutions anchor the maritime world's transition toward a future where environmental stewardship and operational excellence sail in tandem.

FRAMEWORKS FOR ENVIRONMENTAL COMPETENCE DEVELOPMENT

2.1 Defining Green Competencies for the Maritime Workforce

A big part of making the maritime industry more sustainable is training workers with green skills—technical, behavioral, and ethical skills that help seafarers do their jobs in a way that has the least impact on the environment. As the rules for ships and the goal of reducing carbon emissions change around the world, seafarers need to learn more than just how to sail. Today, maritime professionals need to know a lot about complex environmental systems, how to use green technologies, and how to make choices that are good for both the environment and the business.

The most basic part of being green is having technical skills. They include both theoretical and practical knowledge about how to run a business in a way that saves energy, cut down on emissions, avoid pollution, and manage waste. This field includes knowing how to treat ballast water, use fuel more efficiently, use alternative propulsion systems, and make plans for managing ship energy efficiency (SEEMP). As technology has become more digital and automated, technical skills now include being able to use smart sensors and data analytics to keep an eye on how well the environment is doing. Marine engineers and navigators need to know about environmental compliance tools like the Energy Efficiency Existing Ship Index (EEXI) and the Carbon Intensity Indicator (CII) as well as standard safety rules.

Behavioral competencies encompass a range of skills beyond mere technical proficiency. They also include behaviors related to attitudes, teamwork, and leadership that support a culture of sustainability both at sea and on land. To be good stewards of the environment, you need to work together, be aware of your surroundings, and actively participate in sustainable practices. Seafarers need to learn how to be responsible, respect marine life, and work together to keep the ocean clean. MET institutions play a significant role in shaping these behaviors through role modeling, experiential learning, and reflective instruction. Some examples of programs that can help both trainees and professionals have better attitudes toward the environment are environmental campaigns, sustainability clubs, and peer mentoring programs.

Ethical skills are what keep maritime operations going in the right direction. When you have to make moral choices, you have to think about the good and bad sides of economic efficiency and ecological integrity. It makes sailors question how things are done, report environmental violations, and push for things to get better all the time. MET schools make sure that sustainability becomes a professional duty instead of just a legal obligation by teaching ethical literacy based on being open, following the rules, and protecting the environment.

The International Maritime Organization (IMO) helps people learn these skills in a structured way by offering model courses and new green skill taxonomies. Model Course 7.03 (Officer in Charge of an Engineering Watch) and Model Course 7.04 (Chief Engineer Officer) are two examples of courses that follow the STCW Code and the International Convention for the Prevention of Pollution from Ships (MARPOL) and have modules on protecting the environment. Along with these, international organizations like the European Maritime Safety Agency (EMSA) and the International Labour Organization (ILO) are also trying to find ways to define and measure green skills along the maritime value chain.

All of these frameworks agree that being good at maritime work in the 21st century means more than just knowing how to do it well. It also means being able to learn new things, being morally responsible, and being smart about the environment. Teaching these kinds of skills to people who work at sea will not only make them more compliant, but it will also change how things are done, making the seas greener, cleaner, and more sustainable.

2.2 Integrating Climate-Resilient Training Standards

To effectively deal with the increasing number and severity of climate-related disruptions, we need to completely change the way we train maritime workers. Climate change, which shows up in things like cyclones, heatwaves, rising sea levels, and ocean acidification, has a big effect on how global shipping and coastal infrastructure work. Santos et al. (2025). It is important to include climate resilience in Maritime Education and Training (MET) in order to keep global trade safe, sustainable, and going

(Amorim & Chaffe, 2021). MET institutions can help seafarers deal with the uncertainties of a quickly changing maritime environment by including risk management, adaptation strategies, and scenario-based learning into their training programs.

The key to climate-resilient training is being able to manage risk well. Conventional frameworks have primarily concentrated on mechanical failures, human errors, and navigational hazards; however, contemporary methodologies must include climate-related threats such as intensified storms, variable ocean currents, and disruptions to port infrastructure (Amorim & Chaffe, 2021). By adding climate risk management to their courses, MET schools give seafarers the analytical skills they need to find, evaluate, and reduce these new risks. More and more, training programs focus on climate modeling, environmental monitoring, and predictive analytics. This helps mariners make smart choices when things are not clear (Praetorius et al., 2020). Using standardized frameworks like the International Safety Management (ISM) Code makes it easier to use resilience principles in everyday maritime operations.

Incorporating climate adaptation strategies into maritime education is just as important. Such training cultivates a proactive mindset, prompting seafarers and maritime managers to prepare for enduring environmental transformations rather than merely responding to immediate emergencies (Fitzpatrick & West, 2022). Learners examine the ramifications of phenomena such as sea-level rise on port operations, the significance of varied energy sources for vessels, and the sustainable utilization of resources during voyages. This thorough study makes sure that trainees not only understand how adaptation works, but also how to create and put into action adaptive systems, like retrofitting ships to be more environmentally friendly and planning routes that can withstand bad weather. MET institutions, in collaboration with industry and policymakers, can function as experimental platforms for novel adaptive strategies addressing climate threats (Perkovič, 2024).

Scenario-based learning is a very effective way to teach people how to prepare for disasters. In immersive simulations, trainees deal with real-life maritime emergencies like storm surges, flooding, or equipment failures during bad weather. These exercises help people learn how to work together, make decisions, and solve problems under pressure, which are all important skills to have during climate emergencies with high stakes (Bassey et al., 2025). Digital simulation platforms and virtual reality (VR) technologies make these scenarios more realistic, letting trainees practice how to respond to disasters in a controlled, data-rich setting. Debriefing sessions after simulations help students remember what they learned, encourage deep thinking, and improve performance outcomes (Sardar et al., 2022).

Including climate-resilient standards in MET training ensures that being aware of the environment leads to being ready for work. This method trains a group of maritime professionals who are not only good at their jobs but also flexible. They can handle risks, protect marine ecosystems, and keep maritime operations going even when the weather changes (Simanjuntak et al., 2024). In the end, climate-resilient training turns sailors into proactive agents of safety and sustainability on the seas that are changing all the time.

2.3 Curriculum Design and Learning Outcomes

To create an effective curriculum for environmental competence in maritime education, we need to move away from teaching a lot of facts and instead focus on competency-based and experiential learning. Traditional maritime curricula have prioritized technical proficiency and regulatory compliance, but in the era of sustainability and climate uncertainty, learners must also acquire the capacity to think critically, act ethically, and innovate responsibly. A competency-based curriculum ensures that seafarers not only understand environmental theories but can demonstrate tangible skills in pollution prevention, resource management, and eco-efficient operations. This method focuses on measurable learning outcomes—knowledge, skills, and attitudes—that are in line with international environmental standards and the changing needs of the maritime industry.

Competency-based learning lets students solve real-world problems instead of just memorizing facts. Each module is based on certain performance standards, like how to navigate in a way that saves energy, how to separate waste on board, or how to treat ballast water. Assessment is more than just written tests; it also includes simulations, onboard training, and reflective portfolios that show what you can do. This hands-on model is like real-life problems that happen at sea and helps people build confidence, independence, and a sense of professional responsibility. It also fits with the STCW Convention and IMO Model Courses, which call for ongoing skill development and evaluation based on performance.

Experiential learning changes environmental education from theory to real-life experience. Students learn by watching, trying things out, and thinking about what they did. For example, they can work on marine conservation projects, pretend to clean up an oil spill, or do environmental audits of ships. Field trips to ports, shipyards, and coastal towns help students connect what they learn in the classroom to the real world. This kind of exposure makes people feel more responsible for the environment, which supports the idea that protecting the environment is a professional duty that is part of everyday maritime practice.

The curriculum must also include knowledge of ecology, engineering, and policy from different fields. We can't solve sustainability problems by looking at them from just one angle. We need to understand how natural systems, new technologies, and governance frameworks all work together. Marine ecology courses teach students how pollution affects the environment, while green engineering modules teach students about systems that use less energy and technologies that can be used again and again. Policy and law classes teach students how to read and understand international agreements like MARPOL, SOLAS, and the Paris Agreement. This gives them the confidence and integrity to navigate the regulatory landscape.

By combining these fields, MET schools are training a new generation of maritime professionals who are technically skilled, environmentally aware, and aware of policy. The result is a complete learning ecosystem where environmental competence is at the heart of professional identity, making sure that maritime education stays in line with global sustainability goals.

PEDAGOGICAL INNOVATIONS FOR SUSTAINABLE LEARNING

3.1 Simulation and Experiential Learning for Environmental Awareness

The progress of technology has greatly changed maritime education, moving it from traditional teaching methods to immersive, interactive, and hands-on learning environments. To promote a profound understanding of the environment, Maritime Education and Training (MET) institutions are progressively integrating simulation-based and virtual reality (VR) technologies that emulate authentic ecological challenges in secure, regulated environments. These new teaching methods help students connect what they learn in the classroom with real-world situations. This improves their ability to think critically, solve problems, and be responsible for the environment, all of which are important skills for sustainable maritime operations.

Simulation-based pollution control training is a key part of this change. It lets seafarers see how their actions affect marine ecosystems without putting themselves in danger. Using high-fidelity simulators, students do training exercises that are like real-life situations, such as oil spills and managing ballast water. These kinds of virtual experiences can follow international rules like the MARPOL Convention and the Ballast Water Management Convention. This makes sure that trainees not only learn how to do things technically, but also understand what they need to do to stay in compliance (Makransky & Klingenberg, 2022). The interactive aspect of simulations greatly improves memory and emotional involvement, making people more aware of how their decisions affect the environment. For instance, a trainee driving a virtual tanker learns how to plan the best route to save fuel and cut down on emissions while also dealing with emergencies that make it harder to follow the rules.

VR technologies also take these immersive experiences to the next level by putting trainees in three-dimensional spaces where they can interact with digital ecosystems that look like real-life maritime situations. VR can help sailors understand the long-term effects of their operational decisions by showing them how pollutants or climate change affect underwater habitats (Ryan et al., 2022). Some MET schools are using VR-based modules that let students explore a ship's engine room and find problems with waste management or emissions systems. This level of involvement turns abstract environmental data into experiences that people can relate to, effectively connecting cognitive understanding with emotional investment.

Case-based learning, along with simulation and VR, places environmental education in real-life maritime situations based on best practices and incidents in the industry. Learners examine actual cases—such as responses to oil spills or effective measures for reducing emissions—thereby improving their analytical and ethical reasoning abilities (Brammer et al., 2021; Brammer et al., 2021). This method encourages students to think about mistakes made by people, corporate responsibility, and the social and economic effects of pollution at sea. It also encourages teamwork and communication as students work together to come up with practical sustainability strategies based on policy and engineering insights.

The combination of simulation, VR, and case-based learning creates a teaching style that values real change over memorization. This learning environment teaches not only how to do things, but also how to care about the environment, which is important in light of climate change and ocean degradation. Through experiential engagement, seafarers perceive themselves not solely as vessel operators but as stewards of the marine ecosystem, tasked with preserving the fragile equilibrium between technological advancement and environmental conservation.

In conclusion, the use of high-tech tools in maritime education is a big step forward for better training methods. As MET institutions keep training people to handle the complexities of environmental stewardship, the future of maritime operations depends more and more on finding professionals who are not only skilled but also very dedicated to sustainability.

3.2 Digital and Blended Learning Approaches

The digital transformation of education has changed the way maritime schools teach students about sustainability. Digital and blended learning methods are now strong tools for teaching about the environment. They let students access, analyze, and use information in a flexible and interactive way. Maritime Education and Training (MET) institutions can improve both the cognitive and behavioral aspects of environmental competence by using Artificial Intelligence (AI), data-driven platforms, and gamified learning environments. This will help seafarers understand climate data, adopt sustainable practices, and stay motivated as they develop professionally.

AI and e-learning tools are very important for helping people understand climate data, which is a basic skill for living in a time of environmental uncertainty. Students can look at real-time climate data, like ocean temperature, carbon emissions, and wind patterns, and think about how it affects navigation, safety, and operational efficiency through adaptive learning platforms. AI-powered dashboards and digital twins show how ships interact with environmental systems. This lets trainees try out ways to save energy or cut down on waste. Personalized feedback algorithms find areas where students need more help and suggest specific modules to help them better understand sustainability metrics. Also, cloud-based e-learning systems make it possible for people all over the world to access them, which helps seafarers keep learning and growing professionally no matter where they are. By adding climate analytics to technical courses, MET schools turn data into useful information that helps maritime professionals make smart, environmentally friendly choices.

Gamification and interactive assessments make digital learning more fun and engaging by making sustainability education an interactive and fun experience. Game-based modules encourage students to make environmentally friendly choices in fake situations, where they can earn points for lowering emissions, making better use of resources, or stopping pollution. These kinds of systems use intrinsic motivation to encourage green behaviors by giving people positive feedback. Leaderboards and group challenges can encourage healthy competition and teamwork, which are both important for creating a culture of sustainability on ships and in maritime organizations. Interactive quizzes, scenario games, and digital storytelling help students see how their decisions will affect the health of the ocean in the long run.

The blended learning model uses both digital tools and in-person mentoring and simulation training to make sure that technology improves rather than replaces human instruction. Teachers help students think about their actions, make moral decisions, and talk about things from different fields. These are all things that make digital engagement more meaningful.

MET schools bring together AI-driven learning, e-resources, and gamified teaching methods to make learning environments that encourage ongoing awareness, skill mastery, and long-term behavior. This combination of teaching methods not only brings maritime training up to date, but it also creates professionals who are climate-literate and digitally savvy and ready to lead the industry toward a greener future.

3.3 Collaborative and Community-Based Learning

Sustainability in maritime education cannot be attained in isolation from the communities and ecosystems that the sector directly influences. Collaborative and community-based learning connects what students learn in the classroom with what they do in the real world to protect the environment. It lets students learn through working together, taking part, and being responsible for their actions. This teaching method sees Maritime Education and Training (MET) schools as more than just places to learn technical skills; they are also places that help coastal and maritime communities grow in a way that lasts. By working with local groups, non-governmental organizations (NGOs), and marine stakeholders, students gain a well-rounded understanding of the social, ecological, and economic aspects of maritime sustainability.

Working with coastal communities and NGOs gives students real-world learning opportunities where they can see how human health and ocean health are connected. These kinds of partnerships often include things like fixing up coral reefs, restoring mangroves, cleaning up beaches, or working on fishing projects that don't harm the environment. These programs teach trainees about local ecology, traditional maritime practices, and the social and economic effects of climate change. Students learn to be more understanding, culturally aware, and responsible for their own actions by working with community members and NGO facilitators. These are traits that are often missing from traditional maritime training. Also, community partnerships help MET institutions reach regional sustainability goals by aligning academic goals with national blue economy strategies and international frameworks like the UN Decade of Ocean Science for Sustainable Development.

Student-led sustainability projects on maritime campuses are just as important. These programs give students the power to turn what they learn about sustainability into real changes on campus, like programs for recycling waste, energy audits, simulations of green shipping, and systems for keeping track of their carbon footprint. Students learn how to manage projects, work as a team, and solve environmental problems by designing and carrying out these projects. Faculty mentors and industry partners can help these projects even more by setting up innovation incubators or sustainability labs that encourage entrepreneurship in green maritime technologies. Also, campus-wide campaigns like "Plastic-Free Ports" and "Blue Innovation Weeks" encourage everyone to take responsibility and change the culture of the institution.

Collaborative and community-based learning changes maritime education into a process that everyone can take part in and that changes them. Students go from being passive learners to active participants in making social and environmental changes. MET institutions benefit from stronger networks of stakeholders and a bigger impact on society. Communities, on the other hand, get access to experts, resources, and advocacy for sustainable maritime practices. In the end, this model of reciprocal learning creates a new generation of sailors who know that protecting the ocean and the people who depend on it are two sides of the same coin. This makes sustainability a part of both their purpose and their actions.

INSTITUTIONAL AND POLICY INTEGRATION

4.1 Embedding Environmental Education into Institutional Policy

To truly make Maritime Education and Training (MET) schools more sustainable, environmental education needs to be a part of not only the curriculum but also the way the schools are run and the rules they follow. Making sustainability a key part of institutional policy makes sure that the green transformation of MET institutions is a long-term goal, not just a short-term project. This alignment is essential for harmonizing organizational vision, operations, and pedagogy with global sustainability initiatives, especially those specified by the International Maritime Organization (IMO) and the United Nations Sustainable Development Goals (SDGs) (Tsai, 2025).

To create governance models for green transformation in MET institutions, there must be clear leadership commitment and strategic integration. More and more progressive maritime universities are setting up "green steering committees" or sustainability councils to create, keep an eye on, and report on sustainability policies. These governance structures make sure that environmental goals are always a part of planning, budgeting, and accreditation at the institution. For instance, adding environmental performance indicators like lowering the carbon footprint, improving waste management, and saving energy to annual reviews can help create a culture of accountability. Good leadership is very important for showing faculty, staff, and students how to be responsible and for showing them how to be responsible. Strategic partnerships with government agencies and the shipping industry also give institutional green initiatives more credibility and resources (Madiraju & Pamula, 2025).

The change in MET institutions also depends on the use of Environmental Management Systems (EMS) that meet global standards like ISO 14001. These systems help make sustainability goals official, keep track of progress, and encourage ongoing improvement in how people take care of the environment. Institutions that use EMS frameworks can improve their operational efficiency and environmental responsibility at the same time, making sure they follow both national and international maritime environmental standards (Baniaga, 2025).

Sustainable campus initiatives are just as important because they turn institutional policy into real action. These green campus programs focus on making the best use of energy, cutting down on waste, and managing resources. For example, initiatives could include putting in solar panels, smart lighting systems, and switching to renewable energy sources to power student housing and simulation facilities. For an environmentally friendly culture to grow, it's important to have programs that focus on recycling, composting, and cutting down on single-use plastics. Additionally, strategies that promote sustainable water use, eco-friendly procurement, and the inclusion of biodiversity in campus planning are vital parts of a complete environmental strategy (Bashir et al., 2024).

By making sustainability a part of how MET schools run, students and staff can become much more aware of the environment and their social responsibilities. The campus itself becomes a living laboratory, a small example of how to run a sustainable maritime operation. Students see and take part in environmental practices every day. In the end, strong governance and proactive campus initiatives will make environmental education a permanent part of MET institutions. This will make them leaders in climate-conscious leadership and help the maritime sector prepare for a more sustainable and resilient future (Hambon, 2025).

4.2 Accreditation and Quality Assurance Mechanisms

To make sure that Maritime Education and Training (MET) lasts for a long time, environmental values must be built into systems for accreditation and quality assurance. Accreditation serves as both a gatekeeper and a catalyst for educational transformation by delineating the criteria for quality, relevance, and excellence. By adding environmental performance indicators to audits and accreditation frameworks, MET institutions can make sustainability a measurable standard of educational and operational quality, not just an optional feature.

The first step in adding environmental performance to accreditation is to change the benchmarks for institutions. The main things that traditional maritime audits have looked at are safety, technical skill, and following the Standards of Training, Certification, and Watchkeeping for Seafarers (STCW). These are still important, but the new climate realities call for more indicators that measure things like reducing carbon footprints, improving energy efficiency, managing waste, and teaching students and staff about the environment (Madiraju & Pamula, 2025). These standards make sure that MET schools are not only training skilled sailors, but also professionals who care about the environment. Environmental audits might look at how green the campus is, how eco-friendly the training simulators are, and how well sustainability is built into the curriculum.

Regular self-assessment reports and evaluations by outside parties help create a culture of openness and responsibility while also pushing for ongoing improvements in environmental performance.

Accrediting bodies, both national and international, are increasingly aligning their standards with global environmental frameworks. By linking environmental metrics to international standards, institutions can make sure that they are consistent, comparable, and credible. The STCW Convention sets the minimum standards for maritime skills, and its ongoing changes show how important it is to protect the environment and use energy wisely. In the same way, adopting ISO standards like ISO 14001 (Environmental Management Systems) and ISO 50001 (Energy Management) shows that an organization is committed to running in a way that is good for the environment by setting up systematic ways to keep track of, report on, and lower environmental impacts. These certifications show that an institution follows internationally accepted standards for sustainability.

Also, adding Environmental, Social, and Governance (ESG) principles to maritime accreditation makes people more accountable and builds trust among stakeholders. ESG-based evaluation frameworks look at more than just how well an organization does in terms of the environment. They also look at social equity, governance ethics, and institutional transparency, which are all important parts of sustainable maritime leadership.

By adding these mechanisms, accreditation becomes a dynamic process that encourages responsibility and new ideas. Institutions that meet environmental standards have a competitive edge, a better reputation, and more chances to work with other countries and get funding. Ultimately, connecting accreditation to sustainability makes environmental excellence a key part of what makes maritime education high-quality. This will help MET stay accountable, strong, and in line with the rest of the world in the future.

4.3 Public–Private and International Collaborations

For maritime education and operations to be sustainable, academia, industry, government, and international organizations must all work together. Because the maritime industry has a lot of complicated environmental problems to deal with, schools can't solve them on their own. Consequently, public-private partnerships (PPPs) and international collaborations are essential catalysts for eco-innovation, augmenting research capacities, and guaranteeing that environmental education in Maritime Education and Training (MET) institutions adheres to global sustainability standards. These partnerships are the foundation of a climate-resilient maritime ecosystem. They make it easier to share the resources, knowledge, and technologies needed to move toward greener maritime practices (Erstad et al., 2022).

Partnerships in the shipping industry that focus on eco-innovation and sustainable shipping make real-world links between environmental theory and maritime practice. By working with shipping companies, port authorities, and maritime technology companies, MET institutions can include real-world sustainability problems in their research and training programs (Undurraga et al., 2023). Projects like making ships more energy-efficient, using technologies to cut down on emissions, and looking into alternative fuels like hydrogen and ammonia are like living labs for both students and teachers. Students get valuable, hands-on experience in sustainable operations through internships, apprenticeships, and co-funded research. This is important as the maritime industry moves to greener technologies (Tomasi et al., 2021).

Industry partnerships also help schools add eco-innovation to their programs. For instance, working with shipyards or classification societies gives you access to cutting-edge digital tools for monitoring carbon, doing lifecycle assessments, and planning sustainable port logistics. This relationship helps businesses by making sure that MET schools are more relevant and useful in the global maritime value chain (Taghavi et al., 2023). It also gives companies a steady stream of graduates who are knowledgeable about the environment and can help their organizations move forward with sustainability initiatives.

In addition to working together in the industry, regional and international networks focused on climate-resilient maritime education help people share knowledge, work together on research, and make policies that work across borders. The International Maritime Organization's (IMO) World Maritime University partnerships, the ASEAN Maritime Education Network, and the European Maritime Education and Training Network (EMETNET) are all examples of platforms that bring schools together to work on curricula, joint degree programs, and sustainability benchmarks. These kinds of partnerships help make environmental standards more consistent and make it easier for countries to recognize each other's maritime qualifications, which makes it easier for workers to move around the world (Benczi, 2023).

International organizations like the International Maritime Organization (IMO), UNESCO, and the International Labour Organization (ILO) are very important for coordinating these efforts. They give money, training materials, and policy advice. Being part of these networks helps MET institutions stay flexible and competitive on a global scale by using the latest climate science and sustainable practices in their research and teaching (Simanjuntak et al., 2023).

Maritime education goes beyond institutional boundaries by encouraging collaboration between the public and private sectors and between countries. This makes it a movement for ocean stewardship. These partnerships boost innovation, cut down on duplication, and encourage shared responsibility in the quest for carbon-neutral and environmentally friendly shipping. Collaborative ecosystems make sure that maritime education is no longer just about how to steer ships. It's also about how to steer humanity toward a future maritime future that is sustainable and can handle climate change (Caughman et al., 2020).

FUTURE PATHWAYS TOWARD CLIMATE-RESILIENT MARITIME EDUCATION

5.1 Research and Innovation Directions

The future of maritime education hinges on its capacity to adapt through research and innovation that address the pressing global demand for sustainability and climate resilience. As the maritime industry moves toward decarbonization and green transformation, Maritime Education and Training (MET) institutions must take on two roles: they must be both teachers and places where new ideas can grow. This means changing the focus of research to green technologies, renewable energy uses, and data-driven solutions that help make decisions and run operations in an environmentally friendly way all along the global maritime value chain (Brammer et al., 2021).

Research into green technologies and renewable energy is leading the way in this change. More and more, MET institutions are working with shipbuilders, port authorities, and energy companies to look into new ways to power ships and find fuel sources that won't run out. Biofuels, hydrogen fuel cells, wind-assisted propulsion, and electrification of port operations are now the main areas of research. These new ideas are very important for the International Maritime Organization's (IMO) plan to cut greenhouse gas emissions by half by 2050. Research on retrofitting existing ships with eco-friendly systems and improving hull designs to cut down on drag and fuel use is just as important. By doing this kind of research, maritime institutions not only help technology move forward, but they also make themselves more useful as partners in the industry's green transition.

Another important area of innovation is the use of renewable energy on MET campuses. Solar-powered labs, energy-efficient simulators, and smart buildings can all be used as living labs for research on sustainability. By using the same technologies they teach, schools help their students learn while also lowering their carbon footprint. These activities show students how new ideas can have a real effect on sustainability.

In addition to studying technology, climate data analysis, and ocean literacy are becoming important parts of maritime education. Being able to read and use climate data is now essential for safe navigation, predicting risks, and making long-term plans. MET research centers are starting to use satellite data, machine learning, and oceanographic modeling to figure out when environmental hazards will happen, find the best routes, and reduce the risks of severe weather events. Combining data science with maritime knowledge creates a culture based on evidence, where decisions are based on predictions instead of past trends.

Ocean literacy, on the other hand, helps people understand the ocean's ecosystems and how people depend on each other. Research promoting ocean literacy equips seafarers and policymakers with the awareness to balance economic activity with marine conservation.

Through green technology research, renewable energy innovation, and data-driven ocean science, MET institutions can become epicenters of maritime sustainability—driving the intellectual, technological, and ethical transformation necessary for a climate-resilient maritime future.

5.2 Lifelong Learning and Green Workforce Transformation

The maritime industry needs workers who can quickly adapt to new technologies, rules, and environmental needs as it moves toward a more sustainable and climate-resilient future. To deal with these problems, lifelong learning and changing the workforce to be more environmentally friendly have become important parts of Maritime Education and Training (MET) policy. In this changing world, seafarers, engineers, and maritime administrators need to keep learning new things about the environment and how to think about it. Lifelong learning makes sure that sustainability is not just a goal for one training session, but a journey of change and new ideas that never ends.

Upskilling and reskilling programs are important for giving maritime workers the skills they need to work in a way that is good for the environment. As the industry moves toward low-carbon fuels, digital monitoring systems, and green logistics solutions, current workers need specialized training that combines their old skills with new environmental practices. Courses on managing fuel efficiency, carbon accounting, treating ballast water, and reducing waste may be part of upskilling programs. Reskilling, on the other hand, gets workers ready for new jobs in green shipping technology, integrating renewable energy, and auditing environmental compliance. Collaborative efforts between MET schools, shipping companies, and government agencies can make sure that the needs of the industry and the educational offerings are in sync. Short-term certification programs or modular online courses, for instance, can help professionals learn flexibly without having to leave their jobs at sea or in port facilities (Benczi, 2023).

Alongside this, the use of micro-credentials and digital badges is a new way to recognize environmental skills. Micro-credentials are different from regular degrees or certifications because they only show that you have certain skills, like eco-navigation, strategies for reducing emissions, or sustainable port management. These credentials, which can be checked online, let seafarers create personalized learning portfolios that show they are experts in areas related to sustainability. Employers get clearer signs of how capable their workers are, and learners get qualifications that are portable and stackable, which makes it easier for them to move up in their careers in different areas and sectors.

MET institutions can promote a culture of self-directed learning and accountability by including micro-credentials in their continuing professional development programs. Digital badges can also be used in gamified learning systems to motivate people by recognizing their achievements and tracking their progress in real time (Undurraga et al., 2023).

In the end, lifelong learning and recognition based on credentials make the maritime workforce flexible and ready for the green transition. These strategies make education more accessible to everyone, encourage people to keep learning about sustainability, and make sure that developing human capital is in line with the global goal of reducing carbon emissions. MET institutions play a key role in making sure that environmental competence becomes a key part of being a professional in the maritime industry in the twenty-first century.

5.3 Vision for a Sustainable Maritime Future

The goal for a sustainable maritime future goes beyond just improving technology or following the rules. It is really about raising a generation of seafarers who are ethical and care about the environment, and who see taking care of the oceans as both a professional duty and a moral obligation. Integrity, caring about the marine environment, and taking responsibility for one's operational impact are all important human values that are the foundation of maritime sustainability. The future maritime professional must incorporate these values into all decisions—from voyage planning and energy management to waste disposal and resource utilization—recognizing that every action at sea impacts ecosystems and communities.

To teach seafarers about environmental ethics, maritime education needs to include moral reasoning and reflective learning on purpose. In addition to teaching technical skills, teachers need to help students become more aware of the environment through critical discussion, ethical case studies, and service-learning projects. Confronting environmental challenges, like the conflict between economic efficiency and ecological preservation, equips trainees to manage the intricate realities of maritime employment. This ethical foundation encourages lasting changes in behavior, making it so that following environmental rules becomes a natural part of life instead of something that is forced on people. Leadership development programs that stress green values, working together as a team, and working with people from different cultures can help seafarers become better advocates for sustainability in their workplaces.

The maritime education sector is a game-changer when it comes to making the world more resilient to climate change. MET institutions are not just places to learn; they are also strategic agents of change that can affect research, policy, and business practices. These schools teach climate literacy and sustainability science at all levels, from pre-sea training to executive education. This gives graduates the skills they need to work in a maritime economy that is becoming less carbon-intensive. Also, their research and innovation skills help make adaptive technologies, predictive risk tools, and sustainable port management systems that make maritime infrastructure stronger against climate-related problems.

Working together is still the most important part of making this vision a reality. MET institutions can align global training standards and make it easier for people to share best practices in climate adaptation by using international networks, knowledge-sharing platforms, and policy partnerships. This kind of global alignment makes sure that maritime education helps the United Nations' Sustainable Development Goals, especially SDG 13 (Climate Action) and SDG 14 (Life Below Water).

The sustainable maritime future is one where workers are guided by both their conscience and their skills. They don't just work for money; they also work to protect the environment. The maritime industry can help people stay committed to a strong and ecologically balanced ocean economy by teaching ethics, encouraging new ideas, and working together.

CONCLUSION

The incorporation of environmental education and climate-resilient training into maritime education signifies a crucial evolution in equipping future seafarers for an era characterized by sustainability challenges and ecological accountability. Maritime Education and Training (MET) institutions are leading this change by rethinking how they teach, make rules, and work together to create professionals who have both technical skills and a sense of environmental ethics and the ability to adapt. Through simulation-based learning, digital innovation, and community engagement, students learn how to balance maritime operations with environmental protection.

Institutional governance and quality assurance frameworks further reinforce this transformation by embedding sustainability into policy, accreditation, and performance standards. The combination of green campus programs, environmental management systems, and partnerships between the public and private sectors shows that sustainability is not just a goal, but a way of life for institutions. MET institutions help the world work together to lower carbon emissions and encourage eco-innovation by making maritime education fit in with international standards like STCW, ISO, and ESG frameworks.

To have a sustainable maritime future, we need to keep doing research, coming up with new ideas, and learning new things all the time. More research into green technology, more use of renewable energy, and more decisions based on data make sure that maritime professionals stay flexible and up to date. The workforce will be able to adapt to changing environmental needs while still doing a great job, thanks to lifelong learning, micro-credentialing, and partnerships with other countries.

Ultimately, sustainability in maritime education is both an ethical and strategic endeavor. It shows that everyone is committed to protecting the oceans, making the world more resilient, and raising a new generation of sailors who see the sea as more than just a trade route, but as a shared ecosystem that needs to be respected and protected. This change makes maritime education a key part of global efforts to make the ocean cleaner, safer, and more sustainable in the future.

REFERENCES

Amorim, P., & Chaffe, P. (2021). Teaching climate risk for water planning: A pilot training for tertiary students and practitioners in brazil. *Geoscience Communication*, *4*(4), 527–554. DOI: 10.5194/gc-4-527-2021

Badarnah, L. (2025). Holistic education for a resilient future: An integrated biomimetic approach for architectural pedagogy. *Biomimetics*, *10*(6), 369. DOI: 10.3390/biomimetics10060369 PMID: 40558338

Baniaga, J. (2025). Environmental management compliance in the university of the cordilleras. *Cognizance Journal of Multidisciplinary Studies*, *5*(9), 216–228. DOI: 10.47760/cognizance.2025.v05i09.016

Bashir, M., Noor-e-Zahra, S., & Qaisar, Z. (2024). The gig economy and automation: Implications for human resource management in pakistan. *International Journal of Systems and Society*, *3*(3), 41–53. DOI: 10.63544/ijss.v3i3.90

Bassey, G., Ebaretonbofa-okonji, S., Nordby, K., Gernez, E., & Mallam, S. (2025). A systematic curriculum review of ship energy efficiency content across global maritime education and training institutions., 186. DOI: 10.54941/ahfe1006546

Benczi, M. (2023). Sustainable cross-border cooperation? a case-study on the role of national minorities. Észak-Magyarországi Stratégiai Füzetek, 20(4), 74-85. DOI: 10.32976/stratfuz.2023.37

Brammer, S., Regan, S., Collins, C., & Gillespie, G. (2021). Developing innovative virtual reality simulations to increase health care providers' understanding of social determinants of health. *The Journal of Continuing Education in the Health Professions*, *42*(1), 60–65. DOI: 10.1097/CEH.0000000000000400 PMID: 34799522

Butler, M. (2022). Interdisciplinary experiential learning during covid-19: Lessons learned and reflections for the future. *Journal of Environmental Studies and Sciences*, *12*(2), 369–377. DOI: 10.1007/s13412-021-00734-w PMID: 35013697

Caughman, L., Keeler, L., & Beaudoin, F. (2020). Real-time evaluation of city–university partnerships for sustainability and resilience. *Sustainability (Basel)*, *12*(21), 8796. DOI: 10.3390/su12218796

Erstad, E., Lund, M., & Ostnes, R. (2022). Navigating through cyber threats, a maritime navigator's experience.. DOI: 10.54941/ahfe1002205

Fan, L., Yang, H., & Zhang, X. (2024). Targeting the effectiveness assessment of the emission control policies on the shipping industry. *Sustainability (Basel)*, *16*(6), 2465. DOI: 10.3390/su16062465

Fitzpatrick, R. and West, H. (2022). Improving resilience, adaptation and mitigation to cimate change through education in low- and lower-middle income countries.. DOI: 10.19088/K4D.2022.083

Hallinger, P., & Nguyen, V. (2020). Mapping the landscape and structure of research on education for sustainable development: A bibliometric review. *Sustainability (Basel)*, *12*(5), 1947. DOI: 10.3390/su12051947

Hambon, S. (2025). The implementation of iso 9001:2015 quality management systems on the delivery of public services, city government of baguio. *International Journal for Multidisciplinary Research, 7*(4), 50465. Advance online publication. DOI: 10.36948/ijfmr.2025.v07i04.50465

Hananto, P., Trihastuti, N., & Pratama, A. (2025). Advancing international shipping liability on greenhouse gasses emission through port-state jurisdiction. *IOP Conference Series. Earth and Environmental Science, 1537*(1), 012029. DOI: 10.1088/1755-1315/1537/1/012029

Hsu, S., Tzu, F., Chen, Y., & Huang, C. (2024). Navigating safety and compliance in high-voltage shore connection systems: A comprehensive exploration of iec/ieee 80005-1 standards and the guidelines of ship classification societies. *Journal of Marine Science and Engineering, 12*(2), 322. DOI: 10.3390/jmse12020322

İnal, Ö. (2024). Decarbonization of shipping: Hydrogen and fuel cells legislation in the maritime industry. *Brodogradnja, 75*(2), 1–13. DOI: 10.21278/brod75205

Islam, M. (2024). Maritime security in a technological era: addressing challenges in balancing technology and ethics. Mersin University Journal of Maritime Faculty, 6(1), 1-16. DOI: 10.47512/meujmaf.1418239

Madiraju, S., & Pamula, A. (2025). Environmental sustainability: A continuous commitment to living in harmony with the earth. *SustainE, 1*(2). Advance online publication. DOI: 10.55366/suse.v1i2.9

Makransky, G., & Klingenberg, S. (2022). Virtual reality enhances safety training in the maritime industry: An organizational training experiment with a non-weird sample. *Journal of Computer Assisted Learning, 38*(4), 1127–1140. DOI: 10.1111/jcal.12670

Morales, B., Gálvez, S., Aponte, W., Ozejo, A., Molina, R., Lévano, F., & Colos, M. (2025). Integrating education and conservation: A case study of the huaper wetland. *Frontiers in Psychology, 16*, 1517653. Advance online publication. DOI: 10.3389/fpsyg.2025.1517653 PMID: 40115288

Moshiul, A., Mohammad, R., Hira, F., Yesmin, A., & Chelliapan, S. (2021). The evolution of green shipping practices adoption in the international maritime industry. Tem Journal, 1112-1121. DOI: 10.18421/tem103-15

Perkovič, M. (2024). Advances in navigability and mooring. *Journal of Marine Science and Engineering, 12*(9), 1601. DOI: 10.3390/jmse12091601

Praetorius, G., Hult, C., & Österman, C. (2020). Maritime resource management: Current training approaches and potential improvements. *Transnav the International Journal on Marine Navigation and Safety of Sea Transportation, 14*(3), 573–584. DOI: 10.12716/1001.14.03.08

Reddy, C. (2021). Environmental education, social justice and teacher education: Enabling meaningful environmental learning in local contexts. *South African Journal of Higher Education*. Advance online publication. DOI: 10.20853/35-1-4427

Roy, W., Merveille, J., Scheldeman, K., Nieuwenhove, A., & Schallier, R. (2025). Airborne measurements reveal the underestimated impact of black carbon emissions from ships. DOI: 10.21203/rs.3.rs-6411226/v1

Ryan, G., Callaghan, S., Rafferty, A., Higgins, M., Mangina, E., & McAuliffe, F. (2022). Learning outcomes of immersive technologies in health care student education: Systematic review of the literature. *Journal of Medical Internet Research*, *24*(2), e30082. DOI: 10.2196/30082 PMID: 35103607

Santos, R., Abreu, V., & Santos, A. (2025). The rise in sea levels and new maritime routes: challenges and guidelines for global port adaptation., XIII, 473-488. DOI: 10.29183/2596-237x.ensus2025.v13.n1.p473-488

Sardar, A., Garaniya, V., Anantharaman, M., Abbassi, R., & Khan, F. (2022). Comparison between simulation and conventional training: Expanding the concept of social fidelity. *Process Safety Progress*, *41*(S1). Advance online publication. DOI: 10.1002/prs.12361

ŞEREN, N. and GÜL, S. (2022). "an innovative and interdisciplinary perspective on environmental issues through ecological art projects: a mixed methods study". Romanian Review of Geographical Education, 11(1), 73-91. DOI: 10.23741/RRGE120225

Sibarani, M., Junaidi, J., & Wibowo, T. (2025). Advancing green ship design and experiential learning in maritime education. *Research and Development in Education (Raden)*, *5*(1), 88–98. DOI: 10.22219/raden.v5i1.39397

Simanjuntak, M., Rafli, Z., & Utami, S. (2024). Enhancing maritime education for ocean sustainability: a multidisciplinary approach. Bio Web of Conferences, 106, 02006. DOI: 10.1051/bioconf/202410602006

Simanjuntak, M., Sutrisno, S., Putrawan, B., Lumingkewas, M., & Hutabarat, C. (2023). Enhancing environmental literacy through english language education in maritime institutions. Bio Web of Conferences, 79, 11001. DOI: 10.1051/bioconf/20237911001

Simanjuntak, M., Zuriyati, Z., Utami, S., Rahmat, A., & Setiadi, S. (2023). Fostering intercultural understanding and environmental consciousness in maritime education. Bio Web of Conferences, 79, 06004. DOI: 10.1051/bioconf/20237906004

Supangat, S., Sriantini, A., & Malik, D. (2025). Bridge simulator with green technology to enhance critical thinking skills of shipping vocational cadets. *IOP Conference Series. Earth and Environmental Science*, *1473*(1), 012028. DOI: 10.1088/1755-1315/1473/1/012028

Taghavi, S., Ghezavati, V., Bidhandi, H., & Al-e-Hashem, S. (2023). Supply portfolio selection for lead-time sensitive manufacturers under operational and disruption risks. *Kybernetes*, *53*(11), 4253–4282. DOI: 10.1108/K-10-2022-1493

Tomasi, S., Cavicchi, A., Aleffi, C., Paviotti, G., Ferrara, C., Baldoni, F., & Passarini, P. (2021). Civic universities and bottom-up approaches to boost local development of rural areas: The case of the university of macerata. *Agricultural and Food Economics*, *9*(1), 15. Advance online publication. DOI: 10.1186/s40100-021-00185-5 PMID: 35024263

Tran, T., Woo, S., & Yuen, K. (2021). The impacts of sustainable inter-firm collaboration on business performance of shipping companies. *International Journal of Logistics Management*, *32*(3), 766–789. DOI: 10.1108/IJLM-11-2020-0453

Tsai, S., Wang, M.-C., Yao, S.-P., Tsay, G. J., & Lin, C.-P. (2025). Greenhouse gas emissions and mitigation strategies in universities under iso 14064-1: Lessons for global higher education sustainability. *Sustainability (Basel)*, *17*(21), 9462. DOI: 10.3390/su17219462

Tusher, H., Sharma, A., Nazir, S., & Munim, Z. (2021). Exploring the current practices and future needs of marine engineering education in bangladesh. *Journal of Marine Science and Engineering*, *9*(10), 1085. DOI: 10.3390/jmse9101085

Undurraga, T., Mudd, S., Straub, D., Aguirre, G., & Orellana, T. (2023). "they don't understand us, but we have to understand them": Interrogating the making of interdisciplinary research in chilean climate science. *Minerva*, *61*(4), 581–606. DOI: 10.1007/s11024-023-09495-y PMID: 37359302

Werkmeister, A., Carrel, A., Porwal, N., Clemente, C., & Macdonald, M. (2023). Monitoring ship emissions using sentinel-5p and ais data., 10. DOI: 10.1117/12.2678424

Zhen, L., Wu, Y., Wang, S., & Laporte, G. (2020). Green technology adoption for fleet deployment in a shipping network. *Transportation Research Part B: Methodological*, *139*, 388–410. DOI: 10.1016/j.trb.2020.06.004

Chapter 14 Navigating Sustainability: Embedding Environmental Literacy and Climate Resilience in Maritime Education and Training

Randy Ruslan
http://orcid.org/0009-0007-2019-5844
Politeknik Ilmu Pelayaran Makassar, Indonesia

Siti Zulaikah
http://orcid.org/0009-0003-1090-3924
Politeknik Ilmu Pelayaran Makassar, Indonesia

Bruce Rumangkang
Politeknik Ilmu Pelayaran Makassar, Indonesia

ABSTRACT

This study explores the integration of environmental education and climate-resilient training within maritime education to advance sustainability and global climate action. It highlights the transformation of maritime curricula, teaching methods, and governance frameworks to embed ecological literacy, ethical responsibility, and adaptive skills among seafarers. Through interdisciplinary learning, technological innovation, and international collaboration, maritime institutions are redefining professional competencies to meet the challenges of decarbonization and ocean stewardship. The discussion underscores the role of maritime education as a catalyst for green innovation, lifelong learning, and ethical leadership in achieving a sustainable maritime future.

SETTING THE COURSE: THE NEED FOR ENVIRONMENTAL AWARENESS IN MARITIME EDUCATION

1.1 Maritime Industry and the Global Climate Crisis

The maritime industry stands at a crucial intersection between global trade, environmental sustainability, and climate change. Accounting for nearly 90 percent of world trade, the sector is indispensable

DOI: 10.4018/979-8-3373-6670-8.ch014

to the global economy; yet, it also remains a significant contributor to greenhouse gas (GHG) emissions, marine pollution, and ecological degradation (Laskar et al., 2025). Ships burn heavy fuel oil that emits sulfur oxides, nitrogen oxides, and particulate matter, contributing to ocean acidification and air quality deterioration (Ghoneim et al., 2023; Zulfiqar & Chang, 2023). Ballast water discharge, oil spills, and marine litter further exacerbate the strain on fragile marine ecosystems (Melnyk et al., 2023). As the effects of climate change intensify—rising sea levels, increased storm frequency, and temperature anomalies—the maritime sector faces both operational disruptions and ethical responsibilities to transform toward sustainability (Mallouppas & Yfantis, 2021; Kanchiralla et al., 2022).

The urgency of integrating sustainability into seafaring education cannot be overstated. Future maritime professionals must be equipped not only with navigational and technical skills but also with an environmental consciousness that guides their decisions and practices (Wang et al., 2023). Embedding sustainability in maritime education is essential for shaping seafarers who understand the interconnectedness of human activities and marine ecosystems. Such integration moves beyond compliance to cultivate a mindset of stewardship—encouraging seafarers to perceive the ocean as a shared heritage rather than a mere resource (Wu et al., 2022). By instilling awareness of the ecological consequences of navigation, energy consumption, and waste management, maritime institutions can nurture environmentally responsible behavior that extends from training simulators to real-world operations (Fan et al., 2024; Liang et al., 2024).

At the policy level, international frameworks and conventions provide a robust foundation for aligning maritime education with global sustainability agendas. The International Maritime Organization (IMO) has taken decisive steps toward decarbonization through initiatives such as the Initial GHG Strategy and the MARPOL Convention, which aim to cut total annual emissions from shipping by at least 50 percent by 2050 compared to 2008 levels (Vakili et al., 2025; Fan et al., 2022). The integration of the United Nations Sustainable Development Goals (SDGs)—particularly SDG 13 (Climate Action), SDG 14 (Life Below Water), and SDG 4 (Quality Education)—emphasizes the multidimensional nature of this transformation (Caprace et al., 2025). Furthermore, the Paris Agreement reinforces the collective global commitment to limit global warming to 1.5°C, calling for sectoral cooperation and innovation in maritime education and training (Serra & Fancello, 2020).

To meet these international commitments, maritime education institutions must serve as catalysts for green transformation. They need to align curricula, training methodologies, and institutional missions with sustainability standards, bridging the gap between global policy aspirations and local educational realities (Makhtar et al., 2025). By cultivating a generation of climate-conscious seafarers, maritime academies and training centers play a pivotal role in ensuring that the industry navigates the oceans efficiently and responsibly—anchoring the future of shipping in ecological balance and global climate resilience (Huang & Tsai, 2025; İnal, 2024).

1.2 Environmental Literacy as a Core Competence

Environmental literacy has become a fundamental aspect of contemporary maritime professionalism, signifying the increasing acknowledgment that proficient seafarers must comprehend not only navigation and engineering but also the ecological systems in which they function. Maritime professionals who understand ecology know how their choices about routes, fuel management, waste disposal, and ballast water treatment will affect the environment. This literacy connects technical skills with environmental responsibility, making sure that every maritime operation helps protect the oceans for the long term. A seafarer who knows about marine ecosystems can make smart choices that cut down on pollution, save energy, and lower their carbon footprint. This makes operations more efficient while also protecting the environment Sijabat et al., 2025; Cahyadi, 2025).

Adding environmental ethics and making decisions that are good for the environment makes this base even stronger. In maritime settings, ethics means more than just following international rules; it also means making a moral commitment to protect the ocean as a life-supporting system (Vujičić et al., 2020; Filonenko et al., 2023). To make decisions that are good for the environment, the economy, and society all at the same time, you need to be able to weigh all three of these factors at the same time. This is a skill that is important for balancing the competing needs of safety, cost, and environmental impact. For example, when choosing fuel, scheduling maintenance, or running cargo operations, you need to think about more than just making money; you also need to think about how these choices will affect the environment. Maritime education helps people become responsible stewards of the ocean by encouraging them to think about ethics. This makes them aware of their moral duty to protect the planet for the long term.

Including environmental literacy in maritime training also makes maritime safety and operational responsibility better. A lot of maritime accidents, like oil spills or chemical discharges, happen not just because of technical problems but also because people don't know enough about how their actions will affect the environment. By combining safety training with environmental education, seafarers can see how the health of ecosystems affects both human health and safety on the water. For instance, knowing how mangroves, coral reefs, and tidal patterns fit into the ecosystem can help you plan your route and get ready for disasters. In the same way, knowing about marine biodiversity helps keep waste management and ballast operations safer, which lowers the chance of invasive species spreading.

To make this happen, maritime schools and training centers need to include environmental literacy in all of their courses instead of treating it as an extra subject. Marine ecology, environmental management, and sustainability analytics courses should go along with traditional subjects like navigation and engineering. Cadets can learn how to evaluate environmental risks and make data-driven, long-term decisions under pressure through scenario analysis and simulation-based learning.

1.3 Historical and Policy Foundations

The evolution of environmental policy in maritime education reflects a gradual yet decisive transformation from reactive compliance to proactive stewardship. In the early decades of global shipping, maritime education primarily focused on navigation, engineering, and safety, with limited attention to ecological impacts (Purba & Simanjuntak, 2024; Türkistanlı, 2023). However, the environmental crises of the late 20th century—ranging from oil spills to marine biodiversity loss—prompted a paradigm shift. The 1973 International Convention for the Prevention of Pollution from Ships (MARPOL) marked a historic milestone, introducing a regulatory foundation for pollution control and environmental protection at sea (Vujičić et al., 2020; Filonenko et al., 2023). Over the following decades, the International Maritime Organization (IMO) expanded this framework, introducing annexes that addressed air pollution, waste management, and energy efficiency (Lin et al., 2023). These international efforts gradually influenced maritime education and training (MET) institutions, prompting the inclusion of environmental awareness and sustainability as integral components of professional competence (Werkmeister et al., 2023; Yuen et al., 2022).

As the shipping industry moved toward decarbonization, maritime education systems worldwide began to adapt to emerging policy frameworks. The introduction of the IMO's STCW Convention (Standards of Training, Certification, and Watchkeeping for Seafarers) revisions emphasized competence-based education, creating opportunities to embed environmental standards into skill certification (Masodzadeh et al., 2024; Fan et al., 2024). National maritime authorities adopted complementary strategies aligned with the United Nations Sustainable Development Goals (SDGs), particularly SDGs 4, 7, 13, and 14, which address education, clean energy, climate action, and life below water (Purba & Simanjuntak, 2024; Bayotas, 2024). In Europe, the EU Green Deal and the Fit for 55 Package accelerated the green maritime transition by mandating educational reform and innovation in maritime academies (Türkistanlı, 2023). In Asia, countries such as Japan, Singapore, and the Philippines developed maritime sustainability frameworks integrating low-carbon operations and green port initiatives into training standards (Campos et al., 2025; Bokau & Sulistiana, 2024). Indonesia and other ASEAN nations have likewise aligned their national maritime strategies with IMO and regional sustainability roadmaps, emphasizing climate adaptation, marine conservation, and renewable energy integration within their maritime education systems (Lin et al., 2023; Türkistanlı, 2023).

Early environmental initiatives in MET institutions offer valuable lessons for contemporary reform. Programs such as "Green MET," launched in several European maritime academies, pioneered curriculum innovation by linking classroom instruction with real-world environmental challenges, such as emission control zones and ballast water management (Masodzadeh et al., 2024; Werkmeister et al., 2023). Pilot projects in Nordic countries integrated digital tools for monitoring ship emissions, combining environmental science with operational practice (Werkmeister et al., 2023). Similarly, partnerships between universities and shipping companies in Southeast Asia have demonstrated how collaborative training can foster both compliance and innovation (Yuen et al., 2022). These initiatives highlight that sustainable transformation requires not only policy alignment but also institutional will, pedagogical creativity, and industry collaboration (Fan et al., 2024; Meštrović et al., 2023).

Collectively, the historical and policy evolution underscores that maritime education stands at the heart of global sustainability efforts. From MARPOL to modern decarbonization strategies, the trajectory reveals a growing recognition that environmental competence is not ancillary but central to maritime professionalism—anchoring education as both a driver and beneficiary of the green maritime transition (Purba & Simanjuntak, 2024; Palippui, 2024).

EMBEDDING SUSTAINABILITY IN MARITIME CURRICULA

2.1 Curricular Reform and Integration Models

Integrating sustainability into maritime education requires a comprehensive curricular reform that bridges traditional technical training with ecological awareness and responsible practice. Historically, maritime curricula have emphasized navigation, engineering, and safety competencies, but the urgency of climate change and environmental degradation demands a reorientation toward sustainability as a core educational outcome (Simanjuntak & Barus, 2024; Simanjuntak et al., 2024). Embedding sustainability into existing competency frameworks ensures that environmental literacy, ethical reasoning, and sustainable decision-making are not isolated subjects but fundamental dimensions of maritime professionalism (Simanjuntak et al., 2023; Barasa et al., 2025). Through this reform, future seafarers are prepared not only to meet regulatory standards but also to lead the green transformation of global shipping (Winarno et al., 2025).

Embedding sustainability begins with aligning educational goals with international competency frameworks such as the Standards of Training, Certification and Watchkeeping (STCW) Convention, which provides the foundation for global maritime qualification. Sustainability dimensions can be infused into core modules—navigation, ship operations, and marine engineering—by emphasizing eco-efficiency, energy conservation, and pollution prevention (Winarno et al., 2025). For example, navigational training can integrate fuel-optimized route planning and emission reduction strategies, while engineering modules can highlight green propulsion systems and waste-to-energy technologies (Barasa, 2025). Competency-based training (CBT) models enable instructors to measure learners' environmental performance through behavioral indicators such as adherence to pollution control protocols, eco-friendly operational decisions, and participation in environmental audits (Diahyleva et al., 2024).

Cross-disciplinary approaches are essential to bridge the knowledge gap between marine ecology, policy, and technology (Cahyadi et al., 2025). Maritime students should understand how ecological processes interact with human activity, including how ocean currents influence pollution dispersion or how marine biodiversity supports sustainable fisheries. Courses integrating environmental science, maritime law, and green technology encourage holistic thinking, wherein learners recognize that operational choices have far-reaching environmental and socio-economic consequences (Sibarani et al., 2025). Partnerships between departments—engineering, logistics, oceanography, and environmental management—can create multidisciplinary learning environments that mirror real-world maritime operations (Simanjuntak, 2023). Such cross-pollination strengthens ecological understanding and enhances innovation capacity, enabling students to design and evaluate green technologies and operational strategies (Winarno et al., 2025).

Curriculum mapping is a critical step toward systematic integration. It involves identifying where sustainability-related outcomes naturally align with existing subjects and where new modules are required. Through careful mapping, institutions can ensure progressive skill development—from foundational awareness in the early years to advanced application in professional training (Guntoro & Simanjuntak, 2024). This process helps educators design coherent learning trajectories, embedding green skills across levels and disciplines. For instance, early modules may introduce environmental concepts and global conventions, while advanced courses focus on sustainable shipping design, energy transition, and circular economy principles (Barus & Simanjuntak, 2023).

2.2 Teaching Methods for Environmental Engagement

For maritime education to effectively include sustainability, it needs to change the curriculum and the way it teaches environmental concepts. Traditional lecture-based instruction does not adequately foster the critical thinking, problem-solving abilities, and ethical awareness necessary for sustainable maritime operations. Problem-based, project-based, and experiential learning approaches have emerged as crucial pedagogical strategies to foster active engagement and real-world applicability. Problem-based learning (PBL) lets cadets work together and ask questions to come up with good answers to real-world maritime environmental problems like oil spills, ballast water contamination, or cutting down on carbon emissions. Project-based learning (PBL) takes this a step further by having students work on long-term projects like making plans for how to deal with ship waste, designigng green ports, or looking into renewable energy options for ships. These hands-on activities change students from people who just passively take in information to people who actively contribute to the sustainability of the maritime industry.

Experiential learning helps people understand things better by putting education in real-life situations. Field trips to ports, marine conservation areas, and shipyards show students the real-world effects of bad environmental management and the possibilities of eco-innovation. These kinds of experiences help students connect what they learn in class to how things really work in the maritime industry and ecosystems. Teachers can lead discussions where students think critically about how their choices, like how they use fuel or how they take care of things, affect larger ecological systems (Diahyleva et al., 2024).

Simulation and case-based learning are great ways to help people learn how to be more sustainable in a safe setting. Maritime simulators can recreate complex environmental situations, giving students a chance to see how operational choices affect emissions, pollution, and marine safety. For instance, trainees might use real-time data to guide virtual ships through areas where emissions are controlled or to clean up simulated oil spills. Case studies based on events like the Exxon Valdez or Deepwater Horizon disasters help people think about mistakes in decision-making, moral quandaries, and what can be done to avoid them in the future. These methods help people learn not only technical skills, but also how to be responsible for the environment and make good decisions in different situations.

Lastly, using community-based and local ecological knowledge makes maritime education better by linking global sustainability goals with what's really going on in the area. Coastal communities have learned how to manage marine resources, deal with bad weather, and adapt over many generations. Getting students involved in community projects like restoring mangroves, cleaning up beaches, or rehabilitating coral reefs teaches them to care about others and the environment. This partnership connects academic learning with cultural sustainability. It stresses that to protect the ocean, you need to know science and respect local knowledge.

2.3 Assessment and Certification of Green Competence

Assessment and certification systems that recognize and validate learners' environmental skills must be put in place to make sure that sustainability is successfully integrated into maritime education. Most traditional maritime evaluation frameworks have focused on technical skills, safety, and following operational standards. But as the maritime industry moves toward being more environmentally friendly and less carbon-intensive, it's important to find out how well seafarers understand and use sustainability principles in real life. So, assessing environmental competence goes beyond just testing theoretical knowledge; it also means measuring values, attitudes, and behaviors that show a commitment to taking care of the environment.

In contemporary maritime certification frameworks, sustainability-related competencies ought to be integrated into existing qualification standards, such as the STCW Convention. Evaluations may have parts on how to avoid pollution, run your business in a way that saves energy, and eco-navigation. Practical assessments can put cadets in situations where they have to make operational decisions that affect the environment, like choosing fuel-efficient routes, managing waste on board, or responding to oil spills in a responsible way. These tests make sure that certified professionals have both compliance-based knowledge and the ability to make smart decisions under stress that will last. Adding environmental skills to certification is in line with global goals for maritime decarbonization and makes practitioners more accountable.

Green performance metrics give you ways to measure how well you are doing in terms of the environment during training and practice on board. Metrics might include things like fuel efficiency, following plans for energy management, reducing emissions, and separating waste properly. These performance-based measures encourage a culture of constant improvement by giving trainees feedback on how their actions affect the environment and encouraging them to use greener practices. Teachers can use performance dashboards to keep an eye on progress. These dashboards use data analytics and digital tracking systems to objectively assess environmental outcomes. These quantitative and qualitative methods turn sustainability assessment from a one-time test into a process of ongoing behavioral change.

Digital badges and micro-credentials have also become new ways to prove that someone is environmentally literate and has green skills. These portable, verifiable credentials show that you have certain skills, like "Eco-Navigation," "Carbon Management," or "Marine Waste Reduction." They give seafarers the freedom to keep learning and moving up in their careers by letting them update their credentials as sustainability standards change. Digital credentials also make things clearer for employers, who can then find and reward professionals who care about the environment.

CLIMATE-RESILIENT TRAINING AND CAPACITY BUILDING

3.1 Developing Climate Adaptation and Mitigation Skills

In the face of accelerating climate change, maritime education must evolve beyond conventional training to develop professionals who can anticipate, adapt to, and mitigate the effects of environmental disruptions. The maritime sector is directly exposed to the consequences of global warming—rising sea levels, intensified storms, and shifting ocean currents all pose serious risks to navigation, port operations, and coastal infrastructure (Newman & Noy, 2023; Johnson, 2021). Therefore, cultivating climate adaptation and mitigation skills is not merely a policy imperative but a professional necessity. By integrating resilience-building modules into maritime training, institutions can equip seafarers, port managers, and maritime engineers with the knowledge and competencies to operate safely and sustainably in an increasingly volatile environment (Purba & Simanjuntak, 2024).

Integrating resilience-building modules in maritime training begins with embedding climate science, risk management, and sustainability frameworks across the curriculum. Trainees should learn how to assess environmental risks and interpret meteorological data to implement adaptive strategies in navigation and operations (Simanjuntak, 2024). Courses on ship stability can be expanded to include climate-induced variables such as extreme weather events or changes in wave patterns. Scenario-based training—using simulations of storm surges, flooding, or heat stress—can prepare learners to make critical operational decisions under pressure. Beyond technical mastery, resilience training emphasizes adaptability, critical thinking, and leadership—skills that enable maritime professionals to respond effectively to complex climate challenges (Mthuli & Singh, 2024; Giordono et al., 2020).

Coastal risk management, emergency response, and adaptation planning are central to this transformative agenda. Coastal zones host much of the maritime infrastructure, making them particularly vulnerable to sea-level rise and extreme weather. Maritime training should therefore include modules on disaster preparedness, evacuation protocols, and infrastructure resilience planning (Xu et al., 2021). Trainees can learn to use Geographic Information Systems (GIS) for hazard mapping, conduct vulnerability assessments, and design mitigation strategies such as mangrove restoration or the construction of resilient port structures (Sharma & Nazir, 2021). Practical drills simulating oil spill containment, flood response, and vessel stability management during storms enhance readiness and coordination across maritime teams. Integrating these skills strengthens both human and institutional resilience, ensuring that maritime operations remain safe and efficient even under environmental stress (Mthuli & Singh, 2024; Dacosta et al., 2022).

Equally vital is the incorporation of renewable energy systems and eco-operations into maritime training. The transition toward low-carbon shipping requires expertise in alternative fuels, hybrid propulsion systems, and energy efficiency technologies. Trainees must understand how to manage shipboard solar, wind, and hydrogen-based systems, as well as how to implement emission control and waste heat recovery mechanisms (Nikolov, 2024). Training institutions can collaborate with industry partners to create laboratories and pilot projects showcasing green technologies in practice (Dacosta et al., 2022).

Ultimately, developing climate adaptation and mitigation skills positions maritime education as a driver of transformation—producing professionals who are not only competent navigators but also proactive agents of environmental resilience and sustainability in a changing world

3.2 Technological Innovations for Climate-Resilient Training

New technology is at the heart of modern maritime education. It gives us powerful tools to help us become more aware of climate change and how to live in a way that is good for the environment. As environmental problems get bigger and more complicated, the maritime industry is relying more and more on digital transformation to get sailors ready for real-world situations that are both unpredictable and dangerous. By using cutting-edge technologies like virtual reality (VR), augmented reality (AR), artificial intelligence (AI), and smart ship systems, students can better understand, analyze, and respond to climate-related situations. These tools not only improve technical skills, but they also raise awareness of environmental issues and help people make decisions that are good for the long term.

Using VR/AR, AI, and simulators to model climate scenarios lets trainees learn in a hands-on way without putting lives or property at risk. For example, VR-based simulation can recreate extreme weather events like hurricanes, storm surges, or polar navigation when ice is melting. This gives emergency responders and planners a realistic place to practice. AI-powered simulation platforms look at things like sea-state data, temperature changes, and emission levels to help trainees understand how their actions affect the environment. AR overlays can also show real-time data on fuel use, emissions, or route optimization, which helps connect theory and practice in environmental management. Repeated exposure to simulated crises helps seafarers not only learn the technical skills they need, but also how to be flexible and strong enough to keep operations going on the water (Dacosta et al., 2022).

Smart ship technologies and green navigation systems are changing maritime training even more. Smart ships with built-in sensors, digital twins, and energy-efficient automation systems let students see how technology can help cut down on emissions and make things safer. Training modules can show how smart energy grids, optimized propulsion systems, and predictive maintenance tools work to cut down on waste of resources. Using digital twins, which are virtual copies of real ships, in training lets students try out ways to adapt to climate change, like changing the shape of the hull to improve hydrodynamics or using different types of fuel. AI-powered green navigation systems teach cadets how to choose routes that are good for the environment and use less fuel (Newman & Noy, 2023; Emad & Shahbakhsh, 2022).

At the same time, data analytics for tracking carbon and monitoring sustainability makes sure that students know how to measure and improve the environment. Trainees can keep an eye on emission rates, fuel efficiency, and energy use patterns by interpreting real-time data from sensors and ship management systems. Dashboards and analytics software give you useful information that can help you improve your operations and meet regulatory goals like the IMO's decarbonization goals.

3.3 Human Capital Development for a Green Maritime Sector

The strength of the people who work in the maritime industry is the most important thing for making it climate-resilient and sustainable. Without professionals who have the skills, values, and leadership to make green changes, technology, infrastructure, and policy changes will not work. As a result, the goal of human capital development is to give maritime educators, trainers, and professionals the tools they need to include sustainability in their teaching, management, and operational practices. Maritime education can help create a workforce that can lead the way to a more environmentally friendly future by focusing on upskilling, working together across disciplines, and forming partnerships with other institutions.

The basis for this change is teaching trainers and maritime workers about sustainability. Teachers and professionals need to know not only how to use energy-efficient technologies, but also how to teach people about sustainability. Professional development programs can include training on how to manage the environment, how to keep track of carbon emissions, and how to use circular economy practices in shipping. The International Maritime Organization (IMO), World Maritime University (WMU), and regional centers of excellence offer workshops and international certifications that can help trainers teach sustainability in both the classroom and the simulator. Also, ongoing professional development makes sure that teachers know about the newest global standards, new ideas in renewable energy, and ways to reduce carbon emissions in the maritime industry (Simanjuntak, 2024).

It's just as important to build international networks and interdisciplinary teaching teams to ensure a comprehensive approach to maritime sustainability. Climate change is so complicated that experts in marine engineering, oceanography, environmental policy, and data science need to work together. Maritime academies can put together teaching teams from different departments that bring together these different points of view. This helps students understand how technology, ecology, and regulation all work together. Joining global academic networks like the International Association of Maritime Universities (IAMU) or the ASEAN Maritime Education Forum makes it easier to share knowledge, do research together, and come up with new ideas for the curriculum. Collaborative teaching also encourages the joint development of case studies and simulations that represent a variety of operational and environmental situations.

Partnerships between institutions that help build capacity create a framework for keeping these efforts going. When maritime academies, shipping companies, and government agencies work together, they can create shared training resources, joint laboratories, and internships that focus on using green technology. Collaborating with environmental NGOs and local communities also makes sure that sustainability training stays useful for both global standards and local needs. Institutions can get money, research help, and policy support for long-term human capital development by working together in these ways.

In the end, investing in human capital allows the maritime industry to turn sustainability from a legal requirement into a cultural and professional norm. This makes environmental responsibility a key part of maritime education and practice.

POLICY, GOVERNANCE, AND INSTITUTIONAL COLLABORATION

4.1 Regulatory and Accreditation Frameworks

The transition toward sustainable maritime education relies heavily on robust policy frameworks and accreditation systems that embed environmental responsibility into institutional structures (Hardian et al., 2024). Regulatory and accreditation frameworks serve as both a compass and a compliance mechanism, guiding maritime institutions toward the integration of sustainability across all dimensions of education, training, and governance. Effective policy alignment ensures that environmental goals are not treated as supplementary objectives but as central pillars of quality assurance and institutional excellence (Aslam et al., 2025).

Integrating environmental performance indicators in accreditation represents a key innovation in shaping accountable and forward-thinking maritime education systems. Accreditation bodies traditionally assess institutions based on technical proficiency, safety standards, and pedagogical quality (Lobato et al., 2025). However, as global environmental imperatives intensify, there is a growing need to include sustainability benchmarks such as carbon footprint reduction, resource efficiency, and environmental management practices in evaluation criteria (Yu et al., 2025). For maritime academies, this might involve assessing compliance with the International Maritime Organization's (IMO) decarbonization strategy, implementation of pollution prevention measures, or integration of green technologies in training facilities. Institutions that meet or exceed these indicators can be recognized as leaders in sustainable maritime education, inspiring others to follow similar pathways (Omer, 2024). The inclusion of environmental performance metrics also fosters transparency and accountability, motivating institutions to continuously improve their ecological impact (Sahu & Doppalapudi, 2025).

Ensuring policy coherence between maritime education and green transition agendas is equally essential. Fragmented or inconsistent policies often hinder the effective implementation of sustainability initiatives. Maritime education must align with national climate strategies, international agreements such as the Paris Accord, and regional frameworks like ASEAN's Sustainable Shipping Roadmap or the European Green Deal (Verma, 2025). Policy coherence facilitates smooth transitions between regulatory levels—global, national, and institutional—ensuring that maritime education reforms support broader environmental goals. This alignment requires collaboration among ministries of transport, education, and environment, alongside active consultation with industry stakeholders (Joseph et al., 2025). Coherent policy design promotes consistency in curricula, certification standards, and investment priorities, ensuring that education systems evolve in step with green maritime transformations.

Equally important are governance models for sustainability assurance, which define how institutions organize, monitor, and report their environmental commitments. Effective governance integrates sustainability into leadership vision, institutional planning, and operational decision-making. Dedicated sustainability offices, environmental audit committees, and transparent reporting systems can help track progress toward emission reduction and resource conservation (Diaz et al., 2023). Participatory governance—engaging faculty, students, and external partners—fosters a shared sense of responsibility and continuous improvement (Yatsenko, 2025).

4.2 Industry–Academia Partnerships for Sustainability

Working together with businesses and schools has become a key part of the maritime sector's move toward sustainability. While maritime education institutions offer theoretical foundations and research capabilities, industry partners supply technological proficiency, operational perspectives, and financial support. The collaboration between these two areas speeds up innovation, makes it easier to share technology, and makes sure that sustainability principles are not just taught in classrooms but also used in real-world maritime operations (Ilesanmi, 2024).. These kinds of partnerships help create a complete ecosystem that can lead to a greener and less carbon-intensive future for global shipping by working together on research, development, and training.

Working together on research and development in green shipping and decarbonization is one of the most exciting areas of cooperation. Universities, maritime academies, and shipping companies have worked together on research projects to make fuels cleaner, designs better, and energy use more efficient. New research into hydrogen, ammonia, and biofuel propulsion technologies has made it possible for ships to operate in a more environmentally friendly way. Academia gives us the tools to test new materials and systems through analysis and experimentation, while industry gives us data, pilot vessels, and places to put them into action. These partnerships also help make decisions based on facts, which supports international frameworks like the United Nations Sustainable Development Goals (SDGs) and the International Maritime Organization's (IMO) GHG Reduction Strategy. Industry-academia partnerships create scalable solutions that speed up the decarbonization of global shipping by combining scientific innovation with operational validation (Sahu & Doppalapudi, 2025).

Co-funded environmental innovation projects make this collaborative model even stronger by aligning the research goals of institutions with the investment priorities of businesses. Funding from both the public and private sectors lets maritime institutions do applied research and make technologies that are useful to businesses right away. Some examples are partnerships to build ballast water treatment systems, low-emission port infrastructure, and smart energy management software for ships. Co-funded programs also encourage students and faculty to do research together, which helps everyone involved in education and business. These programs are like living labs where theory and practice come together. They help maritime graduates get ready for the job market and make them more employable.

To have a lasting effect, it's important to connect institutional and industrial capacity through shared training. Internships, joint training centers, and co-designed curricula make sure that students learn skills that are useful for the green maritime industry now and in the future. Industry experts can teach as guest instructors, and teachers can help with workforce upskilling programs by sharing their knowledge of how to teach. Collaborative certifications that show skills in energy efficiency, pollution control, and environmental management create a common standard of excellence.

4.3 Global and Regional Collaboration Networks

The maritime industry's sustainability journey is inherently global, demanding collaboration that transcends borders and institutional boundaries. Climate change, marine pollution, and decarbonization challenges cannot be addressed in isolation; they require shared knowledge, coordinated action, and harmonized educational frameworks. Global and regional collaboration networks therefore play a critical role in fostering climate-resilient maritime education and training. By connecting institutions, governments, and industry actors, these networks facilitate capacity building, policy alignment, and innovation diffusion across regions (Lindstad et al., 2023).

IMO-led capacity-building and knowledge-sharing platforms have long served as the backbone of international maritime cooperation. The International Maritime Organization (IMO), through programs such as the *Integrated Technical Cooperation Programme (ITCP)* and *Global Maritime Training Institutes (MTIs)*, supports member states in developing environmental competence and regulatory compliance. Initiatives like the *IMO-Norway GreenVoyage2050 Project* and the *Global Industry Alliance for Low Carbon Shipping (GIA)* exemplify how cross-sector collaboration accelerates the adoption of sustainable practices and technologies. These platforms enable developing nations to access technical assistance, digital learning resources, and research partnerships, bridging gaps in expertise and resources. By embedding environmental awareness and resilience into maritime education systems, IMO-led initiatives strengthen the global foundation for green shipping and sustainable ocean governance (Winarno et al., 2025).

At the regional level, ASEAN, EU, and Pacific initiatives for climate-resilient education have emerged as models of cooperative innovation. The Association of Southeast Asian Nations (ASEAN) promotes regional harmonization of maritime education through its *Sustainable Shipping Roadmap* and *Blue Economy Framework*, which encourages integration of climate adaptation into maritime curricula. The European Union, through its *Horizon Europe* and *EMSA (European Maritime Safety Agency)* programs, funds research and training in decarbonization, digitalization, and maritime sustainability. In the Pacific, collaborative projects under the *Pacific Community (SPC)* and *University of the South Pacific (USP)* strengthen resilience through localized maritime education that addresses rising sea levels and coastal vulnerability. These initiatives reflect how regional cooperation enhances relevance and inclusivity, ensuring that maritime education responds to both global standards and local environmental realities (Lindstad et al., 2023).

Equally significant is the establishment of centers of excellence for green maritime training, which serve as innovation hubs and capacity-building anchors. These centers—often supported by international agencies and regional alliances—facilitate joint research, simulator-based sustainability training, and policy advisory functions. By linking academia, industry, and government, they nurture a networked ecosystem of expertise that advances both environmental and economic goals.

NAVIGATING TOWARD A SUSTAINABLE MARITIME FUTURE

5.1 Emerging Research and Innovation Pathways

As the maritime industry advances toward a low-carbon and climate-resilient future, research and innovation have become critical drivers of transformation. The challenges of decarbonization, pollution control, and ocean health demand scientific discovery, technological creativity, and human-centered approaches that balance efficiency with ethics (Герлянд, 2024). Maritime education and training institutions play a central role in this innovation ecosystem—linking theory, practice, and policy through research that responds to global sustainability imperatives (Bartusevičienė et al., 2023). Emerging research pathways now focus not only on engineering solutions but also on cultivating environmental awareness and social responsibility, ensuring that progress remains equitable and enduring (Cahyadi, 2025).

A major area of focus lies in green technologies, renewable energy, and ocean literacy. Research into alternative propulsion systems—such as hydrogen, ammonia, methanol, and biofuels—continues to reshape the future of sustainable shipping (Doucouré, 2024). Hybrid and electric vessel designs are reducing dependency on fossil fuels while increasing energy efficiency through smart automation and waste-heat recovery systems (Dacosta et al., 2022). Renewable energy applications in ports and ship operations, including wind-assisted propulsion and solar charging infrastructure, further demonstrate the potential of technological innovation to mitigate environmental impact. Parallel to this, promoting ocean literacy has become essential in maritime education, emphasizing the interconnection between human activity and marine ecosystems (Hardian et al., 2024). By fostering understanding of ocean dynamics, biodiversity, and climate systems, maritime professionals develop the scientific awareness needed to operate responsibly within complex ecological networks (Ma et al., 2025).

Climate data analytics and sustainable logistics represent another frontier of maritime research and innovation. The use of big data, AI, and predictive modeling enables more efficient and environmentally conscious decision-making (Doucouré, 2024). Through digital twins and data-driven simulations, maritime operators can forecast weather conditions, optimize fuel consumption, and minimize emissions across shipping routes (NWEKE & Ali, 2025). Research into sustainable logistics explores carbon-neutral supply chains, circular economy models, and port digitalization—key enablers of decarbonized global trade (Moskalenko & POPKOV, 2022). Data analytics also facilitates real-time monitoring of compliance with environmental regulations, such as the IMO's Carbon Intensity Indicator (CII) and Energy Efficiency Existing Ship Index (EEXI), enhancing accountability across the industry.

Equally important are the ethical and social dimensions of the maritime green shift, which ensure that sustainability transitions remain inclusive and just. Research must address the human implications of technological transformation—employment transitions, upskilling, and equitable access to green technologies (Sardinha, 2024). Ethical frameworks guide decision-making in automation, AI adoption, and resource use, preventing environmental progress from reinforcing social inequality. Collaborative research involving social scientists, engineers, and policymakers can help shape a maritime future that values both technological advancement and human dignity (Purba & Simanjuntak, 2024).

5.2 Lifelong Learning and Workforce Transformation

A sustainable maritime future depends on the ongoing growth of human capital through lifelong learning and changes in the workforce. Maritime professionals need to keep their skills and knowledge up to date all the time because technology is changing quickly, environmental rules are getting stricter, and green innovation is happening. The maritime industry is changing, and traditional, one-time certification models can't keep up with the skills it needs. Instead, we need to create dynamic learning ecosystems that are based on flexibility, accessibility, and relevance (Doucouré, 2024). These ecosystems will help seafarers become adaptable, environmentally responsible, and ready for the future (RUBEL et al., 2021).

Upskilling programs for sustainable operations are very important for giving the current workforce the skills they need to make the transition to green. These programs teach people how to be more environmentally friendly in practical and technical ways, like how to use less fuel, navigate in a way that saves energy, control emissions, and deal with waste. Training modules might also cover eco-design principles, how to use digital navigation to find low-carbon routes, and how to use renewable energy systems on board. Maritime professionals can learn while still doing their jobs through modular short courses, simulation-based training, or online platforms. Upskilling programs make sure that the workforce stays in line with global decarbonization goals and regulatory frameworks like the IMO's GreenVoyage2050 and EEXI standards by including environmental awareness and operational efficiency in ongoing professional development (Doucouré, 2024).

Micro-credentials in environmental management and policy compliance are another way to recognize specialized knowledge that is flexible and can be verified. Micro-credentials, which are digital badges or certificates given out after completing certain modules, can be about things like protecting marine ecosystems, managing ballast water, carbon accounting, or sustainable logistics. These stackable credentials encourage people to keep learning and move up in their careers. For example, seafarers, port officers, and teachers can keep getting better at their jobs without having to go back to school for a full degree. Also, they encourage a culture of accountability and openness, which shows employers and regulators that maritime professionals have the most up-to-date skills in sustainability (Dacosta et al., 2022).

Lastly, creating green career paths in the maritime industry makes sure that sustainability is a part of professional growth and the culture of the workplace. Green maritime jobs go beyond traditional roles in navigation and engineering. They also include jobs in environmental auditing, sustainability consulting, designing renewable energy systems, and analyzing climate risk. Institutions, working with businesses, can create clear career paths that reward innovation and environmental performance. The maritime industry can create a virtuous cycle of learning and leadership by connecting education, certification, and jobs. This will make professionals want to help make the industry cleaner, stronger, and more ethical.

5.3 Vision and Commitment for the Future

The path toward a sustainable maritime future requires more than technological innovation or policy reform—it demands a cultural transformation rooted in ethics, awareness, and shared global responsibility Simanjuntak et al. (2024). A long-term vision for maritime education must therefore go beyond producing skilled operators; it must nurture a new generation of professionals who act as stewards of the ocean, advocates of sustainability, and ambassadors of global cooperation (Kanchiralla et al., 2022). This vision aligns maritime progress with the collective commitment to safeguard the planet's ecological balance and ensure prosperity for future generations.

Cultivating a culture of sustainability and ethical responsibility begins within maritime education institutions themselves. Schools and academies must model the values they teach by adopting sustainable campus practices, promoting transparency, and integrating environmental ethics into their organizational culture (Schwartz et al., 2022). Faculty, staff, and students should share a collective understanding that sustainability is not merely a technical requirement but a moral obligation. Courses on maritime law, safety, and management should incorporate discussions on environmental justice, resource equity, and the ethical implications of human activity at sea. Mentorship and leadership programs can further strengthen this ethical foundation, ensuring that future maritime leaders prioritize ecological integrity alongside economic efficiency (Alop & Koit, 2024).

Maritime education's role in global climate resilience is increasingly central to achieving sustainable development. By integrating climate science, risk management, and adaptation strategies into curricula, maritime education institutions can produce graduates capable of responding to the growing threats of sea-level rise, extreme weather events, and ocean degradation (Sun et al., 2022). Through research, simulation training, and collaboration with international organizations, these institutions can develop innovative solutions that enhance the resilience of coastal and shipping communities (Zhang & Feng, 2024). Furthermore, maritime universities can act as hubs for knowledge exchange—bridging science, policy, and industry to inform global efforts toward decarbonization and ocean conservation (Gillingham & Huang, 2020).

Equally vital is fostering global citizenship among future seafarers, empowering them to view their professional responsibilities through a planetary lens. As seafarers navigate across nations and ecosystems, they become key actors in promoting intercultural understanding, environmental diplomacy, and shared stewardship of the seas (Huang et al., 2024). Embedding global citizenship education in maritime training encourages empathy, inclusivity, and respect for diversity—values essential to addressing global environmental challenges collaboratively (Lindstad et al., 2023).

Ultimately, the vision for the maritime sector's future is one of harmony: where economic growth coexists with ecological preservation, and where every maritime professional embodies a deep, enduring commitment to ethical leadership and sustainability. Through education, this vision can become reality—anchoring hope, responsibility, and innovation at the heart of the world's oceans (Müller-Casseres et al., 2022).

CONCLUSION

The journey toward integrating environmental education and climate-resilient training in maritime education signifies a transformative shift in how the global maritime community perceives its role in addressing the climate crisis. Maritime institutions are no longer just places to learn technical skills; they are now important places to train professionals who care about the environment and know how human activity affects ocean health. Sustainability has gone from being on the edge of maritime training to being at its very core through changes to the curriculum, new technologies, better policies, and collaboration between different sectors.

By teaching green skills, how to make ethical choices, and how to understand the environment, future seafarers will be able to not only operate ships well but also protect marine ecosystems in a responsible way. Training that helps people deal with climate change helps them be flexible and think critically, so they can confidently and wisely deal with new environmental problems. Adding digital technologies like AI, VR, and simulation to these efforts makes them even stronger by creating immersive learning experiences that are like real-world ecological problems.

The governance structures, accreditation systems, and international collaborations that support these improvements are just as important. When national and institutional policies are in line with global sustainability goals, maritime education can help both innovation and accountability. Partnerships between universities, businesses, and international groups make capacity-building efforts stronger and help everyone work together to make the maritime transition to a greener future.

In the end, the goal of environmental and climate-resilient maritime education is a long-term commitment to the health of the world. At every level of practice, it calls for ongoing learning, working together across disciplines, and being morally responsible. As the maritime workforce changes, they must all still have the same goal: to find a way to navigate not only through oceans and trade routes, but also toward a future that is fair and sustainable, where progress in the maritime industry goes hand in hand with protecting the sea, which is our planet's most important resource.

REFERENCES

Герлянд, Т. (2024). Екологічна компетентність судноводіїв в умовах сталого розвитку. *Professional Pedagogics*, *1*(28), 152–158. DOI: 10.32835/2707-3092.2024.28.152-158

Alop, A. and Koit, K. (2024). Potential impacts of the deployment of maritime autonomous surface ships on the maritime freight transport process.. DOI: 10.5821/mt.13182

Aslam, F., Bhutta, M., Asghar, M., Khan, M., & Rashid, J. (2025). Environmental sustainability in emerging countries: The role of green energy, green finance and digitalization. *International Journal of Systems and Society*, *4*(3), 215–224. DOI: 10.63544/ijss.v4i3.159

Barasa, L., Cahyadi, T., Malau, A., Simanjuntak, M., Suhartini, S., Herawati, S., Suranta, N., Kurniadi, B., & Simanjuntak, M. (2025). Integrating health, sustainability, and vocational competencies in maritime education for future seafarers. *Physical Therapy Journal of Indonesia*, *6*(1), 6–11. DOI: 10.51559/ptji.v6i1.240

Barasa, L., Cahyadi, T., Simanjuntak, M., Malau, A. G., Suranta, N., Rinaldi, A., & Herawati, S. (2025). Evaluating maritime education effectiveness in preparing port management professionals for green transition. *IOP Conference Series. Earth and Environmental Science*, *1566*(1), 012020. DOI: 10.1088/1755-1315/1566/1/012020

Bartusevičienė, I., Kitada, M., & Valionienė, E. (2023). Rethinking maritime education and training for generation z students. Regional Formation and Development Studies, 16-29. DOI: 10.15181/rfds.v41i3.2543

Barus, I., & Simanjuntak, M. (2023). Integrating environmental education into maritime english curriculum for vocational learners: challenges and opportunities. Bio Web of Conferences, 79, 08001. DOI: 10.1051/bioconf/20237908001

Bayotas, M. (2024). Shifting from global maritime professional to global maritime citizen.. DOI: 10.5821/mt.13183

Bokau, J., & Sulistiana, O. (2024). Reshaping curriculum of indonesian maritime education and training. *International Journal of Social Service and Research*, *4*(6). Advance online publication. DOI: 10.46799/ijssr.v4i6.809

Cahyadi, T., Barasa, L., Riyanto, R., Winarno, W., Suranta, N., Simanjuntak, M., . . . Simanjuntak, M. (2025). Empowering maritime vocational schools for sustainable leadership in port and shipping practices. Bio Web of Conferences, 175, 03002. DOI: 10.1051/bioconf/202517503002

Cahyadi, T., Winarno, W., Barasa, L., Herawati, S., Qodriah, R., & Kardiono, D. E. (2025). Empowering seafarers as key implementers of green maritime technologies. *IOP Conference Series. Earth and Environmental Science*, *1559*(1), 012002. DOI: 10.1088/1755-1315/1559/1/012002

Cahyadi, T., Winarno, W., Barasa, L., Herawati, S., Qodriah, R., & Kardiono, D. E. (2025). Empowering seafarers as key implementers of green maritime technologies. *IOP Conference Series. Earth and Environmental Science*, *1559*(1), 012002. DOI: 10.1088/1755-1315/1559/1/012002

Campos, C., Castells, M., & Altés, C. (2025). Maritime stakeholders' insights on maritime education and training in the autonomous shipping era. a small-scale study in spain. *Pomorstvo*, *39*(1), 80–91. DOI: 10.31217/p.39.1.7

Caprace, J., Marques, C., Assis, L., Lucchesi, A., & Pereda, P. (2025). Sustainable shipping: modeling technological pathways toward zero-emission in maritime transport (part i). DOI: 10.21203/rs.3.rs-5943477/v1

Dacosta, E., Jin, Z., Bowers, J., & Abdul-Salam, R. (2022). Green maritime practices in an emerging economy towards the achievement of sustainable development: A ghanaian context. *Benchmarking*, *30*(9), 3637–3673. DOI: 10.1108/BIJ-10-2021-0629

Diahyleva, O., Kononova, O., & Yurzhenko, A. (2024). Integration of whiteboard use in maritime education and training to enhance environmental awareness of cadets. *Advances in Mobile Learning Educational Research*, *4*(1), 1038–1045. DOI: 10.25082/AMLER.2024.01.014

Diaz, S., Hammadi, N., Nasr, A., Villasuso, F., Prakash, S., Baobaid, O., … & Mills, R. (2023). Green corridor: a feasible option for the uae decarbonization pathway, opportunities & challenges.. DOI: 10.2118/216033-MS

Doucouré, M. (2024). Decarbonisation in shipping and maritime innovation call for readiness in maritime education and skills training in south africa. *SAJMET*, *3*, 31–38. DOI: 10.47348/SAJMET/2024/i1a3

Emad, G. and Shahbakhsh, M. (2022). Digitalization transformation and its challenges in shipping operation: the case of seafarer's cognitive human factor.. DOI: 10.54941/ahfe1002505

Fan, H., Enshaei, H., & Jayasinghe, S. (2022). Formation of dataset for fuzzy quantitative risk assessment of lng bunkering simops. *Data*, *7*(5), 60. DOI: 10.3390/data7050060

Fan, L., Yang, H., & Zhang, X. (2024). Targeting the effectiveness assessment of the emission control policies on the shipping industry. *Sustainability (Basel)*, *16*(6), 2465. DOI: 10.3390/su16062465

Filonenko, V., Tenishcheva, V., ZELENKOV, G., Manetskaya, S., & Genkin, Y. (2023). Deep awareness as a factor of environmental motivation at sea. E3s Web of Conferences, 411, 02028. DOI: 10.1051/e3sconf/202341102028

Ghoneim, N., Colak, A., & Amer, A. (2023). Exploring the regulatory framework of maritime decarbonization to achieve imo ghg emission targets. *Port-Said Engineering Research Journal*, *27*(1), 8–14. DOI: 10.21608/pserj.2023.209426.1234

Gillingham, K., & Huang, P. (2020). Long-run environmental and economic impacts of electrifying waterborne shipping in the united states. *Environmental Science & Technology*, *54*(16), 9824–9833. DOI: 10.1021/acs.est.0c03298

Giordono, L., Boudet, H., & Gard-Murray, A. (2020). Local adaptation policy responses to extreme weather events. *Policy Sciences*, *53*(4), 609–636. DOI: 10.1007/s11077-020-09401-3

Guntoro, R., & Simanjuntak, P.R.Herlan GuntoroPargaulan Dwikora Simanjuntak. (2024). Integration of ship machinery maintenance and control systems in maritime education: Enhancing industry readiness. *Journal of Business Finance and Economics (Jbfe)*, *5*(1), 409–419. DOI: 10.32585/jbfe.v5i1.5687

Hardian, M., Fauzan, A., Taufika, R., Erlande, R., Juri, J., & R, A. (2024). Green maritime education: a framework for cultivating ecological citizenship and sustainable practices in coastal areas. SHS Web of Conferences, 205, 05002. DOI: 10.1051/shsconf/202420505002

Huang, L., Tan, Y., & Yue, X. (2024). Optimizing route and speed under the sulfur emission control areas for a cruise liner: A new strategy considering route competitiveness and low carbon. *Mathematics*, *12*(12), 1847. DOI: 10.3390/math12121847

Huang, S., & Tsai, X. (2025). Exploring decarbonized shipping strategies: a multidimensional analysis using the qfd-based method. DOI: 10.21203/rs.3.rs-6201467/v1

Ilesanmi, J. (2024). Importance of eco-entrepreneurship as a tool for climate action and lowcarbon transition in developing countries: A case study of nigeria. *Journal of Sustainable Development Law and Policy (The)*, *15*(2), 298–327. DOI: 10.4314/jsdlp.v15i2.11

İnal, Ö. (2024). Decarbonization of shipping: Hydrogen and fuel cells legislation in the maritime industry. *Brodogradnja*, *75*(2), 1–13. DOI: 10.21278/brod75205

Johnson, B. (2021). Urban resilience: what role can business improvement areas play in increasing climate change and extreme weather resilience in cities?.. DOI: 10.32920/ryerson.14660514.v1

Joseph, O., Olateji, M., Ijiga, O., Okoli, I., & Frempong, D. (2025). Future-proofing skills in the global south: Strategic directions for transforming technical and vocational education and training (tvet). *IJAMRS*, *5*(2), 2478–2492. DOI: 10.62225/2583049X.2025.5.2.4730

Kanchiralla, F., Brynolf, S., Malmgren, E., Hansson, J., & Grahn, M. (2022). Life-cycle assessment and costing of fuels and propulsion systems in future fossil-free shipping. *Environmental Science & Technology*, *56*(17), 12517–12531. DOI: 10.1021/acs.est.2c03016

Laskar, I., Dowlatabadi, H., & Giang, A. (2025). Expert assessments of maritime shipping decarbonization pathways by 2030 and 2050. *Earth's Future*, *13*(4), e2024EF005255. Advance online publication. DOI: 10.1029/2024EF005255

Liang, C., Sun, W., Shi, J., Wang, K., Zhang, Y., & Lim, G. (2024). Decarbonizing maritime transport through green fuel-powered vessel retrofitting: A game-theoretic approach. *Journal of Marine Science and Engineering*, *12*(7), 1174. DOI: 10.3390/jmse12071174

Lin, C., Wu, P., & Yang, H. (2023). Alternative gaseous fuels for marine vessels towards zero-carbon emissions. *Gases*, *3*(4), 158–164. DOI: 10.3390/gases3040011

Lindstad, E., Lagemann, B., Rialland, A., Acciaro, M., & Eskeland, G. (2023). Smart use of renewable electricity and carbon capture in the transport sector. DOI: 10.21203/rs.3.rs-3726551/v1

Lobato, M., Pradelle, R., Ticona, E., Sánchez, F., Elías, J., Braga, S., … & Pradelle, F. (2025). Decarbonization of maritime engines with alternative fuels: impact of biofuels on autonomy and economicity.. DOI: 10.4043/36188-MS

Ma, X., Ji, Y., Yuan, J., & Zhao, Y. (2025). The exploration of green shipping concepts and ideological education in the context of ecological civilization construction in the maritime economic geography course. *JMBE*, *1*(3). Advance online publication. DOI: 10.70767/jmbe.v1i3.431

Makhtar, M., Rahman, M., Saibani, N., & Ikram, I. (2025). Revolutionising maritime decarbonisation: a synthesis of carbon emission drivers, emerging technology, and global policy pathways. DOI: 10.21203/rs.3.rs-7197877/v1

Mallouppas, G., & Yfantis, E. (2021). Decarbonization in shipping industry: A review of research, technology development, and innovation proposals. *Journal of Marine Science and Engineering*, *9*(4), 415. DOI: 10.3390/jmse9040415

Masodzadeh, P., Baumler, R., Celis, J., Ballini, F., & Ölçer, A. (2024). Stcw requirements in a regulatory and technology landscape change.. DOI: 10.5821/mt.13158

Melnyk, O., Onishchenko, O., & Onyshchenko, S. (2023). Renewable energy concept development and application in shipping industry. *Lex Portus*, *9*(6). Advance online publication. DOI: 10.26886/2524-101X.9.6.2023.2

Meštrović, T., Pavić, I., Androjna, A., & Maljković, M. (2023). Challenges for seafarers education and training in the context of autonomous ships development. Časopis Pomorskog Fakulteta Kotor - Journal of Maritime Sciences, 24(2), 31-42. DOI: 10.56080/jms231103

Moskalenko, O., & Popkov, B. (2022). Environmental education of future navigators as psychological and pedagogical problem. *Scientific Bulletin of Flight Academy Section Pedagogical Sciences*, *12*, 81–86. DOI: 10.33251/2522-1477-2022-12-81-86

Mthuli, S., & Singh, N. (2024). State-led maritime governance, education and training nexus in south africa. *ECMLG*, *20*(1), 401–407. DOI: 10.34190/ecmlg.20.1.2950

Müller-Casseres, E., Szklo, A., Bergman-Fonte, C., Carvalho, F., Portugal-Pereira, J., Baptista, L., & Schaeffer, R. (2022). Are there synergies in the decarbonization of aviation and shipping? an integrated perspective for the case of brazil. *iScience*, *25*(10), 105248. DOI: 10.1016/j.isci.2022.105248

Newman, R., & Noy, I. (2023). The global costs of extreme weather that are attributable to climate change. *Nature Communications*, *14*(1), 6103. Advance online publication. DOI: 10.1038/s41467-023-41888-1

Nikolov, B. (2024). Approach to developing a maritime cybersecurity virtual training environment. Environment Technology Resources Proceedings of the International Scientific and Practical Conference, 2, 220-225. DOI: 10.17770/etr2024vol2.8039

Omer, A. (2024). *Environmental pollution: a growing cancer risk in developing countries*. Barw Medical Journal., DOI: 10.58742/bmj.v2i3.97

Palippui, H. (2024). Integration of technology and regulations for safe and efficient marine logistics. *CBCER*, *2*(1), 1–7. DOI: 10.62012/collaborate.v2i1.53

Purba, D., & Simanjuntak, M. (2024). Sustainable maritime education: Integrating environmental science for global competence. [Jurnal Pendidikan Biologi Indonesia]. *Jpbi*, *10*(1), 310–319. DOI: 10.22219/jpbi.v10i1.32588

Purba, D., & Simanjuntak, M. (2024). Sustainable maritime education: Integrating environmental science for global competence. [Jurnal Pendidikan Biologi Indonesia]. *Jpbi*, *10*(1), 310–319. DOI: 10.22219/jpbi.v10i1.32588

Rubel, O. E., Aghayev, A., & Zhikhareva, A. A.RUBEL. (2021). Institutional-cognitive and nonlinear scientific fundamentals of innovative "smart"-specialization of the maritime economic complex. *Economic Innovations*, *23*(2(79)), 140–151. DOI: 10.31520/ei.2021.23.2(79).140-151

Sahu, R., & Doppalapudi, R. (2025). Blue economy: Framework for integrating economic growth with marine ecosystem. *International Journal of Marine Engineering Innovation and Research*, *10*(1), 165–174. DOI: 10.12962/j25481479.v10i1.4758

Sardinha, A. (2024). Apresentação do centro de competência e desenvolvimento da economia azul. *Revista Internacional Em Língua Portuguesa*, (45), 135–138. DOI: 10.31492/2184-2043.RILP2024.45/pp.135-138

Schwartz, H., Solakivi, T., & Gustafsson, M. (2022). Is there business potential for sustainable shipping? price premiums needed to cover decarbonized transportation. *Sustainability (Basel)*, *14*(10), 5888. DOI: 10.3390/su14105888

Serra, P., & Fancello, G. (2020). Towards the imo's ghg goals: A critical overview of the perspectives and challenges of the main options for decarbonizing international shipping. *Sustainability (Basel)*, *12*(8), 3220. DOI: 10.3390/su12083220

Sharma, A., & Nazir, S. (2021). Assessing the technology self-efficacy of maritime instructors: An explorative study. *Education Sciences*, *11*(7), 342. DOI: 10.3390/educsci11070342

Sibarani, M., Junaidi, J., & Wibowo, T. (2025). Advancing green ship design and experiential learning in maritime education. *Research and Development in Education (Raden)*, *5*(1), 88–98. DOI: 10.22219/raden.v5i1.39397

Sijabat, P., Cahyadi, T., Winarno, W., Riyanto, R., Kuntadi, C., & Simanjuntak, M. (2025). Seafarer readiness for green shipping transition - insights from maritime education and industry professionals. *Jurnal Kajian Dan Penelitian Umum*, *3*(1), 40–58. DOI: 10.47861/jkpu-nalanda.v3i1.1496

Simanjuntak, M. (2023). Enhancing environmental awareness and sustainable communication skills in maritime education. Bio Web of Conferences, 79, 01002. DOI: 10.1051/bioconf/20237901002

Simanjuntak, M., & Barus, I. (2024). Environmental integration in maritime education: A holistic approach. [Jurnal Pendidikan Biologi Indonesia]. *Jpbi*, *10*(2), 366–373. DOI: 10.22219/jpbi.v10i2.32589

Simanjuntak, M.Marudut Bernadtua Simanjuntak. (2024). Exploring the intersection of psychological features and language proficiency in seamen's activity: A qualitative analysis of maritime cadets at maritime institute jakarta (stip jakarta). *Pragmatik*, *2*(1), 216–227. DOI: 10.61132/pragmatik.v2i1.254

Simanjuntak, M., Rafli, Z., & Utami, S. (2024). Enhancing maritime education for ocean sustainability: a multidisciplinary approach. Bio Web of Conferences, 106, 02006. DOI: 10.1051/bioconf/202410602006

Simanjuntak, M., Rafli, Z., & Utami, S. (2024). Enhancing maritime education for ocean sustainability: a multidisciplinary approach. Bio Web of Conferences, 106, 02006. DOI: 10.1051/bioconf/202410602006

Simanjuntak, M., Zuriyati, Z., Utami, S., Rahmat, A., & Setiadi, S. (2023). Fostering intercultural understanding and environmental consciousness in maritime education. Bio Web of Conferences, 79, 06004. DOI: 10.1051/bioconf/20237906004

Sun, L., Ding, P., Xiong, Y., Liu, W., & Hu, Z. (2022). Carbon emission reduction of shore power from power energy structure in china. *Frontiers in Marine Science*, *9*, 1077289. Advance online publication. DOI: 10.3389/fmars.2022.1077289

Türkistanlı, T. (2023). Advanced learning methods in maritime education and training: A bibliometric analysis on the digitalization of education and modern trends. *Computer Applications in Engineering Education*, *32*(1), e22690. Advance online publication. DOI: 10.1002/cae.22690

Vakili, S., İnsel, M., Singh, S., & Ölçer, A. (2025). Decarbonizing domestic and short-sea shipping: A systematic review and transdisciplinary pathway for emerging maritime regions. *Sustainability (Basel)*, *17*(16), 7294. DOI: 10.3390/su17167294

Verma, D., Agrawal, D. S., Sonker, N., & Kori, R. (2025). Sustainable and green pharmacy: Eco-friendly approaches in drug manufacturing. *IJPRA*, *10*(5), 348–351. DOI: 10.35629/4494-1005348351

Vujičić, S., Hasanspahić, N., Car, M., & Čampara, L. (2020). Distributed ledger technology as a tool for environmental sustainability in the shipping industry. *Journal of Marine Science and Engineering*, *8*(5), 366. DOI: 10.3390/jmse8050366

Wang, S., Wang, X., Han, Y., Wang, X., Jiang, H., Duan, J., Hua, R., & Zhang, Z. (2023). Decarbonizing in maritime transportation: Challenges and opportunities. *Journal of Transportation Technologies*, *13*(02), 301–325. DOI: 10.4236/jtts.2023.132015

Werkmeister, A., Carrel, A., Porwal, N., Clemente, C., & Macdonald, M. (2023). Monitoring ship emissions using sentinel-5p and ais data., 10. DOI: 10.1117/12.2678424

Winarno, W., Cahyadi, T., Barasa, L., Permana, A., Kuntadi, C., Martha, Y., & Simanjuntak, M. (2025). Competency development, sustainability practices, and industry preparedness in maritime vocational education. *Digital Innovation*, *2*(1), 130–142. DOI: 10.61132/digitalinnovation.v2i1.180

Winarno, W., Riyanto, R., Kuntadi, C., Malau, A., Herawati, S., Wibowo, T., & Simanjuntak, M. (2025). A qualitative analysis and systematic literature review on enhancing maritime vocational education. *ARJ*, *2*(1), 12–28. DOI: 10.63987/arj.v2i1.170

Wu, Y., Wen, K., & Zou, X. (2022). Impacts of shipping carbon tax on dry bulk shipping costs and maritime trades—The case of china. *Journal of Marine Science and Engineering*, *10*(8), 1105. DOI: 10.3390/jmse10081105

Xu, T., Xiao, Y., & Jiang, Z. (2021). Maritime pilots' risky operational behavior analysis based on structural equation model. *Discrete Dynamics in Nature and Society*, *2021*, 1–11. DOI: 10.1155/2021/3611859

Yatsenko, O. (2025). Development of innovative business and international hydrogen trade: Institutional support for the energy transition to a sustainable post-carbon future. *Ukrainian Journal of Applied Economics*, *2025*(1), 92–103. DOI: 10.36887/2415-8453-2025-1-16

Yu, Y., Lee, C., & Ahn, Y. (2025). Developing a competency-based transition education framework for marine superintendents: A dacum-integrated approach in the context of eco-digital maritime transformation. *Sustainability (Basel)*, *17*(14), 6455. DOI: 10.3390/su17146455

Yuen, K., Tan, L., & Loh, H. (2022). Core competencies for maritime business educators in the digital era. *Frontiers in Psychology*, *13*, 915980. Advance online publication. DOI: 10.3389/fpsyg.2022.915980

Zhang, S. and Feng, C. (2024). A tripartite evolutionary game model for carbon reduction decisions in shipping industry. E3s Web of Conferences, 512, 03027. DOI: 10.1051/e3sconf/202451203027

Zulfiqar, K., & Chang, Y. (2023). Climate change and maritime law: A review of imo governance mechanism. *JAOE*, *11*(1). Advance online publication. DOI: 10.18686/jaoe.v11i1.9511

Chapter 15

Inspiration From the Local Wisdom of Bugis–Makassar Pinisi for the Development of a Sustainable Maritime Curriculum in Indonesia and Southeast Asia

Erma Suryani Sahabuddin
http://orcid.org/0000-0003-4899-0923
Universitas Negeri Makassar, Indonesia

Faidah Faidah Yusuf
Universitas Negeri Makassar, Indonesia

Farhan Fadhiil Ali
Universitas Negeri Makassar, Indonesia

ABSTRACT

Green shipping has become a decisive element in shaping the future of maritime education, particularly in regions like Indonesia where the sea defines both identity and economy. This chapter situates maritime transformation within the realities of climate change, technological disruption, and regional socio-economic pressures, arguing that Maritime Education and Training (MET) must no longer be limited to technical instruction. Instead, it should cultivate ecological awareness, adaptive skills, and a mindset oriented toward sustainability. The discussion draws on the Bugis-Makassar Pinisi tradition, a heritage of low-emission seafaring that demonstrates how indigenous practices can anticipate modern green principles. By proposing curriculum reforms that integrate environmental issues, innovative learning methods, and 21st-century competencies, the article frames green shipping education as a pathway to resilience. It concludes that empowering future seafarers through this approach is key to positioning Indonesia and Southeast Asia as leaders in sustainable maritime development.

DOI: 10.4018/979-8-3373-6670-8.ch015

INTRODUCTION

The global maritime industry is currently undergoing a phase of rapid and multidimensional transformation, triggered by a combination of environmental pressures, technological innovations, and global socio-economic dynamics that increasingly demand efficiency and sustainability. First, the environmental crisis caused by climate change has created a new urgency in maritime sector management. Rising sea levels, the intensity of tropical storms, and the vulnerability of coastal ecosystems not only pose direct risks to port infrastructure and international trade routes but also threaten the continuity of global supply chains. This requires integrated mitigation and adaptation strategies, including the implementation of stricter emission standards, the use of environmentally friendly alternative fuels, and the development of trade routes that are more resilient to climate shocks.

Second, technological disruption through automation, digitalization, and the development of smart ports are major catalysts in changing the maritime industry landscape. The implementation of the Internet of Things (IoT), Artificial Intelligence (AI), and blockchain in maritime logistics systems has increased transparency, security, and efficiency in cross-border distribution of goods. Smart ports equipped with advanced technology not only accelerate the flow of goods but also have the potential to significantly reduce operational costs and carbon emissions. However, this digital transformation also presents new challenges, such as the need for human resources with high digital skills, cybersecurity risks, and the potential for technological inequality between developed and developing countries.

Third, global socioeconomic changes require restructuring in the maritime supply chain. Increased urbanization, the growth of the middle class in Asia, and global consumption patterns that are increasingly shifting towards e-commerce have created enormous pressure on the international logistics system. Consumer demands for speed of distribution, cost efficiency, and sustainability have made the decarbonization of maritime transport a priority

agenda. The International Maritime Organization (IMO), for example, has promoted the ambitious target of the " " to reduce carbon emissions by 50% by 2050 compared to 2008 levels, requiring the global shipping industry to systematically transition to clean energy.

In this context, Indonesia and Southeast Asia hold a strategic role while facing the most complex challenges. The region has the second-longest coastline in the world, vital trade routes such as the Strait of Malacca, and enormous blue economy potential. However, this geographical position also makes the region vulnerable to the direct impacts of climate change, such as coastal erosion, mangrove ecosystem damage, and threats to the food security of coastal communities. As the world's largest archipelagic country, Indonesia is at a crossroads between the need to utilize its maritime potential as a driver of national economic growth and its global obligation to maintain environmental sustainability.

In the context of global maritime industry transformation, maritime education can no longer be understood merely as a means of producing graduates who are technically skilled in navigation, ship engines, or port management. The multidimensional challenges currently faced by the maritime sector demand a strategic role for *Maritime Education and Training* (MET) institutions in producing a workforce that is not only technically competent but also has environmental literacy, high adaptability, and 21st-century skills that include *critical thinking,* cross-disciplinary collaboration, and digital proficiency.

The integration of *green shipping* principles into the MET curriculum is an important step to ensure that the new maritime generation understands the urgency of decarbonization, energy efficiency, and waste management in the shipping sector(E. S. Sahabuddin & Makkasau, 2024). Systematic maritime environmental education is also crucial for building ecological awareness from an early age, especially regarding the interrelationship between shipping activities, marine ecosystem health, and coastal community resilience(Jugović et al., 2025). This is in line with the global agenda that encourages the transition to *a* sustainable *blue economy*, where economic and ecological aspects are no longer positioned as conflicting interests but as complementary dimensions.

In addition, *a climate-resilient training model* needs to be adopted by MET to prepare graduates for increasingly uncertain maritime conditions due to climate change. Adaptive competencies in dealing with storm risks, sea level rise, and global supply chain disruptions are vital skills that determine the future sustainability of the maritime sector. In other words, maritime education must be able to produce human resources who are not only skilled in operating ships and infrastructure, but also function as agents of change in promoting sustainability, green technology innovation, and international maritime diplomacy(Tscholl et al., 2024).

Therefore, MET in Indonesia and Southeast Asia has a greater responsibility, given that this region is the center of global maritime traffic as well as the area most vulnerable to the impacts of climate change. The maritime education reforms that emphasize *green literacy,* digital technology integration, and socio-ecological resilience will be key factors in strengthening the competitiveness of regional maritime labor in the global arena. Without a visionary and sustainability-oriented paradigm shift in education, the region's maritime

sector risks being unable to keep up with the rapidly accelerating global industrial transformation.

The green shipping industry in the contemporary era can no longer be understood merely as an effort to reduce carbon emissions, but rather as a structural transformation that includes changes in work culture, the formulation of progressive regulations, and fundamental reforms in the education system(Gaul & Rutkowski, 2025). Developed countries have responded relatively quickly by adopting low-carbon and alternative fuels *(green fuels)*, electrifying ships to reduce dependence on fossil fuels, and implementing smart navigation systems based on digitalization and artificial intelligence(Zhou et al., 2025). These innovations not only reduce the carbon footprint of the shipping sector but also create new standards in efficiency, safety, and sustainability of maritime operations.

In contrast, Southeast Asia, particularly Indonesia, as the world's largest archipelagic country, still faces significant gaps. These obstacles are evident in the high dependence on fossil fuels, weak enforcement of consistent environmental regulations, and limitations in accessing and implementing digital innovations in the shipping sector. The misalignment between national policies and international regulatory requirements set by the International Maritime Organization (IMO) further highlights the gap between the global vision and regional realities. This places Indonesia in a dilemma: on the one hand, it has enormous maritime potential, but on the other, it is at risk of being left behind in the global transition to clean energy and digitalization.

In this context, maritime education has a very strategic urgency. Curriculum reform in *Maritime Education and Training* (MET) institutions needs to be directed not only at mastering technical skills, but also at building ecological awareness, renewable energy literacy, and adaptive competencies in facing new regulations and technologies. Instilling values of sustainability from an early stage of education will strengthen the capacity of the next generation of maritime professionals to become not only ship operators but also agents of change in promoting green transformation in the shipping sector. Thus, maritime education must be seen as a key instrument in bridging the gap between global demands and local limitations, as well as a fundamental pillar towards a sustainable and inclusive maritime transition in Southeast Asia.

In the context of maritime industry transformation, the integration of environmental education is no longer an option, but an urgent necessity to shape a generation of seafarers and maritime professionals who are globally competitive. Maritime education that emphasizes environmental literacy not only equips students with technical knowledge but also instills ecological awareness and a sense of responsibility for marine sustainability. Thus, a curriculum designed based on environmental literacy and 21st-century skills—such as critical thinking, innovation, interdisciplinary collaboration, and digital literacy—will strengthen the adaptability of the maritime workforce in facing the complexities of climate change, geopolitical uncertainty, and the demands of global shipping industry decarbonization (Minh et al., 2025).

Furthermore, the orientation of maritime education towards sustainability contributes directly to the achievement of *the Sustainable Development Goals* (SDGs), particularly SDG 13 (*Climate Action*) and SDG 14 (*Life Below Water*). SDG 13 emphasizes the importance of concrete actions in mitigating climate change and adapting to its impacts, while SDG 14 stresses the urgency of conservation and sustainable use of marine resources(Minh et al., 2025)(Yang et al., 2025). Maritime education that systematically incorporates the dimension of sustainability into the curriculum will produce graduates who not only understand the theory but are also capable of implementing *green shipping practices* in the field.

By placing green shipping as *a core value* in maritime education, Southeast Asia—especially Indonesia has a strategic opportunity to strengthen its position as a center of world maritime trade as well as a pioneer in producing maritime workers with ecological character(Sagin et al., 2025). This is particularly relevant given Indonesia's geographical position on the most vital international shipping routes, such as the Malacca Strait and IASL (Indonesian Archipelagic Sea Lanes), which make it a key node in the global supply chain. Visionary maritime education reform will position Indonesia not only as a user of green technology but also as an active actor in building a more sustainable global maritime ecosystem.

Thus, the integration of environmental education into MET (Maritime Education and Training) can serve as a dual strategy: first, to enhance the competitiveness of Indonesian and Southeast Asian maritime workers in the global market; second, to ensure a tangible contribution to the transition towards a blue economy that is in line with the sustainable development agenda (Bace et al., 2025). If this strategy is implemented consistently, Indonesia will not only be recognized as the largest archipelagic country but also as a center of excellence in producing a maritime workforce that is resilient, adaptive, and ecologically minded to face the era of global energy transition.

GLOBAL AND REGIONAL CONTEXT

Globally, the International Maritime Organization (IMO) has established a greenhouse gas (GHG) emission reduction strategy as the main framework for promoting clean energy transition in the shipping sector. This strategy, which was revised in 2023, targets a reduction of at least 40% in emissions by 2030 and net-zero by 2050, compared to 2008 emission levels. This policy is an important milestone that affirms the international community's commitment to supporting the decarbonization agenda, while also posing a major challenge for IMO member countries to adjust domestic regulations, technological capacity, and human resource readiness.

Developed countries have responded to this strategy by making massive investments in the development and implementation of green fuel technologies such as ammonia, hydrogen, and new-generation biofuels, which are considered the most promising alternatives to conventional fossil fuels. In addition, the concept of electric shipping is beginning to be adopted through the use of battery-powered ships for short-distance voyages, especially in Scandinavia, which is known for its progressive application of renewable energy in the maritime transport sector. At the same time, the integration of automated navigation systems utilizing *Artificial Intelligence* (AI), *Internet of Things* (IoT), and *blockchain* technologies points to a new direction in operational efficiency and safety in shipping.

The rapid response of developed countries demonstrates a *first mover advantage* that not only strengthens their position in global trade but also in international environmental diplomacy. However, the IMO's strategy and its implementation in developed countries reveal a significant gap with developing countries, including those in Southeast Asia. Unequal access to green technology, high investment costs, and weak enforcement of environmental regulations are major obstacles for developing countries to keep pace with the ongoing transformation in developed countries.

However, in the Southeast Asian region, there is still a significant imbalance in access to green technology in the shipping sector. Most countries in the region, including Indonesia, still rely on conventional fossil fuel-powered ships with relatively high emission standards. This dependence not only increases the maritime sector's contribution to global carbon emissions but also exacerbates the risk of marine pollution and reduces the competitiveness of the regional shipping industry in the face of increasingly stringent international regulatory dynamics.

The main obstacles to accelerating the adoption of green technology include limited port infrastructure that supports the use of *green fuel*, a weak regulatory framework that is in line with IMO strategies, and a lack of fiscal incentive schemes and public investment to support energy transition in the shipping sector. In addition, the shortage of trained workers with environmental literacy and modern maritime technology skills further slows down this transformation process. This gap in human resource capacity reflects the need for fundamental reforms in the maritime education system, particularly through curriculum updates at *Maritime Education and Training* (MET) institutions.

These conditions give rise to multidimensional challenges. From an environmental perspective, the continued use of fossil fuels accelerates the degradation of marine ecosystems and exacerbates the impact of climate change in coastal areas. From a socio- economic perspective, the inability to adapt to global green standards has the potential to reduce export competitiveness, increase logistics costs, and suppress the potential for blue economic growth. Meanwhile, from an educational perspective, delays in integrating sustainability values and green technology into the curriculum will result in a widening *skills gap* between MET graduates in Southeast Asia and graduates from developed countries.

For Indonesia, challenges and strategic opportunities arise from its position as the world's largest archipelago with the second longest coastline after Canada. This geographical location makes Indonesia not only a center of marine biodiversity, but also an important hub in the international trade network connecting the Indian and Pacific Oceans. As a major hub for global shipping routes, Indonesia cannot escape the demands for maritime decarbonization being promoted by the international community through the IMO policy framework. This global pressure requires Indonesia to adjust its domestic policies to align with international sustainability standards, despite facing limitations in infrastructure, technology, and socio- economic disparities between regions.

Indonesia's geographical conditions and socio-economic realities mean that the adaptation of green technology requires a more contextual and inclusive approach. The application of modern innovations such as the use of *green fuel*, ship electrification, and the digitization of shipping systems is indeed a strategic agenda, but its effectiveness cannot be separated from the role of local wisdom. For example, traditional practices of coastal communities in utilizing marine resources sustainably, managing mangrove ecosystems, and traditional navigation systems can be combined with the latest technology to form an energy transition model that is more suited to the characteristics of the Indonesian archipelago. Thus, Indonesia's maritime transformation is not merely the adoption of technology from outside, but a process of hybridization between modernity and local traditions.

In the context of education, the integration of environmental education into the maritime curriculum is a vital instrument for strengthening the competitiveness of human resources while ensuring the sustainability of coastal ecosystems(Yoga & Kesumadiksa, 2022). The *Maritime Education and Training* (MET) institution in Indonesia has the opportunity to become a regional laboratory for the development of *climate-resilient training* models(Alavi-Borazjani et al., 2025)(Iwan et al., 2023). Through this approach, students are not only equipped with technical skills and an understanding of green technology, but also with ecological values and social awareness rooted in the maritime culture of the archipelago. This integration will produce graduates who are able to compete on the global stage, while also being sensitive to local socio-ecological sustainability(E. S. Sahabuddin et al., 2023).

This strategic position places Indonesia in a paradoxical situation: on the one hand, there is enormous pressure to adapt to the global decarbonization agenda; on the other hand, there is an opportunity to become a regional pioneer in developing a maritime education model that is not only adaptive but also distinctive. If managed properly, Indonesia can emerge as a center of sustainable maritime innovation in Southeast Asia—an experimental space where modernity and tradition converge to address the challenges of climate change while strengthening the national maritime identity.

THEORETICAL AND CONCEPTUAL FOUNDATIONS

1. Maritime Environmental Education

Environmental education essentially aims to internalize ecological knowledge, attitudes, skills, and actions into the mindset and behavior of students. In the maritime context, environmental education cannot be separated from the real challenges faced by the maritime sector, such as marine pollution caused by plastic waste and industrial waste, high carbon emissions from maritime transportation, coastal ecosystem degradation, and the urgency of

clean energy transition. Maritime environmental education serves as a strategic instrument to equip the younger generation with ecological awareness and technical competence in facing the complexities of climate change(Sar & Pujiastuti, 2023). This makes maritime education not just a process of transmitting navigation or ship operational skills, but also a means of transforming values that place ecological sustainability as the main foundation of sustainable maritime development.

Figure 1. Maritime Environmental Education

(photo: BBKSDA West Papua, https://bbksda-papuabarat.com/pendidikan-lingkungan-hidup-di-friwend-raja-ampat/)

Furthermore, maritime environmental education also plays a role in building critical awareness of the interconnection between human activities and the balance of marine ecosystems. Students are encouraged to understand that every decision in the maritime sector—from ship design, logistics distribution patterns, to sailing practices—has significant ecological consequences(Sumarmi et al., 2022). With this understanding, they can develop a holistic and systemic perspective in viewing marine issues, so that the solutions designed are not only technical but also oriented towards long-term sustainability.

In addition, environmental education in the maritime field strengthens the ecological identity of the younger generation by integrating (E. S. Sahabuddin et al., 2022) and traditional practices of coastal communities, such as Pinisi sailing or community-based mangrove management. This integration not only increases the relevance of learning but also enriches the cultural values that support sustainability. Thus, graduates of maritime education are expected to have triple capacity: technical skills, ecological sensitivity, and social responsibility.

2. Environmental Literacy And 21st Century Competencies

Environmental literacy in maritime education cannot be understood merely as the accumulation of factual knowledge about marine ecosystems and the impacts of pollution. Furthermore, this literacy requires critical thinking skills, scientific data-based decision making, and the courage to innovate in response to increasingly complex climate crises. Environmental literacy thus not only teaches students to recognize problems, but also trains them to formulate applicable and sustainable solutions.

The integration of environmental literacy with 21st century competencies will produce a maritime workforce that is not only technically reliable, but also has analytical capacity, strategic thinking, and sensitivity to global sustainability issues. This is important considering that the maritime industry is a sector that is closely connected to the dynamics of world trade, geopolitics, and ecology.

Figure 2. Children observe coral reefs while participating in environmental education in Kampung Awat,

Kofiau District, Raja Ampat Regency, West Papua
(photo: Hariandi Hafid, https://data.tempo.co/foto/detail/P2704201500191/kegiatan- pendidikan-lingkungan-hidup-di-kampung-awat-papua)

With this literacy, maritime human resources are no longer positioned merely as operational actors on ships or in ports, but also as agents of change who can drive green innovation, strengthen maritime ethics, and contribute to the achievement of the global agenda of the, such as the Sustainable Development Goals (SDGs), particularly SDG 13 (climate action) and SDG 14 (marine ecosystems).

3. Climate-Resilient Training Model

The climate-resilient training model is one of the important innovations in strengthening the adaptive capacity of maritime human resources amid global climate uncertainty. This model integrates a *simulation-based learning* approach to provide practical experience in dealing with climate change scenarios, *project-based learning* to foster creativity and innovation in solving real problems in the green shipping sector, and collaboration with industry to ensure the relevance of competencies to the needs of the job market. By implementing this training model, students will not only be technically prepared, but also resilient in facing climatic, social, and economic challenges(Zhu et al., 2025). This paves the way for the creation of a maritime education

ecosystem that is more responsive to global dynamics, while strengthening the position of Indonesia and Southeast Asia in the global maritime transformation map.

Furthermore, maritime environmental education cannot be understood solely as an academic instrument oriented towards knowledge transfer, but must be placed as an integral part of cultural transformation in educational institutions and the shipping industry. This education not only changes the way individuals think, but also serves as a catalyst that shapes norms, work ethics, and decision-making patterns in the maritime sector. With a transdisciplinary approach, maritime environmental education is able to bridge the connections between environmental science, maritime technology, public policy, and the local wisdom of coastal communities(García et al., 2023)(Wibowo et al., 2023). This kind of approach allows for a more holistic perspective in interpreting and solving complex problems at sea.

For example, issues such as marine pollution, coastal ecosystem degradation, and ship emissions cannot be understood reductionistically through a technical lens alone. These issues require interpretation within the framework of environmental ethics, social justice, and collective responsibility, so that their resolution involves both ecological and socio- economic dimensions. This shows that 21st-century *Maritime Education and Training* (MET) graduates need more than just operational skills to manage or operate ships.

In addition, the use of digital technology, such as climate simulation, *big data analytics*, and AI-based modeling, opens up opportunities for students to understand the impacts of climate change in a more realistic and in-depth manner. These skills not only foster sensitivity to ecological challenges but also strengthen innovative capacity in designing applicable environmentally friendly solutions in the shipping sector. With the integration of 21st- century competencies, environmental literacy serves as a booster for the global competitiveness of maritime human resources, so that graduates are not only technically superior but also able to adapt to technological disruption, changes in international regulations, and the demands of the transition to a sustainable blue economy.

Finally, the climate-resilient training model requires close collaboration between various strategic actors, including educational institutions, the shipping industry, coastal communities, and national and international regulators. This multi-stakeholder collaboration is not only intended as a form of formal synergy, but also as a substantive strategy to expand the scope and effectiveness of the maritime education process. Concrete implementation can be realized through field practice programs integrated with industry, internships at ports that apply green shipping principles, and digital technology-based climate crisis simulations that allow students to directly experience the complexity of emergency situations caused by climate change (Alavi-Borazjani et al., 2025)(Earsom, 2025).

This approach shifts the educational paradigm from classroom-based activities to contextual experiences in the field, where students can internalize technical skills and sustainability values in real-life situations. Furthermore, the involvement of coastal communities in the educational process provides an essential socio-cultural dimension, given that coastal communities are the most vulnerable to the impacts of climate change. Thus, the maritime human resources produced are not only equipped with the technical competencies to deal with climate uncertainty, but also have social sensitivity, ecological empathy, and high adaptive capacity. Ultimately, this model is expected to produce a maritime workforce that is resilient, inclusive, and ready to contribute to the transition to a sustainable blue economy.

Case Study and Local Wisdom: Bugis-Makassar Pinisi

The Pinisi ship of the Bugis-Makassar tribe is not only recognized as a world cultural heritage by UNESCO, but also represents a form of green sailing based on local wisdom that has existed long before the discourse on maritime decarbonization became a global agenda. Pinisi is not just a means of sea transportation, but a symbol of the maritime philosophy of the archipelago that emphasizes the integration of technical skills, cultural values, and ecological harmony. The ecological values inherent in the Pinisi are evident in the sustainability of the raw materials, which are selectively chosen wood, the use of wind power as a zero-emission propulsion system, and star-based navigation practices that reflect the integration of traditional knowledge with sensitivity to the universe.

Beyond technical aspects, the Pinisi also embodies maritime ethics passed down through generations by the Bugis-Makassar community. These ethics emphasize the importance of balancing the exploitation of marine resources with ecosystem preservation, while shaping the character of sailors to be disciplined, resilient, and sustainability-oriented. In the context of contemporary maritime education, Pinisi can be positioned as a cultural laboratory that demonstrates how local wisdom can offer a model of green sailing that is relevant to today's global challenges (Leirissa & Leirissa, 2000). Thus, integrating the ecological values of Pinisi into the *Maritime Education and Training* (MET) curriculum not only enriches Indonesia's maritime identity but also paves the way for the development of an alternative paradigm in the transition to a sustainable blue economy.

The local wisdom contained in the practice of building and operating Pinisi ships can be strategically integrated as a case study in the *Maritime Education and Training* (MET)

curriculum. Through this approach, students not only learn the technical aspects of sailing but also understand that sustainability can be achieved through traditions that have proven to survive across generations. Pinisi teaches the basic principles of sustainability, from the selection of raw materials that take into account the cycle of nature's regeneration, the use of wind energy as an environmentally friendly source of propulsion, to a star-based navigation system that emphasizes harmony between humans and the universe.

The integration of local wisdom broadens the horizons of maritime education, as students are invited to see the dialectical relationship between tradition and innovation. Thus, the sailing practices of the Bugis-Makassar people are not only understood as cultural heritage, but also as a source of ecological philosophy relevant to the global agenda of decarbonization and clean energy transition(Dunlop et al., 2022). When local wisdom is combined with modern technology, such as digital navigation or the use of green fuel, a comprehensive learning model is formed: rooted in tradition, but visionary towards the future(Nurabdiansyah & Nurabdiansyah, 2019). In this framework, the Bugis-Makassar people not only pass on sailing skills, but also an ecological ethos that is in line with the Sustainable Development Goals (SDGs), particularly those related to climate action (SDG 13) and life below water (SDG 14).

Figure 3. The Pinisi Ship from Bulukumba, South Sulawesi

(Photo: Putu Intan. https://www.detik.com/sulsel/budaya/d-6581846)

Model for Developing a Maritime Environmental Education Curriculum

The proposed curriculum model encompasses four dimensions:

1. Integration of Environmental Issues

The integration of environmental issues into the maritime curriculum is both an epistemological and pedagogical foundation for equipping students with a comprehensive ecological perspective. The curriculum cannot stop at the transfer of technical knowledge alone, but must place environmental issues as the main framework for reading,

understanding, and responding to the dynamics of the maritime sector. The modules developed cover at least three main clusters:

a. Marine Pollution, which includes an in-depth analysis of the impact of plastic waste, oil spills, and ship waste on marine ecosystems and human health. This topic emphasizes the link between shipping industry practices and global environmental degradation.
b. Clean Energy, which discusses the transition from fossil fuels to environmentally friendly alternatives such as *Liquefied Natural Gas (LNG)*, hydrogen, and solar and wind power innovations. This module can be supplemented with comparative studies of green technology implementation in developed countries and the challenges of its adoption in Southeast Asia.
c. Coastal Conservation, focusing on mangrove rehabilitation, coral reef preservation, and marine ecosystem management. Students are trained to understand the role of coastal ecosystems as a natural barrier against climate change and a pillar of the local economy.

As a contextual approach, the case study of the Pinisi ship from the Bugis-Makassar community can be used as a concrete representation of environmentally friendly sailing practices based on local wisdom. Pinisi not only reflects traditional innovations in the use of wind energy and sustainable raw materials, but also embodies an ecological philosophy that emphasizes harmony with nature. By integrating these aspects, students not only master theory but can also interpret and apply this knowledge to real challenges in the field, while understanding that maritime sustainability can stem from the intersection of local traditions and global innovation.

2. Innovative Learning Methods

An environmentally-conscious maritime curriculum requires not only relevant content, but also innovative and participatory learning methodologies. The traditional learning paradigm that emphasizes lectures and memorization is no longer adequate to address the complexity of environmental issues and the dynamics of the global maritime industry. Therefore, a pedagogical approach that is oriented towards experience, critical reflection, and active student involvement in the learning process is needed.

a. **Project-Based Learning (PjBL)** provides space for students to design and execute real projects directly related to maritime sustainability issues. Examples of implementation include creating prototypes of ship waste management systems, designing alternative energy systems for marine transportation, or developing data- driven coastal conservation plans. Through this approach, students learn to solve complex problems in a collaborative, creative, and solution-oriented manner.

b. **Simulation-Based Learning** allows students to interact with digital devices, simulators, and modeling technologies to visualize the impact of climate change on
c. navigation, sea conditions, and ship operations. Such simulations not only improve technical skills in dealing with emergency situations but also equip students with a systemic understanding of the interconnectedness between global climate phenomena and everyday shipping practices.
d. **Community-Based Learning** places students directly in coastal communities to learn about sustainability practices rooted in local wisdom. Activities may include assisting with mangrove forest management, documenting traditional techniques for preserving the ocean, or collaborating with communities to design community-based ecotourism. This approach strengthens the socio-cultural dimension of maritime education while fostering students' ecological empathy.

By integrating these three methods, the learning process is not only theoretical but also practical, reflective, and transformative. Students are encouraged to develop technical skills, analytical capacity, and socio-ecological sensitivity that complement each other, resulting in maritime graduates who are able to respond to environmental challenges while remaining globally competitive(Amir et al., 2023).

3. 21st Century Competencies

The environmentally-conscious maritime curriculum not only focuses on technical aspects but also on strengthening 21st-century competencies, which are a key prerequisite for facing the global maritime industry transformation(Yoga & Kesumadiksa, 2022). These competencies are multidimensional, encompassing cognitive, social, and technological skills that enable graduates to adapt to ecological and digital disruptions.

a. **Green Technology Literacy**: Students are trained to understand, evaluate, and utilize environmentally friendly technologies in shipping practices. Examples include the use of sensor-based ship emission monitoring systems, optimization of shipping routes with energy-efficient software, and the digitization of green ports. This literacy connects technical expertise with ecological awareness, so that students not only master the technology but also understand its sustainability implications.
b. **Creativity and Innovation**: Maritime graduates are required to come up with new solutions to increasingly complex environmental issues. This includes designing ships with higher energy efficiency, developing low-carbon operational protocols, or creating circular economy-based maritime business models. Creativity is positioned not merely as an additional skill, but as the core of global competitiveness.
c. **Adaptation to Climate Change**: This competency is vital given the increasing frequency of storms, extreme waves, and changes in ocean currents due to global warming. Students need to be equipped with the ability to read climate data, design risk mitigation scenarios, and integrate climate adaptation into maritime operations. Thus, graduates will be able to maintain the safety, sustainability, and efficiency of the shipping industry.
d. **Higher-Order Thinking Skills**: Critical thinking, problem solving, and data-based decision making must be at the core of the learning process. These skills enable students to assess environmental risks, analyze maritime policies, and formulate strategies for sustainable marine resource management.

e. **Collaboration and Global Awareness**: The maritime world is transnational, making cross-cultural, cross-linguistic, and cross-regulatory cooperation a necessity. Students need to be trained in collaborative learning with international partners, while also developing global awareness of marine sustainability issues, international maritime law, and the sustainable development agenda (SDGs).

By emphasizing these 21st-century competencies, the maritime curriculum not only produces graduates who are technically superior, but also visionary, adaptive, and globally competitive. They are positioned as agents of change who are able to connect technological innovation, environmental sustainability, and social justice in the maritime context(Karahalil et al., 2024).

4. Assessment and Evaluation

Assessment is a strategic instrument to ensure that environmentally-conscious maritime education produces graduates who are not only academically excellent but also possess practical skills and ecological integrity(Kolb, 1984). In the context of the maritime curriculum, evaluation should not be limited to traditional cognitive tests but should reflect holistic learning outcomes: knowledge, skills, and attitudes.

1. **Performance-Based Assessment**: Performance-based assessment places students in real or simulated situations to measure their applied skills. Forms include ship waste management projects, navigation simulations in extreme weather conditions, coastal conservation strategy presentations, and field practice reports. This model encourages students to integrate theory with practical experience, while honing their communication, collaboration, and leadership skills.
2. **Evaluation Indicators**:
    1) *Level of environmental literacy*: This indicator measures the extent to which students have a comprehensive understanding of maritime ecological issues. Environmental literacy is not only understood as mastery of basic information, but encompasses three main dimensions. First, factual knowledge, which is students' understanding of data, terminology, and real phenomena related to marine pollution, ship emissions, or coastal ecosystem damage. Second, conceptual knowledge, which is the ability to connect various environmental concepts with the maritime context, such as the relationship between shipping activities and global climate change or the relationship between mangrove ecosystem sustainability and coastal resilience. Third, procedural knowledge, which is the mastery of practical steps in identifying, analyzing, and designing solutions to maritime environmental problems, such as coastal ecosystem rehabilitation techniques or ship emission monitoring methods.
    2) *Climate adaptation skills*: This indicator assesses students' capacity to respond to the dynamics of climate change that increasingly affect the global shipping sector. Climate adaptation skills cover three main aspects. First, climate risk data analysis skills, namely the ability to process and interpret information related to sea conditions, extreme weather patterns, sea level rise, and long-term climate phenomena that directly impact shipping routes and maritime safety. Second, the formulation of mitigation strategies, which is the skill of developing preventive measures, such as implementing energy efficiency, diversifying ship energy sources, and environmentally friendly operational designs to reduce vulnerability to climate risks. Third, the design of contingency scenarios, which includes the preparation of emergency protocols and alternative plans

in the event of a crisis, such as tropical storms, high waves, or supply chain disruptions due to climate change.

3) *Maritime ethics*: This indicator serves to assess students' affective and moral dimensions in internalizing sustainability values into maritime practices. Maritime ethics includes three main components. First, ecological awareness, which is students' awareness of the importance of maintaining the balance of marine ecosystems through a proactive attitude in preventing pollution, reducing emissions, and supporting environmentally friendly shipping practices. Second, social responsibility, which emphasizes the moral commitment of maritime workers to the welfare of coastal communities, including involvement in empowerment programs, environmental education, or climate disaster mitigation. Third, commitment to preserving the sea, which is a long-term understanding that the sea is not only an economic space but also an ecological and cultural heritage that must be preserved for future generations.. The evaluation of maritime ethics is carried out through a multi-method approach, such as observing attitudes in academic activities and field practices, written self-reflections that assess the depth of students' ecological awareness, and direct involvement in community-based programs such as mangrove rehabilitation, coral reef conservation, or campaigns to reduce plastic waste in the sea. Thus, the ethical aspect is not treated as an addition, but as an integral dimension that affirms the role of MET students as agents of change with ecological character in the global maritime world.

3. **Multidimensional Approach**: The green maritime curriculum evaluation system must be designed with a multidimensional approach that integrates various assessment instruments to measure students' knowledge, skills, and attitudes in a balanced manner. This can be achieved through a combination of formative assessment and summative assessment. Formative assessment provides continuous feedback during the learning process, for example, through class discussions, reflection journals, project progress reports, or field observations(E. Sahabuddin et al., 2019).

   issues. Through this combination, students are not only measured based on final results, but are also systematically guided to improve their capacity throughout the educational process. Thus, this multidimensional approach ensures that MET graduates have deep environmental literacy, applicable climate adaptation skills, and maritime ethics embedded in their professional practices.

4. **Integrative Assessment**: Assessments not only evaluate students' conceptual understanding of maritime ecological issues, but also the extent to which they are able to connect environmental literacy with 21st-century skills. This includes the use of digital technology in modeling the impact of climate change on the shipping sector, the use of data analytics to formulate mitigation strategies, and the application of cross-disciplinary collaboration in solving real-world case studies. In addition, student creativity can be measured through the design of sustainability solutions, such as environmentally friendly ship design innovations, IoT-based waste management systems, or strategies for educating coastal communities about marine conservation. Thus, assessment serves not only as an evaluation tool, but also as a mechanism to stimulate critical thinking, creativity, collaboration, and digital literacy in the context of green maritime.

Figure 4. Four Dimensions of Green Maritime Curriculum

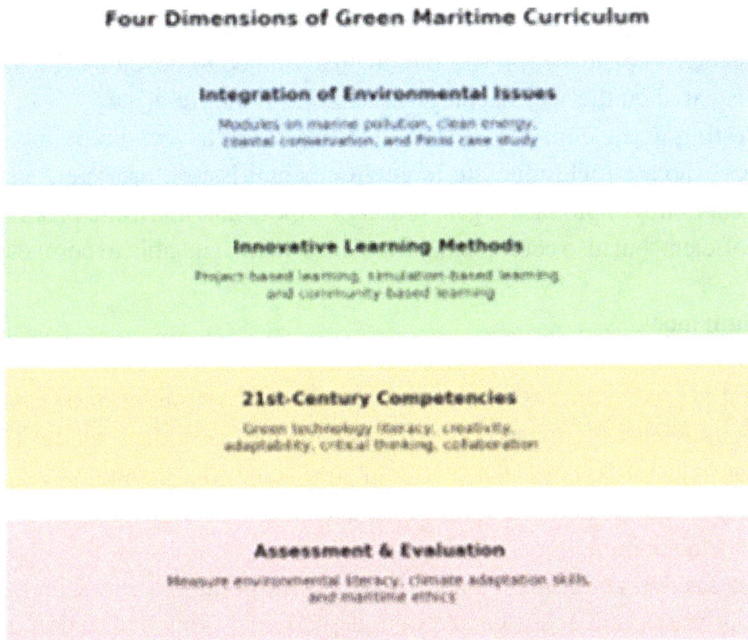

Climate-Resilient Training Model Roadmap

1. Short Term (1–3 years)

The main focus at this stage is to build a strong foundation at the educational institution level.

a. Strengthening the Capacity of MET Lecturers

The main focus at the institutional level is to strengthen the capacity of lecturers and instructors as key actors in the maritime education transformation process. MET lecturers can no longer merely play the role of technical instructors, but must also function as facilitators of contextual learning, researchers, and agents of change in facing the challenges

of climate crisis and green energy transition. Therefore, **intensive training** programs need to be designed to equip educators with a deep understanding of global climate change issues, the latest green technologies (such as the use of *green fuel,* port digitalization, and *smart navigation systems)*, as well as innovative pedagogy methods based on *student-centered learning.*

This training can be carried out through a **sustainable capacity-building** approach, such as thematic workshops, *training of trainers* (ToT), international professional certification, and research collaboration with the green shipping industry and maritime research institutions. In this way, MET lecturers will not only master academic material, but also be able to integrate the latest research results and industry practices into the classroom(Jugović et al., 2025).

In addition, strengthening the capacity of lecturers must include **pedagogical and transdisciplinary** dimensions. This means that lecturers need to have the competence to connect marine science, maritime technology, public policy, and local wisdom into a single, comprehensive learning framework. Thus, students not only receive knowledge transfer but are also trained to develop critical understanding and innovative solutions based on the socio-ecological realities in the field.

Ultimately, **investing in the capacity of MET lecturers** will have a direct impact on the quality of graduates. Lecturers who are highly literate in environmental issues, proficient in digital technology, and adaptive to disruption will produce a generation of sailors and maritime professionals who are not only technically proficient, but also ecologically minded, critical, and able to compete at the global level.

b. Green curriculum modules

The development of green curriculum modules is a strategic step to ensure that the maritime learning process is directly relevant to global ecological challenges and local needs. These modules must be designed with an integrative approach that combines scientific, technological, social, and ethical aspects, so as to produce graduates who not only understand the technical dynamics of sailing but are also committed to sustainability.

The module content covers three main pillars. First, marine pollution, which includes issues of plastic waste, oil spills, ship waste, and coastal ecosystem degradation. This material is important for fostering students' critical awareness of the impact of maritime activities on the environment. Second, clean energy, with a focus on the transition from fossil fuels to environmentally friendly technologies such as LNG, hydrogen, biofuels, and the integration of solar and wind energy in ship propulsion systems. Third, maritime ethics, which emphasizes social responsibility, environmental justice, and a philosophy of sustainability based on local wisdom, including a case study of Pinisi ships as a traditional green shipping practice.

For this module to be effective, its design must follow international standards set by the International Maritime Organization (IMO) and Standards of Training, Certification, and Watchkeeping (STCW), while still considering the local context of Indonesia and Southeast

Asia. This allows students to master global competencies while understanding the ecological, cultural, and socio-economic dynamics of the region. Thus, the green curriculum not only functions as an academic tool but also as an instrument of transformation towards a sustainable blue economy.

c. Pinisi Pilot Project

One innovative approach in developing a green curriculum is to use the local wisdom of Bugis-Makassar as a source of contextual learning and inspiration for sustainable maritime ethics. The case study of Pinisi shipbuilding can be positioned as a concrete representation of traditional environmentally friendly sailing practices. The ecological values embodied in Pinisi—from the selection of sustainable raw materials, the use of wind as a source of energy (zero-emission shipping), to star-based navigation—can be used as learning materials that integrate technical, cultural, and environmental ethical aspects.

In practice, the Pinisi can serve as a model for transdisciplinary learning. Students not only learn shipbuilding techniques from a maritime architecture perspective, but are also invited to understand the ecological philosophy behind it. This integration enriches the learning dimension by connecting marine science, engineering technology, anthropology, and environmental ethics. Thus, maritime education is not stuck in a purely technical dimension, but develops into a vehicle for shaping ecological awareness rooted in local identity(Karahalil et al., 2024).

In addition, the implementation of a Pinisi-based pilot project can be a means of testing the effectiveness of the green curriculum on a small scale before it is adopted more widely. This pilot involves collaboration between educational institutions, traditional boat builders, coastal communities, and regulators(Souppez & Awotwe, 2023). Through this multi-stakeholder collaboration, students gain hands-on learning experiences that are both practical and reflective, while educational institutions can evaluate the feasibility, challenges, and opportunities of implementing green curricula at the national level.

By using Pinisi as a practical learning model, Indonesia not only preserves its world maritime cultural heritage, but also solidifies its position as a pioneer in synergizing local wisdom and modern innovation to support the transition to a sustainable blue economy.

2. Medium Term (4–7 years)

This phase focuses on strengthening networks and standardizing workforce competencies.

- **Green industry partnerships**

Strategic partnerships with industry are an important pillar in strengthening the implementation of sustainable maritime education. Maritime education institutions cannot stand alone in preparing human resources relevant to the needs of the global job market, especially amid the transition to green shipping. Therefore, close collaboration is needed between educational institutions and shipping companies, ports, *shipyards*, and other supporting sectors committed to sustainable practices.

This partnership can be realized through several mechanisms. First, internship programs at green shipping companies or international standard ports, which allow students to experience firsthand the application of low-emission technologies, ship waste management systems, and port operation digitalization. Second, collaborative research, where students and lecturers work together with industry to develop innovations, such as energy-efficient ship design, the use of *green fuel,* or digital technology applications for emissions monitoring. Third, joint field training provides opportunities for students to interact with professionals while understanding the operational dynamics of the industry in the context of sustainability.

- ***Green skills* certification**

The paradigm shift towards green shipping requires the presence of a certification mechanism that can guarantee the quality and competitiveness of the maritime workforce at the global level. An environmentally friendly competency certification system is needed to recognize specific skills relevant to energy transition and marine sustainability. This certification serves not only as an administrative document but also as a tool for professional legitimacy that equates graduate competencies with international standards, particularly *International Maritime Organization* (IMO) regulations and *Standards of Training, Certification, and Watchkeeping* (STCW) requirements.

The areas of skills that can be certified include:

1. Emissions Management

This skill focuses on the ability of maritime workers to monitor, analyze, and control greenhouse gas emissions generated by shipping activities. This competency includes the use of digital-based emission monitoring devices, interpretation of ship operational data, and the development of mitigation strategies in line with the IMO (International Maritime

Organization) decarbonization targets. With certification in this field, maritime human resources are expected to be able to support the achievement *of net-zero shipping*, which is a global agenda.

2. Ship Energy Efficiency

The main focus of this skill is mastery of technical and managerial standards related to improving energy efficiency on ships. Important aspects include understanding the Energy Efficiency Design Index (EEDI) for new ships, implementing the Ship Energy Efficiency Management Plan (SEEMP) for operating ships, and the ability to innovate in the use of fuel-efficient technologies. Certification in this field will produce a workforce that not only understands international regulations but is also capable of implementing practical solutions to reduce operational costs and carbon footprints.

3. Maritime Waste Management

This competency relates to the skills of preventing, managing, and minimizing marine pollution caused by shipping activities. Its scope includes the treatment of liquid, solid, and oil residues on ships, the application of modern *waste treatment* technologies, and compliance with international standards such as the Ballast Water Management Convention. With this certification, maritime human resources are ensured to not only have technical capacity but also ecological awareness to maintain the health of marine ecosystems as an integral part of a sustainable blue economy.

The certification can be designed based on practical competency tests, involving *simulator training*, field practice, and industry case studies. Collaboration with shipping companies, ports, and international certification bodies is key to ensuring that the certification is recognized globally.

- **Integration of national policies**

For the implementation of green curricula in maritime education to have a sustainable impact, strong regulatory support at the national level is required. The results of implementing this curriculum need to be mainstreamed into maritime higher education standards and cross-ministerial policies, particularly those of the Ministry of Transportation, the Ministry of Education, and the Ministry of Environment and Forestry. Integration into the national regulatory framework will provide formal legitimacy, so that

the green curriculum functions not only as a local or experimental initiative, but also as part of state policy in preparing maritime human resources that are adaptive to the climate crisis.

Regulations can take the form of ministerial regulations or graduate competency standards that require mastery of environmentally friendly skills, such as emissions management, energy efficiency, and coastal ecosystem conservation. In addition, this policy can also regulate incentives for educational institutions that successfully implement green training models, for example through funding support, special accreditation, or access to international research networks.

With formal legitimacy, green curriculum-based training models are guaranteed sustainability, as they become part of the national development agenda, in line with Indonesia's commitment to the Sustainable

Development Goals (SDGs) and the IMO's maritime sector decarbonization targets. This also ensures that the transformation of maritime education does not stop at the pilot program level, but is institutionalized as a new standard in the formation of a resilient, green, and globally competitive maritime workforce.

Long Term (8–15 years)

This phase focuses on expanding the impact and replicating environmentally-friendly maritime education models at the international level. The long-term orientation ensures that the green curriculum transformation does not stop at the national level, but becomes part of a global education architecture that supports sustainable maritime transition.

a. ASEAN regional adoption

The first step in international expansion is to initiate cooperation among ASEAN member countries to harmonize green maritime education and training standards. This harmonization is important because each country has different geographical conditions, infrastructure capacities, and regulations, requiring a common framework to reduce gaps between countries. The harmonization process can be facilitated through existing mechanisms, such as the ASEAN Maritime Forum, or through the establishment of a green maritime education consortium focused on research, knowledge exchange, and regional curriculum development.

This collaboration would not only include the exchange of lecturers and students but also the integration of joint research on low-emission ship technology, coastal conservation practices, and port energy management systems. In addition, the development of regional competency certification will strengthen the mobility of ASEAN maritime workers in the global market, while ensuring uniform standards related to environmental literacy and climate adaptation skills.

b. Center of excellence for *green maritime education*

In the long term, the establishment of an international research and training center is a crucial step in strengthening the region's capacity to face global maritime transformation. This center functions not only as an educational institution but also as the main reference for the development of sustainable maritime human resources that integrate the dimensions of technology, the environment, and public policy. Strategically, this center of excellence can perform three main roles. First, as an innovation laboratory, this center will serve as a testing ground for green technologies, ranging from the development of alternative fuel ships (LNG, hydrogen, biofuel) to the application of green port digitization systems that support logistics efficiency and emission reduction. Second, as an international curriculum development center, this institution can produce adaptive, environmentally-based maritime education modules that keep pace with global technological developments while remaining relevant to local needs, enabling adoption by various maritime education institutions worldwide. Third, as a regional certification center, its existence ensures the establishment of cross-border competency standards for green maritime workers, while enhancing the mobility and competitiveness of graduates in the international job market.

Furthermore, the existence of this center of excellence will provide strategic value for Indonesia and ASEAN. In addition to enhancing the region's reputation on the global stage, this center can also strengthen Southeast Asia's position as a global hub for green maritime education and innovation. Thus,

ASEAN will not only be a recipient of technology from developed countries, but also a producer of ideas, curriculum models, and green technology innovations that can be replicated in the Global South. This is in line with the mandate of the International Maritime Organization (IMO) and regional commitments to achieving the Sustainable Development Goals (SDGs), particularly SDG 13 (Climate Action) and SDG 14 (Life Below Water).

c. Replication in the Global South

The final stage of the long-term strategy is to replicate the climate-resilient training model to developing countries in Africa, the Pacific, and Latin America. This replication is important because it reinforces the position of Global South countries not merely as recipients of technology transfer from the Global North, but also as producers of knowledge, innovation, and sustainable maritime education models. Thus, the experience of Indonesia–ASEAN can serve as a concrete example of how local wisdom, modern technology, and public policy can be integrated into an educational framework that is relevant to global climate challenges(Bokau, 2020).

The replication process can be carried out through South-South Cooperation mechanisms that emphasize equality and solidarity among developing countries. To strengthen its legitimacy and scalability, this cooperation needs to involve the support of international institutions, such as the International Maritime Organization (IMO) in the development of global standards, UNESCO–UNEVOC in curriculum and institutional capacity development, and UNDP in financing and advocacy for sustainable development. With this multi-stakeholder involvement, the Indonesia–ASEAN model can be institutionalized as a global best practice, which not only prepares a resilient maritime workforce that is adaptive to climate change, but also upholds the principles of environmental justice and social inclusiveness in international maritime governance.

CONCLUSION

The main conclusion that can be drawn from the above description is that the integration of green shipping, environmental education, and climate-resilient training models that combine global innovation with local wisdom such as the Pinisi heritage is a comprehensive strategy in building a resilient, adaptive, and internationally competitive 21st-century maritime workforce. This approach emphasizes that the development of maritime human resources is no longer sufficient to focus solely on technical and operational aspects, but must also address comprehensive ecological, social, and ethical dimensions.

By making maritime education a venue for cultural transformation, MET graduates are positioned not only as ship operators but also as agents of change who bring sustainability values to their daily work practices. Furthermore, this strategy contributes directly to the achievement of the Sustainable Development Goals (SDG 13: Climate Action and SDG 14: Life Below Water) through emission reduction, marine ecosystem conservation, and strengthening the resilience of coastal communities. This is where the urgency of green maritime education lies, namely in producing a generation of sailors and marine managers who not only master technology but are also committed to preserving marine ecology.

Additionally, this initiative has strategic implications for Indonesia and Southeast Asia's position in the global maritime map. By adopting an approach that combines modernity and tradition, this region has the potential to become not only a global maritime trade route but also a center of excellence for sustainable maritime affairs that can offer models of education, technology, and environmentally friendly governance to other countries, especially in the Global South. Replicating the Indonesia–ASEAN model in Africa, the Pacific, and Latin America confirms that developing countries are not merely recipients of technology but also producers of knowledge and innovation in sustainable maritime education.

Thus, this integration project is not only a response to climate challenges but also a statement of regional identity and leadership in the transition to a global blue economy.

REFERENCES

Alavi-Borazjani, S. A., Adeel, S., Chkoniya, V., & Tarelho, L. A. C. (2025). Sustainability-Oriented Port Management: Biomass Gasification as a Strategic Tool for Green and Circular Maritime Logistics. *Sustainability (Basel), 17*(6), 1–32. DOI: 10.3390/su17062634

Amir, A., Akhmad, A., Abidin, Z., Bunyamin, B., Ansaar, A., & Suryaningsi, T. (2023). Model of Raw Material Inventory Control for Pinisi Shipbuilding in Bulukumba Regency, Indonesia. *European Journal of Business and Management Research.* DOI: 10.24018/ejbmr.2023.8.4.2074

Bace, E., Singh, S., & Gottschalk, S. (2025). Green Financing for Shipping Industry: Results of a Marine Professionals' Survey. *Journal of Environment and Earth Science, 7*(3), 306–315. DOI: 10.30564/jees.v7i3.7733

Bokau, J. R. K. (2020). *The Improvement of Local Shipping Safety in Makassar.* DOI: 10.48192/prc.v1i4.330

Dunlop, L., Dunlop, L., Rushton, E. A. C., Rushton, E. A. C., Atkinson, L., Atkinson, L., Ayre, J., Ayre, J., Bullivant, A., Bullivant, A., Essex, J., Essex, J., Price, L., Price, L., Smith, A. L., Smith, A., Summer, M., Summer, M., Stubbs, J., & Wood, L. (2022). Teacher and youth priorities for education for environmental sustainability: A co-created manifesto. *British Educational Research Journal, 48*(5), 952–973. Advance online publication. DOI: 10.1002/berj.3803

Earsom, J. (2025). Making waves or ripples? The influence of the European Green Deal on the revised IMO GHG strategy. *International Environmental Agreement: Politics, Law and Economics, 25*(2), 231–246. DOI: 10.1007/s10784-024-09661-x

García, M. A., Farías, E. B., & Mendoza, Y. F. (2023). Environmental Education Based on the Analysis of the Social Recovery Mechanisms Implemented Post-Covid. *Revista de Gestao Social e Ambiental, 17*(3), 24857. DOI: 10.24857/rgsa.v17n3-004

Gaul, K., & Rutkowski, G. (2025). Harnessing the Wind: The Rise of Wind-Assisted Ship Propulsion (WASP) in the Transformation of Maritime Transport. *TransNav, 19*(1), 217–225. DOI: 10.12716/1001.19.01.25

Iwan, S. (2023). Environmental Care Attitude Analysis of Prospective Biology Teachers. *Egitim ve Ögretim, 13*(2), 72–78. DOI: 10.47750/pegegog.13.02.09

Jugović, A., Sirotić, M., Jugović, T. P., & Žgaljić, D. (2025). Green Shipping Corridors: A Bibliometric Analysis of Policy, Technology, and Stakeholder Collaboration. *Applied Sciences (Basel, Switzerland), 15*(6), 3304. Advance online publication. DOI: 10.3390/app15063304

Karahalil, M., Lützhöft, M., & Scanlan, J. (2024). Factors impacting curricula in maritime simulator-based education. *WMU Journal of Maritime Affairs, 1.* Advance online publication. DOI: 10.1007/s13437-024-00351-8

Kolb, D. A. (1984). *Experiential learning: Experience as the source of learning and development.* Prentice-Hall.

Leirissa, R. Z., & Leirissa, R. Z. (2000). *The Bugis-Makassarese in the port towns; Ambon and Ternate through the nineteenth century*. DOI: 10.1163/22134379-90003842

Minh, T. T. N., Hoang, H. T. H., Nam, H. S., Alamoush, A. S., & Duong, P. A. (2025). Revisiting Port Decarbonization for Advancing a Sustainable Maritime Industry: Insights from Bibliometric Review. *Sustainability (Basel)*, *17*(10), 4302. Advance online publication. DOI: 10.3390/su17104302

Nurabdiansyah, & Nurabdiansyah. (2019). Semiotic Studies of The Menara Pinisi Symbolization in Visual Identity. *Proceedings of the 1st International Conference on Advanced Multidisciplinary Research (ICAMR 2018)*. DOI: 10.2991/icamr-18.2019.127

Sagin, S., Haichenia, O., Karianskyi, S., Kuropyatnyk, O., Razinkin, R., Sagin, A., & Volkov, O. (2025). Improving Green Shipping by Using Alternative Fuels in Ship Diesel Engines. *Journal of Marine Science and Engineering*, *13*(3), 589. Advance online publication. DOI: 10.3390/jmse13030589

Sahabuddin, E., Irfan, M., & Makkasau, A. (2019). The Knowledge Of Pollution And Preservation In Relation With Environmental Care Attitude In State University Of Makassar. *Proceedings of the Proceedings of the 1st International Conference of Science and Technology in Elementary Education, IC-STEE 2019*, 14 September, Makassar, South Sulawesi, Indonesia. DOI: 10.4108/eai.14-9-2019.2290029

Sahabuddin, E. S., Liskawati, L., & Syamsiah, S. (2023). Teaching Science Through Demonstrations: An Innovative Approach To Improve Students' Environmental Science Literacy. *Klasikasl Journal. Journal Of Education Lenguage Teaching and Science*, *5*(1), 138–147. DOI: 10.52208/klasikal.v5i1.624

Sahabuddin, E. S., & Makkasau, A. (2024). Utilization of virtual reality as a learning tool to increase students' pro-environmental behavior at universities: A maximum likelihood estimation approach. *Eurasia Journal of Mathematics, Science and Technology Education*, *20*(12), em2540. Advance online publication. DOI: 10.29333/ejmste/15654

Sahabuddin, E. S., Syawaluddin, A., & Nurzakinah, S. (2022). Pengembangan Media PAKEM The Box Of Pinisi Dalam 4 Pilar Budaya Bugis-Makassar (Sipakatau, Sipakainge', Sipakalebbi, Dan Sipatokkong) Sebagai Pemberdayaan Karakter Siswa Sekolah Dasar. *Publikasi Pendidikan*, *12*(2), 172. DOI: 10.26858/publikan.v12i2.34333

Sar, R. W., & Pujiastuti, P. (2023). Social studies learning modules to improve concept understanding and attitude of the environmental care. *Journal of Education and Learning*, *17*(1), 127–135. DOI: 10.11591/edulearn.v17i1.20690

Souppez, J. B. R. G., & Awotwe, T. W. (2023). the Conceive Design Implement Operate (Cdio) Initiative - an Engineering Pedagogy Applied To the Education of Maritime Engineers. *International Journal of Maritime Engineering*, *164*(4), 405–413. DOI: 10.5750/ijme.v164iA4.1187

Sumarmi, W. (2022). The Effect of Environmental Volunteer Integrated with Service Learning (EV_SL) to Improve Student's Environment Care Attitudes and Soft Skills. *Egitim ve Ögretim*, *12*(1), 168–176. DOI: 10.47750/pegegog.12.01.16

Tscholl, S., Candiago, S., Marsoner, T., Fraga, H., Giupponi, C., & Egarter Vigl, L. (2024). Climate resilience of European wine regions. *Nature Communications*, *15*(1), 1–12. DOI: 10.1038/s41467-024-50549-w PMID: 39048582

Wibowo, N. A., Sumarmi, S., Utaya, S., Bachri, S., & Kodama, Y. (2023). Students' Environmental Care Attitude: A Study at Adiwiyata Public High School Based on the New Ecological Paradigm (NEP). *Sustainability (Basel)*, *15*(11), 8651. Advance online publication. DOI: 10.3390/su15118651

Yang, L., Chen, D., Chen, Y., & Zhang, Z. (2025). Analyzing the Impact of Government Subsidies on Carbon Emission Mitigation Considering Carriers' Price-and-Service Competition and Green Shippers. *Systems*, *13*(4), 1–21. DOI: 10.3390/systems13040249

Yoga, I. K. D. P., & Kesumadiksa, K. (2022). Maritime Law Subject in Indonesian Law Faculty Curriculum: Supporting Indonesia's Maritime Industry Development. *Media Iuris*, *5*(1), 67–90. DOI: 10.20473/mi.v5i1SpecialIssue.38322

Zhou, D., Yang, Y., & Cai, R. (2025). Dynamic Optimization of Tramp Ship Routes for Carbon Intensity Compliance and Operational Efficiency. *Sustainability (Basel)*, *17*(5), 2280. Advance online publication. DOI: 10.3390/su17052280

Zhu, L., Zhou, R., Li, X., Lu, S., & Liu, J. (2025). Research on the Optimization of Collaborative Decision Making in Shipping Green Fuel Supply Chains Based on Evolutionary Game Theory. *Sustainability (Basel)*, *17*(11), 1–25. DOI: 10.3390/su17115186

Chapter 16
Educating for the Blue Economy:
Integrating Economic Literacy Into Maritime Education

Andi Annisa Sulolipu
http://orcid.org/0009-0007-8212-577X
Universitas Negeri Makassar, Indonesia

Vivit Rosmayanti
http://orcid.org/0000-0002-3648-9878
Universitas Negeri Makassar, Indonesia

St. Wijdanah Ram
http://orcid.org/0009-0005-1890-5355
Universitas Negeri Makassar, Indonesia

Andi Tenri Ampa
Universitas Negeri Makassar, Indonesia

Yati Yati
Universitas Terbuka, Indonesia

Andi Tonra Lipu
Universitas Negeri Makassar, Indonesia

ABSTRACT

This chapter explores the integration of economic literacy into maritime education as essential for developing professionals in the Blue Economy. It highlights the need for maritime education systems to balance technical skills with knowledge in economics, sustainability, and environmental policy. By focusing on cost-benefit analysis, resource efficiency, and long-term economic impacts, the chapter advocates for curriculum reforms that align with global sustainability goals, such as the UN SDGs. It suggests teaching methods like project-based learning, digital tools, and cross-sector partnerships to enhance economic competency, ultimately preparing students for leadership in a sustainable ocean economy.

1. INTRODUCTION

One of the most pressing challenges in maritime education is the mismatch between technical competencies and the broader economic and sustainability demands of the Blue Economy. While maritime professionals are highly trained in operational skills, they often lack the economic reasoning needed to evaluate trade-offs, optimize resources, and respond to global market and environmental pressures. Despite the increasing focus on the Blue Economy and maritime sustainability, current research predominantly addresses these areas separately, with minimal incorporation into organised educational systems. Specifi-

DOI: 10.4018/979-8-3373-6670-8.ch016

cally, there is an absence of definitive models that implement economic literacy in maritime education in a quantitative, competency-oriented manner that aligns with industry and sustainability requirements. This chapter proposes an integrative framework for incorporating economic literacy into maritime education, which includes (1) competency-based curriculum design, (2) Teaching and Learning Approaches, and (3) Assessment and Competency Development. Consequently, the chapter transcends theoretical discourse and offers practical suggestions for curriculum developers, educators, and policymakers.

1.1 Background of the Study

1.1.1 The emergence of the *Blue Economy* as a sustainable economic model emphasizing the responsible use of ocean resources for growth, employment, and environmental health.

The Blue Economy is a dynamic and revolutionary strategy for economic growth, emphasizing the sustainable utilization of ocean resources to foster development while preserving ecological equilibrium. The global world confronts escalating environmental issues, including climate change and resource depletion, necessitating a paradigm that harmonizes economic expansion with environmental sustainability. The Blue Economy provides a means to attain this equilibrium by harnessing the extensive potential of the world's oceans to generate economic value while safeguarding the enduring health of marine ecosystems (Geng et al., 2024).

The Blue Economy fundamentally promotes the sustainable utilization of ocean resources, encompassing fisheries, aquaculture, maritime transportation, renewable ocean energy, and coastal tourism. These sectors substantially impact the global economy, generating millions of employment possibilities and economic prospects, particularly in coastal and island regions. Nonetheless, absent effective management and regard for environmental constraints, the excessive exploitation of marine resources may result in irreparable harm to marine ecosystems, jeopardizing the long-term viability of these enterprises (Elegbede et al., 2023).

In this sense, the Blue Economy encompasses not merely the extraction of resources, but the sustainable utilization of these resources to safeguard the integrity of marine ecosystems for future generations. This encompasses initiatives to mitigate pollution, preserve marine biodiversity, and save essential ocean habitats. The Blue Economy concept aligns with the United Nations Sustainable Development Goals (SDGs), specifically SDG 14, which underscores the conservation and sustainable utilization of oceans, seas, and marine resources (Gouvea & Gutierrez, 2023).

The integration of economic literacy into maritime education is essential for realizing the goals of the Blue Economy. As marine sectors develop and grow, there is a rising demand for experts who comprehend the intricacies of the economic and environmental difficulties confronting ocean industries. Integrating economic principles into maritime education can better prepare future professionals to make educated decisions that reconcile economic growth with the sustainable utilization of ocean resources. This strategy guarantees the sustainability of oceanic industry while also advancing worldwide initiatives aimed at fostering sustainable development and safeguarding marine environments for future generations (Marwa et al., 2024).

1.1.2 The maritime sector's vital role in global trade, logistics, fisheries, energy, and tourism.

The marine sector is essential to the global economy, underpinning international trade, logistics, fisheries, energy, and tourism. It enables the transportation of products and services across extensive distances, with over 80% of global trade by volume and more than 70% by value being conveyed via maritime routes. Maritime trade serves as a fundamental pillar of global supply chains, linking producers and consumers across continents. Ports, shipping lines, and container terminals provide essential infrastructure for international trade, facilitating the interchange of goods from raw materials to finished products (Gurning et al., 2022).

The maritime sector is crucial in logistics for the effective transportation of bulk commodities, including oil, coal, grain, and other natural resources vital to global industrial operations. Shipping routes, such as the Suez Canal and the Strait of Malacca, are crucial chokepoints facilitating the seamless transit of goods and energy resources among major world economies (Haralambides, 2024; Pham et al., 2023).

The maritime industry plays a vital role in fisheries. The global fishing sector is strongly dependent on marine resources, supplying sustenance and employment for millions. Fisheries play a crucial role in global food security, as the seas provide a substantial share of the world's protein requirements. The sustainable management of marine ecosystems and fisheries is crucial for maintaining their support of local economies and the global food supply (Pham et al., 2023). In the energy sector, maritime transportation is essential for the conveyance of crude oil, liquefied natural gas (LNG), and renewable ocean energy resources. Oil tankers and LNG carriers convey energy resources to global markets, while offshore oil and gas platforms use marine resources to satisfy the world's energy requirements. Maritime tourism serves as a significant economic catalyst, with millions of tourists utilizing cruise ships and visiting coastal areas, so bolstering the economies of coastal regions and island nations (Sardá et al., 2022; Setiawan, 2023). Consequently, the maritime sector is critical for the efficient operation of global trade and economic advancement, connecting businesses and nations while delivering vital services across several sectors (van Leeuwen et al., 2024; Yagci & Noordali, 2024).

1.1.3 Connecting maritime education with global economic, environmental, and social sustainability goals (SDGs 4, 8, 13, and 14).

Maritime education is essential for promoting the United Nations' Sustainable Development Goals (SDGs), specifically SDGs 4, 8, 13, and 14, by providing future professionals with the requisite skills and knowledge to tackle the interrelated issues of economic development, environmental conservation, and social equity. By incorporating these sustainability objectives into maritime curricula, educational institutions may cultivate a new generation of maritime professionals that are proficient in technical operations and profoundly dedicated to global sustainability initiatives (Simanjuntak, 2023). SDG 4 (Quality Education) underscores the significance of inclusive and equitable education. Integrating economic literacy into maritime education enables institutions to advance SDG 4 by providing students with a comprehensive education that transcends just technical training. This comprehensive approach guarantees that graduates are equipped to manage the intricacies of the contemporary maritime sector, comprehending the economic, environmental, and social dimensions of their field (Kim et al., 2023; Simanjuntak et al., 2023). SDG 8 (Decent Work and Economic Growth) advocates for the advancement of equitable and sustainable economic development. The maritime sector is a crucial catalyst for global commerce and employment generation, and incorporating economic literacy into maritime education may cultivate a workforce that is more adept at making decisions that promote economic advancement while guaranteeing sustainability. Students can learn to evaluate the economic consequences of their actions, so fostering equitable labor practices, optimal resource utilization, and economic development in maritime communities (Syuzairi, 2023).

SDG 13 (Climate Action) emphasizes the necessity for immediate measures to mitigate climate change and its effects. The marine industry, a major source of global carbon emissions, is essential in combating climate change. Integrating environmental economics and sustainability principles into maritime education enables students to make decisions that mitigate the industry's environmental impact. This include the promotion of energy-efficient technologies, the reduction of emissions, and the endorsement of policies that alleviate climate change (Lau et al., 2024).

Ultimately, SDG 14 (Life Below Water) emphasizes the preservation and sustainable utilization of oceans, seas, and marine resources. Maritime education directly advances SDG 14 by enhancing comprehension of marine ecosystems and the economic and environmental concerns confronting maritime industry. Incorporating the principles of the Blue Economy and sustainable resource management into the curriculum equips maritime professionals to make informed decisions that safeguard marine biodiversity while promoting the responsible utilization of ocean resources (Barus & Simanjuntak, 2023). In summary, linking maritime education with global sustainability objectives guarantees that future maritime professionals are prepared to facilitate the shift towards a more sustainable, economically viable, and socially responsible marine sector. This strategy facilitates the alignment of the maritime industry with the overarching global initiative to attain a sustainable future.

1.2 Objectives

1.2.1 To examine the relevance of economic literacy in maritime education.

This chapter aims to analyze the essential significance of economic literacy in marine education. As the maritime business grows more intricate and intertwined with global economic systems, comprehending economic fundamentals is vital for prospective maritime professionals. Economic literacy provides students with the competencies required to make educated decisions that harmonize operational efficiency, environmental sustainability, and financial viability (Barile et al., 2023; Nõmmela & Kaare, 2022). The marine industry functions within a larger economic context, where elements such as market trends, resource distribution, pricing tactics, and cost management profoundly influence the decisions of maritime professionals. In the absence of a robust understanding of economics, these professionals may find it difficult to tackle the issues presented by volatile global markets, supply chain interruptions, and the increasing focus on sustainability (Koray et al., 2025).

This chapter seeks to underscore the significance of incorporating economic principles into maritime education courses by analyzing the relevance of economic literacy. This examines how comprehension of economic principles such as supply and demand, cost-benefit analysis, and financial management can improve the decision-making skills of marine professionals. This mission aims to pinpoint the precise domains within maritime education where economic literacy can offer the greatest benefit, encompassing shipping logistics, port management, sustainability practices, and resource optimization (Sijabat et al., 2024). The primary aim is to illustrate that economic literacy is not merely a supplementary talent but an essential competency that empowers marine professionals to address the issues of the contemporary maritime industry, promoting growth, sustainability, and resilience within the sector.

1.2.2 To propose pedagogical strategies for embedding Blue Economy principles into maritime curricula.

To successfully incorporate Blue Economy principles into maritime education, it is crucial to implement pedagogical methodologies that impart technical knowledge of maritime industries while also highlighting sustainability, environmental stewardship, and economic responsibility. A major method is to integrate case studies and real-world examples that demonstrate successful implementations of the Blue Economy across maritime businesses. This enables students to comprehend the application of sustainability concepts and economic feasibility across diverse contexts, including sustainable fishing techniques, renewable maritime energy, and eco-friendly shipping systems (Abid & Abid, 2025; Amodu, 2022).

An other beneficial strategy is to employ multidisciplinary learning, wherein maritime students engage collaboratively with peers from economics, environmental science, and policy fields. This enhances their comprehension of the intersection between maritime industry and global environmental objectives. Problem-based learning (PBL) may be implemented, wherein students confront intricate, real-world difficulties associated with the Blue Economy, necessitating the formulation of innovative, sustainable solutions (Whitehill et al., 2022).

Furthermore, incorporating sustainability metrics into the curriculum, including carbon footprint analysis, resource optimization, and life-cycle evaluations, will provide students with the necessary tools to assess the environmental and economic effects of maritime activities. These policies will guarantee that future marine professionals are adequately equipped to contribute to a sustainable Blue Economy (Peña et al., 2024).

1.2.3 Economic To explore how economic awareness supports sustainable maritime workforce development.

Awareness is essential for cultivating a sustainable marine workforce, as it provides professionals with the knowledge necessary to make decisions that reconcile economic growth with environmental and social accountability. In the marine sector, economically astute experts are better equipped to maximize resources, minimize waste, and enhance efficiency, hence contributing to sustainability (Nõmmela & Kaare, 2022).

Economic understanding enables marine professionals to comprehend the enduring financial advantages of investing in environmentally sustainable technologies, including energy-efficient vessels and renewable energy solutions for ports. These investments may necessitate initial expenditures but can result in considerable savings over time, enhancing the financial sustainability of maritime enterprises (Argyriou et al., 2025).

Furthermore, economic acumen equips the workforce to adeptly maneuver through market volatility and worldwide economic trends, including variations in fuel prices and alterations in trade patterns. By comprehending these economic elements, maritime professionals may formulate strategic judgments that safeguard employment, minimize operational expenses, and enhance the resilience of maritime enterprises (Lau et al., 2024). An economically informed workforce is more inclined to promote policies that endorse sustainable maritime practices, so assuring the sector's conformity with global environmental objectives, such as those specified in the Blue Economy framework. Thus, economic awareness not only fosters the expansion of the maritime workforce but also guarantees its capacity to contribute significantly to sustainable development within the maritime sector (Bueger et al., 2024).

2. THE NEXUS BETWEEN MARITIME EDUCATION AND THE BLUE ECONOMY

2.1 Bridging Technical and Economic Knowledge

2.1.1 Why seafarers, port managers, and maritime policymakers need economic literacy.

Economic literacy is crucial for seafarers, port managers, and maritime policymakers to adeptly negotiate the changing dynamics of the marine business (Simanjuntak et al., 2024). For sailors, comprehending economic principles aids in decision-making that transcends operational responsibilities, including optimizing routes based on fuel expenses, discerning market demands, and evaluating the financial feasibility of sustainable technology. These economic insights allow for contributions to cost-efficient and environmentally sustainable operations.

Port managers gain advantages from economic literacy, as they oversee resource management, enhance port operations, and adapt to global economic fluctuations. Understanding economic issues, including supply chain disruptions, international trade rules, and investment strategies, empowers port managers to make informed decisions that optimize operating efficiency, increase profitability, and promote long-term sustainability. Moreover, they can more effectively evaluate the economic ramifications of infrastructure expenditures and the implementation of sustainable technology (Xie & Zhou, 2025).

Economic literacy is essential for marine policymakers to formulate strategies that promote the development of the Blue Economy while maintaining sustainability. Policymakers must comprehend the economic ramifications of regulations, market dynamics, and environmental policies to establish balanced frameworks that foster both economic advancement and environmental conservation. By incorporating economic principles, they can formulate policies that correspond with global sustainability objectives, such as those delineated in the Blue Economy, so ensuring that the marine sector fosters a more sustainable and prosperous future (Nõmmela & Kaare, 2022).

2.1.2 Integrating concepts such as resource efficiency, cost optimization, and green finance in maritime operations.

Integrating principles such as resource efficiency, cost optimization, and green finance into maritime operations is crucial for achieving long-term sustainability and financial viability in the sector. Resource efficiency in maritime operations entails the reduction of resource consumption, including fuel, water, and materials, while optimizing output. Optimizing vessel routes, employing fuel-efficient technologies, and minimizing waste can result in decreased operational costs and a diminished environmental impact.

Effective resource utilization not only diminishes costs but also aids in attaining sustainability objectives by lessening the environmental repercussions of maritime operations (Bai et al., 2025; Buchmann, 2022).

Cost optimization is intricately associated with resource efficiency and aims to enhance the economic performance of maritime enterprises. Through the utilization of data-driven decision-making tools, investment in energy-efficient technologies, and the implementation of lean management methods, marine enterprises can decrease operational expenses while sustaining elevated service standards. Efficient cost optimization enables enterprises to maintain competitiveness in a progressively globalized market, characterized by volatile fuel prices and frequent operational disruptions (Melnyk et al., 2024). Green finance pertains to investments and resources allocated to initiatives that foster environmental sustainability. In the maritime industry, green finance can facilitate the advancement of environmentally sustainable boats, renewable energy sources (such as wind or solar power for ships), and enhancements to port infrastructure designed to mitigate emissions. Integrating green finance into maritime operations enables enterprises to obtain capital for sustainable initiatives, comply with regulatory mandates, and connect their practices with global environmental standards, so ensuring long-term financial and ecological sustainability (Swaty, 2023).

2.2 Blue Economy as an Educational Paradigm

2.2.1 Moving from traditional maritime training to a holistic approach encompassing economic, social, and environmental dimensions.

The transition from conventional maritime training to a more comprehensive approach is essential for meeting the changing requirements of the maritime industry. Historically, maritime education has emphasized technical skills and operational competencies, including navigation, vessel maintenance, and safety standards. Although these abilities are fundamental, they do not adequately prepare maritime professionals to tackle the extensive difficulties presented by the Blue Economy, which encompasses economic, social, and environmental factors in maritime operations.

A comprehensive approach to maritime education underscores the importance of economic literacy, sustainability awareness, and social responsibility in conjunction with conventional technical training. This methodology equips students to comprehend the economic ramifications of maritime operations, including cost-benefit analysis, resource management, and market dynamics. It promotes understanding of the environmental consequences of maritime activities, emphasizing sustainable practices such as emission reduction, energy efficiency, and responsible resource utilization (Singh et al., 2023).

The social aspect of the Blue Economy emphasizes the significance of inclusivity, equitable labor standards, and community involvement in marine development. Maritime education must instruct students on addressing local community needs, fostering equitable economic possibilities, and ensuring the widespread distribution of maritime industry advantages (Nur et al., 2023). By implementing this comprehensive strategy, maritime education may more effectively prepare future professionals to address the intricate, interconnected challenges of the Blue Economy, so ensuring their contribution to sustainable development and the enduring vitality of the seas.

2.2.2 Case examples: circular economy practices in ports, sustainable shipping innovations, and eco-efficient marine logistics.

Circular economy methods in ports are gaining prominence, as numerous ports globally implement waste reduction and resource recycling strategies. The Port of Rotterdam has instituted measures to recycle ship garbage, transform it into useable resources, and minimize landfill disposal. Through the promotion of material reuse and effective waste management, these ports enhance sustainability and reduce environmental impact (Karimpour et al., 2019).

In sustainable shipping advancements, firms such as Maersk are investing in environmentally friendly vessels fueled by renewable energy sources. Maersk's endeavor to create vessels utilizing biofuels or hydrogen as substitutes for conventional fossil fuels exemplifies the increasing movement towards emission reduction in the shipping sector. These advances reduce greenhouse gas emissions, enhancing the sustainability of maritime operations (Roux et al., 2024).

Eco-efficient marine logistics is demonstrated through the implementation of intelligent shipping technologies and data-driven optimization. Companies are progressively implementing technology such as automated systems, real-time data monitoring, and route optimization to diminish fuel usage and enhance operational efficiency. The application of AI to enhance shipping routes by considering weather conditions and traffic congestion decreases fuel consumption, cuts expenses, and mitigates environmental impact, thereby conforming to eco-efficient logistics standards (Chen & Biancardo, 2025).

2.3 Policy and Institutional Support

2.3.1 The role of international and regional organizations (IMO, UNESCO, ASEAN, World Bank) in promoting Blue Economy education.

International and regional organizations are essential in advancing Blue Economy education by offering frameworks, rules, and funding that facilitate the incorporation of sustainability ideas into maritime education and training. The International marine Organization (IMO) is a pivotal entity, establishing global benchmarks for marine safety, environmental conservation, and sustainable practices. The IMO assists member states in formulating educational curricula that adhere to the principles of the Blue Economy, focusing on sustainable maritime practices, resource efficiency, and environmental protection through initiatives such as the STCW Convention and the IMO's Integrated Technical Cooperation Programme. (Dewan & Godina, 2023)

UNESCO, via the Intergovernmental Oceanographic Commission (IOC), facilitates international initiatives to improve marine scientific education and the sustainable stewardship of ocean resources. UNESCO facilitates partnerships among nations and organizations to enhance ocean literacy and incorporates sustainability into maritime educational frameworks. At the regional level, entities such as ASEAN (Association of Southeast Asian Nations) are endeavoring to enhance the Blue Economy in the Asia-Pacific area. ASEAN fosters regional collaboration to enhance maritime governance, advocate for sustainable resource utilization, and incorporate Blue Economy principles into state policies and educational frameworks. (Ting & Yongkun, 2023)

The World Bank offers essential funding and technical support to developing nations, facilitating educational initiatives designed to enhance capabilities in marine conservation, sustainable fisheries, and

Blue Economy sectors, thereby ensuring that economic development is congruent with environmental sustainability. (Tambun et al., 2025)

2.3.2 National strategies and curriculum reform initiatives that embed sustainability and economic awareness.

National initiatives and curriculum revisions are crucial for incorporating ecological and economic knowledge into marine education. Numerous nations are reformulating their educational systems to conform to Blue Economy concepts, guaranteeing that future marine professionals are prepared to balance economic development with environmental conservation. Simanjuntak et al. (2023) The Norwegian government has enacted rules that foster sustainable maritime innovation by including economic literacy and sustainability into maritime training programs.

The Norwegian Maritime Authority has partnered with universities and technical colleges to provide curricula emphasizing green technologies, cost-effective shipping, and sustainable maritime resource management. Similarly, India has announced curriculum modifications in its maritime colleges under the Ministry of Shipping to incorporate concepts like circular economy, energy efficiency, and eco-friendly practices. This reform seeks to cultivate professionals who comprehend the economic ramifications of sustainable shipping, port administration, and coastline conservation. Xiao et al. (2024)

Southeast Asian nations are endeavoring to integrate economic and sustainability knowledge into marine education via ASEAN programs. Regional cooperation emphasize the creation of cooperative curricula that integrate sustainable fisheries management, resource-efficient shipping, and environmental economics to equip students for the increasing demands of a sustainable maritime sector. These reforms ensure that maritime professionals are prepared to tackle the economic problems and environmental obligations of the Blue Economy. (Gavalas, 2025)

3. PEDAGOGICAL INTEGRATION OF ECONOMIC LITERACY

3.1 Curriculum Design Strategies

3.1.1 Incorporating Blue Economy topics into maritime subjects (navigation, shipping management, marine engineering).

Integrating Blue Economy themes into maritime disciplines such as navigation, shipping management, and marine engineering is crucial for equipping future maritime professionals to tackle the interrelated concerns of sustainability, economic development, and environmental conservation (Heirs & Manuel, 2021). Curriculum design for navigation may incorporate modules that examine resource-efficient routing and cost-benefit analysis to optimize shipping routes. Students can learn to evaluate aspects such as fuel usage, environmental effect, and global trade patterns, empowering them to make informed decisions that reconcile operational efficiency with sustainability.

In maritime management, economic literacy can be integrated by incorporating subjects such as sustainable logistics, green financing, and the economic ramifications of environmental regulations (Xiao et al., 2024). This may include case studies on eco-efficient shipping practices, such as the implementation of low-carbon fuels, emissions reduction technology, and the economic advantages of adopting sustainable shipping technologies. Shipping managers can acquire skills to assess market trends, control expenses, and enhance port operations in a way that harmonizes economic development with environmental sustainability.

Integrating green technologies and eco-design principles into the marine engineering curriculum is crucial. Students can explore the economic feasibility of investing in sustainable vessel designs, energy-efficient engines, and renewable energy sources. By integrating economic principles with technical solutions, future marine engineers will be prepared to further the creation of environmentally beneficial maritime technologies that are also commercially viable (Simanjuntak et al., 2024).

3.1.2 Cross-disciplinary modules linking economics, environmental science, and maritime policy.

To adequately equip marine professionals for the problems of the Blue Economy, interdisciplinary programs integrating economics, environmental science, and maritime policy are necessary. These classes amalgamate the ideas of economic analysis, ecological sustainability, and regulatory frameworks to furnish students with a thorough comprehension of the maritime sector. A module on sustainable maritime policy can integrate economic analysis with environmental impact assessments to examine how policy modifications can promote sustainable practices in shipping, port operations, and marine conservation. Students may examine economic incentives for the adoption of green technologies, like subsidies for environmentally friendly boats and carbon pricing, while evaluating their environmental and economic ramifications (Lagouvardou et al., 2023).

Furthermore, environmental economics courses can analyze the economic ramifications of marine conservation, encompassing market-oriented solutions such as carbon credits and eco-labeling within maritime sectors. Students can evaluate how these techniques not only reduce environmental harm but also generate financial incentives for sustainability. These interdisciplinary approaches guarantee that future maritime professionals are prepared to formulate policies, strategies, and technologies that foster economic growth and environmental preservation, thereby connecting maritime operations with sustainable development objectives in the Blue Economy (Gerou & Pantouvakis, 2025).

3.2 Teaching and Learning Approaches

3.2.1 Project-Based Learning (PjBL) on sustainable maritime enterprises.

Project-Based Learning (PjBL) is an efficacious pedagogical method for involving students in the tangible issues of establishing sustainable maritime firms. This experiential learning approach challenges students to utilize theoretical information in practical situations, enhancing critical thinking and problem-solving abilities. Within the framework of sustainable marine companies, Project-Based Learning (PjBL) facilitates student collaboration on initiatives that tackle critical challenges, including resource efficiency, the implementation of green technologies, and sustainable supply chain management in the maritime industry (Astuti et al., 2023).

Students could be assigned to create a business plan for a sustainable shipping enterprise that integrates environmentally friendly boats, renewable energy sources, and carbon offset measures. They must undertake feasibility studies, execute cost-benefit evaluations, and investigate funding alternatives, including green finance or environmental incentives. This method enhances their comprehension of sustainable business practices and elucidates the economic and environmental trade-offs inherent in maritime operations (Buchmann, 2022).

Through Project-Based Learning, students acquire practical experience and learn to navigate the intricacies of balancing profitability with environmental stewardship. This approach fosters a sense of ownership and equips students to meet the increasing demand for sustainable maritime firms, connecting academic knowledge with practical application in the Blue Economy (Eid et al., 2023).

From a critical pedagogy perspective, maritime education should not only transfer knowledge but also encourage students to critically examine the economic and environmental implications of maritime practices. This includes questioning existing industry norms, evaluating unequal resource distribution, and understanding the socio-economic impacts of maritime activities on coastal communities. Integrating critical thinking into economic literacy ensures that students are not only technically competent but also socially and ethically aware decision-makers.

3.3 Assessment and Competency Development

3.3.1 Developing indicators of economic understanding and Evaluating students through research projects, community-based initiatives, or entrepreneurial simulations.

To accurately evaluate economic comprehension in maritime education, it is essential to establish explicit indicators that demonstrate a student's capacity to employ cost-benefit analysis, assess sustainability trade-offs, and make ethical economic choices. An indicator is a student's capacity to perform a cost-benefit analysis, evaluating the long-term advantages of implementing sustainable technologies, such as energy-efficient vessels or renewable energy in ports, in relation to initial expenditures. Students must exhibit the capacity to evaluate both financial viability and environmental consequences, so enhancing their comprehension of the economic ramifications of decisions in the maritime industry (Acciaro & Dirzka, 2023; Dantas & Θεοτοκατος, 2023).

A crucial metric is the assessment of sustainability trade-offs. Maritime professionals frequently encounter the dilemma of reconciling economic development with environmental conservation. Students ought to evaluate situations in which immediate financial benefits may contradict long-term sustainability objectives, such as emission reduction or marine resource conservation. Evaluating how students manage these trade-offs and prioritize sustainable solutions might yield significant insights into their economic decision-making abilities (Fortnam et al., 2023; Ofir & Elmakiess, 2023). Ethical economic choices function as a crucial signal. Students ought to be assessed on their capacity to integrate ethical factors into their decision-making processes. For example, prioritizing equitable labor policies, community welfare, or environmentally sustainable business practices in maritime firms is essential. This underscores the necessity of reconciling profitability with social and environmental accountability, which is vital for sustainable marine advancement (Simanjuntak et al., 2023).

Effective student evaluation can be conducted through research projects, community-based initiatives, or entrepreneurial simulations. These practical examples enable students to exhibit their capacity to implement economic ideas in real-world contexts. A research project on sustainable shipping practices can evaluate a student's comprehension of economic analysis, while community-based initiatives, like formulating sustainable port management strategies, can illuminate students' interactions with local stakeholders and their contributions to the Blue Economy. Through these varied evaluation methodologies, students can demonstrate their economic proficiency in multiple maritime scenarios (Almeida et al., 2025).

4. CHALLENGES AND OPPORTUNITIES

4.1 Institutional and Curriculum Barriers

4.1.1 Limited expertise among maritime educators in economics and sustainability topics.

A major obstacle to incorporating economics and sustainability into maritime education is the insufficient experience of maritime educators in these fields. Historically, maritime educators have concentrated on technical disciplines like as navigation, marine engineering, and safety, while placing minimal emphasis on economic and sustainability issues. Consequently, numerous instructors may be deficient in the specific expertise necessary to instruct on concepts such as cost-benefit analysis, green finance, or sustainability trade-offs within marine contexts (Kim et al., 2023).

The deficiency in expertise is a difficulty for the effective integration of economic literacy and sustainable practices into the curriculum. In the absence of sufficient training in these domains, educators may find it challenging to develop interesting, contemporary curriculum that adheres to the tenets of the Blue Economy. Furthermore, instructors may encounter challenges in incorporating interdisciplinary concepts that connect economics, environmental science, and marine policy (Costa & Faria, 2025).

This challenge also offers an opportunity for professional advancement and curricular enhancement. Investing in training programs for maritime educators that emphasize economics and sustainability enables institutions to enhance capacity and guarantee educators has the requisite knowledge and abilities to teach these essential subjects. Moreover, collaboration with industry professionals, economists, and environmental scientists can yield significant insights and resources to enrich curriculum content, enabling students to get a comprehensive grasp of the Blue Economy and its ramifications for the marine sector.

4.1.2 Overloaded curricula that prioritize technical skills over socio-economic awareness.

A major obstacle to incorporating socio-economic understanding into maritime education is the congested curricula that emphasize technical skills at the expense of broader themes like economics, sustainability, and social responsibility. Maritime education conventionally emphasizes fundamental technical skills such as navigation, marine engineering, and safety procedures. Although these abilities are crucial for operational efficiency, they frequently overshadow the curriculum, restricting the incorporation of economic principles and ecological measures (Lopes et al., 2025).

This focus on technical abilities may lead to graduates possessing robust operational knowledge yet lacking an understanding of the wider economic and environmental issues confronting the maritime industry. Students may find it challenging to negotiate the intricacies of the Blue Economy and sustainable marine practices without comprehending concepts such as cost-benefit analysis, sustainability trade-offs, and ethical decision-making (Lau et al., 2021). This challenge also offers a chance to reform curricula by integrating socio-economic subjects into current programs. Integrating economic literacy and sustainability awareness with technical training in maritime education can provide well-rounded individuals adept at balancing operational, economic, and environmental factors in their decision-making.

However, the integration of economic literacy into maritime education is not without challenges. Critics argue that adding new competencies may overload already dense curricula and place additional burdens on instructors. Furthermore, without proper institutional support, such integration risks becoming superficial rather than transformative.

4.2 Policy and Opportunities

4.2.1 Insufficient funding for curriculum innovation and teacher training.

A primary obstacle to incorporating economic literacy and sustainability into maritime education is the inadequate financing for curriculum development and educator training. Numerous maritime institutions encounter funding limitations that hinder their capacity to revise curricula in accordance with developing trends such as the Blue Economy. Consequently, maritime education frequently depends on antiquated frameworks that emphasize technical skills, with scant resources devoted to integrating socio-economic subjects like sustainability, green finance, and economic decision-making into the curriculum (Jafari et al., 2020).

Likewise, insufficient financing for teacher preparation may result in instructors lacking the requisite ability to instruct these intricate subjects. Due to budget constraints, professional development programs in economics and sustainability are frequently deprioritized. The absence of training for instructors creates a deficiency in effective pedagogy, since educators may find it challenging to assimilate new concepts or utilize novel teaching methodologies that encompass both economic and environmental viewpoints (Seguido et al., 2025).

Increased policy support and funding for curricular reform and professional development are necessary to solve this issue. By directing resources to these domains, maritime institutions may cultivate a more holistic educational experience, equipping students with the requisite skills and knowledge to excel in the dynamic marine business and promote sustainable practices within the Blue Economy (Suparman et al., 2024).

4.2.2 Lack of national policy alignment between maritime and economic education sectors.

A major obstacle in incorporating economic literacy and sustainability into maritime education is the absence of national policy coherence between the marine and economic education sectors. In numerous nations, the maritime sector is frequently seen as a distinct domain from comprehensive economic education, with policies and curricula predominantly emphasizing technical skills and operations. Simultaneously, economic education sometimes neglects the distinct requirements of the maritime sector, including the intricacies of maritime economics, resource management, and sustainable maritime practices (Gavalas, 2025).

The disjunction between rules regulating maritime and economic education results in disjointed curricula that inadequately equip students for the interconnected issues of the Blue Economy. Maritime students may be deficient in the economic acumen required to manage the financial and environmental dimensions of the industry, whilst students in economic disciplines may lack comprehension of the distinctive dynamics inherent to maritime sectors (Syriopoulos & Kafka, 2024). Policy alignment between these sectors is essential to address this issue. Governments and educational institutions must collaborate to formulate unified policies that merge economic and maritime education, guaranteeing that students acquire the competencies necessary to tackle both the technical and economic difficulties of sustainable maritime sectors (Simanjuntak et al., 2023).

4.3 Opportunities for Reform and Innovation

4.3.1 Collaborative programs between universities, maritime academies, and industry stakeholders.

A significant opportunity for transformation in maritime education lies in the establishment of joint programs among universities, maritime academies, and industry partners. These collaborations can connect technical education with economic sustainability by developing curricula that incorporate both operational competencies and economic acumen. Collaborative efforts between educational institutions and industry leaders can guarantee that the forthcoming generation of marine professionals possesses the requisite abilities to adeptly handle the intricacies of the Blue Economy (Sijabat et al., 2024).

Such programs may encompass industry-driven curriculum development, wherein maritime academies and universities partner with shipping companies, port authorities, and environmental organizations to create courses that embody contemporary trends in sustainable maritime practices, economic analysis, and regulatory compliance. Guest lectures, internships, and research partnerships with industry specialists offer students practical experience and understanding of the difficulties and potential in the maritime sector (Rauf et al., 2023). Furthermore, collaborations with international entities such as the IMO and UNESCO can provide global viewpoints and exemplary practices to local educational frameworks. These joint programs may cultivate a comprehensive marine workforce that excels in technical operations while comprehending the economic and environmental facets of the sector, so fostering innovation and sustainability within the Blue Economy (Otero et al., 2019).

4.3.2 Blue Economy innovation hubs and partnerships for entrepreneurship development.

Blue Economy innovation hubs offer a powerful opportunity for fostering entrepreneurship development in the maritime sector. These hubs serve as collaborative spaces where startups, entrepreneurs, and researchers can work together to develop innovative solutions that address the economic and environmental challenges of the Blue Economy. By providing access to resources, expertise, and networking opportunities, these hubs help entrepreneurs develop new green technologies, sustainable shipping solutions, and eco-friendly port operations.(Jamasb & Sornn-Friese, 2024).

Partnerships between universities, maritime academies, and innovation hubs can stimulate entrepreneurial thinking among students and professionals. These collaborations can involve incubators and accelerators that support new ventures focused on sustainability, such as renewable marine energy, waste management solutions, and resource-efficient shipping technologies. Such initiatives help bridge the gap between academic learning and real-world application, encouraging the development of practical, market-driven solutions (Clott & Hartman, 2022). Moreover, industry partnerships can provide mentorship, funding, and market access for entrepreneurs, while academic institutions can offer research-driven insights and technical expertise. By combining innovation hubs with educational and industry collaborations, the maritime sector can cultivate a new generation of entrepreneurs capable of driving economic growth while advancing sustainable practices, ultimately contributing to the long-term success of the Blue Economy (Paipa-Sanabria et al., 2025).

4.3.2 Integration of SDGs and ESG (Environmental, Social, and Governance) indicators into educational practices.

Incorporating Sustainable Development Goals (SDGs) and Environmental, Social, and Governance (ESG) indicators into maritime education effectively aligns the industry with global sustainability aims. By integrating these frameworks into teaching methods, institutions can guarantee that future marine professionals are prepared to tackle the economic, environmental, and social concerns of the Blue Economy. Goals 14 (Life Below Water), 13 (Climate Action), and 8 (Decent Work and Economic Growth) are directly pertinent to maritime industry. Educational programs can include these objectives into curricula by instructing students about the effects of maritime operations on the environment and communities, as well as how these activities might be harmonized with sustainable development (Sulolipu et al., 2022). Students can investigate sustainable shipping, eco-efficient port management, and renewable maritime energy, examining how these practices facilitate the attainment of the SDGs (Noonan-Birch et al., 2024; Tremblay et al., 2024).

Integrating ESG indicators into educational procedures enables students to comprehend the growing assessment of firms based on their environmental impact, social responsibility, and governance standards. Incorporating ESG principles into curricula enables students to evaluate marine operations based on financial performance as well as social and environmental accountability, equipping them for leadership positions in sustainable maritime firms (Tsatsaronis et al., 2024).

5. TOWARD A FRAMEWORK FOR BLUE ECONOMIC LITERACY IN MARITIME EDUCATION

5.1 Curriculum integration model combining economic, environmental, and technical competencies.

In response to evolving industry demands, maritime education is increasingly shaped by several key trends, including the integration of sustainability principles, the adoption of interdisciplinary learning approaches, and the use of digital and simulation-based training. However, these trends are often applied in isolation, without a structured framework that connects economic literacy with technical and environmental competencies.

A comprehensive curriculum integration model for Blue Economic Literacy in maritime education should combine economic, environmental, and technical competencies to prepare students for the complex challenges of the Blue Economy (Costa & Faria, 2025; Syriopoulos & Kafka, 2024). The model emphasizes the interconnectedness of these competencies, ensuring that students can evaluate the financial, environmental, and technical aspects of maritime operations. This integrated approach encourages students to think holistically about the maritime industry and its impact on global sustainability goals.

The economic competencies component of the curriculum should focus on teaching students the fundamentals of economic analysis, including cost-benefit analysis, green finance, and resource management. Students will learn how to assess the financial implications of adopting sustainable practices, such as the cost-effectiveness of renewable technologies and the economic benefits of eco-efficient shipping. Understanding these concepts will allow them to make informed decisions that balance profitability with environmental and social responsibility (Baştuğ et al., 2024; Xiao et al., 2024).

In addition to economic competencies, the curriculum must emphasize environmental competencies, such as carbon footprint reduction, eco-efficient vessel design, and marine conservation. Students should be trained to evaluate the environmental impact of maritime operations and understand how sustainable practices align with global SDGs. The technical competencies must still focus on essential maritime skills, but with an added emphasis on integrating sustainable technologies like renewable energy sources and energy-efficient systems, ensuring students are prepared to meet both operational and environmental challenges (Jeon & Lee, 2025; Pazaver & Kitada, 2025).

5.2 Learning outcomes aligned with sustainability and industry needs.

The learning outcomes of a Blue Economic Literacy curriculum must closely correspond with sustainability objectives and the changing requirements of the maritime sector. These results should guarantee that graduates are both technically adept and able to make informed, sustainable decisions that promote long-term environmental and economic objectives.

Sustainability objectives must emphasize students' capacity to assess the environmental ramifications of maritime operations, encompassing the evaluation of carbon emissions, resource utilization, and the conservation of marine biodiversity. Students must possess the capability to devise and execute eco-efficient shipping solutions, integrate green technology such as renewable marine energy, and employ circular economy ideas in port management and vessel operations. They must have the capacity to reconcile economic development with the conservation of marine habitats, thereby advancing global sustainability objectives, including SDG 14 (Life Below Water) and SDG 13 (Climate Action) (Chua et al., 2024; Lopes et al., 2025; Oloruntobi et al., 2023).

Industry requirements must guarantee that students are equipped to fulfill the practical demands of the maritime sector. Graduates must possess economic literacy to evaluate market circumstances, manage resources, and enhance operations for profitability and sustainability. They must also have the technical expertise to incorporate sustainable practices into maritime technologies, ensuring that firms remain competitive while complying with regulatory frameworks and environmental standards (Chua et al., 2024). These results guarantee that marine professionals can effectuate sustainable transformation within the Blue Economy.

5.3 Teacher training and institutional capacity-building initiatives.

To effectively include Blue Economic Literacy into maritime education, it is crucial to emphasize teacher training and the enhancement of institutional capacities. Educators must possess the requisite knowledge and abilities to impart economic, environmental, and technological competencies pertinent to the Blue Economy. This can be accomplished by professional development programs emphasizing sustainability, green technologies, economic analysis, and maritime policy. Workshops, online courses, and certification programs assist educators in remaining informed about contemporary trends, tools, and pedagogical techniques, so enabling them to proficiently convey knowledge pertaining to sustainable maritime practices (Barus & Simanjuntak, 2023).

Moreover, institutional capacity-building is essential for equipping maritime education institutions with the necessary resources, infrastructure, and support systems to execute these reforms. This encompasses investment in contemporary educational resources, simulation technologies, and research initiatives centeredon the Blue Economy. Collaborative alliances with industry players, international entities, and governmental bodies can furnish essential resources and insights to enhance institutional frameworks. By augmenting the capabilities of educators and institutions, maritime education systems may more effectively prepare students to address the increasing requirements of a sustainable marine economy and contribute to the Blue Economy (Barus & Simanjuntak, 2023).

6. CONCLUSION

6.1 Summary of key arguments: The necessity of embedding economic literacy to support sustainable maritime development.

Incorporating economic literacy into marine education is vital for promoting sustainable maritime development. As the marine sector progressively aligns with the Blue Economy, professionals must possess the competencies to reconcile economic development with environmental sustainability. Economic literacy empowers marine professionals to make informed decisions, evaluate the financial viability of sustainable technology, and enhance operations while reducing environmental effect.

Incorporating economic, environmental, and technological proficiencies into maritime courses guarantees that graduates are equipped to manage the intricacies of the global maritime industry. By comprehending cost-benefit analysis, sustainability trade-offs, and green financing, students may aid in the transition to a more sustainable and resilient maritime business.

Moreover, cooperation across educational institutions, industry, and government agencies is essential for developing a comprehensive and flexible approach to maritime education. This collaborative initiative will cultivate a generation of maritime experts proficient in promoting economic advancement and environmental conservation, so securing the enduring prosperity of the Blue Economy.

6.2 Future directions: preparing a generation of maritime professionals who are *economically informed, environmentally responsible, and globally competent*

The future of maritime education involves cultivating a generation of professionals that are not just technically proficient but also fiscally astute, environmentally conscious, and globally adept. This necessitates a comprehensive educational strategy, wherein students are provided with the resources to make informed economic choices that promote sustainability. Future maritime professionals must possess expertise in cost-benefit analysis, green finance, and the economic ramifications of environmental regulations, enabling them to reconcile economic growth with environmental preservation in their decision-making processes.

Alongside economic literacy, students must cultivate a robust sense of environmental stewardship, recognizing the imperative to safeguard marine ecosystems and mitigate the carbon imprint of maritime activities. The curriculum should fundamentally incorporate sustainable shipping, renewable energy integration, and environmentally friendly activities. Moreover, maritime education must equip students for a worldwide environment by promoting cultural awareness and international collaboration. As global trade and international rules influence the marine industry, experts must be adept at managing intricate cross-border challenges to ensure the sector's sustainability and its role in the Blue Economy.

REFERENCES

Acciaro, M., & Dirzka, C. (2023). The European Policy-mix for the Energy Transition in the Maritime Sector. *Research Portal Denmark*, 148–150. https://local.forskningsportal.dk/local/dki-cgi/ws/cris-link?src=cbs&id=cbs-a83906bc-83a1-4b0e-b902-e20f588d8812&ti=The European Policy-mix for the Energy Transition in the Maritime Sector

Almeida, M., Laranjeiro, D., Costa, R., Lillebø, A. I., & Vieira, H. (2025). Blue economy concepts are lagging behind in ocean literacy. *Frontiers in Marine Science, 12*, 1648508. Advance online publication. DOI: 10.3389/fmars.2025.1648508

Amodu, T. A. (2022). Blue Economy and Foreign Direct Investment to Maritime Nations. In *Practice, progress, and proficiency in sustainability* (pp. 131–147). IGI Global. DOI: 10.4018/978-1-6684-3393-5.ch007

Argyriou, I., Nisiforou, O., & Tsoutsos, T. (2025). Setting Sail for a Sustainable Growth in Small/Medium Ports. *Sustainability (Basel)*, *17*(8), 3330. DOI: 10.3390/su17083330

Astuti, P., Febrian, F., Fera, M., Putri, N. H. S., Azmi, R. D., & Rosmery, L. (2023). Project-based Learning Design: Developing Maritime Context-based Tasks in English for Mathematics Course. *BIO Web of Conferences, 79*, 5002. DOI: 10.1051/bioconf/20237905002

Bai, J., Yan, Y., & Bai, X. (2025). A comprehensive review of ship emission reduction technologies for sustainable maritime transport. In *Frontiers in Marine Science* (Vol. 12). Frontiers Media., DOI: 10.3389/fmars.2025.1576661

Barile, L., Mearman, A., & Plumridge, A. (2023). *Embedding Sustainability in the Economics Curriculum*. DOI: 10.53593/n3626a

Barus, I. R. G., & Simanjuntak, M. B. (2023). Integrating Environmental Education into Maritime English Curriculum for Vocational Learners: Challenges and Opportunities. *BIO Web of Conferences, 79*, 8001. DOI: 10.1051/bioconf/20237908001

Baştuğ, S., Akgül, E. F., Haralambides, H., & Notteboom, T. (2024). A decision-making framework for the funding of shipping decarbonization initiatives in non-EU countries: Insights from Türkiye. *Journal of Shipping and Trade*, *9*(1), 12. Advance online publication. DOI: 10.1186/s41072-024-00172-1

Ben Abid, S., & Abid, N. (2025). Advancing a sustainable blue economy through innovation: a systematic review. In *Discover Sustainability* (Vol. 6, Issue 1). Springer Nature. DOI: 10.1007/s43621-025-01465-6

Buchmann, F. M. (2022). Driving the Green Transition of the Maritime Industry through Clean Technology Adoption and Environmental Policies. *Research Portal Denmark*, 176. https://local.forskningsportal.dk/local/dki-cgi/ws/cris-link?src=cbs&id=cbs-a22ab85e-2f3e-4bf6-b4bf-97f2bf7cfac3&ti=Driving the Green Transition of the Maritime Industry through Clean Technology Adoption and Environmental Policies

Bueger, C., Edmunds, T., & Stockbruegger, J. (2024). Securing the Seas : A comprehensive assessment of global maritime security. In *Research Portal Denmark*. Technical University of Denmark. https://local.forskningsportal.dk/local/dki-cgi/ws/cris-link?src=ku&id=ku-45584bf3-3380-4667-a933-dbe2edc98f2f&ti=Securing the Seas %3A A comprehensive assessment of global maritime security

Chen, X., & Biancardo, S. A. (2025). Smart and Low Carbon Emission-Oriented Maritime Traffic Management and Controlling. *Journal of Marine Science and Engineering*, *13*(9), 1793. DOI: 10.3390/jmse13091793

Chua, C., Li, X., Tan, K. H., & Yuen, K. F. (2024). Building sustainable performance in the maritime industry via digital resources and innovation. *Transport Policy*, *149*, 282–299. DOI: 10.1016/j.tranpol.2024.02.014

Clott, C., & Hartman, B. C. (2022). Do maritime innovation centers produce results? *WMU Journal of Maritime Affairs*, *21*(3), 283–326. DOI: 10.1007/s13437-022-00285-z

Costa, R. L., & Faria, C. (2025). The Blue School Program: A Model for Holistic Ocean Literacy Education. *Sustainability (Basel)*, *17*(2), 661. DOI: 10.3390/su17020661

Dantas, J. L. D., & Θεοτοκατος, R. (2023). A framework for the economic-environmental feasibility assessment of short-sea shipping autonomous vessels. *Ocean Engineering*, *279*, 114420. DOI: 10.1016/j.oceaneng.2023.114420

Eid, J., Aanerud, M., & Enberg, K. (2023). Teaching sustainability at the high sea: The "One Ocean Expedition.". *Sustainability Science*, *19*(1), 347–359. DOI: 10.1007/s11625-023-01419-9

Elegbede, I. O., Fakoya, K. A., Adewolu, M. A., Jolaosho, T. L., Adebayo, J. A., Oshodi, E., Hungevu, R. F., Oladosu, A. O., & Abikoye, O. (2023). Understanding the social–ecological systems of non-state seafood sustainability scheme in the blue economy. *Environment, Development and Sustainability*, *27*(2), 2721–2752. Advance online publication. DOI: 10.1007/s10668-023-04004-3

Fortnam, M., Chaigneau, T., Evans, L., & Bastian, L. (2023). Practitioner approaches to trade-off decision-making in marine conservation development. *People and Nature*, *5*(5), 1636–1648. DOI: 10.1002/pan3.10530

Gavalas, D. (2025). Green finance frameworks for sustainable shipping industry and blue economy: A review. In *Maritime Technology and Research* (Vol. 7, Issue 3). Chiang Mai University. DOI: 10.33175/mtr.2025.277132

Geng, B., Wu, D., Zhang, C., Xie, W., Mahmood, M. A., & Ali, Q. (2024). How Can the Blue Economy Contribute to Inclusive Growth and Ecosystem Resources in Asia? A Comparative Analysis. *Sustainability (Basel)*, *16*(1), 429. DOI: 10.3390/su16010429

Gerou, A., & Pantouvakis, A. (2025). The transition to a sustainable blue economy explored through frameworks and SDG alignment. *Discover Sustainability*, *6*(1), 1039. Advance online publication. DOI: 10.1007/s43621-025-01953-9

Gouvea, R., & Gutierrez, M. (2023). The Sustainable Brazilian Blue Economy: A Blue Powershoring and Blue Watershoring Strategy. *Modern Economy*, *14*(12), 1892–1920. DOI: 10.4236/me.2023.1412099

Gurning, R. O. S., Hutapea, G., Marpaung, E., Malisan, J., Arianto, D., Siahaan, W. J., Bimantoro, B., Sujarwanto, , Suastika, I. K., Santoso, A., Utama, D., Kurniawan, A., Hardianto, S., Aryawan, W. D., Nanda, M. I., Simatupang, E. J., Suhartana, I. K., & Putra, T. P. (2022). Conceptualizing Floating Logistics Supporting Facility as Innovative and Sustainable Transport in Remote Areas: Case of Small Islands in Indonesia. *Sustainability (Basel)*, *14*(14), 8904. DOI: 10.3390/su14148904

Haralambides, H. (2024). The Red Sea crisis and chokepoints to trade and international shipping. *Maritime Economics & Logistics*, *26*(3), 367–390. DOI: 10.1057/s41278-024-00296-y

Heirs, S. B. C., & Manuel, M. E. (2021). Sustainable Maritime Career Development: A case for Maritime Education and Training (MET) at the Secondary Level. *TransNav the International Journal on Marine Navigation and Safety of Sea Transportation*, *15*(1), 91–99. DOI: 10.12716/1001.15.01.08

Jafari, H., Lista, A., Siekapen, M. M., Ghaffari-Bohlouli, P., Nie, L., Alimoradi, H., & Shavandi, A. (2020). Fish Collagen: Extraction, Characterization, and Applications for Biomaterials Engineering. In *Polymers* (Vol. 12, Issue 10, p. 2230). Multidisciplinary Digital Publishing Institute. DOI: 10.3390/polym12102230

Jamasb, T., & Sornn-Friese, H. (2024). Regulatory Economics and the Future of Ports as Energy Hubs. *Research Portal Denmark*, 34–42. https://local.forskningsportal.dk/local/dki-cgi/ws/cris-link?src=cbs&id=cbs-9a3f2b03-6270-4b1c-8c90-51bb39dcd2ae&ti=Regulatory Economics and the Future of Ports as Energy Hubs

Jeon, T.-Y., & Lee, Y.-C. (2025). Energy Saving in Ship Central Cooling Systems: IMC-Tuned PID with Feedforward Control. *Journal of Marine Science and Engineering*, *13*(3), 510. DOI: 10.3390/jmse13030510

Karimpour, R., Ballini, F., & Ölçer, A. I. (2019). Circular economy approach to facilitate the transition of the port cities into self-sustainable energy ports—A case study in Copenhagen-Malmö Port (CMP). *WMU Journal of Maritime Affairs*, *18*(2), 225–247. DOI: 10.1007/s13437-019-00170-2

Kim, J.-K., Lee, C.-H., Jeong, M., Cho, E., & Lee, Y.-G. (2023). Identifying Optimal Approaches for Sustainable Maritime Education and Training: Addressing Technological, Environmental, and Epidemiological Challenges. *Sustainability (Basel)*, *15*(10), 8092. DOI: 10.3390/su15108092

Koray, M., Kaya, E., & Keskin, M. H. (2025). Determining Logistical Strategies to Mitigate Supply Chain Disruptions in Maritime Shipping for a Resilient and Sustainable Global Economy. *Sustainability (Basel)*, *17*(12), 5261. DOI: 10.3390/su17125261

Lagouvardou, S., Lagemann, B., Psaraftis, H. N., Lindstad, E., & Erikstad, S. O. (2023). Marginal abatement cost of alternative marine fuels and the role of market-based measures. *Nature Energy*, *8*(11), 1209–1220. DOI: 10.1038/s41560-023-01334-4

Lau, Y., Chen, Q., Poo, M. C., Ng, A. K. Y., & Ying, C. C. (2024). Maritime transport resilience: A systematic literature review on the current state of the art, research agenda and future research directions. *Ocean and Coastal Management*, *251*, 107086. DOI: 10.1016/j.ocecoaman.2024.107086

Lau, Y., Dragomir, C., Tang, Y. M., & Ng, A. K. Y. (2021). Maritime Undergraduate Students: Career Expectations and Choices. *Sustainability (Basel)*, *13*(8), 4297. DOI: 10.3390/su13084297

Lopes, L. S., Nabais, J. L., Pinto, C. J., Caldeirinha, V., & Pinho, T. (2025). Essential Competencies in Maritime and Port Logistics: A Study on the Current Needs of the Sector. *Sustainability (Basel)*, *17*(6), 2378. DOI: 10.3390/su17062378

Marwa, T., Muizzuddin, M., Bashir, A., Andaiyani, S., & Cahyadi, A. (2024). Determinants of the Blue Economy Growth in the Era of Sustainability: A Case Study of Indonesia. *Economies*, *12*(11), 299. DOI: 10.3390/economies12110299

Melnyk, O., Onyshchenko, S., Rudenko, S., Павлова, H., & Muradian, A. (2024). Embracing Integrated Optimization Strategies for Cost-Effective Port Operations in Marine Logistics. In *Studies in systems, decision and control* (pp. 491–508). Springer International Publishing., DOI: 10.1007/978-3-031-68372-5_27

Nõmmela, K., & Kaare, K. K. (2022). Incorporated Maritime Policy Concept: Adopting ESRS Principles to Support Maritime Sector's Sustainable Growth. *Sustainability (Basel)*, *14*(20), 13593. DOI: 10.3390/su142013593

Noonan-Birch, R., Adams, M., & Ross, M.-C. (2024). Utilizing the SDGs to develop a blue economy capacity framework enabling a shift from an ocean economy to a blue economy in Canada. *Frontiers in Marine Science*, *11*, 1400043. Advance online publication. DOI: 10.3389/fmars.2024.1400043

Nur, M., Nurbayani, S., Mulyana, A., Dermawan, W., Sapriya, S., Supriyadi, A., & Jumadi, J. (2023). Histoire et culture maritimes en Indonésie : Mise en œuvre dans l'apprentissage des études sociales. *Encounters in Theory and History of Education*, *24*, 230–253. DOI: 10.24908/encounters.v24i0.16705

Ofir, M., & Elmakiess, T. (2023). The Eco-Agency Problem and Sustainable Investment. SSRN *Electronic Journal*. DOI: 10.2139/ssrn.4652981

Oloruntobi, O., Mokhtar, K., Gohari, A., Asif, S., & Chuah, L. F. (2023). Sustainable transition towards greener and cleaner seaborne shipping industry: Challenges and opportunities. *Cleaner Engineering and Technology*, *13*, 100628. DOI: 10.1016/j.clet.2023.100628

Otero, R. M. F., Bayliss-Brown, G., & Papathanassiou, M. (2019). Ocean Literacy and Knowledge Transfer Synergies in Support of a Sustainable Blue Economy. *Frontiers in Marine Science*, *6*, 646. Advance online publication. DOI: 10.3389/fmars.2019.00646

Paipa-Sanabria, E., Montoya, D. G., & Coronado-Hernández, J. R. (2025). Green Technologies for Environmental Air and Water Impact Reduction in Ships: A Systematic Literature Review. *Journal of Marine Science and Engineering*, *13*(5), 839. DOI: 10.3390/jmse13050839

Pazaver, A., & Kitada, M. (2025). Integrating twenty-first century skills into STCW competences: Implications for maritime education and training. *WMU Journal of Maritime Affairs*, *24*(3), 397–418. DOI: 10.1007/s13437-025-00368-7

Peña, L. V. D. L., Dewulf, J., Staes, J., Moulaert, I., Vandamme, S., Heymans, J. J., & Taelman, S. E. (2024). Assessing the sustainability of Blue Economy activities using an ecosystem and life cycle-based approach: Possibilities, challenges and implications for an informed policy making. *Ocean and Coastal Management*, *257*, 107360. DOI: 10.1016/j.ocecoaman.2024.107360

Pham, C.-V., Wang, H.-C., Chen, S.-H., & Lee, J. (2023). The Threshold Effect of Overfishing on Global Fishery Outputs: International Evidence from a Sustainable Fishery Perspective. *Fishes*, *8*(2), 71. DOI: 10.3390/fishes8020071

Rauf, U. A. A., Aziz, N. I., Zulkarnaini, N. A. S., Deli, M. M., Asha'ari, M. J., Jamil, A. H., & Abdullah, S. I. N. W. (2023). Strengthening the University-Maritime Industry Collaborations (UMICs): Technology Issues. [JAETS]. *Journal of Applied Engineering and Technological Science*, *5*(1), 515–530. DOI: 10.37385/jaets.v5i1.3211

Roux, M., Lodato, C., Laurent, A., & Astrup, T. F. (2024). A review of life cycle assessment studies of maritime fuels: Critical insights, gaps, and recommendations. In *Sustainable Production and Consumption* (Vol. 50, pp. 69–86). Elsevier BV., DOI: 10.1016/j.spc.2024.07.016

Sardá, R., Pogutz, S., De Silvio, M., Allevi, V., Saputo, A., Daminelli, R., Fumagalli, F., Totaro, L., Rizzi, G., Magni, G., Pachner, J. H. G., & Perrini, F. (2022). Business for ocean sustainability: Early responses of ocean governance in the private sector. *Ambio*, *52*(2), 253–270. DOI: 10.1007/s13280-022-01784-2 PMID: 36260251

Seguido, Á. F. M., Alcaraz, R. S., Ferrero-Punzano, S. M., Miguel-Revilla, D., Vera, J. R. M., Rodríguez-Pizzinato, L. A., & García, Ó. J. (2025). Climate Change, Education, Training, and Perception of Pre-Service Teachers. *Social Sciences (Basel, Switzerland)*, *14*(4), 236. DOI: 10.3390/socsci14040236

Setiawan, A. (2023). Navigating Sustainable Development in ASEAN: A Comprehensive Review of the Blue Economy's Essential Questions. In *BIO Web of Conferences* (Vol. 70, p. 6004). EDP Sciences. DOI: 10.1051/bioconf/20237006004

Sijabat, P. S., Malau, A. G., Mudakir, M., Kurniawan, W. D., & Agustinawati, M. (2024). Integrating Computer Literacy and Social Skills in Maritime Education: Enhancing Cadet Readiness. *Dinasti International Journal of Education Management And Social Science*, *5*(6), 1655–1663. DOI: 10.38035/dijemss.v5i6.2701

Simanjuntak, M. B. (2023). Enhancing Environmental Awareness and Sustainable Communication Skills in Maritime Education. *BIO Web of Conferences, 79*, 1002. DOI: 10.1051/bioconf/20237901002

Simanjuntak, M. B., Rafli, Z., & Utami, S. R. (2024). Enhancing maritime education for ocean sustainability: A multidisciplinary approach. *BIO Web of Conferences, 106*, 2006. DOI: 10.1051/bioconf/202410602006

Simanjuntak, M. B., Zuriyati, Z., Utami, S. R., Rahmat, A., & Setiadi, S. (2023). Fostering Intercultural Understanding and Environmental Consciousness in Maritime Education. *BIO Web of Conferences, 79*, 6004. DOI: 10.1051/bioconf/20237906004

Singh, S., Dwivedi, A., & Pratap, S. (2023). Sustainable Maritime Freight Transportation: Current Status and Future Directions. *Sustainability (Basel)*, *15*(8), 6996. DOI: 10.3390/su15086996

Sulolipu, A. A., Soetjipto, B. E., Wahyono, H., & Haryono, A. (2022). Silk weaving business sustainability as a cultural heritage of Indonesia: A case study in Wajo Regency, South Sulawesi. *Industria Textila (Bucuresti)*, *73*(02), 184–190. DOI: 10.35530/IT.073.02.202056

Suparman, J., Fahcruddin, I., Malau, A. G., Kurniawan, W. D., Sayakfika, M., & Geboy, G. (2024). Bridging The Gap Between Maritime Education and Industry Needs: Enhancing Human Resource Development. *Epaper Bisnis, 1*(4), 33–49. DOI: 10.61132/epaperbisnis.v1i4.113

Swaty. (2023). Green Finance and Sustainable Development: Exploring Dynamic Causal Links and Global Implications. *E3S Web of Conferences, 453*, 1053. DOI: 10.1051/e3sconf/202345301053

Syriopoulos, T., & Kafka, K. I. (2024). Pathways to Resilient and Sustainable Economic Development Through the Blue Economy. In *Business, management and economics*. DOI: 10.5772/intechopen.1005480

Syuzairi, M. (2023). Strategic Management in the Maritime Sector in Mitigating Climate Change in Indonesia. *BIO Web of Conferences, 79*, 3002. DOI: 10.1051/bioconf/20237903002

Tremblay, D., Villeneuve, C., & Faubert, P. (2024). Alignment of the 2030 Agenda to the port industry. *Sustainable Development*. Advance online publication. DOI: 10.1002/sd.3108

Tsatsaronis, M., Syriopoulos, T., Karamperidis, S., Boura, G., & Dimopoulos, A. (2024). Quality assessment of ESG reporting among listed maritime companies. *Maritime Economics & Logistics, 26*(4), 592–611. DOI: 10.1057/s41278-024-00299-9

van Leeuwen, J., van Tatenhove, J. P. M., Coelho, N. F., Adjei, M., Pereira, H., Haapasaari, P., Varjopuro, R., Dodd, L., Toonen, H., Hegland, T. J., Prato, G., West, L., Flannery, W., Farrington, N., Dyremose, S. C. S., Pagani, D., van den Brink, T., Knol-Kauffman, M., Nielsen, K. N., . . . Lafitte, A. (2024). Deliverable D2.2 : Multi- layered Marine Governance Arrangements to support the European Green Deal. In *Research Portal Denmark*. Technical University of Denmark. https://local.forskningsportal.dk/local/dki-cgi/ws/cris-link?src=aau&id=aau-061fabde-9971-43c8-ac28-2b9e1a63f335&ti=Deliverable D2.2%3A Multi- layered Marine Governance Arrangements to support the European Green Deal

Whitehill, S., Hayles, C., Jenkins, S. E., & Taylour, J. (2022). Engagement with Higher Education Surface Pattern Design Students as a Catalyst for Circular Economy Action. *Sustainability (Basel), 14*(3), 1146. DOI: 10.3390/su14031146

Xiao, G., Wang, Y., Wu, R., Li, J., & Cai, Z. (2024). Sustainable Maritime Transport: A Review of Intelligent Shipping Technology and Green Port Construction Applications. In *Journal of Marine Science and Engineering* (Vol. 12, Issue 10, p. 1728). Multidisciplinary Digital Publishing Institute. DOI: 10.3390/jmse12101728

Xie, F., & Zhou, Z. (2025). Port green investment strategy under government subsidization and regulation policy. *Frontiers in Marine Science, 12*, 1661382. Advance online publication. DOI: 10.3389/fmars.2025.1661382

Yagci, M., & Noordali, M. (2024). *Maritime Trade: Riding the Waves of Commerce and Weathering the Storms of Disruption*. DOI: 10.55780/Re24043

Chapter 17
Aligning Global Standards:
International Frameworks and Regional Cooperation in Maritime Education Reform

Nurul Fadliana
http://orcid.org/0009-0003-1867-5532
Politeknik Ilmu Pelayaran Makassar, Indonesia

Nurul Hatifah
Politeknik Ilmu Pelayaran Makassar, Indonesia

Nur Alfahira
Politeknik Ilmu Pelayaran Makassar, Indonesia

Dzakiyah Ulya Yusuf
Politeknik Ilmu Pelayaran Makassar, Indonesia

ABSTRACT

This study examines the synchronization of global standards and regional collaboration in enhancing maritime education and training (MET). It examines how international frameworks, particularly those established by the IMO, ILO, and UNESCO, collaborate with regional organizations such as ASEAN and the European Union to promote competence, safety, sustainability, and inclusivity. Curriculum reform, accreditation, and technology-enabled learning are all seen as ways to bring things together. The analysis shows how important multi-stakeholder governance, capacity building, and policy innovation are for creating a unified, flexible, and future-ready maritime education system that promotes ethical and environmentally responsible human capital development.

DOI: 10.4018/979-8-3373-6670-8.ch017

SETTING THE COURSE: THE IMPERATIVE OF GLOBAL ALIGNMENT IN MARITIME EDUCATION

1.1 Evolving Global Maritime Landscape

Globalization, digitalization, and decarbonization are all having a big impact on the maritime industry. These changes are changing how the shipping industry works and how maritime education and training (MET) is set up. Globalization has made maritime trade networks bigger, brought in more people from different countries to work on ships, and made it even more important for countries to agree on safety and competency standards. As ships travel more complicated routes around the world, maritime education needs to prepare people to work well in places that are multicultural, high-tech, and focused on sustainability. The traditional focus on navigation, engineering, and seamanship has now been complemented by emerging areas such as cybersecurity, environmental stewardship, and data analytics for smart shipping systems. Safety awareness, ethical behavior, and leadership are all important traits that cadets need to develop in order to become professionals in basic maritime education. This is in line with the IMO-STCW guidelines that aim to promote safe and environmentally friendly maritime operations (Sijabat et al., 2024; Sihombing et al., 2024).

Digitalization, which combines AI, automation, and big data, has changed the maritime ecosystem in a big way. Smart ports, autonomous ships, and digital twins are changing how ships work, which means that curricula and training methods need to be changed. Using simulation-based methods in maritime training makes future maritime professionals more skilled and ready for their jobs, which is in line with the International Maritime Organization's (IMO) international standards (Ala et al., 2024). Schools and colleges need to find a balance between teaching theory and giving students hands-on digital learning experiences. This will help them develop skills like human-machine collaboration and critical thinking, which are important for the transition to Industry 5.0 (Sharma et al., 2022; Tusher et al., 2022).

Decarbonization makes things even more complicated, so MET schools need to make sustainability and environmental literacy important parts of their education. The International Maritime Organization's goal of having no greenhouse gas emissions by 2050 makes it clear that maritime education needs to include new skills related to green technologies, energy management, and environmental compliance (Bartusevičienė et al., 2023; Purba & Simanjuntak, 2024). As seafarers are increasingly expected to understand principles related to alternative fuels and emission control systems, maritime education must equip learners with both technical proficiency and a sense of ecological responsibility (Dacosta et al., 2022; Barus & Simanjuntak, 2023). The incorporation of environmental education into curricula signifies the increasing acknowledgment of the necessity for maritime professionals to be both proficient practitioners and custodians of the marine environment (Ghalwash et al., 2022).

The growing reliance on education, regulation, and technology shows how important it is to take a global and comprehensive approach. Regulatory frameworks need to change as new teaching methods are developed to make sure that the skills outlined in global conventions are actually used in schools (Sarjito, 2024; Demirel, 2020). As the maritime industry becomes more digital and accountable for the environment, it is important for policymakers, educators, and industry stakeholders to work together to keep maritime education relevant and high-quality. Ultimately, global alignment in educational standards will steer the sector towards safety, sustainability, and human-centered advancement, positioning maritime education as both a catalyst and a beneficiary of global transformation (Vio & Brdar, 2022; Yıldırım et al., 2022).

1.2 Rationale for International Standardization

The rationale for international standardization in maritime education lies at the core of ensuring competence, safety, and sustainability within a highly interconnected global industry. As maritime operations transcend national borders, the need for harmonized training and certification systems becomes essential to guarantee uniform levels of professionalism and operational reliability. Seafarers from different regions must share a common understanding of safety protocols, navigational procedures, and environmental obligations to maintain seamless coordination in international waters. The International Maritime Organization's (IMO) Standards of Training, Certification, and Watchkeeping for Seafarers (STCW) Convention serves as the foundational framework for achieving this alignment. By establishing clear guidelines for competence and certification, the STCW ensures that all maritime personnel possess the necessary knowledge, skills, and attitudes to perform their duties safely and efficiently (Rahmawati et al., 2025; Karahalil et al., 2024).

Beyond operational competence, international standardization supports the broader goals of sustainability and environmental responsibility. The maritime industry's transition toward green shipping and decarbonization requires a globally coherent approach to training on alternative fuels, emission control, and sustainable vessel operation. Without standardized curricula, uneven capacity building across nations could lead to disparities in safety, compliance, and environmental outcomes. Harmonization ensures that every seafarer—whether trained in an advanced maritime nation or a developing coastal state—contributes equally to achieving the IMO's sustainability targets and the United Nations Sustainable Development Goals (SDGs) (Bayotas, 2024; Matacera et al., 2024). Moreover, standardized practices enhance interoperability between nations, enabling ships and crews to operate seamlessly under multiple jurisdictions and regulatory systems. This interoperability is critically emphasized in the research discussing the legal characteristics of maritime safety (Dopilka et al., 2023).

Equally vital is the role of international benchmarks in maintaining quality assurance and institutional accountability. Global standards act as reference points against which the effectiveness of maritime education and training (MET) programs can be evaluated. Organizations such as the European Maritime Safety Agency (EMSA), the ASEAN Maritime Education and Training Network, and the International Association of Maritime Universities (IAMU) contribute to creating mechanisms for peer review, accreditation, and continuous improvement (Barus et al., 2024; Sihombing et al., 2024). These benchmarks not only uphold consistency in educational outcomes but also encourage innovation through global best practices and mutual recognition agreements. They foster a culture of transparency and trust among stakeholders, ensuring that MET institutions meet internationally recognized thresholds of excellence (Nhleko, 2023; Masuku, 2021).

Ultimately, international standardization is more than a bureaucratic necessity—it is a strategic instrument for cultivating a globally competent, ethical, and adaptable maritime workforce. By embedding harmonized quality benchmarks across all levels of maritime education, the sector secures its long-term resilience and competitiveness. In an era of rapid technological change and environmental imperatives, shared standards function as the common language of global maritime collaboration, steering the industry toward safety, sustainability, and continuous improvement (Fabian-Perona, 2025; Simanjuntak, 2023).

1.3 Challenges in Educational Fragmentation

Even though global conventions and frameworks have helped, maritime education still has problems with fragmentation that threaten the quality and consistency of workforce competence around the world. Different regions have different curricula, accreditation processes, and qualification systems, which makes a big difference in how maritime professionals are trained, tested, and certified. The International Maritime Organization (IMO) and the International Labour Organization (ILO) set general standards, but how they are put into action can vary from country to country, depending on national priorities, institutional capacities, and regional governance structures. These inconsistencies can make it hard for people to develop their skills evenly, make it hard for people to follow safety and environmental rules, and make it hard for people to recognize each other's qualifications across borders. All of these things make it harder to achieve the goal of a globally unified maritime education system.

One of the most obvious signs of fragmentation is differences in the curriculum. In many developing countries, maritime education institutions still use old syllabi that focus on traditional seamanship and technical operations while ignoring new areas like digital navigation, autonomous vessels, and green energy management. On the other hand, schools in places with advanced technology, like Northern Europe or East Asia, have added cutting-edge material on AI, cybersecurity, and environmental ethics. This difference in training makes it harder for seafarers from different regions to find work and makes operations less safe. Accreditation systems make things even more complicated. Some countries use strict external quality assurance that meets international standards, while others use national accreditation systems that don't do much to compare themselves to others. The lack of frameworks for mutual recognition makes this problem worse by making it harder for workers to move between countries and making qualifications less credible across borders.

The gap between developed and developing maritime nations is due to more than just differences in their curricula. It is also due to differences in access to infrastructure, technology, and funding. Institutions in low- and middle-income countries frequently encounter challenges due to insufficient resources for simulation-based learning, digital laboratories, and ongoing professional development. As a result, their graduates might not have had much experience with real-world maritime technologies or global compliance systems. Also, the gap gets bigger because of regional instability, policy fragmentation, and not enough money being spent on maritime research. These problems have led to a two-tiered maritime workforce: one that is ready for the needs of Industry 5.0 and sustainable shipping, and another that is stuck in old ways of doing things.

To fix these differences, we need a comprehensive and cooperative approach that includes building capacity, transferring technology, and making policies more inclusive. The ASEAN Mutual Recognition Arrangement (MRA) for maritime professionals, IAMU's global education partnerships, and IMO-led technical cooperation programs are all good ways to close the gap. But these efforts need to be bigger and more relevant to the situation in each country so that developing countries can fully take part in setting global maritime standards. Bridging the educational divide is not solely an issue of fairness; it is a strategic necessity for safeguarding global maritime safety, environmental conservation, and economic viability in an ever-more interconnected world.

GLOBAL GOVERNANCE AND REGULATORY FRAMEWORKS

2.1 The International Maritime Organization (IMO)

The International Maritime Organization (IMO) is the main organization that makes rules for international shipping. It makes sure that shipping is safe, secure, and good for the environment. The Standards of Training, Certification, and Watchkeeping for Seafarers (STCW) Convention is one of the most important tools for competence-based maritime education and training (MET) (Fabian-Perona, 2025). The STCW has changed over time to meet the changing needs of the maritime industry. It was first adopted in 1978 and then changed again in 1995 and 2010 (the Manila Amendments). It sets clear minimum standards for the education, certification, and watchkeeping of seafarers of all ranks. This makes sure that people working in international waters have the right technical and professional skills. This harmonization makes sure that safety and efficiency are always kept up, no matter what nationality the seafarer is or what flag the ship flies (Vujičić et al., 2020).

The STCW Convention has stayed relevant in the face of rapid changes in technology and rules because it has been constantly changed. The IMO's competency-based framework changes the focus of education from input-based to measurable performance outcomes. It stresses applying knowledge, making decisions in the field, and solving problems critically (Nyairo et al., 2025). This method encourages a culture of ongoing learning, where seafarers are not only trained to follow the rules, but also to adapt to changes in the maritime world. IMO's recent push to use blended learning, simulation-based assessments, and digital verification systems shows that it is committed to bringing training methods up to date with 21st-century standards (Atik, 2020). The organization also encourages global cooperation by doing evaluations, creating model courses, and offering capacity-building programs to help member states implement STCW in a consistent and effective way (Yu et al., 2025).

The IMO has taken the lead in adding environmental and digital skills to seafarer training as part of its response to the need for global sustainability. The International Convention for the Prevention of Pollution from Ships (MARPOL) and the International Maritime Organization's (IMO) greenhouse gas (GHG) strategy have a direct impact on how environmental stewardship is taught in MET classes. Seafarers must now learn how to run ships in a way that uses less energy, handle ballast water, and use alternative fuels like LNG, methanol, and hydrogen (Kut & Pietrucha-Urbanik, 2023). The rise of smart shipping, automation, and digitalization has led the IMO to put more emphasis on e-navigation, data analytics, and cyber risk management in the competency matrix (Kim et al., 2021).

The IMO makes sure that maritime education keeps up with changes in the industry by including sustainability and digital skills in its rules. These global standards create a generation of sailors who know how to use technology, care about the environment, and are good at math. In this way, the IMO reaffirms its important role in guiding maritime education toward a safer, smarter, and more sustainable future for the world (Konon, 2022).

2.2 The International Labour Organization (ILO)

The International Labour Organization (ILO) has a big impact on the moral, social, and human sides of the marine business. The 2006 Maritime Labour Convention (MLC), which is commonly nicknamed the "seafarers' bill of rights," is a notable example of this. The MLC pulls together and modifies more than 65 previous marine labor standards to make a whole set of rules for the rights, working conditions, and health of seafarers around the world. It sets the bare minimums for shelter, food, medical care, social protection, and jobs. This makes sure that those who work on ships are treated with respect and fairness. The MLC stipulates that competency must go together with an understanding of human rights, labor ethics, and the social obligations that come with being a sailor. This is part of the bigger picture of maritime education and training (MET). This human-centered approach to maritime training teaches both technical and moral abilities, making it a full process. This gets experts ready to not only run ships, but also make sure that maritime workplaces are fair and compassionate.

The MLC is a crucial aspect of the ILO's plan to improve human resources as a key part of maritime growth. It realizes that the marine business needs to keep growing over the long term, and that means not only using new technologies and following environmental standards, but also making sure that workers' skills, health, and professional integrity are always getting better. The ILO helps ensure that seafarers stay motivated, talented, and tough in an industry that is changing swiftly by enforcing equitable hiring practices, access to training, and opportunities for professional progression. The ILO is made up of three parts: governments, employers, and workers. This makes it easier for everyone to speak and come to an agreement on policy decisions. This makes sure that everyone can see, understand, and follow the rules for workers. The ILO's Guidelines for Training in Occupational Safety and Health (OSH) and partnerships with the IMO also help to make safety, health, and professional advancement a bigger part of MET frameworks.

Not only do people have to observe labor rights, welfare, and social protection standards, but they also need to learn about them. MET schools are more and more accountable for teaching these principles in their classes on marine law, labor conventions, ethical leadership, and mental health awareness. This form of education teaches future sailors about their rights and responsibilities, how to stand up for themselves, and how to help make the ship a better place to be. The COVID-19 pandemic made it increasingly evident how weak mariners are and how crucial it is to teach them how to be strong in times of crisis, such as when they are lonely, have mental health problems, or need social protection (Fabian-Perona, 2025).

The ILO gives maritime education a new meaning by using the MLC and other programs that go along with it to give people more authority. It makes sure that shipping businesses can compete with each other around the world without hurting anyone's dignity. By making sure that workers' rights and well-being are in line with training goals, the ILO supports a vision of maritime development that is fair, moral, and long-lasting. This makes the future of seafaring depend on fairness and shared accountability.

2.3 UNESCO and Sustainable Development Goals (SDGs)

The United Nations Educational, Scientific and Cultural Organization (UNESCO) is an important link between global education policies and the sustainable development agenda. It makes sure that maritime education is in line with the goals of the Sustainable Development Goals (SDGs). SDG 4—Quality Education—and SDG 14—Life Below Water—are two of these that are especially important for the maritime industry. UNESCO's support for learning that is open to everyone, fair, and lasts a lifetime is very important to the global maritime community, where education, caring for the environment, and being socially responsible all come together. UNESCO is a key player in embedding sustainability and human development principles into maritime education and training (MET) frameworks by encouraging international cooperation, new ideas in the curriculum, and the sharing of knowledge.

To connect maritime education with SDG 4 and SDG 14, the skills of sailors and other maritime professionals must be in line with the larger global goal of sustainable oceans and fair access to education.

SDG 4 stresses the need for quality education that is open to everyone and teaches skills that are useful for getting a job, doing decent work, and starting a business. In the maritime context, this means that programs not only teach sailors how to be technically and operationally excellent, but they also teach them how to care about the environment, think ethically, and work well with people from other cultures. UNESCO's Education for Sustainable Development (ESD) framework tells MET schools to include sustainability literacy in their classes. This includes marine ecology, pollution control, and climate resilience. This connection makes maritime professionals stronger protectors of the oceans, making sure that their daily work shows a deep respect for marine ecosystems.

SDG 14, which is about protecting ocean resources and using them in a way that is good for the environment, makes maritime education even more important as a way to protect the environment. The Intergovernmental Oceanographic Commission (IOC) of UNESCO supports ocean literacy programs that give seafarers, policymakers, and coastal communities the tools they need to make smart choices about how to manage the ocean. UNESCO encourages a culture of stewardship that goes beyond the classroom and into the real world of global shipping by promoting marine science education, research collaboration, and community outreach (Dacosta et al., 2022).

At the same time, UNESCO's commitment to lifelong and inclusive learning helps seafarers deal with the problems they face when trying to get continuing education and professional development. The group supports open and distance learning platforms and other flexible, technology-enabled learning systems to make sure that everyone can get training, no matter where they live or how much money they have. It helps member states and MET institutions build sustainable, competency-based learning ecosystems through programs like the Global Education Monitoring Report and the UNESCO-UNEVOC network.

By incorporating UNESCO's educational philosophy and the Sustainable Development Goals (SDG) framework into maritime reform, the sector progresses towards a vision of comprehensive human development, where technical proficiency coexists with ethical consciousness, environmental stewardship, and continuous learning. This synergy makes maritime education a driving force behind global sustainability, and it is based on both human and ecological values that will help the industry change.

REGIONAL COOPERATION AND POLICY HARMONIZATION

3.1 ASEAN and Regional Maritime Networks

The Association of Southeast Asian Nations (ASEAN) has become an important place for improving cooperation in maritime education and training (MET) in the region. This effort is driven by the shared belief that aligning standards is essential for the maritime industry's competitiveness, safety, and long-term viability (Sijabat et al., 2024). Southeast Asia is one of the world's most important maritime corridors, connecting the Pacific and Indian Oceans. Its shipping, port, and logistics sectors depend heavily on skilled workers. However, the differences in educational systems and rules between ASEAN member states have made it hard to achieve consistency in training and certification. To address this, the ASEAN Maritime Education and Training Cooperation Framework has been established to promote integration, reciprocal learning, and regional standardization in accordance with global benchmarks such as the International Maritime Organization's Standards of Training, Certification, and Watchkeeping for Seafarers (STCW) (Sihombing et al., 2024).

The ASEAN MET Cooperation Framework provides a systematic method to synchronize national training systems with global and regional goals. It encourages member states to work together on things like developing curricula, exchanging faculty, and doing joint research projects, which improve both quality and relevance (Ala et al., 2024). The creation of regional Centers of Excellence in Maritime Education is a key part of this framework. These centers will bring together experts, share resources, and encourage new ideas in maritime pedagogy and technology. These centers are regional hubs for building capacity, offering technical help, quality assurance, and support in new areas like digital navigation, green shipping, and maritime cybersecurity (Sharma et al., 2022). ASEAN's commitment to aligning MET with its Blueprint for the ASEAN Economic Community (AEC) 2025 further demonstrates the region's objective of developing a globally competitive maritime workforce that adheres to international standards while addressing local requirements (Tusher et al., 2022).

Another important part is that Southeast Asian countries recognize each other's maritime qualifications. This is a key part of making it easier for workers to move around and for economies to come together. The ASEAN Qualifications Reference Framework (AQRF) and the ongoing development of sector-specific mutual recognition arrangements (MRAs) in maritime professions seek to guarantee that certificates and competencies acquired in one member state are recognized in others (Bartusevičienė et al., 2023). Not only does this harmonization make it easier for workers to move around, but it also cuts down on unnecessary training, which in turn increases trust in regional certifications. This means that seafarers and maritime professionals will have better chances to work and move up in their careers across borders, which will make the regional labor market more open and strong (Purba & Simanjuntak, 2024).

3.2 European Union and Other Regional Models

The European Union (EU) has one of the most complete and powerful models for regional cooperation in maritime education, training, and governance. The EU's European Maritime Transport Policy has successfully brought together goals for education, safety, and sustainability into a single set of rules and goals for development (Ala et al., 2024). This policy stresses both the competitiveness of Europe's shipping industry and its duty to the environment and society. This vision is based on the idea that Europe can stay at the top of the global shipping and logistics industry by having a skilled, flexible, and creative maritime workforce. The EU's approach includes coordinating policies, forming partnerships between institutions, and creating funding mechanisms that make the connection between maritime education and industry needs stronger. This is useful for other areas, such as ASEAN and the Pacific.

The Erasmus+ mobility model is one of the EU's most important projects in this area. It encourages academic collaboration across borders, the exchange of students and staff, and the creation of joint degrees in maritime-related fields. European maritime academies have formed strong partnerships through Erasmus+ and its earlier programs. These partnerships make it easier for seafarers and maritime professionals to recognize each other's qualifications, share curricula, and improve their intercultural skills. The model encourages a culture of internationalization, where students learn about different maritime practices and rules from around the world. This prepares them to work well in the global fleet. Erasmus+ supports more than just student mobility. It also supports collaborative research, updating the curriculum, and innovation projects like the EMSHIP+ Master Program in Advanced Ship Design, which combines digitalization, environmental protection, and engineering excellence. This focus on shared learning and mutual growth shows how educational mobility can help bring regions together and make people more employable around the world.

Another important strength of the EU model is that it has the best ways to work together on research and get joint accreditation. The European Quality Assurance Register for Higher Education (EQAR) and the European Association for Quality Assurance in Higher Education (ENQA) make sure that maritime schools in all EU member states meet the same high standards. Joint accreditation systems help maritime academies make their programs more open, easier to compare, and better over time. This lets them follow both the Standards of Training, Certification, and Watchkeeping for Seafarers (STCW) and the Bologna Process framework for higher education. EU-funded research platforms like Horizon Europe and the European Maritime, Fisheries, and Aquaculture Fund (EMFAF) also make it easier for people from different countries to work together on new projects in areas like green technologies, autonomous shipping, and ocean governance (Fabian-Perona, 2025).

All of these projects show how regional cooperation, supported by strong policy alignment and trust in institutions, can turn maritime education into a system of innovation that connects the whole world. The EU experience shows that harmonization doesn't mean everyone is the same; it means everyone is committed to quality, flexibility, and long-term growth. The European model shows how to create a global maritime education ecosystem that connects policy, practice, and innovation by encouraging academic mobility, joint accreditation, and collaborative research.

3.3 South–South Cooperation and Cross-Regional Learning

South–South cooperation has become an increasingly powerful mechanism for strengthening maritime education and training (MET) among developing nations, especially in regions across Asia, Africa, Latin America, and the Pacific. Rooted in the principles of solidarity, equality, and mutual benefit, this collaborative approach allows nations with shared developmental challenges to exchange knowledge, resources, and best practices without relying solely on traditional North–South assistance. In the maritime sector, South–South cooperation promotes regional self-reliance and enhances global equity by enabling developing nations to collectively build capacity, modernize educational systems, and meet international standards such as those established by the International Maritime Organization (IMO) and the International Labour Organization (ILO) (Bartusevičienė et al., 2023)..

Partnerships among developing maritime nations have become instrumental in advancing capacity building through shared institutional expertise and joint training programs. Initiatives led by organizations such as the *Indian Ocean Rim Association (IORA)*, *ASEAN Maritime Education Network*, and *Africa's Regional Maritime University Consortium* have created structured pathways for cooperation in curriculum development, faculty training, and maritime safety research. For example, collaboration between Indonesia, the Philippines, and Malaysia has strengthened regional maritime training standards and facilitated the sharing of best practices in seafarer education, environmental compliance, and digital learning integration. Similarly, partnerships between African maritime academies and counterparts in Asia—supported by technical assistance from IMO's Integrated Technical Cooperation Programme (ITCP)—have enhanced competence-based education and simulation-based training capabilities. These alliances foster not only knowledge transfer but also institutional resilience, helping developing nations strengthen their human capital and policy alignment with global maritime conventions (Purba & Simanjuntak, 2024).

Equally important is the creation and sharing of joint training resources and innovation initiatives, which amplify the collective capacity of partner nations. Joint simulation centers, online learning platforms, and open-access digital repositories enable resource-limited institutions to access modern training tools and standardized instructional materials. Collaborative innovation hubs—such as those emerging in Ghana, Indonesia, and Vietnam—promote applied research in green shipping, port sustainability, and maritime digitalization. By pooling financial, technical, and intellectual resources, developing nations can collectively bridge the technology gap that has historically limited their participation in global maritime advancements. Moreover, these initiatives contribute to inclusive innovation by contextualizing maritime education to local realities, ensuring that solutions are culturally relevant and economically feasible.

Cross-regional learning within the Global South also encourages policy innovation through peer dialogue and adaptive governance. Countries learn from each other's reforms—whether in safety management, curriculum modernization, or accreditation systems—creating a dynamic ecosystem of mutual growth. In essence, South–South cooperation redefines maritime education as a shared enterprise of empowerment rather than dependency. By promoting collaboration, inclusivity, and innovation among developing maritime nations, it paves the way for a more balanced global maritime order—one in which all regions contribute meaningfully to safety, sustainability, and the future of ocean stewardship.

INSTITUTIONAL AND PEDAGOGICAL INTEGRATION

4.1 Curriculum Reform and Competency Mapping

At the heart of institutional and pedagogical change in maritime education and training (MET) are changes to the curriculum and mapping of competencies. As the maritime sector adapts to globalization, digitalization, and environmental demands, aligning national curricula with global and regional standards has become a crucial step in ensuring coherence, relevance, and employability (Sijabat et al., 2024). The International Maritime Organization's (IMO) Standards of Training, Certification, and Watchkeeping for Seafarers (STCW) Convention is the basis for global consistency in maritime competence. Regional frameworks, like the ASEAN Maritime Education and Training Cooperation Framework, add more layers of contextual alignment (Edar et al., 2024). But to make these benchmarks work in national education systems, schools need to make systematic changes to their curricula that bring together theory, practice, and values in a way that is based on results.

To make sure that national curricula are in line with global and regional standards, we need to use an evidence-based method that finds the gaps between current skills and the needs of the industry. Competency mapping is a strategic tool that helps MET institutions fill this gap by looking at job roles, performance expectations, and technological trends to create curricula that are both compliant and forward-looking (Mke, 2024). To make sure that training results meet the needs of the real world, this process requires working with regulatory bodies, shipping companies, and professional associations. Countries like the Philippines, Indonesia, and Singapore have shown good alignment by using modular, flexible learning paths that follow international standards while also taking into account the needs of local industries (Bokau & Sulistiana, 2024). By combining standardized learning outcomes and shared assessment frameworks, national curricula become tools for both following the rules and competing in the global job market.

Incorporating sustainability, ethics, and digital literacy as core components of maritime education is just as important for changing the curriculum. In the age of green and smart shipping, sailors must not only sail the seas but also deal with environmental risks and complicated socio-technical systems (Kim et al., 2021). Embedding sustainability means including marine ecology and pollution control in core courses. This will help future maritime professionals take care of the environment (Fasoulis, 2021). Ethical education guarantees that seafarers assimilate principles of integrity, equity, and human dignity, in alignment with the International Labour Organization's Maritime Labour Convention (MLC) and the overarching ethical obligations of global citizenship.

At the same time, digital literacy is now a must-have in modern MET, which includes knowing how to use e-navigation systems, simulation technologies, artificial intelligence (AI), and cybersecurity management (Mke, 2024). By creating curricula that combine digital skills with knowledge of ethics and the environment, schools help students become well-rounded professionals who are ready for Industry 5.0 and the blue economy. In short, curriculum reform and competency mapping are the guiding principles for the growth of maritime education. They make sure that learning stays relevant around the world, adaptable to new technologies, and based on strong moral principles in a maritime world that is changing quickly.

4.2 Accreditation and Quality Assurance Mechanisms

Accreditation and quality assurance serve as the backbone of credibility, accountability, and excellence in maritime education and training (MET). As maritime operations become increasingly complex and transnational, the need for globally consistent benchmarks to assess the quality of maritime institutions has never been more urgent. Accreditation ensures that MET providers not only comply with international conventions such as the *Standards of Training, Certification, and Watchkeeping for Seafarers* (STCW) but also demonstrate continuous improvement, innovation, and responsiveness to evolving industry needs. Global benchmarks provide a structured framework through which educational quality, institutional governance, and training outcomes can be systematically evaluated. These benchmarks—developed by organizations such as the International Maritime Organization (IMO), the International Labour Organization (ILO), and the International Association of Maritime Universities (IAMU)—promote a shared understanding of competence, performance, and ethical responsibility across national boundaries.

Global benchmarks for assessing maritime education institutions emphasize a combination of input, process, and outcome indicators. Inputs include faculty qualifications, training facilities, and curriculum relevance; processes focus on instructional design, student assessment, and stakeholder engagement; while outcomes evaluate graduate competence, employability, and compliance with international safety standards. The IMO Model Course series, for example, serves as a key instrument for standardizing curricula and teaching methodologies worldwide. IAMU further complements this by establishing the *Global Maritime Professional Framework (GMP)*, which defines competencies for the next generation of maritime professionals in line with technological and environmental transitions. These frameworks guide institutions in designing self-assessment mechanisms, peer reviews, and external evaluations that ensure transparency and global comparability (Mke, 2024).

In addition to these international instruments, ISO standards and regional accreditation bodies play a pivotal role in supporting the alignment of quality assurance systems. The ISO 9001:2015 Quality Management System has been widely adopted by maritime academies to standardize institutional processes and ensure a culture of continual improvement. This framework emphasizes leadership accountability, evidence-based decision-making, and stakeholder satisfaction—principles that are critical to maintaining institutional integrity and trust. On a regional level, bodies such as the *European Quality Assurance Register for Higher Education (EQAR)*, *ASEAN Quality Assurance Network (AQAN)*, and *Asia-Pacific Accreditation and Certification Commission (APACC)* foster harmonization across member states through peer evaluation, benchmarking exercises, and capacity-building initiatives. These regional and global mechanisms create a multilayered quality ecosystem that promotes mutual recognition and mobility within the maritime profession.

4.3 Technology-Enabled Learning and Cross-Border Collaboration

The digital transformation that is happening in education around the world has had a big impact on maritime education and training (MET), changing how knowledge is shared, delivered, and tested. As the maritime industry moves toward smart shipping and automation, schools and businesses are using technology to make learning environments that are dynamic and connected, going beyond geographical and institutional limits. Learning through technology and working together across borders are now important ways to promote innovation, inclusivity, and resilience in the development of maritime human capital. By bringing together digital platforms, simulators, and artificial intelligence (AI), MET institutions are creating shared learning ecosystems that connect classroom theory with real-world maritime practice and encourage cooperation between countries.

Using digital platforms, simulators, and AI to create shared learning ecosystems has greatly increased the ability of maritime schools to offer flexible, high-quality training. Students and professionals can learn interactively and based on their skills from anywhere in the world with the help of digital learning platforms like cloud-based learning management systems (LMS), virtual reality (VR) environments, and online simulation tools. Advanced maritime simulators create very realistic scenarios for navigating ships, running engines, handling cargo, and managing emergencies. This lets people learn by doing without the risks or costs of live training. Adaptive learning analytics, personalized feedback, and predictive performance tracking are all ways that artificial intelligence makes this ecosystem even better. They make sure that each learner moves at the best pace for them. AI-driven systems are also being used for remote testing and certification, which makes skill evaluation more open and consistent. These technologies make maritime education more accessible to everyone, especially developing countries and learners who are already at a disadvantage.

The rise of virtual maritime training networks that connect institutions, industries, and regulators across borders is also a big change. These networks make it easier for people to work together on programs, share curricula, and do research that leads to mutual recognition and ongoing professional growth. The International Association of Maritime Universities (IAMU) has led the way in creating digital cooperation models like virtual conferences, global e-classrooms, and shared research repositories. The ASEAN Maritime Education and Training Network and the European Maritime University Alliance, for example, have also used virtual exchange programs and online accreditation platforms to make sure that learning continues and that quality is guaranteed. These shared ecosystems make it easier for people to share knowledge, promote cultural exchange, and build up institutions by sharing their expertise and digital infrastructure (Edar et al., 2024).

The move toward technology-enabled and collaborative maritime education is a big change in how seafarers and other maritime professionals get ready for the future. By embracing digital innovation, MET institutions are not just keeping up with technological progress; they are also creating a new way of learning that focuses on connectivity, inclusivity, and lifelong learning. Virtual maritime networks, powered by AI and immersive technologies, will make sure that the next generation of seafarers is globally competent, technologically savvy, and morally sound. This will set the maritime industry up for a sustainable, knowledge-driven future.

STEERING THE FUTURE: STRATEGIES FOR GLOBAL–REGIONAL SYNERGY

5.1 Multi-Stakeholder Governance and Policy Innovation

The future of maritime education and training (MET) depends on the effectiveness of multi-stakeholder governance and policy innovation that unites global, regional, and national actors in a shared commitment to quality, inclusivity, and sustainability. As maritime challenges grow increasingly interconnected—ranging from digital transformation and decarbonization to labor mobility and social equity—no single institution or organization can address them in isolation. A collaborative governance framework that integrates the perspectives and expertise of the International Maritime Organization (IMO), the International Labour Organization (ILO), regional blocs such as ASEAN and the European Union (EU), and academic and industry partners has become essential. This convergence not only strengthens global maritime standards but also fosters innovation in policy design, ensuring that education systems remain relevant and resilient in the face of rapid change.

Collaborative governance involving IMO, ILO, regional blocs, and academia promotes an integrated approach to maritime policy formulation and implementation. The IMO continues to guide technical and environmental standards, ensuring that seafarer training aligns with evolving conventions such as the *STCW* and *MARPOL*. The ILO complements this by embedding labor rights, social protection, and welfare principles into educational and institutional frameworks through the *Maritime Labour Convention (MLC)*. Regional organizations such as ASEAN, the African Union (AU), and the EU play a crucial role in contextualizing these global standards within local governance systems, bridging global commitments with regional realities. Academia, meanwhile, functions as both a think tank and an implementation hub—translating international conventions into curriculum innovation, pedagogical reform, and evidence-based research. Universities and maritime academies provide the intellectual infrastructure necessary to analyze emerging trends, design responsive training models, and prepare policymakers with the analytical tools required for adaptive governance (Benstaali, 2024).

Policy alignment for inclusive and future-ready maritime education demands that stakeholders move beyond compliance-based systems toward adaptive, innovation-driven governance. This includes harmonizing standards across jurisdictions, integrating digital competencies into educational policy, and embedding sustainability and ethical leadership into the maritime learning agenda. Cross-sectoral collaboration—linking ministries of transport, labor, education, and environment—ensures that policy initiatives are coherent and mutually reinforcing. For instance, policies that incentivize green shipping must be accompanied by training reforms that develop corresponding environmental skills. Similarly, initiatives promoting digital transformation in ports and logistics require complementary education policies that prioritize digital literacy and data-driven decision-making.

At its core, multi-stakeholder governance is about shared accountability and collective innovation. By fostering dialogue among international bodies, regional networks, and educational institutions, the maritime sector can create a future-oriented ecosystem that balances competitiveness with sustainability. Policy innovation, grounded in inclusivity and collaboration, will ensure that maritime education evolves not as a fragmented system but as a globally aligned, regionally adaptive framework—capable of navigating the complexities of a rapidly changing world while upholding safety, equity, and excellence at sea and ashore.

5.2 Capacity Building and Knowledge Exchange

Building capacity and sharing knowledge are two of the most important parts of making a maritime education system that is ready for the future, competitive on a global scale, and adaptable to the needs of the region. In a time when technology is changing quickly, the environment is important, and the job market is changing, developing countries often have capacity gaps that make it hard for them to fully participate in global maritime standards. To fix these differences, we need to work together to come up with plans that encourage shared learning, resource sharing, and long-term strengthening of institutions. Joint research projects, programs that let professors move around, and networks for faculty development, all backed by long-term funding, are important tools for making maritime education a dynamic system of innovation and inclusion.

Joint research, mobility programs, and networks for faculty development help maritime institutions around the world share ideas and knowledge with each other. Joint research not only bolsters scientific investigation but also guarantees that policy and curriculum reforms are guided by empirical evidence and optimal practices. Collaborative projects within frameworks like the International Association of Maritime Universities (IAMU), ASEAN Maritime Education Network, and the European Maritime University Alliance have illustrated the advantages of consolidating intellectual and technical resources. Research domains such as green shipping, autonomous navigation, and maritime cybersecurity illustrate how international collaborations foster both knowledge enhancement and innovation.

Academic and professional mobility programs make this exchange even better by giving students, faculty, and maritime professionals the chance to work in different kinds of operational environments and governance systems. Programs like Erasmus+ in Europe or ASEAN International Mobility for Students (AIMS) have helped a lot with making maritime skills more similar and recognizing each other's qualifications. These exchanges also help people from different cultures understand each other better and build professional networks that last beyond formal training. At the same time, faculty development networks are very important for making sure that teaching is of high quality and new ideas are used. Workshops for continuous professional development (CPD), peer mentoring programs, and digital teaching fellowships help teachers stay up to date on new technologies, standards for sustainability, and ways to teach that are open to everyone (Benstaali, 2024).

Financing mechanisms for regional training excellence centers are just as important because they provide the institutional infrastructure needed to keep these programs going. Setting up Centers of Excellence with the help of public-private partnerships, regional development funds, and international donors makes sure that people can use the latest facilities, simulators, and e-learning platforms. The IMO's Integrated Technical Cooperation Programme (ITCP), the World Maritime University (WMU), and the Asian Development Bank's (ADB) Education and Skills Development Fund have all set great examples of how to give money to build capacity in maritime education. Sustainable financing mechanisms also include getting national governments to set aside money for maritime education, giving businesses incentives to invest in their workers, and starting scholarship programs for groups that aren't well represented.

5.3 Vision for a Unified Maritime Education Ecosystem

The future of maritime education lies in the creation of a unified global ecosystem—one that harmonizes international standards with regional adaptability while nurturing resilient, ethical, and future-oriented human capital. As the maritime industry confronts rapid technological change, environmental challenges, and evolving workforce expectations, a coherent and interconnected education system becomes vital (Simanjuntak, 2023). A unified maritime education ecosystem does not imply uniformity; rather, it embraces diversity within a framework of shared values, competencies, and strategic objectives. It envisions a maritime community where institutions, industries, and governments collaborate seamlessly to ensure that every seafarer and maritime professional—regardless of origin—meets common standards of excellence, innovation, and integrity (Bayotas, 2024).

Toward a globally coherent yet regionally adaptive maritime education system, the first step is building structural alignment among international conventions, regional frameworks, and national policies. The Standards of Training, Certification, and Watchkeeping for Seafarers (STCW), the Maritime Labour Convention (MLC), and the Sustainable Development Goals (SDGs) form the foundation of global coherence, ensuring universal quality, welfare, and sustainability benchmarks (Simanjuntak, 2023). Regional organizations—such as ASEAN, the African Union (AU), and the European Union (EU)—should contextualize these standards through localized curricula, regional accreditation mechanisms, and mutual recognition arrangements. Such layered alignment allows flexibility while maintaining global consistency. It ensures that developing nations can adopt international standards without compromising their unique socio-economic and cultural contexts. Digital platforms, shared learning repositories, and AI-driven maritime databases can further facilitate global-regional coordination, enabling continuous knowledge exchange and standardized competency verification across borders (Quintão et al., 2025).

At the heart of this vision is the roadmap for cultivating resilient, ethical, and future-oriented human capital. The maritime workforce of tomorrow must embody adaptability, ecological consciousness, and technological fluency. Training institutions should embed lifelong learning pathways that integrate technical proficiency with digital literacy, emotional intelligence, and cross-cultural communication (Kamal, 2024). Emphasizing ethical leadership ensures that future maritime professionals act responsibly in safeguarding both human life and the marine environment. Moreover, resilience must be cultivated through psychological preparedness, health and safety education, and equitable career development opportunities. These human-centered competencies position seafarers as agents of sustainable change rather than passive participants in global trade (Simanjuntak, 2023).

This unified vision also calls for inclusive governance and collaborative investment. Governments, industries, and academia must co-develop strategic roadmaps supported by financing for Centers of Excellence, research innovation hubs, and digital learning networks (Ma, 2025). By fostering a globally coherent yet regionally responsive system, the maritime education community can navigate future uncertainties with confidence and solidarity. Ultimately, a unified maritime education ecosystem is not only an educational reform—it is a collective commitment to shaping a maritime future that is safe, sustainable, and grounded in shared human values and global responsibility (Benstaali, 2024).

CONCLUSION

The shift of maritime education and training (MET) toward global–regional alignment is a key step in getting the maritime industry ready for the future by making sure that workers are skilled, moral, and ready for change. As globalization, digitalization, and decarbonization change the industry, it is more important than ever to have consistent educational standards. International organizations like the IMO, ILO, and UNESCO set the rules and help things grow, while regional groups like ASEAN and the European Union make sure that things fit in with their own cultures and work together to come up with new ideas. They work together to create a framework for developing maritime human capital that is based on competence, safety, sustainability, and inclusivity.

Institutional reforms, such as updating the curriculum, getting accreditation, and making sure quality, let MET providers include environmental literacy, ethical awareness, and digital skills in their teaching and testing. The use of technology in learning, such as simulators, artificial intelligence, and virtual collaboration platforms, has made learning more accessible and created a learning environment that is connected to the rest of the world. Multi-stakeholder governance, on the other hand, makes sure that educational change is based on evidence and includes everyone. It also makes sure that global standards are met in local situations.

The goal of a unified maritime education ecosystem shows how important it is for things to be consistent and flexible. Countries can create maritime education systems that are strong, fair, and able to handle future problems by making sure that international standards match local needs. This ecosystem needs more than just policies and partnerships; it also needs ongoing funding for research, mobility, and faculty development.

In the end, the goal of global–regional synergy in maritime education shows a shared desire to build a maritime future based on working together, coming up with new ideas, and acting ethically. It calls for a constant, group effort to train maritime professionals who are not only skilled but also aware of the environment and responsible in their actions. This will help keep the seas safe, sustainable, and a place of global solidarity.

REFERENCES

Ala, A., Hamidi, N., Yoniessa, S., Masito, F., & Muis, M. (2024). Simulation-based learning in maritime training: Enhancing competency and preparedness. *Meteor Stip Marunda*, *17*(1), 95–102. DOI: 10.36101/msm.v17i1.361

Atik, O. (2020). Eye tracking for assessment of situational awareness in bridge resource management training. *Journal of Eye Movement Research*, *12*(3). Advance online publication. DOI: 10.16910/jemr.12.3.7 PMID: 33828730

Bartusevičienė, I., Kitada, M., & Valionienė, E. (2023). Rethinking maritime education and training for generation z students. Regional Formation and Development Studies, 16-29. DOI: 10.15181/rfds.v41i3.2543

Barus, I., & Simanjuntak, M. (2023). Integrating environmental education into maritime english curriculum for vocational learners: challenges and opportunities. Bio Web of Conferences, 79, 08001. DOI: 10.1051/bioconf/20237908001

Barus, I., Simanjuntak, R., Siahaan, R., Toko, G., & Resmayasari, I. (2024). Cultural and linguistic challenges in global maritime education (navigating english usage). *Meteor Stip Marunda*, *17*(1), 121–130. DOI: 10.36101/msm.v17i1.358

Bayotas, M. (2024). Shifting from global maritime professional to global maritime citizen.. DOI: 10.5821/mt.13183

Benstaali, B. (2024). Internationalisation of higher education in middle east and africa., 341-366. DOI: 10.4018/979-8-3693-6849-7.ch013

Bokau, J., & Sulistiana, O. (2024). Reshaping curriculum of indonesian maritime education and training. *International Journal of Social Service and Research*, *4*(6). Advance online publication. DOI: 10.46799/ijssr.v4i6.809

Dacosta, E., Jin, Z., Bowers, J., & Abdul-Salam, R. (2022). Green maritime practices in an emerging economy towards the achievement of sustainable development: A ghanaian context. *Benchmarking*, *30*(9), 3637–3673. DOI: 10.1108/BIJ-10-2021-0629

Demirel, E. (2020). Maritime education and training in the digital era. *Universal Journal of Educational Research*, *8*(9), 4129–4142. DOI: 10.13189/ujer.2020.080939

Dopilka, V., Zagorodnyuk, S., & Osadtsa, R. (2023). Legal characteristics of maritime safety. *Uzhhorod National University Herald Series Law*, *2*(76), 96–100. DOI: 10.24144/2307-3322.2022.76.2.16

Edar, A., Tongco, A., Arizalita, B., Baldomar, L., Leon, N., Manlimos, J., & Parami, M. (2024). Teaching strategies in simulator-based courses: Basis for faculty development program. *Jpair Institutional Research*, *22*(1), 112–129. DOI: 10.7719/irj.v22i1.885

Fabian-Perona, E. (2025). Maritime education and language as the acting link between bridge and engine room – a report. Educational Role of Language Journal, 2025-1(13), 64-67. DOI: 10.36534/erlj.2025.01.07

Fabian-Perona, E. (2025). Maritime education and language as the acting link between bridge and engine room – a report. Educational Role of Language Journal, 2025-1(13), 64-67. DOI: 10.36534/erlj.2025.01.07

Fasoulis, I. (2021). Investigating the effectiveness of the maritime regulatory regime to address a socially responsible shipping industry: A content analysis study. *International Journal of Sustainable Development and Planning*, *16*(4), 629–640. DOI: 10.18280/ijsdp.160403

Ghalwash, G., El-Bawab, M., Swidan, A., Rowihil, M., Ibrahim, A., & Farag, Y. (2022). A proposed protocol for gmp-bok gap analysis: case study at aastmt. Maritime Research and Technology, 1(1), 025. DOI: 10.21622/mrt.2022.01.1.025

Kamal, M. (2024). Labour market skills for seafarers: a comparative analysis of saudi arabia and the global context. pst, 48(4), 5866-5891. DOI: 10.52783/pst.1383

Karahalil, M., Lützhöft, M., & Scanlan, J. (2024). *Factors impacting curricula in maritime simulator-based education.* Wmu Journal of Maritime Affairs., DOI: 10.1007/s13437-024-00351-8

Kim, T., Sharma, A., Bustgaard, M., Gyldensten, W., Nymoen, O., Tusher, H., & Nazir, S. (2021). The continuum of simulator-based maritime training and education. *Wmu Journal of Maritime Affairs*, *20*(2), 135–150. DOI: 10.1007/s13437-021-00242-2

Konon, N. (2022). Prospects for modern maritime education and training practices in terms of distance learning. *Shipping & Navigation*, *33*(1), 54–66. DOI: 10.31653/2306-5761.33.2022.54-66

Kut, P., & Pietrucha-Urbanik, K. (2023). Bibliometric analysis of renewable energy research on the example of the two european countries: Insights, challenges, and future prospects. *Energies*, *17*(1), 176. DOI: 10.3390/en17010176

Ma, R., Li, T., & Yuan, X. (2025). The characteristics, paths and challenges of china participating in global vocational education governance. *EIR*, *3*(4), 262–266. DOI: 10.18063/eir.v3i4.1043

Masuku, M. (2021). Enhancing maritime education through online distance learning in developing environments: case study of south africa., 143-154. DOI: 10.1007/978-3-030-64088-0_13

Matacera, A., Tola, F., Tarantino, M., Gianvincenzi, M., & Mosconi, E. (2024). A comparative analysis of european sustainability reporting practices: the role of esg standards and sdg's in enhancing effectiveness. jlsdgr, 5(2), e01918. DOI: 10.47172/2965-730X.SDGsReview.v5.n02.pe01918

Mke, D. (2024). Assessment of digital competencies in south african maritime education and training institutions: A study of evaluation methods for future seafarers. *SAJMET*, *3*, 103–120. DOI: 10.47348/SAJMET/2024/i1a8

Nhleko, Y. (2023). Challenges in international convention on the standards of training, certification and watchkeeping compliance: A case study of the south african maritime education and training system. *SAJMET*, *2*(1), 121–131. DOI: 10.47348/SAJMET/2023/i1a8

Nyairo, F., Haavardtun, P., Lindroos, E., Munim, Z., Lampiola, J., Salokorpi, M., ... & Krabbel, H. (2025). Instructional approaches for simulator-based maritime education and training., 120-131. DOI: 10.1007/978-3-031-84170-5_11

Purba, D., & Simanjuntak, M. (2024). Sustainable maritime education: Integrating environmental science for global competence. [Jurnal Pendidikan Biologi Indonesia]. *Jpbi*, *10*(1), 310–319. DOI: 10.22219/jpbi.v10i1.32588

Quintão, V., Sousa, G., Lino, L., Alves, F., Gonçalves, A., & Carlos, R. (2025). Building a competency-based curriculum in pediatric anesthesia in latin america. *Revista Chilena De Anestesia*, *54*(5), 551. DOI: 10.25237/revchilanestv54n5-10

Rahmawati, M., Pitana, T., Handani, D., & Siswantoro, N. (2025). Utilization of ais data and ship simulator integration in maritime safety: A systematic literature review. *IOP Conference Series. Earth and Environmental Science*, *1461*(1), 012049. DOI: 10.1088/1755-1315/1461/1/012049

Sarjito, A. (2024). Sailing towards excellence: Revamping the education policy to foster maritime leadership in indonesia. *Saintara Jurnal Ilmiah Ilmu-Ilmu Maritim*, *8*(1), 32–43. DOI: 10.52475/saintara.v8i1.262

Sharma, A., Undheim, P., & Nazir, S. (2022). Design and implementation of ai chatbot for colregs training. *Wmu Journal of Maritime Affairs*, *22*(1), 107–123. DOI: 10.1007/s13437-022-00284-0

Sihombing, D., Dwiyani, N., Martha, Y., Hutabarat, C., & Sutrisno, S. (2024). Impact of international standards on maritime education: Perspectives of junior cadets. *Meteor Stip Marunda*, *17*(1), 7–15. DOI: 10.36101/msm.v17i1.357

Sihombing, D., Dwiyani, N., Martha, Y., Hutabarat, C., & Sutrisno, S. (2024). Impact of international standards on maritime education: Perspectives of junior cadets. *Meteor Stip Marunda*, *17*(1), 7–15. DOI: 10.36101/msm.v17i1.357

Sijabat, P., Simanjuntak, M., Mudakir, M., Putrawan, B., & Lumingkewas, M. (2024). Empowering literacy in maritime education: Strategies and professionalism alignment. *Meteor Stip Marunda*, *17*(1), 42–50. DOI: 10.36101/msm.v17i1.359

Simanjuntak, M. (2023). Elevating maritime competence: A qualitative analysis of semester 3 cadets' perspectives at maritime institute jakarta (stip jakarta). *Morfologi*, *1*(6), 192–203. DOI: 10.61132/morfologi.v1i6.255

Tusher, H., Nazir, S., Mallam, S., & Munim, Z. (2022). Artificial neural network (ann) for performance assessment in virtual reality (vr) simulators: from surgical to maritime training., 0334-0338. DOI: 10.1109/IEEM55944.2022.9989816

Vio, I., & Brdar, M. (2022). Maritime autonomous surface ships – international and national legal framework. *Journal of Maritime & Transportation Science*, *62*(1), 141–155. DOI: 10.18048/2022.62.09

Vujičić, S., Hasanspahić, N., Gundić, A., & Hrdalo, N. (2020). Assessment for ensuring adequately qualified instructors in maritime education and training institutions. *Athens Journal of Sciences*, *7*(2), 115–126. DOI: 10.30958/ajs.7-2-4

Yıldırım, U., Şükür, F., & İnegöl, G. M. (2022). Quality criteria in maritime education and training. *Dokuz Eylül Üniversitesi Denizcilik Fakültesi Dergisi*, *14*(2), 236–263. DOI: 10.18613/deudfd.1058625

Yu, Y., Lee, C., & Ahn, Y. (2025). Developing a competency-based transition education framework for marine superintendents: A dacum-integrated approach in the context of eco-digital maritime transformation. *Sustainability (Basel), 17*(14), 6455. DOI: 10.3390/su17146455

Chapter 18
Cross-Cultural Understanding in Maritime Education for Globally Competent Seafarers

Yuniar Ayu Hafita
http://orcid.org/0009-0002-1300-226X
Politeknik Pelayaran Sorong, Indonesia

Agus Sulistiono
Universitas Negeri Semarang, Indonesia

Ryan Puby Sumarta
http://orcid.org/0009-0008-9889-5928
Politeknik Pelayaran Sorong, Indonesia

Muhammad Idris
Politeknik Pelayaran Sorong, Indonesia

Dwi Haryanto
Politeknik Pelayaran Sorong, Indonesia

Dodik Widarbowo
Politeknik Pelayaran Sorong, Indonesia

ABSTRACT

This study investigates the effectiveness of the Cross Cultural Understanding (CCU) course in maritime higher education and its role in preparing cadets for multicultural workplaces. Using a mixed methods design, data from 157 students and four lecturers were analyzed. Survey results showed high satisfaction, with CCU Comprehension (M = 4.36) and Benefit of the Course (M = 4.41) rated highest. Interviews revealed that cadets understand basic concepts but struggle with abstract topics such as cultural bias. Experiential learning methods such as role plays, case studies, and group projects were effective in improving intercultural communication. Overall, the CCU course successfully enhances intercultural competence, though further improvements are needed to strengthen critical thinking and institutional recognition of its relevance to maritime safety and operational performance.

INTRODUCTION

One of the most dynamic and multinational sectors is the maritime industry. With over 90% of world trade involving maritime transport, the industry plays a central role in global economic connectivity and development (UNCTAD, 2021). Professionals in this field, including seafarers, port operators, and maritime managers, are often required to work in multicultural environments where effective communication

DOI: 10.4018/979-8-3373-6670-8.ch018

and collaboration are essential. Cross-cultural understanding (CCU) has therefore become a fundamental competency for maritime professionals to ensure operational efficiency, safety, and harmonious teamwork in diverse contexts (Phanphichit & Bartusevičienė, 2024).

In Indonesia, the maritime sector has experienced rapid growth, reflecting the country's strategic position as the world's largest archipelagic state. The government's "Global Maritime Fulcrum" initiative emphasizes the strategic importance of the seas as connectors and unifiers across the nation (Irwan, 2020). Consequently, maritime education and training (MET) programs in Indonesia must prepare seafarers not only in technical and navigational skills but also in the cultural competencies required for multinational work environments. Developing cross-cultural awareness among cadets is therefore a pressing educational priority (Lau & Ng, 2015).

Traditional MET programs in Indonesia have primarily emphasized operational skills such as navigation, seamanship, and safety management. While these competencies are critical to maritime safety, the focus on developing cross-cultural communication skills remains limited. This gap in the curriculum may hinder the ability of cadets to interact effectively with multinational crews and adapt to the human and social dimensions of maritime operations (Riyanto et al., 2023).

Indonesian seafarers often face significant challenges in intercultural communication when working on ships with multinational crews. Language differences, varying communication styles, and cultural norms frequently lead to misunderstandings, which are sometimes mitigated only through nonverbal cues (Riyanto et al., 2023). These challenges underscore the need for structured training in CCU, as informal or on-the-job learning alone is insufficient to prepare seafarers for complex, multicultural maritime environments.

The integration of cross-cultural understanding into MET is particularly relevant in ensuring safety and operational efficiency within Indonesia's vast archipelago. Given the country's sovereign rights over its maritime territory, competent and culturally aware seafarers contribute not only to operational success but also to national security and unity (Irwan, 2020). Enhancing cadets' CCU skills ensures that they can effectively collaborate, resolve conflicts, and navigate the diverse social dynamics on board ships.

The post-pandemic recovery period has further highlighted the importance of CCU in maritime education. With sectors such as cruise shipping increasingly prioritizing sustainable development, global citizenship, and crew competence, seafarers are expected to operate in multicultural teams while adhering to international standards and ethical practices (Yoon, 2023). This development necessitates that MET institutions equip students with both technical proficiency and intercultural competence.

Improving language proficiency is another key component of preparing maritime students for multicultural environments. Task-based learning, multimodal communication strategies, and cultural awareness training have been shown to enhance students' ability to interact effectively across cultural boundaries (Simanjuntak et al., 2024). Such pedagogical interventions provide cadets with the practical skills needed to navigate diverse communication scenarios onboard.

Crew resource management (CRM) training also emphasizes the critical role of effective communication in mitigating human error, which is often exacerbated by intercultural misunderstandings (Simanjuntak et al., 2024). By integrating CCU and communication strategies into MET curricula, cadets can better prevent operational errors and enhance overall maritime safety, complementing the technical training provided in conventional courses (Dominguez-Péry et al., 2021).

Despite these imperatives, the current MET curriculum in Indonesia remains heavily oriented toward technical competencies, with limited structured courses explicitly targeting intercultural skills. As a result, many cadets acquire cultural awareness informally, which may result in inconsistent preparedness for the complexities of international maritime operations. Compared to best practices in other maritime nations, Indonesian MET institutions are still developing systematic approaches to teaching intercultural competence (Lau & Ng, 2015).

The introduction of a dedicated CCU course offers a strategic solution to these challenges. By incorporating language development, cultural awareness, and collaborative strategies into the formal curriculum, such a course can systematically prepare cadets to work effectively in multicultural settings. This approach ensures that learning outcomes are standardized, measurable, and aligned with the competencies required in modern global shipping operations (Phanphichit & Bartusevičienė, 2024).

A structured CCU course also aligns with the International Maritime Organization's (IMO) emphasis on the human element and effective resource management. By emphasizing the development of interpersonal, intercultural, and problem-solving skills alongside technical knowledge, MET programs can produce globally competent seafarers capable of meeting international standards and improving operational performance (UNCTAD, 2021).

Ultimately, integrating cross-cultural understanding into Indonesian MET represents not only an educational innovation but also a strategic investment in maritime safety, professionalism, and competitiveness. Equipping cadets with the knowledge, skills, and attitudes to navigate diverse cultural environments ensures that they are prepared for the complex social and operational challenges of modern seafaring, contributing to both national and global maritime objectives.

METHOD

This study employed a mixed-methods design, integrating both quantitative and qualitative approaches to comprehensively examine the implementation of the Cross-Cultural Understanding (CCU) course in Maritime Education and Training. The quantitative component consisted of a survey administered to 157 students across various semesters. The survey was designed to capture students' perceptions of multiple dimensions of the course, including comprehension of CCU concepts, relevance of course materials, clarity of teaching, readiness for multicultural environments, lecturer competence, internalization of values, assessment systems, learning challenges, and perceived benefits of the course. Data collection was conducted during the semester in which the CCU course was delivered, ensuring that responses reflected students' immediate learning experiences.

The qualitative component involved in-depth interviews with four lecturers who had teaching experience ranging from six to fifteen years. These interviews aimed to provide deeper insights into pedagogical methods, student engagement, perceived learning barriers, and suggestions for course improvement. Interviews were conducted both face-to-face and online, with each session lasting between 45 and 60 minutes. This approach allowed for flexibility in scheduling while capturing rich, contextualized information regarding the instructional practices and challenges associated with teaching CCU in a maritime educational setting.

Quantitative data were analyzed using descriptive statistics to determine central tendencies, variations, and trends in students' responses, providing a clear overview of the overall effectiveness and reception of the course. Meanwhile, qualitative data were examined through thematic analysis, identifying recurring patterns and key themes related to teaching strategies, student comprehension, and the integration of cross-cultural content into the curriculum. The integration of both datasets strengthened the validity and reliability of the findings, enabling a nuanced interpretation of how CCU education contributes to cadets' intercultural competence and highlighting areas requiring pedagogical refinement.

RESULT

Survey Findings

The survey results indicate a generally positive evaluation of the Cross-Cultural Understanding (CCU) course by the students, with mean scores above 4.0 for most aspects, reflecting strong approval of the course's content, instructional quality, and perceived benefits. This section will provide a detailed breakdown of the student evaluations across nine key aspects of the course, offering an in-depth analysis of the findings and contextualizing them within existing research on intercultural competence and maritime education. Additionally, we will explore possible interpretations of the data, linking it to potential pedagogical improvements and furthering the discourse on intercultural education within Maritime Education and Training (MET).

Table 1 presents the descriptive statistics for students' evaluations across nine aspects of the CCU course. These aspects include various dimensions such as comprehension, relevance, teaching clarity, preparedness for multicultural environments, lecturer competency, internalization of values, assessment practices, learning challenges, and perceived benefits of the course. The table below provides the mean scores (M) and standard deviations (SD) for each aspect, allowing for a quantitative understanding of how students perceived each element of the course:

Table 1. Student Perceptions of the CCU Course (Scale 1–5)

Aspects	Mean	Std. Deviation
CCU Comprehension	4.25	.65
Relevant Material	4.12	.72
Clarity of Teaching	4.35	.58
Readiness to Face a Multicultural Environment	4.08	.69
Lecturers' Competency	4.30	.61
Internalization of Values and Attitudes of Tolerance	4.05	.71
Assessment System	3.95	.74
Learning Challenges	3.72	.80
Benefit of the Course	4.20	.63

The results from the survey provide insightful feedback on the Cross-Cultural Understanding (CCU) course, shedding light on both its strengths and areas for improvement. The overall findings indicate that students gave high ratings to certain aspects of the course, suggesting their strong appreciation for the teaching process, instructional quality, and the course's utility in preparing them for future professional roles.

Clarity of Teaching (M = 4.35, SD = 0.58)

The highest rating in the survey was given to the clarity of teaching, with a mean score of 4.35 and a standard deviation of 0.58, reflecting high student satisfaction with how clearly the course material was delivered. This suggests that the instructional strategies employed by the lecturers were highly effective in making the content comprehensible and accessible. Students appreciated the well-structured delivery of the material, as it played a critical role in understanding abstract concepts such as cross-cultural communication and intercultural competence. The low standard deviation indicates that most students found the lessons easy to follow, contributing to an overall positive evaluation of the teaching process.

A mean score of 4.35 indicates that the course structure and teaching methodology significantly contributed to students' understanding of the theoretical frameworks underpinning intercultural issues. Since cross-cultural communication often involves complex and abstract ideas, such as cultural norms, communication styles, and societal expectations, clear presentation of these topics is crucial for maintaining student engagement. The relatively low standard deviation further suggests a consensus among students regarding the clarity of the teaching, meaning that the majority of students found the lessons to be consistent in quality and effective in conveying the material.

An essential factor in the success of the teaching process is the ability of instructors to convey difficult concepts in an understandable and relatable manner. Effective teaching goes beyond transferring knowledge—it requires the ability to engage students in ways that resonate both personally and professionally. For students studying intercultural communication, understanding the theory and practice behind core concepts is vital but can often be challenging. Lecturers who provided clear explanations, real-life examples, and facilitated interactive discussions likely played a significant role in bridging the gap between theory and practice, making the subject more tangible for students (Saray et al., 2021).

Moreover, the clarity of the teaching process was enhanced by the instructors' ability to simplify complex concepts without oversimplifying them; maintaining academic rigor while ensuring the material was approachable. Clear communication of learning objectives and expectations at the beginning of the course further alleviated potential anxieties, giving students a sense of direction. This approach is consistent with the emphasis on clear communication in motivating students to actively engage with intercultural education programs (Saray et al., 2021). Structured lessons and transparent objectives created an environment where students felt confident in exploring difficult content and engaging in meaningful dialogue about intercultural issues.

Lecturer Competence (M = 4.30, SD = 0.61)

Another highly rated aspect of the course was lecturer competence, with a mean score of 4.30 and a standard deviation of 0.61. This suggests that students not only perceived their lecturers as knowledgeable but also as skilled in delivering intercultural education. The relatively low standard deviation indicates that there was widespread agreement among students regarding their lecturers' ability to effectively communicate and impart the essential knowledge and skills related to cross-cultural understanding. Given the complexity of teaching intercultural competence, this positive feedback points to the lecturers' success in facilitating a learning environment where students felt supported and encouraged to engage with challenging content.

In the maritime industry, where global collaboration is the norm, lecturers play a crucial role in fostering a learning environment that emphasizes both the understanding and application of intercultural principles. Seafarers frequently work in multinational and culturally diverse teams, and their ability to navigate these differences effectively is essential for maintaining operational efficiency and team harmony. Therefore, lecturers who are not only experts in their respective fields but also skilled in facilitating intercultural learning are vital in preparing students for such environments. The success of the course in this regard reflects the lecturers' competence in creating an inclusive and culturally sensitive educational setting, where students feel safe to explore and challenge their own cultural biases and assumptions.

The role of lecturer competence goes beyond just having knowledge of the subject matter. It also encompasses the ability to communicate complex ideas clearly, the use of diverse teaching strategies, and the ability to foster a dynamic classroom environment. In intercultural education, it is important for lecturers to not only present facts but also engage students through interactive teaching methods. These can include group discussions, case studies, and role-playing exercises, which help students better understand and practice the intercultural skills they need to apply in the real world. Moreover, competent lecturers also serve as role models for students, demonstrating how to communicate respectfully and effectively across cultures, setting the tone for the professional behavior expected in the global maritime industry.

The positive feedback regarding lecturer competence underscores how important teacher effectiveness is in the success of the course. The ability of instructors to model intercultural competence and offer practical support to students as they engage with complex cultural issues plays a key role in helping students internalize the values of tolerance, respect, and global citizenship. These skills are vital not only in the maritime industry but also in any profession where workers are likely to interact with individuals from different cultural backgrounds.

In addition to knowledge and practical skills, lecturers must possess a deep understanding of the theoretical frameworks that inform intercultural education. The ability to explain complex concepts such as cultural relativism, power distance, and communication styles requires not only familiarity with these theories but also the ability to contextualize them within students' personal experiences and professional futures. This depth of understanding is critical in helping students see the relevance of the course content to their careers and motivating them to engage with the material more deeply.

The high rating for lecturer competence in the survey suggests that students felt their lecturers were successful in facilitating these learning processes. These findings are consistent with existing literature, which highlights the crucial role of lecturer competence in ensuring student success, particularly in subjects that involve both theoretical knowledge and practical application (Fong, 2020). Lecturers who possess a high level of expertise and a passion for intercultural education can significantly enhance the learning experience, ensuring that students not only gain a solid understanding of intercultural concepts but are also equipped with the skills needed to apply those concepts effectively in real-world situations. In this sense, lecturer competence directly contributes to the course's ability to prepare students for the cultural complexities they will face in their professional careers.

Moreover, the feedback suggests that the lecturers were able to balance theoretical and practical elements of the course, providing students with a robust framework of knowledge while also equipping them with the tools to apply that knowledge in a multicultural maritime setting. As the global shipping industry continues to grow and diversify, the need for competent and culturally aware leaders in the maritime field will only increase. Therefore, the ability of instructors to teach effectively in this area is not just beneficial—it is critical to the development of future maritime professionals who can successfully navigate the increasingly complex, multinational working environments they will encounter.

In conclusion, the positive evaluation of lecturer competence underscores the importance of teaching effectiveness in intercultural education, particularly in the context of the maritime industry. The high mean score for this aspect reflects students' recognition of the lecturers' role in preparing them for the challenges they will face in multicultural environments. To continue building on this success, it is essential to further support lecturers with professional development opportunities, allowing them to stay informed about the latest developments in both intercultural communication theories and teaching methodologies. This will ensure that the course remains relevant and effective in preparing students for an increasingly globalized and interconnected maritime workforce.

Perceived Benefits (M = 4.20, SD = 0.63)

The perceived benefits of the Cross-Cultural Understanding (CCU) course received a strong mean score of 4.20, reflecting the students' recognition of the course's value in preparing them for future careers in the globalized maritime industry. This high rating demonstrates that students viewed the course not just as an academic requirement, but as a crucial component of their professional development. In an era where the maritime industry is increasingly globalized, the ability to navigate cultural differences and work effectively in multinational teams is essential. With a standard deviation of 0.63, the relatively low variation in responses indicates that the majority of students found the course both useful and relevant to their professional needs, further emphasizing its alignment with their expectations.

This score suggests that students felt well-prepared to meet the challenges of working in multicultural environments, a core aspect of the maritime industry. As the industry diversifies, there is an increasing need for workers who can collaborate across cultural lines, manage cross-cultural conflicts, and understand the dynamics of international maritime operations. Intercultural competence involves more than just theoretical knowledge; it requires real-world application in environments where effective communication and teamwork are crucial. The high perceived benefits rating indicates that students believe the course helped them develop practical skills such as effective communication, problem-solving, and conflict resolution in diverse teams, all of which are critical for success in a globalized maritime context.

Additionally, the course's perceived benefits underscore the importance of relevance in the curriculum. Students are more likely to engage with the content and appreciate its value when they see a direct connection to their future careers (Ahmed, 2022). In industries like maritime, where cross-cultural teams are the norm, students who perceive the course as an investment in their future—helping them understand cultural nuances and adapt to diverse work environments—are more motivated and committed. The practical skills gained through the course not only help students grasp the mechanics of working in multicultural environments, but they also foster a sense of preparedness and confidence in handling real-world challenges as they enter the workforce.

A key element contributing to the perceived benefits of the course lies in its emphasis on global citizenship and cultural sensitivity. The global nature of maritime operations requires a workforce that not only understands the technical aspects of the job but also possesses the cultural intelligence necessary for effective collaboration across cultural boundaries. The CCU course, by focusing on these principles, empowers students to become global professionals who can navigate diverse cultures with respect and understanding. This aligns with Ahmed's (2022) assertion that when students view a course as directly linked to their future careers, they are more likely to engage with and appreciate the content. The perceived benefits, therefore, extend beyond theoretical knowledge—they include the development of social competencies and leadership qualities, which are indispensable in today's interconnected world.

Moreover, the interdisciplinary approach to teaching cross-cultural understanding likely enhanced the perceived benefits by bridging the gap between theory and practice. Instead of focusing solely on theoretical knowledge, the course incorporated real-life scenarios, interactive workshops, and simulations that allowed students to engage with the material in a more active way. These hands-on activities help students deepen their understanding of cultural dynamics and practice applying the concepts they've learned in real-world settings. By emphasizing key professional skills such as teamwork, leadership, and conflict management, the course equipped students with essential tools for success in multicultural environments. The high perceived benefits score of 4.20 suggests that students felt the course contributed to their emotional and social development, giving them the confidence to work effectively with people from diverse backgrounds.

Comprehension of CCU Concepts (M = 4.25, SD = 0.65)

The comprehension of CCU concepts received a strong score of 4.25, indicating that students generally had a solid understanding of the key principles of intercultural communication and global cultural awareness. This suggests that the course was effective in delivering the core concepts that are foundational to fostering cultural competence, particularly for those entering the maritime industry. The relatively low standard deviation (0.65) indicates that most students had a good grasp of the course content. However, the small variation suggests that a few students found certain concepts more challenging, which is common when dealing with abstract ideas that require a shift in perspective and cognitive adjustment.

The ability to understand these concepts is crucial for students' engagement in cross-cultural interactions and for understanding the cultural dynamics that influence behavior and decision-making in diverse environments. For maritime professionals, these skills are particularly vital since they often work with colleagues from various cultural backgrounds. Understanding intercultural communication allows students to navigate differences in communication styles, hierarchical structures, and value systems—all essential for fostering teamwork and ensuring operational efficiency. Without this comprehension, there could be communication breakdowns, misunderstandings, and conflicts, which could ultimately affect the safety and success of maritime operations.

The comprehension of CCU concepts provides students with the intellectual framework needed to appreciate the significance of cultural differences in the workplace. It helps them understand how these differences influence leadership, teamwork, and decision-making. As students transition into their professional roles, their ability to apply these concepts will enhance their effectiveness when working with multinational crews, clients, and stakeholders. The course likely emphasized the application of theoretical knowledge, not just in academic contexts, but in real-world situations, reinforcing that cultural competence is a practical skill that extends beyond theoretical learning.

These findings align with research emphasizing the importance of a strong foundational understanding of intercultural concepts as the first step toward achieving cultural competence (Saray et al., 2021). A deep understanding of theoretical principles like cultural relativism, ethnocentrism, and cultural dimensions provides students with the tools to recognize and adapt to cultural differences in professional settings. While the course's positive feedback on comprehension is promising, the slight variation in responses highlights the need for more innovative teaching methods. Using case studies, role-playing exercises and real-world simulations could further enhance the students' ability to connect theoretical concepts with practical, intercultural communication challenges they will face in maritime environments.

Relevance of Materials (M = 4.12, SD = 0.72)

The relevance of the course materials received a positive rating, with a mean score of 4.12, indicating that students perceived the materials as aligned with their professional needs and the real-world challenges they will face in multicultural maritime settings. This suggests that the course was successful in providing practical content applicable to their future careers, where cultural awareness and communication are key. The maritime industry, with its international scope and diverse workforce, demands a high level of intercultural competence, and the fact that students found the materials relevant suggests that they recognized the importance of these skills for their professional development. The course's alignment with industry needs further underscores its practical value in preparing students for the complexities of global maritime operations.

The relatively higher standard deviation of 0.72 indicates that while most students found the materials useful, some may have felt that certain content could be further refined to meet their specific learning needs. This variation may reflect individual learning preferences or varying levels of prior knowledge on intercultural topics. Students with previous exposure to cross-cultural training might have found some content easier, while others encountering these concepts for the first time could have struggled. This diversity in experience highlights the need for curriculum design that addresses the varying levels of student experience, perhaps through personalized resources or interactive materials tailored to different learning styles—whether visual, auditory, or kinesthetic.

The relevance of the materials plays a crucial role in maintaining student engagement, which is essential for success in any educational program, especially one involving abstract concepts like intercultural communication. Students who see the materials as directly applicable to their careers are more likely to be motivated to engage with the content (Chen et al., 2025). By incorporating real-world scenarios and case studies from actual maritime operations, the course helps students understand the practical implications of what they are learning, enhancing their ability to handle challenges in cross-cultural communication, conflict resolution, and teamwork—all of which are central to the maritime profession.

To ensure the course remains relevant, it is crucial to align the materials not just with theoretical knowledge but with the practical expectations of the maritime industry. As the industry continues to globalize, understanding cultural norms, leadership styles, and communication techniques is essential. Incorporating multicultural case studies and digital tools—such as virtual cross-cultural simulations—would provide interactive, real-time practice for students, enhancing their preparedness for multicultural work environments. Refining the course materials to cater to diverse learning needs ensures that all students, regardless of their prior exposure, benefit fully from the course's content, equipping them with the skills necessary to thrive in the global maritime industry.

Aspects with Lower Ratings

While the positive feedback on most aspects of the course is encouraging, the survey results also highlight two areas that received lower ratings: learning challenges and the assessment system. These aspects have implications for the course's overall effectiveness and suggest areas for improvement.

Learning Challenges (M = 3.72, SD = 0.80)

The learning challenges aspect received the lowest score in the survey, with a mean of 3.72 and a standard deviation of 0.80, indicating that students faced significant difficulties engaging with the course material. This relatively low score highlights barriers to understanding and applying the complex intercultural concepts introduced in the Cross-Cultural Understanding (CCU) course. The high standard deviation suggests a wide range of experiences among students, with some finding the material particularly challenging, while others grasped it more easily. This variation points to the diverse backgrounds and learning styles of students, with some having prior exposure to intercultural concepts, while others encountered these ideas for the first time.

The challenges students faced are likely due to the cognitive complexity of intercultural competence, which often requires a shift in worldview. Concepts such as cultural relativism, power distance, and contextual communication challenge students' assumptions about culture, behavior, and communication. These concepts ask students to rethink their own cultural norms and personal biases, which can be a challenging mental exercise. This aligns with literature that highlights the difficulty students experience when learning abstract intercultural issues that demand a significant restructuring of thought (Okoye et al., 2022). In the maritime context, this shift is particularly important as students need to understand not only the theories but also their application in diverse, dynamic maritime environments.

Another significant challenge is the application of theoretical knowledge to real-world scenarios. While students may understand intercultural communication principles in theory, they often struggle to apply these concepts in complex, real-world settings. This is especially true in the maritime industry, where interactions with people from diverse backgrounds are routine. Students may find it difficult to foresee how cultural differences affect the day-to-day operations of ships, ports, and international trade. The abstract nature of intercultural competence makes it hard to bridge the gap between classroom learning and practical, multicultural maritime environments.

The difficulties in mastering intercultural competence may also stem from the lack of experiential learning opportunities, which are crucial for reinforcing theoretical understanding. Intercultural competence is a skill-based ability, and while students may grasp cultural differences conceptually, they may not be fully equipped to navigate these differences in real-world situations without practice. Abstract concepts like cultural sensitivity, ethnocentrism, and communication styles can be difficult for students to translate into actionable strategies without hands-on experience in multicultural settings.

To address these challenges, future iterations of the CCU course should incorporate more interactive learning activities and practical experiences that allow students to engage with the material in dynamic and contextualized ways. For instance, role-playing exercises can simulate multicultural interactions, providing students the opportunity to practice applying intercultural theories to real-world scenarios. These activities would also give students immediate feedback on their communication and conflict management strategies. Additionally, cultural simulations could immerse students in virtual or physical environments where different cultural values and communication norms are at play, helping them practice interpreting cultural cues and making decisions with cultural context in mind.

In conclusion, while the learning challenges score highlights the difficulties students face in mastering intercultural concepts, it also provides an opportunity for enhancing the course. By integrating experiential learning, role-playing, cultural simulations, and real-world case studies, the course can better support students in developing the practical intercultural skills needed for success in multicultural maritime environments. These changes would help bridge the gap between theory and practice, preparing students to handle real-world challenges and excel in their careers within the global maritime industry.

Assessment System (M = 3.95, SD = 0.74)

The assessment system received a mean score of 3.95, suggesting that while students found the assessments generally satisfactory, there was some room for improvement. The standard deviation of 0.74 indicates a degree of dissatisfaction or uncertainty regarding the assessment methods used. This variability in feedback points to the fact that while many students were comfortable with the assessments, others felt the methods did not fully capture the complexity of the skills and knowledge necessary for navigating multicultural environments in the maritime industry.

This score suggests a potential misalignment between the theoretical and practical aspects of the course. While traditional exams or quizzes can measure theoretical knowledge, they may not adequately assess how well students can apply these principles in dynamic, multicultural environments. Intercultural competence involves not only understanding concepts but also translating that understanding into effective communication, problem-solving, and teamwork in diverse, real-world settings. This highlights the gap in how the current assessment system evaluates core skills necessary for success in a globalized maritime workforce.

Additionally, the traditional assessment format may not fully capture the cognitive and emotional aspects of intercultural competence. In a multicultural work environment, success depends on factors like empathy, adaptability, and conflict management. These qualities are integral to intercultural communication and are difficult to assess through traditional tests, which tend to measure factual recall rather than practical application. This points to the need for more diverse and interactive assessments that can evaluate students' ability to function effectively in multicultural settings.

To address these concerns, future iterations of the CCU course could benefit from more interactive and practical learning activities, such as peer evaluations, self-reflective assignments, and real-world problem-solving scenarios. Peer evaluations would allow students to assess each other's intercultural communication skills in group settings, providing valuable feedback on interpersonal effectiveness. Self-reflective assignments could help students identify and address their own cultural biases, while real-world problem-solving scenarios—such as case studies—would give students the opportunity to apply their knowledge to simulated, real-world challenges, preparing them for the complexities of professional multicultural environments.

Incorporating digital tools and virtual simulations into assessments could also enhance the learning experience. These tools could simulate cross-cultural interactions in a controlled yet immersive environment, allowing students to practice their intercultural skills in real-time and receive instant feedback. By engaging in virtual simulations or interactive online platforms, students can experience the challenges of working in diverse teams without leaving the classroom. This can reinforce learning and improve practical skills, better preparing students for their future roles in the global maritime industry.

In conclusion, the relatively low rating of the assessment system suggests that more diverse, interactive, and practical assessments are needed. While traditional assessments may be useful for evaluating theoretical understanding, they do not fully capture the complexity of intercultural competence. By incorporating authentic assessments such as peer evaluations, self-reflection exercises, and real-world simulations, the course can more comprehensively evaluate students' ability to navigate the complex cultural dynamics they will face in their professional careers.

Interview Findings

Three central themes emerged from the lecturer interviews, providing qualitative depth to the survey data. These themes reflect the challenges and strategies in teaching Cross-Cultural Understanding (CCU) to maritime cadets, offering a clearer picture of the obstacles and successes in the pedagogical approach.

Basic vs. Abstract Understanding

Lecturers observed that while cadets had a solid grasp of basic intercultural concepts like tolerance and cultural awareness, they struggled with more abstract constructs such as cultural bias and intercultural conflict. As Lecturer A explained, "They still need guidance when discussing abstract issues, such as cultural bias and intercultural conflict." This observation aligns with the survey's lower score for Learning Challenges (M = 3.72), which suggests that students find it difficult to engage with these complex topics. While many students can understand fundamental ideas, they often encounter challenges when asked to tackle concepts that are less tangible and harder to apply in real-world contexts.

The difficulty in understanding and applying abstract intercultural concepts suggests that students need structured support to deepen their understanding. Cultural bias and intercultural conflict are multifaceted issues that require a shift in perspective—something that can be mentally challenging for students who may not have had prior exposure to such topics. Addressing these more abstract intercultural issues effectively requires instructors to provide students with frameworks and structured discussions that help them engage critically with these complex challenges (Ungureanu, 2014). Such structured learning environments allow students to move beyond surface-level comprehension and begin processing and resolving deeper, more nuanced intercultural conflicts.

Developing higher-order intercultural competence involves understanding the dynamics of cultural biases, stereotypes, and conflict resolution, which is key to fostering a deeper level of intercultural communication skills. This development is especially vital in fields like maritime education, where professionals must work in diverse, often multicultural settings. Providing students with structured pedagogical scaffolding is essential for helping them make deeper connections and apply these abstract concepts effectively. In the context of the CCU course, this suggests that while students are introduced to essential intercultural concepts, there is a need for ongoing guidance and practice to help them master these advanced communication skills.

Experiential Learning

All lecturers emphasized the effectiveness of experiential methods such as role-play, case studies, and group discussions in helping students apply theoretical knowledge to practical, real-world scenarios. Lecturer B noted, "Role play and group discussion were effective for practicing cross-cultural communication directly." These interactive pedagogies allowed students to move beyond just understanding intercultural concepts and instead engage in dynamic learning that mirrors real-life situations. The hands-on approach encouraged students to practice communication skills that are vital for successfully navigating cultural differences, and provided them with opportunities to experiment with various strategies for conflict resolution, negotiation, and teamwork. By participating in role-play exercises, students were able to experience firsthand the complexities of intercultural interaction and learn how to manage cultural diversity effectively. This approach fosters a deeper level of understanding, as it helps students contextualize theoretical concepts within the environment they will face in their professional careers.

This finding aligns with the survey's high ratings for Clarity of Teaching and Perceived Benefits, indicating that students recognized the practical relevance and clarity of these methods in improving their learning experience. The incorporation of these experiential learning strategies not only enhanced students' comprehension of intercultural communication but also made the content more relevant to their future careers. In the context of maritime education, where professionals routinely collaborate with people from different cultural backgrounds, these interactive techniques are especially valuable in preparing students for the challenges they will encounter in multinational teams. By practicing cross-cultural communication directly, students gain practical experience that helps them transition from theoretical understanding to real-world application, thus enhancing their ability to work effectively in diverse and often challenging environments.

Prior research supports the role of experiential learning in providing tangible contexts for intercultural communication (Nikonorova & Kemalova, 2021; Simanjuntak et al., 2024). Experiential learning has long been recognized as a powerful tool in intercultural education because it engages students in active learning, which has been shown to significantly enhance their critical thinking and problem-solving skills. Unlike traditional methods that may focus solely on theoretical instruction, experiential learning encourages students to confront real-world challenges and make decisions based on the intercultural principles they have learned. This process helps solidify their understanding and enables them to translate their knowledge into actionable strategies that they can use in the workplace. By incorporating activities such as case studies and group discussions, students are given the opportunity to evaluate real intercultural scenarios, make decisions, and reflect on their experiences, thus better preparing them for the complex realities of working in global maritime operations.

Challenges of Perception

Lecturers also highlighted that students' limited prior exposure to diverse cultures and a tendency to undervalue CCU compared to more technical subjects posed significant challenges in engaging students with the course. Lecturer D remarked, "Some students are less interested because CCU is not considered a technical course." This perspective reveals a common issue in maritime education, where technical skills are often seen as more directly linked to career success, overshadowing the importance of intercultural communication training. The technical nature of maritime programs frequently leads to the perception that CCU is less relevant to future maritime professionals. This view was reflected in the survey's lowest scores, highlighting a disconnect between students' perception of the value of intercultural education and its importance in their professional roles (Policy & Theotokas, 2019).

This perspective resonates with broader trends in maritime education, where technical proficiency has traditionally been prioritized over skills such as intercultural communication, leadership, and conflict resolution. However, this emphasis on technical skills alone can create a gap in essential competencies that are crucial in the increasingly globalized maritime industry. While maritime professionals need to understand navigation, safety, and engineering, they also need the interpersonal skills to manage a multinational workforce. Communication, teamwork, and the ability to navigate cultural differences are essential for ensuring safety and operational effectiveness in diverse environments. The challenge remains in shifting the focus to include cultural competence as a fundamental skill for the modern maritime workforce.

Yet, literature shows that communication breakdowns remain a major cause of maritime accidents and operational failures, particularly in multicultural teams where misunderstandings can arise due to cultural differences (Galešić & Coslovich, 2019; Riyanto et al., 2023). These studies underscore the critical need for intercultural training to address and prevent such communication issues. Without a solid foundation in cultural awareness, seafarers may struggle to communicate effectively across cultural boundaries, potentially leading to misunderstandings or conflict. This reinforces the importance of integrating cross-cultural communication into maritime education, ensuring that students not only acquire technical expertise but also develop the soft skills necessary for successful collaboration in a diverse global workforce. By recognizing and addressing this gap in maritime training, educational programs can better prepare students for the realities of a multicultural maritime environment.

Integrated Findings

The survey and interviews together reveal a coherent pattern that highlights both strengths and areas for improvement in the CCU course. The quantitative results emphasize students' appreciation for the course's clarity, lecturer competence, and practical benefits, suggesting that students generally find the course well-structured and relevant to their future careers. However, these results also point to challenges students face with more abstract concepts and the assessment system, which fails to fully capture the complexity of intercultural competence. The survey's lower scores for areas like Learning Challenges suggest that students struggle with concepts such as cultural bias, intercultural conflict, and the practical application of theoretical knowledge in multicultural environments.

The qualitative data from the interviews reinforce these findings, offering deeper insights into students' experiences. Lecturers highlighted that experiential learning methods, such as role-play, case studies, and group discussions, were highly effective in helping students engage with the material and apply intercultural concepts in real-world contexts. This aligns with the high ratings for Clarity of Teaching and Perceived Benefits, confirming that interactive, hands-on pedagogies significantly enhance student comprehension and retention. However, lecturers also pointed out that students' limited prior exposure to diverse cultures and a tendency to undervalue CCU compared to technical subjects hindered deeper engagement with the course content.

This integration of both quantitative and qualitative findings suggests that the CCU course is effective and valued, but improvements are necessary to enhance its impact. Specifically, the findings indicate the need to strengthen pedagogical strategies for teaching abstract intercultural concepts, which many students find difficult to internalize and apply. The difficulty in grasping more advanced topics like cultural bias and intercultural conflict suggests that further scaffolding and structured support are required to help students bridge the gap between theory and practice. Additionally, there is a need to make CCU more central within the maritime curriculum, positioning it as a core competence that directly contributes to safety, operational effectiveness, and global employability in the maritime industry.

In conclusion, while the CCU course is effective in providing foundational intercultural knowledge, the integration of survey and interview findings reveals that areas for growth remain. By refining pedagogical strategies to address the challenges with abstract concepts and ensuring CCU's relevance in the broader curriculum, the course can better equip students with the necessary skills to navigate complex multicultural environments. This approach will not only enhance maritime safety and team cohesion but also improve students' global employability in the increasingly interconnected maritime industry.

DISCUSSION

The findings from this mixed-methods study provide a comprehensive understanding of the Cross-Cultural Understanding (CCU) course's implementation in a maritime higher education institution. The quantitative survey data, which indicated overwhelmingly positive student evaluations, are enriched by the qualitative insights derived from lecturer interviews. This integrated perspective affirms the course's overall efficacy while identifying areas of strength and potential refinement, aligning with contemporary discussions in maritime education regarding intercultural competence (Pazaver & Kitada, 2025).

The consistently high mean scores across most survey aspects, particularly Comprehension of CCU Concepts (M = 4.25), demonstrate that students generally acquire a solid foundational understanding of cross-cultural principles. However, lecturers noted that while cadets grasped basic ideas such as tolerance and cultural awareness, they often struggled with abstract constructs like cultural bias and intercultural conflict. As Lecturer A explained, "They still need guidance when discussing abstract issues." This indicates that while the course successfully conveys essential knowledge, fostering deeper critical thinking and analytical skills for navigating complex intercultural dynamics remains a pedagogical challenge. Such findings align with research emphasizing the need for intercultural training that extends beyond awareness to cultivate higher-order cognitive engagement in diverse professional contexts (Cheng et al., 2021). The relatively lower mean score for Learning Challenges (M = 3.72) supports this interpretation, suggesting that abstract concepts may be a source of difficulty for some students.

A significant strength of the CCU course lies in its teaching methods. Survey results revealed particularly high ratings for Clarity of Teaching (M = 4.35) and Perceived Benefits (M = 4.20), which correspond closely with lecturers' observations. Interview participants consistently highlighted the value of experiential approaches such as role-play, case studies, and group discussions. As Lecturer B emphasized, "Role play and group discussion were effective for practicing cross-cultural communication directly." This affirms that interactive and participatory pedagogies enhance both clarity and applicability of the course, aligning with scholarship that underscores the importance of active learning for developing communication skills in multicultural crews (Simanjuntak et al., 2024). Modern maritime education increasingly supports simulator-based and experiential learning as vital for transforming theoretical knowledge into applied skills (Hjellvik & Mallam, 2023; Kim et al., 2021). These strategies provide authentic contexts for cadets to practice teamwork and communication, directly contributing to their readiness to work in multicultural environments (Murai et al., 2017).

Nevertheless, challenges remain in fully embedding CCU within the maritime curriculum. Lecturers pointed to students' limited exposure to diverse cultural contexts and the tendency to undervalue CCU compared to technical subjects. Lecturer D remarked, "Some cadets are less interested because CCU is not considered a technical course," highlighting a persistent perception issue. Maritime training has traditionally emphasized operational skills, often relegating intercultural competence to a secondary role (Manuel, 2017; Pazaver & Kitada, 2025). This undervaluation risks undermining engagement, despite growing recognition that effective communication and cultural understanding are crucial to maritime safety and efficiency. A robust body of literature confirms that communication breakdowns—often rooted in cultural and linguistic differences—are significant contributors to maritime accidents (Galešić & Coslovich, 2019; Nikonorova & Kemalova, 2021).

As Jeon et al. (2022) and Saeed (2015) further argue, CCU is not merely a "soft skill" but an essential dimension of professional competence and risk management in the global maritime industry (Jeon et al., 2022; Saeed, 2015). Effective intercultural communication is integral to managing multinational crews, ensuring smooth operations, and reducing the risk of miscommunication. This aligns with the broader maritime educational shift that increasingly recognizes intercultural competence as a necessary skill for successful international maritime operations. Fostering such competence in students will enable them to handle complex intercultural interactions and navigate the challenges posed by global maritime environments.

In the context of the maritime industry, where global collaboration is the norm, lecturers play a crucial role in fostering a learning environment that emphasizes both the understanding and application of intercultural principles. Seafarers frequently work in multinational and culturally diverse teams, and their ability to navigate these differences effectively is essential for maintaining operational efficiency and team harmony. Lecturers who are not only experts in their respective fields but also skilled in facilitating intercultural learning are vital in preparing students for such environments. The success of the Cross-Cultural Understanding (CCU) course in this regard reflects the lecturers' competence in creating an inclusive and culturally sensitive educational setting, where students feel safe to explore and challenge their own cultural biases and assumptions.

Despite these challenges, the survey findings and interview insights underscore the effectiveness of the CCU course in equipping students with essential intercultural skills. The combination of explicit instruction and experiential learning strategies—such as simulations, case studies, and virtual interactions with native speakers or multicultural professionals—has proven effective in developing students' intercultural awareness and communication skills (Cizer & Lungu, 2015; Hidayati et al., 2024; Simanjuntak et al., 2024). Integrating local cultural elements into CCU materials also deepens students' understanding and engagement, enhancing their adaptability in real-world interactions (Aristia et al., 2025; Permatasari & Andriyanti, 2021).

However, lecturers' observations suggest that to enhance the course's impact, greater emphasis should be placed on abstract intercultural concepts, such as cultural values and critical reflection, which remain underdeveloped in many maritime programs (Ragab, 2024; Yarosh et al., 2018). Many maritime institutions have begun integrating intercultural education, yet the main challenge lies in the continuous development of curricula that remain relevant to the evolving dynamics of the global industry (Dirgayasa, 2022; Ragab, 2024; Simanjuntak et al., 2023). Formal recognition of CCU as a core competence within maritime curricula, aligned with international standards such as the STCW Convention, is essential to ensuring graduates' professional readiness (Dirgayasa, 2022; Lyu, 2024; Simanjuntak et al., 2023).

The current curriculum's focus on technical subjects, while necessary, often leads to a narrower educational perspective that overlooks the significance of intercultural competence in global maritime operations. To address this gap, it is crucial to reframe CCU as a critical component of professional readiness that directly impacts operational safety, teamwork, and efficiency. As the maritime industry becomes increasingly interconnected, the importance of cross-cultural understanding cannot be understated. By embedding these competencies more deeply into the maritime curriculum, students will be better equipped to manage the complexities of working in multicultural teams and international trade.

Moving forward, maritime educational institutions must build upon the successes of the CCU course while addressing the pedagogical gaps identified in this study. Strengthening the understanding of abstract intercultural concepts and positioning CCU as a central part of the curriculum will ensure that students not only acquire technical expertise but are also prepared to thrive in an increasingly globalized maritime workforce. This approach will not only enhance maritime safety but also foster a more inclusive, effective, and harmonious international maritime community.

CONCLUSION

This study highlights the crucial role of the Cross-Cultural Understanding (CCU) course in preparing cadets at maritime higher education institutions for the realities of working in multicultural environments. The quantitative survey results demonstrated consistently high ratings across key aspects such as comprehension, teaching clarity, lecturer competence, readiness for diversity, and course benefits, suggesting that the course is effective in meeting its objectives. These findings are reinforced by the qualitative data from lecturer interviews, which emphasized the course's strengths, particularly the use of experiential learning methods like role-plays, case studies, and group discussions. These methods significantly enhance students' understanding of intercultural dynamics and their ability to apply this knowledge in real-world contexts.

However, the study also identifies several challenges that need to be addressed. While cadets generally grasp basic concepts such as cultural awareness and tolerance, they often struggle with more abstract concepts such as cultural bias and intercultural conflict. This gap in comprehension was reflected in the relatively lower survey score for Learning Challenges ($M = 3.72$), suggesting that these topics require further pedagogical support. Lecturers noted that students' limited exposure to diverse cultural contexts and the tendency to undervalue CCU compared to technical subjects posed barriers to deeper engagement with the course content. The maritime curriculum traditionally emphasizes technical skills, often relegating intercultural competence to a secondary role.

To overcome these challenges, it is crucial for maritime higher education institutions to reframe CCU as a core competence that directly contributes to safety, operational effectiveness, and global employability. Integrating intercultural competence more fully into the maritime curriculum will help students recognize its importance in preventing communication breakdowns and improving collaboration in multinational teams. As the maritime industry continues to globalize, the ability to navigate cultural differences effectively is becoming increasingly vital. The study underscores the need for curriculum innovation, focusing not only on technical proficiency but also on developing interpersonal skills and cross-cultural communication abilities.

In conclusion, while the CCU course has proven effective in providing students with essential intercultural skills, the study identifies the need for ongoing refinement to address the challenges students face with abstract concepts. By strengthening the pedagogical approach to abstract intercultural concepts and repositioning CCU as a core component of maritime education, institutions can better equip cadets to thrive in multicultural work environments. This approach will help ensure that students are not only technically proficient but also capable of contributing effectively to maritime safety, team cohesion, and global operational efficiency in the increasingly interconnected maritime industry.

REFERENCES

Ahmed, I. N. E.-D. (2022). Raising University Students' Level of Academic and Professional Readiness through Teaching Intercultural Communication and Digital War. *Advances in Journalism and Communication, 10*(02), 253–277. DOI: 10.4236/ajc.2022.102016

Aristia, E. S., Siswantara, E., & Ismiati, I. (2025). Developing CCU Instructional Materials Integrated with Local Cultures in Improving EFL Learners' Communicative Competences. *Journal of Languages and Language Teaching*, *13*(2), 863. DOI: 10.33394/jollt.v13i2.13082

Chen, F., Cheng, J., Huang, X., Zhao, W., Zhuo, X., & Zhao, Y. (2025). The Value, Challenges and Path of Integrating Chinese Culture into Higher Foreign Language Teaching from the Perspective of Students. *English Language Teaching*, *18*(3), 1. DOI: 10.5539/elt.v18n3p1

Cheng, M. M., Lacaste, A. V., Saranza, C., & Chuang, H. H. (2021). Culturally responsive teaching in technology-supported learning environments in marine education for sustainable development. *Sustainability (Basel)*, *13*(24), 13922. Advance online publication. DOI: 10.3390/su132413922

Cizer, L., & Lungu, D. (2015). PRACTICING INTERCULTURAL COMMUNICATIVE COMPETENCES THROUGH BLENDED LEARNING. *11th International Conference ELearning and Software for Education*. DOI: 10.12753/2066-026X-15-154

Dirgayasa, I. W. (2022). Maritime English Learning Materials Based on Standard Training Certification and Watchkeeping for Seafarers (STCW) Curriculum and Intercultural Competence (IC). *World Journal of English Language*, *12*(4), 65. DOI: 10.5430/wjel.v12n4p65

Dominguez-Péry, C., Vuddaraju, L. N. R., Corbett-Etchevers, I., & Tassabehji, R. (2021). Reducing maritime accidents in ships by tackling human error: A bibliometric review and research agenda. *Journal of Shipping and Trade*, *6*(1), 20. DOI: 10.1186/s41072-021-00098-y

Galešić, A. D., & Coslovich, S. T. (2019). Working with multinational and multicultural crews: A Croatian Seafarers' perspective. *Pomorstvo*, *33*(1), 56–62. DOI: 10.31217/p.33.1.6

Hidayati, F. N., Fatmawati, N. L., & Muntaha, M. (2024). Promoting Intercultural Communication in CCU Classroom of EFL students by Using VCT. *Script Journal: Journal of Linguistics and English Teaching*, *9*(2), 67–85. Advance online publication. DOI: 10.24903/sj.v9i2.1773

Hjellvik, S., & Mallam, S. (2023). Integrating motivated goal achievement in maritime simulator training. In *WMU Journal of Maritime Affairs* (Vol. 22, Issue 2). Springer Berlin Heidelberg. DOI: 10.1007/s13437-023-00309-2

Irwan, . (2020). The Role of the Institution of Navigation Education Regarding Safety Navigation. 443. *Iset*, *436–440*. Advance online publication. DOI: 10.2991/assehr.k.200620.084

Jeon, T. Y., Kim, B. G., Kim, N., & Lee, Y. C. (2022). Have Non-Native English-Speaking Marine Cadet Engineers Been Educated Appropriately? *Journal of Marine Science and Engineering*, *10*(8), 1018. Advance online publication. DOI: 10.3390/jmse10081018

Kim, T. eun, Sharma, A., Bustgaard, M., Gyldensten, W. C., Nymoen, O. K., Tusher, H. M., & Nazir, S. (2021). The continuum of simulator-based maritime training and education. *WMU Journal of Maritime Affairs, 20*(2), 135–150. DOI: 10.1007/s13437-021-00242-2

Lau, Y. yip, & Ng, A. K. Y. (2015). The motivations and expectations of students pursuing maritime education. *WMU Journal of Maritime Affairs, 14*(2), 313–331. DOI: 10.1007/s13437-015-0075-3

Lyu, X. (2024). The Necessity and Suggestions for Cultivating Intercultural Communication Skills of Maritime Students. *Advances in Social Development and Education Research, 1*(3), 84. DOI: 10.61935/asder.3.1.2024.P84

Manuel, M. E. (2017). Vocational and academic approaches to maritime education and training (MET): Trends, challenges and opportunities. *WMU Journal of Maritime Affairs, 16*(3), 473–483. DOI: 10.1007/s13437-017-0130-3

Murai, K., Wang, J., Wang, Y., & Qilei, Y. (2017). Toward evaluation of mixed culture's team works: Case study of ship bridge simulator-based training for cadets. *2017 Joint 17th World Congress of International Fuzzy Systems Association and 9th International Conference on Soft Computing and Intelligent Systems (IFSA-SCIS)*, 1–5. DOI: 10.1109/IFSA-SCIS.2017.8023343

Nikonorova, M., & Kemalova, L. (2021). Technology of training future seafarers to work in a multinational ship crew. *E3S Web of Conferences, 258*. DOI: 10.1051/e3sconf/202125810015

Okoye, K., Daruich, S. D. N., & De La, O. (2022, December). A Text Mining and Statistical Approach for Assessment of Pedagogical Impact of Students' Evaluation of Teaching and Learning Outcome in Education. *IEEE Access : Practical Innovations, Open Solutions*, *11*, 9577–9596. DOI: 10.1109/ACCESS.2023.3239779

Pazaver, A., & Kitada, M. (2025). Integrating twenty-first century skills into STCW competences: Implications for maritime education and training. *WMU Journal of Maritime Affairs*, *24*(3), 397–418. DOI: 10.1007/s13437-025-00368-7

Permatasari, I., & Andriyanti, E. (2021). Developing students' intercultural communicative competence through cultural text-based teaching. *Indonesian Journal of Applied Linguistics*, *11*(1), 72–82. DOI: 10.17509/ijal.v11i1.34611

Phanphichit, T., & Bartusevičienė, I. (2024). Perspectives of stakeholders on onboard training: A thematic analysis of qualitative interviews. *Journal of International Maritime Safety, Environmental Affairs, and Shipping*, *8*(4), 2408698. DOI: 10.1080/25725084.2024.2408698

Policy, M., & Theotokas, I. (2019). *Cultural diversity, manning strategies and management practices in Greek shipping. February*. DOI: 10.1080/03088830701539198

Ragab, A. (2024). *Intercultural competence and communication on board of merchant vessels* [University of Antwerp]. DOI: 10.63028/10067/2079220151162165141

Riyanto, B., Nurmala, E., Agustina, I., & Maidari, S. R. (2023). Indonesian Seafarers' Intercultural Communication Challenges With Multinational Crews. *Journal of Intercultural Communication*, *23*(1), 76–81. DOI: 10.36923/jicc.v23i1.92

Saeed, F. (2015). FSA Based Analysis of Deck Officers' Non-Technical Skills in Crisis Situations [Liverpool John Moores University]. DOI: 10.24377/LJMU.t.00004489

Saray, S., Satır, T., & Doğan-Sağlamtimur, N. (2021). Proficiency of Maritime English Course: An Investigation in Istanbul, Turkey. *Heritage and Sustainable Development*, *3*(1), 6–15. DOI: 10.37868/hsd.v3i1.48

Simanjuntak, M. B., Selasdini, V., Malau, A. G., Barasa, L., Cahyadi, T., Winarno, , & Herawati, S. (2024). Development of maritime english communication learning model based on multiliteracy pedagogy. *Multidisciplinary Science Journal*, *7*(5), 2025237. DOI: 10.31893/multiscience.2025237

Simanjuntak, M. B., Zuriyati, Z., Utami, S. R., Rahmat, A., & Setiadi, S. (2023). Fostering Intercultural Understanding and Environmental Consciousness in Maritime Education. *BIO Web of Conferences, 79*. DOI: 10.1051/bioconf/20237906004

UNCTAD. (2021). Review of Maritime Report 2021. In *United Nations Publications*.

Ungureanu, C. C. (2014). Intercultural Education, a Response to Contemporary Multilingual Societies and a New Challenge for Maritime Education and Training (MET) Institutions. *Procedia: Social and Behavioral Sciences*, *116*, 4260–4263. DOI: 10.1016/j.sbspro.2014.01.928

Yarosh, M., Lukic, D., & Santibáñez-Gruber, R. (2018). Intercultural competence for students in international joint master programmes. *International Journal of Intercultural Relations*, *66*, 52–72. https://doi.org/https://doi.org/10.1016/j.ijintrel.2018.06.003. DOI: 10.1016/j.ijintrel.2018.06.003

Yoon, Y. (2023). Improving Cruise Crew Competency and Cultivating Global Citizenship: A Sustainable Development Approach for the Cruise Industry. *Sustainability (Basel)*, *15*(17), 13208. Advance online publication. DOI: 10.3390/su151713208

Chapter 19
Exploring Factors Impacting the Academic Achievement of Maritime Students in Learning English

Andi Anto Patak
http://orcid.org/0000-0001-8417-0493
Universitas Negeri Makassar, Indonesia

Fatimah Hidayahni Amin
http://orcid.org/0009-0001-5826-627X
Universitas Negeri Makassar, Indonesia

Lely Novia
http://orcid.org/0009-0009-7654-9255
Universitas Negeri Makassar, Indonesia

Indrawaty Asfah
http://orcid.org/0000-0001-9989-745X
Universitas Negeri Makassar, Indonesia

Seny Luhriyani Sunusi
http://orcid.org/0009-0004-3194-8651
Universitas Negeri Makassar, Indonesia

ABSTRACT

This study aims to explore the factors that affect the academic achievement of maritime students in English learning. The study employed a narrative inquiry design. To obtain the desired data, this chapter used the semi-structured interview guide. Ten participants were selected conveniently to take part in interviews. Participants were encouraged to share their ideas, experiences, and stories during the interviews. The entire story recorded was then analyzed using the narrative analysis. It involves interpreting both how the participants make sense of their own lives through narrative and how the researchers interpret that narrative. This chapter identifies key factors that affect maritime students' academic success in master-

DOI: 10.4018/979-8-3373-6670-8.ch019

ing English. Support from parents, lecturers, peers, and learners' self-awareness emerged as the most pivotal contributors to their overall achievement in English learning. These elements serve as driving forces that not only inspire students to engage deeply with the material but also instill confidence to comprehend and communicate effectively in English.

INTRODUCTION

In the vast and dynamic maritime world, effective communication is the cornerstone of successful operational activities, playing a critical role in ensuring shipping safety (Baig et al., 2025). The potential repercussions of communication errors or misunderstandings can be profoundly detrimental. For instance, if crew members misinterpret a ship's captain's vital instructions, the safety of the entire crew, along with the precious cargo or passengers aboard, can be severely compromised. As the maritime industry evolves and expands, seafarers' horizons are no longer confined to domestic waters; they now encompass a wide range of opportunities worldwide. This wide array of job prospects in the international maritime sector necessitates that seafarers, both seasoned professionals and those aspiring to enter the field, possess not only the required qualifications and competencies but also a keen adaptability to diverse working environments.

One paramount competency in this multicultural and multilingual arena is proficiency in international languages. Recognizing the significance of effective communication across borders, the International Maritime Organization (IMO) designated English as one of the official languages of the maritime industry back in 1995. This decision underscores the importance of a common linguistic framework in enhancing collaboration and safety in an industry that bridges nations and cultures. However, IMO data show that communication failures cause sea accidents due to the crew's lack of proficiency in English (Sampson & Zhao, 2003). Seeing this problem, shipping colleges, of course, realize that their graduates must have strong English communication skills, especially in the maritime sector, to carry out their duties professionally later. It requires the crew in the maritime industry to be trained in standard marine communication (Gabedava & Hu, 2025).

Numerous researchers have underscored the major impact of the school environment and the overall learning experience on student achievement (Edgerton & McKechnie, 2023; Gietz & McIntosh, 2014; Samdal et al., 1999). One compelling study posits that various school components—most notably teachers and the nature of learning and teaching activities—play a critical role in determining student success (Idkhan & Idris, 2023; Stronge et al., 2011). English teachers, in particular, exemplify this stimulus through their profound expertise in the subject matter, adept teaching strategies, and ability to customize material to resonate with students' diverse needs. When teachers engage students with stimulating lessons and relatable content, students often become more intrigued and enthusiastic about learning English (Hidayat et al., 2024). Conversely, a lack of classroom discipline can lead to a marked decline in students' academic performance. When English teachers fail to maintain order and instill character development among their students, the fabric of learning is disrupted, and students' achievements tend to suffer. Thus, a disciplined environment and the cultivation of strong character traits are vital components that significantly shape students' learning outcomes (Lamada et al., 2022; Lickona, 2013; Riouch et al., 2025).

In addition to the crucial role of teachers, the influence of learning resources on student performance is undeniably significant. When students have access to a wide range of English-learning materials, they are immersed in an enriching environment that fosters their academic growth, whether they are studying independently or engaging with teachers in a dynamic classroom (Hossain, 2024; Idkhan & Idris, 2021). However, research indicates that parents' educational backgrounds are also pivotal in shaping their children's academic success (Davis-Kean et al., 2021; Hill & Taylor, 2004; Steinmayr et al., 2010; Yamamoto & Holloway, 2010). Parents are uniquely positioned as the primary educators at home, spending the most time with their children and serving as key supporters in their educational journeys. This proximity allows parents to actively guide and influence their children's learning experiences, making their own educational levels an essential factor in their ability to nurture and direct their children's academic pursuits. Thus, the interplay among educational resources, parental guidance, and teacher involvement creates a multifaceted environment crucial to enhancing student achievement.

Several researchers contend that the environmental conditions in which individuals are raised significantly influence their academic performance. For instance, students from rural areas often exhibit lower academic achievement than their urban counterparts (Rachmaniar et al., 2021; Wells et al., 2023; Xiang & Stillwell, 2023). This disparity may stem from a variety of factors, including access to educational resources and extracurricular opportunities. In contrast, urban students tend to achieve more favorable outcomes in English learning, likely benefiting from a richer array of educational tools, diverse cultural experiences, and more qualified instructional support that urban settings typically provide.

Conversely, certain researchers contend that external influences, including parents' educational backgrounds, family and community environmental conditions, educators, and school infrastructure, do not determine students' academic achievement, particularly in domains of learning and mastery of the English language. Students possessing high levels of confidence, robust self-esteem, and minimal anxiety generally find it easier to acquire a second language (Habrat, 2018; Onwuegbuzie et al., 1999). Likewise, knowledge, skills, and confidence are intricately interconnected with academic success. Consequently, an individual's increasing confidence correlates with improved learning performance. Beliefs and self-confidence determine how a person behaves, thereby indicating their level of understanding. Confidence in learning English as a foreign language can be interpreted as a person's personal views and thoughts about the surrounding environment, including teachers, classmates, classroom interactions, and English learning activities.

In addition, other critical internal elements play a significant role, namely motivation and interpersonal interactions. Motivation represents an individual's intrinsic desire to pursue and achieve specific objectives, particularly in the context of learning a foreign language (Lăpădat & Lăpădat, 2023; Natsir et al., 2023). This drive is not uniform; rather, it is profoundly shaped by aspects inherent to the individual, such as their educational background, environmental conditions, and the values that influence them. Furthermore, interpersonal interactions also contribute to the motivation levels one experiences in learning English as a foreign language (Chew & Ng, 2021). Additionally, the overall quality of the learning experience and the dynamics between the learner and their instructor significantly impact the effectiveness of language acquisition. With this multifaceted understanding, the primary objective of this research is to identify and analyze the most influential factors impacting cadets and maritime students in their journey towards mastering English, the essential lingua franca of the maritime industry.

RESEARCH METHODS

Research Design

To gain a deeper insight into the intricate factors influencing cadets' success in learning English, we employed a Narrative Inquiry research design. This innovative approach is particularly practical for exploring an individual's life through a series of personal stories that reveal their unique journeys. Narrative Inquiry is a qualitative research methodology dedicated to the collection and analysis of these compelling narratives, allowing us to understand how individuals derive meaning from their diverse life experiences (Barkhuizen & Consoli, 2021; Clandinin, 2022; Kutsyuruba & Stasel, 2023; Pino Gavidia & Adu, 2022). A key aspect of this approach is the collaborative construction of meaning between the researchers and the participant, which requires the researchers to remain conscious of their own biases and preconceptions.

Research Participants

Ten cadets, who have been attending lectures for approximately two years and have fulfilled their obligation to reside in the dormitory, participated in this research. These cadets have considerable experience and are well aware of the importance of English proficiency for their academic pursuits. To select these 10 participants, convenience sampling was employed, focusing on the types of stories and experiences that aligned with the research objectives. The aim is to ensure that the data obtained from these narratives remains consistent with the research goals.

Research Instruments

To gather the necessary data, the researchers employed a semi-structured interview guide (Wilson, 2014). Semi-structured interviews allow the researchers to delve deeper into participants' rich narratives. By offering flexibility in questioning, these interviews facilitate a more comprehensive exploration of the stories and experiences shared. Each participant is encouraged to elaborate on their responses, providing a nuanced understanding that may not emerge from rigid questioning formats. Throughout this process, all conversations are meticulously recorded using a high-quality recording device, ensuring that no detail is overlooked. Once the data has been collected through the instrument, the researchers diligently transcribe the recorded stories, building a vivid tapestry of insights that reflect the participants' voices and experiences.

Data Collection

Through thoughtful, immersive interactions with participants, we conducted in-depth interviews to delve into their subjective realities. This qualitative framework not only captures values and identities but also highlights the ways these elements evolve, shaped by their social environments. Through our efforts, we gathered rich and layered stories from each participant. Our primary aim was to comprehend their personal worlds, uncover their distinctive viewpoints, and explore how they interpret and navigate their own experiences. Building a trusting and intimate rapport with the participants was essential, as it encouraged them to candidly share their narratives, transforming their lived experiences into profound stories of resilience, challenge, and triumph.

Data Analysis

Narrative analysis is a rich and nuanced qualitative research method that delves into the art of storytelling to unravel how individuals construct meaning from their unique lived experiences (Cissé & Rasmussen, 2022). This approach involves a meticulous examination of the structure, content, and context of personal narratives, whether derived from interviews, written accounts, or other expressive forms. The goal is to uncover profound themes and recurring patterns that illuminate the human experience. In this analytical framework, we focus on the intricate ways in which individuals craft their stories, striving to make sense of significant events and navigate their social environments. Narrative serves as a powerful tool for understanding individual phenomena; it reveals the inner workings of how people articulate their lives and experiences. At its core, narrative analysis rests on the belief that storytelling is fundamental to how individuals organize their lives and derive meaning from them. This analysis not only scrutinizes how participants interpret their own narratives but also explores how researchers interpret these intricate accounts. By examining these narratives, we gain valuable insights into the human condition, connection, and the diverse ways people understand their paths through life.

RESEARCH RESULTS

Following a series of in-depth interviews and meticulous analysis of the collected narrative information, the findings were organized and presented in alignment with the key themes that emerged from the data. Furthermore, it was essential to refine and adapt the data to ensure its suitability for the research objectives at hand. In addition to addressing the overarching theme, the explanations and analyses of the research findings presented the factors impacting cadet achievement and learning outcomes in maritime education and identified the most significant contributing factors in learning English.

Parents Support

Overall, the respondents' interest and motivation to learn English were significantly influenced by their parents' behavior and attitudes. The parents' conduct and mindset are not always evident from the direct instructions or financial support provided to the participants. Instead, they were reflected in daily actions and behaviors. For instance, Participant 2's father, a lecturer, frequently invites Participant 2 to observe his work environment, thereby potentially fostering a positive influence on the academic working environment. Furthermore, his father often conveys concrete messages and guidance.

> My father told me that my English skills had improved. Yesterday, I particularly informed my father that my TOEFL results are satisfactory. He also remarked that if he were sailing, his English skills would be effectively utilized (Participant 2)

Participant 2's father has been a constant source of guidance, instilling in his son the vital importance of mastering the English language. He not only emphasizes this essential skill but also champions practical steps to foster his son's progress, providing support and resources along the way. Meanwhile, the father of Participant 1 has taken a more challenging approach, pushing his son to strive for excellence in English, encouraging him to embrace the language with determination and confidence.

"My decision to attend the English village was not my own; rather, it was influenced by my father. He drew inspiration from his colleagues who were selected to represent the TNI in Wellington, New Zealand, for a comparative study." (Participant 1)

Participant 1's father experienced an English-speaking environment in Wellington, New Zealand, during the comparative study activity representing TNI. He encourages his son to master English so he can communicate more easily with English speakers in the future. Participant 3 also received tangible support from his parents, though the nature of this support differed from that provided by the parents of Participants 1 and 2.

My parents consistently supported my participation in English tutoring throughout my elementary and high school years (Participant 3).

The attitudes and approaches of the parents of these three respondents differed significantly from those of participants 4 and 5. Participant 4's parents are employed as factory workers. Due to their demanding work schedules. Participant 4 did not receive explicit guidance regarding the importance of learning English. While Participant 4 was encouraged by his parents to pursue schooling and higher education, the support was primarily verbal and lacked tangible follow-up or practical examples.

"My parents provided considerable support for my education, which contributed to my success. However, they did not place particular emphasis on the mastery of English, possibly due to their own educational backgrounds and experiences." (Participant 4)

The behavior of Participant 4's parents closely resembles that of Participant 5's parents. Participant 5 revealed that his parents encouraged their son to pursue higher education and broaden his knowledge. The support primarily takes the form of verbal encouragement and financial assistance. Due to limited educational attainment, they are unable to offer specific guidance or serve as practical role models.

"My parents have been offering me considerable support to pursue my education. However, my parents have not completed academic or university studies; my father graduated only from junior high school. Despite this, he hopes that his son will attain an academy or bachelor's degree. Their primary role is to provide a challenge by saying, You may wish to consult your peers for further advice. Regarding financial matters, if it becomes necessary, my parents are prepared to help, God willing." (Participant 5)

A participant reported that the family assumes a vital and supportive role as their child commences the educational journey. Although parents have not had the opportunity to pursue higher education themselves—his father only completed junior high school—he harbors a profound hope that his son will attain an academic diploma or even a bachelor's degree. Parents' steadfast support is rooted in the aspiration to guide children toward success, despite their own academic limitations. They encourage children to seek counsel from peers, acknowledging the significance of collaboration and shared experiences. Concerning financial matters, should the need arise, parents are more than willing to assist, trusting that circumstances will align favorably, with a bit of assistance from above.

Since elementary school, he has been receiving educational lessons. Initially, I was obliged to accompany my mother. As both my father and mother were engaged in their respective employment commitments, I had no alternative activities. Subsequently, I was enrolled in a tutoring program alongside my mother. Over time, I adapted to this routine and continued tutoring until the third year of high school. (participant 3)

Learners' Self-awareness

In the course of the interview, three participants showcased a remarkable enthusiasm and notable accomplishments in their language learning journeys. They revealed a deep learners' self-awareness regarding the importance of acquiring the English language, a realization that began to take shape during their formative school years. For example, Participant 8 recounted how, from a young age, he recognized the pivotal role that English would play in his aspirations to become a sailor. This awareness was intricately linked to his personal interests, driving his commitment to mastering the language in order to navigate the seas he so passionately longed to explore.

> "Proficiency in English is essential for maritime communication, particularly with individuals from diverse backgrounds. This insight highlighted to me the significance of learning English, which led me to begin self-study." (Participant 8)

This excerpt illustrates that Participant 8's aspirations have been significantly shaped by his own interests. As a result, he developed a strong motivation to learn English, recognizing it as a valuable skill for achieving his professional goals. Similarly, Participant 7 has maintained a long-standing interest in English since elementary school, albeit for different reasons. Participant 7's enthusiasm for English was initially sparked by the independence parade that exhibited a sailor parade in Elementary School and further reinforced during his shipping education, where his commitment to learning English grew as he gained clarity regarding his objectives.

> "From a young age, I have nurtured a deep and enduring fascination with the English language, a journey that began in the vibrant classroom of my elementary school. My initial spark of interest was ignited by a colorful independence parade that showcased the impressive coordination of a sailor parade, capturing my imagination and instilling a sense of wonder. As I progressed through my educational journey, particularly during my studies in shipping, this initial enthusiasm blossomed into a profound commitment to mastering English. Each lesson revealed new layers of the language, and with that, my goals became clearer, driving me ever forward in my pursuit of fluency and understanding." (Participant 7)

The maritime student shared that his fascination with the English language started at a young age. It all began in the lively classroom of his elementary school, where a colorful independence parade showcasing sailors' coordination sparked his interest. This moment sparked his imagination and curiosity. As he continued his education, especially during his shipping studies, his initial interest grew into a strong desire to master English. Each lesson uncovered new aspects of the language, helping him clarify his goals and motivating him to achieve fluency and deeper understanding.

Although it is not a regular occurrence, Participant 10 often finds himself drifting into the realm of reading, driven by an enduring self-awareness about vocabulary. The questions that appear on English tests frequently use perplexing terminology, which captures his attention and sparks a desire to delve deeper into their meanings. This puzzling language not only challenges him but also ignites a fascination that compels him to explore and truly grasp the rich nuances of words.

> It is not a frequent occurrence; I typically read around and maintain a persistent curiosity about vocabulary. Usually, questions in the English test use confusing terminology, which piques my interest in understanding their meanings (Participant 10).

Though it may not happen often, Participant 10 occasionally drifts into the captivating world of reading, propelled by a deep-seated self-awareness regarding the intricacies of vocabulary. The questions posed in English tests often contain enigmatic terminology that not only piques his curiosity but also ignites a fervent desire to unravel their meanings. This challenging and perplexing language serves not only as a puzzle but also as a doorway to a fascinating exploration, compelling him to dive into the rich tapestry of words and genuinely appreciate the subtle nuances they harbor.

When it comes to my speaking abilities, Participant 2 would not classify himself as exceptionally fluent. He genuinely believes that effective speaking often thrives on interaction; having a conversation partner can significantly accelerate his progress. Nevertheless, he remains committed to enhancing his speaking skills, whether through practicing with a partner or engaging in self-directed study. This continuous effort reflects his determination to grow and refine his abilities, striving for greater confidence and proficiency in his communication.

> Regarding speaking skills, I do not consider myself highly fluent. Truly, effective speaking requires a partner, which facilitates quick progress. However, I continually endeavor to improve my speaking skills, either with a speaking partner or self-study (Participant 2).

Participant 2 would not describe his speaking skills as exceptionally fluent. He genuinely believes that effective speaking often depends on interaction; practicing with a conversation partner can significantly speed up his progress. However, he stays dedicated to improving his speaking abilities, whether through partner practice or self-study. This ongoing effort shows his commitment to growth and refinement, aiming for increased confidence and proficiency in communication.

Similarly, another participant revealed that from the very beginning, his journey with the English language has been intertwined with his passion for gaming. Engaging in countless online games with players from around the globe, he found himself navigating the vibrant and diverse arena of multiplayer environments where English became not just a tool, but an essential lifeline for communication.

> I have been fluent in English from the outset through playing games, often online with external players. Consequently, irrespective of personal preference, communication in English is necessary in these contexts. Throughout this period, my English learning has been largely self-directed through gaming, as effective communication in English is essential for participation. (Participant 1)

Participant 1 reported that in these dynamic, often fast-paced contexts, the ability to articulate thoughts and strategies clearly in English shifted from a mere preference to a necessity. His learning process has been primarily self-guided, fueled by the immersive experiences gaming offers. Through interactions with virtual teammates and opponents alike, he has developed a deeper understanding of the language, recognizing that effective communication is crucial to engage and thrive within these virtual communities fully.

Lecturer Support

Participants 6 demonstrate enthusiasm for learning English upon entering the shipping education program. Participant 6 considered that he was late in developing enthusiasm for learning English due to interactions with English teachers who had a poor teaching style during his secondary school. The motivation in learning English was heightened after receiving guidance from lecturers and seniors during lectures and training sessions. In an interview, Participant 6 expressed that during his school years, he found English uninteresting and difficult to learn. He ultimately concluded that it was unnecessary to dedicate excessive effort to learning English.

> I previously did not enjoy English lessons and found the subject to be difficult. Ultimately, I prefer to focus on learning other subjects. This preference may also be influenced by the teacher's less

> engaging teaching style. Lucky me, I have become motivated to learn English since I was accepted into maritime education. I have received guidance from my lecturers during lectures (participant 6).

Participant 6 exuded a newfound enthusiasm for learning English upon entering the shipping education program, a stark contrast to his previous experiences. He reflected on his secondary school years, where his interactions with English teachers, whose ineffective teaching methods left much to be desired, stifled his initial interest in the language. This lack of inspiration led him to feel that he was too late to cultivate a genuine passion for English. However, a turning point came during his time in the program, when the support and guidance from engaging lecturers and encouraging seniors transformed his perspective. Their infectious passion for the subject sparked a renewed motivation within him, making the learning experience not only more enjoyable but also more meaningful. In a candid interview, Participant 6 candidly shared his previous struggles, revealing how he once found English unappealing and tedious. The complexities of the language felt overwhelming, overshadowing his desire to learn. As he reflected on his journey, he concluded that he had previously underestimated the importance of dedicating effort to mastering English. This awareness emerged only after he experienced the invigorating environment of the shipping education program.

Next, participant 9 reported that throughout his years in elementary and high school, he often struggled to grasp the nuances of the English language. The complexity of grammar, vocabulary, and pronunciation felt like an insurmountable barrier. However, his perspective changed dramatically when he stumbled upon a vibrant and engaging learning method during his time on campus.

> Honestly, from elementary through high school, I still found it hard to understand English. However, after experiencing a fun learning method on campus, I realized that English is no longer difficult (participant 9)

Throughout participant 1's years in elementary and high school, he often struggled to grasp the nuances of the English language. The complexity of grammar, vocabulary, and pronunciation felt like an insurmountable barrier. However, his perspective changed dramatically when he stumbled upon a vibrant and engaging learning method during his time on campus. This innovative approach transformed his experience, making the process enjoyable and interactive. Suddenly, what once seemed daunting became accessible, and he discovered that English was no longer a source of frustration, but rather a medium for communication and expression that he could embrace with confidence.

Peers Support

Offering tutoring by seniors in training sessions can be incredibly beneficial, particularly when there are gaps in understanding that need to be filled. During classroom studies, Participant 3 often finds that he requires additional time and support to grasp the nuances of the English subject fully. Simply listening during lectures does not suffice; his comprehension often feels fragmented or lacking depth. As a result, he seeks personalized guidance that can help him explore the material more thoroughly and solidify my understanding. This tailored assistance is essential for unlocking his full potential in the subject.

> Providing tutoring by seniors in training sessions is advantageous, especially if something necessary is still missing. When I engage in classroom study, I need extra time for assistance to learn the English subject. If one merely listens during class, comprehension remains incomplete. Therefore, I need guidance to deepen my understanding of the material (participant 3)

Similarly, participant 9 reported that he often finds himself reaching out to friends for valuable assistance. For example, he sometimes asks them the English word for a "dipper" and seeks guidance on how to start a natural conversation. While these tasks can feel daunting at first, he holds onto the hope that, with patience and practice, he will gradually internalize these words and skills. Moreover, he regularly welcomes feedback from his friends, who generously offer it whenever he stumbles or makes mistakes, helping him grow and improve.

> I often seek assistance from friends. For instance, I inquire about the English term for a dipper and ask how to initiate small talk. Although these may seem somewhat challenging initially, I believe that with time, I will remember them. Additionally, I frequently receive feedback from friends if I make mistakes. (Participant 9)

Correspondingly, participant 10 reported that mastering the English language continues to present a considerable challenge for him. Whenever he faces obstacles in his learning journey, he usually turns to his classmates or friends at the mess, where they often engage in lively discussions that spark insights and help clarify his doubts. Moreover, he recognizes that it is his responsibility to take charge of his own education, and at this stage, he has not yet enrolled in a formal course. However, he is considering enrolling in a structured course in the future to enhance his language skills further.

> Learning English remains a significant challenge for me. When I encounter difficulties, I typically seek assistance from my classmates or friends at the mess. Additionally, it is my responsibility to ensure that I have not yet enrolled in a formal course. Considering enrolling in a course at a later time (participant 10)

Similarly, participant 10 said that mastering English remains a big challenge for him. When he faces difficulties in learning, he usually talks with his classmates or friends at the mess, where they often have lively discussions that generate ideas and help clear up his doubts. He also understands that it is his job to take charge of his own learning, and he has not enrolled in a formal course yet. However, he is thinking about signing up for a structured course in the future to improve his language skills.

DISCUSSION

Upon reviewing the study's findings, it is evident that a distinction exists in mindset and behavior between cadets who demonstrate interest in learning, enthusiasm, and notable achievements, and those who lack these attributes. Cadets who excelled in English have accordingly attained success in their prior educational endeavors. Students possessing existing competence and prior knowledge are better equipped to comprehend new material and to acquire more advanced knowledge (Winget & Persky, 2022). Additionally, apart from the competencies and knowledge already held, four other factors contribute significantly to cadets' success in learning English: parents' support, self-awareness, lecturer support, and peer support.

Concerning parents' support, cadets are also influenced by their competence and achievements in learning English. The levels of education, occupation, and parental associations significantly influence cadets' success in acquiring a foreign language. This is because these factors can impact parental behavior and mindset, which should extend beyond mere guidance to support and foster better learning outcomes actively. The research findings indicate that parental involvement and educational background play a significant role in supporting students' English language development. Cadets whose parents set exemplary standards or provide guidance exhibit a more positive mindset and greater motivation to learn English. In contrast, cadets whose parents have limited educational attainment tend to receive primarily verbal encouragement and financial assistance, lacking specific guidance on English language learning. This study suggests that parents' educational levels and their ability to serve as role models and provide practical support are crucial factors in shaping their children's enthusiasm and success in mastering English.

The findings of this study further indicate a strong interest and motivation in learning English, which results in significantly higher scores during schooling and college education, as well as on the TOEFL examination. Students with initially low motivation and achievement developed an appreciation for English upon entering the shipping education program. Individuals' motivation to engage in certain activities is shaped by two principal factors: internal drivers (Intrinsic motivation) and environmental influences (Extrinsic motivation) (Fitria et al., 2024; Morris et al., 2022; Padalia & Natsir, 2022). The former encompasses interest, enjoyment, and a sense of achievement derived from the activity or its outcome. Conversely, the latter is predominantly affected by the satisfaction of needs, rewards, and punishments, and the enhancement of self-esteem through interactions with the surrounding environment.

This research supports the previous studies that extrinsic motivation to learn English is supported by parents, lecturers, and peers (Wang & Neihart, 2015) as well as learners' self-awareness (Castro & Shelton-Strong, 2024). This is exemplified by their aspiration to become successful sailors. Recognizing the significance of English language proficiency for pursuing a career at sea, they consequently endeavor to develop a greater liking for and a more serious approach to learning the language. However, among all participants with the same type of motivation, some students possessed both motivations. Her interest in learning English initially stemmed from being compelled to attend lessons from elementary through high school. This habitual engagement with tutoring may have further cultivated their fondness for English, irrespective of their intended career objectives. Conversely, after recognizing the advantages of English proficiency within the maritime industry, their enthusiasm for improving their English skills has intensified. Additionally, they have achieved success in several English competitions. These dual motivations set her apart from other cadets.

Additional findings from this research indicate that lecturers' teaching methods and practices significantly influence cadets' enthusiasm for learning English. Several participants cited the instructor's inadequate teaching style as one reason for their lack of interest in English (Tran & Moskovsky, 2022). Consequently, deficiencies in teacher discipline, commitment, and morality are identified as primary factors contributing to students' inadequate proficiency in English. The research shows that instructors' teaching methods greatly affect students' motivation to learn English. Several participants mentioned that poor teaching styles are a main reason for their lack of interest. Issues such as lack of discipline, commitment, and morality among teachers are seen as critical factors behind students' low English proficiency. To boost enthusiasm and improve learning results, it is essential to use engaging teaching methods that connect with students' varied backgrounds and experiences.

The journey towards mastering the English language among maritime cadets is shaped by a multitude of factors that intertwine to influence their learning outcomes. The research reveals a noticeable correlation between the educational backgrounds of the cadets' parents and their enthusiasm for language acquisition. It appears that parental principles and perspectives play a pivotal role in molding their children's attitudes towards learning English (Tong et al., 2021). Cadets who exhibit a passionate interest in the language often soar academically, outperforming peers who may lack that drive. Interestingly, while many cadets start their English education with a sense of trepidation, often scoring below expectations, they almost universally acknowledge the essential role that English proficiency will play in their future maritime careers.

This study aims to provide cadets with fresh insights and innovative perspectives on effective English-learning strategies tailored to their individual needs. They are encouraged to draw inspiration from their peers who have excelled in English, using these successful individuals as sources of motivation and guidance. Moreover, the findings offer valuable reflections for lecturers and educators, enhancing their understanding of the diverse backgrounds and experiences that shape each cadet's learning journey. As educators analyze these results, they are better equipped to identify and deploy the most fitting and effective teaching methods, approaches, and techniques that resonate with the unique dynamics of their classrooms (Badolo et al., 2025; Dajang et al., 2024; Rajaram, 2021, 2023).

The study found that several teaching practices and methods effectively enhance students' interest and performance in learning English. First, engaging teaching strategies demonstrate that when English teachers use stimulating lessons and relatable content, students often become more intrigued and enthusiastic about learning the language. Second, a disciplined classroom environment is essential; it shows that a structured atmosphere and the development of strong character traits among students are crucial components that significantly influence their learning outcomes in English. Third, access to diverse learning resources is important. When students have a wide range of English-learning materials at their disposal, they are immersed in an enriching environment that fosters their academic growth. Finally, parental involvement plays a crucial role. Parents' educational backgrounds greatly impact their children's academic success in English, as they are uniquely positioned to guide and influence their children's learning experiences.

This research proposes that more effective English teachers employ several strategies to engage and motivate their students. This research stimulates lessons and relatable content. This study states that when teachers engage students with stimulating lessons and relatable content, students often become more intrigued and enthusiastic about learning English. This suggests that effective teachers use engaging teaching methods and tailor the material to resonate with students' interests and experiences (Goyibova et al., 2025). This research also suggests maintaining classroom discipline: "A disciplined environment and the cultivation of strong character traits are vital components that significantly shape students' learning outcomes." Effective teachers maintain order and foster positive character development in their students, creating a conducive learning environment. Finally, this research leverages diverse learning resources. This study notes that "when students have access to a wide range of English-learning materials, they are immersed in an enriching environment that fosters their academic growth." Effective teachers likely provide their students with a variety of engaging learning resources to support their English language development.

Effective English teachers exemplify their expertise through adept teaching strategies and the ability to tailor material to students' diverse needs (Feng et al., 2025). When teachers engage students with stimulating lessons and relatable content, students often become more intrigued and enthusiastic about learning English. The research also highlights that a disciplined environment and the cultivation of strong character traits are vital components that significantly shape students' learning outcomes. This research discusses the significant influence of learning resources on student performance in English. It states that when students have access to a wide range of English learning materials, they are immersed in an enriching environment that fosters their academic growth, whether they are studying independently or engaging with teachers in a dynamic classroom. This research highlights that the availability of diverse English-learning resources is a crucial factor in enhancing students' academic achievement in English.

This research discusses several learning resources that can benefit students' English language development. Access to a wide range of English-learning materials can foster academic growth when students engage with them independently or in the classroom (Parker, 2023). Guidance and support from English teachers, who can leverage their expertise, teaching strategies, and ability to customize content to students' needs. Parental involvement and educational background are key factors, as parents serve as key supporters and educators at home. This research suggests that the interplay among these educational resources, parental guidance, and teacher involvement creates a multifaceted environment that is crucial for enhancing student achievement in English language learning.

In addition to parental educational background, other family-related factors that can influence students' motivation and performance in learning English include parental behavior and attitudes. This research notes that parents' conduct and mindset, as reflected in their daily actions and behaviors, can serve as sources of inspiration and guidance for their children's English learning. This study found that cadets whose parents actively supported and encouraged their English learning, whether through practical actions, verbal guidance, or financial assistance, tended to exhibit higher motivation and achievement compared to those whose parents provided limited support.

CONCLUSION

The research findings presented in the article provide valuable insights into the factors that influence maritime cadets' success in learning English, the essential lingua franca of the maritime industry. Cadets whose parents actively supported and encouraged their English learning, whether through practical actions, verbal guidance, or financial assistance, tended to exhibit higher motivation and achievement compared to those whose parents provided limited support. Cadets who demonstrated a strong interest and enthusiasm for learning English from a young age, often driven by their aspirations to become successful sailors, achieved significantly higher scores during schooling and college education, as well as on the TOEFL examination. Engaging teaching methods and a disciplined classroom environment were found to be crucial in enhancing students' interest and performance in learning English. Finally, seeking guidance and assistance from classmates and friends was also identified as a valuable strategy for maritime cadets to improve their English language skills.

The educational background and involvement of parents significantly impact their children's enthusiasm and achievement in English language learning. Cadets whose parents provided guidance, role modeling, and practical support tended to exhibit higher motivation and performance compared to those with limited parental involvement. Cadets who recognized the importance of English proficiency for their future maritime careers developed a strong intrinsic motivation to master the language. This self-awareness and goal-oriented mindset contributed to their academic success in English. Engaging teaching methods and a disciplined classroom environment fostered by lecturers were found to enhance students' enthusiasm and learning outcomes in English significantly. Receiving guidance and feedback from classmates and senior students helped fill gaps in understanding and boosted cadets' confidence in their English language skills.

REFERENCES

Badolo, M., Malik, M. A., Nur, R., & Latifa, A. (2025). The Impact of Metacognitive Strategy Training on Higher-Order Thinking Skills (HOTS) in High School Mathematics: A Quasi-Experimental Study. *International Journal of Environment. Engineering and Education*, *7*(2), 146–157. DOI: 10.55151/ijeedu.v7i2.302

Baig, M. Z., Lagdami, K., & Mejia, M. Q.Jr. (2025). Safeguarding maritime transport: Disclosing the paradox of safety in domestic ferry operations. *Australian Journal of Maritime and Ocean Affairs*, *17*(3), 496–525. DOI: 10.1080/18366503.2024.2354558

Barkhuizen, G., & Consoli, S. (2021). Pushing the edge in narrative inquiry. [). Elsevier.]. *System*, *102*, 102656. DOI: 10.1016/j.system.2021.102656

Castro, E., & Shelton-Strong, S. J. (2024). Exploring emotions in language learning: Learners' self-awareness, personal growth, and transformation on a CLIL course. *Language Teaching Research*, •••, 13621688241267366. DOI: 10.1177/13621688241267366

Chew, S. Y., & Ng, L. L. (2021). *Interpersonal Interactions and Language Learning*. Springer. DOI: 10.1007/978-3-030-67425-0

Cissé, A., & Rasmussen, A. (2022). Qualitative Methods. In *Comprehensive Clinical Psychology* (pp. 91–103). Elsevier., DOI: 10.1016/B978-0-12-818697-8.00216-8

Clandinin, D. J. (2022). *Engaging in narrative inquiry*. Routledge. DOI: 10.4324/9781003240143

Dajang, I. N., Ayuba, M. M., & Mahanan, S. (2024). Innovation and Implementation of Online Learning Technology in Enhancing Learning Experience Post-COVID-19. *International Journal of Environment. Engineering and Education*, *6*(3), 181–189. DOI: 10.55151/ijeedu.v6i3.170

Davis-Kean, P. E., Tighe, L. A., & Waters, N. E. (2021). The role of parent educational attainment in parenting and children's development. *Current Directions in Psychological Science*, *30*(2), 186–192. DOI: 10.1177/0963721421993116

Edgerton, E., & McKechnie, J. (2023). The relationship between student's perceptions of their school environment and academic achievement. *Frontiers in Psychology*, *13*, 959259. DOI: 10.3389/fpsyg.2022.959259

Feng, X., Zhang, N., Yang, D., Lin, W., & Maulana, R. (2025). From awareness to action: Multicultural attitudes and differentiated instruction of teachers in Chinese teacher education programmes. *Learning Environments Research*, *28*(2), 345–386. DOI: 10.1007/s10984-024-09518-9

Fitria, F., Yahya, M., Ali, M. I., Purnamawati, P., & Mappalotteng, A. M. (2024). The Impact of System Quality and User Satisfaction: The Mediating Role of Ease of Use and Usefulness in E-Learning Systems. *International Journal of Environment. Engineering and Education*, *6*(2), 119–131. DOI: 10.55151/ijeedu.v6i2.134

Gabedava, G., & Hu, Y. (2025). Enhancing maritime safety through linguistic analysis: a case study of communication failures in maritime accidents. *WMU Journal of Maritime Affairs*, 347–361. DOI: 10.1007/s13437-025-00371-y

Gietz, C., & McIntosh, K. (2014). Relations between student perceptions of their school environment and academic achievement. *Canadian Journal of School Psychology, 29*(3), 161–176. DOI: 10.1177/0829573514540415

Goyibova, N., Muslimov, N., Sabirova, G., Kadirova, N., & Samatova, B. (2025). Differentiation approach in education: Tailoring instruction for diverse learner needs. *MethodsX, 14*, 103163. DOI: 10.1016/j.mex.2025.103163

Habrat, A. (2018). *The role of self-esteem in foreign language learning and teaching*. Springer. DOI: 10.1007/978-3-319-75283-9

Hidayat, L. E., Basthomi, Y., & Afrilyasanti, R. (2024). Exploring secondary school teachers' creativity in differentiated instruction (DI) practices across Indonesian EFL classrooms. *Thinking Skills and Creativity, 53*, 101620. DOI: 10.1016/j.tsc.2024.101620

Hill, N. E., & Taylor, L. C. (2004). Parental school involvement and children's academic achievement: Pragmatics and issues. *Current Directions in Psychological Science, 13*(4), 161–164. DOI: 10.1111/j.0963-7214.2004.00298.x

Hossain, K. I. (2024). Literature-based language learning: Challenges, and opportunities for English learners. *Ampersand (Oxford, UK), 13*(July), 100201. DOI: 10.1016/j.amper.2024.100201

Idkhan, A. M., & Idris, M. M. (2021). Dimensions of Students Learning Styles at The University with The Kolb Learning Model. *International Journal of Environment. Engineering and Education, 3*(2), 75–82. DOI: 10.55151/ijeedu.v3i2.60

Idkhan, A. M., & Idris, M. M. (2023). The Impact of User Satisfaction in the Use of E-Learning Systems in Higher Education: A CB-SEM Approach. *International Journal of Environment. Engineering and Education, 5*(3), 100–110. DOI: 10.55151/ijeedu.v5i3.91

Kutsyuruba, B., & Stasel, R. S. (2023). Narrative inquiry. In *Varieties of Qualitative Research Methods: Selected Contextual Perspectives* (pp. 325–332). Springer.

Lamada, M. S., Sanatang, S., Ifani, A. Z., & Hidayat, D. H. (2022). Evaluation in Assessment of Student Competence: Application of the Indonesian Student Competency Assessment (AKSI) in Elementary Schools. *International Journal of Environment. Engineering and Education, 4*(2), 66–75. DOI: 10.55151/ijeedu.v4i2.81

Lăpădat, L. C., & Lăpădat, M.-M. (2023). The importance of motivation in foreign language learning. *Scientific Bulletin of the Politehnica University of Timişoara Transactions on Modern Languages, 22*(1), 142–152.

Lickona, T. (2013). Character education: The cultivation of virtue. In *Instructional-design theories and models* (pp. 591–612). Routledge. DOI: 10.4324/9781410603784-28

Morris, L. S., Grehl, M. M., Rutter, S. B., Mehta, M., & Westwater, M. L. (2022). On what motivates us: A detailed review of intrinsic v. extrinsic motivation. *Psychological Medicine, 52*(10), 1801–1816. DOI: 10.1017/S0033291722001611

Natsir, T., Rasyid, A. R., & Bassey, S. A. (2023). The SAVI Learning Model and the 21st Century Skills: Developing Critical Thinking, Collaboration, and Creativity in Students Vocational High School. *International Journal of Environment. Engineering and Education, 5*(1), 27–34. DOI: 10.55151/ijeedu.v5i1.96

Onwuegbuzie, A. J., Bailey, P., & Daley, C. E. (1999). Factors associated with foreign language anxiety. *Applied Psycholinguistics, 20*(2), 217–239. DOI: 10.1017/S0142716499002039

Padalia, A., & Natsir, T. (2022). End-User Computing Satisfaction (EUCS) Model: Implementation of Learning Management System (LMS) on Students Satisfaction at Universities. *International Journal of Environment. Engineering and Education, 4*(3), 100–107. DOI: 10.55151/ijeedu.v4i3.72

Parker, L. L. (2023). Technology in support of young English learners in and out of school. *Technology-Mediated Learning Environments for Young English Learners*, 213–250.

Pino Gavidia, L. A., & Adu, J. (2022). Critical narrative inquiry: An examination of a methodological approach. *International Journal of Qualitative Methods, 21*, 16094069221081594. DOI: 10.1177/16094069221081594

Rachmaniar, R., Yahya, M., & Lamada, M. (2021). Evaluation of Learning through Work Practices Industry Program at University with the CIPP Model Approach. *International Journal of Environment. Engineering and Education, 3*(2), 59–68. DOI: 10.55151/ijeedu.v3i2.55

Rajaram, K. (2021). *Evidence-based teaching for the 21st century classroom and beyond.* Springer. DOI: 10.1007/978-981-33-6804-0

Rajaram, K. (2023). Future of learning: Teaching and learning strategies. In *Learning Intelligence: Innovative and Digital Transformative Learning Strategies: Cultural and Social Engineering Perspectives* (pp. 3–53). Springer.

Riouch, A., Benamar, S., Ezzeri, H., & Cherqi, N. (2025). Post-COVID Environmental Education in Morocco: School Clubs as Drivers of Student Engagement and Sustained Self-Reported Sustainable Practices. *International Journal of Environment. Engineering and Education, 7*(2), 119–134. DOI: 10.55151/ijeedu.v7i2.303

Samdal, O., Wold, B., & Bronis, M. (1999). Relationship between students' perceptions of school environment, their satisfaction with school and perceived academic achievement: An international study. *School Effectiveness and School Improvement, 10*(3), 296–320. DOI: 10.1076/sesi.10.3.296.3502

Sampson, H., & Zhao, M. (2003). Multilingual crews: Communication and the operation of ships. *World Englishes, 22*(1), 31–43. DOI: 10.1111/1467-971X.00270

Steinmayr, R., Dinger, F. C., & Spinath, B. (2010). Parents' education and children's achievement: The role of personality. *European Journal of Personality, 24*(6), 535–550. DOI: 10.1002/per.755

Stronge, J. H., Ward, T. J., & Grant, L. W. (2011). What makes good teachers good? A cross-case analysis of the connection between teacher effectiveness and student achievement. *Journal of Teacher Education, 62*(4), 339–355. DOI: 10.1177/0022487111404241

Tong, F., Zhang, H., Zhen, F., Irby, B. J., & Lara-Alecio, R. (2021). Supporting home literacy practices in promoting Chinese parents' engagement in their children's English education in low-SES families: An experimental study. *International Journal of Educational Research*, *109*, 101816. DOI: 10.1016/j.ijer.2021.101816

Tran, L. H., & Moskovsky, C. (2022). Students as the source of demotivation for teachers: A case study of Vietnamese university EFL teachers. *Social Psychology of Education*, *25*(6), 1527–1544. DOI: 10.1007/s11218-022-09732-4

Wang, C. W., & Neihart, M. (2015). How do supports from parents, teachers, and peers influence academic achievement of twice-exceptional students. *Gifted Child Today*, *38*(3), 148–159. DOI: 10.1177/1076217515583742

Wells, R. S., Chen, L., Bettencourt, G. M., & Haas, S. (2023). Reconsidering rural-nonrural college enrollment gaps: The role of socioeconomic status in geographies of opportunity. *Research in Higher Education*, *64*(8), 1089–1112. DOI: 10.1007/s11162-023-09737-8

Wilson, C. (2014). *Interview Techniques for UX Practitioners: A User-Centered Design Method*. Newnes. https://books.google.co.id/books?id=2h3SDP7xSLIC

Winget, M., & Persky, A. M. (2022). A practical review of mastery learning. *American Journal of Pharmaceutical Education*, *86*(10), ajpe8906. DOI: 10.5688/ajpe8906

Xiang, L., & Stillwell, J. (2023). Rural–urban educational inequalities and their spatial variations in China. *Applied Spatial Analysis and Policy*, *16*(2), 873–896. DOI: 10.1007/s12061-023-09506-1

Yamamoto, Y., & Holloway, S. D. (2010). Parental expectations and children's academic performance in sociocultural context. *Educational Psychology Review*, *22*(3), 189–214. DOI: 10.1007/s10648-010-9121-z

Chapter 20

Officer Trainees' Attitudes Toward Online Learning Across Class Levels

Ryan Puby Sumarta
http://orcid.org/0009-0008-9889-5928
Politeknik Pelayaran Sorong, Indonesia

Yuniar Ayu Hafita
http://orcid.org/0009-0002-1300-226X
Politeknik Pelayaran Sorong, Indonesia

Dodik Widarbowo
Politeknik Pelayaran Sorong, Indonesia

Muhammad Idris
Politeknik Pelayaran Sorong, Indonesia

Dwi Haryanto
Politeknik Pelayaran Sorong, Indonesia

Oktovianus Cristian Karubaba
Politeknik Pelayaran Sorong, Indonesia

Ahmad Hamir
Politeknik Pelayaran Sorong, Indonesia

ABSTRACT

This study explores officer trainees' attitudes toward online learning within hybrid maritime education and examines differences across class levels. A quantitative survey involving 170 trainees from Nautical and Marine Engineering programs at Sorong Merchant Marine Polytechnic was conducted using a 28 item questionnaire. Descriptive statistics, one way ANOVA, and Tukey HSD tests were used for data analysis. Results revealed significant differences among class levels: Class III trainees showed the most positive attitudes, Class IV moderate, and Class V the least favorable. These variations reflect differences in digital literacy, motivation, and learning experience. The findings highlight the importance of level specific strategies that provide digital support for lower levels, reinforcement for mid-levels, and advanced digital integration for seniors to enhance readiness, engagement, and professional competency in maritime education.

DOI: 10.4018/979-8-3373-6670-8.ch020

BACKGROUND

Maritime education plays a critical role in preparing professional seafarers capable of meeting global shipping industry demands. The maritime sector represents a multifaceted system in which requires highly skilled personnel to conduct vessel operations safely, productively, and in an environmentally sustainable way. The preparation of professional seafarers involves a combination of theoretical knowledge, practical skills, and the cultivation of critical soft skills such as leadership, communication, teamwork, problem-solving, and intercultural competence. In recent decades, the globalization of the shipping industry has increased the demand for seafarers who are not only technically competent but also culturally sensitive and capable of operating in multi-national environments. This trend has necessitated the evolution of maritime education to encompass not only traditional classroom instruction but also innovative methods that can equip cadets with the skills needed to thrive in dynamic, technology-driven maritime workplaces.

The ongoing rapid growth of digital technology has transformed learning systems across educational fields, including maritime education. Digital platforms have introduced new avenues for delivering content, facilitating communication, and supporting the development of professional competencies. Hybrid learning, which integrates face-to-face instruction with online modalities, has emerged as a prominent pedagogical model in maritime education (Boulougouris et al., 2019; Fedorova & Bobrysheva, 2021; Galić et al., 2020; Shvetsova et al., 2021). This approach provides cadets with flexible learning schedules, personalized learning paths, and opportunities for self-directed study. The hybrid model is particularly valuable for maritime students who often balance academic responsibilities with practical onboard training, making conventional, rigid class schedules less feasible.

Hybrid learning offers multiple benefits for maritime education. By combining synchronous activities such as live discussions and workshops with asynchronous learning through recorded lectures and digital exercises, cadets can engage in meaningful learning experiences without being constrained by time and space. This flexible approach supports independent learning, critical thinking, and reflective practices, all of which are vital for developing decision-making abilities in real-world maritime scenarios. Studies have shown that hybrid learning contributes to increased student satisfaction, reduced dropout rates, and improved learning outcomes, highlighting its potential to support professional development and career readiness among maritime students (Boulougouris et al., 2019; Shvetsova et al., 2021).

The successful implementation of hybrid learning in maritime contexts depends heavily on the effective use of digital platforms. Learning Management Systems (LMS) such as Moodle, combined with tools like Zoom and Google Classroom, provide cadets through availability of learning resources and facilitation of communication with instructors and peers, and create opportunities for collaborative learning (Mansur & Asmawati, 2021; Shurygin et al., 2021). LMS platforms also allow instructors to monitor student progress, provide timely feedback, and tailor content to meet individual learning needs. In addition, these platforms can bridge the discrepancy between theoretical knowledge and practical application by integrating multimedia, simulations, and interactive modules that replicate real-world maritime operations. The use of digital platforms is thus integral to creating a learning environment that is responsive, adaptive, and conducive to professional skill development.

In addition to LMS and communication platforms, technological innovations such as simulation software and virtual reality (VR) have become critical in maritime education. Simulation-based training enables cadets to practice navigational maneuvers, engine operations, and emergency response procedures in a controlled virtual environment, reducing the risk of errors in real-life scenarios (Mallam et al., 2019; Voloshynov et al., 2022). VR technology further enhances experiential learning by providing immersive scenarios where cadets can engage with realistic shipboard environments, simulate complex problem-solving situations, and develop procedural memory. These technologies not only complement traditional hands-on training but also allow cadets to experience rare or high-risk scenarios that are difficult to reproduce in physical settings.

Despite these technological advances, cadets' readiness to engage with hybrid learning remains a critical determinant of its effectiveness. Research has identified several challenges that affect engagement and learning outcomes, including uneven digital literacy, lack of motivation, limited self-regulation, and difficulties in time management (Andiansyah et al., 2025; Belev et al., 2022; Kumar & Rajini, 2024; Wang et al., 2023). These challenges are particularly pronounced in maritime education due to the intensive nature of cadet training, which often involves strict schedules, high physical and cognitive demands, and adherence to discipline. Cadets who lack preparedness for digital learning may experience frustration, reduced engagement, and suboptimal learning outcomes, which can negatively impact their professional development.

Cadets with positive attitudes toward hybrid learning, such as perceived usefulness, ease of use, and intrinsic interest, tend to exhibit higher levels of engagement and achievement (Andromeda & Fatimah, 2025; Boulougouris et al., 2019; Shvetsova et al., 2021). These students are more likely to participate actively in online discussions, complete digital assignments on time, and apply learned concepts to practical training. Conversely, cadets with lower digital literacy or poor self-regulation often struggle to navigate online platforms effectively, resulting in diminished learning outcomes and underutilization of available resources (Jutaite et al., 2021; Karagul et al., 2021; Tandrayen-Ragoobur et al., 2023). This highlights the importance of assessing and supporting cadet readiness when implementing hybrid learning models.

Class level has also been identified as a significant factor influencing cadets' attitudes and readiness for digital learning. Lower-level cadets generally display limited familiarity with online platforms, lower motivation, and less confidence in using digital tools, which can hinder their engagement in hybrid learning (Shi & Fan, 2021; Sulistyono et al., 2024). These students may require additional support, guidance, and scaffolding to navigate online environments effectively. In contrast, higher-level cadets typically possess stronger digital skills, greater self-efficacy, and a clearer understanding of how hybrid learning aligns with their professional development goals (Johansen, 2023; Karahalios, 2025; Pratiwi et al., 2023; Simanjuntak, 2024). Recognizing these differences is essential for designing instructional strategies that accommodate diverse learning needs and optimize outcomes across all levels.

Although existing research provides valuable insights into cadets' experiences with hybrid learning, most studies focus on general cadet populations without differentiating between officer trainees and regular cadets. Officer trainees undergo specialized training that emphasizes leadership, decision-making, and adherence to international standards, which may influence their perceptions and readiness for hybrid learning. Understanding officer trainees' attitudes toward online learning, particularly across class levels, is crucial for developing instructional strategies that enhance engagement, foster skill acquisition, and prepare students for the complex responsibilities of maritime leadership.

Hybrid learning tailored for officer trainees has significant implications for maritime education quality. By addressing class-level differences in digital readiness, motivation, and learning preferences, instructors can implement level-specific interventions, design appropriate scaffolding, and provide personalized feedback. This approach not only improves academic performance but also supports the development of professional competencies essential for officer roles, including leadership, crisis management, and team coordination. Moreover, effective hybrid learning can bridge gaps between theory and practice, ensuring that officer trainees acquire both technical knowledge and practical skills aligned with international maritime standards.

The integration of hybrid learning in officer training is also consistent with global trends in maritime education. International regulations and conventions, such as the STCW (Standards of Training, Certification, and Watchkeeping for Seafarers), emphasize competency-based training, continuous professional development, and the use of modern technology to enhance learning outcomes. By leveraging online and digital learning tools, maritime institutions can provide officer trainees with accessible, flexible, and immersive learning experiences that align with these standards, while simultaneously fostering adaptability and lifelong learning skills.

Therefore, this study aims to examine officer trainees' attitudes toward online learning in hybrid maritime education and to analyze whether significant differences exist across class levels. Investigating these attitudes will provide valuable insights into how instructional strategies can be optimized to improve engagement, learning outcomes, and competency development. The findings are expected to inform the design of more effective, level-specific teaching methods, thereby enhancing the overall quality of maritime education and preparing officer trainees to meet the evolving demands of the global shipping industry.

METHOD

This study employed a quantitative survey research design to investigate maritime officer trainees' attitudes toward online learning during their training and education programs. Quantitative survey research is particularly suitable for this type of study as it allows for the systematic collection of numerical data, which can then be used to describe, compare, and analyze the perceptions and attitudes of participants. The use of a survey design facilitates a structured approach to gathering information, providing both breadth and generalizability within the target population. This approach is also advantageous in capturing objective measures of attitudes and in identifying potential differences across demographic and academic variables, such as class level or study program. By utilizing a survey, the researchers aimed to obtain a comprehensive overview of officer trainees' experiences with online learning in the context of hybrid maritime education, ensuring that the findings could inform future instructional strategies and policy decisions.

The population targeted in this study consisted of 170 maritime officer trainees enrolled at Sorong Merchant Marine Polytechnic. These trainees represented two primary programs: Nautical Studies (ANT) and Marine Engineering (ATT). The inclusion of both programs allowed the study to capture a diverse perspective on online learning attitudes, reflecting differences in curriculum focus, practical training demands, and prior exposure to digital learning tools. The participants spanned multiple diploma-level cohorts, which provided a basis for examining variations in attitudes across different levels of academic and professional experience. Specifically, participants included 24 officer trainees from ANT IV Batch XXIII, 23 from ATT IV Batch XXII, 13 from ANT V Batch XXIV, 14 from ATT V Batch XXIV, 48 from ATT III Batch XIV, and 48 from ANT III Batch XV. The detailed distribution across program and class levels allowed the researchers to perform meaningful comparisons and infer the potential influence of class level on attitudes toward online learning.

A total sampling technique was employed in this study, meaning that all officer trainees enrolled in the selected classes were included as participants. This method guaranteed thorough coverage of the population, reducing potential sampling bias and increasing the reliability of the findings. Total sampling is particularly appropriate in educational research settings where the population size is manageable and where the aim is to obtain a complete representation of specific cohorts. The researchers emphasized voluntary participation, ensuring that officer trainees were able to opt out of the study without any repercussions, thereby adhering to ethical research practices and fostering a sense of trust and cooperation among participants.

Data were collected using a structured questionnaire adapted from Obaid Ullah's (2018) instrument on students' attitudes toward online learning at the tertiary level. The original instrument was chosen for its demonstrated reliability and validity in measuring multiple dimensions of online learning attitudes. Since officer trainees at Sorong Merchant Marine Polytechnic participate in a hybrid learning system, the questionnaire was adjusted to ensure relevance and clarity for the target population. Modifications were made to reflect the specific nature of maritime officer training, including references to simulation exercises, online maritime training modules, and blended instruction involving both classroom and online sessions. The adaptation process involved consultation with maritime education experts to ensure that the content was accurate, culturally appropriate, and reflective of the trainees' learning experiences.

The instrument consisted of two main sections. The first section collected demographic and background information, including study program, class level, prior experience with online learning, internet access, and devices used for participation. These variables provided contextual information that could influence officer trainees' attitudes and help interpret patterns observed in the data. For instance, prior exposure to online learning platforms or the type of devices used may affect comfort levels, perceived ease of use, and overall engagement. Collecting this information also allowed the researchers to control for potential confounding variables during analysis and to better understand how demographic and technological factors intersect with attitudes toward hybrid learning.

The second section of the questionnaire contained a 28-item attitude scale covering three dimensions: interest in computers and adoption of online learning (7 items), perceived effectiveness of online learning (11 items), and ease of using online learning (10 items). Each item was rated on a 5-point Likert scale ranging from strongly disagree (1) to strongly agree (5). The interest dimension measured participants' intrinsic motivation and enthusiasm toward digital learning, while the effectiveness dimension assessed perceptions regarding learning outcomes, knowledge acquisition, and practical applicability. The ease-of-use dimension focused on perceived user-friendliness, technical challenges, and comfort in navigating online platforms. This multidimensional approach allowed for a nuanced understanding of officer trainees' attitudes and identified specific areas for improvement in instructional design and technological support.

The original instrument demonstrated high internal consistency, with a reported Cronbach's Alpha of 0.90, indicating excellent reliability. To ensure the instrument's suitability for maritime officer trainees, it underwent expert review and a pilot trial prior to full deployment. Maritime education specialists assessed each item for clarity, relevance, and contextual appropriateness, providing feedback to refine wording and enhance interpretability. The pilot trial involved a small group of officer trainees outside the main sample, allowing the researchers to identify potential ambiguities, adjust instructions, and confirm that respondents could understand and respond to items consistently. These steps ensured the validity and reliability of the data collected in the main study.

The finalized questionnaire was distributed electronically via Google Forms, a platform that allowed for efficient, secure, and accessible data collection. Participants were provided with clear instructions regarding the purpose of the study, their rights as participants, and the voluntary nature of participation. Anonymity was strictly maintained, with no personally identifying information collected, ensuring that officer trainees could respond candidly without concern for privacy or repercussions. The use of an online survey also aligned with the study's focus on online learning, providing participants with a familiar digital interface and minimizing potential barriers to participation.

Data collection was conducted over a two-week period, providing officer trainees sufficient time to complete the questionnaire while accommodating their training schedules. Regular reminders were sent to participants to encourage timely responses, and technical support was offered to address any difficulties encountered during submission. The researchers monitored response rates to ensure that the sample was representative of the targeted cohorts, and follow-up communications helped maximize participation while maintaining ethical standards.

Collected data were analyzed using the Statistical Package for the Social Sciences (SPSS), which enabled both descriptive and inferential analyses. Descriptive statistics, including mean, standard deviation, and frequency, were employed to summarize overall attitudes, highlighting trends and patterns within the sample. These statistics provided an overview of officer trainees' perceptions of online learning, including areas of strength, such as perceived effectiveness, and areas for potential improvement, such as ease of use or technical support needs.

Inferential analyses were conducted using one-way Analysis of Variance (ANOVA) to examine potential differences in attitudes across class levels. This method allowed the researchers to test whether observed differences in mean scores were statistically significant, providing evidence for the impact of academic seniority or experience on online learning attitudes. When significant differences were detected, Tukey HSD post hoc tests were performed to identify specific pairwise differences between class levels, providing a detailed understanding of how attitudes varied among groups. This analytic approach ensured rigor in evaluating the influence of class level and supported evidence-based recommendations for instructional strategies and interventions.

Ethical considerations were strictly observed throughout the research process. Participation was entirely voluntary, with officer trainees informed of their right to withdraw at any time without consequence. Anonymity and confidentiality were maintained to protect participants' privacy, and no identifying information was collected or reported. Data were stored securely, and only the research team had access to raw responses. These measures aligned with international standards for research ethics, ensuring respect, integrity, and transparency in the conduct of the study.

RESULTS

1. Descriptive Statistics

Before conducting inferential analyses, descriptive statistics were examined to provide a detailed overview of officer trainees' attitudes toward online learning across three class levels: Class III, Class IV, and Class V. Descriptive statistics are essential as they summarize the central tendencies, variability, and range of responses, offering insights into general trends within the population before testing for statistically significant differences. This preliminary analysis enables researchers to identify patterns, highlight potential issues, and frame interpretations in the context of maritime officer training. In the present study, descriptive measures included the mean, standard deviation, minimum, and maximum scores for attitudes toward online learning, providing a comprehensive snapshot of trainees' perceptions. Table 1 presents the descriptive statistics of attitudes toward online learning for the three class levels.

Table 1. Descriptive Statistics of Attitudes toward Online Learning

Class Level	N	Mean	SD	Minimum	Maximum
Class III	96	3.71	0.50	2.70	4.80
Class IV	47	3.62	0.48	2.50	4.70
Class V	27	3.45	0.52	2.40	4.60

The results indicate that Class III trainees (N = 96) had a mean score of 3.71 with a standard deviation of 0.50, indicating relatively high positive attitudes. Class IV trainees (N = 47) reported a slightly lower mean of 3.62 with a standard deviation of 0.48, while Class V trainees (N = 27) had the lowest mean score of 3.45 with a standard deviation of 0.52. The minimum and maximum scores for each group ranged from 2.40 to 4.80, showing that while most trainees responded positively, there were variations in individual perceptions. The range of responses indicates that some trainees may experience challenges or reservations toward online learning, reflecting the diversity of experiences in a hybrid maritime education environment.

The trend observed in the mean scores suggests a gradual decline in positive attitudes as class level increases. Class III trainees, who are generally at the intermediate stage of their training, reported the most favorable perceptions of online learning. This may be attributed to their novelty in experiencing hybrid education and their enthusiasm for engaging with digital platforms and interactive learning modalities. As officer trainees advance to higher class levels, their exposure to professional responsibilities, practical shipboard training, and complex academic content increases, potentially shifting their focus from general engagement with online learning to prioritizing practical skills and experiential training.

Class IV trainees exhibited moderately positive attitudes, with a mean slightly lower than that of Class III. This cohort is typically in a transitional phase, balancing advanced theoretical coursework with practical training aboard vessels. The slight decrease in mean attitude scores may reflect an increased awareness of the limitations of online learning in replicating hands-on experiences. While online platforms provide accessibility and flexibility, officer trainees in Class IV may encounter challenges in applying theoretical knowledge to practical contexts without direct supervision or onboard practice. Their responses suggest a nuanced understanding of both the benefits and constraints of hybrid learning in maritime officer training.

Class V trainees, representing the most advanced cohort, reported the lowest positive attitudes toward online learning (M = 3.45). This decline may be influenced by several factors, including heightened academic expectations, greater exposure to real-world shipboard operations, and the increasing importance of leadership and decision-making competencies that are more effectively developed through practical engagement rather than virtual simulations. As officer trainees near the completion of their programs, they may perceive online learning as supplementary rather than central to their professional development. The lower mean score highlights the need for instructional designers to integrate online learning with hands-on experiences that address the specific needs of advanced trainees.

The standard deviations across the three class levels, ranging from 0.48 to 0.52, indicate a relatively consistent distribution of responses within each group. While the overall trend shows a decline in mean attitudes with higher class levels, individual variation persists within each cohort. Some trainees in Class V may still hold positive perceptions of online learning due to personal motivation, digital literacy, or previous successful experiences with hybrid instruction. Conversely, a subset of Class III trainees may express reservations or lower engagement due to unfamiliarity with online platforms or external factors such as limited internet access. These variations underscore the importance of considering individual differences alongside class-level trends when evaluating the effectiveness of online learning interventions.

The minimum and maximum scores provide further insight into the variability of attitudes toward online learning. Trainees' scores ranged from 2.40 to 4.80, suggesting that while the majority hold moderately to highly positive perceptions, there are instances of lower engagement or skepticism. Such findings are critical for maritime education stakeholders, as they indicate that even within structured training programs, not all officer trainees equally benefit from online learning initiatives. Addressing the factors contributing to lower scores, such as limited digital readiness, time management challenges, or preference for practical instruction, may help enhance the overall efficacy of hybrid learning models.

In summary, the descriptive statistics highlight a clear pattern in officer trainees' attitudes toward online learning: a generally positive perception across all cohorts, with a gradual decrease in positivity as class level advances. These findings suggest that while hybrid learning is broadly accepted and valued, its perceived relevance and effectiveness may diminish for trainees with more advanced practical responsibilities and professional expectations. The results provide a foundation for further inferential analysis, offering insights into potential differences between class levels and informing strategies to tailor online learning experiences to the developmental and professional needs of maritime officer trainees. Understanding these patterns is essential for optimizing hybrid instructional models, ensuring that online learning continues to support both theoretical comprehension and the practical competencies required for successful maritime careers.

2. Normality Test

Before proceeding with inferential statistical analyses, it is crucial to examine whether the data meet the assumptions required for parametric tests. One of the fundamental assumptions in parametric statistics is normality, which refers to the degree to which the data distribution approximates a normal, bell-shaped curve. Normality ensures that statistical procedures, such as the Analysis of Variance (ANOVA), yield valid and reliable results, including accurate estimates of means, variances, and significance levels. In the context of this study, testing normality is particularly important because officer trainees' attitudes toward online learning are measured on a Likert scale, and parametric techniques assume that the dependent variable is normally distributed within each group.

To assess the assumption of normality, the Shapiro–Wilk test was employed. The Shapiro–Wilk test is widely recognized as one of the most powerful tests for normality, particularly for small to medium sample sizes, which is relevant for this study where individual class sizes ranged from 27 to 96 officer trainees. Unlike visual inspection of histograms or Q-Q plots, which can be subjective, the Shapiro–Wilk test provides a quantitative assessment, generating a W statistic and an associated p-value that indicate whether the data significantly deviate from a normal distribution. A p-value greater than the significance threshold (typically 0.05) suggests that the null hypothesis—that the data are normally distributed—cannot be rejected. Table 2 presents the results of the Shapiro–Wilk normality test for Class III, Class IV, and Class V officer trainees.

Table 2. Shapiro–Wilk Test of Normality

Class Level	W	p-value	Interpretation
Class III	0.98	0.075	Normal distribution
Class IV	0.97	0.062	Normal distribution
Class V	0.96	0.084	Normal distribution

Class III yielded a W value of 0.98 with a p-value of 0.075, Class IV had a W of 0.97 with a p-value of 0.062, and Class V produced a W of 0.96 with a p-value of 0.084. All p-values exceeded the conventional threshold of 0.05, indicating that the null hypothesis of normality could not be rejected for any of the three class levels. This means that the distributions of attitudes toward online learning for all groups are approximately normal, allowing for the use of parametric tests such as ANOVA to examine differences across class levels.

The findings of the Shapiro–Wilk test hold practical significance in the context of hybrid maritime education. Given the structured nature of online and blended learning programs for officer trainees, the assumption of normality suggests that the data do not contain extreme skewness or outliers that could distort the analysis. Normality in this context implies that trainees' perceptions and attitudes toward online learning are distributed in a balanced manner, with most individuals' responses clustering around the mean, while fewer trainees report extremely high or low attitudes. Such a distribution is consistent with the expectation that while online learning is generally accepted, individual experiences vary depending on factors such as digital literacy, motivation, access to technology, and prior exposure to hybrid learning modalities.

Furthermore, confirming normality ensures the robustness of subsequent inferential analyses. Parametric tests like ANOVA rely on the assumption that residuals are normally distributed to produce valid F-statistics and p-values. If the data were non-normal, the results of the ANOVA could be misleading, potentially inflating Type I or Type II errors. In maritime officer training research, where accurate assessment of attitudes across class levels informs instructional strategies, leadership development programs, and curriculum design, maintaining methodological rigor is essential. The Shapiro–Wilk results provide confidence that the parametric analyses to follow are appropriate and that comparisons between Class III, Class IV, and Class V officer trainees will yield meaningful insights.

In summary, the normality test confirmed that the attitudes of officer trainees toward online learning across all class levels are approximately normally distributed. This validation supports the use of parametric inferential statistics, ensuring that the subsequent ANOVA and post hoc analyses can accurately detect differences in mean attitudes among the class levels. By establishing the suitability of the data for parametric testing, the researchers can proceed with greater confidence in interpreting the influence of class level on trainees' perceptions of hybrid learning environments. This step not only strengthens the reliability of the findings but also provides a methodological foundation for drawing evidence-based conclusions about optimizing online learning strategies in maritime officer training programs.

3. Homogeneity of Variances

After confirming the normality of the data, the next assumption to be tested was the homogeneity of variances, which is a critical prerequisite for conducting parametric tests such as ANOVA. Homogeneity of variances, also known as homoscedasticity, refers to the extent to which the variability of scores is similar across different groups. In the context of this study, it is essential to ensure that Class III, Class IV, and Class V officer trainees exhibit comparable levels of dispersion in their attitudes toward online learning. If variances were substantially unequal, the results of ANOVA could be biased, leading to incorrect conclusions about the differences in mean attitudes among the groups.

To assess this assumption, Levene's test of homogeneity of variances was applied. Levene's test evaluates whether the variance of the dependent variable is equal across groups by testing the null hypothesis that the variances are the same.

Table 3. Levene's Test of Homogeneity of Variances

Test	F	df1	df2	p-value	Interpretation
Levene's	1.10	2	167	0.337	Equal variances

In this study, the Levene's test yielded an F value of 1.10 with degrees of freedom df1 = 2 and df2 = 167, and a p-value of 0.337. Since the p-value exceeds the conventional significance threshold of 0.05, the null hypothesis cannot be rejected. This indicates that the variances of attitudes toward online learning are statistically equivalent across Class III, Class IV, and Class V officer trainees.

Meeting the homogeneity assumption has important implications for the validity of the subsequent one-way ANOVA. Because the groups exhibit comparable variance levels, the ANOVA can reliably determine whether there are significant differences in mean attitudes among the class levels without the risk of heteroscedasticity distorting the F-statistic. In practical terms, this finding suggests that the variability in officer trainees' responses is consistent, allowing the researchers to confidently interpret any observed differences in mean attitudes as reflective of true group-level distinctions rather than artifacts of unequal dispersion. Ensuring homogeneity, therefore, strengthens the methodological rigor and credibility of the study's inferential analyses in the context of hybrid maritime education.

4. One-Way ANOVA

With the assumptions of normality and homogeneity of variances confirmed, the study proceeded to conduct a one-way Analysis of Variance (ANOVA) to determine whether significant differences exist in officer trainees' attitudes toward online learning across three class levels: Class III, Class IV, and Class V. One-way ANOVA is appropriate for comparing the means of three or more independent groups and assessing whether observed differences are statistically significant rather than due to random variation. This method is particularly useful in educational research to explore how factors such as class level influence learners' perceptions and engagement in hybrid or online learning environments. The results of the one-way ANOVA are summarized in Table 4.

Table 4. One-Way ANOVA Results

Source	SS	df	MS	F	p
Between Groups	1.92	2	0.96	3.80	0.025*
Within Groups	42.50	167	0.254		
Total	44.42	169			

*p < 0.05

The analysis revealed a between-groups sum of squares (SS) of 1.92, a mean square (MS) of 0.96, and an F-statistic of 3.80 with degrees of freedom df1 = 2 and df2 = 167. The associated p-value was 0.025, which is below the conventional significance level of 0.05. This finding indicates that the null hypothesis—that the mean attitudes toward online learning are equal across all class levels—can be rejected. Therefore, the differences observed in mean scores are statistically significant, suggesting that class level indeed influences officer trainees' attitudes.

Interpretation of these results in the context of maritime education provides meaningful insights. Class level in officer training programs often reflects differences in experience, exposure to practical shipboard operations, and cognitive development. The significant ANOVA result suggests that these developmental and experiential factors contribute to variations in attitudes toward online learning. For example, trainees in lower classes may perceive online learning more positively due to its novelty and flexibility, whereas senior trainees may prioritize hands-on, practical training that cannot be fully replicated in a virtual environment. This highlights the interplay between educational stage and the perceived value of hybrid instructional methods.

Furthermore, the statistical significance detected in the ANOVA emphasizes the need for level-specific instructional strategies in maritime officer training. Recognizing that Class III, IV, and V trainees experience and value online learning differently allows educators to tailor course content, technology integration, and engagement techniques to match the developmental needs of each cohort. For instance, interactive simulations and virtual reality tools may be highly effective for junior trainees, while advanced trainees may benefit from online modules that complement onboard practical exercises or leadership development programs.

It is also important to note that while ANOVA confirms the existence of significant differences, it does not identify which specific groups differ from each other. To address this, post hoc analyses such as Tukey HSD are required to determine pairwise differences between class levels. These subsequent tests are critical for providing actionable insights, guiding curriculum designers in refining hybrid learning approaches to enhance effectiveness across all stages of officer training.

In conclusion, the one-way ANOVA demonstrates that officer trainees' attitudes toward online learning vary significantly by class level, confirming that experience, exposure, and stage of training influence perceptions of hybrid education. This finding underscores the importance of considering class-level differences when designing and implementing online learning initiatives in maritime institutions. By leveraging these insights, educators can optimize learning outcomes, increase engagement, and ensure that online learning contributes meaningfully to the professional development of maritime officer trainees.

5. Post Hoc Test

Following the significant results of the one-way ANOVA, a Tukey HSD (Honestly Significant Difference) post hoc test was conducted to identify which specific class levels differed in their attitudes toward online learning. While ANOVA establishes the presence of a statistically significant difference among group means, it does not indicate which pairs of groups contribute to this significance. The Tukey HSD test is a robust post hoc procedure designed to compare all possible pairs of means while controlling for Type I error, making it particularly suitable for studies involving multiple class levels, such as Class III, Class IV, and Class V officer trainees in this research. Table 5 presents the results of the Tukey HSD post hoc test.

Table 5. Tukey HSD Post Hoc Test

Comparison	Mean Difference	p-value	Interpretation
III vs IV	0.09	0.420	Not significant
III vs V	0.26	0.018*	Significant
IV vs V	0.17	0.120	Not significant

*p < 0.05

The comparison between Class III and Class IV trainees revealed a mean difference of 0.09, with a p-value of 0.420, indicating no statistically significant difference between these two groups. Similarly, the comparison between Class IV and Class V yielded a mean difference of 0.17 and a p-value of 0.120, which is also not significant. These findings suggest that the attitudes of Class IV trainees are relatively similar to both their immediate junior and senior counterparts, highlighting a transitional nature in perceptions as trainees progress through the program.

In contrast, the comparison between Class III and Class V trainees showed a mean difference of 0.26, with a p-value of 0.018, which is statistically significant at the 0.05 level. This result indicates that Class III trainees hold significantly more positive attitudes toward online learning compared to the most advanced cohort, Class V. The difference may reflect a combination of factors, including novelty effects, enthusiasm for digital learning, and the decreasing relative importance of online modules for advanced trainees who are increasingly focused on practical shipboard experience, leadership responsibilities, and career-oriented competencies.

The significance of the difference between Class III and Class V has important implications for hybrid maritime education. It suggests that as officer trainees progress to higher levels, they may perceive online learning as less central to their development, potentially due to the increasing emphasis on hands-on training and real-world operational skills that cannot be fully replicated in a virtual environment. Understanding this trend allows maritime educators to design differentiated learning experiences that maintain engagement and perceived relevance across all class levels, ensuring that online learning continues to complement practical training effectively.

Moreover, the lack of significant differences between Class III and IV or IV and V indicates that middle-level trainees (Class IV) occupy a transitional stage where attitudes toward online learning are neither as positive as juniors nor as diminished as seniors. This intermediate position provides an opportunity for educators to implement bridging strategies that sustain engagement while gradually integrating practical, career-focused content. For example, online modules for Class IV trainees could include virtual simulations of ship operations combined with leadership scenarios, preparing them for the more hands-on responsibilities expected in Class V.

The post hoc findings also underscore the importance of monitoring individual differences within each class. Although significant differences were detected between Class III and Class V on average, individual variability within each group exists, as shown by prior descriptive statistics. Some advanced trainees may still express highly positive attitudes toward online learning due to strong digital literacy, motivation, or prior success with hybrid instruction. Similarly, a subset of junior trainees may experience challenges or limited engagement. Recognizing these individual differences allows for targeted support, personalized interventions, and adaptive instructional strategies that maximize learning outcomes across the entire cohort.

In conclusion, the Tukey HSD post hoc test confirms that officer trainees' attitudes toward online learning vary significantly between the earliest and most advanced class levels, while intermediate differences are not statistically significant. This pattern highlights the influence of training stage, practical experience, and perceived relevance on learners' engagement with hybrid education. The results provide evidence for the need to design class-level-specific online learning interventions that maintain positive attitudes, enhance motivation, and ensure that all trainees—regardless of level—benefit from the full potential of hybrid maritime education programs. By addressing these differences, maritime institutions can optimize learning experiences, strengthen professional competency development, and better prepare officer trainees for the complex demands of global maritime careers.

6. Interpretation

Taken together, the results of this study reveal a nuanced progression in officer trainees' attitudes toward online learning as they advance through class levels. Across all three cohorts—Class III, Class IV, and Class V—trainees generally reported positive perceptions of hybrid learning, indicating broad acceptance of online platforms as a complementary educational tool in maritime training. This overall positivity reflects the successful integration of digital technologies in the curriculum, enabling trainees to access course materials, participate in virtual discussions, and engage in interactive simulations that reinforce theoretical knowledge and practical competencies essential for their future maritime careers.

The significant difference observed between Class III and Class V trainees suggests that senior trainees may possess greater adaptability and confidence in navigating online and hybrid learning systems. This can be attributed to several interrelated factors, including extended exposure to digital learning environments, accumulated academic experience, and the development of self-regulation and time management skills over the course of their training. Senior trainees' higher comfort level with technology-enhanced learning indicates that repeated engagement with online platforms helps reduce barriers to adoption, increasing their perceived usefulness and fostering a more positive attitude toward these instructional methods.

Interestingly, the absence of significant differences between adjacent class levels (Class III vs IV and Class IV vs V) indicates that changes in attitudes occur incrementally rather than abruptly. This gradual shift may reflect the layered nature of maritime officer training, where each class level introduces new theoretical and practical challenges, allowing trainees to progressively adjust to hybrid learning. Early-stage trainees, particularly in Class V, may still encounter difficulties related to digital literacy, familiarity with learning management systems, or balancing online study with practical training obligations. In contrast, intermediate and senior trainees demonstrate a steady increase in competence and acceptance, suggesting that repeated exposure over time plays a critical role in shaping attitudes.

From a practical perspective, these findings underscore the importance of level-specific instructional strategies in hybrid maritime education. For junior trainees, targeted support such as orientation sessions on online platforms, guided tutorials, and scaffolded assignments can facilitate smoother adaptation. For senior trainees, educators might focus on advanced applications of technology, including simulation-based exercises, virtual collaboration, and scenario-based problem solving that complement real-world onboard experiences. By aligning instructional design with the developmental stage and technological readiness of each cohort, maritime institutions can maximize engagement, sustain positive attitudes, and enhance the effectiveness of hybrid learning for officer trainees across all class levels.

DISCUSSION

The results of this study revealed that officer trainees across class levels demonstrated significantly different attitudes toward online learning in hybrid maritime education. This finding indicates that class level is a crucial factor shaping perceptions of online learning, reflecting differences in experience, maturity, and exposure to digital platforms. It aligns with prior research emphasizing that academic maturity and accumulated learning experiences influence students' digital readiness, motivation, and engagement with online learning environments (Shi & Fan, 2021; Sulistyono et al., 2024). The presence of significant differences across class levels confirms that hybrid learning cannot be applied uniformly; instead, it must be adapted to the specific developmental and professional needs of each cohort.

The lowest-level trainees, classified as Class V, exhibited the least favorable attitudes toward online learning. This group often faces challenges related to limited digital literacy, unfamiliarity with learning management systems, and lower self-regulation. These obstacles hinder their ability to engage effectively with online components of hybrid learning. Similar patterns have been observed in prior studies, where junior cadets struggled with independent online tasks and adapting to technology-enhanced learning environments (Jutaite et al., 2021; Karagul et al., 2021). The weaker readiness of Class V trainees suggests a critical need for institutions to implement supportive measures, such as introductory digital skills workshops, step-by-step guidance, and scaffolded online activities to build confidence and competence gradually.

In contrast, mid-level trainees (Class IV) demonstrated moderately positive attitudes toward online learning. This group occupies a transitional stage where they have accumulated some experience with digital platforms but may still be developing full confidence in their abilities. The moderate attitudes of Class IV trainees reflect growing adaptability and comfort with hybrid learning processes, highlighting the developmental role of repeated exposure. Consistent engagement with online tools fosters digital literacy, self-efficacy, and motivation, enabling trainees to navigate learning platforms with increasing ease (Pratiwi et al., 2023; Shvetsova et al., 2021). For Class IV trainees, instructional strategies should focus on gradually increasing the complexity of online tasks while maintaining guidance and mentorship to support progressive skill development.

At the highest level, Class III trainees displayed the most positive attitudes toward online learning. Their favorable perceptions reflect advanced digital literacy, well-developed time management skills, and a clear understanding of the relevance of online learning to their future maritime careers. Studies have shown that senior cadets who have experienced multiple hybrid learning cycles tend to appreciate the practicality and direct professional applicability of online learning tools (Johansen, 2023; Karahalios, 2025). Class III trainees' readiness indicates they are well-positioned to leverage advanced digital resources, such as simulation-based exercises, virtual reality, and problem-based learning modules, to refine technical and leadership competencies.

The progression observed across class levels underscores that attitudes toward online learning are dynamic rather than static, as officer trainees advance through their academic journey, their confidence, motivation, and ability to self-regulate in online learning environments increase. This developmental trajectory demonstrates how cumulative exposure to digital platforms and structured hybrid instruction contributes to the gradual acquisition of skills necessary for effective engagement and independent learning. Attitudes toward online learning also tend to become more positive over time as trainees gain experience with digital environments, and students often show improved attitudes and sustained intention to continue online learning after completing blended courses, influenced by self-regulation and social interaction (Zhu et al., 2020). The integration of intelligent technologies such as ChatGPT within peer learning has been shown to increase learner satisfaction and engagement (Younis, 2024). Moreover, goal-setting and meta-regulation abilities develop progressively with age and experience in digital learning contexts (Yaban & Gaschler, 2025), while well-designed online platforms can accelerate the development of autonomous learning skills and enhance active engagement (Alshammary & Alhalafawy, 2023).

The results also highlight the importance of designing level-specific learning interventions to optimize hybrid learning outcomes. For lower-level trainees, foundational support is essential, encompassing hands-on orientation with online platforms, explicit assignment instructions, and time management guidance. Such orientation should include familiarization with digital tools and platforms, simulation of online learning experiences, and explanation of necessary skills (Abdous, 2019; Christopoulos et al., 2018; Rotar, 2022). Clear and structured instructions—such as checklists, weekly announcements, and step-by-step guidance—help learners understand expectations and reduce confusion (Christopoulos et al., 2018; Lapitan et al., 2021; Ren et al., 2023). Training and reminders on time management, including progress trackers and task scheduling, have been proven to enhance learners' consistency, autonomy, and academic outcomes (Abdous, 2019; Faza & Lestari, 2025; Lapitan et al., 2021; Reyes-Millán et al., 2023). Digital literacy training is also crucial, as not all learners—even digital natives—possess sufficient technological competence; therefore, such training should be provided regardless of background (Abdous, 2019; Reyes-Millán et al., 2023).

For mid- and higher-level trainees, instructional design should shift toward fostering autonomy, collaboration, and professional readiness through advanced learning strategies. Structured reinforcement with partially self-directed, project-based tasks—such as collaborative writing using wikis or group video projects—enhances learners' independence, communication, and motivation while maintaining teacher facilitation as a source of guidance and support (Huang, 2021; Sadaghıan & Marandı, 2020). Collaborative online activities further promote leadership, time management, and teamwork tolerance (Ateş & Köroğlu, 2024; Olefirenko & Dobrunov, n.d.), while teacher autonomy support strengthens self-efficacy, self-regulation, and engagement (Ito et al., 2024; Miao & Ma, 2023). For higher-level trainees, scenario-based learning (SBL) and immersive simulations such as Maritime Leaders at Sea (ML@S) develop leadership and teamwork skills through realistic maritime challenges (Ala et al., 2024; Gurbuz & Celik, 2024; Kim et al., 2021). Virtual reality (VR) environments further enhance intrinsic motivation, behavioral change, and safe procedural training (Makransky & Klingenberg, 2022; Thach & Van Hung, 2024). These learning scenarios must be designed with clear learning goals, appropriate complexity, and balanced attention to both technical and non-technical skills such as communication, collaboration, and reflection (Harrington, 2024; Harrington et al., 2025). Tailoring instructional design in this manner maximizes the effectiveness of hybrid learning across all cohorts.

Another key implication of these findings relates to digital readiness and motivation. Junior trainees' lower attitudes toward online learning highlight the need for institutions to focus on building core competencies in technology use, self-directed learning, and online communication. Providing scaffolded learning experiences, peer mentoring, and feedback mechanisms can improve engagement and help trainees overcome initial barriers. This approach ensures that all trainees develop the foundational digital skills necessary to benefit from hybrid maritime education fully.

The significant difference between Class III and Class V further underscores the influence of experience and exposure. Senior trainees' higher positivity reflects accumulated familiarity with online platforms and the ability to integrate theoretical knowledge with practical applications. As trainees progress, repeated interaction with hybrid tools enhances their confidence, reduces anxiety associated with technology use, and strengthens perceived relevance. This pattern suggests that integrating online learning gradually and consistently throughout the curriculum is essential for promoting positive attitudes and long-term engagement.

These findings also contribute to the broader discourse on hybrid learning in maritime education, where the balance between online instruction and practical shipboard training is critical. While digital tools offer flexibility, accessibility, and opportunities for independent learning, their perceived effectiveness varies depending on trainees' developmental stage and prior exposure. Institutions should carefully design hybrid programs that complement hands-on training rather than replace it, ensuring that officer trainees at all levels recognize the value of online learning in enhancing professional competence.

Moreover, the study highlights the importance of leadership and professional skills development within hybrid learning. Senior officer trainees' positive attitudes suggest that advanced digital tools can be used to simulate leadership scenarios, emergency decision-making, and team management exercises. These applications not only enhance engagement but also prepare trainees for the complex responsibilities of shipboard operations, bridging the gap between theory and practice.

Taken together, the results emphasize that class-level differentiation is key to maximizing the impact of hybrid maritime education. By acknowledging the developmental and experiential differences among trainees, educators can implement targeted interventions, provide appropriate support, and design challenging learning experiences that align with each cohort's readiness. Such an approach ensures that hybrid learning contributes meaningfully to technical competence, leadership skills, and professional preparedness.

In conclusion, this study confirms that attitudes toward online learning evolve as officer trainees progress through class levels, influenced by digital literacy, exposure, and professional development needs. Tailoring hybrid learning strategies to accommodate these differences can enhance engagement, motivation, and skill acquisition, ultimately supporting the development of competent, confident, and career-ready maritime officers. The findings provide practical guidance for maritime institutions seeking to optimize the design and delivery of hybrid education programs in alignment with international standards and industry expectations.

CONCLUSION

This study concludes that officer trainees' attitudes toward online learning in hybrid maritime education vary significantly across class levels, highlighting the role of educational progression in shaping perceptions of digital learning. Lower-level trainees (Class V) generally encounter challenges such as limited digital literacy, unfamiliarity with online platforms, and weaker self-regulation, which collectively contribute to less favorable attitudes toward hybrid learning. These findings underscore the need for targeted support to help junior trainees build foundational skills and develop confidence in navigating technology-enhanced learning environments.

Mid-level trainees (Class IV) exhibit transitional attitudes, reflecting partial familiarity with online learning systems and increasing adaptability. Their moderate engagement indicates that repeated exposure to hybrid learning gradually fosters digital competence, self-efficacy, and motivation. This transitional stage suggests that structured reinforcement, incremental complexity in online tasks, and continuous mentoring are crucial to facilitate their progression toward greater confidence and readiness. Such interventions can bridge the gap between basic competence and the advanced skills required at higher levels of officer training.

Higher-level trainees (Class III) demonstrate the most positive attitudes, reflecting higher confidence, stronger digital literacy, effective time management, and recognition of the relevance of hybrid learning to professional development. This group is well-positioned to take advantage of advanced digital tools, such as virtual simulations and scenario-based problem-solving exercises, to refine technical and leadership competencies. Their attitudes indicate that cumulative experience with hybrid learning enhances both engagement and perceived usefulness, reinforcing the value of integrating online components throughout the maritime training curriculum.

Overall, the results emphasize the importance of level-specific instructional strategies in hybrid maritime education. Maritime institutions should implement interventions tailored to trainees' developmental stages: strengthening digital foundations and providing scaffolded support for lower-level trainees, offering structured reinforcement and gradual autonomy for mid-level trainees, and integrating advanced tools and challenging tasks for higher-level trainees. By adopting this differentiated approach, institutions can optimize engagement, foster readiness, and ensure the comprehensive development of professional competencies in line with international maritime standards, ultimately preparing officer trainees for the demands of a digitally evolving global shipping industry.

REFERENCES

Abdous, M. (2019). Well Begun is Half Done: Using Online Orientation to Foster Online Students' Academic Self-Efficacy. *Online Learning, 23*(3 SE-Section II). DOI: 10.24059/olj.v23i3.1437

Ala, A., Hamidi, N., Yoniessa, S., Masito, F., & Muis, M. A. (2024). Simulation-Based Learning in Maritime Training: Enhancing Competency and Preparedness. *Meteor STIP Marunda, 17*(1), 95–102. DOI: 10.36101/msm.v17i1.361

Alshammary, F. M., & Alhalafawy, W. S. (2023). Digital Platforms and the Improvement of Learning Outcomes: Evidence Extracted from Meta-Analysis. In *Sustainability* (Vol. 15, Issue 2). DOI: 10.3390/su15021305

Andiansyah, M., Yuliasri, I., & Wahyuni, S. (2025). Blended Task-Based Language Teaching in Maritime English: Voices of Indonesian Seafarer Upgrading Program Students. *Language Teaching Research Quarterly, 49*, 151–169. DOI: 10.32038/ltrq.2025.49.08

Andromeda, V. F., & Fatimah, F. (2025). Attitude Behavior Tendencies and Knowledge Orientation as Antecedents of Maritime English Learning: Practical Implications for the International Maritime Industry. *World Journal of English Language, 15*(2), 309–317. DOI: 10.5430/wjel.v15n2p309

Ateş, H., & Köroğlu, M. (2024). Online collaborative tools for science education: Boosting learning outcomes, motivation, and engagement. *Journal of Computer Assisted Learning, 40*(3), 1052–1067. DOI: 10.1111/jcal.12931

Belev, B., Nikolov, N., Dorigatti, J., & Mrčelić, G. J. (2022). Students' Attitude to Online Emergency Remote Teaching (ERT) at Nikola Vaptsarov Naval Academy and Faculty of Maritime Studies Split during COVID-19 crisis. *Transactions on Maritime Science, 11*(1), 294–306. DOI: 10.7225/toms.v11.n01.024

Boulougouris, E., Mizythras, P., Chrysinas, L., Vavourakis, G., Theotokatos, G., Aymelek, M., & Kurt, I. (2019). Developing multidisciplinary blended learning courses for maritime education with cross-European collaboration. *WMU Journal of Maritime Affairs, 18*(2), 319–340. DOI: 10.1007/s13437-019-00167-x

Christopoulos, A., Conrad, M., & Shukla, M. (2018). Increasing student engagement through virtual interactions: How? *Virtual Reality (Waltham Cross), 22*(4), 353–369. DOI: 10.1007/s10055-017-0330-3

Faza, A., & Lestari, I. A. (2025). Self-Regulated Learning in the Digital Age: A Systematic Review of Strategies, Technologies, Benefits, and Challenges. *The International Review of Research in Open and Distributed Learning, 26*(2 SE-Research Articles), 23–58. DOI: 10.19173/irrodl.v26i2.8119

Fedorova, O., & Bobrysheva, N. (2021). Methodology of blended learning for maritime officers of senior courses with involvement of the latest informational technologies. *Humanities Science Current Issues, 3*(44), 227–234. DOI: 10.24919/2308-4863/44-3-36

Galić, S., Lušić, Z., & Stanivuk, T. (2020). E-learning in maritime affairs. *Journal of Naval Architecture and Marine Engineering, 17*(1), 38–50. DOI: 10.3329/jname.v17i1.42203

Gurbuz, S. C., & Celik, M. (2024). An Experimental Study to Explore the Effectiveness of a 3D Maritime Serious Game Prototype: Maritime Leaders at Sea. *Transactions on Maritime Science, 13*(2). 10.7225/toms.v13.n02.019

Harrington, S. (2024). Enhancing Scenario Design in Maritime Education and Training. *Advances in Human Factors of Transportation, 148*, 740–748. DOI: 10.54941/ahfe1005266

Harrington, S., Sellberg, C., & Lindwall, O. (2025). Crafting congruence: Towards systematic scenario design in maritime simulator training and assessment. *WMU Journal of Maritime Affairs, 24*(2), 157–178. DOI: 10.1007/s13437-024-00356-3

Huang, H.-W. (2021). Effects of smartphone-based collaborative vlog projects on EFL learners' speaking performance and learning engagement. *Australasian Journal of Educational Technology, 37*(6 SE-Articles), 18–40. DOI: 10.14742/ajet.6623

Ito, T., Umemoto, T., & Nakaya, M. (2024). Providing and receiving of autonomy support promotes self-efficacy and value for group activities in university and the workplace. *International Journal of Educational Research Open, 7*, 100339. DOI: 10.1016/j.ijedro.2024.100339

Johansen, K. (2023). Challenges regarding digital distance learning of operationally- oriented professions, due to Covid-19 pandemic. *International Journal of Educational Research Open, 4*(September 2022), 100225. DOI: 10.1016/j.ijedro.2023.100225

Jutaite, R., Janiunaite, B., & Horbacauskiene, J. (2021). The challenging aspects of digital learning objects usage in a primary school during the pandemics. *Journal of Educational and Social Research, 11*(5), 201–215. DOI: 10.36941/jesr-2021-0118

Karagul, B. I., Seker, M., & Aykut, C. (2021). Investigating students' digital literacy levels during online education due to covid-19 pandemic. *Sustainability (Basel), 13*(21), 11878. Advance online publication. DOI: 10.3390/su132111878

Karahalios, H. (2025). Enhancing maritime education for digital sustainability. *International Journal of Innovation Science, 17*(4), 901–913. Advance online publication. DOI: 10.1108/IJIS-06-2024-0156

Kim, T. eun, Sharma, A., Bustgaard, M., Gyldensten, W. C., Nymoen, O. K., Tusher, H. M., & Nazir, S. (2021). The continuum of simulator-based maritime training and education. *WMU Journal of Maritime Affairs, 20*(2), 135–150. DOI: 10.1007/s13437-021-00242-2

Kumar, N., & Rajini, G. (2024). Reimaging maritime education and training using latest technologies. *Salud, Ciencia y Tecnologia - Serie de Conferencias, 3*. DOI: 10.56294/sctconf2024895

Lapitan, L. D. S.Jr, Tiangco, C. E., Sumalinog, D. A. G., Sabarillo, N. S., & Diaz, J. M. (2021). An effective blended online teaching and learning strategy during the COVID-19 pandemic. *Education for Chemical Engineers, 35*, 116–131. DOI: 10.1016/j.ece.2021.01.012

Makransky, G., & Klingenberg, S. (2022). Virtual reality enhances safety training in the maritime industry: An organizational training experiment with a non-WEIRD sample. *Journal of Computer Assisted Learning, 38*(4), 1127–1140. DOI: 10.1111/jcal.12670

Mallam, S. C., Nazir, S., & Renganayagalu, S. K. (2019). Rethinking Maritime Education, Training, and Operations in the Digital Era: Applications for Emerging Immersive Technologies. In *Journal of Marine Science and Engineering* (Vol. 7, Issue 12). DOI: 10.3390/jmse7120428

Mansur, A. A., & Asmawati, D. N. (2021). The Utilization of Zoom, Google Classroom, and Quizizz in Maritime English Learning. *English Review Journal of English Education, 10*(1), 113–120. DOI: 10.25134/erjee.v10i1.5361

Miao, J., & Ma, L. (2023). Teacher Autonomy Support Influence on Online Learning Engagement: The Mediating Roles of Self-Efficacy and Self-Regulated Learning. *SAGE Open, 13*(4), 21582440231217736. DOI: 10.1177/21582440231217737

Olefirenko, N., & Dobrunov, O. (n.d.). DIGITAL PEDAGOGICAL TOOLKIT FOR SUPPORTING COLLABORATIVE STUDENT ACTIVITIES IN COMPUTER SCIENCE EDUCATION. *Information Technologies and Learning Tools, 106*(2 SE-ICT and learning tools in secondary education), 1–14. DOI: 10.33407/itlt.v106i2.5974

Pratiwi, D. I., Prayogo, D., & Runadi, T. (2023). Pursuing Maritime Education in Digital Era: Students' Voices. *Jurnal Pendidikan Progresif, 13*(3), 1174–1189. DOI: 10.23960/jpp.v13.i3.202321

Ren, L., Fu, K., & Cao, R. (2023). Influence of Learning Intervention on Online Learners' Performance. *International Journal of Emerging Technologies in Learning (IJET), 18*(16 SE-Papers), 198–209. DOI: 10.3991/ijet.v18i16.42297

Reyes-Millán, M., Villareal-Rodríguez, M., Murrieta-Flores, M. E., Bedolla-Cornejo, L., Vázquez-Villegas, P., & Membrillo-Hernández, J. (2023). Evaluation of online learning readiness in the new distance learning normality. *Heliyon, 9*(11), e22070. Advance online publication. DOI: 10.1016/j.heliyon.2023.e22070 PMID: 38034679

Rotar, O. (2022). Online student support: A framework for embedding support interventions into the online learning cycle. *Research and Practice in Technology Enhanced Learning, 17*(1), 2. DOI: 10.1186/s41039-021-00178-4

Sadaghıan, S., & Marandı, S. (2020). FOSTERING LANGUAGE LEARNER AUTONOMY THROUGH INTERDEPENDENCE: THE POWER OF WIKIS. *Turkish Online Journal of Distance Education, 22*(1), 194–208. DOI: 10.17718/tojde.849907

Shi, J., & Fan, L. (2021). Investigating Teachers' and Students' Perceptions of Online English Learning in a Maritime Context in China. *SAGE Open, 11*(3), 21582440211040800. DOI: 10.1177/21582440211040800

Shurygin, V., Saenko, N., Zekiy, A. O., Klochko, E., & Kulapov, M. (2021). Learning Management Systems in Academic and Corporate Distance Education. *International Journal of Emerging Technologies in Learning, 16*(11), 121. DOI: 10.3991/ijet.v16i11.20701

Shvetsova, I., Fediaieva, V., & Moroz, O. (2021). Education and professional training: Blended learning in maritime english teaching. *LAPLAGE EM REVISTA, 7*(3D), 175–188. DOI: 10.24115/S2446-6220202173D1705p.175-188

Simanjuntak, M. B. (2024). Navigating the Seas of Knowledge: Cognitive Load Management for Maritime Cadets. *Journal for Maritime Research*, *21*(3), 328–334. https://www.scopus.com/inward/record.uri?eid=2-s2.0-85215105535&partnerID=40&md5=4770a500dbb50e5ea7c87a40f45928c5

Sulistyono, N. J., Suparji, S., Wiyanto, T., Suhartini, R., & Ilham, I. (2024). Understanding Maritime Subjects in Vocational High Schools Through Online Learning. *Jurnal of Pedagogi : Jurnal Pendidikan*, *1*(5), 1–13. DOI: 10.62872/dvfypx37

Tandrayen-Ragoobur, V., Seetanah, B., Fauzel, S., & Teeroovengadum, V. (2023). Digital Learning Response in the Midst of the Covid-19 Pandemic: The Case of Mauritius. *Africa Development. Afrique et Developpement*, *48*(2), 129–158. DOI: 10.57054/ad.v48i2.5083

Thach, N. D., & Van Hung, N. (2024). Research and Design a Lifeboat Virtual Reality Simulation System for Maritime Safety Training in Vietnam. *Journal of Marine Science and Technology (Taiwan)*, *32*(2), 146–156. DOI: 10.51400/2709-6998.2739

Voloshynov, S. A., Popova, H. V., Dyagileva, O. S., Bobrysheva, N. N., & Fedorova, O. V. (2022). Formation of professional competency in life saving appliances operation of future seafarers by means of online and simulation VR technologies. *CEUR Workshop Proceedings*, *3085*, 365–380. DOI: 10.55056/cte.126

Wang, H., Lin, W., & Wang, W. (2023). A Study on the Influence of Hybrid Teaching on Students' Learning Attitude and Learning Confidence. *International Journal of Emerging Technologies in Learning (IJET), 18*(19 SE-Short Papers), 277–285. DOI: 10.3991/ijet.v18i19.43923

Yaban, E. H., & Gaschler, R. (2025). Developmental regulation processes and age-related motivation of distance education students. *Higher Education*, *90*(1), 177–197. DOI: 10.1007/s10734-024-01316-9

Younis, B. K. (2024). Examining Students ' Self -Regulation Skills, Confidence to Learn Online, and Perception of Satisfaction and Usefulness of Online Classes in Three Suggested Online Learning Environments that Integrates ChatGPT. *Online Learning : the Official Journal of the Online Learning Consortium*, *28*(2), 1–23. DOI: 10.24059/olj.v28i2.4397

Zhu, Y., Zhang, J. H., Au, W., & Yates, G. (2020). University students' online learning attitudes and continuous intention to undertake online courses: A self-regulated learning perspective. *Educational Technology Research and Development*, *68*(3), 1485–1519. DOI: 10.1007/s11423-020-09753-w

Chapter 21
Carting Competence:
Redisigning Maritime Education Through Competency-Based Training Frameworks

Tony Santiko
http://orcid.org/0009-0008-9279-8799
Politeknik Ilmu Pelayaran Makassar, Indonesia

Edi Abdurachman
Trisakti University, Indonesia

Novita Widyaningrum
Sea Transportation Department, Trisakti University, Indonesia

ABSTRACT

This chapter examines the imperative shift in maritime education towards competency-based training (CBT) to address the changing industry requirements influenced by automation, sustainability, and global mobility. It analyzes how performance-driven standards, STCW-compliant curriculum, simulation-based education, and micro-credential frameworks might enhance operational preparedness and employability. The study emphasizes essential components such authentic assessment, faculty development, digital learning analytics, and industry-academia relationships that facilitate competence development. It also recognizes institutional challenges—spanning cultural opposition to resource deficiencies—and suggests solutions for cultivating flexible, technology-enhanced learning environments. The article contends that maritime education should adopt innovation, lifelong learning, and robust regulatory alignment to develop resilient, future-ready workers by delineating routes for harmonized global competency frameworks.

INTRODUCTION: THE IMPERATIVE FOR COMPETENCY-BASED REFORM IN MARITIME EDUCATION

1.1 Evolving Demands of the Maritime Industry

The maritime industry is undergoing a transformation marked by an urgent need for educational reform to align with modern competencies. This transition underscores a pivotal shift from task-based

DOI: 10.4018/979-8-3373-6670-8.ch021

to performance-based professional standards. Traditionally, maritime training programs were structured around the completion of predefined tasks. However, as maritime operations evolve, there is a growing recognition that professionals must demonstrate a broader spectrum of competencies that encompass problem-solving, decision-making, and adaptability to varied operational scenarios. This performance-based approach is paramount, as emphasized by Belabyad et al., who identify critical crossover skills like 'Operational Skills' and 'Digital Skills' as essential for navigating the complexities of maritime Autonomous Shipping Systems (MASS) (Belabyad et al., 2025). The shift to competency-based frameworks thus not only bridges the gap between education and industry needs but also enhances the employability of graduates by ensuring that they can perform effectively in real-world scenarios (Riyanto et al., 2025).

Concurrently, technological disruptions are reshaping maritime operations, necessitating the integration of advanced digital tools and autonomous systems into training programs. The emergence of technologies such as artificial intelligence and robotics within maritime contexts demands that maritime education also covers these modern competencies explicitly (Riyanto et al., 2025). This aligns with findings from Riyanto et al., highlighting that marine engineering technicians must be adept in emerging technologies, including AI and robotics, to fulfill the industry's evolving requirements (Riyanto et al., 2025). Moreover, as industries across the globe grapple with rapid transformations, there is an enhanced focus on labor mobility. This global trend has been noted for its influence on educational standards, prompting maritime institutions to adopt international benchmarks (Winarno et al., 2025). Ensuring that education systems are responsive to global demands requires institutions to establish curricula that are not merely reflective of local industry needs but that also provide graduates with a competitive edge internationally (Winarno et al., 2025).

In addition to the technological advancements, the maritime sector is faced with sustainability challenges, further complicating the requirement for reform. Incorporating sustainability practices within the competency framework will ensure that the emergence of green technologies is adequately addressed in maritime training (Winarno et al., 2025). There arises a particular need for graduates who are not only competent in key technological areas but also aware of environmental impacts and capable of implementing sustainable practices. This is especially critical given the maritime industry's significant contribution to global trade and its environmental footprint (Winarno et al., 2025).

1.2 Understanding Competency-Based Training (CBT)

Competency-Based Training (CBT) represents a paradigm shift in educational philosophy, particularly within the maritime industry, where the demand for skilled professionals is constantly evolving. In essence, CBT can be defined as an educational framework that focuses on equipping students with specific competencies necessary for effective performance in their respective fields (Dagore & Singh, 2025). It diverges from traditional education models that emphasize the mere acquisition of knowledge within a set timeframe, instead fostering a learning environment where achievement is measured by the attainment and demonstration of predetermined competencies. The philosophy underpinning CBT centers on learner autonomy and mastery, encouraging students to engage with the material actively and to progress at their own pace.

At its core, CBT is grounded in several pedagogical foundations, notably outcome orientation, mastery learning, and authentic assessment. Outcome orientation is a defining characteristic, where educational objectives are explicitly stated and aligned with real-world requirements (Maulahela et al., 2022). This orientation ensures that the skills imparted during training translate directly into the competencies needed in professional settings. The salient aspect of this approach is its focus on mastery learning; students must achieve sufficient proficiency in one competency before progressing to the next. This sequential approach is particularly effective in vocational training contexts and aligns with simulation-based mastery learning (SBML) methodologies, which have shown considerable success in ensuring that learners achieve consistent levels of knowledge and skill acquisition (Tappan et al., 2024; Jensen et al., 2022).

Mastery learning promotes an educational atmosphere where students are encouraged to engage in repeated practice and receive formative feedback until they reach a defined level of competence. This principle not only supports individual learning styles and paces but also reinforces the importance of thorough understanding and skillfulness in practical applications, which is critical in maritime training where the environment is complex and often unpredictable (Maulahela et al., 2022).

Furthermore, authentic assessment plays a pivotal role in CBT, as it focuses on evaluating students' capabilities through real-world applications rather than standardized tests alone. Authentic assessments allow educators to gauge how well students can transfer their skills and knowledge to practical tasks relevant to industry standards (C, 2025). This aligns with contemporary movements in educational research advocating for performance-based evaluations over traditional assessments, emphasizing critical thinking, collaboration, and problem-solving skills crucial in today's maritime sector (Maulahela et al., 2022).

Ultimately, the integration of CBT in maritime education not only addresses the immediate skills gap observed in industry but also prepares students for lifelong learning and adaptability in the face of continuous technological advancements and shifting labor market demands. By fostering a comprehensive understanding of competencies through a structured framework, maritime institutions can significantly enhance the quality and relevance of their training programs, thus shaping proficient maritime professionals equipped for the challenges ahead.

1.3 Rationale for Competence-Oriented Maritime Education

The need for a competence-oriented maritime education model arises in response to significant gaps and shortcomings observed in conventional maritime training frameworks. Traditional methods have primarily emphasized rote learning and rigid adherence to established curricula, often neglecting the dynamic nature of the maritime industry (Sijabat et al., 2024). Such an approach can lead to inadequately prepared maritime professionals who may struggle with real-world challenges. For instance, conventional maritime training has not sufficiently integrated modern technologies and operational complexities, resulting in graduates lacking the requisite competencies to handle evolving maritime operations, including those associated with environmental sustainability and technological advancements (Çağlayan & Aymelek, 2024). Furthermore, Sijabat et al. highlight that key attributes such as safety awareness and ethical conduct are often under-emphasized in traditional models, which directly contradict vital requirements defined by international maritime standards like the International Convention on Standards of Training, Certification, and Watchkeeping (STCW) (Sijabat et al., 2024). Linking competence with safety, efficiency, and employability is crucial, especially in the context of global ports, a hub for international trade reliant on quality maritime operations. Competence-oriented maritime education systems are tasked with ensuring that graduates possess competencies aligned with safety protocols and operational efficiency (Barus et al., 2024). This is particularly evident in aspects such as navigational safety, where studies indicate that inadequate training and competencies have contributed to maritime accidents (Xue et al., 2024). Ensuring that maritime cadets acquire essential skills is not merely an educational concern but a global imperative, given the potential repercussions on human safety and environmental sustainability. Moreover, a competence-oriented approach emphasizes employability in a highly competitive global job market. As the maritime sector increasingly adopts advanced technologies and operational models, such as the integration of artificial intelligence and automation, the expectations for skilled professionals are evolving (Çağlayan & Aymelek, 2024). Competency-based training allows educational institutions to tailor curricula that meet the distinct needs of the maritime industry, thereby enhancing the employability of graduates in global ports. Research conducted by Vujičić et al. advocates for the assessment of teaching methodologies to ensure a high level of qualifications among instructors, which subsequently translates into the expertise imparted to students (Vujičić et al., 2020). This connection between training quality and industry standards underpins the rationale for competency-oriented maritime education. Furthermore, by equipping maritime professionals with competencies associated with safety and operational effectiveness, the competence-oriented model enhances overall efficiency within port operations. Efficient maritime practices contribute significantly to global trade by reducing delays, thereby increasing productivity and logistics sustainability (Çağlayan & Aymelek, 2024; Bayotas, 2024). This aligns with efforts to implement integrated decision support models in port operations, emphasizing competency in achieving broader organizational goals of reducing environmental impacts while optimizing operational workflows (Çağlayan & Aymelek, 2024). Frameworks and Models of Competency-Based Maritime Education

2.1 International Standards and Policy Frameworks

The field of maritime education is profoundly influenced by international standards, notably those established by the International Maritime Organization (IMO) and the Standards of Training, Certification, and Watchkeeping (STCW). The STCW serves as the cornerstone for competency-based certification in maritime education, setting mandatory minimum requirements for the competencies that seafarers must demonstrate before obtaining certification (Kim et al., 2023; Mudakir et al., 2024). This framework ensures a baseline of safety, efficiency, and professionalism while integrating critical elements of maritime operations encompassing technical knowledge, practical skills, and soft skills necessary for effective performance at sea. As articulated by Kim et al., the philosophy of STCW emphasizes education based on knowledge, understanding, and proficiency (KUPs) to effectively prepare future maritime professionals for the complexities of modern maritime operations (Kim et al., 2023). Moreover, the IMO's guidelines advocate for an adaptive approach to maritime training, where educational programs are regularly updated in light of emerging technologies and operational shifts within the industry. The need for continuous alignment with such standards is underscored by research indicating that cadets and maritime professionals perceive their training programs as integral to their preparedness for real-world challenges (Sihombing et al., 2024; Sijabat et al., 2024). This alignment with international standards helps ensure that graduates are capable of operating in diverse maritime environments and contributing to global maritime safety and efficiency. In examining the regional adoption of these international standards, particularly in contexts such as ASEAN, the European Union, and Anglo-American systems, significant patterns emerge. The ASEAN bloc has made strides in harmonizing its maritime standards to align with STCW, evidenced by various member states striving to improve the quality and consistency of maritime education and training across the region (Barus et al., 2024). This push aligns with broader ASEAN initiatives aimed at fostering educational coherence and improving labor mobility within the regional maritime sector. Conversely, the European Union has taken a more directive approach, mandating compliance with STCW while simultaneously implementing additional regional regulations to address specific local challenges. For example, EU maritime policy emphasizes the integration of sustainability and technological advancements within training frameworks, illustrating a model that not only adapts STCW but enhances it in the context of European maritime priorities (Ala et al., 2024). This proactive stance reflects a commitment to excellence and innovation in maritime education. In contrast, the Anglo-American systems, particularly the United States and the United Kingdom, maintain robust maritime training programs that are largely compliant with STCW yet reflect localized adaptations that address national maritime practices and regulatory environments (Charlo et al., 2023; Mansyur et al., 2021). The emphasis in these countries tends to align with comprehensive assessments of competency that include a broader focus on leadership, decision-making, and crisis management skills essential for navigating the complexities of modern maritime operations.

2.2 Institutional and Curriculum Design Models

The transformation of maritime education necessitates innovative institutional and curriculum design models that embrace competency-based frameworks. A fundamental aspect of this design is the mapping of learning outcomes to operational tasks and performance standards. This alignment enables educational programs to directly reflect the skills and competencies required for effective maritime practice, thereby enhancing the relevance and applicability of training (Peters et al., 2023). The establishment of precise learning outcomes tied to real-world operational tasks ensures that students are not merely absorbing theoretical knowledge but are preparing to enact requisite competencies in their future roles on board ships or in port operations. For instance, competency-based education (CBE) incorporates performance criteria that reflect professional expectations within the maritime industry, facilitating a more meaningful connection between academic learning and industry standards (Siddique et al., 2020). Furthermore, as highlighted by Siddique et al., the alignment process plays a vital role in ensuring that maritime curricula not only meet local requirements but also conform to international guidelines such as those set by the STCW (Desmarchelier & Cary, 2022). When institutions map their curricula to these competencies, they effectively enhance the employability of graduates by providing them with demonstrable skills aligned with industry demands, which is crucial in a highly competitive job market (OECD, 2023).

In addition to mapping learning outcomes, employing modular and micro-credentialed structures presents an innovative approach to curriculum design, facilitating flexible learning pathways. Modular design allows for the segmentation of educational content into smaller, manageable units, or modules, which students can complete independently. This flexibility is particularly beneficial in maritime education, where learners often balance academic pursuits alongside practical training and employment. Micro-credentials amplify this flexibility by providing students with opportunities to earn recognition for specific skills or competencies without committing to a full program (Clausen, 2021). Such a system recognizes the varied and often non-linear educational journeys of maritime professionals, catering to those who seek to enhance their qualifications in specific areas, such as navigation, safety management, or cargo handling.

Micro-credentials also work synergistically with lifelong learning initiatives by allowing learners to continually upskill and reskill throughout their careers. The OECD emphasizes that micro-credentials can contribute significantly to enhancing employability and labor market participation, especially among individuals engaged in maritime professions requiring continuous professional development (OECD, 2023). By providing learners the option to accumulate micro-credentials that are relevant to operational demands, maritime educational institutions can promote a culture of lifelong learning that aligns with contemporary industry practices.

Moreover, design models that incorporate modular and micro-credentialed formats foster collaboration between educational institutions and maritime industries. Such collaborations can result in tailored learning experiences that reflect actual workplace challenges and competencies, thereby enriching the educational outcomes for students and ensuring that the curriculum remains responsive to evolving maritime demands (Brown et al., 2023).

2.3 Assessment and Quality Assurance Mechanisms

In competency-based maritime education, establishing effective assessment and quality assurance mechanisms is crucial to ensure that educational programs meet their intended outcomes. Evidence-based assessment methods, including simulation and portfolio evaluation, play a significant role in validating learner competencies and aligning educational practices with industry requirements. The use of simulation in maritime training allows students to engage in realistic operating scenarios that mirror the complexities of maritime environments. According to Winarno et al., simulation-based assessments have been shown to improve the competency levels of maritime professionals by providing hands-on experiences that traditional assessments cannot replicate Winarno et al. (2025). These simulations help learners develop situational awareness, decision-making skills, and technical proficiency, all of which are integral to successful maritime operations.

Alongside simulation, portfolio evaluation serves as another robust evidence-based assessment method, enabling students to document their learning journey, reflect on their experiences, and showcase their competencies to potential employers. Portfolios can include records of completed projects, feedback from instructors, and evidence of acquired skills. This method not only promotes self-directed learning but also allows educators to gather insights into learner progression and areas needing improvement. Although the specific application of portfolio assessments in maritime education may not be extensively covered in Alshahrani's work, the concept of effective portfolio assessments serving as a tool for continuous quality assurance is widely supported in educational literature (Alshahrani, 2025).

Moreover, benchmarking and continual improvement processes are essential components of quality assurance mechanisms in maritime education. Benchmarking involves comparing educational programs against established standards, other institutions, or industry best practices to identify gaps in performance and areas for enhancement. This approach is vital for maintaining relevance and quality in the rapidly changing maritime educational landscape. Barbour-Tuck et al. utilized benchmarking to examine research competencies within their residency program and successfully identified areas for quality improvement, demonstrating the applicability of benchmarking across various fields, including health and education (Barbour-Tuck et al., 2023).

Continual improvement, which involves systematically reviewing and refining educational practices based on assessment results, is crucial for validating competencies in maritime education. The development of quality assurance frameworks, as proposed by Batt et al., stipulates that ongoing evaluation should be incorporated into the curriculum design process (Batt et al., 2021). This iterative process allows educational institutions to adapt to emerging trends, integrate feedback, and ensure their programs remain aligned with the evolving demands of the maritime sector.

Lastly, the incorporation of stakeholder feedback, including that from industry partners, educators, and students, into the assessment and quality assurance processes enhances the credibility and responsiveness of maritime training programs. Regular engagement with stakeholders ensures that programs not only meet regulatory requirements but also effectively prepare graduates for successful careers in maritime professions (Mills et al., 2020).

REDESIGNING PEDAGOGY FOR COMPETENCE DEVELOPMENT

3.1 Experiential and Simulation-Based Learning Approaches

Experiential and simulation-based learning approaches have taken center stage in maritime education, offering dynamic platforms for cadets to acquire and refine essential skills crucial for navigating complex maritime environments. The integration of advanced technologies, particularly simulation tools, virtual reality (VR), and augmented reality (AR), enhances the learning experience by providing realistic representations of onboard scenarios that cadets may face in their professional careers. Notably, simulation-based learning (SBL) has emerged as a pivotal component of contemporary maritime training, effectively mimicking operational conditions without the inherent risks associated with real-life situations. As highlighted by Ala et al., SBL not only enhances competency development but also fosters preparedness among cadets for the challenges of the maritime industry (Ala et al., 2024).

Simulators allow for the safe practice of various critical skills ranging from navigation to crisis management. For instance, maritime simulators present learners with intricate situations that require rapid decision-making and effective communication, skills essential for maritime professionals (Ala et al., 2024). This training methodology encourages reflective learning, as cadets can analyze their performance and improve on identified weaknesses. The value of this immersive learning experience is further bolstered when coupled with scenario-based training, which emphasizes real-world applications within simulated environments. By engaging in scenario-based activities, cadets can better bridge the gap between theoretical knowledge acquired in the classroom and practical skills needed on board vessels or at ports.

Moreover, the use of VR and AR technologies offers remarkable opportunities for enhancing engagement and interactivity in maritime education. These technologies can immerse students in lifelike simulations that portray a range of maritime operations, including navigation through adverse weather conditions and undertaking safety drills (Reyes, 2025). By utilizing VR and AR, cadets can explore operational environments without physical limitations, thereby broadening their understanding of maritime practices and enhancing their situational awareness before entering the field. This approach aligns well with the trend in maritime education that prioritizes digital transformation and innovative pedagogies.

Bridging classroom theory with on-board and portside practices is another crucial aspect of effective maritime education. This connection is essential to prepare students adequately for their future roles, as the maritime industry demands that professionals understand not only theoretical concepts but also their application in real-world settings. Educational institutions that strategically integrate experiential learning opportunities—such as internships and practical training on vessels—foster a seamless transition from academic rigour to professional practice (Sihombing et al., 2024). The direct involvement of cadets in maritime environments allows for firsthand exposure to industry dynamics, enhancing their competencies and fostering a deeper understanding of operational challenges.

Furthermore, aligning simulation-based and experiential learning with outcome-oriented evaluations ensures that graduates are effectively prepared to meet industry standards. As noted by Sihombing et al., adherence to international standards such as those outlined by the STCW is crucial for ensuring consistency and recognition of qualifications across educational institutions and industry stakeholders (Sihombing et al., 2024). By structuring curriculum design around competencies tied to practical experiences, maritime institutions can optimize graduate readiness and improve overall industry performance.

3.2 Mentoring, Coaching, and Reflective Learning

The implementation of effective mentoring and coaching programs, alongside reflective learning practices, is are vital component in fostering the competence development of maritime cadets. Central to these processes are the feedback loops established through peer interactions and instructor evaluations, which serve to reinforce competencies and promote continuous improvement. Research indicates that structured feedback, particularly when delivered in a timely and constructive manner, enhances learners' self-efficacy and motivation (Cameron et al., 2025). In maritime education, where precision and teamwork are paramount, peer feedback can provide an authentic context for skill reinforcement. Utilizing well-defined criteria and expert oversight for peer reviews can bolster the reliability of feedback, as emphasized by Xie et al., who highlight the importance of structured guidance in promoting effective peer dialogue (Xie et al., 2025).

Moreover, mentorship plays a critical role in helping learners navigate the challenges of both educational and subsequent professional environments. As noted in research by Cameron et al., well-implemented mentor training programs can enhance the effectiveness of mentoring relationships, leading to significant improvements in mentee competencies (Cameron et al., 2025). The relationships built between mentors and cadets provide substantial opportunities for informal learning and the sharing of tacit knowledge, which is invaluable in maritime contexts where hands-on experience is crucial.

Reflective practice, defined as the process of critically examining one's own experiences and learning, is another cornerstone of effective competence development within maritime education. It encourages students to assess their own skills, behaviors, and attitudes in relation to their learning objectives and the real-world application of competencies. Research reveals that reflective practice enhances autonomy and professional growth among learners in various fields, including maritime education (Pace et al., 2025). Through self-assessment, cadets can identify areas for improvement, set personal learning goals, and engage more deeply with their coursework and practical experiences.

The iterative nature of self-reflection aligns seamlessly with competence reinforcement. According to Henriquez et al., fostering a culture of ongoing reflection requires continuous mentorship and practice rather than sporadic training (Henriquez et al., 2025). As students incorporate feedback from their instructors and peers into their reflective practices, they develop a more nuanced understanding of their competencies and how these translate into on-the-job performance.

Furthermore, the incorporation of video-based reflections, as explored by Shaaban, provides another avenue for reflective learning. This approach allows cadets to review recordings of their own performances, analyze their actions, and evaluate their decision-making processes in real-time scenarios, reinforcing their learning through visual feedback (Shaaban, 2022). Such practices are particularly significant in maritime education, where real-time navigation and teamwork skills are critical for success.

3.3 Integration of Technology and Learning Analytics

The integration of advanced technology and learning analytics into maritime education represents a significant evolution in pedagogy, facilitating innovative approaches for tracking student performance and enhancing learning experiences. Digital portfolios, AI-driven performance tracking, and adaptive feedback mechanisms are essential components of this approach. Digital portfolios allow cadets to collect, showcase, and reflect on their achievements over time. As indicated by Ifenthaler and Yau, such portfolios play a critical role in supporting students' learning by providing personalized contexts for understanding individual growth and competency development (Ifenthaler & Yau, 2020). The incorporation of AI technologies further amplifies this effect by enabling real-time performance tracking and personalized feedback tailored to learners' specific needs.

AI-driven performance tracking offers comprehensive insights into students' engagement, progress, and areas needing improvement, allowing educators to intervene proactively. For instance, by utilizing AI algorithms to analyze student interactions with learning materials, institutions can identify patterns potentially indicating challenges in specific competencies. Motz et al. suggest that AI-based tools can significantly enhance performance assessment through automated feedback, which is timely and context-specific, thereby fueling students' learning processes (Motz et al., 2023). This automation in performance tracking not only reduces the burden on instructors but also allows for a personalized learning experience that adapts to the unique pace and needs of each learner.

Furthermore, adaptive feedback mechanisms are integral to the learning process. As learners engage with content, sophisticated learning analytics systems can provide instant feedback based on their inputs and performance metrics, promoting continuous improvement. According to Stoyanov and Kirschner, leveraging adaptive learning analytics facilitates a more customized educational experience by addressing the distinct characteristics and learning styles of each student (Stoyanov & Kirschner, 2023). This ability to offer personalized responses supports engagement and ensures that cadets remain aligned with their learning objectives.

In addition to performance tracking, data-informed instructional decisions are paramount for developing personalized learning progressions. By analyzing data garnered from learning analytics, educators can make informed decisions about curriculum adjustments and instructional methods that align with students' needs. For instance, insights gained from learning analytics can help educators identify effective teaching strategies or misconceptions that need addressing, as discussed by Li and Wong (Li & Wong, 2020). This targeted approach ensures that instruction is not only relevant but also effective in fostering competence among students.

Moreover, the analysis of data can reveal broader trends within cohorts, allowing institutions to refine their curricula strategically. This is particularly crucial in maritime education, where industry requirements continuously evolve. By aligning curriculum adjustments with insights gleaned from student data and learning analytics, educational institutions can remain responsive to changes in the maritime sector while enhancing the preparedness of graduates for the workforce (Motz et al., 2022).

INSTITUTIONAL READINESS AND IMPLEMENTATION CHALLENGES

4.1 Organizational Culture and Change Management

The successful implementation of competency-based maritime education necessitates an organizational culture conducive to change and innovation. Institutional resistance often emerges as a significant barrier to pedagogical innovation within maritime training institutions. This resistance may stem from entrenched traditional practices, concerns about the potential disruption of established curricula, or a lack of understanding of the benefits associated with competency-oriented approaches. To navigate these challenges, educational institutions must cultivate an environment that embraces change and values continuous improvement. Strategies for fostering this environment include promoting open communication among stakeholders, engaging faculty in the decision-making process, and providing professional development opportunities to enhance educators' capabilities in implementing new instructional strategies.

Leadership plays a pivotal role in promoting outcome-based maritime education. Leaders within these institutions must articulate a clear vision for the integration of competency-based frameworks and communicate the rationale behind such shifts. As noted by Mthuli and Singh, effective leadership in maritime governance and education is critical for aligning all stakeholders with the institutional goals and strategies. Leaders must demonstrate commitment to change by actively supporting initiatives that promote competency development, such as incorporating innovative teaching methods and fostering an inclusive culture that values diverse perspectives.

Building an adaptive organizational culture also requires that leaders emphasize collaborative practices that break down silos among departments. This collaboration can aid in creating interdisciplinary programs that address the multifaceted nature of maritime education, integrating technical skills with essential soft skills such as leadership and teamwork. According to Cahyadi et al., embedding sustainability across curricula while providing hands-on learning opportunities can encourage future maritime leaders. Collaborative efforts in curriculum design not only enhance the relevance of education but also foster a sense of collective ownership among educators and administration.

Change management strategies must also consider stakeholders' perceptions and attitudes toward competency-based education. Engaging stakeholders, including faculty, industry representatives, and students, early in the planning and implementation phases can help mitigate resistance by ensuring their voices are heard and their experiences are valued. According to research by Winarno et al., stakeholder involvement leads to the development of educational programs that better meet the evolving demands of the maritime industry, thus improving overall educational quality. Engaging these stakeholders can also facilitate the alignment of training programs with industry expectations, thereby enhancing graduates' workplace readiness.

Furthermore, ongoing support and resources must be made available to assist faculty and staff during the transition to competency-based education. Professional development programs can equip educators with the skills necessary to integrate innovative teaching strategies, utilize technology effectively, and assess student learning in ways that reflect competency outcomes. They can also provide opportunities for faculty to share best practices and learn from one another, fostering a culture of collaboration and continuous learning.

4.2 Faculty Development and Competence Alignment

The successful implementation of competency-based education in maritime training requires a strategic focus on faculty development and alignment with emerging pedagogical methodologies. One key aspect of this focus is the reorientation of instructors toward competence-based methodologies. The transition from traditional teaching methods to competency-oriented approaches mandates that educators are equipped with the knowledge and skills necessary to facilitate this change effectively. A study by Henríquez et al. demonstrated the importance of faculty training programs aimed at enhancing instructors' understanding of competency-based education principles (Belabyad et al., 2025). By engaging in professional development initiatives that focus on effective teaching strategies, assessment methods, and student-centered learning, maritime educators can cultivate an environment that emphasizes the acquisition of competencies essential for students' future careers.

Additionally, the alignment of faculty competencies with the desired outcomes of maritime education is crucial. Educators need to reflect not only on their subject matter expertise but also on their pedagogical practices to ensure that students achieve the intended learning outcomes. Continuous professional certification opportunities serve as a vital mechanism for achieving this alignment, allowing instructors to stay abreast of evolving industry standards and educational practices. As noted by Aboobaker and Zakkariya, fostering a continuous learning culture among educators enhances their capabilities to deliver high-quality education tailored to the needs of students and the maritime industry (Riyanto et al., 2025).

The emphasis on continuous learning extends beyond initial training; it involves an ongoing commitment to professional development. Development programs must resonate with the practical realities of maritime education, incorporating current industry practices, emerging technologies, and pedagogical innovations. For instance, professional development initiatives that focus on digital pedagogy can greatly benefit maritime educators. Schumann et al. suggest that these programs can enhance faculty competence in using technology effectively to create engaging learning experiences for cadets (Winarno et al., 2025).

Moreover, institutions must cultivate an environment that supports faculty development by providing access to resources and learning opportunities. Opportunities for collaboration among faculty can also enhance the collective knowledge pool within institutions. Faculty-led workshops, peer mentoring programs, and collaborative teaching initiatives can significantly contribute to a culture of shared learning and collective growth. This idea aligns with findings from Kaqinari, indicating that fostering a supportive climate where educators share experiences and best practices is crucial for enhancing teaching methods and overall educational quality (Dagore & Singh, 2025).

Finally, aligning evaluation and assessment practices with competency frameworks is essential for ensuring that educators not only deliver content effectively but also facilitate the development of essential skills and competencies within students. This alignment is supported by continuous feedback mechanisms that encourage faculty to engage in reflective practices regarding their teaching methodologies and student outcomes (Maulahela et al., 2022).

4.3 Infrastructure, Resources, and Industry Linkages

The effective transformation of maritime education into a competency-based framework relies heavily on the establishment of robust infrastructure, the effective allocation of resources, and strong industry linkages. One critical aspect of this transformation is the creation of learning laboratories and digital ecosystems that support the practical training and technological advancement required for modern maritime operations. Innovative learning laboratories equipped with advanced simulators create immersive environments where students can acquire hands-on experience in safe yet realistic settings. This experiential learning approach helps bridge theoretical knowledge with practical skills essential in maritime work settings. Cahyadi et al. highlight that integrating technology into educational practices not only enhances cadet preparedness but is also paramount for aligning educational outcomes with industry expectations (Suranta et al., 2025).

In addition to physical laboratories, fostering a digital ecosystem that encompasses digital learning platforms, simulation technologies, and e-learning resources is crucial for modern maritime education. The use of these technologies facilitates access to information, enhances learner engagement, and allows for the personalization of educational experiences. Suparman et al. emphasize the importance of incorporating technological advancements into maritime curricula to meet evolving industry demands and improve human resource development in maritime professions (Suparman et al., 2024). These resources not only better prepare students for real-world challenges but also ensure that curricula remain relevant amidst rapid technological changes.

Another vital component for enhancing the quality of maritime education involves strengthening industry-academia partnerships. Collaborations between educational institutions and maritime industry stakeholders are essential for ensuring that training programs closely align with current industry needs. By collaborating with industry partners, educational institutions can gain insights into labor market trends, technological advancements, and regulatory requirements, ensuring that their curricula are responsive to the latest developments. Winarno et al. highlight how deepening collaborations between educational institutions and industry stakeholders results in curricula that reflect the latest industry practices and technological advancements (Winarno et al., 2025).

Moreover, effective partnerships with the maritime industry facilitate internships, apprenticeships, and real-world project experiences. These experiential learning opportunities allow students to apply their theoretical knowledge in practice, fostering both competence development and readiness for employment. Chauhan's findings indicate that embedding skill-based learning within the curriculum while establishing regional industry links can enhance employability by providing students with the chance to develop the competencies sought by employers (Chauhan, 2025).

In addition to internships, industry linkages can enhance faculty development by providing educators access to professional development opportunities and insights into industry practices. Such collaborations enable educators to understand the competencies valued by employers and to adapt their teaching methodologies accordingly.

FUTURE DIRECTIONS AND GLOBAL IMPLICATIONS

5.1 Toward a Global Competency Framework for Maritime Education

The pursuit of a global competency framework for maritime education is increasingly critical in an era defined by globalization, technological advancements, and evolving industry demands. This framework seeks to harmonize training standards across international institutions, thereby ensuring that graduates possess the skills and knowledge necessary to succeed in diverse maritime environments. The harmonization of standards can mitigate discrepancies in training methodologies and outcomes across different countries, enhancing the global recognition of maritime qualifications. As multiple sources highlight, such alignment fosters a shared understanding of competency expectations, facilitating smoother international careers for maritime professionals.

Achieving harmonization requires concerted efforts among international maritime training institutions, regulatory bodies, and industry stakeholders to promote uniformity in curriculum design, assessment frameworks, and competency benchmarks. The International Maritime Organization (IMO), through the Standards of Training, Certification, and Watchkeeping (STCW) convention, has laid a foundation for these efforts. However, even with established frameworks, institutions often face challenges related to cultural differences, administrative protocols, and varying interpretations of training standards. To navigate these complexities, stakeholders should prioritize collaborative partnerships, share best practices, and invest in capacity-building initiatives aimed at fostering consistency across educational frameworks.

One of the significant steps toward achieving a global competency framework is the cross-recognition of maritime credentials through global collaborations. As educational institutions strive to align with international standards, establishing partnerships with foreign institutions can enhance the transferability of credentials and facilitate academic mobility. Such collaborations can lead to mutual recognition agreements that assure the equivalency of qualifications and competencies, enabling maritime professionals to pursue opportunities internationally without redundant retraining. Recognizing STCW Certificates of Competency (CoCs) as equivalent to academic master's degrees would significantly enhance professional mobility and facilitate shore-based career transitions for mariners.

Additionally, the integration of technology plays a vital role in standardizing and facilitating credential recognition. Digital credentials and blockchain technology can provide secure, verifiable certification that enhances trust in international training programs. The use of digital records enables seamless exchanges of qualifications across borders, ensuring that employers can reliably assess candidates' competencies. This technological integration not only supports the verification of qualifications but also contributes to a more agile response to changing industry requirements by enabling rapid updates to credentialing processes.

5.2 Innovations and Research Opportunities

As the maritime industry undergoes significant transformation due to technological advancements and the complexities of a globalized environment, innovations and research opportunities in competency-based maritime education are becoming increasingly relevant. One critical area of emerging study is competence modeling, which involves defining the knowledge, skills, and behaviors essential for success in maritime professions. Research in this area provides valuable insights into structuring curricula, assessment practices, and instructional strategies that align with industry needs. This enables educators to develop more tailored educational experiences that facilitate better learning outcomes for students.

Cognitive analytics, which combines cognitive science and data analytics, offers another innovative approach to enhance competency-based learning. By analyzing learning behaviors and performance data, educational institutions can gain insights into learners' cognitive processes. This information can help identify areas where students struggle, informing targeted interventions and personalized learning paths. The application of cognitive analytics in maritime education can be instrumental in designing adaptive learning environments that respond to individual student needs, thus improving overall competency development and preparedness for real-world challenges.

In addition to competence modeling and cognitive analytics, there is a pressing need for a well-defined future research agenda that addresses gaps in competency-based maritime learning. Scholars emphasize the necessity of a holistic framework that incorporates various dimensions of maritime education, including pedagogical practices, assessment methodologies, and technological integration. Future research should explore the implementation of innovative pedagogies like simulation-based learning as foundational elements for enhancing competencies among students. This aligns with ongoing studies that indicate that immersive, hands-on experiences effectively enhance students' engagement and skill acquisition, preparing them for practical scenarios in maritime industries.

Moreover, researchers should focus on the role of industry partnerships in shaping maritime education to ensure its relevance and effectiveness. Cross-institutional collaborations that engage industry stakeholders can yield critical insights into the evolving competencies needed in the workforce. The identification of emerging skills and competencies through industry feedback can inform curriculum design, ensuring maritime education aligns with job market demands. For instance, studies propose that recognizing industry qualifications and adjusting curricula accordingly could significantly improve the alignment of educational outcomes with professional expectations.

5.3 Conclusion: Navigating the Path to Professional Excellence

In the pursuit of professional excellence within maritime education, a synthesis of strategies, outcomes, and a transformative vision is paramount. As the maritime industry continues to evolve amid technological advancements and increasing global competition, educational institutions must embrace innovative approaches to cultivate competent and adaptable professionals. A focus on competency-based education is central to this transformation, as it aligns learning outcomes with industry needs, ensuring that graduates are equipped with the requisite skills and knowledge to navigate the complexities of maritime operations.

The integration of immersive learning experiences, such as simulation-based training, reflects a commitment to innovative pedagogical practices that enhance students' preparedness for real-world challenges. Moreover, embracing cognitive analytics enables educators to tailor learning pathways for individual students, fostering engagement and mastery of critical competencies (Ala et al., 2024). Institutions that prioritize such advancements not only empower their graduates to excel but also contribute significantly to strengthening the maritime workforce.

Equally crucial is the commitment to lifelong learning and sustainable workforce development. As articulated by Dacosta et al., the necessity of continuous professional development is underscored in the context of a rapidly changing maritime landscape (Dacosta et al., 2022). Emphasizing the importance of ongoing upskilling in technology and sustainable practices fosters a culture of continuous improvement that benefits both individuals and the maritime sector as a whole.

Moving forward, fostering institutional readiness through strong leadership and a culture that embraces change will play an essential role in implementing competency-based education. Educators must possess the skills necessary to rethink traditional teaching methodologies and adapt to innovative practices that resonate with the needs of today's maritime economy (Purba & Simanjuntak, 2024). By establishing strong partnerships with industry stakeholders, educational institutions can further enhance the relevance of their curricula, creating pathways for meaningful industry engagement and facilitating the recognition of maritime credentials across borders.

Ultimately, navigating the path to professional excellence in maritime education requires a multifaceted approach that intertwines innovative teaching, sustainable practices, and robust industry linkages. By fostering a commitment to lifelong learning and integrating competencies that reflect both technical skills and environmental awareness, maritime institutions can produce professionals who not only succeed in their careers but also contribute positively to the global maritime community at large. The journey toward excellence is ongoing, and the opportunities for research and innovation in this field are vast and promising (Sihombing et al., 2024; Xue et al., 2024).

CONCLUSION

As maritime education continues to evolve in response to technological advancements and industry demands, the alignment of curricula with competency-based education is essential for developing proficient professionals. The synthesis of innovative strategies, such as simulation-based learning and cognitive analytics, presents a viable pathway toward achieving educational outcomes that resonate with real-world applications (Perales & Ruíz, 2020). By fostering a commitment to lifelong learning and nurturing industry relationships, maritime institutions can ensure their graduates are not only technically skilled but also adaptable in a rapidly changing global environment (Öztürk et al., 2022).

Furthermore, the promotion of professional development among educators remains a cornerstone of this transformation, enabling them to embrace new teaching methodologies and engage effectively with students. Empowering faculty through continuous training is crucial in disseminating the significance of technological integration within educational practices.

Additionally, establishing a global competency framework for maritime education is vital for promoting standardized training and cross-recognition of certifications. This approach can enhance the mobility of maritime professionals and address the skills gap evidenced in various studies (Lechner, 2023). With strong industry linkages, educational programs can remain relevant, thereby producing graduates poised to meet the challenges of the maritime sector.

In conclusion, navigating the future of maritime education necessitates a proactive stance toward integrating innovative practices, a commitment to lifelong learning, and the establishment of strong industry partnerships. By focusing on these key areas, maritime institutions can prepare competent professionals who excel in their careers and contribute significantly to sustaining workforce development globally (Lee & Witchel, 2022). Through such dedicated efforts, the maritime sector can thrive, fostering an ecosystem of continuous improvement, skill enhancement, and enhanced professional excellence.

REFERENCES

Ala, A., Hamidi, N., Yoniessa, S., Masito, F., & Muis, M. (2024). Simulation-based learning in maritime training: Enhancing competency and preparedness. *Meteor Stip Marunda, 17*(1), 95–102. DOI: 10.36101/msm.v17i1.361

Alshahrani, S. (2025). Ahp-moora framework for longitudinal evaluation of pharm.d program learning outcomes: A tool for saudi pharmacy programs accreditation and curriculum enhancement. *Frontiers in Medicine, 12*, 1628510. Advance online publication. DOI: 10.3389/fmed.2025.1628510 PMID: 40842539

Barbour-Tuck, E., Mutter, T., O'Brien, J., Girling, L., Choo, E., & Gamble, J. (2023). Benchmarking a canadian anesthesiology resident research program against national norms using a logic model framework: A quality improvement study. *Canadian Medical Education Journal*. Advance online publication. DOI: 10.36834/cmej.75306 PMID: 36998486

Barus, I., Simanjuntak, R., Siahaan, R., Toko, G., & Resmayasari, I. (2024). Cultural and linguistic challenges in global maritime education (navigating english usage). *Meteor Stip Marunda, 17*(1), 121–130. DOI: 10.36101/msm.v17i1.358

Barus, I., Simanjuntak, R., Siahaan, R., Toko, G., & Resmayasari, I. (2024). Cultural and linguistic challenges in global maritime education (navigating english usage). *Meteor Stip Marunda, 17*(1), 121–130. DOI: 10.36101/msm.v17i1.358

Batt, A., Williams, B., Rich, J., & Tavares, W. (2021). A six-step model for developing competency frameworks in the healthcare professions. *Frontiers in Medicine, 8*, 789828. Advance online publication. DOI: 10.3389/fmed.2021.789828 PMID: 34970566

Bayotas, M. (2024). Shifting from global maritime professional to global maritime citizen.. https://doi.org/DOI: 10.5821/mt.13183

Belabyad, M., Kontovas, C., Pyne, R., Shi, W., Li, N., Szwed, P., & Chang, C. (2025). *The human element in autonomous shipping: a study on skills and competency requirements*. Wmu Journal of Maritime Affairs., DOI: 10.1007/s13437-025-00366-9

Brown, M., McGreal, R., & Peters, M. (2023). A strategic institutional response to micro-credentials: key questions for educational leaders. Journal of Interactive Media in Education, 2023(1). https://doi.org/DOI: 10.5334/jime.801

C, M. (2025). Reimagining assessment: alternatives to standardized testing that better measure 21st-century competencies. IJTERS, 56-61. https://doi.org/DOI: 10.63090/IJTERS/3049.1614.0015

Çağlayan, Ö., & Aymelek, M. (2024). An integrated multi-criteria decision support model for sustainable ship queuing policy application via vessel traffic service (vts). *Sustainability (Basel), 16*(11), 4615. DOI: 10.3390/su16114615

Cahyadi, T., Winarno, W., & Malau, A. (2025). Leadership and management training for future-ready engineers: Transforming maritime education. *Research and Development in Education (Raden), 5*(1), 111–120. DOI: 10.22219/raden.v5i1.39398

Cameron, K., Carnethon, M., Barrowman, M., & Welty, L. (2025). Development and assessment of a mentor training workshop series and certificate program. *Journal of Clinical and Translational Science, 9*(1), e98. Advance online publication. DOI: 10.1017/cts.2025.71 PMID: 40395397

Charlo, R., Ancela, J., & Corbacho, F. (2023). Analyzing port state control data to explore future improvements to gmdss training. *Journal of Marine Science and Engineering, 11*(12), 2379. DOI: 10.3390/jmse11122379

Chauhan, P. (2025). A study of skill development challenges and opportunities in higher education in uttarakhand. *International Journal for Multidisciplinary Research, 7*(5), 56798. Advance online publication. DOI: 10.36948/ijfmr.2025.v07i05.56798

Clausen, J. (2021). Learning to fly: Development and design of a micro-credentialing system for an educator preparation program in the absence of a required educational technology course. *TechTrends, 66*(2), 276–286. DOI: 10.1007/s11528-021-00673-x PMID: 34664042

Dacosta, E., Jin, Z., Bowers, J., & Abdul-Salam, R. (2022). Green maritime practices in an emerging economy towards the achievement of sustainable development: A ghanaian context. *Benchmarking, 30*(9), 3637–3673. DOI: 10.1108/BIJ-10-2021-0629

Dagore, A., & Singh, N. (2025). Effectiveness of competency-based education on student academic performance. *International Journal for Multidisciplinary Research, 7*(3), 45151. Advance online publication. DOI: 10.36948/ijfmr.2025.v07i03.45151

Desmarchelier, R., & Cary, L. (2022). Toward just and equitable micro-credentials: An australian perspective. *International Journal of Educational Technology in Higher Education, 19*(1), 25. Advance online publication. DOI: 10.1186/s41239-022-00332-y PMID: 35669714

Henriquez, G., Ulloa, J., Carranza, F., Castro, G., Guillen, M., Ramos, G., & Solano, J. (2025). Faculty training to enhance medical education: Evaluating laboratory instructors at the national autonomous university of honduras (unah). *Cureus*. Advance online publication. DOI: 10.7759/cureus.82535 PMID: 40385923

Ifenthaler, D., & Yau, J. (2020). Utilising learning analytics to support study success in higher education: A systematic review. *Educational Technology Research and Development, 68*(4), 1961–1990. DOI: 10.1007/s11423-020-09788-z

Jensen, G., Jette, D., Timmerberg, J., Chesbro, S., Dole, R., Kapasi, Z., & Lotshaw, A. (2022). Competency-based education in physical therapy: Developing a framework for education research. *Journal, Physical Therapy Education, 36*(4), 334–340. DOI: 10.1097/JTE.0000000000000254

Kim, J., Lee, C., Jeong, M., Cho, E., & Lee, Y. (2023). Identifying optimal approaches for sustainable maritime education and training: Addressing technological, environmental, and epidemiological challenges. *Sustainability (Basel), 15*(10), 8092. DOI: 10.3390/su15108092

Lechner, C. (2023). Patterns and predictors of literacy and numeracy development during adulthood: insights from two longitudinal assessment surveys., 87-112. https://doi.org/DOI: 10.1007/978-3-031-27007-9_4

Lee, M., & Witchel, H. (2022). Intentional innovation in educational technology and media to promote students' holistic development. *The FASEB Journal*, *36*(S1), fasebj.2022.36.S1.0R800. Advance online publication. DOI: 10.1096/fasebj.2022.36.S1.0R800

Li, K., & Wong, B. (2020). Trends of learning analytics in ste(a)m education: A review of case studies. *Interactive Technology and Smart Education*, *17*(3), 323–335. DOI: 10.1108/ITSE-11-2019-0073

Mansyur, M., Sagitasari, R., Wangge, G., Sulistomo, A., & Kekalih, A. (2021). Long working hours, poor sleep quality, and work-family conflict: Determinant factors of fatigue among indonesian tugboat crewmembers. *BMC Public Health*, *21*(1), 1832. Advance online publication. DOI: 10.1186/s12889-021-11883-6 PMID: 34627227

Maulahela, H., Annisa, N., Konstantin, T., Syam, A., & Soetikno, R. (2022). Simulation-based mastery learning in gastrointestinal endoscopy training. *World Journal of Gastrointestinal Endoscopy*, *14*(9), 512–523. DOI: 10.4253/wjge.v14.i9.512 PMID: 36186944

Mills, J., Middleton, J., Schafer, A., Fitzpatrick, S., Short, S., & Cieza, A. (2020). Proposing a re-conceptualisation of competency framework terminology for health: A scoping review. *Human Resources for Health*, *18*(1), 15. Advance online publication. DOI: 10.1186/s12960-019-0443-8 PMID: 32085739

Motz, B., Bergner, Y., Brooks, C., Gladden, A., Gray, G., Lang, C., Li, W., Marmolejo-Ramos, F., & Quick, J. (2023). Lak of direction. *Journal of Learning Analytics*, •••, 1–13. DOI: 10.18608/jla.2023.7913

Motz, B., Quick, J., Brooks, C., Bergner, Y., Gray, G., Lang, C., & Marmolejo-Ramos, F. (2022). A lak of direction: misalignment between the goals of learning analytics and its research scholarship. https://doi.org/DOI: 10.35542/osf.io/bzahw

Mudakir, M., Jogo, B., Krismawati, I., Pambudiyatno, N., & Santoso, A. (2024). Pedagogical approaches in maritime cadet teaching: Enhancing learning outcomes. *Meteor Stip Marunda*, *17*(1), 25–33. DOI: 10.36101/msm.v17i1.360

Остенда, A. and Nestorenko, O. (2025). Education, economy, and ai: multidisciplinary perspectives for a digital future.. https://doi.org/DOI: 10.54264/M051

Öztürk, B., Akarsu, R., Kayıhan, H., Çelik, Y., & Kayhan, S. E. (2022). Investigation of the factors affecting the e-learning process in occupational therapy education during the pandemic with principal component analysis. *British Journal of Occupational Therapy*, *85*(9), 694–703. DOI: 10.1177/03080226211070472 PMID: 38603093

Pace, J., Bartlett, A., Iu, T., La, J., & Penm, J. (2025). Exploring pharmacy students' perceptions of feedback and self-reflection in patient counselling simulations: Implications for professional development. *Pharmacy (Basel, Switzerland)*, *13*(3), 74. DOI: 10.3390/pharmacy13030074 PMID: 40560019

Perales, R., & Ruíz, A. (2020). Education in programming and mathematical learning: Functionality of a programming language in educational processes. *Sustainability (Basel)*, *12*(23), 10129. DOI: 10.3390/su122310129

Peters, M., Aubert, C., Rochet, F., Pagés, C., & Bullini, F. (2023). *Skills alignment for lifelong learners in higher education: smart catalogues for reskilling and upskilling pathways.* Ubiquity Proceedings., DOI: 10.5334/uproc.71

Purba, D., & Simanjuntak, M. (2024). Sustainable maritime education: Integrating environmental science for global competence. [Jurnal Pendidikan Biologi Indonesia]. *Jpbi, 10*(1), 310–319. DOI: 10.22219/jpbi.v10i1.32588

Reyes, S. (2025). Status, applications, and prospects of ai in maritime education: basis for curriculum planning. https://doi.org/DOI: 10.21203/rs.3.rs-7827795/v1

Riyanto, R., Tampubolon, B., & Herawati, S. (2025). Transforming maritime education through a competency-based framework for marine engineering technicians. *Research and Development in Education (Raden), 5*(1), 593–604. DOI: 10.22219/raden.v5i1.39399

Shaaban, S. (2022). Video-based reflection and peer coaching in enhancing tefl student-teachers' teaching practices of receptive skills. *Journal of Education and e-learning Research, 9*(2), 103–109. DOI: 10.20448/jeelr.v9i2.3991

Siddique, G., Lodhi, H., Anwer, M., & Zubair, M. (2020). Effectiveness of traditional and competency based curricula: Perspective of graduates, trainers and employers. *Review of Education Administration and Law, 3*(2), 307–314. DOI: 10.47067/real.v3i2.68

Sihombing, D., Dwiyani, N., Martha, Y., Hutabarat, C., & Sutrisno, S. (2024). Impact of international standards on maritime education: Perspectives of junior cadets. *Meteor Stip Marunda, 17*(1), 7–15. DOI: 10.36101/msm.v17i1.357

Sijabat, P., Simanjuntak, M., Mudakir, M., Putrawan, B., & Lumingkewas, M. (2024). Empowering literacy in maritime education: Strategies and professionalism alignment. *Meteor Stip Marunda, 17*(1), 42–50. DOI: 10.36101/msm.v17i1.359

Stoyanov, S., & Kirschner, P. (2023). Text analytics for uncovering untapped ideas at the intersection of learning design and learning analytics: Critical interpretative synthesis. *Journal of Computer Assisted Learning, 39*(3), 899–920. DOI: 10.1111/jcal.12775

Suparman, J., Fahcruddin, I., Malau, A., Kurniawan, W., Sayakfika, M., & Geboy, G. (2024). Bridging the gap between maritime education and industry needs: enhancing human resource development. ePaper Bisnis, 1(4), 33-49. https://doi.org/DOI: 10.61132/epaperbisnis.v1i4.113

Suranta, N., Simanjuntak, M., & Sijabat, P. (2025). Transforming marine engineering education through industry 4.0 integration and sustainability-driven curriculum design. *Research and Development in Education (Raden), 5*(1), 519–527. DOI: 10.22219/raden.v5i1.39402

Tappan, R., Roth, H., & McGaghie, W. (2024). Using simulation-based mastery learning to achieve excellent learning outcomes in physical therapist education. *Journal, Physical Therapy Education, 39*(1), 40–48. DOI: 10.1097/JTE.0000000000000358 PMID: 38954765

Vujičić, S., Hasanspahić, N., Gundić, A., & Hrdalo, N. (2020). Assessment for ensuring adequately qualified instructors in maritime education and training institutions. *Athens Journal of Sciences*, *7*(2), 115–126. DOI: 10.30958/ajs.7-2-4

Winarno, W., Cahyadi, T., Barasa, L., Permana, A., Kuntadi, C., Martha, Y., & Simanjuntak, M. (2025). Competency development, sustainability practices, and industry preparedness in maritime vocational education. *Digital Innovation*, *2*(1), 130–142. DOI: 10.61132/digitalinnovation.v2i1.180

Winarno, W., Riyanto, R., Kuntadi, C., Malau, A., Herawati, S., Wibowo, T., & Simanjuntak, M. (2025). A qualitative analysis and systematic literature review on enhancing maritime vocational education. *ARJ*, *2*(1), 12–28. DOI: 10.63987/arj.v2i1.170

Xie, X., Zhang, L., & Wilson, A. (2025). Comparing chatgpt feedback and peer feedback in shaping students' evaluative judgement of statistical analysis: A case study. *Behavioral Sciences (Basel, Switzerland)*, *15*(7), 884. DOI: 10.3390/bs15070884 PMID: 40723668

Xue, H., Røds, J., Haugseggen, Ø., Christensen, A., Batalden, B., & Gudmestad, O. (2024). A study on the effects of rapid training method related to ship handling in decision-making skills under stressful situations. *Journal of Navigation*, *77*(3), 395–414. DOI: 10.1017/S0373463324000213

Chapter 22
Educational Innovations in Maritime Architecture:
Digital Transformation and E-Learning Approaches

Juvrianto Chrissunday Jakob
http://orcid.org/0000-0002-5267-3448
Politeknik Negeri Ambon, Indonesia

Rudi Serang
http://orcid.org/0009-0007-9321-2019
Politeknik Negeri Ambon, Indonesia

Isak Lilipory
http://orcid.org/0009-0009-2531-9724
Politeknik Negeri Ambon, Indonesia

Margie Civitaria Siahay
http://orcid.org/0009-0002-8575-1171
Politeknik Negeri Ambon, Indonesia

Henriette Dorothy Titaley
http://orcid.org/0009-0003-1610-6889
Politeknik Negeri Ambon, Indonesia

Maslan Abdin
http://orcid.org/0009-0006-9670-437X
Politeknik Negeri Ambon, Indonesia

ABSTRACT

Digital transformation is reshaping educational paradigms, including maritime architecture education, which covers the design of ships, ports, and coastal structures. E-learning models, synchronous, asynchronous, and blended-support the integration of maritime design software, hydrodynamic simulations, and structural analysis into curriculum. Effective strategies involve technology-based curriculum design, project-based learning, online collaboration, digital competence development, and adaptive assessment. Yet, challenges persist, such as infrastructure gaps, limited digital literacy, resistance to change, data security issues, and the technical complexity of simulations. Opportunities include flexible learning, international collaboration, cost efficiency, and innovation through field data and digital models. Future trends, including AI, digital twins, metaverse applications, and big data, offer transformative potential. This chapter provides analysis and recommendations to optimize digital transformation while preparing adaptive maritime graduates.

DOI: 10.4018/979-8-3373-6670-8.ch022

INTRODUCTION

Technological integration is reshaping global higher education, transcending mere classroom gadgets to redefine learning methods, student-teacher interactions, and delivery models. Within maritime architecture, this shift offers distinct advantages and hurdles. The discipline demands a rigorous blend of technical proficiency, design theory, and intricate practical application. Consequently, integrating digital tools requires a nuanced approach to maintain the field's complex standards. Navigating this evolution ensures that future architects are equipped with both traditional expertise and modern technological fluency to excel in a digitizing industry (Karahalios, 2025).

According to Alop (2019), marine engineering education encompasses diverse disciplines, including ship design, port planning, and coastal engineering for structures like piers and breakwaters. Effective learning in this field necessitates a rigorous blend of theoretical knowledge, computer-aided simulations, and hands-on field practice. Consequently, digital integration must transcend simple online lectures. To be truly effective, technology must facilitate advanced visualization, precise technical simulations, and project-based evaluations that mirror real-world maritime environments. This holistic digital approach ensures students master the complex practical skills required to design and construct resilient infrastructure in challenging coastal and oceanic conditions.

The development of technologies such as the Internet of Things (IoT), artificial intelligence (AI), virtual reality (VR), augmented reality (AR), and cloud computing has provided a new dimension in the teaching and learning process (Mallam et al., 2019). IoT allows for the real-time collection of data from sensors placed in maritime facilities or laboratory models, AI can assist in optimizing design and structural analysis, while VR and AR provide immersive learning experiences that were previously only possible in the field. The integration of these technologies forms an important foundation for efforts to renew learning methods in maritime architecture education.

E-learning represents a tangible outcome of digital transformation by enabling learners to access educational resources at any time and from any location. This approach supports synchronous learning, where teachers and students engage in live, real-time interaction, as well as asynchronous learning, which gives students the freedom to explore materials independently according to their own schedules. Furthermore, blended learning integrates traditional face-to-face instruction with online components, creating a balanced model that maintains meaningful personal interaction while also offering the convenience and adaptability of digital learning environments for diverse educational needs and preferences (Muthmainnah et al., 2023).

In the context of maritime architecture, e-learning can leverage various platforms such as Moodle, Canvas, Microsoft Teams, and Google Classroom for online class management. However, more importantly, is the integration of specialized software such as AutoCAD, Rhino, ShipConstructor, and Maritime Building Information Modeling (BIM) into the learning process. This software can be used to teach ship design, port planning, and coastal building analysis in detail with the aid of hydrodynamic simulations (Koh et al., 2023; Bolbot et al., 2022).

Coastal structures have become one of the topics that require special attention in maritime architecture education. The design of docks, breakwaters, jetties, or coastal protection structures requires a deep understanding of environmental conditions, waves, tides, and material strengths. Through e-learning, students can utilize data-driven simulations to model the interactions between coastal structures and sea conditions. This not only facilitates the learning process but also allows for the exploration of various scenarios without risks and high costs.

Voloshynov et al. (2021) state that to implement e-learning effectively, the curriculum design must adapt to technological developments. Courses must be designed to maximize the potential of digital technology, whether in the form of 3D simulations, parametric modeling, or the use of digital twins to monitor design performance. Additionally, project-based learning that requires students to work collaboratively in online teams can foster communication skills, project management, and problem-solving.

Strengthening digital skills among lecturers and students is essential for successful transformation. If educators and learners lack sufficient ability to operate software and navigate online platforms effectively, the benefits of digital innovation in education cannot be fully realized. For this reason, ongoing training initiatives and continuous capacity-building programs are necessary to ensure sustainable improvement. In addition, evaluation methods should evolve to align with digital learning environments, such as implementing electronic portfolios, project-oriented assessments, and automated evaluation systems supported by artificial intelligence to enhance accuracy, efficiency, and meaningful feedback in the learning process (Ducruet, 2015).

Despite the great opportunity, the implementation of e-learning and digital transformation in maritime architecture education is not without challenges. Limited infrastructure, especially high-speed internet access and adequate hardware, remains an obstacle in many areas. Additionally, the digital literacy gap among students and lecturers can hinder the adaptation process (Pruyn, 2024).

Resistance to change often arises, especially among educators who are accustomed to conventional methods. There are also concerns about data security, particularly related to technical design and sensitive project information. A more specific challenge for coastal building learning is the need for high-spec software and hardware to run complex simulations, which is not always available in all institutions (Yu et al., 2025).

However, behind these challenges, there are great opportunities that can be leveraged. The flexibility of time and location in learning allows students from various regions to access quality education. International collaboration through online projects can broaden perspectives and expand students' professional networks. The use of field data combined with digital models can also enrich the learning process and encourage design innovation.

Long-term cost savings are also an important benefit, as e-learning can reduce the need for travel, accommodation, and practical logistics (Kolarevic, 2003; Jamil & Bhuiyan, 2021). Additionally, students can conduct design experiments and simulations without having to build expensive physical models. For coastal building education, this is very beneficial as it allows for the rapid and efficient testing of various design alternatives.

Looking ahead, technological trends such as AI, machine learning, digital twin, and metaverse will increasingly influence maritime architecture education. AI can be used to assist in optimizing ship designs and coastal structures, while digital twin allows for real-time monitoring of the condition and performance of structures. The metaverse even has the potential to create virtual classrooms where students can interact and conduct simulations together as if they were at the project site.

Based on the research conducted by Miyusov et al. (2022), the integration of big data also presents an important opportunity, especially in port planning and coastal management. Wave data, ocean currents, tides, and weather conditions can be processed to support design and operational decision-making. With the support of this technology, maritime architecture education can produce graduates who not only master theory but are also able to apply knowledge in real contexts with the support of cutting-edge technology.

The success of digital transformation in maritime architecture education will heavily depend on the synergy between the curriculum, technology, human resources, and institutional policies. Strategic recommendations include enhancing digital infrastructure, developing technological competencies for lecturers and students, as well as integrating project-based learning that is relevant to the needs of the maritime industry. Thus, digital transformation is not just a fleeting trend, but a foundation for shaping an adaptive, innovative, and globally-ready generation of maritime professionals.

CONTEXT OF MARITIME ARCHITECTURE EDUCATION

Definition and scope of maritime architecture

Maritime architecture education is a field that combines engineering, design art, and a deep understanding of the marine environment and its supporting infrastructure. Its scope includes the design of ships with various types and functions, port planning as a maritime logistics hub, the development of supporting facilities such as docks, shipyards, and the construction of shoreline buildings that include piers, breakwaters, and coastal protection structures. Each subfield has unique technical challenges, ranging from hydrodynamic aspects, material strength, to integration with navigation and safety technologies (Mallam et al., 2019). This diversity in scope makes maritime architecture a complex discipline, requiring a multidisciplinary approach, and involving cross-disciplinary collaboration, such as civil engineering, marine engineering, architecture, and environmental science.

The characteristics of learning in this field are very distinctive because it requires a combination of conceptual theory, technical skills, and hands-on experience in the field. Ducruet (2015) stated that theory provides the foundational knowledge of design principles, fluid mechanics, structures, and safety regulations. Meanwhile, technical skills are trained through the use of design software, 3D modeling, hydrodynamic simulations, and structural analysis. Field practice becomes an important element because students must understand real conditions in ports, shipyards, and coastal areas. This blend of theory, practice, and technology shapes the competency excellence of graduates, ensuring they are capable of designing and implementing functional, efficient, and safety-compliant projects.

With the development of technology, learning in the field of maritime architecture increasingly relies on the integration of digital devices to accelerate the design process, validate concepts, and test the performance of structures before the construction phase. Computer-based simulations allow students to test various design scenarios of ships or coastal buildings without having to build expensive physical models (Theunissen et al., 2024). Furthermore, virtual reality (VR) and augmented reality (AR) technologies can create immersive learning experiences that demonstrate the impact of waves, currents, or extreme weather on the designed structures. This transformation not only accelerates the learning process, but also enhances accuracy, efficiency, and creativity in designing solutions.

The competency needs in the 21st century require maritime architecture graduates to possess more than just technical skills. They must have critical thinking abilities to analyze complex problems, collaborative skills to work in multidisciplinary teams, and digital literacy to leverage cutting-edge technological tools. Visual communication and presentation skills are also crucial, as the design outcomes must be understood by various parties, including clients, engineers, and regulatory authorities. Furthermore, awareness of sustainability issues and environmental impact becomes an important aspect, especially in coastal building design that must consider coastal ecosystems and disaster mitigation.

Characteristics of learning in maritime architecture

Maritime architecture education, according to Papanikolaou (2014), is a learning process that integrates engineering design knowledge with maritime studies, aiming to produce graduates capable of designing and constructing safe, efficient, and sustainable marine transportation systems as well as supporting infrastructure. This field encompasses not only ship design but also port planning, offshore structures, and maritime logistics facilities integrated within global trade networks.

Bertram (2012) emphasizes that education in maritime architecture carries a high degree of complexity, as it requires the integration of physics, fluid mechanics, materials engineering, and hydrodynamic analysis with creative design skills. Consequently, maritime education demands an approach that combines theoretical lectures, computer-based simulations, project-based learning, and hands-on practice in shipyards or port facilities.

Carlton (2019) highlights the importance of mastering cutting-edge technologies in maritime architecture education, including Computer-Aided Design (CAD), Computational Fluid Dynamics (CFD), and maritime-specific Building Information Modeling (BIM). He argues that these competencies have become critical in the digital era, as maritime design and construction increasingly rely on high-precision simulations to optimize vessel performance and safety (Benavides et al., 2020).

From an industry management perspective, Stopford (2020) observes that maritime architecture education must also equip students with knowledge of maritime economics, international regulations, and environmental sustainability issues. Thus, graduates are expected not only to serve as technical designers but also as decision-makers who incorporate economic, social, and ecological considerations into their designs.

Wright & Crosbie (2021) add that twenty-first century maritime architecture education requires the integration of technological innovation and environmental awareness. Students should be encouraged to develop ship and maritime facility designs that are low in carbon emissions, energy-efficient, and adaptive to climate change. This aligns with global trends toward green shipping and the development of smart ports.

Thus, the context of maritime architecture education is currently shifting towards a more integrated, innovative, and solution-oriented approach to sustainability. This change reflects the demands of the increasingly competitive and dynamic global maritime industry. Educational institutions need to respond by updating curricula, enhancing access to technology, and strengthening partnerships with industry to provide relevant learning experiences. Only in this way can graduates be prepared to become designers and innovators who not only understand theory and techniques, but are also able to apply them effectively in a complex and ever-changing real world.

DIGITAL TRANSFORMATION IN HIGHER EDUCATION

Technological developments affecting education

Digital transformation in higher education has become a major driver of change in the way teaching and learning occur across various disciplines, including maritime education. Technological advancements such as the Internet of Things (IoT), artificial intelligence (AI), virtual reality (VR), augmented reality (AR), and cloud computing have paved the way for more interactive, personalized, and data-driven learning methods. These technologies not only replace conventional learning media but also create new learning models that were previously difficult to implement, particularly in fields that require visualization and technical simulation, such as maritime architecture.

IoT, for example, enables the integration of real-time data from equipment and sensors installed on ships, ports, or marine laboratories (Benavides et al., 2020). This data can be directly used in the learning process to analyze ship performance, monitor weather conditions, or measure wave strength. Students can study real scenarios without having to be on-site, thus expanding the scope of learning experiences. AI then plays a role in processing this data, providing design recommendations, performance predictions, or operational efficiency analyses that can help students understand the complexities of technical decision-making in the maritime world.

VR and AR technology are key elements in creating immersive learning experiences. With VR, students can 'enter' a ship or port environment virtually and interact with various components such as the engine room, navigation bridge, or dock structures. AR, on the other hand, allows the integration of virtual elements with the real environment, so instructors can display coastal building models on a laboratory table or project ship designs directly into the classroom. This visual experience helps students understand the scale, proportions, and functions of each design element.

Cloud computing supports all these innovations by providing a data storage and processing platform that can be accessed anytime and anywhere. Online platforms allow students to upload simulation-based assignments, access interactive learning modules, and collaborate on ship design or coastal structure projects simultaneously. This not only enhances efficiency but also eliminates geographical boundaries in maritime education (Gkrimpizi et al., 2023).

The role of digital transformation in improving access, efficiency, and quality of learning

The influence of digital transformation on improving access, efficiency, and quality of learning in maritime education is very significant. Sebaaly (2019) stated that with the presence of e-learning and digital platforms, students in remote areas or island countries can attend the same classes as students in urban centers. Learning time becomes more flexible, allowing students to adjust their study pace according to their needs. In terms of quality, learning materials can be enhanced with simulations, interactive videos, and real-time data, making the learning process more relevant to current industry conditions (Mohamed Hashim et al, 2022).

Several international maritime colleges have demonstrated success in leveraging digital transformation (Soares & Santos, 2022). For example, maritime academies in Europe and Asia have integrated world-class bridge simulators, allowing students to practice ship navigation in various weather conditions and maritime traffic. Other institutions have developed engine room simulators that replicate ship engine room operations in detail, enabling students to learn operational procedures and handle disturbances without real risks. Such digitalization not only enhances technical skills but also strengthens decision-making under pressure.

According to Kennedy & de Sousa Moreira (2022), simulation-based training is also extending to coastal building design. Hydrodynamic simulations allow students to test breakwater or dock designs against extreme waves, strong currents, and tides. This provides a deep understanding of the interaction between coastal structures and the marine environment, which is crucial for sustainable coastal infrastructure planning and development. With the support of technology, students can explore various design options and perform optimizations before the physical construction stage is carried out.

In addition, the utilization of remote sensing has brought a new dimension to the learning of port planning, navigation, and maritime disaster mitigation. Satellite imagery, radar data, and ocean sensors enable the collection of accurate spatial information about sea conditions, sedimentation, or vessel movements. This data can be analyzed to identify potential hazards, plan safe navigation routes, or assess the environmental impacts of maritime projects. For students, the ability to interpret remote sensing data becomes a relevant value-added skill in the modern job market. Real-time marine data integration also reinforces the concept of problem-based learning (Vysochan et al., 2024). For example, students can be asked to design a port operation strategy during a tropical storm using the latest weather data. This approach not only tests technical skills but also trains analytical skills, quick decision-making, and teamwork. Thus, technology not only serves as a supportive tool but also acts as a catalyst for the formation of holistic professional competencies.

Digital transformation in higher maritime education is a continuous and adaptive process. Technology will continue to evolve, and educational institutions need to be responsive to these changes so that the curriculum remains relevant to the needs of the global industry. The success of implementing digital transformation depends on infrastructure readiness, the capabilities of teaching staff, and policy support that encourages innovation. If all these factors work synergistically, maritime education will be able to produce graduates who are ready to compete in the increasingly digitized maritime industry era.

INNOVATIONS IN MARITIME EDUCATION AND WORKFORCE DEVELOPMENT

Ship Design

Ship design encompasses the development of hull forms, propulsion systems, spatial layouts, stability, safety, and energy efficiency. This field requires a deep understanding of hydrodynamics, materials engineering, and international regulations such as those established by the International Maritime Organization (IMO). According to Pan et al. (2020), innovation in ship design education demands the integration of co-design methods and advanced simulation technologies to enrich the learning process. This approach involves active collaboration among students (Baya, 2014), faculty, industry practitioners, and regulators, thereby creating a learning environment that is realistic and responsive to the needs of the maritime industry. By utilizing sophisticated simulators and 3D visualization technologies, students are able to interactively explore hull forms, propulsion systems, and spatial configurations while simultaneously developing an understanding of the technical, operational, and safety implications of their designs. This model of learning has proven effective not only in strengthening technical competence but also in enhancing soft skills such as communication and cross-disciplinary problem solving.

Meanwhile, Zhu et al. (2024) emphasize that the emergence of Simulation-Based Design Optimization (SBDO) and intelligent optimization algorithms has transformed the paradigm of ship design in maritime education. Through the integration of Computational Fluid Dynamics (CFD), digital twins, and surrogate models, students are now able to design ships that are more energy-efficient, environmentally friendly, and capable of optimal performance under a wide range of sea conditions. These innovations align with the global push toward green shipping and sustainability, ensuring that graduates acquire not only technical expertise in ship design but also the capacity to address environmental challenges, comply with international regulations, and adapt to evolving maritime technologies.

Ports and Maritime Facilities

Ports and maritime facilities constitute critical components of the global maritime transportation system, functioning as nodes for cargo handling, passenger movement, and various support services for ship operations. According to the United Nations Conference on Trade and Development (UNCTAD, 2021), modern ports no longer serve merely as berthing locations but have evolved into integrated logistics hubs interconnected with land, air, and multimodal transport networks. Thus, operational efficiency and connectivity have become key determinants of port competitiveness (Monteiro et al., 2021).

In general, maritime facilities include berths, warehouses, container yards, cargo-handling equipment (such as cranes, forklifts, and conveyors), ship repair yards, navigation and safety systems, as well as supporting areas like administrative offices, quarantine zones, and passenger terminals. Notteboom & Rodrigue (2022) highlight that current port development trends increasingly embrace the concept of the *smart port*, which leverages digital technologies, the Internet of Things (IoT), and big data analytics to enhance security, reduce waiting times, optimize ship scheduling, and minimize environmental impacts.

Offshore Structures and Supporting Facilities

Offshore structures and supporting facilities are vital elements in the maritime and energy industries, serving to enable exploration, production, and distribution of marine resources such as oil, gas, and renewable energy. According to Chakrabarti (2005), offshore structures encompass a variety of installations, including fixed platforms, compliant towers, semi-submersible platforms, jack-up rigs, and Floating Production Storage and Offloading (FPSO) units. Their design must take into account extreme environmental conditions such as high waves, strong currents, and intense winds, while ensuring operational safety and environmental sustainability.

Supporting facilities include marine transport assets (such as supply vessels and crew boats), communication and navigation systems, energy storage and distribution infrastructure, and maintenance and repair facilities. Bai and Bai (2018) note that technological advancements have enabled offshore operations in increasingly deeper waters through the use of dynamic positioning systems, subsea production systems, and high-performance composite materials. Furthermore, recent trends emphasize the development of offshore renewable energy structures, including offshore wind turbines and wave energy converters, which are designed to support the global transition toward clean energy. The scope of maritime architecture, therefore, is inherently multidisciplinary, integrating aspects of civil engineering, mechanical engineering, industrial design, marine technology, and marine environmental studies.

21st-Century Competency Requirements in the Maritime Sector

In the era of digital transformation and increasing sustainability demands, the maritime sector requires a workforce with capabilities that extend far beyond traditional technical operations. Koh and colleagues argue that the core competencies now essential include digitalization, maritime business knowledge, social competence, environmental awareness, and supply chain management. Kapalidis et al. (2022) aligned that this aligns with findings from the SkillSea report, which highlights the necessity of integrating digital skills, green competencies, and managerial soft skills into seafarer training standards in order to remain aligned with evolving technologies and regulatory frameworks.

In parallel, Maritime Education and Training (MET) is progressively moving toward a balanced approach that combines hard skills—such as navigation and engineering—with soft skills (Barston & Birnie, 2024), including leadership, teamwork, and decision-making. This orientation is reflected in the 2010 Manila Amendments to the STCW Convention and further reinforced by sustainability competency frameworks that integrate systems thinking, future-oriented thinking, normative reasoning, as well as strategic and interpersonal competencies. Such an approach underscores the pressing need for maritime professionals who are not only proficient in ship operations but also capable of exercising vision and ethical judgment in addressing environmental and operational challenges.

Finally, the rapid evolution of international regulations and the adoption of green technologies—such as alternative fuels (hydrogen, ammonia), automation, e-navigation, and digitalized port and ship operations—are driving an urgent demand for reskilling and upskilling programs among seafarers and maritime workers. On a global scale, it is estimated that up to 800,000 seafarers will require retraining by the mid-2030s in order to safely operate new technologies and manage high-risk fuels, thereby ensuring the continued resilience and sustainability of the maritime industry.

Innovation and Sustainability

Innovation and sustainability in the maritime sector are manifested through the application of environmentally friendly technologies such as alternative fuel propulsion systems (LNG, hydrogen, or biofuels), energy-efficient ship designs, and the integration of digital technologies including smart shipping, the Internet of Things (IoT), and big data analytics to monitor operational performance in real time (Wright & Crosbie, 2021). In addition, the concept of a circular economy has begun to take shape through ship material recycling, responsible waste management, and the utilization of renewable energy in both ports and vessels (Stopford, 2020). These forms of innovation not only reduce carbon footprints but also enhance cost efficiency and industry competitiveness, while supporting the achievement of sustainability targets set by the International Maritime Organization (IMO).

According to Wright and Crosbie (2021), innovation and sustainability represent the key pillars of maritime sector transformation in the twenty-first century, driven by global pressures to reduce emissions, improve energy efficiency, and minimize marine environmental impacts. Innovations in ship design, eco-friendly propulsion systems, and digital technologies such as smart shipping are regarded as strategic solutions for achieving IMO's sustainability goals. This approach not only promotes operational efficiency but also creates new economic opportunities for the maritime industry.

It can therefore be argued that sustainability in the maritime sector cannot be achieved solely through technological advancements, but also requires a paradigm shift in resource management, logistics planning, and operational behavior. Pazaver & Kitada (2025) stated that this includes the adoption of circular economy principles in ship material utilization, responsible waste treatment, and the integration of renewable energy sources such as wind and solar power into shipping operations.

E-LEARNING IN MARITIME ARCHITECTURE EDUCATION

Definition and models of e-learning in maritime architecture education

The shift in learning paradigms from conventional to digital is one form of educational adaptation to technological developments. Bolmsten et al. (2021) stated that one rapidly growing innovation is electronic learning or e-learning. E-learning is the use of internet technology to deliver a range of solutions that can enhance knowledge and skills. E-learning is not just about the use of digital media, but also encompasses flexible, interactive, and outcome-oriented learning strategies. There are three main models in the implementation of e-learning, namely asynchronous, synchronous, and blended learning. Garrison & Vaughan (2008) emphasize that blended learning serves as an effective bridge between face-to-face interaction and the flexibility of online learning. On the other hand, synchronous learning can enhance social engagement through real-time interaction, while asynchronous learning provides participants with the freedom to access materials according to their own timing and learning pace. Furthermore, Hrastinski (2008) states that the integration of these learning models can improve the quality of higher education by offering a more adaptive learning experience in the higher education environment.

The development of information technology has brought significant changes to the education sector, particularly in the implementation of e-learning. Since the COVID-19 pandemic, the utilization of Learning Management Systems (LMS) has become increasingly widespread as a solution for both distance and hybrid learning. LMS serves to support learning activities, ranging from the delivery of materials, interaction, to the evaluation of learning outcomes. Maritime architecture education requires students to master technical skills in planning, modeling, and designing ships as well as maritime infrastructure. As digital technology evolves, design software has become an essential instrument that cannot be separated from the curriculum.

The integration of this software in e-learning is of very high urgency (Sadeghi, 2024). First, because modern maritime education requires digital skills that are relevant to global industry standards. Second, digital platforms facilitate students to practice independently, access modules, and collaborate across locations using the same software employed in the industry. Third, this integration supports student-centered learning (Bolmsten et al., 2021), where students can learn adaptively, according to their pace and needs. Thus, the importance of integrating maritime design software in e-learning is not only to support the achievement of learning outcomes but also to address the challenges of competitive maritime workforce needs in the digital era.

E-learning in maritime architecture education has become one of the main strategies to address the challenges of learning in the digital era (Sadeghi, 2024). The development of information technology allows the learning process to no longer be restricted to physical classrooms, but can take place anytime and anywhere. In the context of maritime architecture, e-learning not only serves as a medium for delivering theory, but also as a means to develop technical skills through simulations, design software, and online collaboration. The advantage of e-learning lies in its flexibility, allowing students to access materials at their own learning pace, while also providing ample interactive space through discussion forums, video conferences, and project collaborations based on digital platforms.

The e-learning model used in maritime architecture education can take the form of both synchronous and asynchronous. Synchronous learning allows students and instructors to interact directly via video conferencing (Abid et al., 2024), providing space for Q&A, discussion, and real-time feedback. Conversely, the asynchronous model gives students the flexibility to study the material independently through digital modules, learning videos, and assignments that can be submitted at any time. Many institutions also adopt a blended learning approach, which is a combination of face-to-face and online learning, integrating the benefits of direct interaction with the flexibility of technology. This approach is highly relevant in maritime architecture, where some practical skills still require direct demonstration, while conceptual understanding can be gained online (Soares & Santos, 2022).

Commonly used platforms and tools

The integration of specialized software is a crucial element in e-learning in this field. Applications such as AutoCAD, Rhino, ShipConstructor, and maritime BIM platforms allow students to learn about ship design processes, port planning, and coastal development. Hydrodynamic simulations, for example, can show the impact of waves on a breakwater or dock, enabling students to test and modify designs before they are implemented in the field. Barston & Birnie (2024) explained that through project-based learning that utilizes such software, students can develop technical skills while enhancing their analytical and problem-solving abilities. This makes e-learning not just a tool for delivering information, but also a virtual laboratory that enriches the learning experience.

However, the implementation of e-learning in maritime architecture education faces its own challenges. Adequate technology infrastructure is a primary requirement, both in the form of a stable internet connection and high-spec hardware to run technical simulations. In addition, the digital competence of lecturers and students must also be improved to optimally utilize technology (Barston & Birnie, 2024; Loh et al., 2024). Another challenge is how to ensure the active involvement of students in online learning, considering that this model requires a high level of autonomy and discipline. Institutions need to design interactive and project-based learning strategies to keep students engaged and motivated.

Nevertheless, the opportunities offered by e-learning in maritime architecture education are vast. Through the utilization of field data, digital models, and advanced simulations, students can access learning experiences that were previously only possible at project sites or specialized training facilities. Zou et al. (2025) stated that cross-country collaboration also becomes easier, allowing students to engage in international projects without the need for physical travel. With an adaptive curriculum design, appropriate technological support, and student-centered learning strategies, e-learning can be a key catalyst in producing innovative, adaptive graduates in maritime architecture who are ready to meet the demands of the global industry.

EFFECTIVE E-LEARNING IMPLEMENTATION STRATEGIES

Technology-based curriculum design

The implementation strategy of effective e-learning in maritime architecture education requires a curriculum planning specifically designed to maximize the use of digital technology. The curriculum should consider the balance between the delivery of theory (Barston & Birnie, 2024), technical skills, and mastery of relevant industry software. The utilization of online learning platforms integrated with interactive modules can facilitate students in accessing materials, completing exercises, and receiving immediate feedback. This approach also opens opportunities for integrating cross-disciplinary learning, for example by combining coastal civil engineering knowledge with maritime architectural design in a single integrated project.

The use of 3D simulations, Virtual Reality (VR), and Augmented Reality (AR) has become an important component in creating learning experiences that closely resemble real conditions. This technology allows students to explore models of ships, docks, or ports virtually, understand proportions and layouts, and visualize interactions between structures and the marine environment. Through VR, for example, students can experience how their designs will function in extreme weather conditions or when facing large waves, which cannot be safely done in the real world. This helps to develop a deep understanding before the designs are realized in the field.

The integration of coastal structure design learning with hydrodynamic simulation software and structural analysis provides significant added value. Students not only learn to draw or model structures such as piers, breakwaters, and harbors, but also analyze how these designs will respond to wave forces, currents, and tides (Ni & Irannezhad, 2024). This process trains both analytical skills and the technical skills needed in the workforce. Software such as MIKE 21, SWAN, or ANSYS can be used to test various design scenarios, making the learning outcomes more comprehensive and data-driven.

Several models of digital or e-learning can be identified, including the following:

Asynchronous Learning

The asynchronous model allows students to access learning materials, discussion forums, and assignments at any time, according to their own schedules. According to Hrastinski (2008), the main advantage of this model lies in its flexibility and the opportunity for deeper reflection before providing a response. However, it presents challenges such as limited direct interaction and the risk of low learning motivation if not supported by effective management.

Synchronous Learning

The synchronous model relies on real-time communication, typically through video conferencing, chat platforms, or webinars. Its strength lies in enhanced social interaction, collaboration, and active student engagement (Limbong et al., 2022). Nevertheless, technical barriers such as internet stability and differences in time zones can pose significant challenges to its implementation.

Blended Learning

Blended learning represents a combination of asynchronous and synchronous learning, supplemented by face-to-face interaction. Boulougouris et al. (2019) explains that this approach combines the flexibility of self-directed learning with the interactivity of direct engagement. Within higher education, this model is often regarded as the most effective because it accommodates diverse academic needs while maintaining the quality of pedagogical interaction.

E-learning has become one of the most critical strategies in modern education. The asynchronous model provides flexibility, the synchronous model fosters interactivity, and the blended learning model offers a balance between the two (Diahyleva et al., 2025). Selecting the most appropriate model requires careful consideration of students' needs, learning objectives, and available technical resources. Ultimately, the integration of these three models may serve as an optimal solution to support adaptive, inclusive, and effective learning processes.

Online collaboration has become an important strategy that can enhance students' communication and teamwork skills (Durlik et al., 2024). Through project-based learning, students from various locations can work together on a single ship design or coastal facility. Digital project management platforms allow for clear task allocation, uploading of work results, and well-documented discussions. These collaborative projects can also involve industry partners, allowing students to receive direct feedback from professional practitioners while also building a beneficial work network for their future careers.

The development of digital competencies for both lecturers and students is one of the foundations for the success of e-learning (Diahyleva et al., 2025). Lecturers need to master techniques for creating digital content, using simulation software, and interactive online teaching methods. Students, on the other hand, must be able to operate various digital platforms, understand online communication ethics, and manage their study time independently. Educational institutions can facilitate ongoing training, provide technology help centers, and build supportive online learning communities.

Digital-based assessment has become a strategic step to ensure that learning outcomes are achieved objectively and transparently. The assessment system can incorporate online tests, digital portfolios, simulation reports, and recorded project presentations. Learning analytics can also be used to monitor student progress in real-time, identify areas needing improvement, and provide faster feedback. With this method, assessment is not just a tool for evaluation but also a means of learning that encourages continuous improvement (Okafor-Yarwood et al., 2024).

The implementation of this strategy also requires adequate infrastructure. High-speed internet connection, high-spec computer labs, and professional software licenses are prerequisites that must be met. In addition, according to Kennedy & de Sousa Moreira (2022), responsive technical support will help address technical obstacles that may hinder the smoothness of learning. Institutions that successfully provide these facilities will have a greater appeal to prospective students, while also enhancing their academic reputation both nationally and internationally.

The success of e-learning implementation in maritime architecture education depends on the synergy between curriculum design, technology, human resources, and institutional support. Each component must complement each other and work harmoniously to create a relevant, effective learning experience that prepares graduates to face the challenges of the global maritime industry. With a strong commitment, this strategy can transform the way maritime architecture education is conducted (Diahyleva et al., 2025), from mere information delivery to a process of innovative and sustainable competency building.

In the context of maritime architecture, e-learning not only serves as a medium for transferring theoretical knowledge but is also starting to be used to teach technical skills through digital simulations, design software, and 3D visualization (Bačnar et al., 2025). However, the integration of e-learning in maritime architecture education still faces various challenges, particularly in teaching practical skills that have previously relied heavily on laboratory-based learning and hands-on practice. Therefore, innovative approaches and supporting technologies are needed to bridge these limitations, such as the use of CAD-based design platforms, Maritime BIM, and virtual simulations.

CHALLENGES AND BARRIERS

Infrastructure and internet access

Challenges in implementing digital transformation and e-learning strategies in maritime architecture education cannot be regarded as simple, as they involve technical, social, and institutional dimensions. One of the primary barriers lies in infrastructural limitations, particularly unequal internet access across regions, especially in coastal and island areas. Maritime education is inherently linked to these regions, and thus the digital divide may lead to inequities in learning opportunities. Asrifan (2025) explained that this condition forces some students to exert greater effort to follow online courses, while institutions are expected to provide alternative solutions to ensure that learning processes remain uninterrupted.

In addition to infrastructure, the gap in digital literacy has emerged as another critical issue that requires attention. Not all students or lecturers are familiar with online learning technologies, design software, or digital simulations. Some possess only basic technological skills, whereas maritime architecture education demands proficiency in advanced applications such as hydrodynamic simulations or three-dimensional modelling. This gap can slow the learning process and diminish the effectiveness of e-learning, thereby necessitating continuous training programs for all stakeholders to strengthen their digital competencies.

Resistance to change among lecturers and students

Resistance to change also frequently becomes an obstacle. For some lecturers, the transition from conventional to digital teaching methods generates concerns about losing authority, difficulties in adapting, or perceptions that technology merely adds to their workload (Faruq, 2025). For students, on the other hand, such a transition demands higher levels of self-directed learning, which not all are able to maintain consistently. This condition indicates that digital transformation in maritime education is not merely about technology, but also about shifting mindsets, academic culture, and the psychological readiness of all participants involved.

Data security and academic ethics

Another equally important issue is data security and academic integrity. Online learning requires the storage of substantial amounts of data, including student design outputs, research findings, and academic administrative records. If not managed properly, these data are vulnerable to breaches or misuse. Furthermore, Slyusarenko & Zadorozhnya (2021) explained that digital learning environments are prone to academic integrity issues such as plagiarism or cheating during online examinations. Institutions must therefore enforce robust cybersecurity policies while instilling values of academic integrity that align with the digital era.

Within the context of maritime architecture education, particularly concerning coastal structures, the complexity of technical simulations presents an additional challenge. Simulating the design of breakwaters, piers, or ports demands high-specification hardware and expensive licensed software (Notteboom et al., 2022). Without access to such technology, students may be limited to theoretical knowledge without opportunities for realistic digital experimentation. This situation risks lowering the quality of education, as students' technical competencies required in professional practice remain underdeveloped. Hence, investment in state-of-the-art digital laboratories has become an indispensable necessity.

In conclusion, the challenges and barriers in the digital transformation of maritime architecture education are multidimensional and interrelated (Masuku, 2021). Inadequate infrastructure, digital literacy gaps, resistance within academic culture, data security concerns, and the complexity of simulation technologies all have the potential to hinder learning if not addressed properly. However, each challenge simultaneously presents an opportunity to strengthen the education system through innovation, training, and policies oriented toward quality improvement. With strategic measures (Kim et al., 2023), these challenges can be transformed into momentum for creating maritime architecture education that is more inclusive, modern, and globally competitive (Maruf et al., 2024).

OPPORTUNITIES AND BENEFITS

Increased flexibility in learning time and location

The opportunities and benefits arising from the implementation of digital transformation and e-learning strategies in maritime architecture education represent a crucial area of discussion, given their significant impact on the quality of learning and the relevance of graduates to the needs of the global industry (Al Yakin et al., 2024). One of the most tangible benefits is the flexibility of time and place, which was previously difficult to achieve in conventional education systems. Students are no longer bound to physical classrooms but can instead access learning materials, simulations, and design software from anywhere and at any time. This flexibility is particularly advantageous for students living in coastal or island regions, where access to campus facilities may be limited, enabling them to fully participate in the learning process without being constrained by geographical distance.

Beyond flexibility, e-learning also paves the way for broader international collaboration and knowledge exchange. Chen et al. (2017) stated that through digital platforms, students and lecturers from various countries can connect directly, share insights, and work together on joint projects without the need for physical relocation. Such interaction provides a cross-cultural learning experience while enriching perspectives in designing maritime architectural solutions that are adaptive to global contexts (Karahalios, 2025). This form of collaboration also allows students to gain feedback from international experts who might previously have been difficult to reach, thereby enhancing the overall quality of education.

Another equally important benefit lies in the potential for long-term cost efficiency. While significant investments are required at the initial stage for digital infrastructure, software, and training, operational costs can be substantially reduced over time. For example, the use of digital simulations can minimize the need for large-scale field practice, which typically involves complex logistics and high expenses. Similarly, digital materials can be reused, updated quickly, and distributed to many students without additional printing costs. This efficiency is particularly relevant for educational institutions seeking to maintain high-quality learning outcomes within limited budgetary frameworks (Boulougouris et al., 2019).

International collaboration and knowledge exchange

Digital transformation also acts as a catalyst for design innovation within maritime architecture. By leveraging advanced software, students can experiment with various design approaches for ships, ports, and coastal structures using simulation data and 3D modeling. This process not only enhances technical proficiency but also fosters bold and creative ideas. The innovations emerging from such technology-driven learning environments have the potential to make a tangible contribution to the maritime industry, particularly in terms of efficiency, sustainability, and adaptation to climate change and environmental challenges.

Limbong et al. (2022) explained that an increasingly relevant aspect of maritime architecture education is the integration of field data and digital models into the learning process. With access to marine big data, satellite imagery, and real-time sensor information, students can study actual conditions faced by coastal infrastructure such as piers, breakwaters, and harbors. These datasets can then be utilized in simulations to test structural resilience against waves, currents, and other extreme natural phenomena. Learning experiences grounded in real-world data not only strengthen conceptual understanding (Liu et al., 2025) but also sharpen students' critical analytical skills in designing practical and context-sensitive solutions.

In addition to enriching technical knowledge, digital transformation in maritime architecture education cultivates a more independent learning culture. With abundant access to digital resources, students can explore beyond the boundaries of the formal curriculum, delve into the latest literature, and utilize online tutorials aligned with their specific needs. This independent learning capability is essential for shaping graduates who are adaptive and capable of responding to rapid changes in an increasingly digitalized maritime industry.

Moreover, the application of e-learning in this field broadens opportunities for collaboration with industry stakeholders. Maritime companies can participate in the learning process by providing digital case studies, field data (Maruf et al., 2024), or even real-world projects that can be integrated into the curriculum. Such collaboration benefits students by offering practical experience, while also benefiting industry players by exposing them to potential innovations from younger generations. In this way, education and industry can progress hand in hand in building a sustainable maritime ecosystem (Durlik et al., 2024).

Another noteworthy contribution lies in the promotion of environmental sustainability. By utilizing digital simulations, the need for direct field testing that may potentially damage marine ecosystems can be significantly reduced. Students can conduct preliminary trials in digital environments before designs are implemented in real-world settings, thereby minimizing negative environmental impacts. This approach aligns with global trends toward sustainable development while instilling a strong ecological awareness among students from an early stage.

Encouraging technology-based maritime design innovation

Digital transformation in maritime architecture education also creates opportunities to strengthen alumni networks and global academic communities. Through digital platforms, graduates can remain connected with their institutions, share professional experiences, and contribute to curriculum development (Liu et al., 2025). Such networks enrich the educational ecosystem by enabling continuous knowledge exchange that extends beyond the formal period of study. This global community also serves as an inspiration for current students, showing them that their education is directly relevant to professional practice.

Overall, the opportunities and benefits of adopting digital transformation and e-learning strategies in maritime architecture education extend far beyond technical aspects. They encompass social, cultural, economic, and environmental dimensions, all of which contribute to shaping a more inclusive, efficient, and competitive education system (Shih, 2024). By leveraging technology appropriately, educational institutions can prepare graduates who not only master theory and practice but also possess global awareness, ecological responsibility, and innovative capacity to contribute to sustainable maritime development.

FUTURE TRENDS OF EDUCATIONAL INNOVATIONS IN MARITIME ARCHITECTURE

AI and machine learning in ship and coastal structure design optimization

The future of maritime architecture education cannot be separated from the rapid advancement of digital technologies that have increasingly permeated various aspects of life, including academia and industry. As the maritime sector faces growing complexity, there is a pressing need for learning strategies that fully leverage technology to prepare competent and adaptive graduates (Maruf et al., 2024). Emerging technological trends are no longer confined to serving as auxiliary tools for teaching (Boulougouris et al., 2019); rather, they are redefining the ways of thinking, designing, and innovating within maritime architecture.

One of the most prominent trends is the application of Artificial Intelligence (AI) and machine learning to optimize the design of ships and coastal structures. Abid et al. (2024) stated that through these technologies, students can learn how intelligent algorithms process marine environmental data, predict structural loads, and recommend more efficient designs. AI not only simplifies complex calculations but also trains students to understand sustainable design patterns. In this way, AI plays a dual role: as an academic exploration tool and as a bridge to modern industry practices.

The use of machine learning in hydrodynamic simulations represents another breakthrough. By analyzing thousands of datasets on currents, waves, and tides, systems can predict the impacts of breakwater or pier designs with far greater accuracy than conventional methods. For students, this provides opportunities to gain deeper insight into the complex interactions between technical design and environmental dynamics (Bačnar et al., 2025). Education thus becomes more contextual, as students learn directly from realistic, data-driven scenarios.

In addition to AI, the concept of digital twins is gaining significant relevance in maritime education. Digital twins create virtual representations of real-world objects, such as ships, piers, or ports (Ni & Irannezhad, 2024). Students can study the operation and performance of these structures digitally, as though interacting with their physical counterparts. This technology makes learning more interactive and allows students to conduct experiments without real-world risks, such as testing structural resilience to storms or simulating vessel collisions.

Digital twins and real-time simulations for maritime training

Digital twins also hold great potential in supporting real-time maritime training. With the integration of sensors and live data from the field, students can study actual conditions without needing to be physically present. For example, the operational activities of a port can be visualized through a digital twin (Boulougouris et al., 2019), allowing students to observe ship movements, cargo handling, and weather responses. This approach redefines field practice, making it safer, more cost-efficient, yet equally rich in learning experiences.

Another increasingly relevant trend is the emergence of the metaverse as a virtual classroom. The metaverse enables students to participate in lectures, discussions, and simulations within immersive three-dimensional environments. Through digital avatars, students and instructors can interact as if in a physical classroom, but with limitless simulation possibilities. In the context of maritime architecture, students can virtually "visit" port models or coastal structures, engage in real-time discussions with peers, and collaborate internationally within an integrated platform.

Metaverse as a virtual maritime classroom

The implementation of the metaverse in maritime education also supports multidisciplinary collaborative learning (Liu et al., 2025). For example, students in civil engineering, architecture, and urban planning can enter the same virtual space to jointly design port development scenarios. This trains students to engage in multidisciplinary collaboration from the outset, a skill highly demanded in the complex global maritime industry. This demonstrates that the metaverse is not merely a technological trend, but a transformative learning environment (Gkrimpizi et al., 2023).

Moreover, the integration of big data is becoming increasingly critical in advancing maritime architecture education and research. Big data enables students and lecturers to access and analyze vast datasets related to ocean conditions, port activities, and climate change. Such analyses provide essential foundations for port planning, coastal project management, and disaster mitigation. By employing big data, students move beyond theory into practicing data-driven decision-making, a vital skill in the digital era.

Jamil & Bhuiyan (2021) explained that the use of big data further strengthens predictive capabilities for long-term planning. For instance, climate data spanning several decades can be analyzed to project the impact of sea-level rise on coastal infrastructure. Through this type of learning, students are encouraged to think more visionary and with a sustainability-oriented mindset. Big data thus functions not only as an analytical tool but also as an educational instrument that shapes new perspectives in maritime planning.

The synergy of AI, digital twins, the metaverse, and big data creates a more dynamic and adaptive educational ecosystem. Students become active participants in simulations, analyses, and explorations rather than passive recipients of knowledge. Such an environment fosters creativity, critical thinking, and technical skills aligned with the demands of modern industry. Maritime architecture education therefore becomes more contextual, rooted in real-world challenges approached through technology-driven solutions.

Although these trends are still in their early stages of implementation across many institutions, their potential to reshape the future of maritime education is immense. Their success will largely depend on the readiness of infrastructure, the digital competence of educators, and the policy support provided by academic institutions and governments (Liu et al., 2025). When these three factors align, digital transformation in maritime architecture education will move beyond rhetoric to become a reality with tangible impact.

Case studies on the implementation of Digital Twin technology in maritime training have been carried out in several developed countries. For instance, Smart Port Singapore employs real-time simulation to predict berth congestion and to train crews in safety procedures (Wei et al., 2024). The application of this technology not only enhances training effectiveness but also prepares the maritime workforce to adapt to technological advancements, thereby supporting safety, operational efficiency, and innovation within the maritime sector. Despite its many advantages, however, implementation faces significant challenges, including the need for advanced sensor infrastructure, stable data connectivity, high initial investment costs, and user adaptation to new technologies (Mallam et al., 2019).

In addition, environmental data such as ocean currents, waves, and channel depths are continuously analyzed to support more efficient dredging operations while simultaneously safeguarding the sustainability of coastal ecosystems. For example, in the Indonesian context, the application of big data has begun to take shape at Tanjung Priok Port through the Inaportnet program developed by the Ministry of Transportation. This system functions as a Maritime Single Window, integrating licensing data, cargo manifests, and vessel arrival schedules. Although still in the development stage toward full integration, this initiative serves as a foundation for the digital transformation of national ports, positioning them to become more competitive within the ASEAN region.

Big data integration for port planning and coastal project management

Meanwhile, Monteiro et al. (2021) stated that the integration of big data into port planning and coastal project management offers significant opportunities to formulate development strategies that are more accurate, predictive, and resource-efficient. The combination of these four trends demonstrates that technological innovation is no longer a mere complement but has become a fundamental foundation for building a resilient, adaptive, and sustainable maritime sector. Thus, the trajectory of future technological development in the maritime field is not merely a matter of digital transformation, but rather a paradigm shifts toward an intelligent ecosystem capable of integrating technical, environmental, social, and economic dimensions within a unified development framework (Liu et al., 2025).

Ultimately, the future of digital technologies will elevate maritime architecture education to a more advanced, modern, and globally competitive stage. By strategically adopting AI, digital twins, the metaverse, and big data, educational institutions can prepare graduates who not only master theoretical and practical knowledge but also possess digital literacy, innovative thinking, and a vision for sustainability. This transformation is expected to strengthen academic standing on a global scale while making tangible contributions to inclusive and sustainable maritime development.

CONCLUSION

To make a long story short, the discussion on digital transformation and e-learning strategies in maritime architecture education highlights that the use of digital technologies is no longer optional but an absolute necessity. The integration of technologies such as Artificial Intelligence, digital twins, big data, and the metaverse has opened new learning spaces that are more interactive, adaptive, and aligned with the needs of the global maritime industry. From an academic perspective, these technologies enrich pedagogical methods, accelerate the transfer of knowledge, and enhance students' capacity to confront real-world maritime challenges.

The main findings indicate that digitalization in maritime education generates dual benefits. On one hand, it enhances the quality of learning by providing realistic simulations, data-driven analyses, and access to limitless learning resources beyond geographical boundaries. On the other hand, digital transformation strengthens the connection between academia and industry through applied research oriented toward practical needs. This creates an educational ecosystem that is more integrated, dynamic, and solution-oriented.

Nevertheless, the adoption of digital technologies in maritime education is not without challenges. Limitations in infrastructure, low levels of digital literacy among educators and students, and disparities in access across maritime regions remain significant barriers. Equally important is the readiness of educational institutions to accommodate this transformation, particularly in terms of regulations, curriculum design, and teaching models aligned with new technologies. Without well-prepared strategies, digital transformation risks remaining superficial without producing substantive impact.

Strategic recommendations for maritime education institutions include strengthening investment in digital infrastructure, encompassing hardware, software, and reliable networks. In addition, building faculty capacity through intensive training is an urgent necessity to enable instructors to utilize technology effectively in teaching. Curricula should also be adjusted to emphasize digital skills, data analysis, and technology-based simulations, ensuring that students not only master theory but also apply it in real-world contexts.

Furthermore, educational institutions should expand collaborations with industry and international research bodies to ensure that adopted technologies are consistent with the latest developments and global needs. Such collaborations may take the form of joint research, exchange programs, and the establishment of virtual laboratories that grant students access to global best practices. Through this approach, maritime education becomes not only nationally relevant but also internationally competitive.

Beyond practical recommendations, future research directions should focus on developing digital learning models tailored to the specific characteristics of maritime education. Studies on the effectiveness of digital twins, the metaverse, and big data in maritime training must continue to identify the most effective approaches for competency development. Further inquiry is also needed into the social and cultural impacts of digitalization in education to ensure that transformation remains inclusive and does not widen regional disparities.

In conclusion, digital transformation in maritime architecture education represents a strategic step toward a more advanced, adaptive, and sustainable learning ecosystem. Technology has evolved beyond its role as a supporting tool to become a foundational pillar underpinning the vision of future maritime education. If strategic recommendations and research directions are consistently implemented, maritime education will be well-positioned to produce graduates who are competitive, innovative, and prepared to address global challenges.

REFERENCES

Abid, M., Suhrab, M. I. R., Osnin, N. A., Nik, W. M. N. S. W., & Hammad, M. (2024). Assessing the impact of self-e-learning, classroom teaching, and simulation training on learning of COLREG: A survey-based analysis among maritime students at the Universiti Malaysia Terengganu. *Australian Journal of Maritime and Ocean Affairs*, •••, 1–18. DOI: 10.1080/18366503.2024.2398282

Al Yakin, A., Asrifan, A., & Elngar, A. A. (2024). Social Media and Technology Instruction Design in Teaching Amid COVID-19. In *Global Digital Transformation and the Covid-19 Pandemic* (pp. 205-236). Apple Academic Press. http://dx.doi.org/DOI: 10.1201/9781032716862-11

Alop, A. (2019, April). The challenges of the digital technology era for maritime education and training. In *2019 European Navigation Conference (ENC)* (pp. 1-5). IEEE. DOI: 10.1109/EURONAV.2019.8714176

Asrifan, A. (2025). Navigating Ethical Dilemmas in AI-Powered Translation: Challenges and Solutions. In Al Aqad, M. (Ed.), *Role of AI in Translation and Interpretation* (pp. 327–356). IGI Global Scientific Publishing., DOI: 10.4018/979-8-3373-0060-3.ch012

Bačnar, D., Barić, D., & Ogrizović, D. (2025). Charting the Future of Maritime Education and Training: A Technology-Acceptance-Model-Based Pilot Study on Students' Behavioural Intention to Use a Fully Immersive VR Engine Room Simulator. *Applied System Innovation*, *8*(3), 84. DOI: 10.3390/asi8030084

Bai, Y., & Bai, Q. (2018). *Subsea engineering handbook* (2nd ed.). Gulf Professional Publishing., DOI: 10.1016/C2016-0-04557-7

Barston, R., & Birnie, P. (Eds.). (2024). *The maritime dimension*. Taylor & Francis., DOI: 10.4324/9781003477877

Baya, W. T. (2014). Education for career-building: How women in the maritime industry can use education to improve knowledge, skills, organizational learning and development, and knowledge transfer. In *Maritime Women: Global Leadership* (pp. 167-178). Berlin, Heidelberg: Springer Berlin Heidelberg. DOI: 10.1007/978-3-662-45385-8_13

Benavides, L. M. C., Tamayo Arias, J. A., Arango Serna, M. D., Branch Bedoya, J. W., & Burgos, D. (2020). Digital transformation in higher education institutions: A systematic literature review. *Sensors (Basel)*, *20*(11), 3291. DOI: 10.3390/s20113291 PMID: 32526998

Bertram, V. (2012). *Practical ship hydrodynamics* (2nd ed.). Butterworth-Heinemann.

Bolbot, V., Methlouthi, O., Chaal, M., Valdez, O., BahooToroody, A., Tsetkova, A., ... & Basnet, S. (2022). Identification and analysis of educational needs for naval architects and marine engineers in relation to the foreseen context of Maritime Autonomous Surface Ships (MASS).

Bolmsten, J., Manuel, M. E., Kaizer, A., Kasepõld, K., Sköld, D., & Ziemska, M. (2021). Educating the Global Maritime Professional—A case of collaborative e-learning. *WMU journal of maritime affairs*, *20*(3), 309-333. DOI: 10.1007/s13437-020-00224-w

Boulougouris, E., Mizythras, P., Chrysinas, L., Vavourakis, G., Theotokatos, G., Aymelek, M., & Kurt, I. (2019). Developing multidisciplinary blended learning courses for maritime education with cross-European collaboration. *WMU Journal of Maritime Affairs*, *18*(2), 319–340. DOI: 10.1007/s13437-019-00167-x

Carlton, J. (2019). *Marine propellers and propulsion* (4th ed.). Butterworth-Heinemann., DOI: 10.1016/C2014-0-01177-X

Chakrabarti, S. K. (2005). *Handbook of offshore engineering* (Vol. 1–2). Elsevier., DOI: 10.1016/B978-0-08-044381-6.X5000-4

Chen, X., Bai, X., & Xiao, Y. (2017). The application of E-learning in maritime education and training in China. *TransNav: International Journal on Marine Navigation and Safety of Sea Transportation*, *11*(2), 349–354. DOI: 10.12716/1001.11.02.19

Diahyleva, O. S., Yurzhenko, A. Y., & Kononova, O. Y. (2025, March). Exploring the effectiveness of online learning tools and technologies while teaching Maritime English to future ship engineers. In *CTE Workshop Proceedings* (Vol. 12, pp. 350-362). DOI: 10.55056/cte.711

Ducruet, C. (Ed.). (2015). *Maritime Networks: Spatial structures and time dynamics* (1st ed.). Routledge., DOI: 10.4324/9781315692852

Durlik, I., Miller, T., Kostecka, E., & Tuński, T. (2024). Artificial intelligence in maritime transportation: A comprehensive review of safety and risk management applications. *Applied Sciences (Basel, Switzerland)*, *14*(18), 8420. DOI: 10.3390/app14188420

Faruq, Y. A. (2025). Role Of Information And Communication Technology (ICT) In Enhancing The Quality Of Maritime Education And Training In Maritime Colleges In Nigeria.

Garrison, D. R., & Vaughan, N. D. (2008). *Blended Learning in Higher Education: Framework, Principles, and Guidelines*. Jossey-Bass.

Gkrimpizi, T., Peristeras, V., & Magnisalis, I. (2023). Classification of barriers to digital transformation in higher education institutions: Systematic literature review. *Education Sciences*, *13*(7), 746. DOI: 10.3390/educsci13070746

Hrastinski, S. (2008). Asynchronous and synchronous e-learning. *EDUCAUSE Quarterly*, *31*(4), 51–55.

Jamil, M. G., & Bhuiyan, Z. (2021). Deep learning elements in maritime simulation programmes: A pedagogical exploration of learner experiences. *International Journal of Educational Technology in Higher Education*, *18*(1), 18. DOI: 10.1186/s41239-021-00255-0

Kapalidis, C., Karamperidis, S., Watson, T., & Koligiannis, G. (2022). A vulnerability centric System of Systems Analysis on the maritime transportation sector most valuable assets: Recommendations for port facilities and ships. *Journal of Marine Science and Engineering*, *10*(10), 1486. DOI: 10.3390/jmse10101486

Karahalios, H. (2025). Enhancing maritime education for digital sustainability. *International Journal of Innovation Science*, *17*(4), 901–913. Advance online publication. DOI: 10.1108/IJIS-06-2024-0156

Kennedy, G., & de Sousa Moreira, W. (Eds.). (2022). *Power and the maritime domain: A global dialogue*. Taylor & Francis., DOI: 10.4324/9781003298984

Kim, J., Lee, C., Jeong, M., Cho, E., & Lee, Y. (2023). Identifying optimal approaches for sustainable maritime education and training: Addressing technological, environmental, and epidemiological challenges. *Sustainability (Basel)*, *15*(10), 8092. DOI: 10.3390/su15108092

Koh, L. Y., Li, K., Chia, Y. Y., & Yuen, K. F. (2023). Quality design for maritime studies programme in the digital era. *Maritime Policy & Management*, *50*(3), 301–320. DOI: 10.1080/03088839.2021.1983220

Kolarevic, B. (2003). *Architecture in the digital age. Design and Manufacturing*. Spon Press-Taylor & Francis Group., DOI: 10.4324/9780203634561

Limbong, S., Jabu, B., & Basri, M. (2022). The Impact of Synchronous Learning of Marlins in Teaching Maritime English. *Journal of Learning and Development Studies*, *2*(3), 06-13. DOI: 10.32996/jlds.2022.2.3.2

Liu, J., Lyu, Y., Wu, J., & Wang, J. (2025). Adoption strategies of carbon abatement technologies in the maritime supply chain: Impact of demand information sharing. *International Journal of Logistics*, *28*(1), 70–97. DOI: 10.1080/13675567.2022.2115025

Loh, H. S., Lee, J. L., Gu, Y., Chen, H. S., & Tay, H. L. (2024). The effects of digital platforms on customers' satisfaction in international shipping business. *Review of International Business and Strategy*, *34*(2), 231–244. DOI: 10.1108/RIBS-07-2023-0072

Mallam, S. C., Nazir, S., & Renganayagalu, S. K. (2019). Rethinking maritime education, training, and operations in the digital era: Applications for emerging immersive technologies. *Journal of Marine Science and Engineering*, *7*(12), 428. DOI: 10.3390/jmse7120428

Maruf, M., Chang, Y. C., & Yang, L. (2024). Managing institutional interlinkages for the protection of marine environment in the East Asian seas region and beyond: The case of marine plastic pollution. *Ocean and Coastal Management*, *255*, 107232. DOI: 10.1016/j.ocecoaman.2024.107232

Masuku, M. B. (2021, March). Enhancing maritime education through online distance learning in developing environments: Case study of South Africa. In *The 1st International Conference on Maritime Education and Development: ICMED* (pp. 143-154). Cham: Springer International Publishing. DOI: 10.1007/978-3-030-64088-0_13

Miyusov, M. V., Nikolaieva, L. L., & Smolets, V. V. (2022). The future perspectives of immersive learning in maritime education and training. *Transactions on Maritime Science*, *11*(02), 14–14. DOI: 10.7225/toms.v11.n02.014

Mohamed Hashim, M. A., Tlemsani, I., & Matthews, R. (2022). Higher education strategy in digital transformation. *Education and Information Technologies*, *27*(3), 3171–3195. DOI: 10.1007/s10639-021-10739-1 PMID: 34539217

Monteiro, J. L., Santoso, P. I., & Prabowo, R. (2021). Maritime industry-ports and supporting activities: literature review. In *IOP Conference Series: Materials Science and Engineering* (Vol. 1010, No. 1, p. 012019). IOP Publishing. DOI: 10.1088/1757-899X/1010/1/012019

Muthmainnah, A. Y. A., Gochhait, S., Asrifan, A., Elngar, A. A., & Cardoso, L. (2023). Satisfaction of Students Toward Media and Technology Innovation Amidst COVID-19. *Handbook of Computational Sciences: A Multi and Interdisciplinary Approach*, 365-390. DOI: 10.1002/9781119763468.ch17

Ni, L., & Irannezhad, E. (2024). Performance analysis of LogisticChain: A blockchain platform for maritime logistics. *Computers in Industry*, *154*, 104038. DOI: 10.1016/j.compind.2023.104038

Notteboom, T., Pallis, A., & Rodrigue, J. P. (2022). *Port economics, management and policy*. Routledge., DOI: 10.4324/9780429318184

Okafor-Yarwood, I., Eastwood, O., Chikowore, N., & de Oliveira Paes, L. (2024). Technology and maritime security in Africa: Opportunities and challenges in Gulf of Guinea. *Marine Policy*, *160*, 105976. DOI: 10.1016/j.marpol.2023.105976

Pan, Y., Oksavik, K., & Hildre, H. P. (2020). Co-designing ship's bridge simulators for competence development. *Proceedings of the 29th International Conference on Offshore Mechanics and Arctic Engineering* (OMAE 2020).

Papanikolaou, A. (2014). *Ship design: Methodologies of preliminary design*. Springer., DOI: 10.1007/978-94-017-8751-2

Pazaver, A., & Kitada, M. (2025). Integrating twenty-first century skills into STCW competences: implications for maritime education and training. *WMU Journal of Maritime Affairs*, 1-22. DOI: 10.1007/s13437-025-00368-7

Pruyn, J. (2024). The use of digital games in academic maritime education: A theoretical framework and practical applications. *Maritime Policy & Management*, *51*(4), 558–571. DOI: 10.1080/03088839.2023.2174608

Sadeghi, S. H. (2024). The effect of gamified e-learning on marine ecology education: Insights from Iranian maritime students. *Environmental Education Research*, •••, 1–18. DOI: 10.1080/13504622.2024.2415944

Sebaaly, M. (2019). Digital transformation and quality, efficiency, and flexibility in Arab universities. In *Major challenges facing higher education in the Arab World: Quality assurance and relevance* (pp. 167–177). Springer International Publishing., DOI: 10.1007/978-3-030-03774-1_8

Shih, Y. C. (2024). Ocean governance in practice: A study of the application of marine science and technology research techniques to maritime law enforcement in Taiwan. *Marine Policy*, *163*, 106081. DOI: 10.1016/j.marpol.2024.106081

Slyusarenko, N., & Zadorozhnya, O. (2021, March). Usage of information and communication technologies in maritime educational institutions. In *International Conference on Economics, Law and Education Research (ELER 2021)* (pp. 257-262). Atlantis Press. DOI: 10.2991/aebmr.k.210320.044

Soares, C. G., & Santos, T. A. (Eds.). (2022). *Trends in Maritime Technology and Engineering*: Proceedings of the 6th International Conference on Maritime Technology and Engineering (MARTECH 2022, Lisbon, Portugal, 24-26 May 2022) (1st ed.). CRC Press. DOI: 10.1201/9781003320289

Stopford, M. (2020). *Maritime economics* (4th ed.). Routledge.

Theunissen, H., van Niekerk, T., & Pretorius, J. H. (2024). A study of naval architecture and marine engineering higher education to build a foundation of future engineering managers in the South African maritime industry. *Southern Journal of Engineering Education*, *3*, 96–118. DOI: 10.15641/sjee.v3i1.1554

Voloshynov, S. A., Riabukha, I. M., Dobroshtan, O. O., Popova, H. V., & Spychak, T. S. (2021). Adaptive learning environment design in the system of future maritime specialits' training. *Educational Dimension*, *5*, 126–143. DOI: 10.31812/educdim.4722

Vysochan, L., Koziar, M., Stelmah, N., & Vasylyuk-Zaitseva, S. (2024). Digital transformation in education: Using technologies for enhancement of efficiency of teaching. *Futurity Education*, *4*(1), 186–209. DOI: 10.57125/FED.2024.03.25.10

Wei, P., Li, C., Jiang, Z., & Wang, D. (2024). Real-Time Digital Twin of Ship Structure Deformation Field Based on the Inverse Finite Element Method. *Journal of Marine Science and Engineering*, *12*(2), 257. DOI: 10.3390/jmse12020257

Wright, P., & Crosbie, T. (2021). *Sustainable ship design and construction*. Elsevier.

Yu, Y. U., Lee, C. H., & Ahn, Y. J. (2025). Developing a Competency-Based Transition Education Framework for Marine Superintendents: A DACUM-Integrated Approach in the Context of Eco-Digital Maritime Transformation. *Sustainability (Basel)*, *17*(14), 6455. DOI: 10.3390/su17146455

Zhu, X., Zhang, J., Wang, J., & Guo, C. (2024). Intelligent hull form optimization using surrogate models and evolutionary algorithms for energy efficiency. *arXiv preprint*.

Zou, Y., Xiao, G., Li, Q., & Biancardo, S. A. (2025). Intelligent Maritime Shipping: A Bibliometric Analysis of Internet Technologies and Automated Port Infrastructure Applications. *Journal of Marine Science and Engineering*, *13*(5), 979. DOI: 10.3390/jmse13050979

Chapter 23
Transforming Maritime Education in the Digital Era:
A Bibliometric Mapping of Research Trends

Rudi Salam
Universitas Negeri Makassar, Indonesia

Muh. Darwis
http://orcid.org/0000-0002-2573-7709
Universitas Negeri Makassar, Indonesia

Indra Dharma Wijaya
Politeknik Negeri Malang, Indonesia

Sovia Rosalin
http://orcid.org/0000-0001-9560-6440
Universitas Brawijaya, Indonesia

Hillman Wirawan
http://orcid.org/0000-0002-0160-3108
Universitas Hasanuddin, Indonesia

ABSTRACT

This study provides a bibliometric analysis of research trends in maritime education within the context of digital transformation. The objectives are to identify current and emerging research streams through bibliographic coupling analysis and evaluate key co-words analysis. The study analyzed 857 documents published between 2015 and 2025. The bibliographic coupling analysis revealed five major clusters: (1) Maritime Simulation, VR/AR, and Technology-Enhanced Learning; (2) Maritime Education Evaluation Models and Quantitative Analysis; (3) Adapting Maritime Education: Digital Literacy and Collaborative Learning; (4) E-Learning and Online Platforms in Maritime Training; and (5) Innovation in Maritime Learning. Co-word analysis identified key themes such as Autonomous Shipping, E-Learning, Gamification, and Simulator-Based Training. These findings highlight the ongoing transformation of maritime education, driven by digital technologies, offering insights for future developments.

DOI: 10.4018/979-8-3373-6670-8.ch023

1. INTRODUCTION

Maritime education is undergoing a significant transformation in response to the rapid advancements in digital technologies. As the maritime industry becomes increasingly interconnected, educational institutions are adopting innovative technological solutions to enhance learning, improve operational processes, and better prepare students for the future workforce. Digital tools such as e-learning platforms, virtual simulators, and data analytics are revolutionizing the way maritime education is delivered, creating new opportunities for skill development and knowledge dissemination (De Água et al. 2020; Laquiores and Yarte 2016; Pruyn 2023; Renganayagalu, Mallam, and Hernes 2022). The integration of digital technologies is reshaping traditional pedagogies, enabling maritime programs to deliver more personalized, interactive, and practical training (Bačnar, Barić, and Ogrizović 2024; Lopes et al. 2025; Ramaraju, Vairavan, and Manigandan 2025; Sokolov et al. 2020).

In the digital era, maritime education is no longer confined to classroom-based learning; it now encompasses a range of online and hybrid models that offer flexibility and accessibility to students worldwide (Diksė 2024; Karahalios 2025). Technologies like augmented reality (AR) and virtual reality (VR) are being used to simulate real-world maritime environments, allowing students to gain hands-on experience without the constraints of physical space or resources (Dakeev et al. 2021; Sridevi et al. 2024). Additionally, big data and artificial intelligence (AI) are being employed to optimize course content, improve student assessments, and track performance in real-time, ensuring that education in this field remains both relevant and forward-thinking (Battineni et al. 2024; Demirel 2024; Ferguson, van den Broek, and van Oostendorp 2022; Galán Hernández, Marín Díaz, and Galdón Salvador 2024).

However, despite these technological advancements, the widespread adoption of digital tools in maritime education faces several challenges. Issues related to technological infrastructure, digital literacy, and faculty training remain prevalent in many institutions. Furthermore, the effectiveness of these technologies in enhancing educational outcomes and industry relevance has not been fully explored, particularly in the context of emerging economies (Jo and D'agostini 2020; Sharma and Gupta 2024; Yashalova and Ruban 2023). There is also a need for a comprehensive understanding of how digital tools are integrated into existing curricula, how they affect student engagement, and how they contribute to bridging the gap between academic learning and industry requirements.

This study seeks to address these gaps by providing a bibliometric mapping of research trends in the field of maritime education and digital transformation. Through an analysis of existing literature, this study aims to identify key research themes, emerging technologies, and the evolving relationship between digital tools and curriculum development in maritime education. By synthesizing the current body of research, this study will provide insights into how digital transformation is reshaping the maritime education landscape and highlight areas that require further exploration (Miao, Wang, and Xu 2023; Renganayagalu et al. 2022; Yang, Gao, and Cui 2024).

Through this bibliometric analysis, the research not only presents a clear overview of the existing literature but also proposes future research directions that can further enhance the integration of digital technologies in maritime education. These future directions include investigating the impact of digital tools on student outcomes, exploring the role of policy and institutional support in driving digital adoption, and examining cross-sector collaborations that could foster innovation in maritime education (Karahalios 2025; Kim et al. 2019; Nadiya 2020). This study is intended to serve as a resource for educators, policymakers, and industry leaders looking to harness the potential of digital technologies to shape the future of maritime education in the digital age.

The main objectives of this research are:

1. To map current and emerging research trends in the digital transformation of maritime education through bibliometric coupling analysis; and
2. To provide insights into future research directions using a co-word analysis approach, highlighting key areas for further investigation and development.

2. METHODOLOGY

2.1 Bibliometric approach

The bibliometric method is a quantitative research technique that analyzes bibliographic data in a structured way, utilizing science mapping tools to depict the underlying patterns, structures, and interconnections within a specific academic area. This approach allows researchers to discover dominant research themes, prominent scholars, and emerging trends, offering a broad perspective on the intellectual evolution of a given field. Through the application of various metrics such as citation analysis, co-citation, and co-authorship networks, bibliometrics reveals the growth of knowledge over time and helps evaluate the influence of academic contributions within the scholarly community. In the context of maritime education, this method provides valuable insights into the digital transformation and its impact on research trends in the field (Donthu et al. 2021).

2.2 Research design and data collection procedure

To gather relevant publications, we used the search string shown in Table 1, which incorporated key terms to ensure a thorough collection of articles that align with the study's main themes. This search strategy was carefully crafted to encompass a wide range of research by targeting specific keywords and their variations across bibliographic databases. Through this methodical approach, we successfully filtered and selected the publications that most effectively addressed the research goals and offered valuable insights into the subject of study.

Table 1. Search string in Scopus Indext database

No	Keywords	Justification
1	(“maritime education” OR “maritime training” OR “seafarer training” OR “nautical education” OR “nautical studies” OR “marine engineering education” OR “marine engineering training” OR “shipping education” OR “shipping training” OR “maritime safety training” OR “naval education” OR “naval training” OR “offshore training”)	To identify literature related to maritime education.
2	(“digital transformation” OR digitali* OR “e-learning” OR “online learning” OR “virtual learning” OR “technology-enhanced learning” OR “blended learning” OR “simulation-based learning” OR “virtual reality” OR “augmented reality” OR “distance learning” OR “remote learning” OR “immersive learning” OR “serious games” OR “ICT” OR “learning technology” OR “digital technology” OR “educational technology” OR “EdTech”)	To identify literature related to digital transformation.

Sources: Scopus Index Database, 2025.

3. FINDINGS AND DISCUSSION

3.1 Findings

A bibliometric analysis was conducted using Scopus, focusing on documents from 2000 to 2025, with the search performed on September 24, 2025. The dataset comprises 2,243 documents and 47,751 citations, showcasing a steady increase in publications, particularly since 2016, and a sharp rise in citations from 2021 to 2024. The analysis reveals an h-index of 94, indicating a significant number of highly-cited articles in the field. This citation overview highlights the growth trajectory of the research area, emphasizing the increasing impact and influence of publications over time, and provides valuable insights into the trends and gaps within the literature.

Figure 1. Number of publications and citations on Transforming Maritime Education in the Digital Era

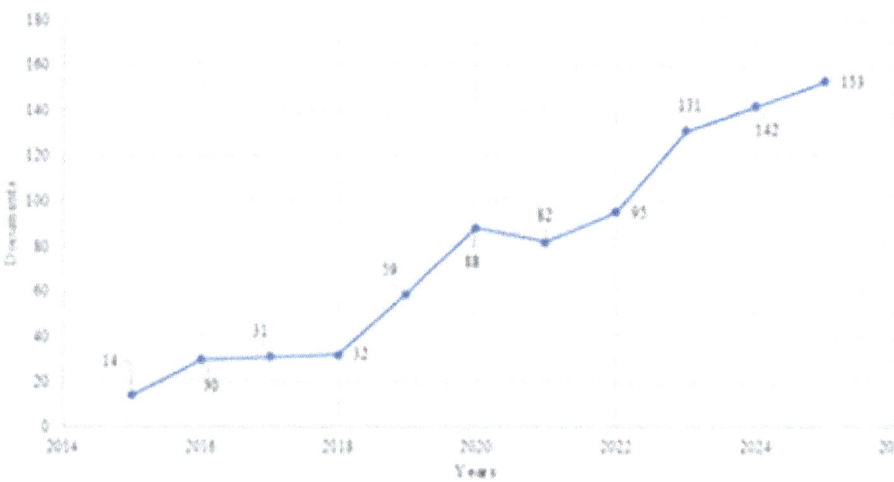

(source: Scopus Index Databased)

3.1.1 Bibliographic coupling

From a total of 857 documents, 54 met the threshold of 27 citations, forming a distinct group of influential works within the field. Among these, the top three documents based on total link strength (TLS) are Wróbel, Gil, and Montewka (2020), with 56 citations and a TLS of 27, followed by Sharma and Kim (2022), which also has 56 citations and a TLS of 23, and Sellberg (2018), with 28 citations and a TLS of 37, the highest in the dataset. These documents, marked by their strong citation counts and high TLS values, play a central role in the research network, indicating their significant impact and connectivity in shaping the academic landscape of the field.

Table 2. Top 10 documents in bibliographic coupling analysis

Rank	Publication	Citation	Total link strength
1.	Sellberg (2018)	28	37
2.	Sharma and Kim (2022)	36	28
3.	Wróbel, Gil, and Montewka (2020)	56	27
4.	Hontvedt and Øvergård (2020)	36	25
5.	Hontvedt and Øvergård (2020)	27	24
6.	Wróbel et al. (2023)	28	23
7.	Kim et al. (2022)	56	23
8.	Kim et al. (2021)	55	22
9.	Sellberg (2017)	50	22
10.	Shahbakhsh, Emad, and Cahoon (2022)	61	17

Figure 2 illustrates the network visualization of bibliographic coupling, where four distinct clusters are clearly separated from each other. The following section explores the current trends and future directions of Transforming Maritime Education in the Digital Era. The clusters are named through an inductive analysis, revisiting key articles within each cluster and synthesizing them based on shared themes and research trajectories.

Figure 2. Bibliographic coupling Transforming Maritime Education in the Digital Era

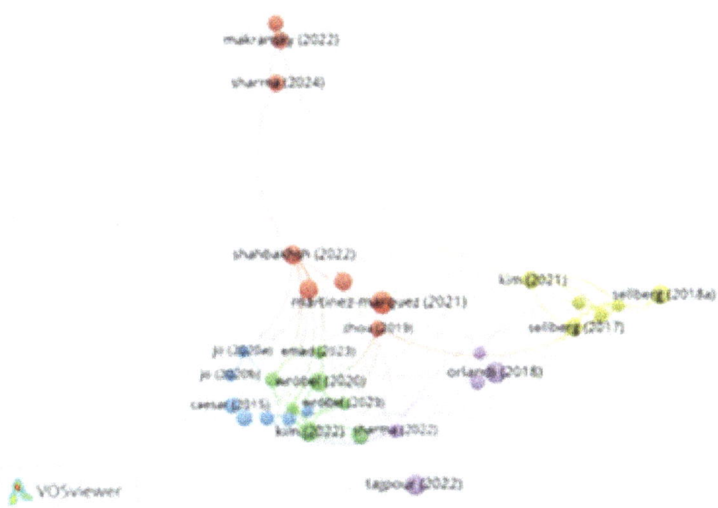

Cluster 1 (red): Maritime Simulation, VR/AR, and Technology-Enhanced Learning

This cluster explores the integration of advanced technologies such as simulation, virtual reality (VR), and augmented reality (AR) in maritime education, emphasizing how these tools enhance the learning experience. It examines the role of immersive technologies in creating realistic training environments that simulate real-world maritime operations, enabling students to acquire practical skills in a controlled, virtual setting (Dinh Thach et al. 2024; Makransky and Klingenberg 2022; Martinez-Marquez et al. 2021; Ogrizovic 2024; Shahbakhsh et al. 2022; Voloshynov et al. 2022). The adoption of these technologies not only improves the quality of maritime education but also allows for cost-effective and scalable training solutions, crucial for developing competencies without the need for extensive physical infrastructure. This cluster highlights the potential of VR/AR to transform traditional maritime training by offering interactive, hands-on experiences that improve student engagement and learning outcomes. Moreover, it addresses the challenges and opportunities of incorporating such innovative technologies into maritime curricula, aiming to align educational practices with the rapidly evolving technological landscape of the maritime industry (Alnagrat, Ismail, and Idrus 2021; Makransky and Klingenberg 2022; Sharma and Gupta 2024).

Cluster 2 (green): Maritime Education Evaluation Models and Quantitative Analysis

This cluster delves into the evaluation models used in maritime education, focusing on the application of quantitative analysis to assess the effectiveness of educational programs. It explores various metrics and methodologies for evaluating student performance, teaching strategies, and overall program success in the maritime domain (Emad and Ghosh 2023; Kim et al. 2022; Liu et al. 2020; Wróbel et al. 2020; Zhou et al. 2019). The cluster emphasizes the importance of using data-driven approaches to continuously improve educational outcomes, ensuring that maritime institutions adapt to evolving industry standards and student needs. It also highlights the role of statistical tools and models in identifying key factors that contribute to successful learning experiences, offering insights into the impact of different teaching methods and technologies on student learning in maritime education. By integrating quantitative analysis into the evaluation process, this cluster advocates for evidence-based decision-making that can guide curriculum development and pedagogical improvements in the maritime field (James et al. 2018; Simanjuntak, Rafli, and Utami 2024).

Cluster 3 (Blue): Adapting Maritime Education: Digital Literacy and Collaborative Learning

This cluster focuses on the adaptation of maritime education to the digital age, highlighting the critical role of digital literacy and collaborative learning in modernizing the curriculum. It explores how integrating digital skills into maritime training enhances students' ability to engage with technology and participate in global maritime networks (Lauronen, Sakari, and Lehtonen 2021; Liu et al. 2025; Odéen et al. 2025; Wu et al. 2024). The cluster emphasizes the importance of fostering collaborative learning environments where students can work together, leveraging digital tools to solve complex maritime problems and share knowledge. By focusing on digital literacy, this cluster advocates for the development of a workforce capable of navigating the increasing digitalization of the maritime industry, ensuring that graduates are prepared for the technological challenges ahead (Kjeldsberg et al. 2025; Sharma et al. 2024).

- Cluster 4 (Yellow): E-Learning and Online Platforms in Maritime Training

This cluster highlights the growing significance of e-learning and online platforms in maritime training, focusing on the use of digital tools to deliver flexible and accessible learning experiences. It examines how online platforms enable maritime students to engage with course content, participate in virtual simulations, and collaborate with peers and instructors, regardless of their physical location (Carballo Piñeiro and Kitada 2020; Jo and D'agostini 2020; Jo, D'agostini, and Kang 2020). The cluster discusses the benefits and challenges of integrating e-learning into maritime education, including the potential for greater accessibility to training materials and reduced logistical costs. It also explores how e-learning can support continuous professional development in the maritime industry, offering a pathway for lifelong learning and skill enhancement for maritime professionals (Karahalios 2025; Miao et al. 2023).

- Cluster 5 (Purple): Innovation in Maritime Learning: Conceptual and Organizational Approaches

This cluster explores innovative approaches to maritime education, focusing on conceptual and organizational changes required to meet the evolving needs of the industry. It examines how maritime institutions are rethinking their pedagogical strategies to incorporate new learning paradigms, such as blended learning, project-based learning, and industry partnerships (Orlandi and Brooks 2018; Tajpour et al. 2022). The cluster also addresses the organizational challenges in implementing these innovative approaches, including the need for institutional support, faculty development, and the alignment of curricula with the rapidly changing demands of the maritime sector. By integrating innovative concepts into the learning process, this cluster emphasizes the role of organizational change in fostering a more dynamic and forward-thinking maritime education system (Cao 2016; Johar 2021; Oliveira, Costa, and Torvatn 2016).

Table 3 below provides a summary of the bibliographic coupling analysis, including the cluster number and color, labels, the number of publications, and the key representative publications.

Table 3. Bibliographic coupling analysis on Transforming Maritime Education in the Digital Era

Cluster No and colour	Cluster label	Number of publications	Representative publication
1 (red)	Maritime Simulation, VR/AR, and Technology-Enhanced Learning	13	(Alnagrat et al. 2021; Makransky and Klingenberg 2022; Martinez-Marquez et al. 2021; Shahbakhsh et al. 2022; Sharma and Gupta 2024)
2 (green)	Maritime Education Evaluation Models and Quantitative Analysis	8	(Emad and Ghosh 2023; Kim et al. 2022; Liu et al. 2020; Wróbel et al. 2020; Zhou et al. 2019)
3 (blue)	Adapting Maritime Education: Digital Literacy and Collaborative Learning	7	(Kim et al. 2021; Renganayagalu et al. 2019; Sellberg 2017, 2018)
4 (yellow)	E-Learning and Online Platforms in Maritime Training	6	(Jo and D'agostini 2020)(Jo et al. 2020)(Carballo Piñeiro and Kitada 2020)
5 (Purple)	Innovation in Maritime Learning: Conceptual and Organizational Approaches	5	(Orlandi and Brooks 2018)(Tajpour et al. 2022)

3.1.2 Co-word analysis

Applying the same dataset, the co-word analysis identified 5,290 keywords, of which 141 met the minimum occurrence threshold of 8, resulting in the formation of several key themes. This analysis grouped keywords based on their frequency and co-occurrence patterns, shedding light on the prominent research trends and thematic focus within maritime education. The top keywords, including maritime education, e-learning, ships, and personnel training, reflect the critical areas of investigation in the field, revealing the growing emphasis on integrating digital tools and innovative training methodologies into maritime curricula. This clustering provides valuable insights into the ongoing evolution of maritime education, offering a deeper understanding of how these terms and concepts are interlinked in shaping the future of maritime training and learning environments.

Table 4. Top 15 keywords in the co-occurrence of keywords analysis

Rank	Keyword	Occurrences	Total link strength
1.	Maritime education	121	688
2.	E-learning	108	582
3.	Ships	98	555
4.	Personnel training	79	541
5.	Students	89	531
6.	Virtual reality	104	484
7.	Maritime training	55	415
8.	Teaching	58	370
9.	Education and training	47	366
10.	Engineering education	58	363
11.	Marine education	42	314
12.	Maritime education and training	58	312
13.	Education	55	295
14.	Simulators	34	237
15.	Curricula	41	231

Figure 3 displays the network structure derived from the co-word analysis, showcasing three separate clusters, each representing distinct thematic areas. Through the author's interpretive approach, each cluster is labeled according to the primary concepts and patterns observed in the data. The graphical representation of these clusters offers a comprehensive view of the relationships between the keywords, enhancing the understanding of the underlying thematic organization within the research domain.

Figure 3. Co-word analysis on Technology Adoption in Digital Startups

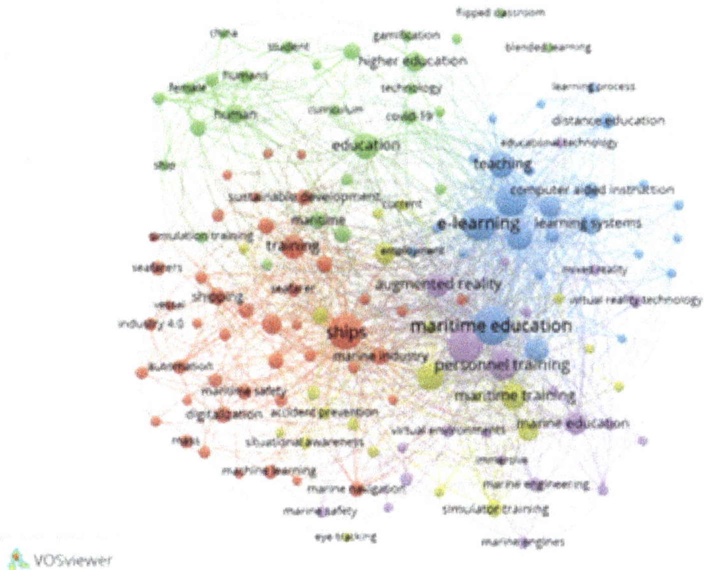

Cluster 1 (red), labeled Autonomous Shipping & Digital Transformation, includes 42 keywords that illustrate the growing integration of autonomous technologies in maritime transport. This cluster highlights key advancements in artificial intelligence, automation, and machine learning, all of which are transforming the maritime industry by enhancing safety and operational efficiency (Li et al. 2024; Shahbakhsh et al. 2022). The inclusion of terms such as autonomous ships, cyber security, and industry 4.0 underlines the crucial role of digital technologies in enabling the next generation of shipping solutions, ensuring safer and more efficient maritime operations (Belabyad et al. 2025; Zhang and Yu 2025). The keyword "maritime safety" reflects the importance of technology in improving risk management and preventing accidents at sea (Karahalios 2025; Rooks, Progoulaki, and Szwed 2020). Together, these keywords emphasize the ongoing digital transformation in the maritime sector, which is leading to the development of more autonomous, sustainable, and efficient shipping practices.

Cluster 2 (green), labeled E-Learning & Educational Systems, is composed of 30 keywords focusing on the role of e-learning and digital education systems in maritime training. This cluster captures the shift towards more flexible and accessible learning models, with keywords like active learning, e-learning, and distance education emphasizing the increasing use of digital platforms to deliver maritime education (Galić, Lušić, and Stanivuk 2020; Kitada et al. 2017; Roy 2015; Sjöberg et al. 2025). Marine education and engineering education suggest a focus on specialized training for future maritime professionals, with an emphasis on integrating technology to improve the learning process (Bharatan, Swan, and Oborn 2022; Raicu and Raicu 2015). The terms knowledge management and information systems indicate a growing interest in the use of digital tools to manage and disseminate knowledge effectively, ensuring that maritime training programs stay up-to-date with technological advancements (Roy 2015). This cluster underscores the significance of e-learning and digital systems in enhancing the reach and effectiveness of maritime education and training

Cluster 3 (blue), labeled Gamification & Higher Education, includes 27 keywords that explore the application of gamification and innovative teaching methods in higher education, particularly within the maritime context. Keywords such as blended learning, flipped classroom, and gamification highlight the integration of interactive and student-centered teaching approaches that aim to engage students and improve learning outcomes (Freeman 2015; Nikitakos et al. 2017). The inclusion of serious games and motivation suggests a focus on leveraging game-based learning to increase student participation and interest in maritime training (De Água et al. 2020; Renganayagalu et al. 2022). The impact of COVID-19 on education is also reflected in this cluster, which demonstrates the rapid shift to online and hybrid learning environments during the pandemic (Renganayagalu et al. 2022). Overall, this cluster emphasizes the role of gamified learning experiences in fostering motivation, engagement, and deeper learning within maritime education.

Cluster 4 (yellow), labeled Simulator-Based Training & Human Factors, consists of 22 keywords related to the use of simulators in maritime training and the consideration of human factors in this process. Keywords such as eye tracking, simulation-based training, and maritime simulators reflect the growing reliance on advanced simulation technologies to replicate real-world maritime scenarios and provide students with hands-on experience (Hjellvik and Mallam 2024; Silva et al. 2025). Human engineering and situation awareness emphasize the importance of understanding human behavior and decision-making in maritime contexts, particularly in high-stress environments like navigation (Sellberg and Sharma 2025). The inclusion of debriefing and assessment indicates a focus on post-simulation analysis, allowing for critical reflection and feedback to improve performance and decision-making in real-world maritime operations (Mraković et al. 2025). This cluster underscores the importance of simulation technologies in developing critical skills and human factors awareness for maritime professionals.

Cluster 5 (purple), labeled Immersive Technologies in Maritime Training, comprises 20 keywords that highlight the integration of immersive technologies, such as virtual reality (VR) and augmented reality (AR), into maritime training. Keywords such as virtual reality, augmented reality, and immersive technologies point to the use of these cutting-edge tools to create realistic and interactive learning environments (Berki and Sudár 2024; Dakeev et al. 2021; Konon, Pipchenko, and Kazak 2023). The term experiential learning reflects the growing emphasis on hands-on, immersive training methods that allow students to experience maritime operations in a virtual setting, enhancing their understanding and skills without the need for physical resources (Bueta and David 2018). Safety training and ship simulators suggest a focus on using these technologies to improve safety protocols and operational efficiency, ensuring that maritime professionals are better prepared for real-world challenges (Simanjuntak et al. 2025). This cluster underscores the potential of immersive technologies to revolutionize maritime training by providing students with engaging, realistic, and impactful learning experiences.

A summary of the co-word analysis is presented in table 5, comprising cluster number and color, cluster labels, number of keywords, and representative keywords.

Table 5. Summary of co-word analysis on Technology Adoption in Digital Startups

Cluster No and color	Cluster label	Number of keywords	Representative Keywords
1 (red)	Autonomous Shipping & Digital Transformation	42	artificial intelligence, automation, autonomous ships, cyber security, industry 4.0, machine learning, maritime safety, maritime transport
2 (green)	E-Learning & Educational Systems	30	active learning, e-learning, distance education, engineering education, knowledge management, information systems, learning process, marine education
3 (blue)	Gamification & Higher Education	27	blended learning, flipped classroom, gamification, higher education, serious games, motivation, curriculum, COVID-19
4 (yellow)	Simulator-Based Training & Human Factors	22	eye tracking, simulation-based training, human engineering, maritime simulators, debriefing, situation awareness, navigation, assessment
5 (Purple)	Immersive Technologies in Maritime Training	20	virtual reality, augmented reality, immersive technologies, experiential learning, mixed reality, ship simulators, safety training, marine engineering

3.3 Discussion

The results of this study provide a comprehensive view of the current state of maritime education in the digital age, reflecting a significant transformation in response to the integration of digital technologies. The bibliometric analysis revealed five prominent clusters: Maritime Simulation, VR/AR, and Technology-Enhanced Learning, Maritime Education Evaluation Models and Quantitative Analysis, Adapting Maritime Education: Digital Literacy and Collaborative Learning, E-Learning and Online Platforms in Maritime Training, and Innovation in Maritime Learning: Conceptual and Organizational Approaches. These clusters not only reflect the diverse areas of research within maritime education but also emphasize the ongoing efforts to adapt and innovate through digitalization.

When comparing these findings with previous research, there is a clear alignment with studies emphasizing the importance of technology in modernizing education. For instance, the integration of virtual reality (VR) and augmented reality (AR) in maritime training is consistent with previous studies by Berki and Sudár (2024) and Dakeev et al. (2021), who highlighted the potential of these immersive technologies to enhance practical training experiences and improve learning outcomes. These studies, along with our findings, underscore the growing role of simulation-based learning in maritime education, offering students a risk-free environment to gain hands-on experience.

In contrast, previous literature on digital transformation in maritime education, such as that from Sharma and Kim (2022), emphasized the challenges of integrating new technologies into traditional curricula, particularly in emerging economies. These findings echo the results of this study, which highlights ongoing issues such as infrastructure limitations, digital literacy, and the need for faculty training. Furthermore, this study adds to the discourse by suggesting the need for a more structured evaluation of digital tools' impact on learning outcomes, an area that has not been extensively addressed in past research.

Moreover, the cluster on E-Learning and Online Platforms in Maritime Training aligns with the growing trend of digital platforms facilitating global access to maritime education, as discussed by Shahbakhsh et al. (2022). The use of these platforms for continuous professional development and lifelong learning is a critical step in adapting to the digital era (Muna and Judiarni 2021; Puteh et al. 2024; Zhou et al. 2024). While this trend has been noted in prior studies, this research emphasizes the importance of addressing the logistical challenges and enhancing the accessibility of digital training materials to support diverse learner populations.

The study also highlights the need for organizational change within maritime education institutions, as reflected in the cluster on Innovation in Maritime Learning: Conceptual and Organizational Approaches. This finding supports previous research by Koh et al. (2023) and Zhou et al. (2024), which suggested that the adoption of innovative pedagogical strategies, including blended and project-based learning, is essential for aligning curricula with industry demands. However, the gap between innovation and institutional readiness remains a critical issue. Organizational and structural challenges in adopting new teaching methods are often underestimated, an aspect that requires further attention from both policymakers and educators.

While much of the prior research has focused on technological advancements and the integration of digital tools into educational frameworks, this study expands the scope by integrating the analysis of key trends such as digital literacy and collaborative learning. This aligns with Kim et al. (2021) emphasis on the importance of fostering digital competencies among maritime students, ensuring they are equipped to navigate the increasingly digitalized maritime industry.

4. CONCLUSION

The study on transforming maritime education in the digital era offers valuable insights into the evolving trends and challenges faced by maritime educational institutions as they integrate digital technologies. Through bibliometric mapping, the research identified several key themes, including the integration of immersive technologies like VR and AR, the evaluation of educational effectiveness through quantitative analysis, and the role of digital literacy and collaborative learning in modernizing maritime curricula. The findings reveal five major research clusters: maritime simulation and technology-enhanced learning, educational evaluation models, digital literacy and collaborative learning, e-learning and online platforms, and organizational innovation in maritime learning. These results underscore the importance of further exploration into the impact of digital transformation on student outcomes, as well as the role of institutional support in driving technology adoption. Additionally, the study emphasizes the need to address the challenges of digital infrastructure, faculty training, and the alignment of maritime education with industry demands. The research contributes to the growing body of knowledge on maritime education and provides critical insights for educators, policymakers, and industry leaders looking to enhance the quality, accessibility, and relevance of maritime training in the digital age.

5. REFERENCES

Alnagrat, A. J. A., Ismail, R. C., & Idrus, S. Z. S. 2021. 'Extended Reality (XR) in Virtual Laboratories: A Review of Challenges and Future Training Directions'. in *Journal of Physics: Conference Series*. Vol. 1874, edited by A.-S. S.Z.S.I., M. W.A.W., and J. J. Faculty of Applied and Human Sciences, Universiti Malaysia Perlis (UniMAP), Perlis, Malaysia: IOP Publishing Ltd. DOI: 10.1088/1742-6596/1874/1/012031

Bačnar, D., Barić, D., & Ogrizović, D. (2024). 'Exploring the Perceived Ease of Use of an Immersive VR Engine Room Simulator among Maritime Students: A Segmentation Approach'. *Applied Sciences (Basel, Switzerland), 14*(18), 8208. Advance online publication. DOI: 10.3390/app14188208

Battineni, G., Chintalapudi, N., Ricci, G., Ruocco, C., & Amenta, F. (2024). 'Exploring the Integration of Artificial Intelligence (AI) and Augmented Reality (AR) in Maritime Medicine'. *Artificial Intelligence Review, 57*(4), 100. Advance online publication. DOI: 10.1007/s10462-024-10735-0

Belabyad, M., Kontovas, C., Pyne, R., & Chang, C. H. (2025). 'Skills and Competencies for Operating Maritime Autonomous Surface Ships (MASS): A Systematic Review and Bibliometric Analysis'. *Maritime Policy & Management*. Advance online publication. DOI: 10.1080/03088839.2025.2475177

Berki, B., & Sudár, A. 2024. 'Virtual and Augmented Reality in Education Based on CogInfoCom and CVR Conference Insights'. Pp. 115–20 in *2024 IEEE 15th International Conference on Cognitive Infocommunications, CogInfoCom 2024*. Corvinus Institute for Advanced Studies, Institute of Data Analytics and Information Systems, Corvinus University of Budapest, Budapest, Hungary: Institute of Electrical and Electronics Engineers Inc. DOI: 10.1109/CogInfoCom63007.2024.10894726

Bharatan, I., Swan, J., & Oborn, E. (2022). 'Navigating Turbulent Waters: Crafting Learning Trajectories in a Changing Work Context'. *Human Relations, 75*(6), 1084–1112. DOI: 10.1177/00187267211010366

Bueta, R. D., & David, L. C. G. 2018. 'Context and Input Evaluations of Physical Fitness Training Programs in Maritime Schools'. Pp. 950–54 in *Proceedings of 2018 IEEE International Conference on Teaching, Assessment, and Learning for Engineering, TALE 2018*, edited by L. M.J.W., N. S., R. M., S. J., L. L.C.U., W. G.K.W., and V. N. College of Marine Engineering, Maritime Academy of Asia and the Pacific, Mariveles, Bataan, Philippines: Institute of Electrical and Electronics Engineers Inc. DOI: 10.1109/TALE.2018.8615140

Cao, F. H. (2016). 'A Ship Driving Teaching System Based on Multi-Level Virtual Reality Technology'. *International Journal of Emerging Technologies in Learning, 11*(11), 26–31. DOI: 10.3991/ijet.v11i11.6249

Carballo Piñeiro, L., & Kitada, M. (2020). 'Sexual Harassment and Women Seafarers: The Role of Laws and Policies to Ensure Occupational Safety & Health'. *Marine Policy, 117*, 103938. Advance online publication. DOI: 10.1016/j.marpol.2020.103938

Dakeev, U., Pecen, R. R., Yildiz, F., & Luong, Y. 2021. 'Augmented Reality Computer-Aided Design Education (ARCADE) Tool to Improve Student Motivation, Engagement, and Spatial Cognition'. in *ASEE Annual Conference and Exposition, Conference Proceedings*. Sam Houston State University, United States: American Society for Engineering Education. DOI: 10.18260/1-2--36730

De Água, P. M. G. B., da Silva Frias, A. D., de Jesus Carrasqueira, M., & Daniel, J. M. M. (2020). 'Future of Maritime Education and Training: Blending Hard and Soft Skills'. *Pomorstvo*, *34*(2), 345–353. DOI: 10.31217/p.34.2.15

Demirel, E. 2024. 'The Use of Artificial Intelligence Applications in Maritime Education and Training'. Pp. 186–95 in *Proceedings of the International Association of Maritime Universities Conference*. Piri Reis University, Turkey: International Association of Maritime Universities.

Diksė, I. 2024. 'Digital Competences on Board. Perspectives in Educating Future Seafarers''. Pp. 531–35 in *Transport Means - Proceedings of the International Conference*. Vols 2024-Octob. Lithuanian Maritime Academy, I. Kanto str. 7, Klaipeda, 92123, Lithuania: Kauno Technologijos Universitetas. DOI: 10.5755/e01.2351-7034.2024.P531-535

Dinh Thach, N., Hung, N. V., Tuan, D. A., Khanh, D. H., & Tam, L. V. (2024). 'Research and Design of Fire Alarm Systems Using Virtual Reality Technology Enhance Safety Training in the Maritime'. *Journal for Maritime Research*, *21*(1), 193–200.

Donthu, N., Kumar, S., Mukherjee, D., Pandey, N., & Lim, W. M. (2021). 'How to Conduct a Bibliometric Analysis: An Overview and Guidelines'. *Journal of Business Research*, *133*(April), 285–296. DOI: 10.1016/j.jbusres.2021.04.070

Emad, G. R., & Ghosh, S. (2023). 'Identifying Essential Skills and Competencies towards Building a Training Framework for Future Operators of Autonomous Ships: A Qualitative Study'. *WMU Journal of Maritime Affairs*, *22*(4), 427–445. DOI: 10.1007/s13437-023-00310-9

Ferguson, C., van den Broek, E. L., & van Oostendorp, H. (2022). 'AI-Induced Guidance: Preserving the Optimal Zone of Proximal Development'. *Computers and Education: Artificial Intelligence*, *3*, 100089. Advance online publication. DOI: 10.1016/j.caeai.2022.100089

Freeman, M. B. 2015. 'Refining Learning Outcomes in Multicultural ICT Classrooms: The Development of a Structured Framework'. in *AIS SIGED: IAIM International Conference*. School of Computing and Information Technology, University of Wollongong, Faculty of Engineering and Information Sciences, Australia: Association for Information Systems.

Galán Hernández, J. J., Marín Díaz, G., & Galdón Salvador, J. L. 2024. 'Artificial Intelligence Applied to Human Resources Management: A Bibliometric Analysis'. Pp. 269–77 in *Lecture Notes in Networks and Systems*. Vol. 932 LNNS, edited by R. A., D. J.H., F. C., and R. M.D. Faculty of Statistics, Universidad Complutense, Puerta de Hierro, Madrid, 28040, Spain: Springer Science and Business Media Deutschland GmbH. DOI: 10.1007/978-3-031-54235-0_25

Galić, S., Lušić, Z., & Stanivuk, T. (2020). 'E-Learning in Maritime Affairs'. *Journal of Naval Architecture and Marine Engineering*, *17*(1), 39–50. DOI: 10.3329/jname.v17i1.42203

Hjellvik, S., & Mallam, S. (2024). 'Training Transfer Validity of Virtual Reality Simulator Assessment'. *Virtual Reality (Waltham Cross)*, *28*(4), 165. Advance online publication. DOI: 10.1007/s10055-024-01058-0

Hontvedt, M., & Øvergård, K. I. (2020). 'Simulations at Work—A Framework for Configuring Simulation Fidelity with Training Objectives'. *Computer Supported Cooperative Work, 29*(1–2), 85–113. DOI: 10.1007/s10606-019-09367-8

James, A. J., Schriever, U. G., Jahangiri, S., & Girgin, S. C. (2018). 'Improving Maritime English Competence as the Cornerstone of Safety at Sea: A Focus on Teaching Practices to Improve Maritime Communication'. *WMU Journal of Maritime Affairs, 17*(2), 293–310. DOI: 10.1007/s13437-018-0145-4

Jo, S., & D'agostini, E. (2020). 'Disrupting Technologies in the Shipping Industry: How Will MASS Development Affect the Maritime Workforce in Korea'. *Marine Policy, 120*, 104139. Advance online publication. DOI: 10.1016/j.marpol.2020.104139

Jo, S., D'agostini, E., & Kang, J. (2020). 'From Seafarers to E-Farers: Maritime Cadets' Perceptions towards Seafaring Jobs in the Industry 4.0'. *Sustainability (Basel), 12*(19), 1–18. DOI: 10.3390/su12198077

Johar, R. (2021). 'Examining Students' Intention to Use Augmented Reality in a Project-Based Geometry Learning Environment'. *International Journal of Instruction, 14*(2), 773–790. DOI: 10.29333/iji.2021.14243a

Karahalios, H. (2025). 'Enhancing Maritime Education for Digital Sustainability'. *International Journal of Innovation Science, 17*(4), 901–913. Advance online publication. DOI: 10.1108/IJIS-06-2024-0156

Kim, T. E., Perera, L. P., Sollid, M. P., Batalden, B. M., & Sydnes, A. K. (2022). 'Safety Challenges Related to Autonomous Ships in Mixed Navigational Environments'. *WMU Journal of Maritime Affairs, 21*(2), 141–159. DOI: 10.1007/s13437-022-00277-z

Kim, T. E., Sharma, A., Bustgaard, M., Gyldensten, W. C., Nymoen, O. K., Tusher, H. M., & Nazir, S. (2021). 'The Continuum of Simulator-Based Maritime Training and Education'. *WMU Journal of Maritime Affairs, 20*(2), 135–150. DOI: 10.1007/s13437-021-00242-2

Kim, T. E., Sharma, A., Gausdal, A. H., & Chae, C. J. (2019). 'Impact of Automation Technology on Gender Parity in Maritime Industry'. *WMU Journal of Maritime Affairs, 18*(4), 579–593. DOI: 10.1007/s13437-019-00176-w

Kitada, M., Bolmsten, J., Zeya, K., Hieu Pham, T., & Aung, M. S. 2017. 'Learning Theories Meet Virtual Classroom Technologies: Understanding New Educational Opportunities in Maritime Education and Training'. Pp. 72–81 in *18th Annual General Assembly of the International Association of Maritime Universities - Global Perspectives in MET: Towards Sustainable, Green and Integrated Maritime Transport, IAMU 2017*. Vol. 1. World Maritime University, Fiskehamnsgatan 1, Malmö, 20124, Sweden: Nikola Vaptsarov Naval Academy.

Kjeldsberg, F., Munim, Z. H., Bustgaard, M., Bhagat, S., Lindroos, E., & Haavardtun, P. 2025. 'Sensitivity of Predictive Performance Assessment Accuracy in Varying K-Fold Cross Validation'. Pp. 71–82 in *Lecture Notes in Networks and Systems*. Vol. 1274 LNNS, edited by K. T.E., M. M., and R. I. Faculty of Technology, Natural and Maritime Sciences, University of South-Eastern Norway, Horten, Norway: Springer Science and Business Media Deutschland GmbH. DOI: 10.1007/978-3-031-84170-5_7

Koh, L. Y., Li, K., Chia, Y. Y., & Yuen, K. F. (2023). 'Quality Design for Maritime Studies Programme in the Digital Era'. *Maritime Policy & Management, 50*(3), 301–320. DOI: 10.1080/03088839.2021.1983220

Konon, N., Pipchenko, O., & Kazak, Yu. 2023. 'Virtual Reality Application and Usability in the Context of Maritime Education and Training: Assessment and Perspectives'. Pp. 680–84 in *Transport Means - Proceedings of the International Conference*. Vols 2023-Octob. National University "Odessa Maritime Academy", Didrikhson str. 8, Odesa, 65052, Ukraine: Kauno Technologijos Universitetas.

Laquiores, R. L., & Yarte, M. M. 2016. 'Communicating at Sea: Flexible Learning for Maritime Education'. Pp. 146–50 in *Proceedings of the 6th International Conference on Information Communication and Management, ICICM 2016*. Technological Institute of the Philippines, Quezon City, Philippines: Institute of Electrical and Electronics Engineers Inc. DOI: 10.1109/INFOCOMAN.2016.7784232

Lauronen, J., Sakari, L., & Lehtonen, T. 2021. 'How Simulation Training Can Benefit from Virtual Reality Extensions? Case: A Virtual Reality Extension to a Simulated Ship Bridge for Emergency Steering Training'. Pp. 149–56 in *Lecture Notes in Networks and Systems*. Vol. 275, edited by A. T.Z. and F. C.S. Novia University of Applied Sciences, Turku, Finland: Springer Science and Business Media Deutschland GmbH. DOI: 10.1007/978-3-030-80091-8_18

Li, J., Dong, W., Yan, X., Shi, L., & Lv, C. (2024). 'A Study on Digital Literacy and Influencing Factors among Chinese Seafarers'. *Scientific Reports*, *14*(1), 29574. Advance online publication. DOI: 10.1038/s41598-024-81069-8 PMID: 39609499

Liu, L., Khan, R. U., Afzaal, M., & Asad, M. (2025). 'A Corpus-Based Quantitative Risk Assessment of Language Barriers in Maritime Safety'. *Maritime Policy & Management*. Advance online publication. DOI: 10.1080/03088839.2025.2507218

Liu, Y., Lan, Z., Cui, J., Krishnan, G., Sourina, O., Konovessis, D., Ang, H. E., & Mueller-Wittig, W. (2020). 'Psychophysiological Evaluation of Seafarers to Improve Training in Maritime Virtual Simulator'. *Advanced Engineering Informatics*, *44*, 101048. Advance online publication. DOI: 10.1016/j.aei.2020.101048

Lopes, L. S., Nabais, J. L., Pinto, C., Caldeirinha, V., & Pinho, T. (2025). 'Essential Competencies in Maritime and Port Logistics: A Study on the Current Needs of the Sector †'. *Sustainability (Basel)*, *17*(6), 2378. Advance online publication. DOI: 10.3390/su17062378

Makransky, G., & Klingenberg, S. (2022). 'Virtual Reality Enhances Safety Training in the Maritime Industry: An Organizational Training Experiment with a Non-WEIRD Sample'. *Journal of Computer Assisted Learning*, *38*(4), 1127–1140. DOI: 10.1111/jcal.12670

Martinez-Marquez, D., Pingali, S., Panuwatwanich, K., Stewart, R. A., & Mohamed, S. (2021). 'Application of Eye Tracking Technology in Aviation, Maritime, and Construction Industries: A Systematic Review'. *Sensors (Basel)*, *21*(13), 4289. Advance online publication. DOI: 10.3390/s21134289 PMID: 34201734

Miao, C., Wang, L., & Xu, X. (2023). 'Enhancing Maritime Professional Training: Integrating Digital Health Perspectives for Improved Outcomes'. *Journal of Commercial Biotechnology*, *28*(4), 215–225. DOI: 10.5912/jcb1613

Mraković, I., Stanovčić, I., Petrović, I., Kapetanović, V., & Pudar, D. (2025). 'Pilot Research of AI-Generated Scenarios in Nautical Simulator Training Using ChatGPT Plus'. *TransNav*, *19*(1), 309–315. DOI: 10.12716/1001.19.01.36

Muna, N., & Judiarni, J. A. (2021). 'Digital Leadership in Facing Challenges in the Era Industrial Revolution 4.0'. *Webology*, *18*(Special Issue), 975–990. DOI: 10.14704/WEB/V18SI05/WEB18275

Nadiya, D. 2020. 'Innovative Approaches and Techniques in Maritime English Study Pack Development'. Pp. 95–100 in *Proceedings of 14th Annual General Assembly and Conference of the International Association of Maritime Universities, IAMU AGA 2013*. Kyiv State Maritime Academy, Ukraine: Muntenia Publishing.

Nikitakos, N., Sirris, I., Dalaklis, D., Papachristos, D., & Tsoukalas, V. D. (2017). 'Game-Based Learning for Maritime Education and Training: The Case of Trader of the World'. *WMU Journal of Maritime Affairs*, *16*(2), 265–291. DOI: 10.1007/s13437-016-0119-3

Odéen, M., Sellberg, C., Praetorius, G., Lindwall, O., Englund, L., & Andersson, A. 2025. 'Intelligent Learning Systems for Simulator-Based Professional Training: A Systematic Literature Review'. Pp. 109–19 in *Lecture Notes in Networks and Systems*. Vol. 1274 LNNS, edited by K. T.E., M. M., and R. I. The Swedish National Road and Transport Research Institute (VTI), Regnbågsgatan 1, Gothenburg, 417 55, Sweden: Springer Science and Business Media Deutschland GmbH. DOI: 10.1007/978-3-031-84170-5_10

Ogrizovic, D. 2024. 'Computer Simulation of a Marine Engine Room Using Fully Immersive and Interactive Virtual Reality'. in *International Conference on Artificial Intelligence, Computer, Data Sciences, and Applications, ACDSA 2024*. University of Rijeka, Faculty of Maritime Studies, Rijeka, Croatia: Institute of Electrical and Electronics Engineers Inc. DOI: 10.1109/ACDSA59508.2024.10467297

Oliveira, M., Costa, J., & Torvatn, H. 2016. 'Tomorrow's on-Board Learning System (TOOLS)'. Pp. 528–38 in *Lecture Notes in Computer Science (including subseries Lecture Notes in Artificial Intelligence and Lecture Notes in Bioinformatics)*. Vol. 9753, edited by Z. P. and I. A. Sintef, Technology and Society, S.P. Andersensv. 5, Trondheim, 7465, Norway: Springer Verlag. DOI: 10.1007/978-3-319-39483-1_48

Orlandi, L., & Brooks, B. (2018). 'Measuring Mental Workload and Physiological Reactions in Marine Pilots: Building Bridges towards Redlines of Performance'. *Applied Ergonomics*, *69*, 74–92. DOI: 10.1016/j.apergo.2018.01.005 PMID: 29477333

Pruyn, J. 2023. 'BSc Maritime Technology Curriculum Revision: What Will the Future Naval Architect Look Like?' in *ASEE Annual Conference and Exposition, Conference Proceedings*. Delft University of Technology, Netherlands: American Society for Engineering Education. DOI: 10.18260/1-2--43268

Puteh, A., Dharma, Y., Selian, R. S., & Mahera, U. (2024). 'The Mediation and Moderation Roles in the Influence of Digital Competence and Religious Values on the Sustainability of Sharia Economic Businesses'. *Journal of Ecohumanism*, *3*(7), 5283–5300. DOI: 10.62754/joe.v3i7.4638

Raicu, A., & Raicu, G. 2015. 'Innovation in Engineering Education through Computer Assisted Learning and Virtual University Model'. in *IOP Conference Series: Materials Science and Engineering*. Vol. 95, edited by C. V., O. E., P. M., C. C., T. P., C. R., and N. D. Constanta Maritime University, Faculty of Naval Electro-Mechanics, 104 Mircea cel Batran Street, Constanta, 900663, Romania: Institute of Physics Publishing. DOI: 10.1088/1757-899X/95/1/012126

Ramaraju, S., Vairavan, C., & Manigandan, K. (2025). 'Digital Dystopia: The Challenges and Opportunities for the Budding Mariners in the Present Scenario'. *Journal for Maritime Research, 22*(1), 192–196.

Renganayagalu, S. K., Mallam, S. C., & Hernes, M. (2022). 'Maritime Education and Training in the COVID-19 Era and Beyond'. *TransNav, 16*(1), 59–69. DOI: 10.12716/1001.16.01.06

Renganayagalu, S. K., Mallam, S. C., Nazir, S., Ernstsen, J., & Haavardtun, P. (2019). 'Impact of Simulation Fidelity on Student Self-Efficacy and Perceived Skill Development in Maritime Training'. *TransNav, 13*(3), 663–669. DOI: 10.12716/1001.13.03.25

Rooks, M., Progoulaki, M., & Szwed, P. 2020. 'Delivering and Assessing a Cross-cultural Module for Seafarers and Maritime University Students'. Pp. 317–22 in *Proceedings - 16th Annual General Assembly and Conference of the International Association of Maritime Universities, IAMU AGA 2015*. Graduate School of Maritime Sciences, Kobe University, Japan: University of Rijeka.

Roy, S. S. K. 2015. 'Skill Development in the Maritime Sector through E-Learning'. Pp. 27–35 in *RINA, Royal Institution of Naval Architects - Education and Professional Development of Engineers in the Maritime Industry 2015, Papers*. Aries International Maritime Research Institute, Sharjah, United Arab Emirates: Royal Institution of Naval Architects.

Sellberg, C. (2017). 'Simulators in Bridge Operations Training and Assessment: A Systematic Review and Qualitative Synthesis'. *WMU Journal of Maritime Affairs, 16*(2), 247–263. DOI: 10.1007/s13437-016-0114-8

Sellberg, C. (2018). 'From Briefing, through Scenario, to Debriefing: The Maritime Instructor's Work during Simulator-Based Training'. *Cognition Technology and Work, 20*(1), 49–62. DOI: 10.1007/s10111-017-0446-y

Sellberg, C., & Sharma, A. (2025). 'Toward Multimodal Learning Analytics in Simulation-Based Collaborative Learning: A Design Ethnography of Maritime Training'. *International Journal of Computer-Supported Collaborative Learning, 20*(2), 201–221. DOI: 10.1007/s11412-024-09435-2

Shahbakhsh, M., Emad, G. R., & Cahoon, S. (2022). 'Industrial Revolutions and Transition of the Maritime Industry: The Case of Seafarer's Role in Autonomous Shipping'. *Asian Journal of Shipping and Logistics, 38*(1), 10–18. DOI: 10.1016/j.ajsl.2021.11.004

Sharma, A., Harrington, S., Sellberg, C., Ihlström, J., & Praetorius, G. 2024. 'Turning the Gaze Inwards: Exploring Simulator Instructors' Professional Vision Through Eye-Tracking and Stimulated Recall Interviews'. Pp. 231–42 in *Lecture Notes in Networks and Systems*. Vol. 1171 LNNS, edited by H. C., P. S., S. C., M. M., O. N., V. P., G. R., D. M. T., T. M., and D. la P. F. Department of Psychosocial Sciences, University of Bergen, Bergen, Norway: Springer Science and Business Media Deutschland GmbH.

Sharma, A., & Kim, T. E. (2022). 'Exploring Technical and Non-Technical Competencies of Navigators for Autonomous Shipping'. *Maritime Policy & Management, 49*(6), 831–849. DOI: 10.1080/03088839.2021.1914874

Sharma, R., & Gupta, H. (2024). 'Harmonizing Sustainability in Industry 5.0 Era: Transformative Strategies for Cleaner Production and Sustainable Competitive Advantage'. *Journal of Cleaner Production, 445*, 141118. Advance online publication. DOI: 10.1016/j.jclepro.2024.141118

Silva, J., Cardoso, J. C. S., Pereira, L. L., & Roque, L. 2025. 'A Virtual Reality Simulator for Enhancing Marine Pollution Control Efforts'. Pp. 121–34 in *Lecture Notes in Computer Science (including subseries Lecture Notes in Artificial Intelligence and Lecture Notes in Bioinformatics)*. Vol. 15192 LNCS, edited by F. P., D. I. A., G. del R. D., C. R. L., and G. C. E.W. University of Coimbra, DEI, Coimbra, 3030-290, Portugal: Springer Science and Business Media Deutschland GmbH. DOI: 10.1007/978-3-031-74353-5_9

Simanjuntak, M. B., Rafli, Z., & Utami, S. R. 2024. 'Enhancing Maritime Education for Ocean Sustainability: A Multidisciplinary Approach'. in *BIO Web of Conferences*. Vol. 106, edited by M. H.M., Z. N.P., G. J.L., A. A.S., M. C. O., and O. T. Doctoral Program, State University of Jakarta, Jakarta, 13950, Indonesia: EDP Sciences. DOI: 10.1051/bioconf/202410602006

Simanjuntak, M. B., Simanjuntak, M., Selasdini, V., Hutagaol, M. N., Malau, A. G., Herawati, S., Simanjuntak, P. D., Purba, D., & Sihombing, D. W. (2025). 'Enriching Maritime Vocational Education with Physical-Sports Activities'. *Retos*, *64*, 338–347. DOI: 10.47197/retos.v64.109713

Sjöberg, C., Jildenstål, P., Ringdal, M., Amorøe, T. N., Sjöstedt, V., & Cederwall, C. J. (2025). 'Simulation-Based Learning in Postgraduate Critical Care and Anaesthesia Nursing: An Interview Study from Postgraduate Nurses' Perspectives'. *BMC Nursing*, *24*(1), 816. Advance online publication. DOI: 10.1186/s12912-025-03336-x PMID: 40598121

Sokolov, S. S., Saveleva, M. N., Mitrofanova, A. V., Kolesnichenko, S. V., & Logunov, N. S. 2020. 'Implementation of Training Programs Using Digital Distance Education Technologies for Seafarers'. Pp. 521–25 in *Proceedings of the 2020 IEEE Conference of Russian Young Researchers in Electrical and Electronic Engineering, EIConRus 2020*, edited by S. S. and P. P. str. 5 Saint Petersburg Electrotechnical University 'LETI' Saint Petersburg. Admiral Makarov State University of Maritime and Inland Shipping, St. Petersburg, Russian Federation: Institute of Electrical and Electronics Engineers Inc. DOI: 10.1109/EIConRus49466.2020.9039034

Sridevi, V., Azath, H., Vijayakumar, R., Anbuselvan, N., Amirthalingam, V., & Arunkumar, S. 2024. 'Augmented Reality Shopping and IoT-Enabled Virtual Try-On with Cloud Services for Interactive Product Displays'. Pp. 880–85 in *Proceedings of the 2024 10th International Conference on Communication and Signal Processing, ICCSP 2024*. Academy of Maritime Education and Training, Deemed To Be University, Electrical and Electronics Engineering, Tamil Nadu, Chennai, India: Institute of Electrical and Electronics Engineers Inc. DOI: 10.1109/ICCSP60870.2024.10543476

Tajpour, M., Hosseini, E., Mohammadi, M., & Bahman-Zangi, B. (2022). 'The Effect of Knowledge Management on the Sustainability of Technology-Driven Businesses in Emerging Markets: The Mediating Role of Social Media'. *Sustainability (Basel)*, *14*(14), 8602. Advance online publication. DOI: 10.3390/su14148602

Voloshynov, S. A., Popova, H. V., Dyagileva, O. S., Bobrysheva, N. N., & Fedorova, O. V. 2022. 'Formation of Professional Competency in Life Saving Appliances Operation of Future Seafarers by Means of Online and Simulation VR Technologies'. Pp. 365–80 in *CEUR Workshop Proceedings*. Vol. 3085, edited by S. S.O., S. M.P., and K. A.E. Kherson State Maritime Academy, 20 Ushakova Ave., Kherson, 73000, Ukraine: CEUR-WS. DOI: 10.55056/ceur-ws.org/Vol-3085/paper28.pdf

Wróbel, K., Gil, M., Krata, P., Olszewski, K., & Montewka, J. (2023). 'On the Use of Leading Safety Indicators in Maritime and Their Feasibility for Maritime Autonomous Surface Ships'. *Proceedings of the Institution of Mechanical Engineers. Part O, Journal of Risk and Reliability*, *237*(2), 314–331. DOI: 10.1177/1748006X211027689

Wróbel, K., Gil, M., & Montewka, J. (2020). 'Identifying Research Directions of a Remotely-Controlled Merchant Ship by Revisiting Her System-Theoretic Safety Control Structure'. *Safety Science*, *129*, 104797. Advance online publication. DOI: 10.1016/j.ssci.2020.104797

Wu, X., He, Z., Liu, S., & Yu, Z. (2024). 'Visual Modeling Method for Ship Piping Network Programs in Engine Simulators'. *Applied Sciences (Basel, Switzerland)*, *14*(20), 9194. Advance online publication. DOI: 10.3390/app14209194

Yang, Z., Gao, Q., & Cui, J. 2024. 'Exploration and Practice of Competency-Based Digital Transformation in Maritime Education : Intelligent Navigation and Intelligent Ship Micro-Specialty'. Pp. 329–33 in *2024 5th International Conference on Information Science and Education, ICISE-IE 2024*. Tianjin University of Technology, Maritime College, Tianjin, China: Institute of Electrical and Electronics Engineers Inc. DOI: 10.1109/ICISE-IE64355.2024.11025521

Yashalova, N. N., & Ruban, D. A. (2023). 'Content of Corporate Vision Statements in Maritime Logistics: A Case Study of the Largest Companies'. *Economies*, *11*(3), 87. Advance online publication. DOI: 10.3390/economies11030087

Zhang, M., & Yu, S. (2025). 'A Review on the Preparedness of Chinese Maritime Law Education for Emerging Industry and Technology Trends: Sustainable Net-Zero Shipping, Maritime Digitalization, and Application of Artificial Intelligence Technologies'. *Sustainable Futures : An Applied Journal of Technology, Environment and Society*, *9*, 100752. Advance online publication. DOI: 10.1016/j.sftr.2025.100752

Zhou, F., Yu, K., Xie, W., Lyu, J., Zheng, Z., & Zhou, S. (2024). 'Digital Twin-Enabled Smart Maritime Logistics Management in the Context of Industry 5.0'. *IEEE Access : Practical Innovations, Open Solutions*, *12*, 10920–10931. DOI: 10.1109/ACCESS.2024.3354838

Zhou, X. Y., Liu, Z. J., Wu, Z. L., & Wang, F. W. (2019). 'Quantitative Processing of Situation Awareness for Autonomous Ships Navigation'. *TransNav*, *13*(1), 25–31. DOI: 10.12716/1001.13.01.01

About the Contributors

Andi Asrifan, S.Pd., M.Pd. is a dedicated scholar and educator specializing in English Language Education. He currently serves as a lecturer in the Doctoral Program in English Language Education, Graduate School of Universitas Negeri Makassar (UNM), Indonesia. Before this role, he held the position of Head of the Institute for Cooperation and International Affairs at Universitas Muhammadiyah Sidenreng Rappang. Dr. Asrifan earned his Doctor of Education in English Language Education and has established himself as an active researcher in areas including English as a Foreign Language (EFL) pedagogy, the impact of the COVID-19 pandemic on educational practices, and the integration of digital technologies into language teaching. He has authored numerous scholarly publications and presented his work at international conferences and academic forums in countries such as India, Pakistan, and the Philippines. Dr. Asrifan is certified in professional competencies including public speaking, personal branding, and literacy instruction. His leadership extends to roles as a peer reviewer for academic journals and an external examiner for doctoral dissertations. He is also an active member of several professional organizations and contributes to global education through ambassadorial roles, aligning his work with the United Nations' Sustainable Development Goals (SDGs).

Syahruddin, M.Kes., AIFO, is a distinguished professor and senior academic at Universitas Negeri Makassar (UNM), Indonesia, currently serving as Vice Rector for Planning and Cooperation. His academic expertise lies in Physical Education, Health, and Recreation, with a strong interdisciplinary foundation in sports science and health physiology. Throughout his career, he has made significant contributions to education, research, and community service, with a focus on developing sport education models, kinesthetic learning, adaptive physical education, and performance optimization strategies for athletes. Prof. Syahruddin is an active lecturer in both undergraduate and postgraduate programs, having supervised numerous theses and dissertations. His scholarly works include multiple research projects, scientific publications in national and international journals, and the authorship of various academic books. Additionally, he has held leadership roles in national sports organizations and served as an assessor for educational accreditation bodies. Prof. Syahruddin continues to champion innovation, quality assurance, and academic excellence in sports education.

***

Maslan Abdin completed his Bachelor's degree in Civic Education at Pattimura University (UNPATTI), Ambon, in 2014, and earned his Master's degree in Civic Education from the Graduate Program of Universitas Pendidikan Indonesia (UPI) in 2018. He is currently a permanent lecturer at Politeknik Negeri Ambon in the Department of Civil Engineering, where he teaches courses in Civic Education, Pancasila Education, and Anti-Corruption Education for the study programs of

Construction Project Management (D4), Civil Engineering (D3), and Road and Bridge Construction Engineering (D4).

Fatimah Hidayahni Amin has been serving and teaching for 18 years in the English Department at Universitas Negeri Makassar. Specializes in Linguistics, particularly in Pragmatics, Discourse Analysis, and English for Specific Purposes (ESP). Skilled in designing project-based and case-based curricula, able to communicate and collaborate cooperatively within a team, and demonstrates strong interest and integrity in developing practical English language teaching, especially in professional and workplace contexts.

Andi Tenri Ampa, S.Pd., M.Pd was born in Ujung Pandang on May 06, 1991. She Has a distinguished lecturer in the Doctoral Program in Economics Education at Makassar State University. Her academic journey began with a Bachelor's degree at Makassar State University, where she laid the groundwork for her expertise in education and economics. She then advanced her studies, earning both her Master's and Doctoral degrees at the esteemed State University of Malang, further solidifying her scholarly credentials. Passionate about empowering future educators and researchers, Andi Tenri Ampa is dedicated to fostering innovative learning and contributing to the development of Economics Education in Indonesia. Email: a.tenriampa@unm.ac.id

Amriani is a dedicated academic currently pursuing her Doctorate in General Education and Character Development at Universitas Pendidikan Indonesia. She holds a Master's degree in Islamic Studies from Universitas Muhammadiyah Malang, obtained in 2014, and a Bachelor's degree in Islamic Education from Sekolah Tinggi Agama Islam Negeri Palopo, completed in 2010. Her professional experience spans various educational institutions, where she has demonstrated a commitment to teaching and curriculum development. Amriani has taught at several schools, including SD Benteng Palopo and SMK Negeri 4 Palopo, and has been a faculty member at Universitas Muhammadiyah Palopo since 2016. Her teaching philosophy emphasizes the importance of character education in fostering holistic student development. Amriani is actively engaged in professional development, having participated in numerous workshops and seminars focused on educational innovation, literacy, and community empowerment. Her contributions to the field of education are underscored by her involvement in various training programs aimed at enhancing pedagogical practices. Through her academic and professional endeavors, Amriani continues to impact the educational landscape positively.

Indrawaty Asfah is a lecturer at Universitas Negeri Makassar (UNM) in Indonesia, specializing in English language education. Her academic focus includes Business English, English for Specific Purposes (ESP), English as a Foreign Language (EFL), and writing instruction. She has contributed to numerous research projects aimed at enhancing English language teaching methodologies. Her work often explores innovative strategies such as AI-based sentence combining to improve student writing quality and accuracy. She has collaborated on projects involving interactive reading models, guided writing, and curriculum development for ESP programs in higher education.

Muh. Darwis is a doctoral at Universitas Negeri Makassar, Indonesia and a lecturer at Universitas Negeri Makassar, Indonesia. He is currently studying Education Policy in Public Administration.

Agussalim Djirong is a distinguished Professor at Universitas Negeri Makassar, dedicated to the advancement of engineering and education. He earned his Engineering degree (Ir.) from Universitas Hasanuddin in 1990, marking the beginning of his academic journey. Driven by a passion for knowledge, he pursued a Master's degree in Engineering at the same institution, successfully completing it in 2004. His commitment to research and education led him to achieve a Doctorate from Universitas Negeri Makassar in 2015. With years of experience in academia, Agussalim Djirong continues to inspire and contribute to the development of future engineers and scholars.

Yuniar Ayu Hafita is a lecturer at Politeknik Pelayaran Sorong, Indonesia. She earned her Master's degree in English Education from Makassar State University and her Bachelor's degree in English Education from Semarang State University. Her academic and professional expertise centers on English for Specific Purposes (ESP), particularly Maritime English, with additional teaching experience in Cross-Cultural Understanding and Research Methodology. Her research interests include English for Specific Purposes (ESP), English Language Teaching (ELT), pedagogy and curriculum development, communicative competence, and digital and technology-enhanced language learning. Hafita has published numerous research papers in national and international journals on topics such as digital integration in maritime English instruction, e-learning, and innovation in maritime education. She is also actively involved in writing several English textbooks, particularly focused on maritime English and professional communication for seafarers. Her scholarly engagement includes participation in international conferences and professional development programs in human resource management and instructional techniques. Her professional dedication reflects a strong commitment to advancing maritime English education through innovation, interdisciplinary collaboration, and research-based pedagogical practice.

Sajed S. Ingilan is an Associate Professor V and AB English Language Program Head at the University of Southeastern Philippines (USeP), where he teaches linguistics and Mindanao studies. He is the Chief Editor of the Southeastern Philippines Journal of Research and Development, the Scopus-indexed journal of USeP. He is a certified Writer and Editor by the National Book Development Board-Philippines and regular member of the National Research Council of the Philippines. To give voice to what has been silenced in the discourse of the majority, he has been involved with government-funded research and extension projects about and for the indigenous cultural communities, which he has presented in onsite fora in the United States of America, Malaysia, Thailand, Taiwan, Vietnam, Indonesia, and the Philippines and published in Scopus and Web of Science-indexed journals and books.

Suryadi Ishak, M.Pd., is an academic and researcher in the field of Mathematics Learning Assessment and Evaluation with more than 15 years of experience. Born in Madatte on January 19, 1986, he completed his undergraduate studies at Al Asyariah Mandar University, earned his Master's degree in Mathematics Education from Makassar State University, and obtained his Doctorate in Educational Research and Evaluation from Yogyakarta State University in 2022. Currently, Dr. Suryadi Ishak, M.Pd., serves as a home-based lecturer at the Postgraduate Program of Makassar State University since 2024. Previously, he served as a lecturer at Al Asyariah Mandar University. His main expertise lies in the field of Mathematics Learning Assessment and Evaluation. Dr. Suryadi Ishak, M.Pd., has actively published scientific works in national and international journals. He also contributes as an editorial board member and reviewer in several educational journals. As a member of HEPI (Indonesian Educational Evaluation Association) and the Indonesian Mathematics Educators Society (I-MES), he continues to contribute to the advancement of mathematics education in Indonesia through research, publications, and community service.

Juvrianto Chrissunday Jakob is a dedicated English lecturer at the Civil Engineering Department of Ambon State Polytechnic, Indonesia. With a strong academic background and a passion for education, his areas of expertise encompass Teaching English as a Foreign Language (TEFL), integrating Technology in Language Learning, Discourse Analysis, and English for Specific Purposes (ESP). These fields reflect his commitment to equipping students with language skills tailored to their professional and academic needs. He holds a master's degree in English Education from Universitas Negeri Makassar, Indonesia, where he honed his skills in pedagogy and research. His scholarly pursuits focus on exploring innovative teaching methodologies and the application of modern tools in language instruction, ensuring his teaching methods align with the evolving demands of education in the digital era. Beyond his role as a lecturer, he is an active contributor to academic communities. He serves as a tutor and language instructor, helping learners enhance their English proficiency. His dedication to academic excellence is further evident in his role as a reviewer for several local and international journals, where he evaluates and supports the dissemination of research in his field. His professional journey is driven by his belief in lifelong learning and his desire to foster effective communication skills in students and professionals alike. His contributions to the intersection of language, technology, and education underscore his impact as an educator and scholar.

Isak Lilipory is a lecturer at Civil Engineering Department, Politeknik Negeri Ambon. He earned his Bachelor's degree in Naval Architecture from Pattimura University (UNPATTI), Ambon, in 1995, and completed his Master's degree in Coastal Engineering and Coastal Management at the Sepuluh Nopember Institute of Technology (ITS), Surabaya, in 2004. He currently serves as a permanent faculty member at Politeknik Negeri Ambon. His academic contribution includes authoring the reference book Prediction of Ocean Wave Dynamics Using ECMWF Wind Data.

Andi Tonra Lipu, S.E., M.M. is Born in Ujung Pandang on June 15, 1987, he holds a Master's degree in Management from Universitas Hasanuddin (2014) and a Bachelor's degree in Management from Universitas Negeri Makassar (2009). His academic career is marked by significant contributions to research, including studies on using YouTube for enhancing motivation in economics learning, the impact of student development on education, and the importance of student development in increasing learning interest. He has published several articles in reputable journals, including the International Journal of Education, Vocational and Social Science and Jurnal Perspektif Pendidikan dan Keguruan. His research and scholarly work continue to contribute to the field of education and management.

Seny Luhriyani Sunusi is a prolific academic affiliated with Universitas Negeri Makassar, known for her interdisciplinary contributions across education, technology, and digital innovation. Her work spans from hybrid learning models and smart campus frameworks to multimedia-based literacy tools and quantum-enhanced clustering applications.

Masud Muhammadiah is a highly accomplished senior lecturer at Universitas Bosowa, specializing in Indonesian Language Studies. With a career spanning over three decades, he has significantly contributed to academia and community service since beginning his professional journey in 1991. Born on

October 10, 1963, in Barru, he holds a Bachelor's degree in Indonesian Language and Literature, a Master's in Mass Communication, and a PhD in Language Sciences. His professional qualifications include certifications in editing and journalism, all obtained in 2023. Dr. Muhammadiah's extensive involvement in community initiatives focuses on promoting literacy and cultural heritage through various training programs. He actively guides students in community service and empowers local artisans through entrepreneurial projects. In research, he has led numerous projects aimed at developing educational materials that incorporate cultural values, enhancing language skills. His published works address critical issues in education, journalism, and language theory, emphasizing the integration of local cultural elements into language education. Dr. Muhammadiah's lifelong commitment to education and community service underscores his influential role in Indonesian language studies, making him a valuable asset to both the academic community and society at large.

Lely Novia is a lecturer at the English Applied Undergraduate Program, Faculty of Languages and Literature, Universitas Negeri Makassar. She holds a Bachelor's degree in English Education from Universitas Riau and a Master's degree in Applied English Linguistics from Universitas Katolik Atma Jaya Indonesia. Her academic interests include professional skills development, English for specific purposes, and intercultural communication. She has authored several books focusing on language education and workplace readiness.

Andi Anto Patak has been Associate Professor since 2024. He has been working as an academic staff since 2007 at the Department of English, faculty of Languages and Literature, Universitas Negeri Makassar, Indonesia. His research interests are Writing Assessment, Research Design, Educational Technology, Applied Linguistics, and Spirituals Group Training, and Plagiarism.

I Ketut Patra is a dedicated lecturer in the Economic and Business Faculty at Universitas Muhammadiyah Palopo, where she has been teaching since 1998. Born on April 4, 1968, in Jembrana, Bali, she holds degrees in Economics from both Hasanuddin University and STIE Muhammadiyah Palopo. Throughout her career, she has held various academic leadership positions, including the Head of the Development Economics Study Program and the Deputy Chair for Academic Affairs at STIE Muhammadiyah Palopo. In addition to her teaching responsibilities, I Ketut is actively involved in several professional organizations, such as the Muhammadiyah Economic Council and the Association of Indonesian Economic Development Studies. Her research interests focus on economic growth, inequality, and community empowerment, with recent studies examining the impact of human capital on poverty levels and the role of digital-based SMEs in job creation. I Ketut is proficient in various software tools, including SPSS and Microsoft Office, and is committed to continuous professional development. Her analytical skills, combined with her strong sense of responsibility and team-oriented approach, make her a valuable asset in the academic community.

Ryan Puby Sumarta is a lecturer at Politeknik Pelayaran Sorong, Indonesia. His academic background and professional expertise are primarily related to English language education, English for Specific Purposes (ESP), and Maritime English within maritime vocational education. His research interests include Maritime English, English language teaching, vocabulary acquisition and learning strategies, language needs analysis, digital and technology-enhanced language learning, maritime education, and professional communication.

Sumiati Putri Natalia is an accomplished academic and educator, currently serving as a Lektor at the Institut Agama Kristen Negeri Toraja. Born on December 29, 1990, in Rattebuttu, she holds a Bachelor's degree in Indonesian Language and Literature and a Master's degree in Language Education from Universitas Negeri Makassar. With a strong commitment to enhancing educational standards, Sumiati has participated in various professional training programs, including workshops on learning design and competency improvement for novice lecturers. Her teaching experience spans multiple subjects across different academic programs, including Indonesian Language, General Psychology, and Citizenship Education. Sumiati has also led significant research projects focusing on leadership and cultural traditions in her community, which DIPA IAKN Toraja has funded. In addition to her teaching and research roles, Sumiati is actively involved in community service and has held various leadership positions within her institution, including serving as the Coordinator of the Christian Leadership Study Program. She fosters academic excellence and promotes cultural understanding through her scholarly publications and community engagements.

Nasaruddin R, S.Pd., M.Pd. is a dedicated lecturer specializing in Early Childhood Education at Universitas Islam Makassar. Born on August 18, 1986, in Gowa, he completed his Bachelor's degree in German Language Education at Universitas Negeri Makassar in 2004 and later earned a Master's degree in Early Childhood Education in 2012 from the same institution. Since 2016, Nasaruddin has been a permanent faculty member, actively contributing to the academic community through various roles, including serving on committees for semester examinations and accreditation preparations. He has also participated in numerous seminars and training sessions aimed at enhancing educational quality and addressing critical issues such as child protection and literacy. His research interests focus on language development and storytelling in early childhood, leading to impactful community service initiatives that promote local cultural heritage among young learners. Notable projects include workshops on reading skills enhancement and parenting programs in local kindergartens. Nasaruddin's commitment to education is evident in his teaching of courses such as Basic Concepts of Early Childhood and Teaching Media for Young Learners. He continues to inspire future educators through his innovative approaches and dedication to fostering a nurturing learning environment.

Annisa Rahmah is a lecturer at PIP Makassar with a background in transport management and maritime operations. Annisa contributes to competency assurance as Chair of the Scheme Committee within PIP's LSP framework and is registered as a MET assessor, underscoring her role in certification and skills standards. Her academic work includes co-authored studies on AIS effectiveness and verified containers in shipping, and she also supervises undergraduate research within the institution, reflecting a blend of teaching, quality assurance, and applied research.

Wijdanah Ram, S.S., M.Si, is a prominent scholar in the fields of sociology and Arabic literature, born in Ujungpandang on December 17, 1988. She completed her undergraduate studies in Arabic Literature at Hasanuddin University in 2010, followed by a Master's degree in Sociology in 2013, and a Ph.D. in Sociology in 2021 from the same institution. Her academic career encompasses over six years of teaching experience at various universities, including a significant tenure at Universitas Hasanuddin, where she has contributed to the development of sociological studies. Dr. Wijdanah has also served as a lecturer at Universitas Cut Nyak Dien Langsa and Universitas Negeri Islam Makassar, demonstrating her commitment to education across diverse academic environments. Dr. Wijdanah's research primarily focuses on the dynamics of polygamous marriages within Islamic boarding schools, exploring their implications for women's roles and status in society. Her notable publications include studies on the motivations for polygamous marriages and their social consequences, which have been presented at international conferences and published in reputable journals. Through her extensive research and teaching endeavors, Dr. Wijdanah has established herself as a knowledgeable and influential figure in the discourse surrounding gender roles and family dynamics in contemporary Muslim societies. Email: st.wijdanah.ram@unm.ac.id

Sovia Rosalin is a doctoral at Universitas Brawijaya, Indonesia and a lecturer at Universitas Brawijaya, Indonesia. He is currently studying Business Resilience in Startups

Vivit Rosmayanti, S.Pd.I., M.Pd was born in Botta on June 26, 1987. She has over 10 years of experience teaching at the University. She obtained a bachelor's degree in English Education from Alauddin State Islamic University. She completed her master's and doctoral degrees in English Education from Makassar State University. She is currently a lecturer in the Post Graduate Program, Department of English Education at Makassar State University, South Sulawesi, Indonesia. She is also actively writing research articles to be published in nationally and internationally accredited journals. She has written in some chapter books, monographs, and reference books. She is interested in teaching methods for teaching English. Her research interests include language teaching methodology, ICT instruction, and ESP teaching. She can be contacted at email: rosmayantivivit@gmail.com

Muh. Ihsan Said Ahmad, SE., M.Si. is a lecturer in the Economics Education Program at Universitas Negeri Makassar. He holds a Master's in Economics from Universitas Hasanuddin (2006) and a Doctorate in Economics Education from Universitas Negeri Makassar (2019). He teaches a wide range of courses, including Business Introduction, Entrepreneurship, Marketing Management, and Economic Public Policy. Dr. Ihsan has contributed extensively to research in fields such as business strategy, entrepreneurship, and economic behavior, with numerous publications in national and international journals. He has also written several books on management, economics, and entrepreneurship, with works published by renowned Indonesian publishers. Additionally, he has been involved in various community service projects and received notable awards, including the "Dosen Teladan III" award in 2018 and a "Satya Lencana" for 10 years of service from the President of Indonesia in 2019. Email: m.ihsan@unm.ac.id

Rudi Salam is a doctoral at Universitas Brawijaya, Indonesia and a lecturer at Universitas Negeri Makassar, Indonesia. He is currently studying Transformational Leadership in service industries and has published his works in high-impact journals, such as the International Journal of Public Sector Management.

Faisal Saransi is a Nautical studies academic and maritime professional serving as Vice Director I (Pudir I) at PIP Makassar. Trained as a master mariner with a master's in engineering, he supports academic leadership and program quality while engaging in scholarship related to sea transportation. His research profile is indexed on SINTA and Google Scholar, and his leadership role is reflected in PIP's official channels and institutional updates.

Rudi Serang earned his Bachelor's degree in Civil Engineering from UKIM in 1999 and his Master's degree in Water Resources Engineering from the Graduate Program at Brawijaya University in 2011. He is currently a lecturer in the Civil Engineering Department at Politeknik Negeri Ambon. His academic publications, both national and international, have been active since 2018. He has also authored several books, including Environmental Pollution, Water Pollution, Precast Concrete, Global Climate Crisis in Indonesia, and Hydrology.

Margie Civitaria Siahay earned her Bachelor's degree in Architecture from the Faculty of Civil Engineering and Planning, Gunadarma University, in 2012. She subsequently completed her Master's degree in Architecture at the Faculty of Engineering, Universitas Indonesia, in 2015, specializing in Urban Design. She is currently a permanent lecturer at the Civil Engineering Department, Politeknik Negeri Ambon. In addition to her teaching responsibilities, she is actively engaged in research, scientific writing, and publishing in national journals. Her academic contributions include journal articles and book chapters such as Evaluation of the Master Plan of Politeknik Negeri Ambon, Identification of Interior Space Needs at Politeknik Negeri Ambon, Infrastructure Development in Indonesia, Introduction to Urban Planning, and Urban Transformation. Her research interests include architecture, urban planning, and urban design.

Oktavera Sulistiana, M.Mar., M.T. is an Associate Professor at the Merchant Marine Polytechnic of Makassar (Politeknik Ilmu Pelayaran Makassar). The research interests include maritime safety, ship systems, and human resource development in traditional shipping, focusing on optimizing training ship utilization in maritime education and professional training.

Agus Sulistiono is an educator, researcher, and creative content developer from Indonesia. He is currently a doctoral student in English Language Education at Universitas Negeri Semarang (UNNES) under the LPDP Scholarship Program. His academic interests center around language learning innovation, educational technology integration, and reflective English teaching within maritime and vocational education contexts. Before pursuing his doctoral degree, Agus served at Politeknik Pelayaran Sorong, and later at Politeknik Pelayaran Sulawesi Utara, where he contributed to curriculum development, language training, and English proficiency enhancement programs for maritime cadets. He also coordinated English immersion activities such as English Morning Training and Intensive Conversation Programs in collaboration with educational organizations like Dejavato Foundation. Beyond academia, Agus is a multifaceted creator. He runs a YouTube music channel called Melody Playground, which produces uplifting, educational, and feel-good music projects such as Skyline Melodies. His works combine pop, indie, and tropical EDM elements with meaningful storytelling aimed at inspiring youth and promoting positivity. Agus is passionate about using technology, music, and storytelling as tools for education and empowerment. He believes that innovation in both classroom and creative fields can transform how people learn, express, and connect across cultures.

Andi Annisa Sulolipu is a lecturer in the Doctoral Program in Economics Education at Universitas Negeri Makassar. She earned her Bachelor's degree from Universitas Negeri Makassar and completed both her Master's and Doctoral studies at Universitas Negeri Malang.

Henriette Dorothy Titaley is a lecturer at Civil Engineering Department, Politeknik Negeri Ambon. She earned her Bachelor's degree in Civil Engineering from Sam Ratulangi University (UNSRAT) in 2008 and completed her Master's degree in Civil Engineering at the Bandung Institute of Technology (ITB) in 2014. She currently serves as a permanent faculty member and Coordinator of the Bachelor of Applied Science Program in Construction Project Management at Politeknik Negeri Ambon. Her academic contributions include authoring several books, such as Environmental Engineering, Geotechnical Engineering, and Urban Drainage.

Wahyuniar, S.Pd., M.Pd., is a distinguished academic and lecturer at Universitas Musamus, where she specializes in Indonesian Language and Literature. Born on February 22, 1992, in Pinrang, she completed her undergraduate studies at Universitas Negeri Makassar in 2014, followed by a Master's degree in 2017, focusing on Indonesian Language Education. Wahyuniar's academic career is marked by her commitment to enhancing educational practices through innovative teaching strategies and research. She teaches a variety of courses, including Language Development and Teaching Strategies, and has actively participated in numerous research projects aimed at improving student learning outcomes. Her scholarly contributions include publications in national journals and presentations at international conferences, addressing topics such as digital literacy and the effectiveness of project-based learning. In addition to her teaching and research, Wahyuniar is involved in community engagement initiatives, conducting workshops to enhance students' skills in public speaking and computer literacy. She also serves as an editor for the Jurnal Ilmiah Nasional RESONA. Her professional affiliations include membership in the Indonesian Journal Managers Association and serving as the Secretary of the Faculty Senate. Wahyuniar's multifaceted contributions reflect her dedication to fostering a transformative educational environment.

Fathullah Wajdi is an academic with an extensive and distinguished track record in the field of Indonesian Language Education. Born in Serang, Indonesia, on April 10, 1978, he has devoted more than two decades to the world of education, beginning his career as an educator in 2001. His intellectual journey spans academic achievements from Sultan Ageng Tirtayasa State University, Semarang State University, and culminated in a doctoral degree from the Indonesia University of Education in 2017. Currently, he serves as a lecturer at Makassar State University and is actively engaged in various academic and higher education development initiatives. Fathullah is recognized as a prolific writer, with scholarly publications focusing on innovations in teaching methodology, such as the implementation of authentic assessment in drama learning and contextual approaches in literary studies. All of his works and dedication stem from a strong commitment to enrich pedagogical practices and promote educational transformation in Indonesia. Beyond the academic sphere, he also expresses his creative side through his novel Telegram Titik Habis, which stands as part of his contribution to literacy and cultural development.

Indra Dharma Wijaya is a doctoral at Universitas Brawijaya, Indonesia and a lecturer at Politeknik Negeri Malanag, Indonesia. He is currently studying Business Administration in service industries.

Hillman Wirawan is a lecturer in Organizational Psychology at the Department of Psychology, Universitas Hasanuddin, Indonesia, and a PhD at the School of Psychology, Deakin University. His research focuses on ethical leadership, abusive supervision, and dark personality traits. His work has been published in reputable journals, including Human Resource Development International and the Leadership & Organization Development Journal.

Yati, M.Pd. is a lecturer in the Economics Education program at the Faculty of Teacher Training and Education at Universitas Terbuka. She completed her PhD in Economics Education at Universitas Negeri Malang, her Master's degree at Universitas Kuningan, and her Bachelor's degree at Universitas Swadaya Gunung Jati. Since 2023, Dr. Yati has been actively involved in teaching and is committed to the Tri Dharma of Higher Education. She is also actively engaged in various professional organizations, such as the Forum Komunikasi Dosen (FKD), the Indonesian Association of Economic Education Professionals (Aspropendo), and the Indonesian Association of Distance Education Professionals (APPJJI). From 2023 to 2027, Dr. Yati serves as the Coordinator for the Field of Economic Tourism and Culture at FKD. With expertise in digital learning, qualitative research, academic writing, and book chapter writing, she also has research profiles on platforms like Scopus, Sinta, Google Scholar, Garuda, and WOS. Email: yati.official@ecampus.ut.ac.id

Dzakiyah Ulya Yusuf is an educator with a strong professional interest in teaching and maritime education. She holds a Master's degree in Education, which has strengthened her academic foundation and commitment to developing competent maritime human resources. With more than six years of teaching experience at a maritime higher education institution, she has been actively involved in guiding students to integrate theoretical knowledge with practical maritime applications. Her teaching philosophy emphasizes applied learning, professional competence, and readiness for real-world maritime challenges. Through her academic and instructional roles, she contributes to the continuous improvement of maritime education and workforce development in Indonesia.

Index

A

B

C

D

E

G

H

I

L

M

O

www.ingramcontent.com/pod-product-compliance
Lightning Source LLC
LaVergne TN
LVHW062156200926
848484LV00007B/1918